A guide to digital painting in

Procreate™

Landscapes & Plein Air

3dtotal Publishing

3dtotal Publishing

Correspondence: publishing@3dtotal.com
Website: www.3dtotal.com

A Guide to Digital Painting in Procreate: Landscapes & Plein Air © **2023**, 3dtotal Publishing. All rights reserved. No part of this book can be reproduced in any form or by any means, without the prior written consent of the publisher. Any images that remain copyright of the artist are marked accordingly.

iPad is a trademark of Apple Inc.

Savage Interactive Pty Ltd is the registered owner of the mark PROCREATE and has authorized the use of the mark PROCREATE.

Every effort has been made to ensure the credits and contact information listed are present and correct. In the case of any errors that have occurred, the publisher respectfully directs readers to the 3dtotalpublishing. com website for any updated information and/or corrections.

First published in the United Kingdom, 2023, by 3dtotal Publishing.

Address: 3dtotal.com Ltd, 29 Foregate Street, Worcester, WR1 1DS, United Kingdom.

Soft cover ISBN: 978-1-912843-63-3
Printing and binding: Gutenberg Press, Ltd (Malta) www.gutenberg.com.mt

Visit 3dtotalpublishing.com for a complete list of available book titles.

Managing Director: Tom Greenway
Studio Manager: Simon Morse
Lead Editor: Samantha Rigby
Lead Designer: Joseph Cartwright
Editor: Marisa Lewis
Designer: Fiona Tarbet

Cover images by individual artists as credited throughout the book.

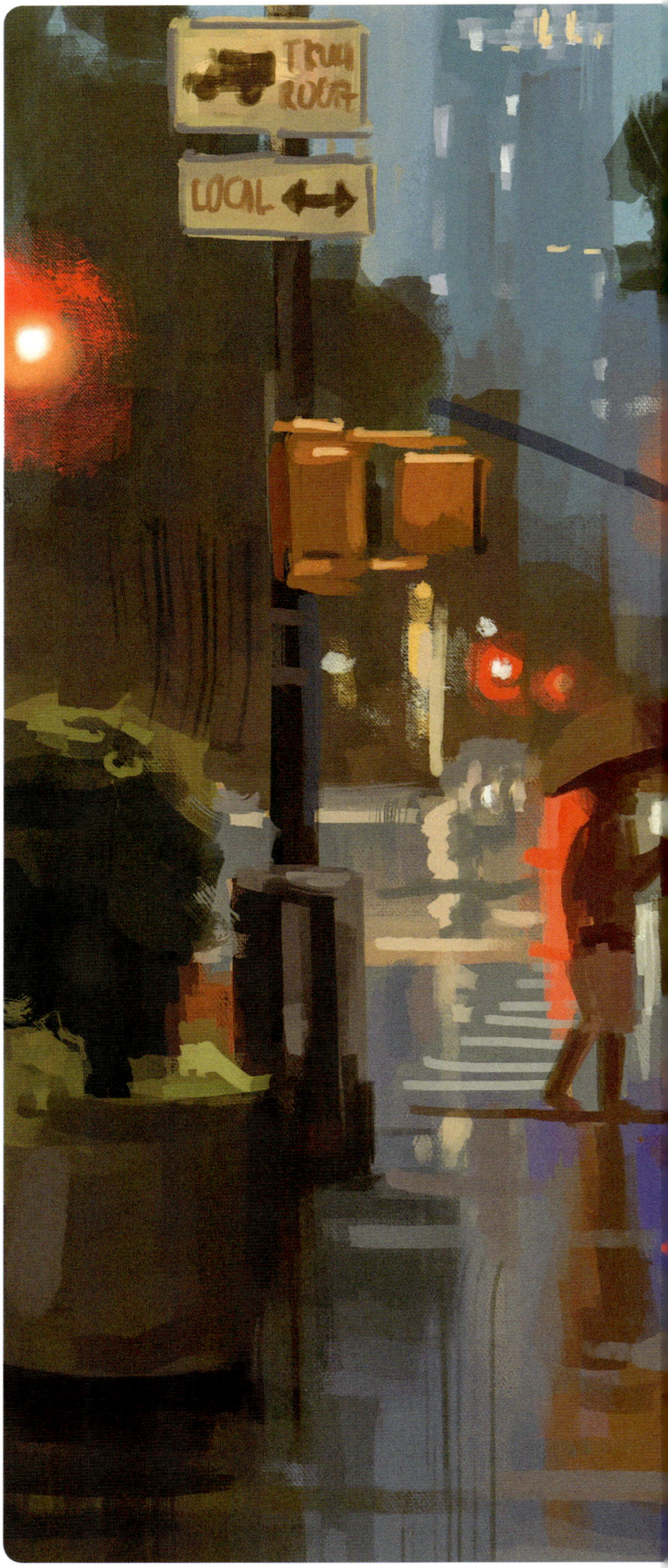

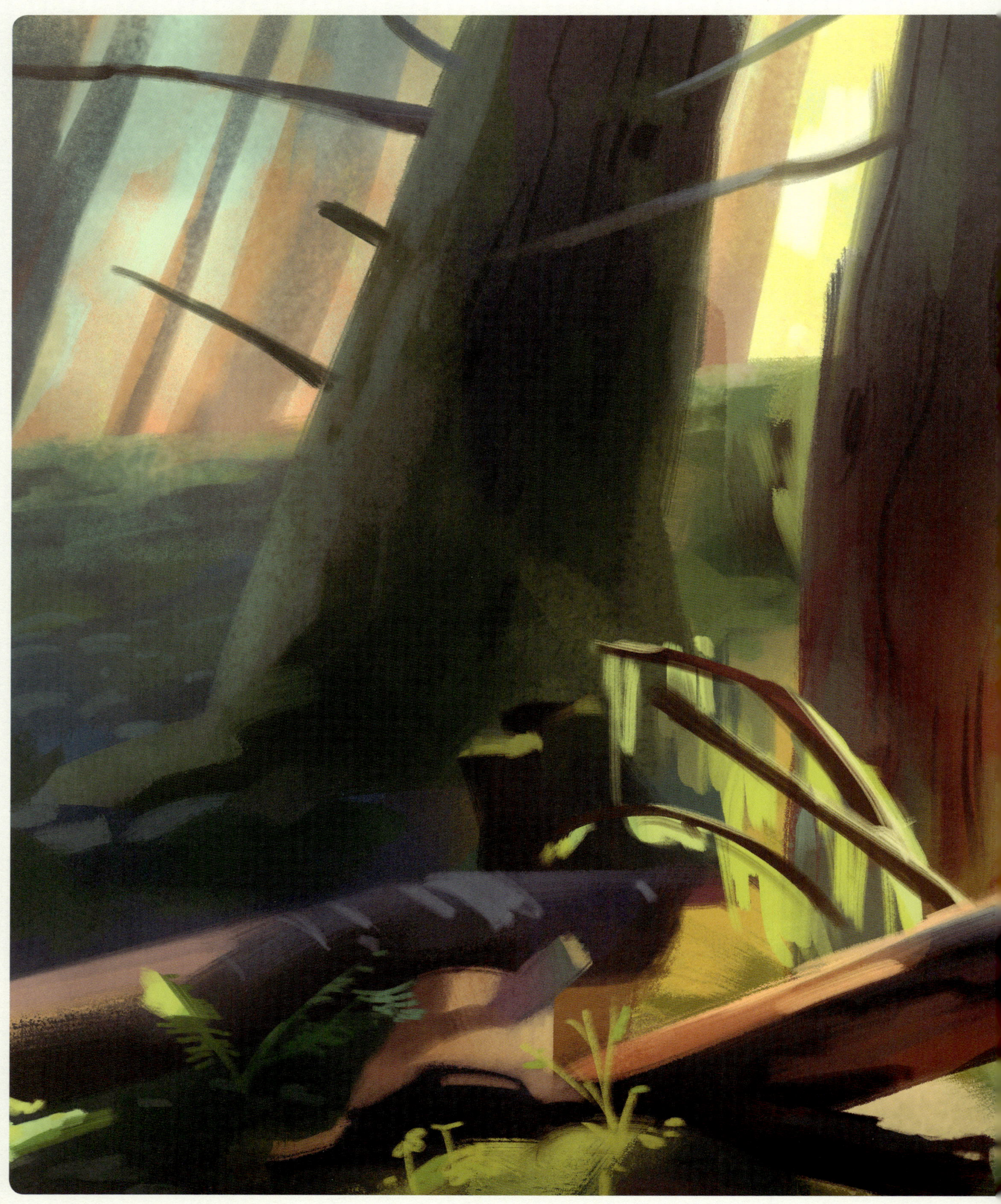

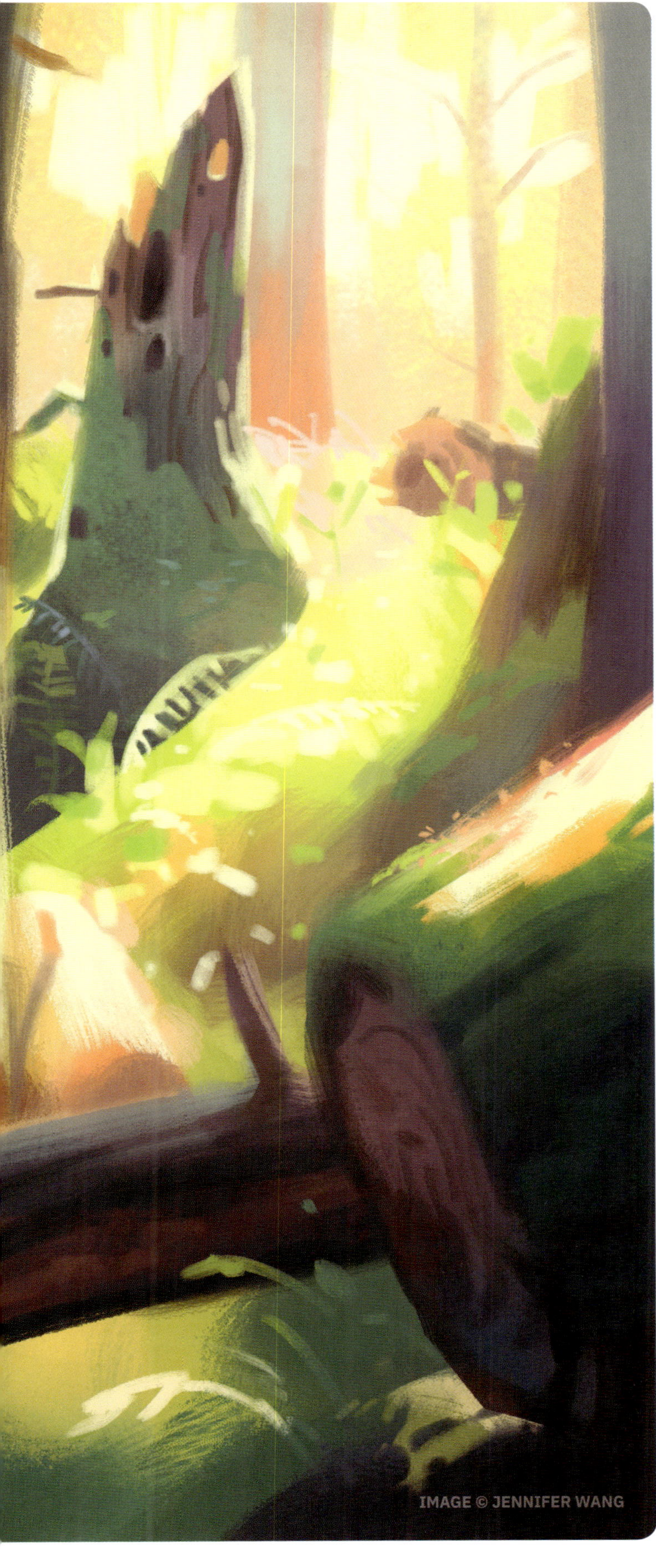

CONTENTS

HOW TO USE THIS BOOK

This book is the ideal companion for Procreate users keen to step into the wide world of environment art and plein-air painting. If you have ever wanted to paint a vibrant landscape scene, attempted an iPad sketch on a road trip, or wished you could recapture a special travel memory in your own style, these pages are the place to begin your journey with environment painting in Procreate.

The Introduction chapter (page 8) will fire up your creative engines, as Mike McCain shares some of the insights and lessons he has learned on his landscape-painting path. His studies of grand vistas, bustling streets, and serene gardens will have you reaching for your iPad and hiking shoes!

The Tutorials chapters (page 29) show how ten artists create an environment step by step in Procreate. They cover a range of approaches to painting, including from real-life observation, photo reference, imagination, and a mix of all three. Some artists have a minimalist approach that's almost like using real paint in your sketchbook; others dig into Procreate's adjustment sliders, blend modes, and powerful brush settings. There are so many ways a beautiful, immersive environment or landscape can be painted – with practice and the help of these tutorials, you'll be sure to find your own unique approach.

At the back of the book, you will find a guide to the Downloadable Resources (page 215) available with this title, and a Glossary (page 216) and Tool Directory (page 217) for the terms and tools commonly used throughout.

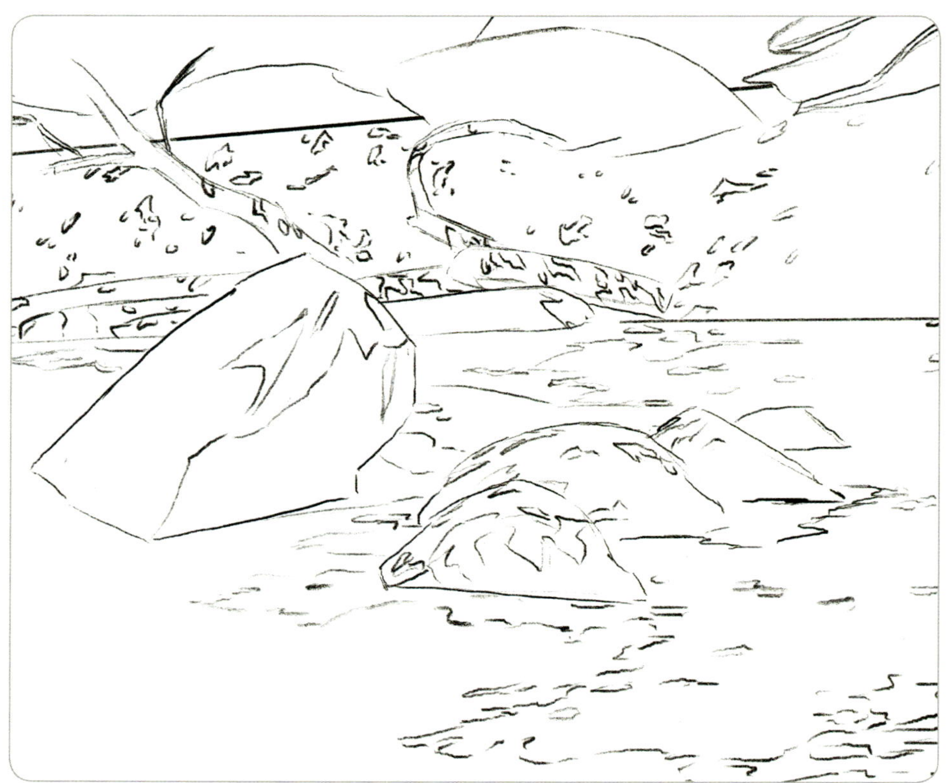

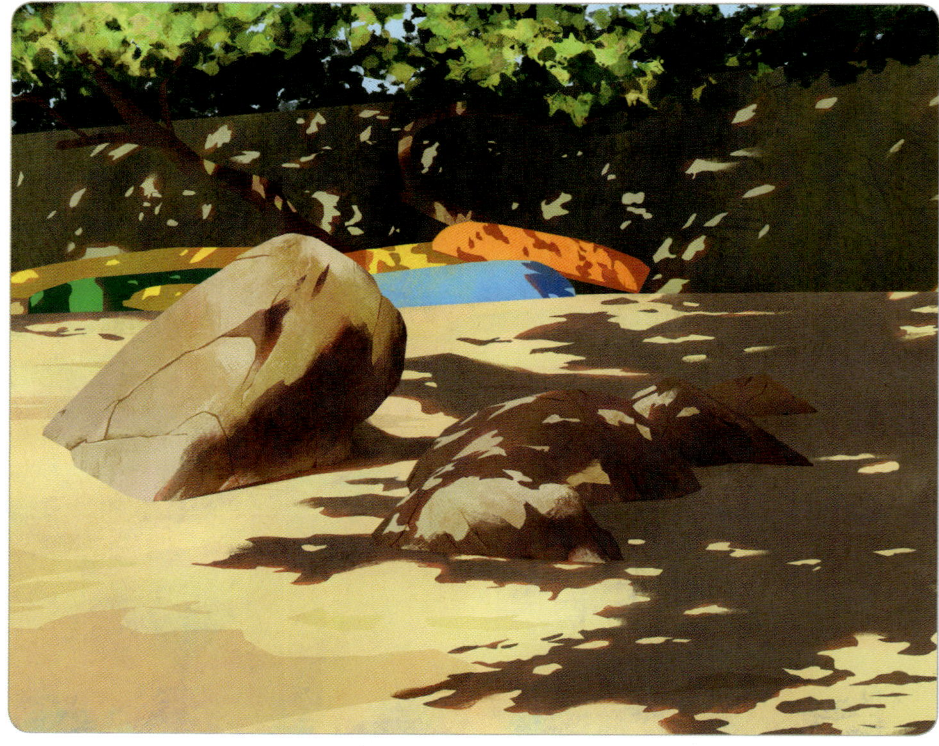

IMAGES BY KARIN BRANDENBERG

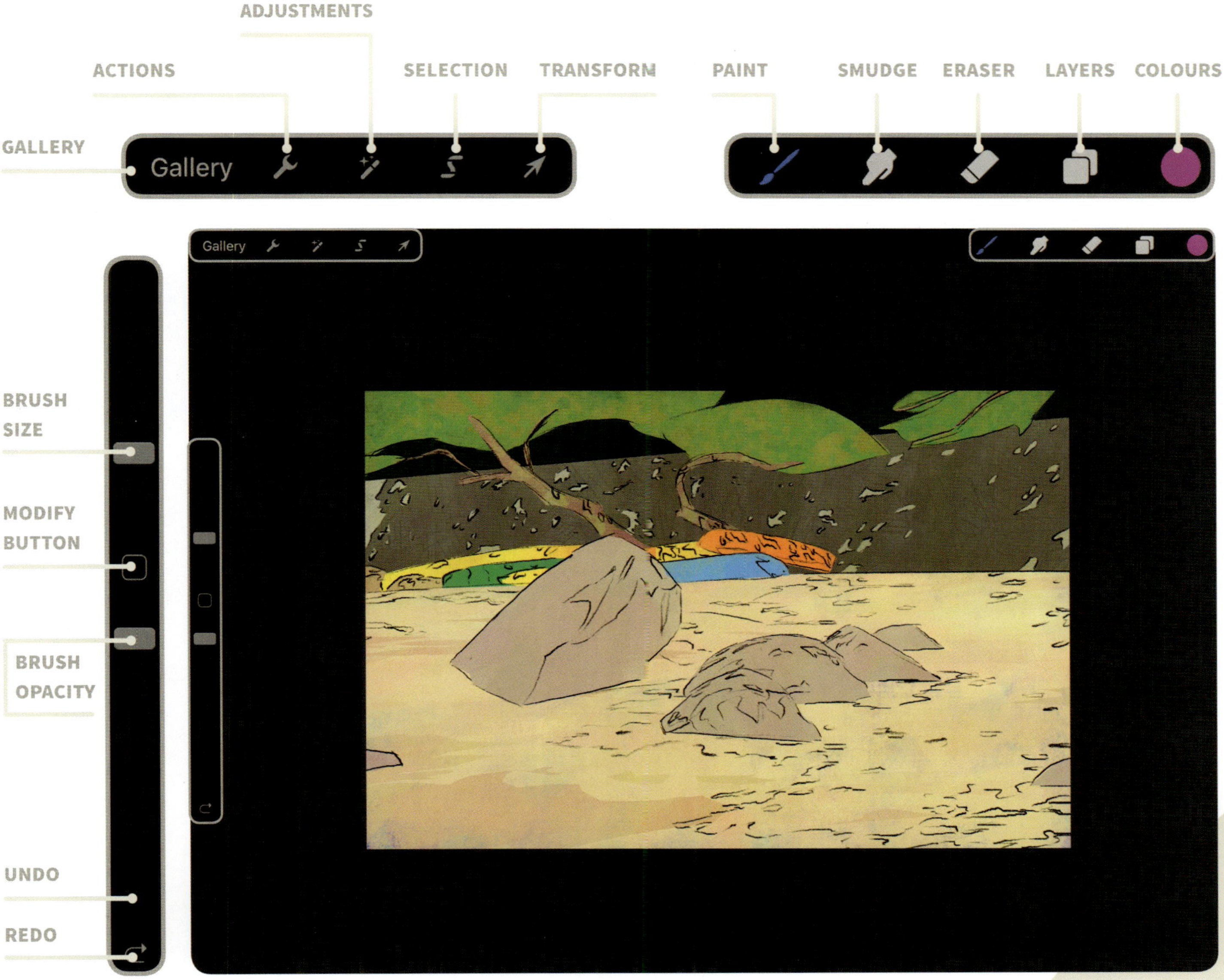

ADJUSTMENTS

ACTIONS SELECTION TRANSFORM PAINT SMUDGE ERASER LAYERS COLOURS

GALLERY

Gallery

BRUSH SIZE

MODIFY BUTTON

BRUSH OPACITY

UNDO

REDO

For the latest information on Procreate's interface, shortcuts, and tools, you can learn more from the official Procreate Handbook (procreate.com/handbook). If you are a total beginner to Procreate, it's highly recommended to browse the Handbook to get a feel for the software and its basic tools.

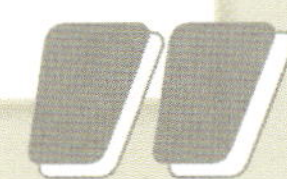

As you read the tutorials, look out for helpful quote bubbles such as this one. In these, the artists offer useful advice, software tips, personal insights, and recaps of subjects you have learned so far.

INTRODUCTION
BY MIKE MCCAIN

Whether you want to paint a simple everyday scene or something imaginary and fantastical, a strong sense of reality will help transport the viewer into your painting's world. As is true when capturing any subject, your landscape paintings will be hugely improved if you take the time to observe from reality and paint from life.

Throughout history, artists have enjoyed and benefitted from the process of going outdoors to paint the world around them – a technique called *en plein air* or plein-air painting. This practice encourages you to observe natural colour and light, pay close attention to your surroundings, and use all your resourcefulness to capture a living environment.

Concept artists and illustrators today still enjoy the benefits of plein-air painting, especially combined with the portability of a digital app such as Procreate. In this chapter, Mike McCain will take you through his landscape-painting journey, from getting into plein-air painting, to unlocking the potential of Procreate, to creating environments from his imagination.

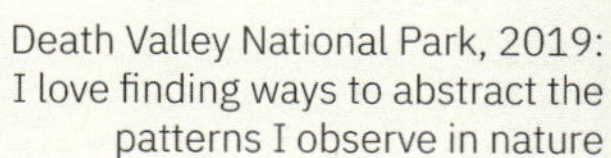

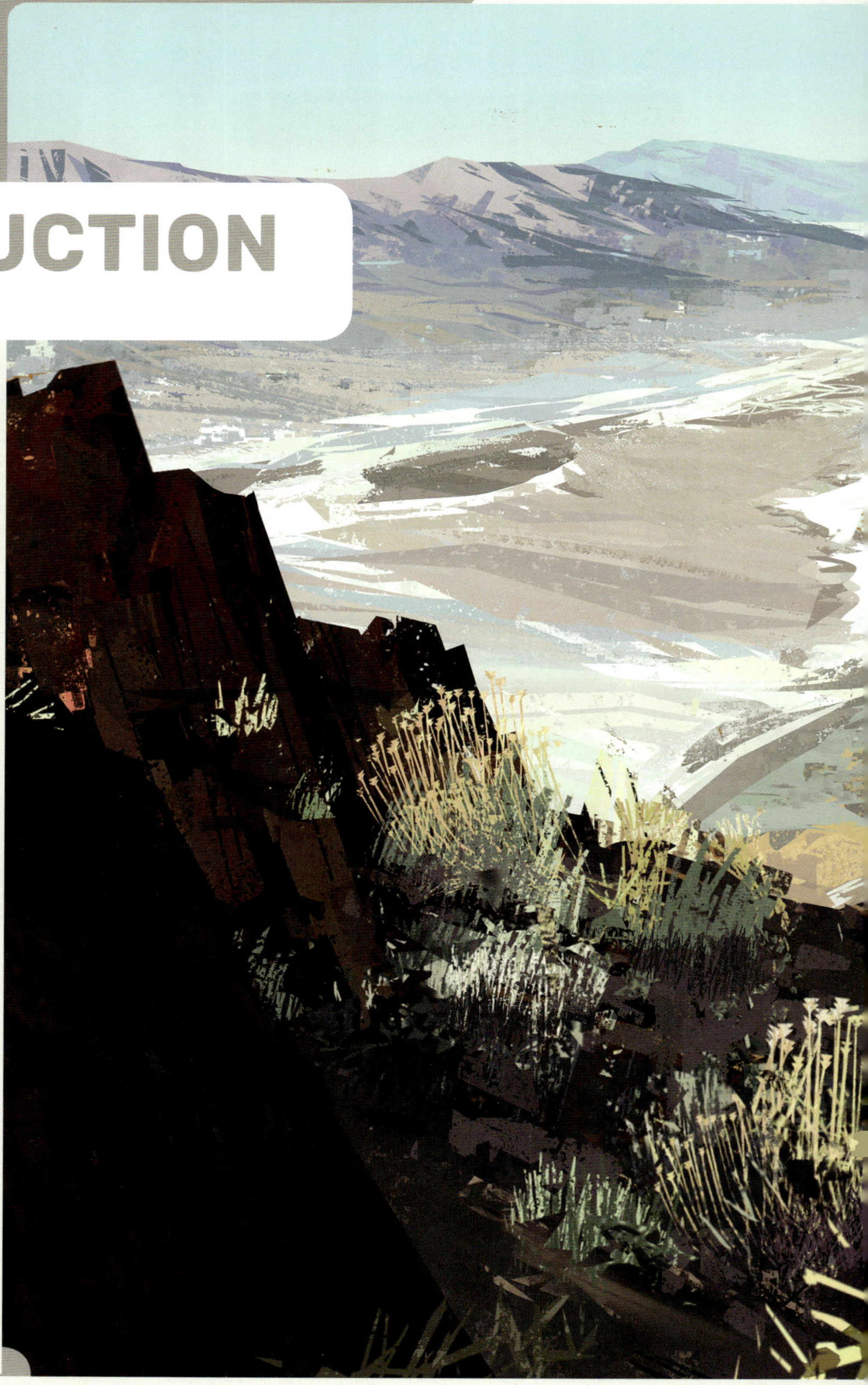

Death Valley National Park, 2019: I love finding ways to abstract the patterns I observe in nature

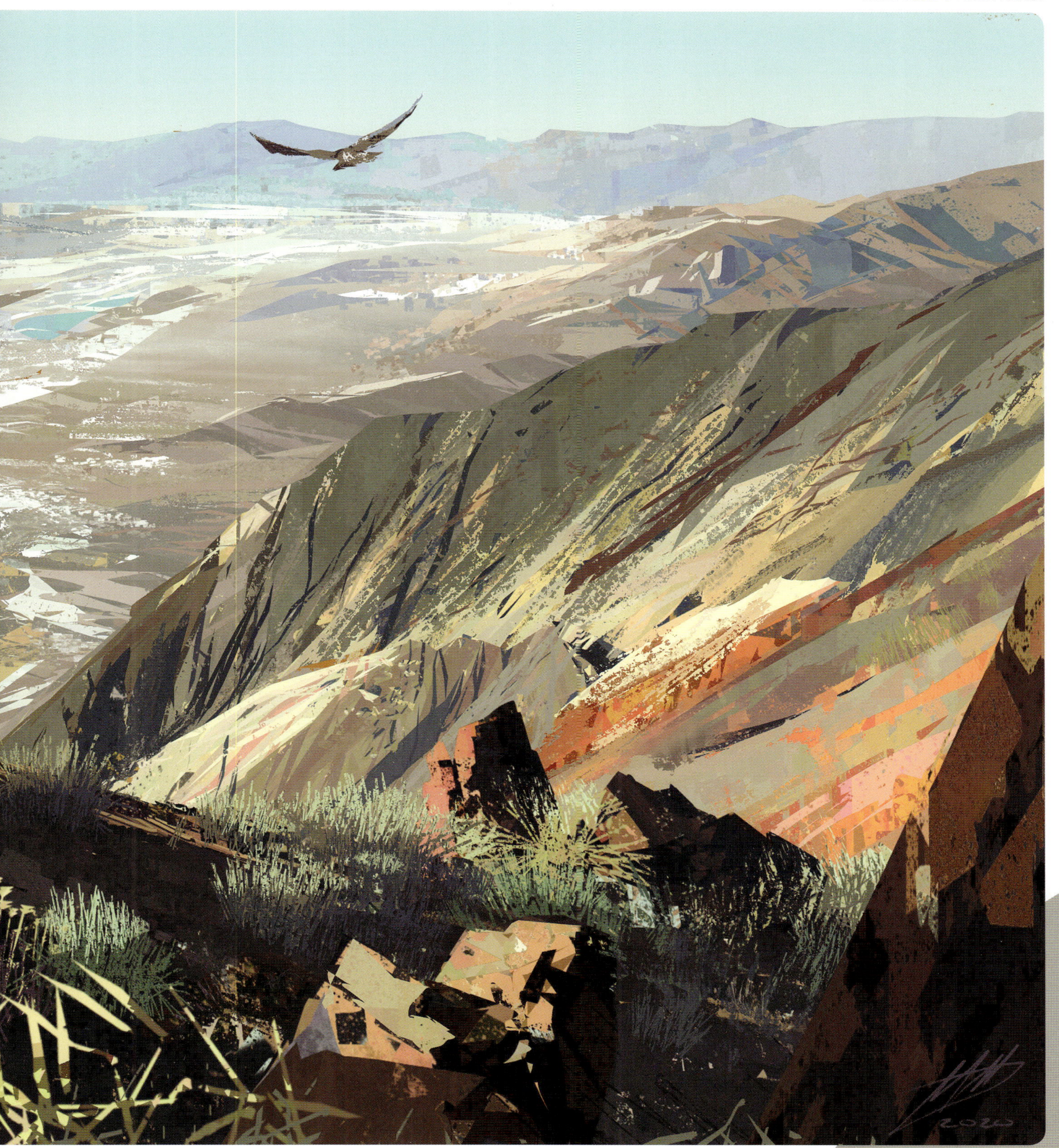

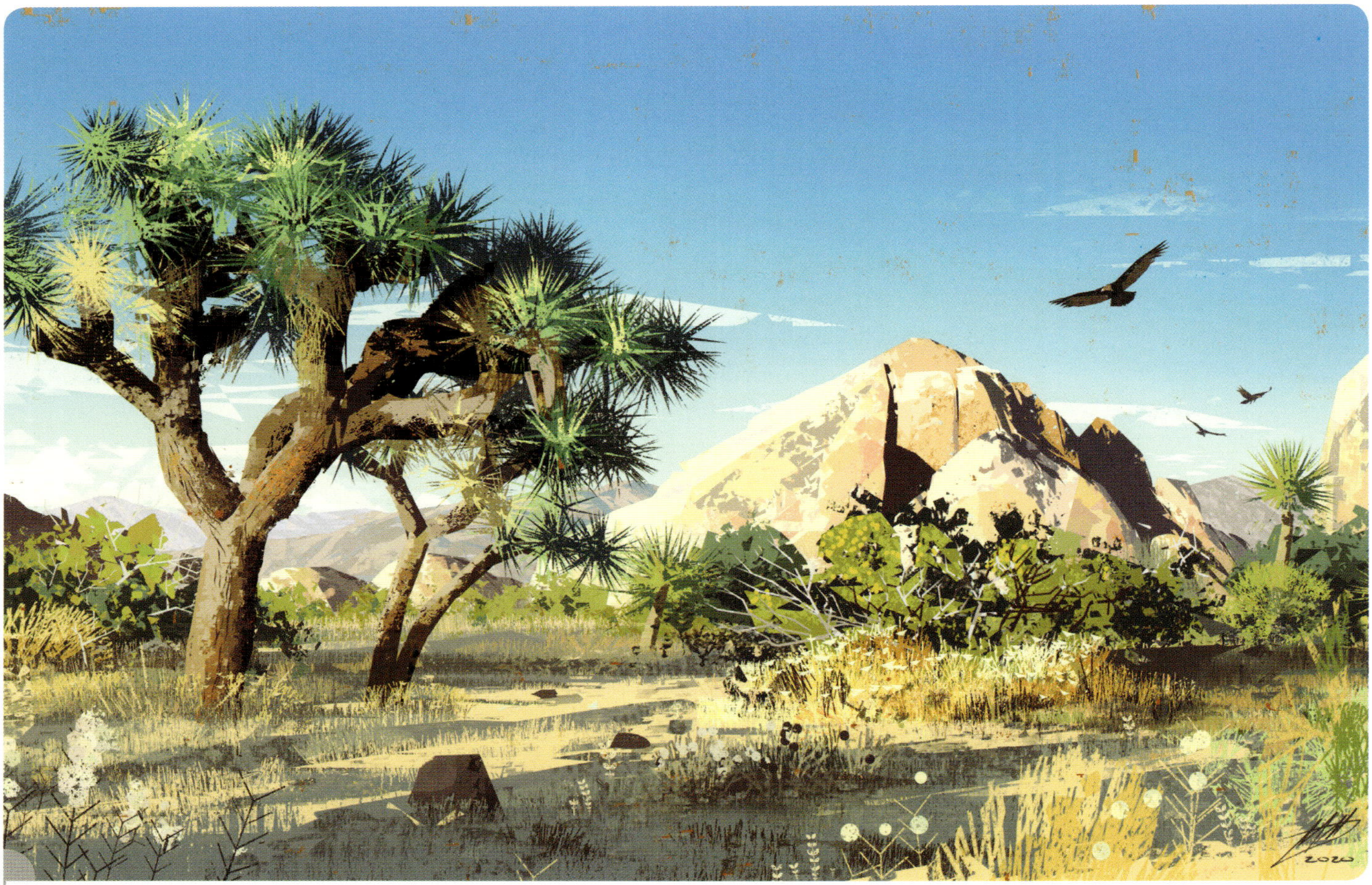

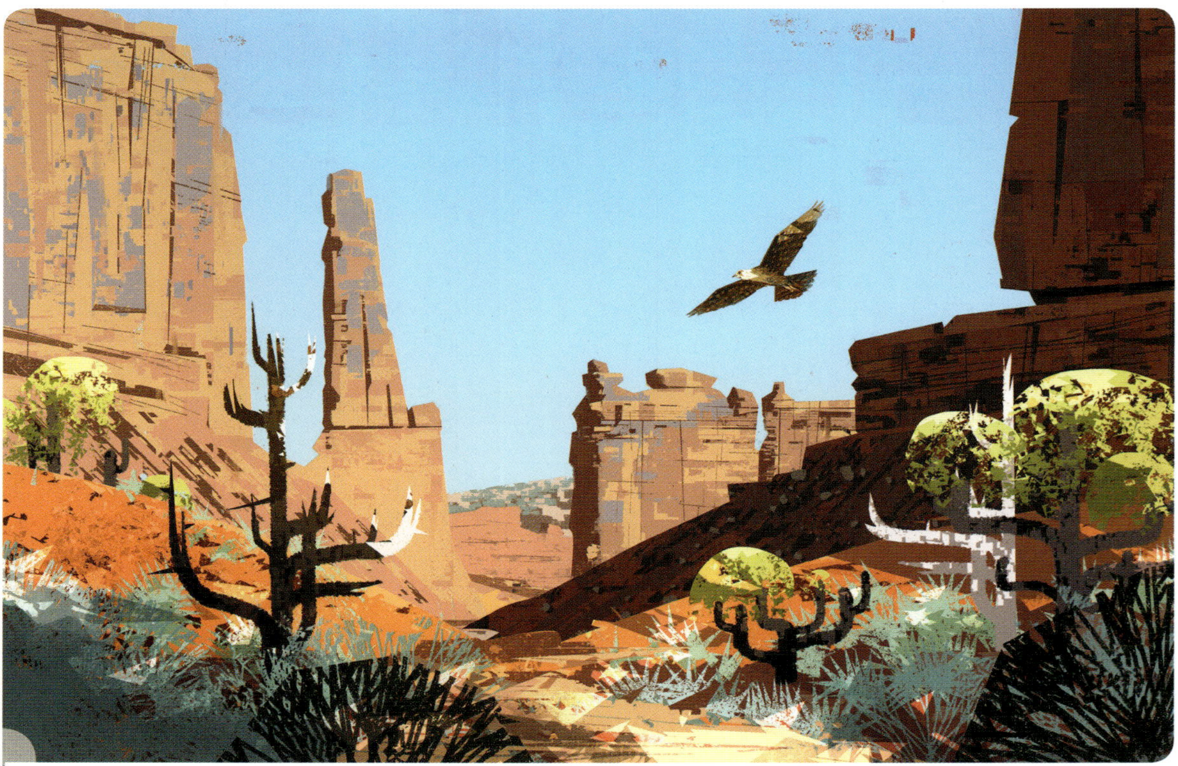

Joshua Tree National Park, 2020: more experimentation with custom brushes in Procreate

Arches National Park, 2018: this was one of the first paintings in which I started to find my voice and process

DISCOVERING PLEIN-AIR PAINTING

To paint *en plein air* just means to paint outdoors, from direct observation of the landscape. Artists have been making plein-air paintings since at least the early 1800s! It is a wonderful way to practise art, improve our sensitivity to colour and light, and enjoy the beauty of the world around us. And with today's digital tools, it has never been more convenient to get outside and paint.

I was thrilled to be asked to write the introduction for this book, because plein-air painting in Procreate was a huge breakthrough for me as an artist. It is where I developed the majority of the painting style, brushes, and workflow I use in my work today. In 2018, I took a month-long road trip through some of America's most beautiful National Parks and fell in love with plein-air painting. This wasn't the first time I had tried it, but it was the first time the magic of it really clicked for me. I had painted traditionally in the past, but it never developed into a comfortable routine for me, so plein-air painting always felt like an uphill struggle. Painting on the iPad opened up a new world of art for me, and I realized how fun and relaxing painting out in nature can be. It felt like play. I started experimenting a lot more with my approach. This led to more exciting results, which in turn encouraged me to get out and paint more. As artists, we can push ourselves really hard sometimes, but I think we often grow the most when we have space to paint just for the enjoyment of it.

This book is filled with great advice and insights for painting environments in Procreate. I hope it will inspire and guide you to go out and try plein-air painting – and I hope you will discover how much fun it can be, like I did!

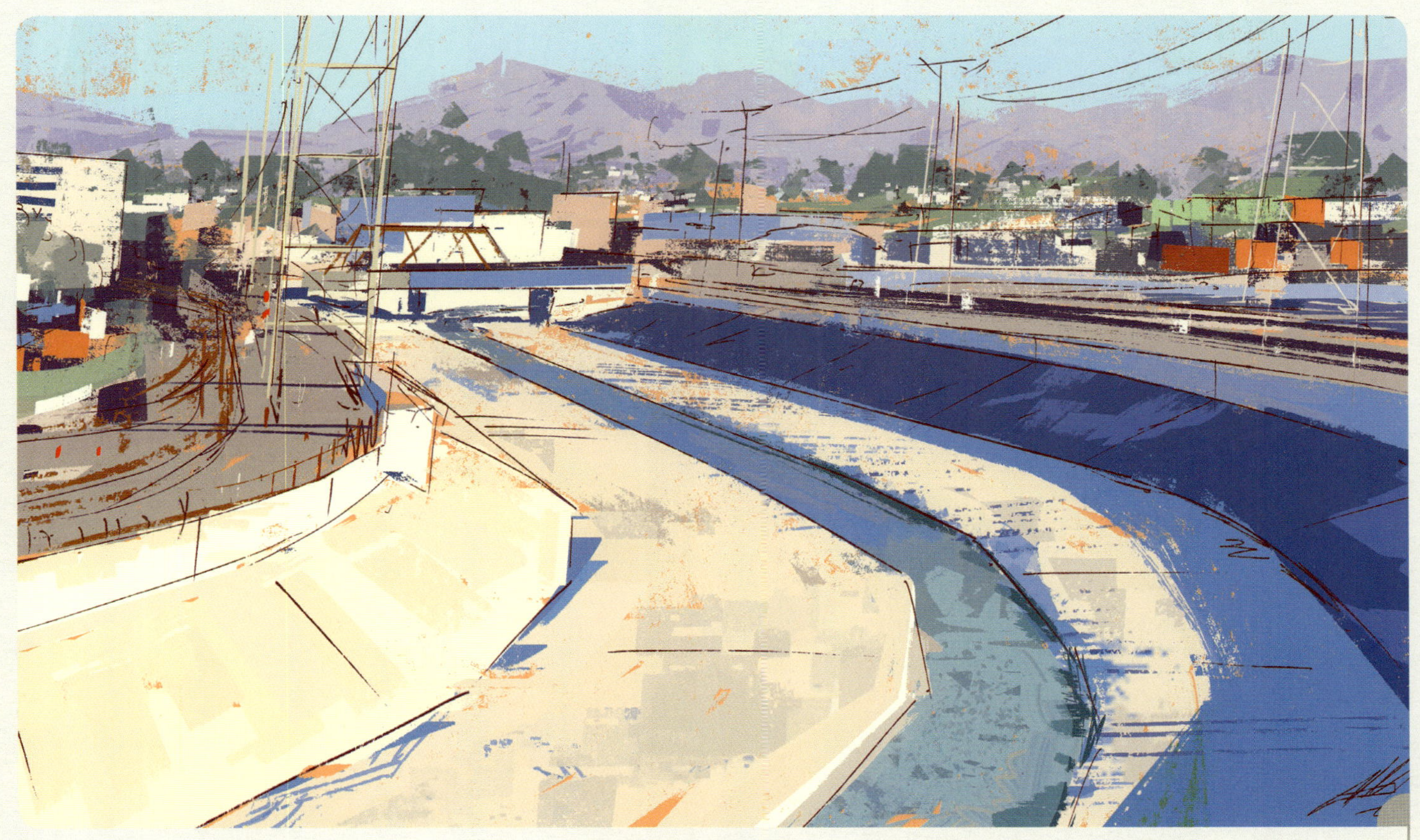

Cesar Chavez Bridge, 2023: a recent plein air where I tried experimenting with a different approach

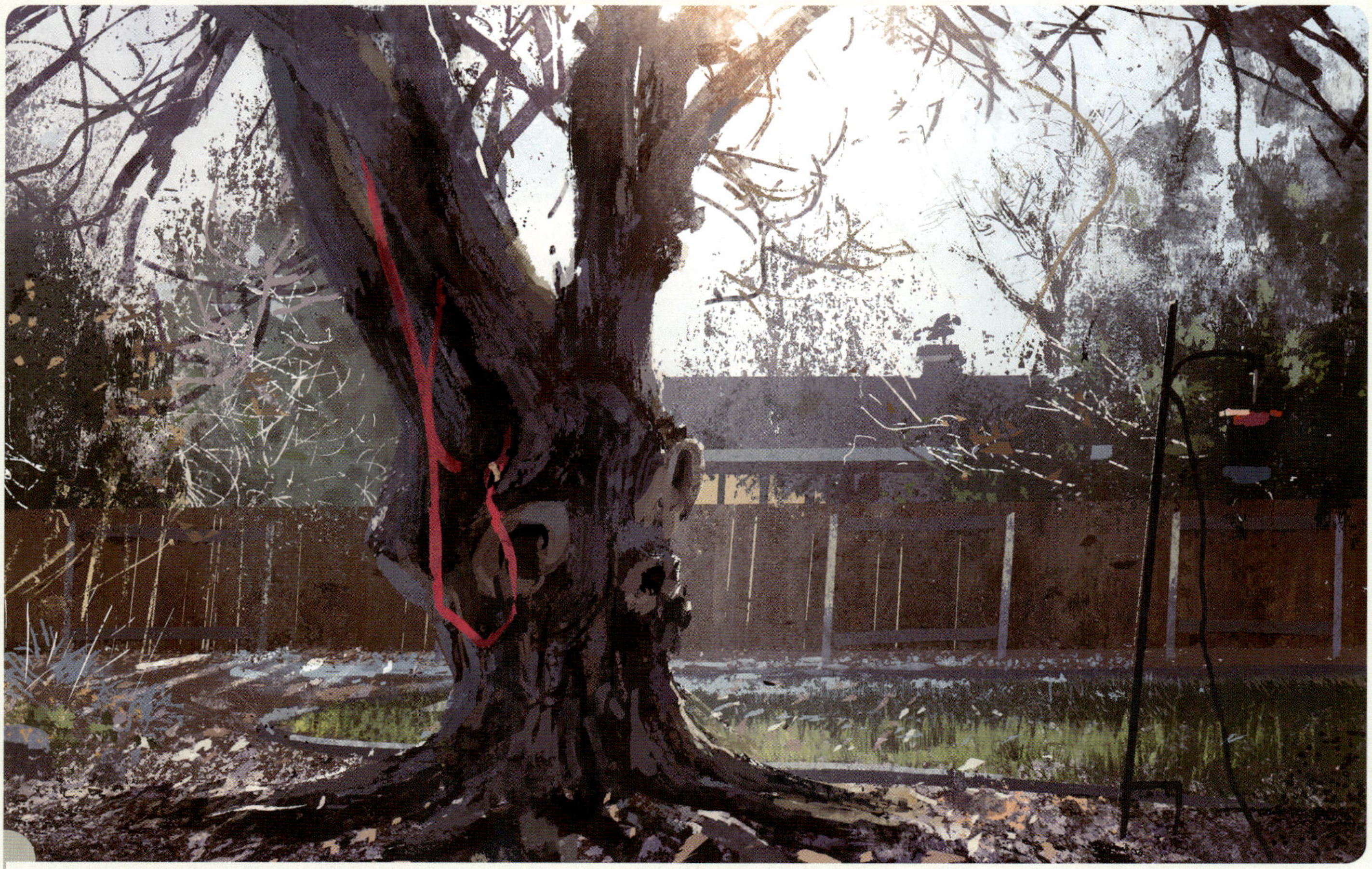

Backyard, 2022: one last painting of this yard before the tree had to be removed due to storm damage

BUILDING CONFIDENCE

If you think plein-air painting sounds scary, that's okay! The idea of painting in public made me really anxious for years. Just like anything else, it was scariest when I wasn't used to it. The more I practised, the more comfortable I became. You can start by painting at home, in private – perhaps painting the view from a window or doing a virtual plein-air study (more on that later, on page 21). Here you can build confidence in your plein-air process without worrying about passers-by or the elements. Try to use the same tools and approach you'll eventually use outdoors.

You can also start by doing greyscale value studies. That way, you don't have to think about colour temperatures and can focus purely on studying the light and value structure of the scene. You will still learn a lot this way, and it can really help you hone your skills with value, composition, and plein-air mark-making. Note that I do not recommend trying to turn plein-air value studies into full-colour paintings using layer blending modes, because in this approach you are no longer picking exact colours from observation. If you are motivated to create a colour painting after completing a value sketch, just repaint it in colour using your value sketch as a drawing guide.

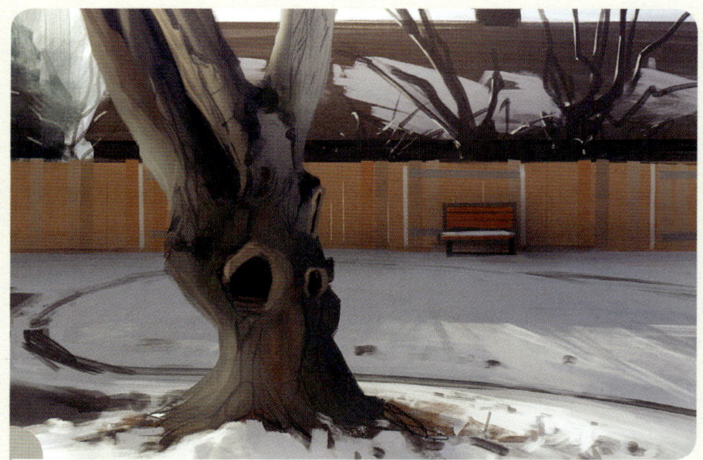

Backyard, 2016: my first plein-air painting in Procreate, getting to know the program in the comfort of my parents' yard

When you are ready to go out painting, bring some friends! I always feel less anxious painting outdoors when I'm not the only one doing it. It takes some of the pressure off if passers-by ask questions, and there is nothing better than grabbing some food and drink with friends after a good painting session.

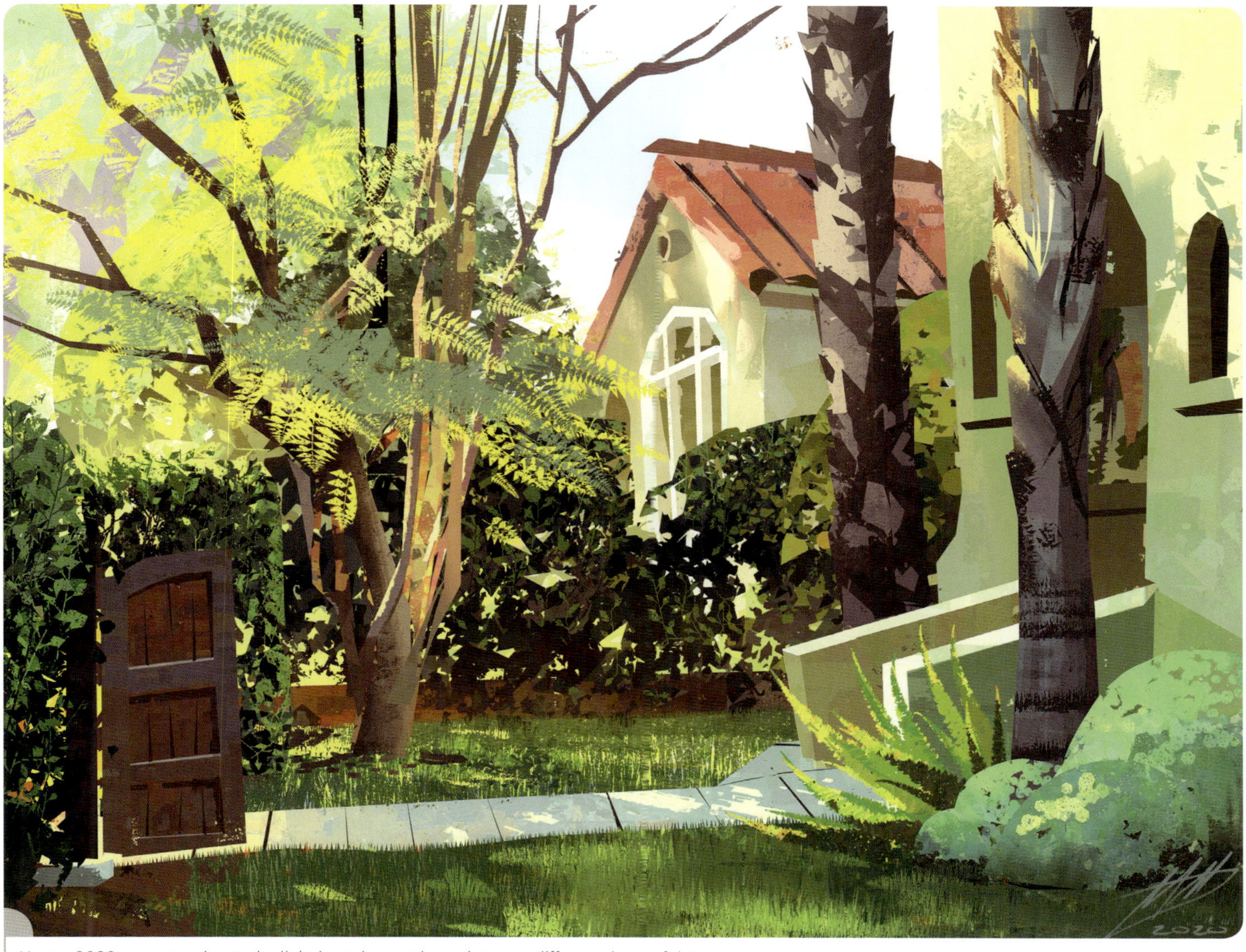

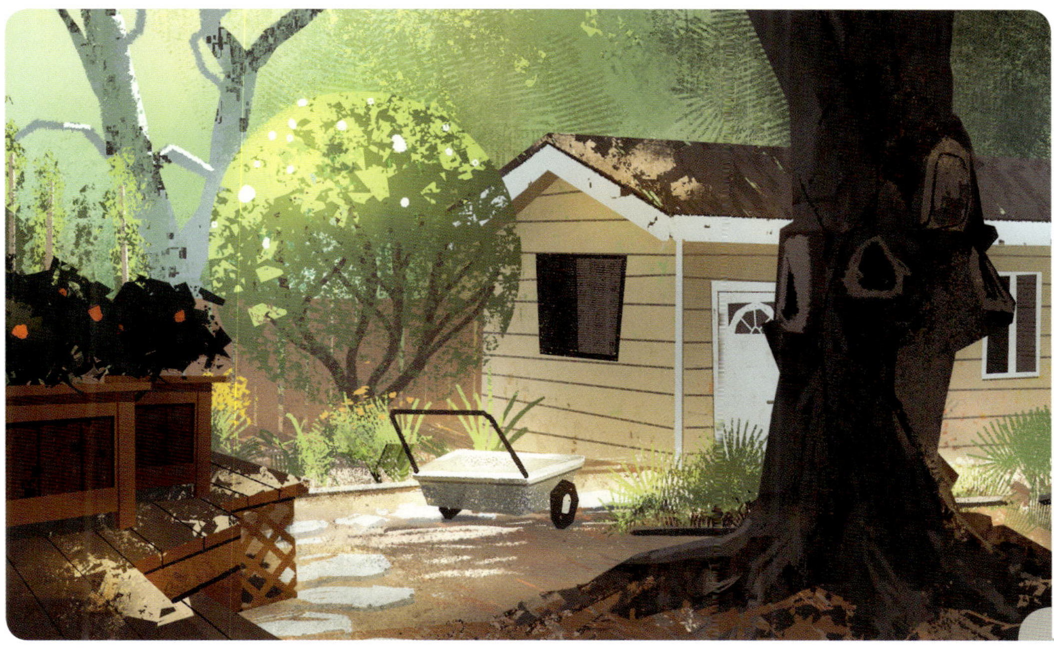

Home, 2020: pay attention to the light in and around your home at different times of day

Backyard, 2018: another painting of the same yard – again, feeling comfortable to experiment on a slow morning at home

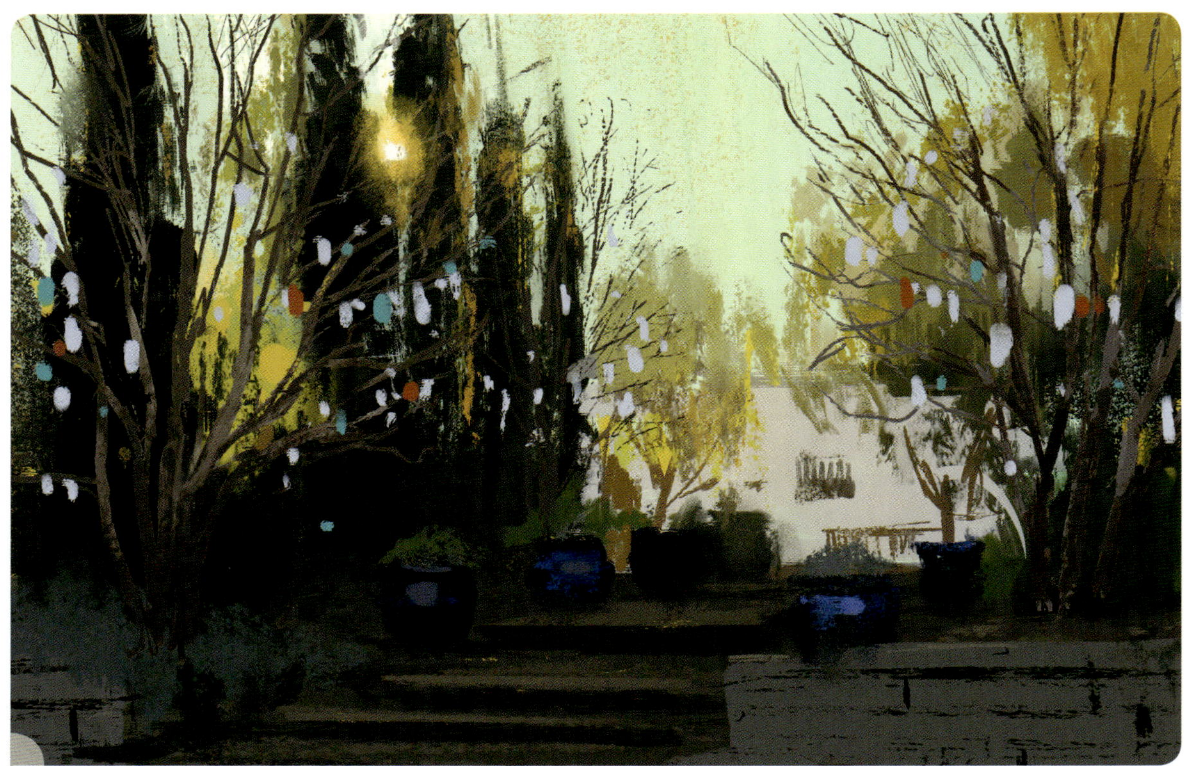

You don't need any fancy brushes to get started – this is a study I did using just a few default Procreate brushes

WHY PROCREATE?

Artists have been plein-air painting for over 200 years, so you definitely don't *need* Procreate to go painting outdoors. But for digital plein air, I like Procreate best for its accessibility and versatile brush engine. The user interface is clean and intuitive, with lots of touch gestures to speed up your workflow. I also love having the automatic time-lapse recordings of your paintings to share and refer back to later.

Procreate comes with a variety of excellent built-in brushes, and there is also a huge online marketplace for artist-created brushes, which you can find on Gumroad and elsewhere. For amazing watercolour brushes and other natural-media styles, check out Max Ulichney's brushes (*maxpacks.com*). For a more graphic, stylized set, you can try mine – there is a free starter set on my website (*mikemccain.art*). Procreate even allows you to import brushes made for Adobe Photoshop, though be aware that more complex Photoshop brushes may behave differently when imported.

Lastly, if you don't have an iPad (or you left it at home), there is an iPhone version of the app called Procreate Pocket. It is surprisingly fun and effective for painting quick little colour studies using just your finger. Sometimes I use it to capture lighting and colour ideas on location that I can further refine at home on the iPad or in Photoshop.

That all said, there *is* a learning curve if you are new to Procreate, especially if you are coming to it after years of familiarity with another program. It took me a couple of months to get really comfortable with it, but this in turn helped me to slow down my process a little. Learning a new way of doing things can force you to be more thoughtful in your choices, and can lead you to try things you might not have normally tried. I recommend diving right in. Familiarize yourself with the basics and then start painting and experimenting. The official Procreate Handbook and Beginners Series videos are excellent resources to consult if you can't figure out how something works, and the tutorials in this book offer great tips and advice for improving your painting workflow. Remember: if you can do it in Photoshop, you can likely do it in Procreate, too.

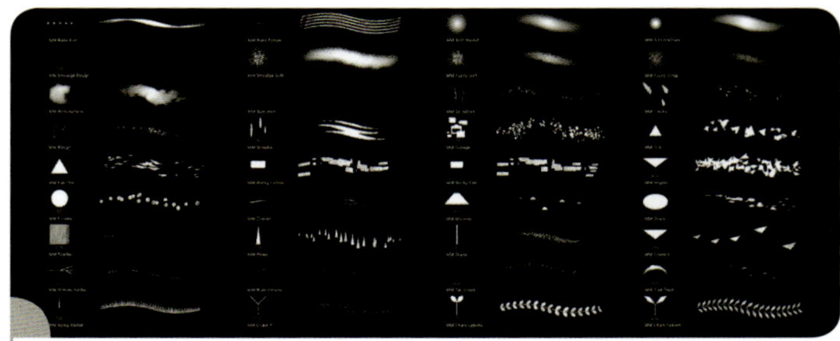

Some of the custom brushes I have created over time to use in my plein-air paintings and illustrations

GET COMFORTABLE

My number one tip is: get comfortable! We are more likely to reach a deeper level of focus in our work when we feel physically and emotionally comfortable. So when I am deciding where to paint, I am not just looking for inspiring scenery, but also looking for a relaxing spot where I'll be able to enjoy simply being present and appreciating the scenery around me. If faced with the choice, I will usually choose a quiet, comfortable spot over the most impressive view. If I am enjoying being somewhere, I can usually find something interesting to paint.

These days I usually prefer sitting while I paint, so I bring a comfortable folding camp chair. If you prefer to stand, there's a variety of iPad tripod mounts available online. Headphones can be helpful if you are worried about questions from passers-by (I recommend more obvious-looking headphones for that). Be sure to bring plenty of water on hot days, and extra layers on chilly days – even if you are warm enough at first, you will get significantly colder after standing or sitting still for a while. Hand-warmers can be really helpful, too.

Last but not least: use the bathroom before you head out, or know where one is nearby!

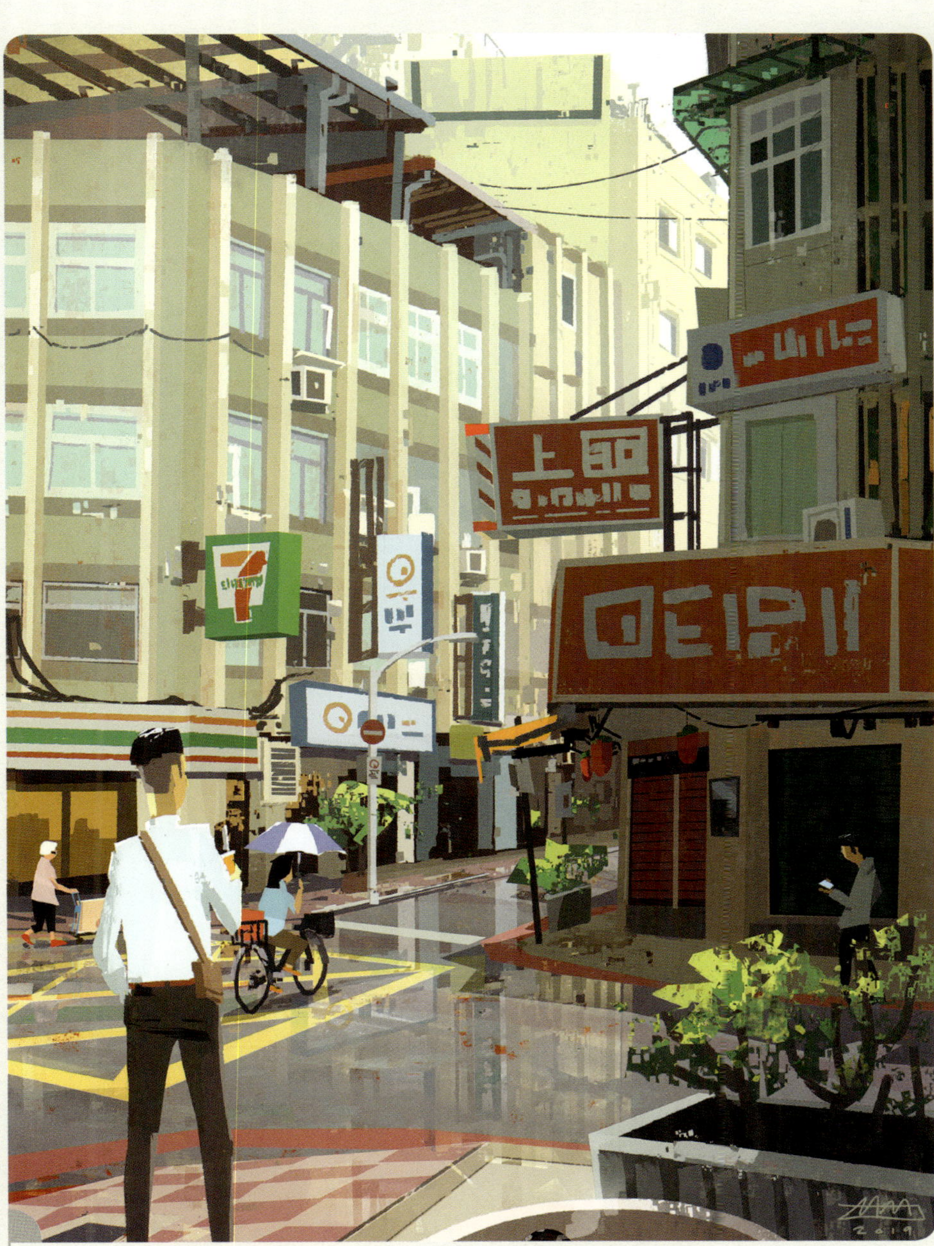

Taipei, 2019: I painted this study over coffee, a couple of mornings in a row

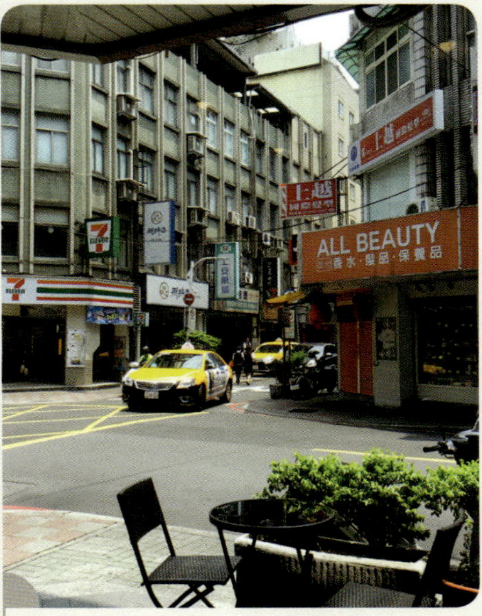

This wasn't the best view around... but it was the best view from the comfy table at the coffee shop downstairs

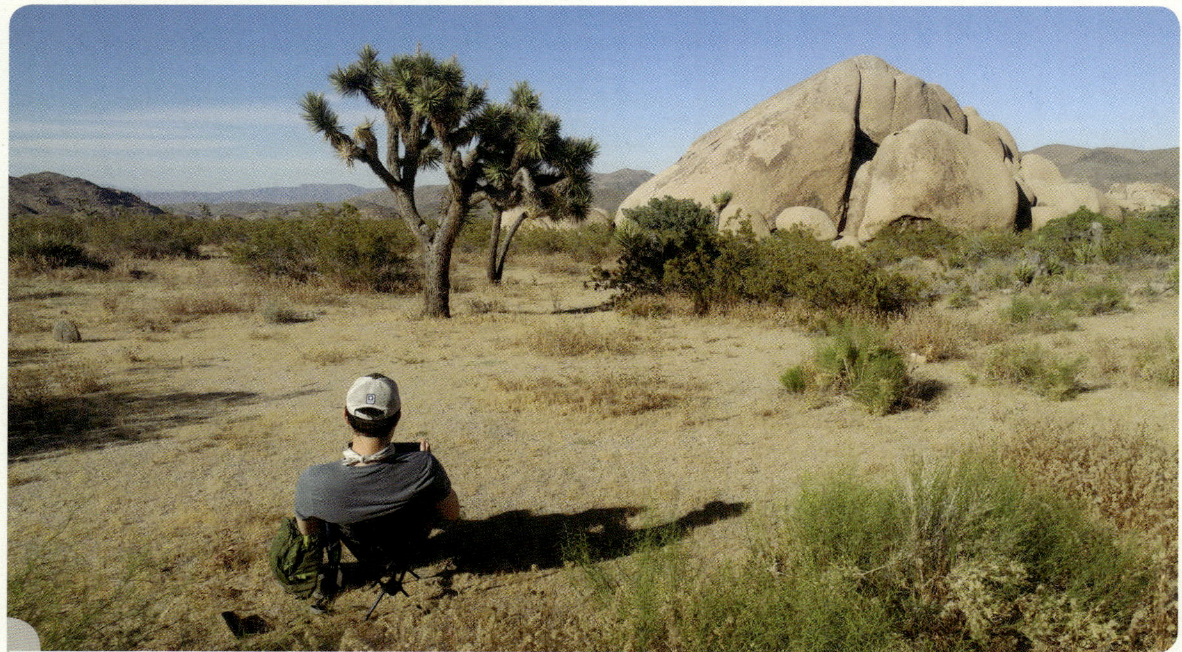

This is more or less what it looks like when I'm painting these days

SCREEN VERSUS SUN

'How do you deal with all the glare?' is probably the question I get asked most about plein-air painting on the iPad. Anyone who has tried to use a smartphone outside on a summer's day will know that screens and sunshine can be a frustrating combination.

Some days are worse than others, but mostly I just try not to let a little glare bother me. Look for spots that will be fully shaded for a couple of hours – check which way is west, as the sun will be moving in that general direction. Have some sort of cover above you, such as a tree canopy, to help reduce glare from the sky. Some painters take a small umbrella along; you can find a variety online by searching for 'plein-air umbrella'. Make sure to crank your iPad's brightness all the way up and disable the 'True Tone' feature if your iPad has it (under **SETTINGS > DISPLAY & BRIGHTNESS**).

Another helpful accessory is a matte screen protector. In addition to reducing glare, these paper-like covers give the iPad's surface a little more resistance, making it feel more like drawing on paper. Just make sure to order the correct cover for the size and year of your iPad, and carefully follow the application instructions to avoid any bubbling under the surface.

Despite all this, though, you may still encounter some glare when plein-air painting. I have found it's best to focus on picking the best colours and colour temperatures based on what is visible on the screen. If this results in the painting being too washed out, you can adjust the contrast and make some quick colour fixes if needed once you are indoors again.

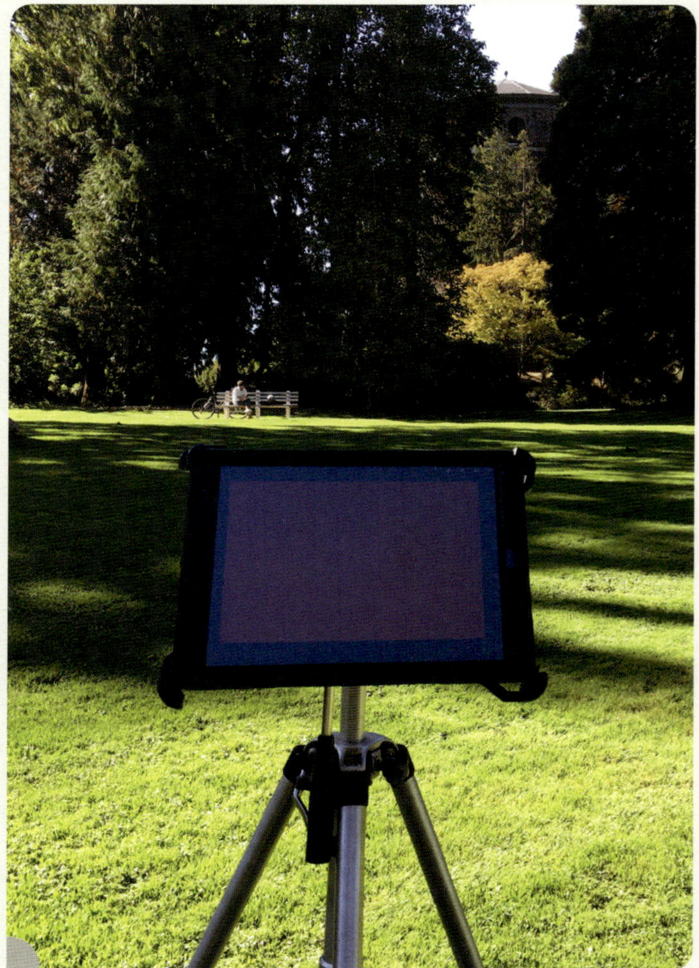

Here, I have set up far enough under a tree to give me a couple of hours of shade

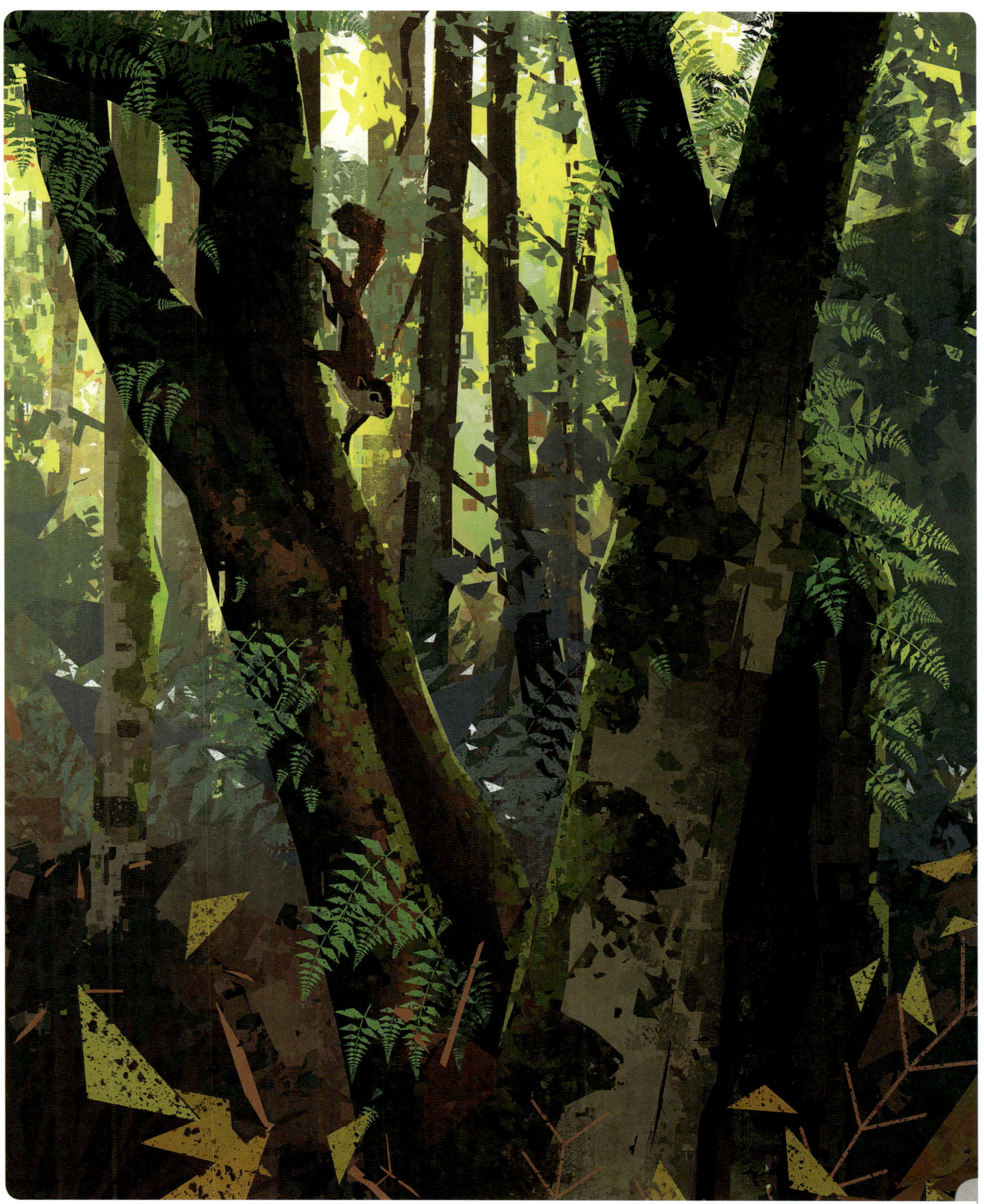

Just a Tree, 2019: observing and understanding the light can make a simple scene interesting

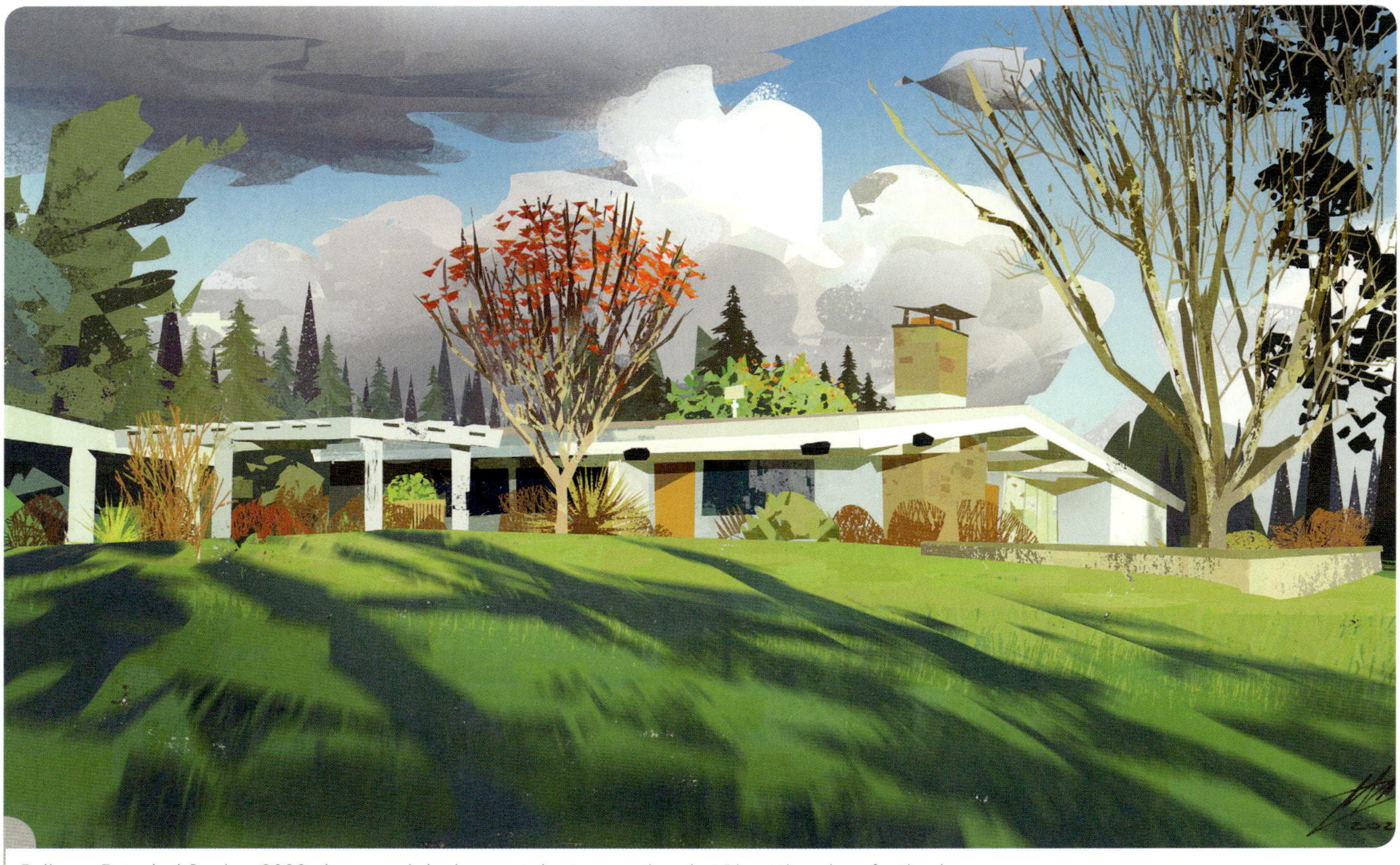

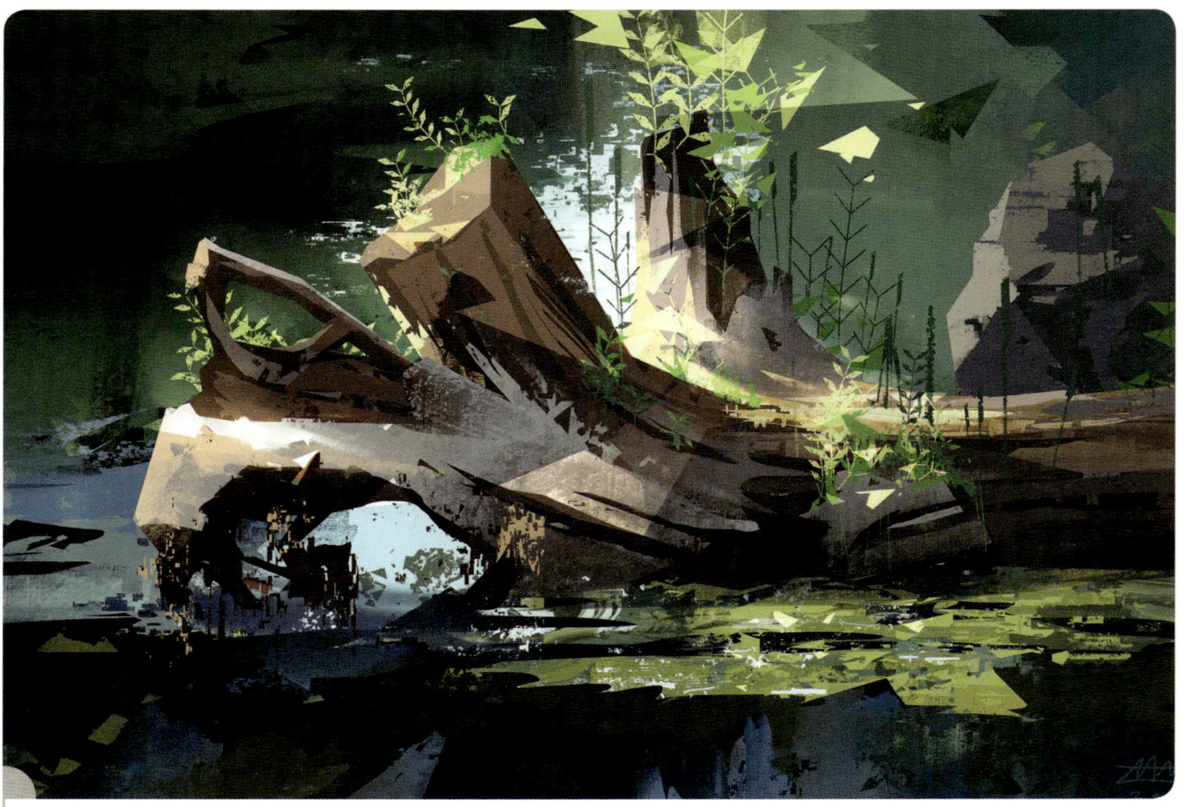

Bellevue Botanical Garden, 2020: the ground shadows got shorter over time, but I kept them long for the drama

Just a Log, 2019: you don't need to paint everything you can see – try focusing on something small

PLEIN-AIR OBSERVATION

I believe the best plein-air paintings come from the deepest understanding of the scene. What's the big story of this place? How does it make you feel? Where is the light strongest? How is the atmosphere affecting colour and value? Where are the big temperature shifts from warm to cool? How do all of these ideas relate to each other – what has the biggest impact, what's more subtle, or how cool is one shadow relative to another?

Achieving this careful, *relative* understanding of a scene takes time and close, thoughtful observation. I have often made the mistake of simply copying what I am seeing, without trying to really understand it. At other times I have focused too much on rendering, at the expense of observation. I still sometimes get caught up drawing the individual things in a scene, instead of painting my impressions of the scene as a whole. These things happen! Once I realize this, I make myself stop painting for a few minutes and simply study the scene again. Patient observation is the heart of plein-air painting.

Of course, the other challenge is that the scene itself will change over time. Your observations after an hour can sometimes be very different from your observations at the start. The first step is to recognize what has changed – otherwise, you can end up stuck chasing your observations, as the scene shifts faster than you can paint. Try to capture your initial lighting impressions early and loosely, then take stock periodically to see if the light has changed significantly. Taking a photo for reference when you start can help. Once you understand what has changed, simply decide whether you like it better or not. The more you understand, the more you can selectively incorporate the changing light into your painting. You just need to decide if the result is believable or not.

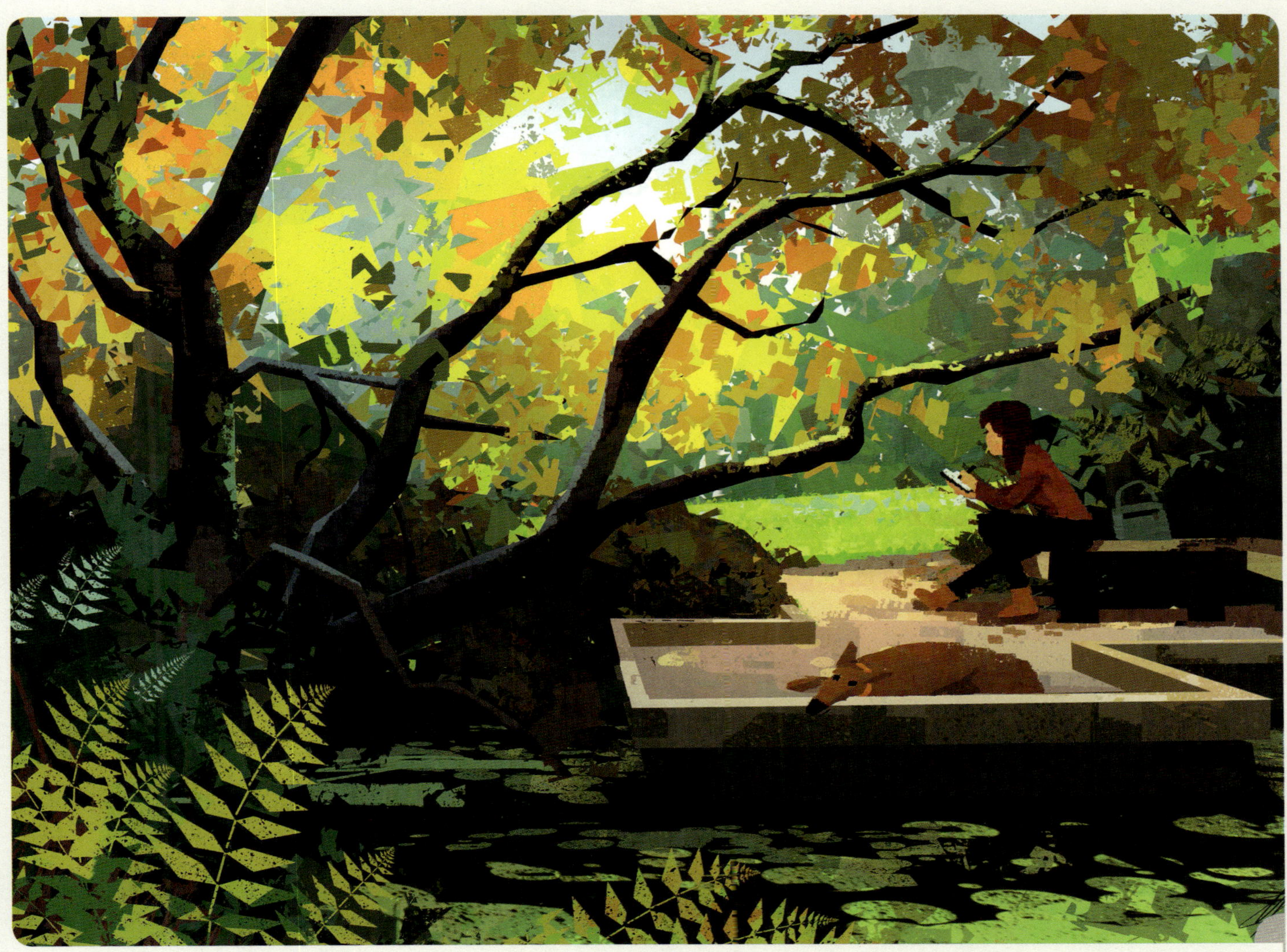

Arboretum, 2019: again, plein-air painting is all about capturing colour and light

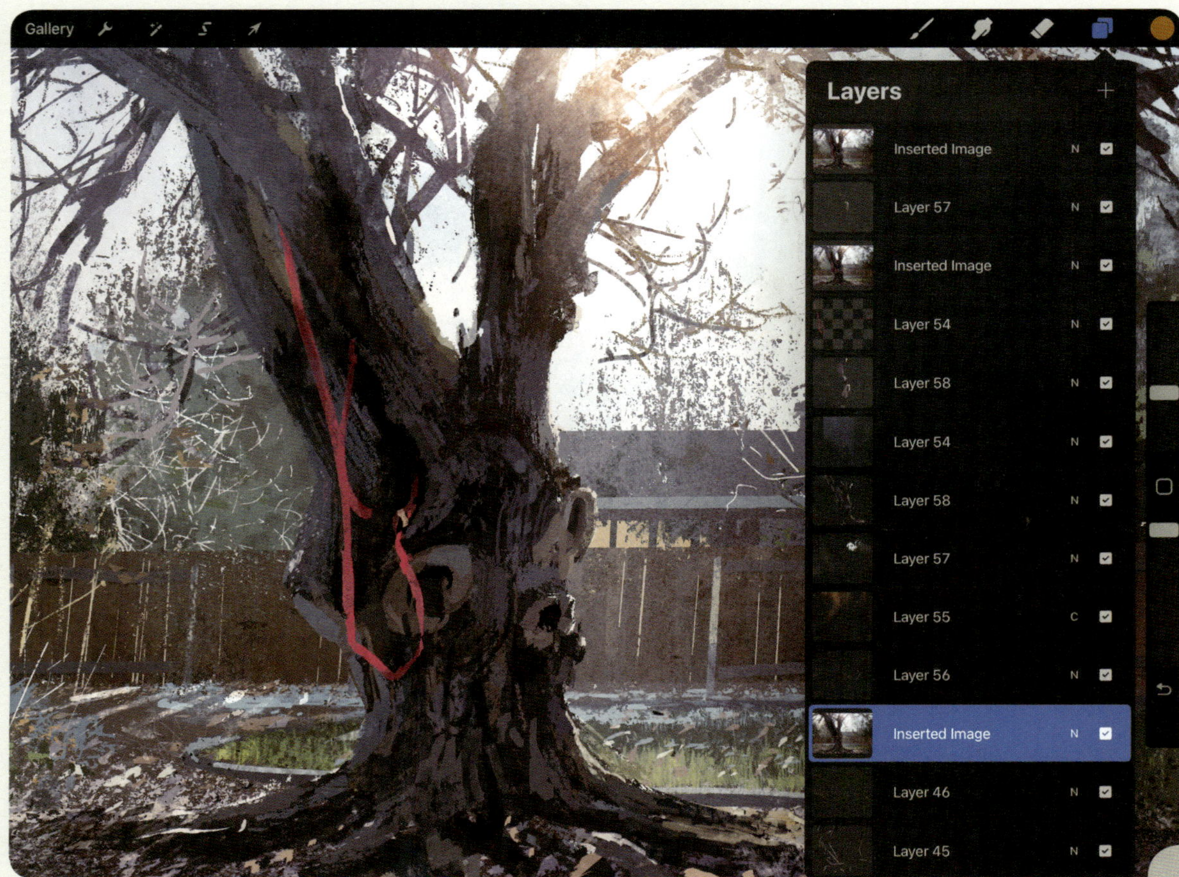

Sometimes I use layers as a way to try new ideas; once I'm happy, I merge them into a new combined layer using **ACTIONS > COPY CANVAS** and **PASTE**

STAY NIMBLE!

I encourage you to keep your plein-air process flexible, and your painting itself loose and malleable. Something will surprise you on almost every outing, whether it's the changing light, a car blocking your view, or a belated observation. If your approach is too rigid or tightly rendered, it can be difficult (and more frustrating) to react to these surprises. It has taken me a while to learn this, but these days I am always willing to make big changes in a painting, even late in a painting session, and even if it means getting rid of something I thought I liked. I don't try to 'finish' any part before the whole, and I expect to have to fix some things as my understanding of the scene builds over time.

Some Procreate tools can help with big adjustments – you can quickly select elements to reposition them, scale them, and transform perspective. Similarly, you can use the Hue, Saturation, and Curves adjustments on a selection or layer to easily react to colour and value issues in your piece. It is common for me to revisit some colour choices in this way as my observations deepen.

On the flip side, if you're not careful, digital conveniences can make your painting harder to adjust! The biggest culprits are layers and blending modes. When you use too many layers and try to keep them organized, especially with blending modes in the mix, it becomes tedious to make big changes across all those layers. This will either slow you down or discourage you from making those changes at all. Either way, your tools have become a hindrance instead of a help. I recommend frequently flattening down layers as you go, or simply being willing to 'break' your layer stack by painting on top of it all.

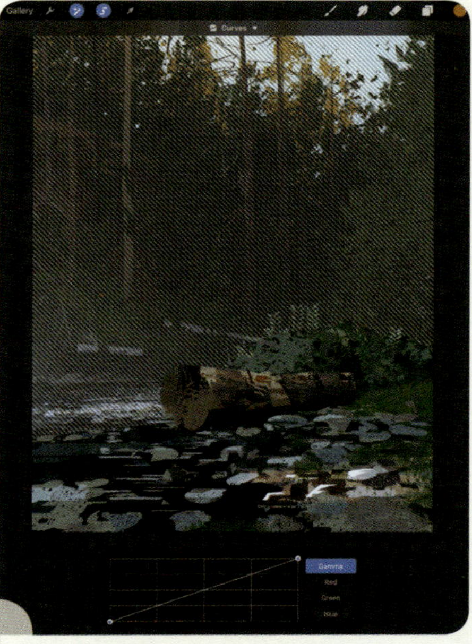

Using the Curves tool to adjust the values in my ground layer

VIRTUAL PLEIN AIR

You can also practise landscape painting virtually. In the last several years, artists have been using mapcrunch.com to find and paint random Google Street View locations from around the world. I did a lot of this 'virtual plein-air' painting during the early part of the Covid pandemic. Being able to 'walk' around a Street View location to find your own composition makes it feel a little more like the real thing than a photo study might. I also really enjoy the random and unstaged nature of the scenery that Street View provides.

Virtual plein-air painting can be a great way to build confidence and refine your observational painting workflow. Since you don't have to worry about the light changing, you can use virtual plein-air studies to explore new rendering techniques, experiment with stylization, and study different subject matter you might not normally encounter. Just keep in mind that any time you are painting from a photo, you are limited to the colour and light information that the camera was able to capture. Cameras can't capture as wide a range of light and dark as our eyes can, and colours that we might perceive richly in person can often appear muted or be lost altogether in a photo. On site, you can feel, hear, and smell the location – all of these senses can subconsciously contribute to how a scene makes you feel, and how you express that in your painting. Still, I recommend virtual plein-air studies – they have really helped me hone my painting process. Just don't forget to go out and enjoy real plein-air painting, too!

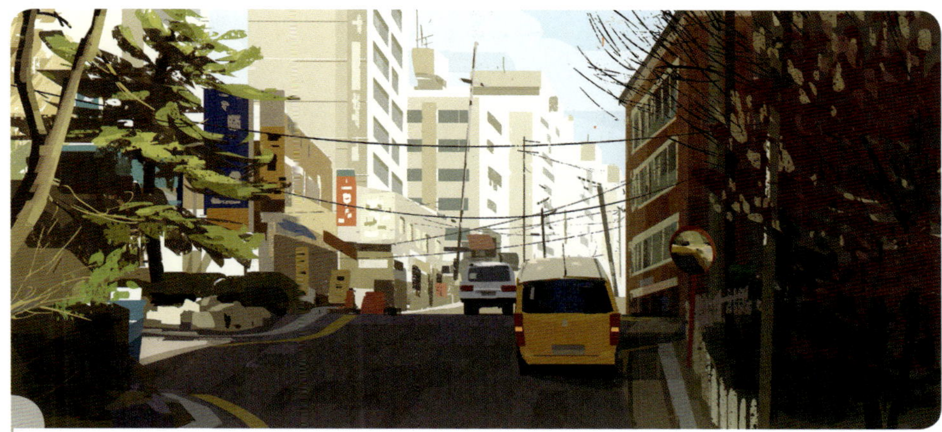

Seoul, South Korea, 2022: in th s one I challenged myself to only use a plain, flat brush – very valuable practice

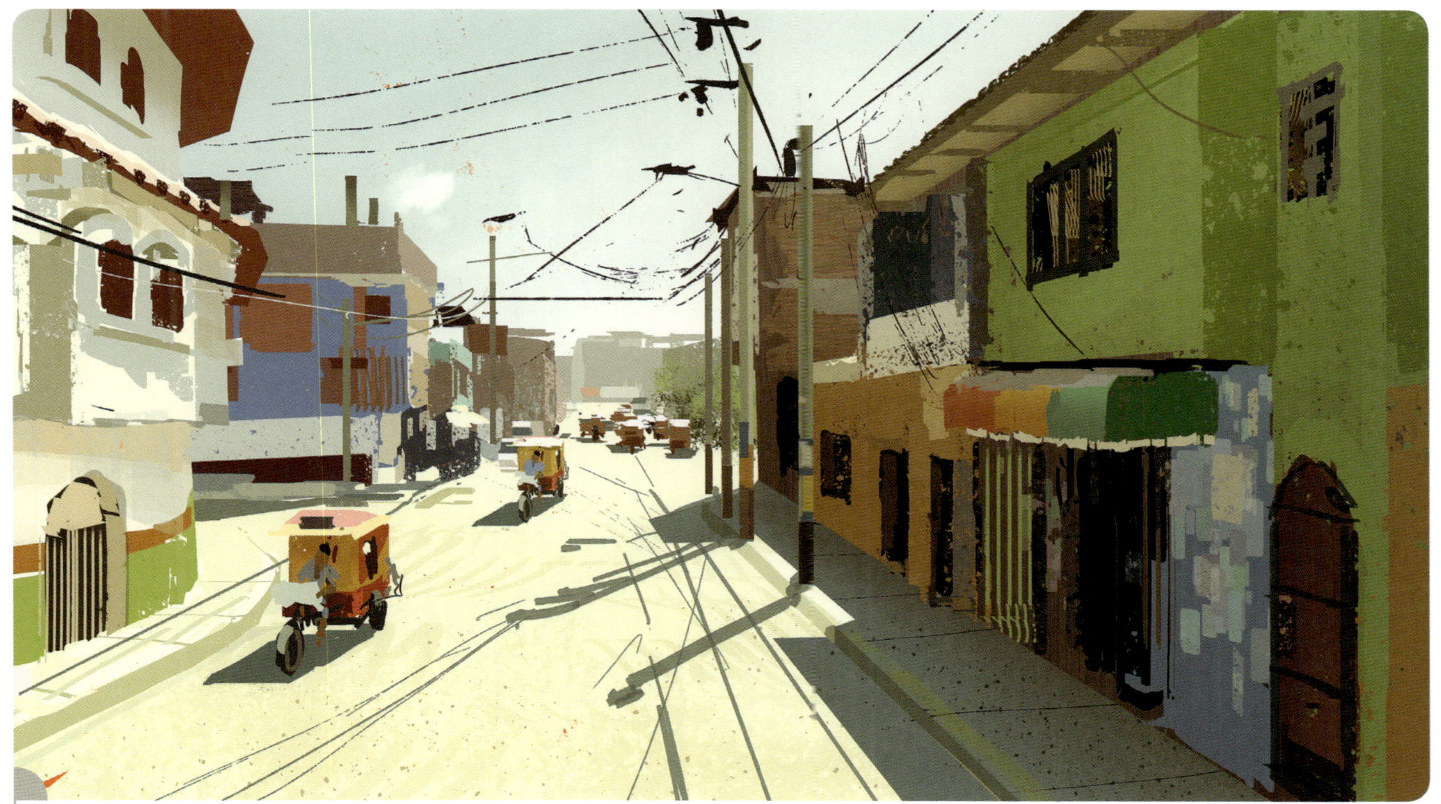

Tumbes, Peru, 2021: I painted this one for a class demo and I think it's one of my favourites so far

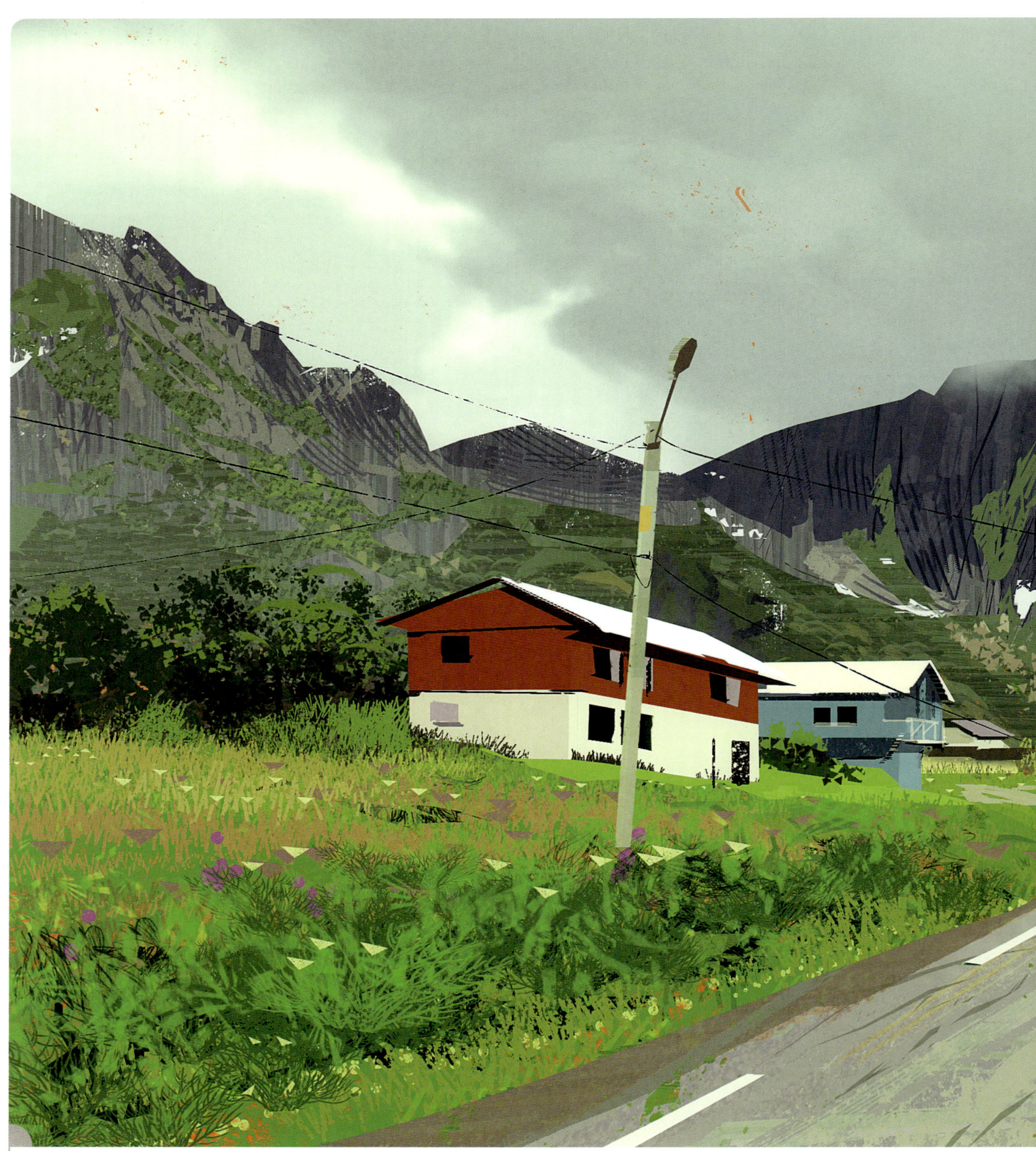

Senjahopen, Norway, 2021: one of the first virtual plein-air paintings I did during lockdown at the start of 2021

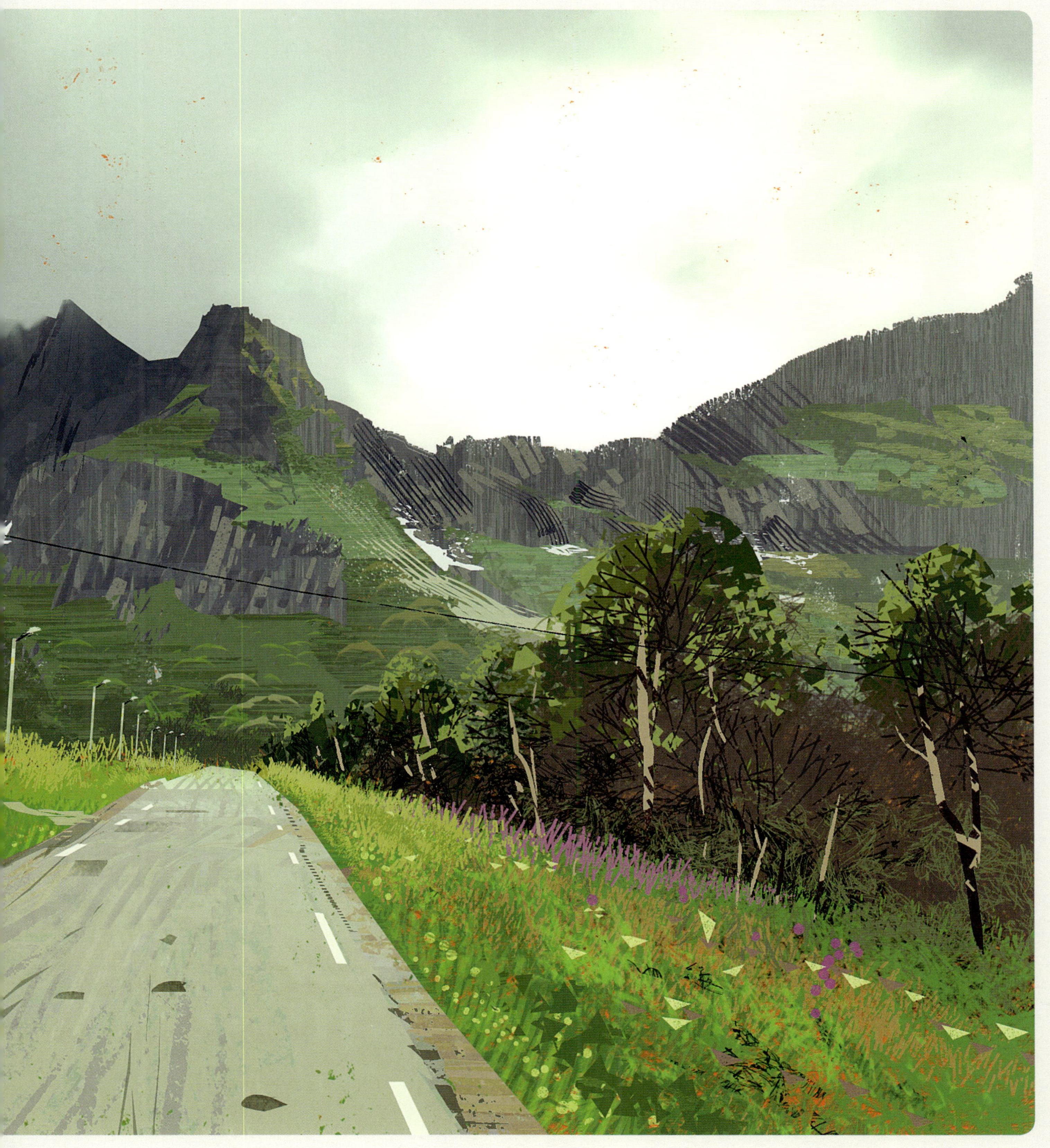

FROM PLEIN AIR TO IMAGINATION

Plein-air painting can help you improve your imaginative work, too. You will become more accurate in your colour choices, value structure, and perspective with time and practice. As you learn what makes an observational painting feel believable, you will learn to look for the same things in your imaginative work.

A big part of painting is problem-solving and plein air is a great way to practise how you solve different problems in your work. I am always looking for ways to communicate more with fewer moves. When I find a shorthand for something

I'm happy with in my plein-air paintings, I can carry that shorthand idea directly into my imaginative and professional work. For example, how I use a certain brush to indicate the grooves of tree bark, or the way I paint the shadowed sides of distant mountains as a single pattern. I find it is easier to arrive at these solutions when I'm doing plein-air paintings, because I'm studying the subject directly and the only goal is to capture it well. When working on a challenging illustration or concept piece, it's great to be able to draw on this existing library of techniques that I have honed while plein-air painting.

Plein-air painting can also train us to use reference more effectively in our imaginative work. The more we are able to observe in the reference, just like we do during plein-air study, the better we can apply and adjust those observations to fit our own painting. I will often work from one piece of reference for overall mood and lighting, and other pieces of reference for the actual subject matter in my piece. With this approach, you draw and compose the scene guided by your subject-matter reference where needed, but you paint the light and atmosphere of the scene guided by your lighting reference.

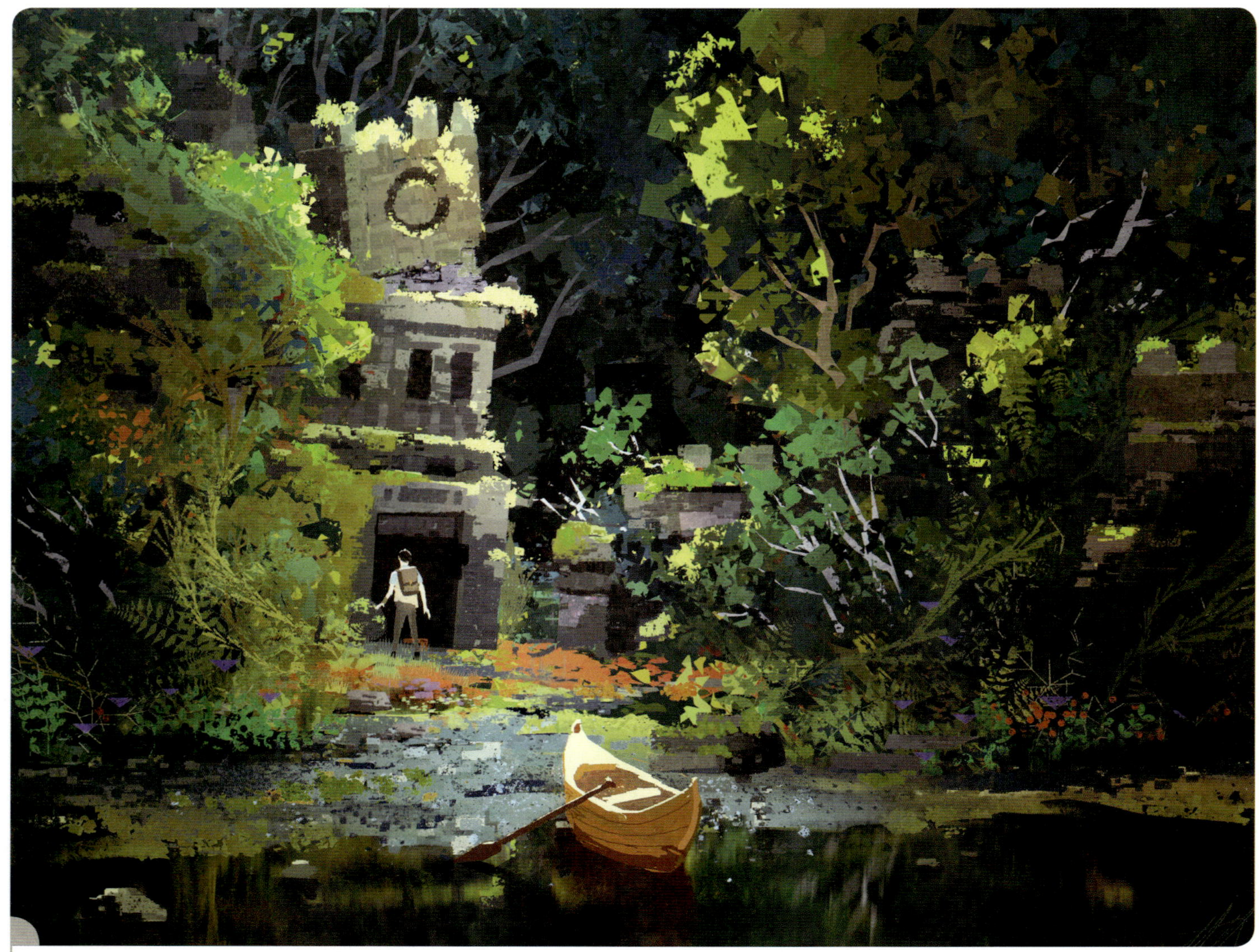

Exploring the Ruins, 2019: all of the custom brushes I used for the foliage here were first developed on plein-air painting trips

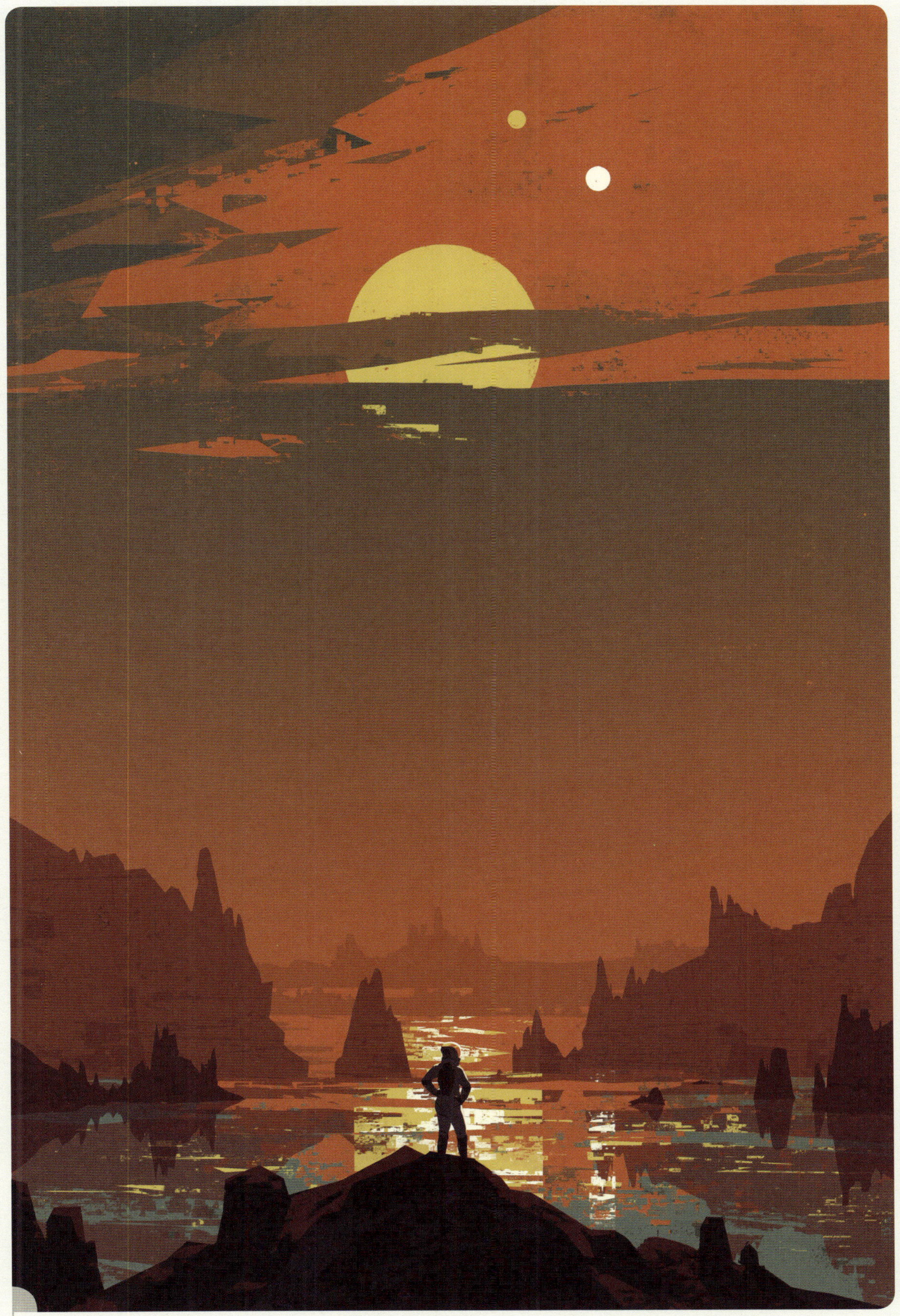

Praxima, 2019: in this illustration, I applied techniques I first found through plein-air painting canyon environments

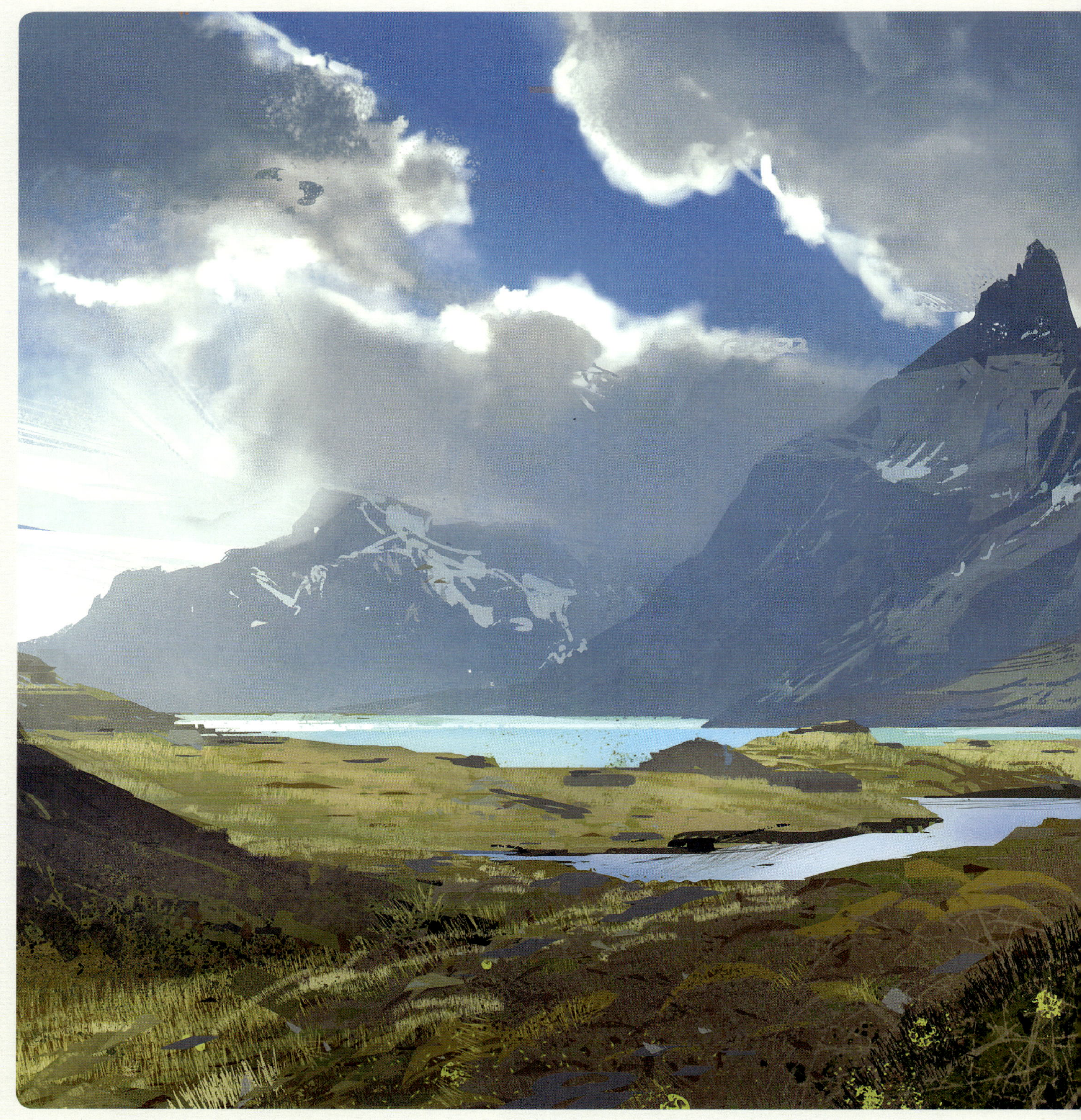

NOW GO AND PAINT!

If it is your first time painting digital landscapes or trying plein-air painting, I encourage you to take it slow and be patient with yourself. Keep your subjects and compositions simple, and focus on the fun. The way I see it, if you are outdoors painting somewhere beautiful, you have already won. This book contains a wealth of useful information to help you on your landscape-painting journey. You don't need to absorb it all at once, though. With a book like this, I recommend reading

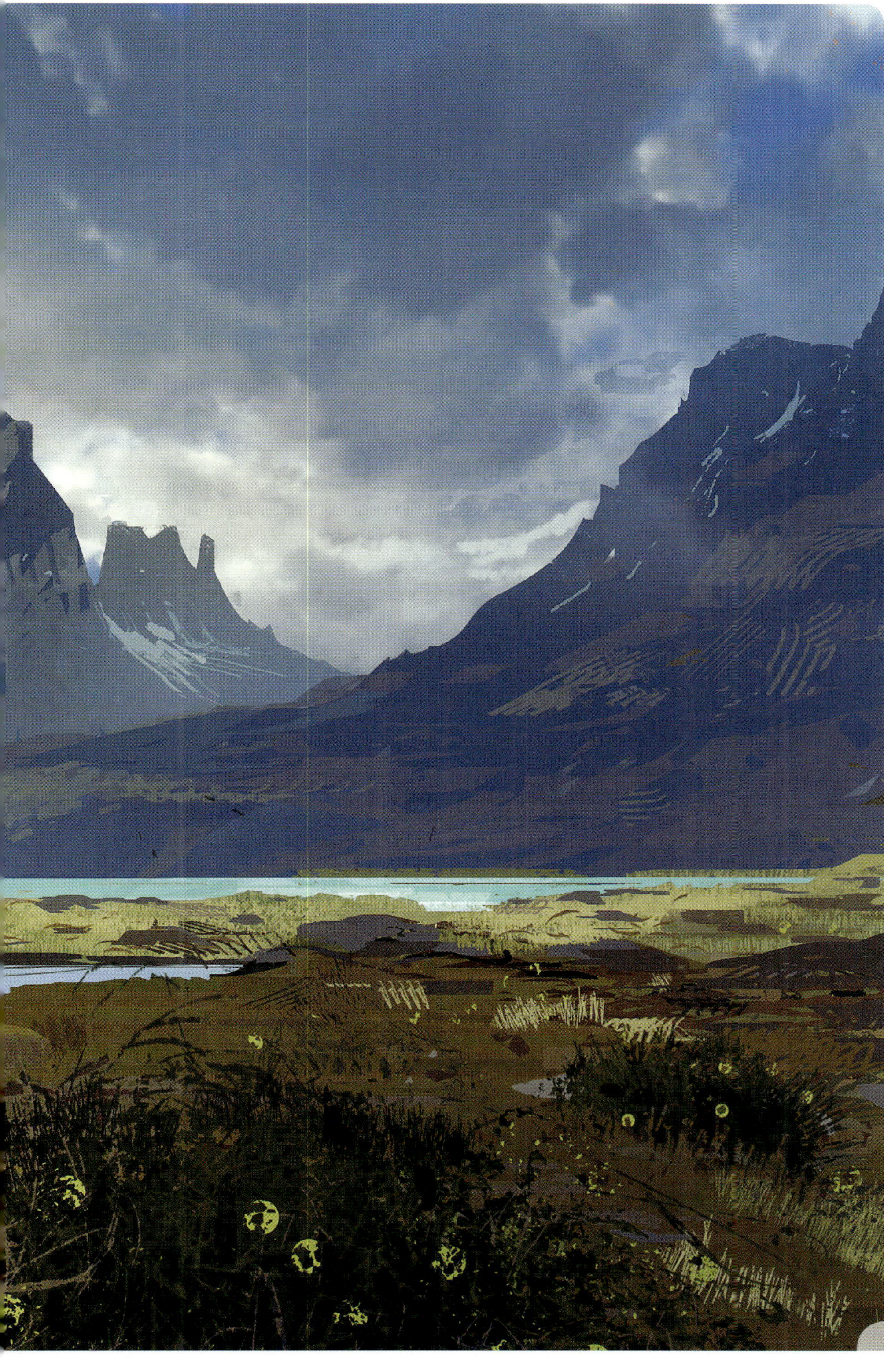

Torres del Paine National Park, 2022:
this is a landscape I painted based on photos
I took and my memory of the light

a little bit, then going out to paint, then reading a little more. This way, each time you paint, you will be armed with a few more ideas for things to try. Perhaps on each outing, you can experiment with the techniques of a different artist featured in these pages. Each time you return to this book, you will have a fresh memory of your last painting experience to help deepen your understanding of these lessons.

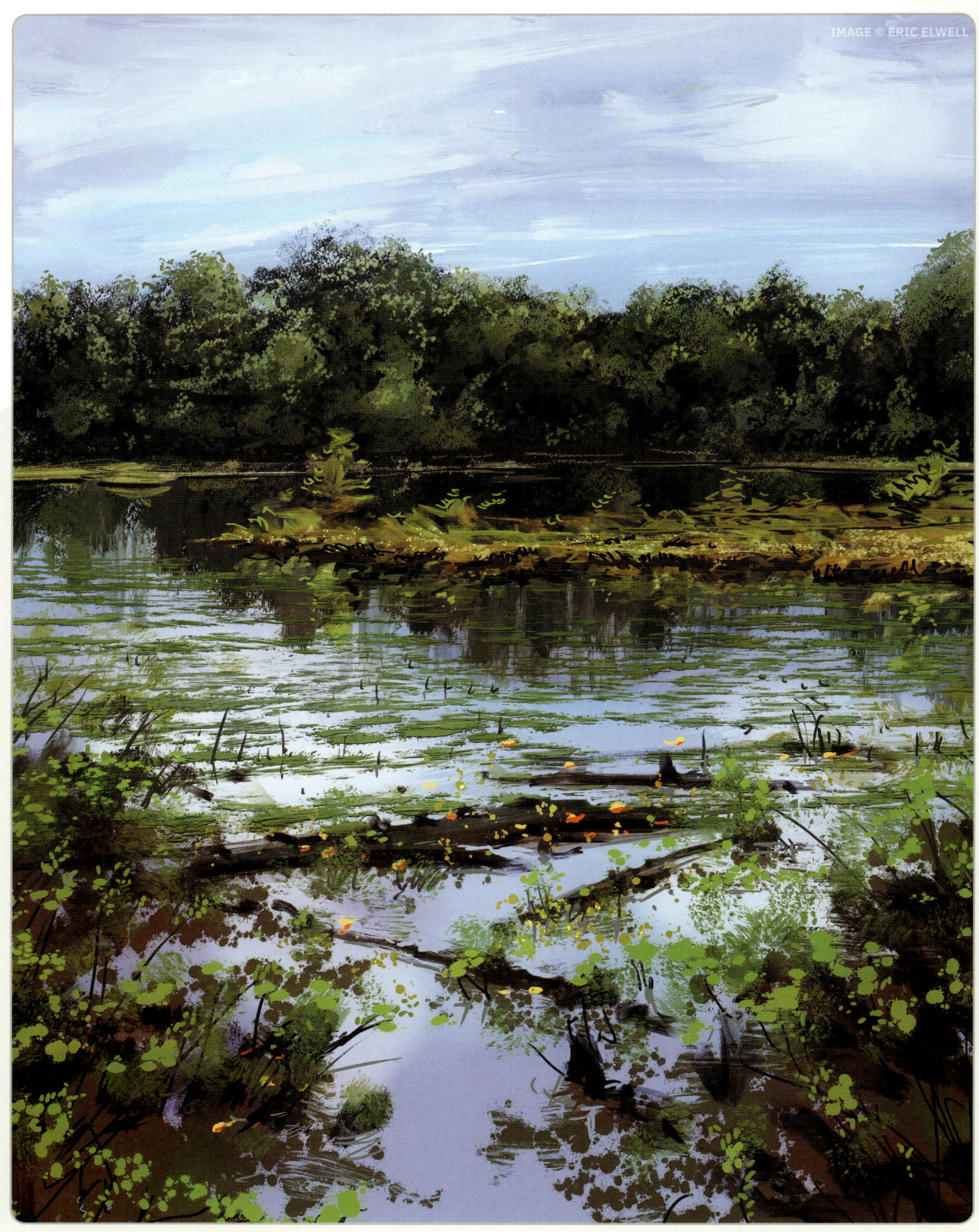
IMAGE © ERIC ELWELL

TUTORIALS

HOUGHTON AUTUMN

BY ERIC ELWELL

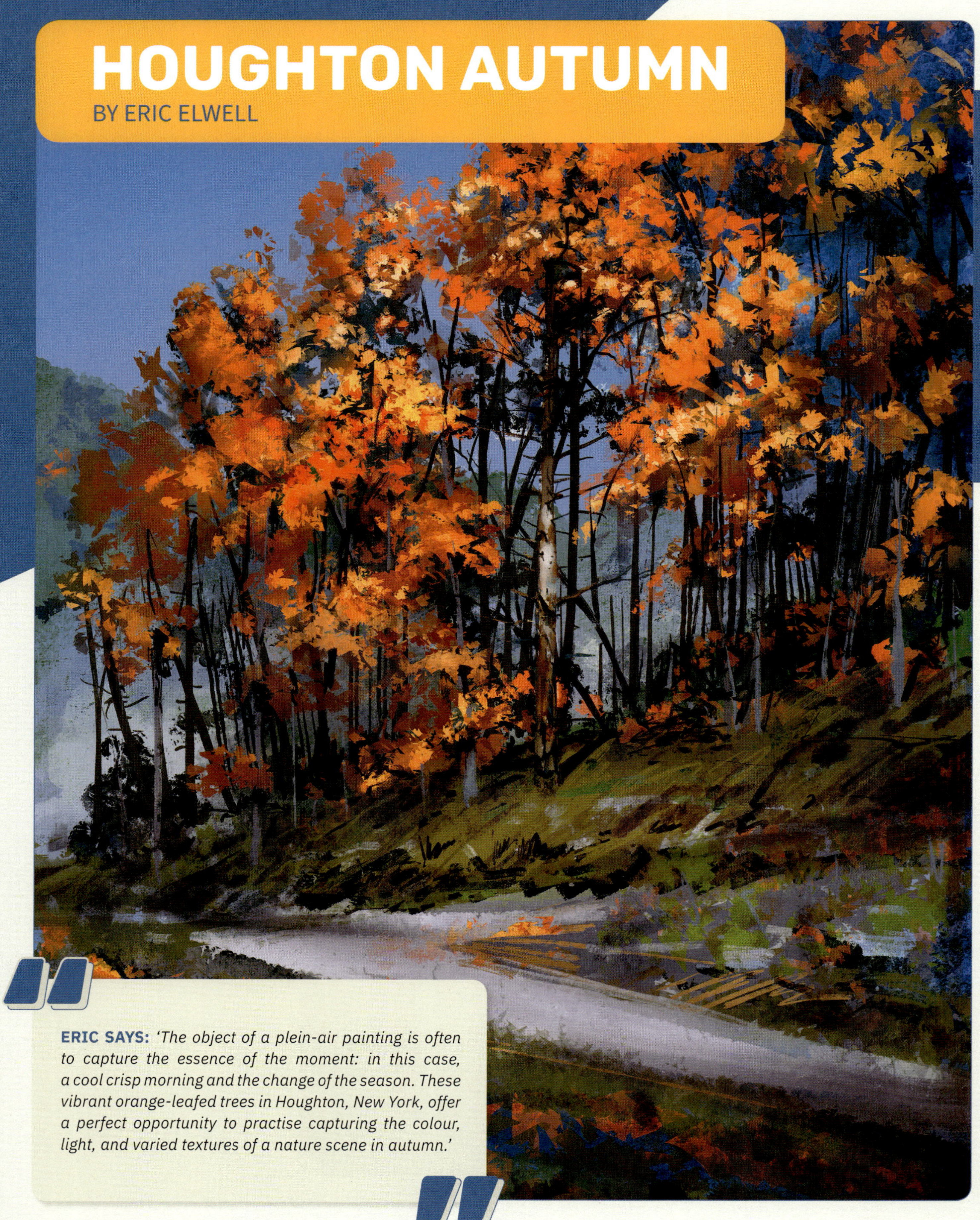

ERIC SAYS: 'The object of a plein-air painting is often to capture the essence of the moment: in this case, a cool crisp morning and the change of the season. These vibrant orange-leafed trees in Houghton, New York, offer a perfect opportunity to practise capturing the colour, light, and varied textures of a nature scene in autumn.'

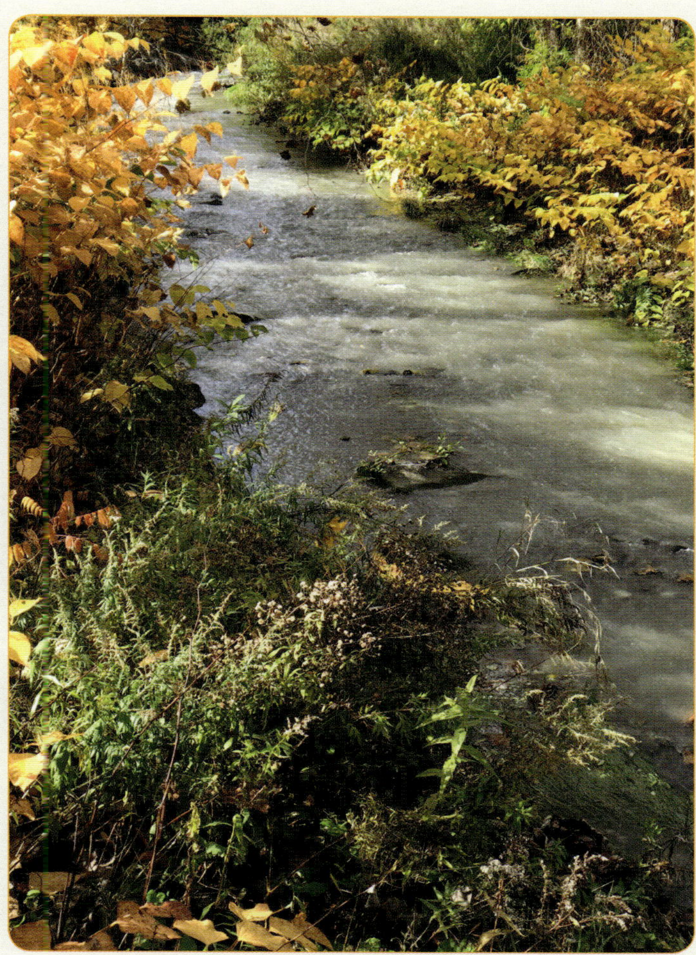

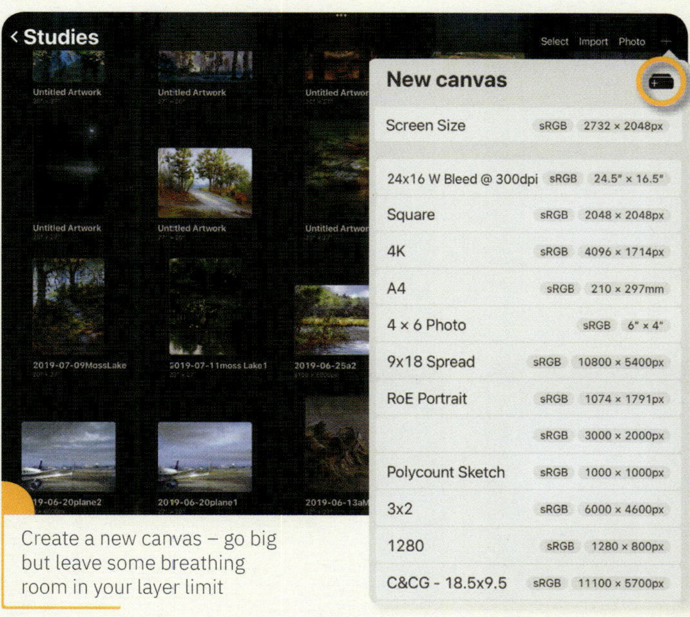

Create a new canvas – go big but leave some breathing room in your layer limit

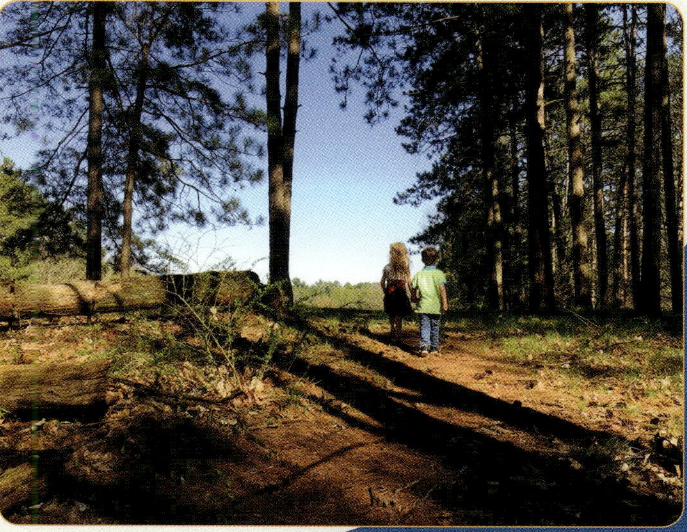

01

You have a location and you are ready to paint. Great! First you need to set up your canvas for a successful session. If you would like to see your painting as a fine-art print, you will need to increase the canvas size. However, in order to ensure a smooth and responsive experience, Procreate limits the number of layers relative to the canvas size. On a first-generation iPad Pro, a canvas 27 inches tall × 20 inches wide, at 300 dpi, will allow for 7 layers. That is enough space to crop and print, and 7 layers are all you will need for this project. So, select the New Canvas icon from the top right and set its size and resolution.

02

You are now set up and ready to go, but you will need to stay organized to manage your layer limit. Don't let that get in the way of what is important: the painting. Block out your sky colour using the Background colour fill – tap on the 'Background Colour' layer in the Layers stack and choose a light blue. This helps keep one more layer free in your limited stack. Open the Brush Library and select **VINTAGE > RAD** – a rough, blotchy brush. On a new layer, use this to block in the foliage masses with a dark grey-blue. Make big, smooth brushstrokes using your elbow and shoulder rather than your wrist.

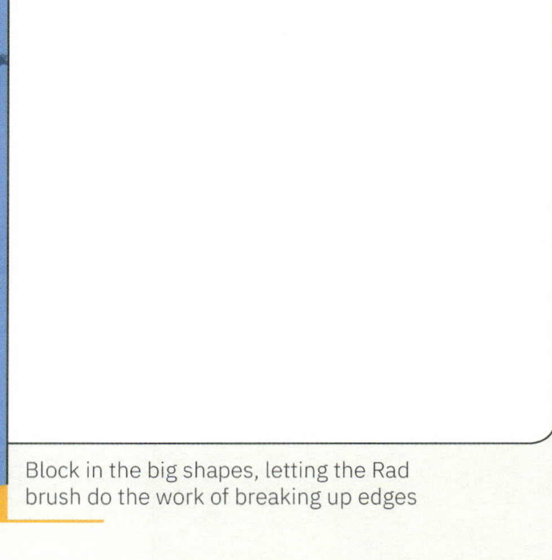

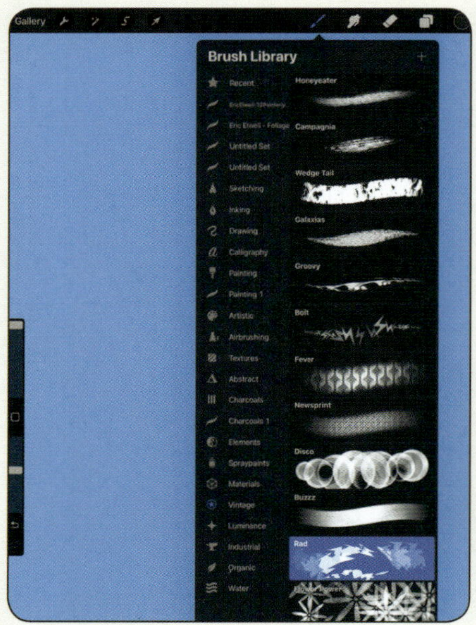

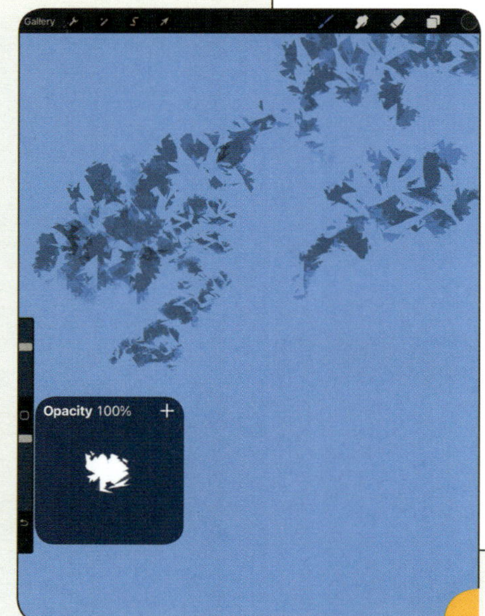

Block in the big shapes, letting the Rad brush do the work of breaking up edges

03

Vary the brush size as you block in the tree canopy. Be mindful of the opacity – too little opacity will lead to a muddy image as the layers build up. Now you need to enable 'Alpha Lock' to prevent you painting outside the layer's existing shapes and opacity. Open the Layers menu, tap the layer, and select Alpha Lock. A chequered background on the layer preview confirms the lock. If you want a shortcut, simply place two fingers on the layer in the stack and swipe to the right! Start adding patches of yellow foliage and you'll find that painting on this layer will only apply where you have previously painted.

Alpha Lock your layer to preserve edges and opacity as you add colour

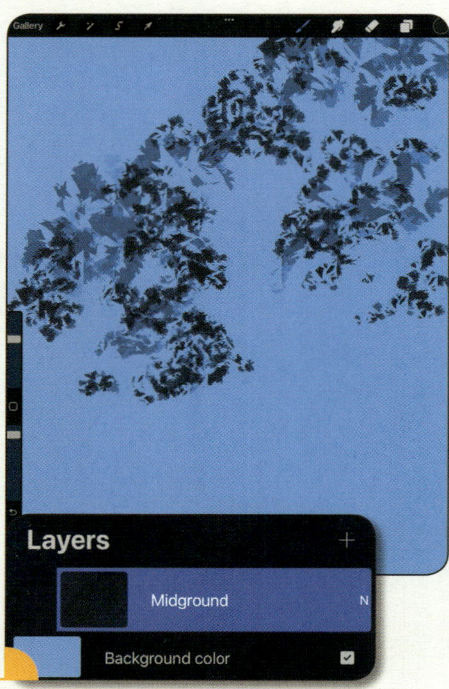

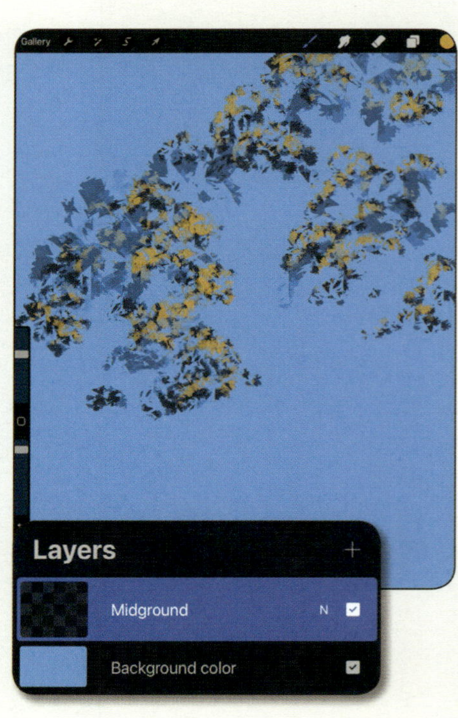

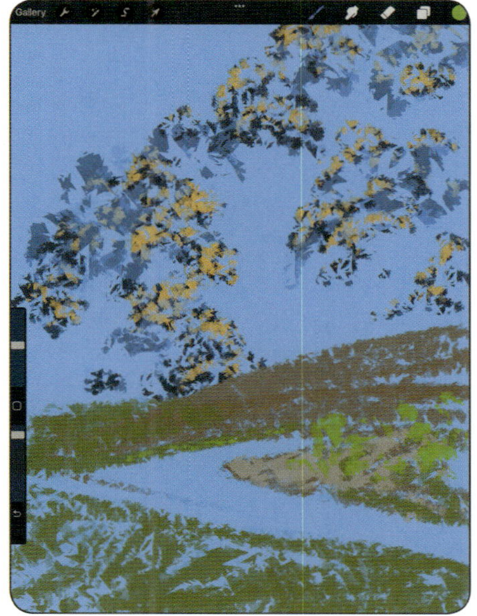
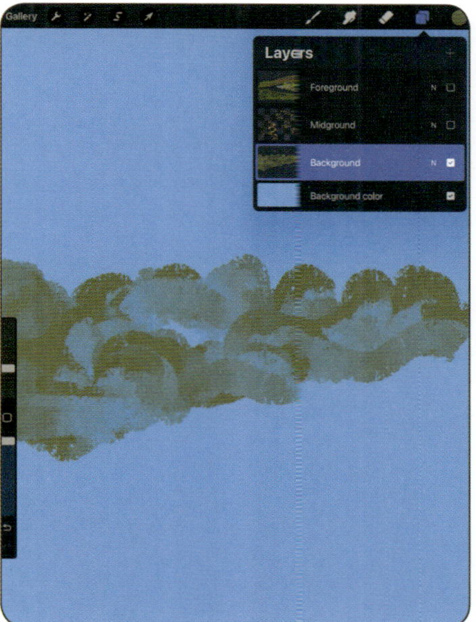
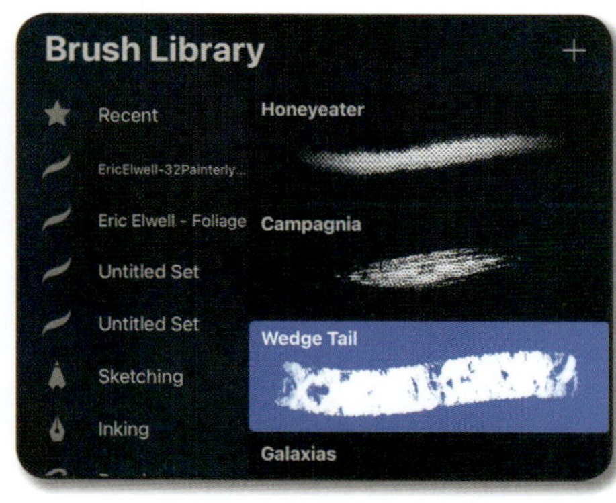

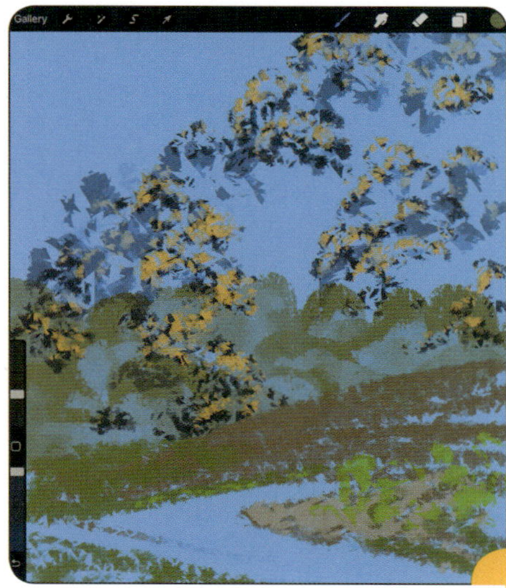

Loosely block in the foreground colours and background bushes on two new separate layers

04

Now you can develop the foreground and background to get an idea of where this composition is going. Set up a new layer for your foreground and lay in some colour: greens and browns, leaving a gap for a path. Switch to the **VINTAGE > WEDGE TAIL** brush, a textured brush with a softer edge that is perfect for the background bushes. Block those in on another layer using a medium green-brown colour. Keep your layer stack tidy and tight — it only takes three layers to separate these important elements. You can title them 'Foreground', 'Midground', and 'Background' (separate from the blue 'Background Colour' layer) as shown. The separation will come in handy as you begin to build up the sense of space.

05

You can begin to fill out the scene by painting behind the landmarks of your initial layers. Utilize your lower layers to paint behind the road and the lower half of the canvas. This allows you to separate the road and easily make adjustments. Create a new layer called 'Tree BG' between the 'Background' and 'Midground' layers. Here, fill in the shadowy back sides of the tree canopy behind the foliage you painted earlier. Utilize a rake-like brush, such as **INKING > THYLACINE**, to lay in a quick mass of tree trunks. This stage is abstract and textural, so a few quick strokes should be enough to create the general impression of tree trunks.

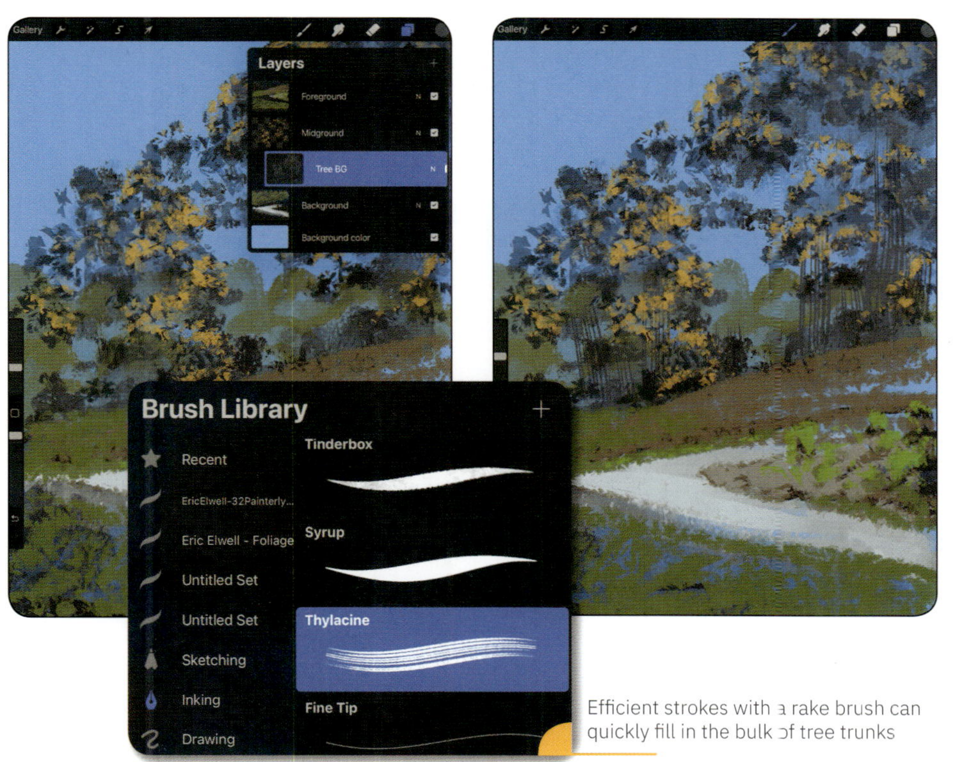

Efficient strokes with a rake brush can quickly fill in the bulk of tree trunks

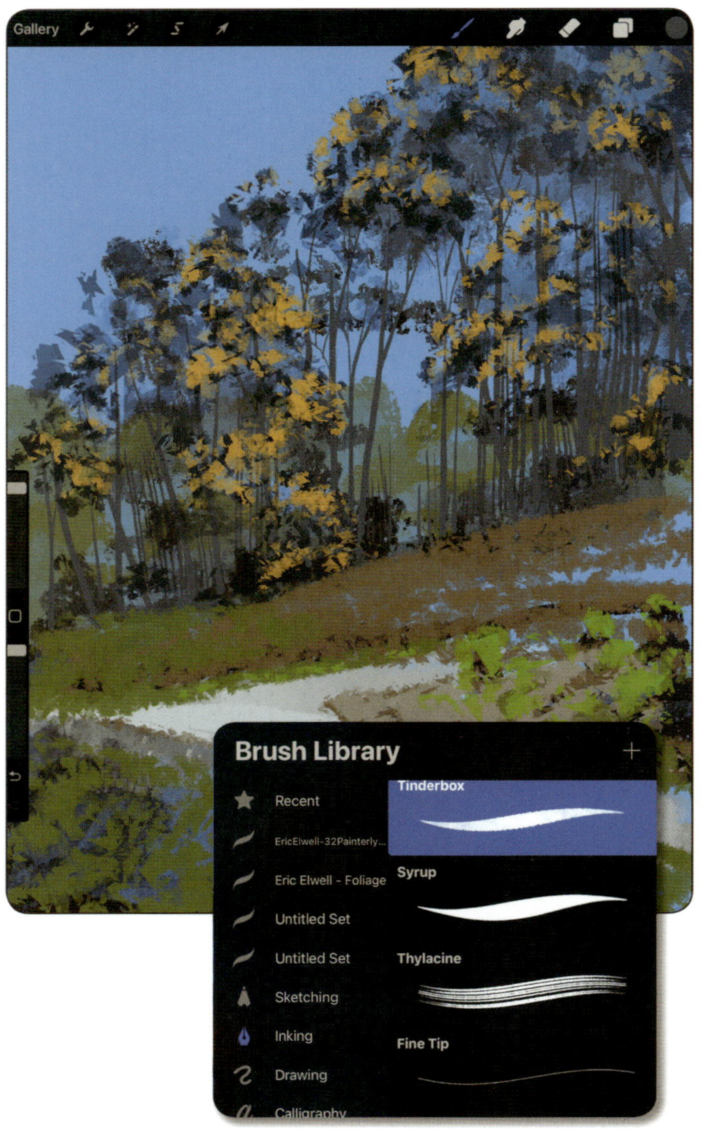

06

At this point you can start to incorporate some tighter brush strokes. Switch to an opaque inking brush, such as **INKING > TINDERBOX**, to paint in more detailed and intentional tree-trunk silhouettes. Pay attention both to what you see on site and how you are integrating new marks on the canvas with the canopy landmarks you previously painted. You may hide the other layers to view this in isolation, but avoid adding too much without all the layers visible. Painting is a balancing act of relationships between parts, so it's important to keep the whole scene in sight.

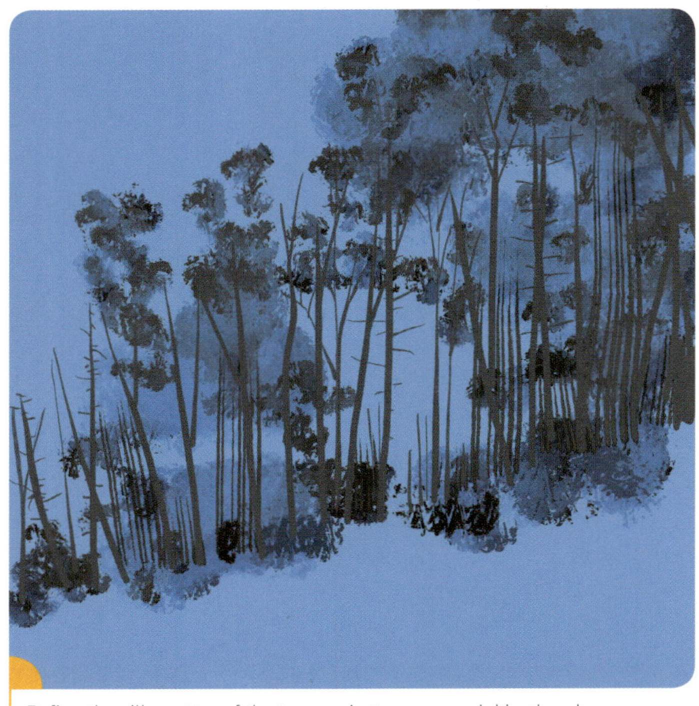

Refine the silhouettes of the trees using an opaque inking brush

07

Now you can loosely lay in an underpainting that will pop through the voids of your 'Foreground' layer. To do this, you may want to hide a few layers to isolate your background. One of the great benefits of working with digital layers is that you can adjust your underpainting at any point in the process. Add a light greyish colour to fill out the road area and some darker browns for dirt and soil. Then switch to the 'Tree BG' layer and refine the silhouettes of the foliage. A relatively rough inking brush, such as **INKING > INKA**, should do the trick; with a little arc and a flick, you can capture the gesture of branches reaching up for sunlight. You can test on the side before committing.

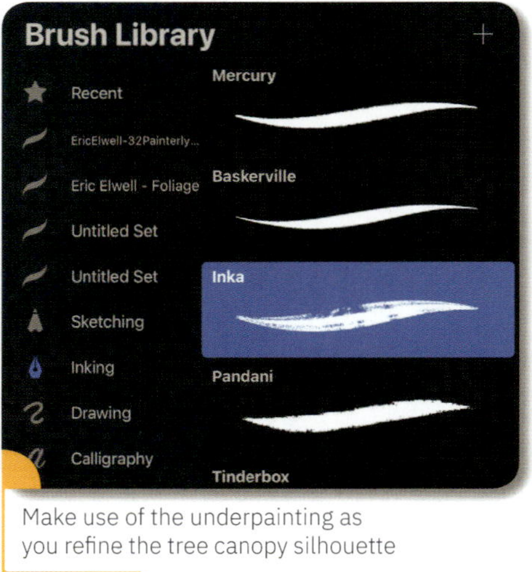

Make use of the underpainting as you refine the tree canopy silhouette

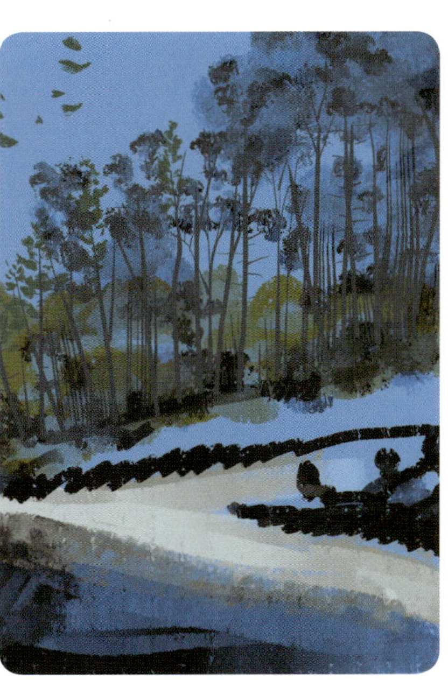

08

Continue to develop the background silhouette until you have captured the overall effect of tall autumn trees. Now that the canvas is filled with colour and the major shapes are in place, you may want to pause to assess the direction of the painting. Unhide all of your layers and evaluate the shapes and their relationships to each other. Look for shapes that could be clarified, edges that are too strong, or leading lines that guide the viewer nowhere. Evaluate where your eye is being led and where you would prefer it to be led. Determine the adjustments you would like to make.

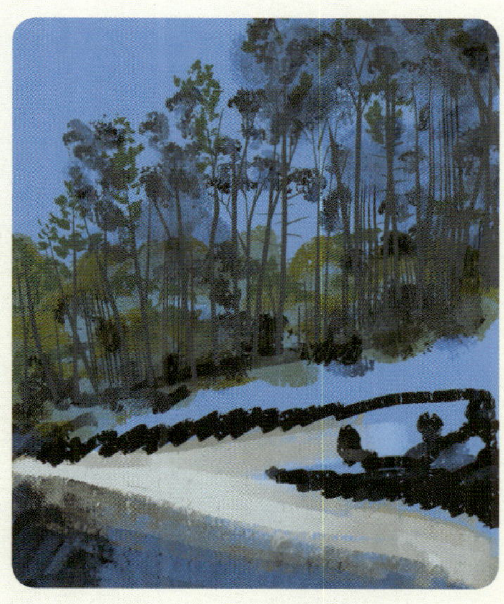

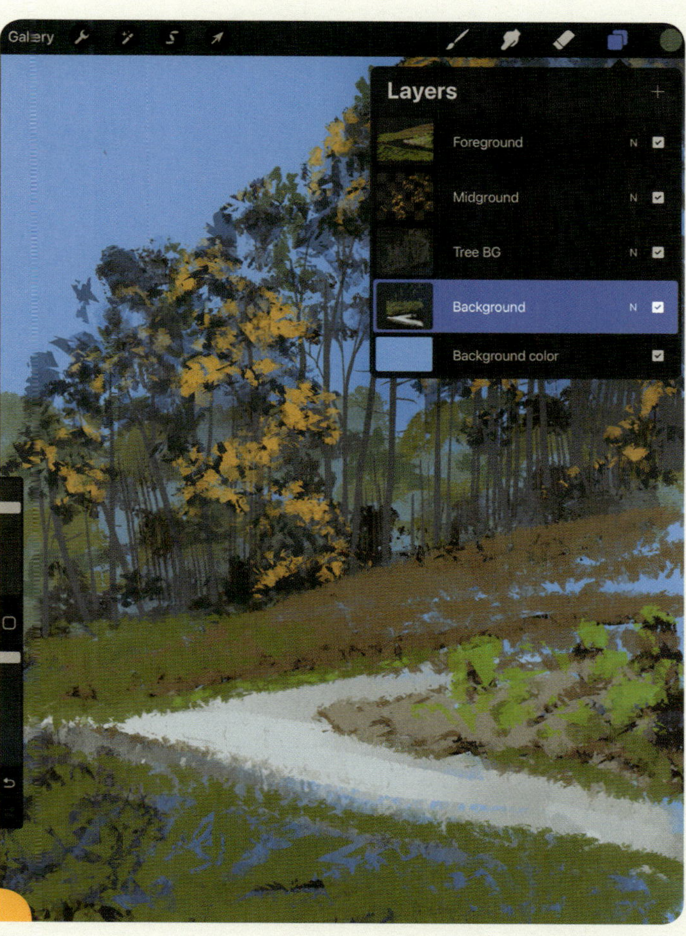

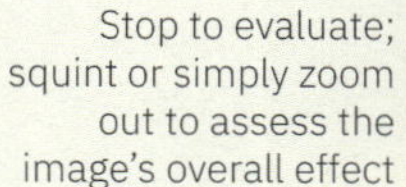

Stop to evaluate; squint or simply zoom out to assess the image's overall effect

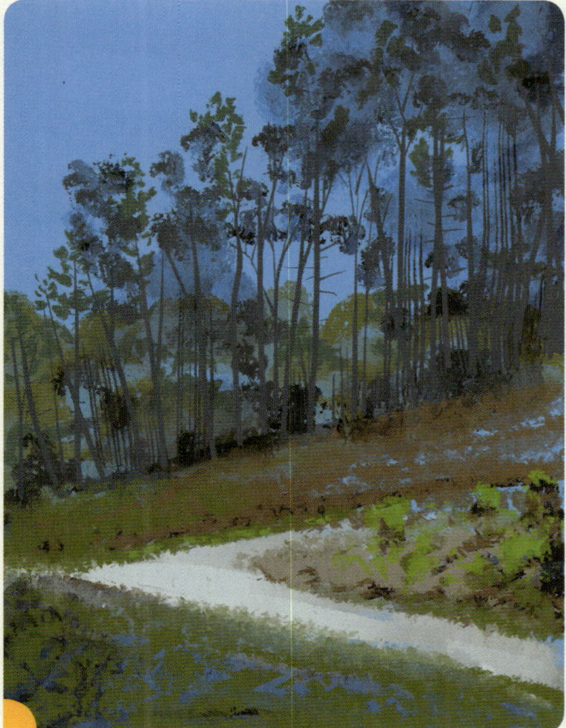

Utilize the Smudge tool with a hard-edged brush to maintain texture while you reshape and blend

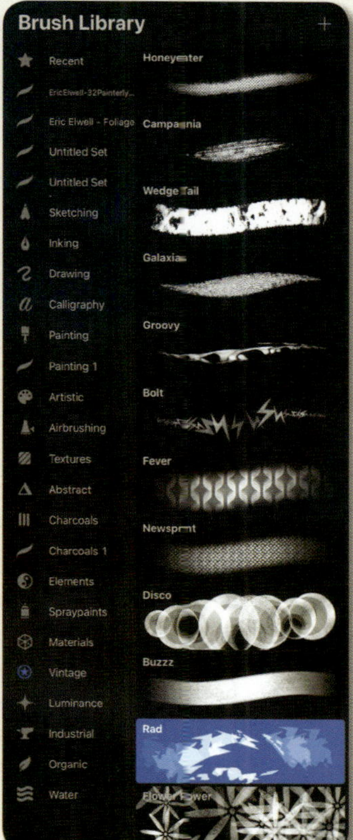

09

As you evaluate, it may be adequate simply to look for the parts that bother you and begin fixing them. However, while many paintings can be improved this way, you should always be mindful of the relationship between all the parts — that is more important than their individual details. That said, you can start by refining the shape of the road, giving it a clearer angle and better perspective. You can do this by utilizing the Smudge tool to reshape or soften edges where necessary. You might consider setting it to a brush type that has hard, broken edges, such as **VINTAGE > RAD**, to maintain textured edges as you nudge and blend.

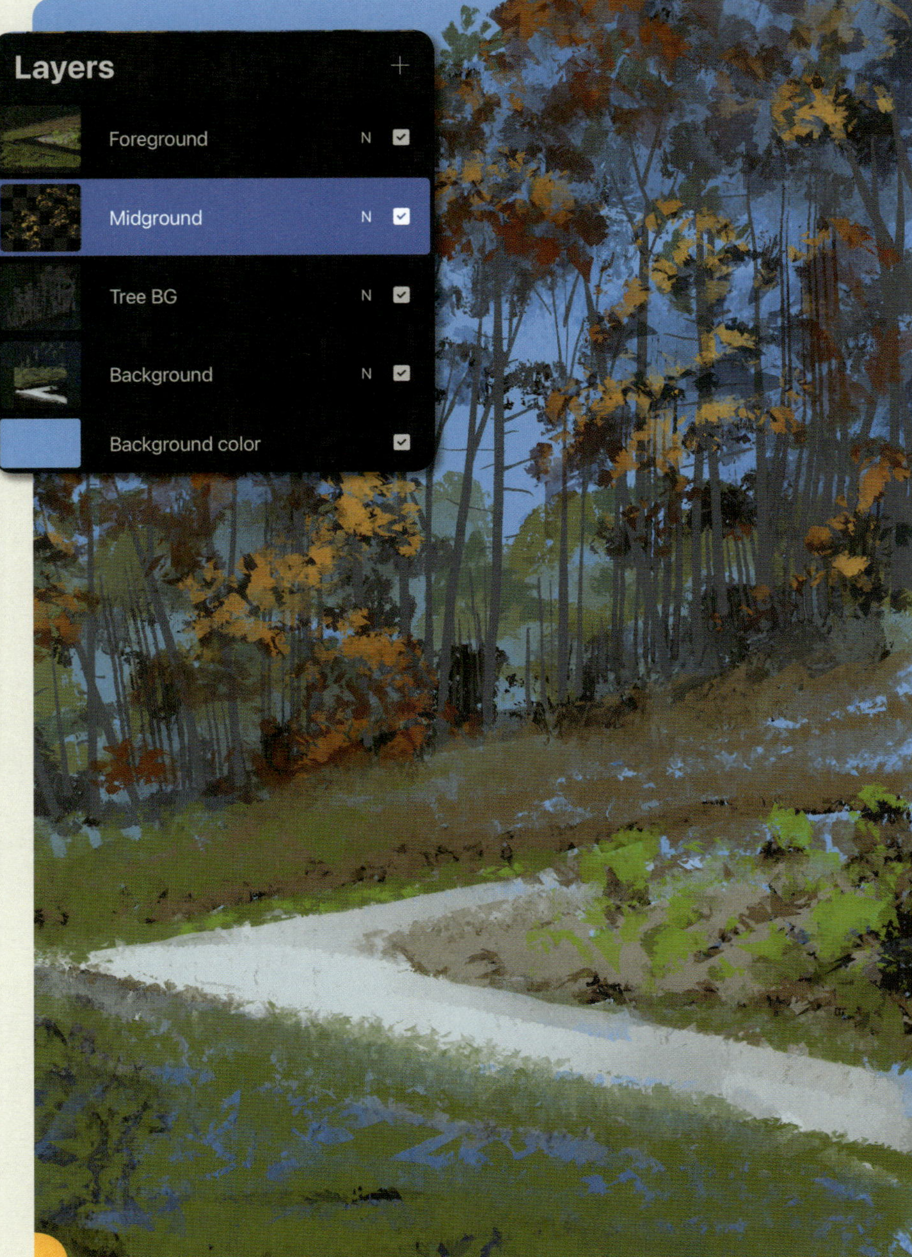

Incorporate blended colour gradations within the shapes of the trees

10

In addition to evaluating shape, you need to consider the use of colour in your composition. Those pops of yellow are feeling lonely! You could strengthen the image's colour relationships with blended gradations that lead the eye down the abstract forms of cascading branches. Now would also be a good time to bring in some autumn colours. So, to capture the vibrancy of autumn leaves, return to the 'Midground' layer and use **AIRBRUSHING > SOFT BRUSH** to create a fade from golden yellow to a warm, muted red-orange. This will pop nicely against the blue sky, as blue and orange form a complementary pair. The Alpha Lock on that layer will help maintain the clean edges and shapes of your canopy as you add and mix colour.

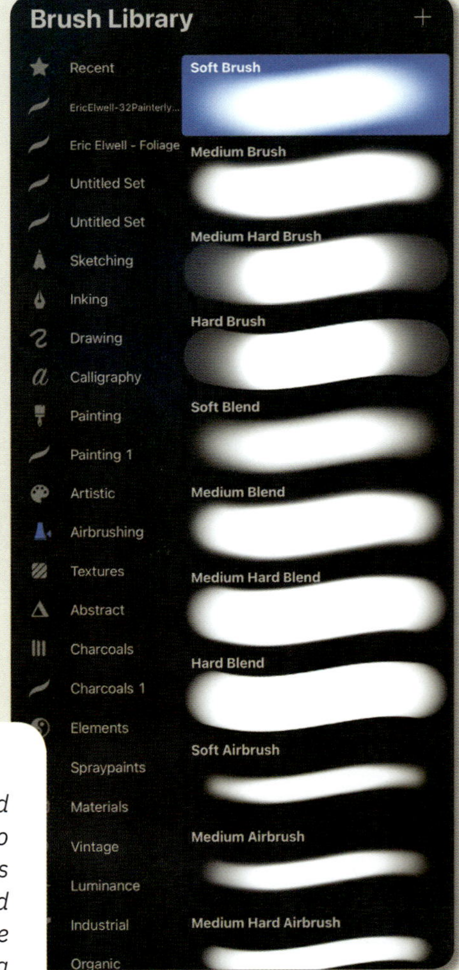

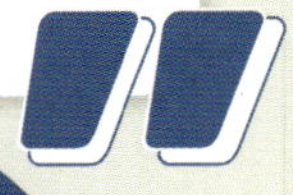

ERIC SAYS: *'So far you have learned to manage your project for increased editing and printing options. You have focused on a clean and concise layer stack, but remember to stay loose! Explore ideas. Be quick, gestural, and open to making mistakes. Specific tools and processes can increase your efficiency, but the ultimate goal is a well-communicated image. At this stage you are building up a base. You can respond to what you see on the canvas and compare to what you see on location. The tools and processes are simply a means to help you communicate what captures your attention.'*

11

You now have a strong structural base laid down, to which you can respond. Having evaluated what you see on canvas, what strikes you as important compared to what you see on location? Perhaps it is time to start intensifying and drawing attention to those orange and yellow leaf structures. In terms of colour and shape, the localized leaf colours of the 'Midground' layer's tree canopy could benefit from a fuller shape and simplified form. Take your choppy Rad brush and paint some more hard-edged patches of autumn leaves cascading down the greater form of the tree canopy.

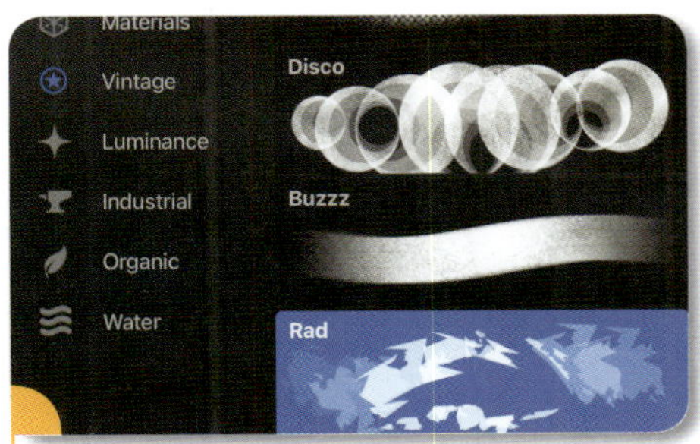

Brush in hard-edged shapes to build up the 'Midground' layer's autumn leaves

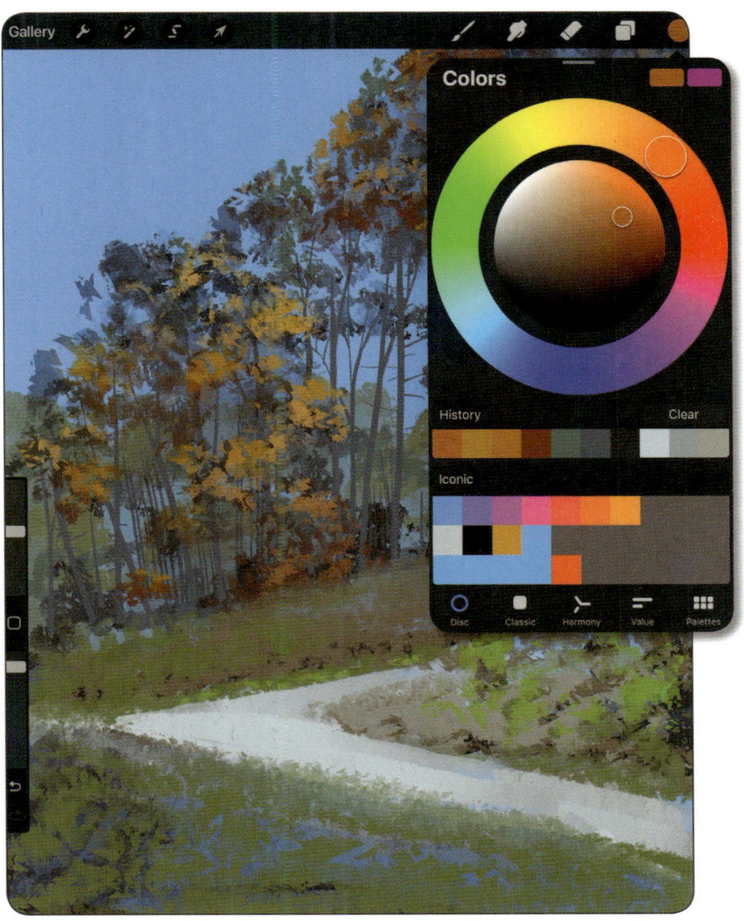

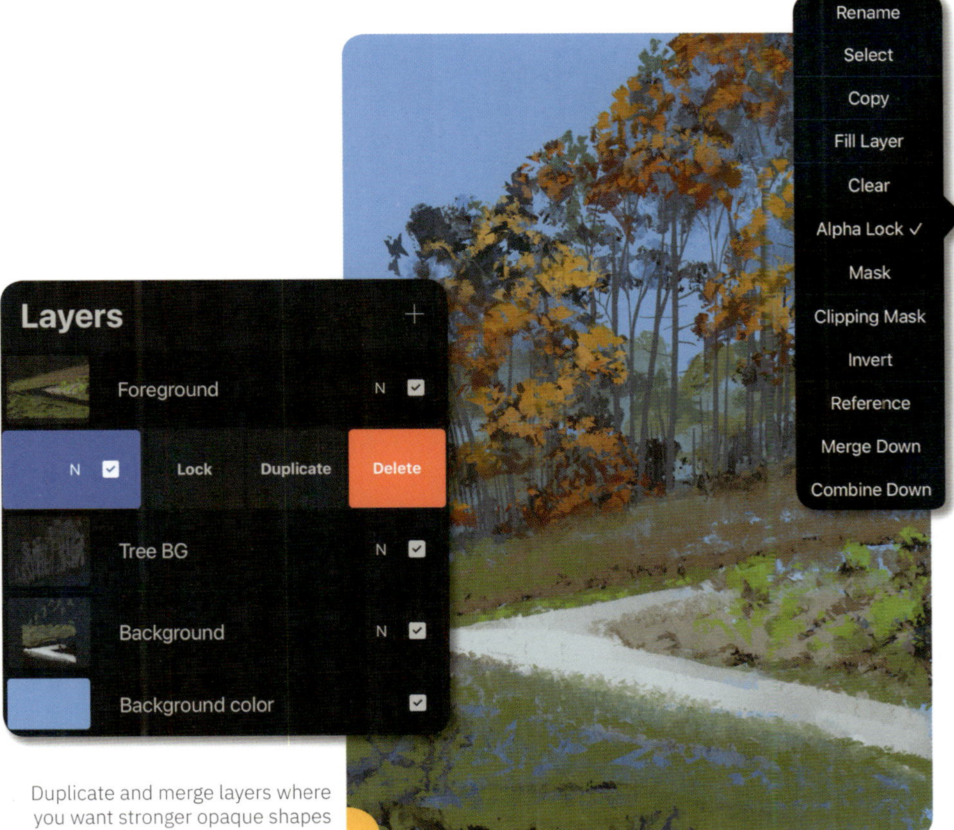

Duplicate and merge layers where you want stronger opaque shapes

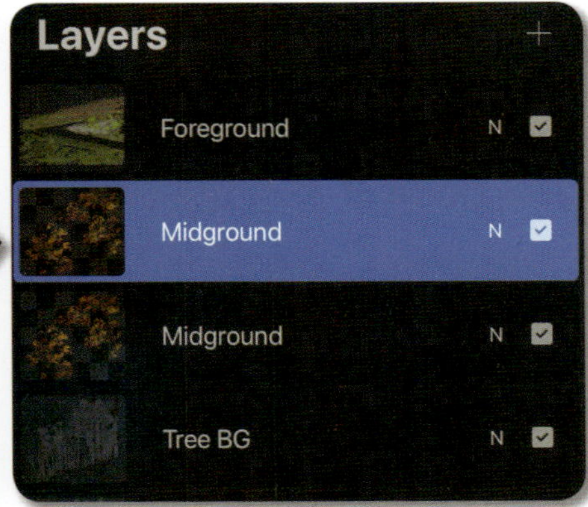

12

If you find the opacity of your block-in lacks intensity, you can leverage another convenient aspect of digital software. In the layer stack, swipe the layer to the left and select Duplicate. Tap on the duplicate and select Merge Down. The results are crisper, stronger colours. Strong opacity helps prevent muddy images. You are successfully clarifying the image one colour-shape at a time!

13

As you continue to focus on the middle ground, you must be sure to control the value range of the rest of the image. Keep the background and foreground comparatively low in contrast, as they are less important to the viewer. Reserve the darkest and lightest values for later stages. You can decrease the contrast of your painted background by lowering the layer opacity, blending it into the blue 'Background Colour' fill. To do this, go to the Layers menu and soften the background trees by tapping the N next to the Show/Hide checkbox and lowering the Opacity slider. The gesture shortcut for Opacity is a two-finger tap on the layer (and again to dismiss). Now create a new layer named 'Main Tree' at the top of your stack, where you will isolate one tree as a focal point. Paint the trunk using a light grey-brown and a solid textured brush, such as **INKING > INKA.**

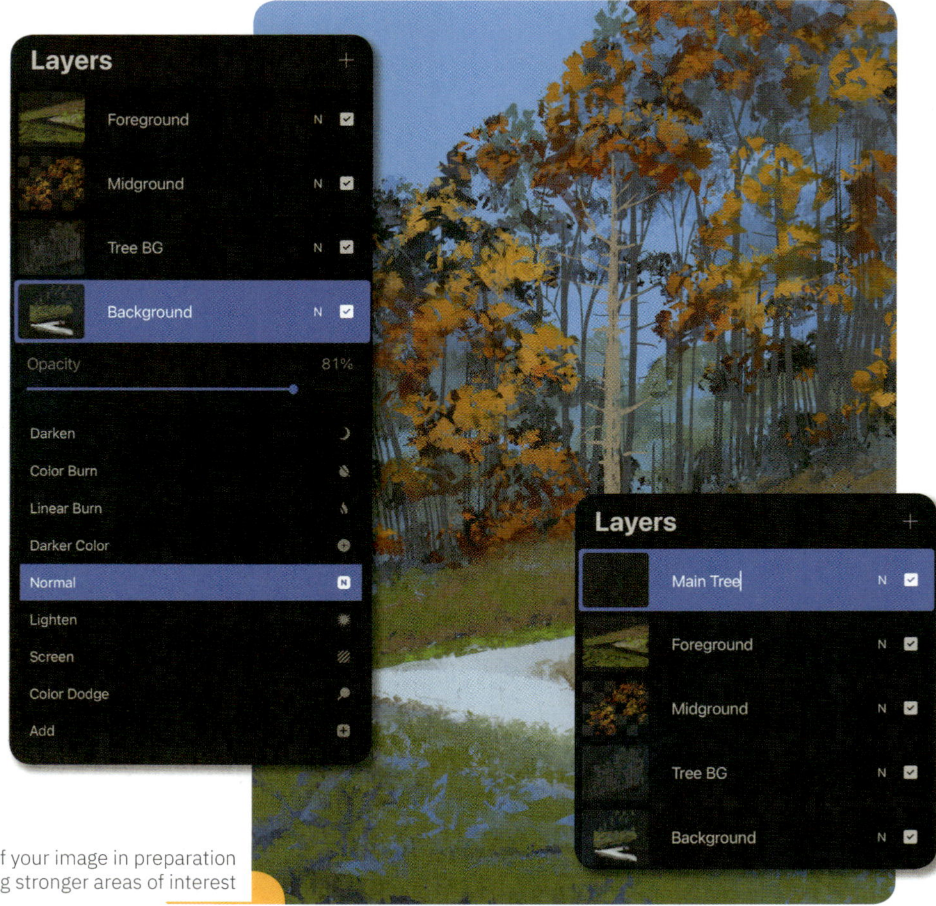

Balance the contrast of your image in preparation for creating stronger areas of interest

14

Now you have painted the silhouette of your 'Main Tree' with some finer detailed branches. Next, Alpha Lock the layer and begin painting in a gradation of colour and value that will integrate the shape into the canopy and ground plane. You can alternate between warm and cool tones, with occasional fine pops of intense saturation. Incorporate the shadows of the branches to provide breaks in the gradation through a variety of hard and soft edges. These techniques will help make this area visually exciting. Be mindful to compare the contrast of this area to the bright orange leaves nearby, so the tree stands out distinctly in shape and colour without looking like it doesn't belong.

Employ contrast of colour, value, edge, and form to develop a focal point

15

Now that a focal point has begun to emerge, evaluate the relationships on your canvas once more. How is the ground plane interacting with your trees? You could add more life to this part of the canvas by picking out more small, light tree trunks that will help solidify the ground plane. Use the 'Foreground' layer to do this, adding small tree trunks and scribbling some autumnal yellow onto the ground. Remember to stay loose and maintain a high level of energy.

It's too early in the process to tighten up. A healthy balance between measured intentionality and 'messy' irreverence can help capture an exploratory liveliness and gesture that make it into the final image.

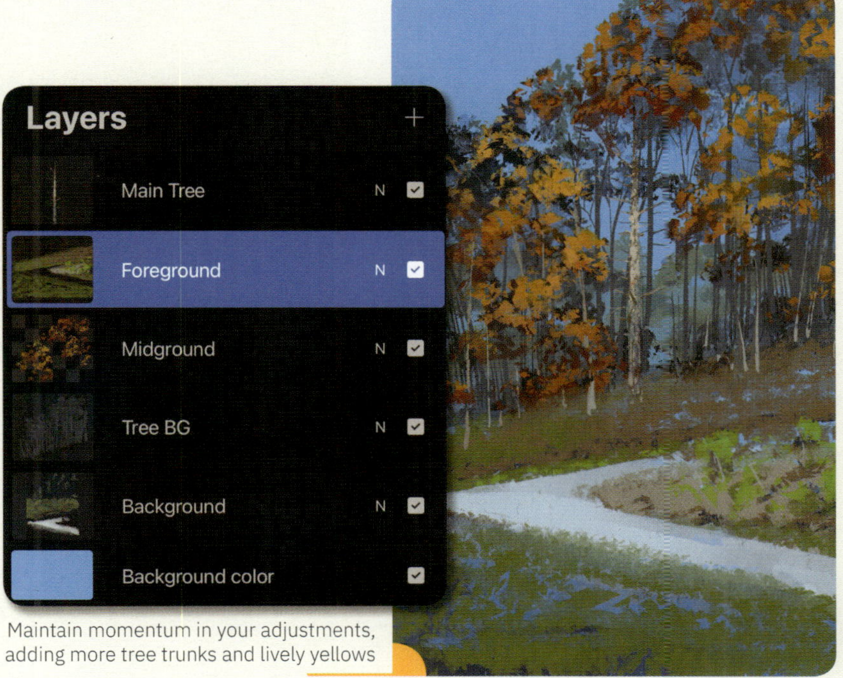

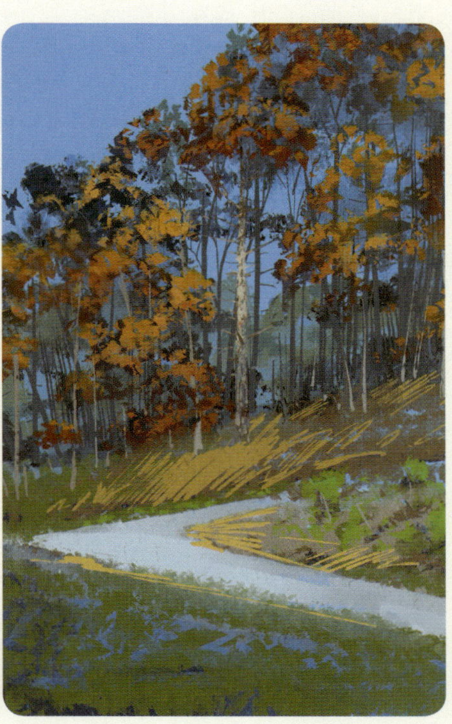

Maintain momentum in your adjustments, adding more tree trunks and lively yellows

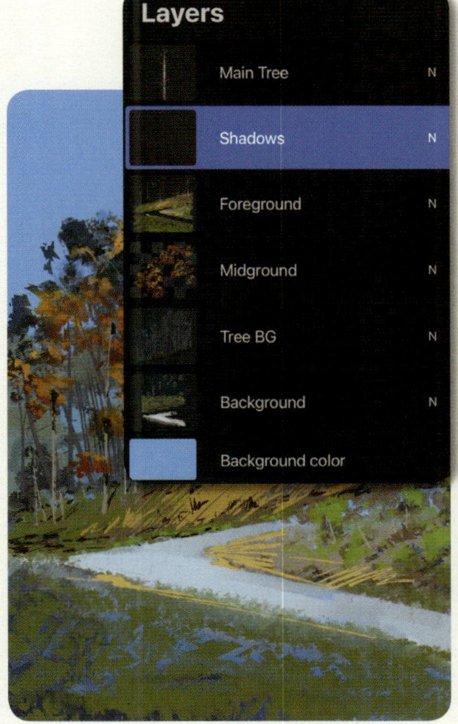

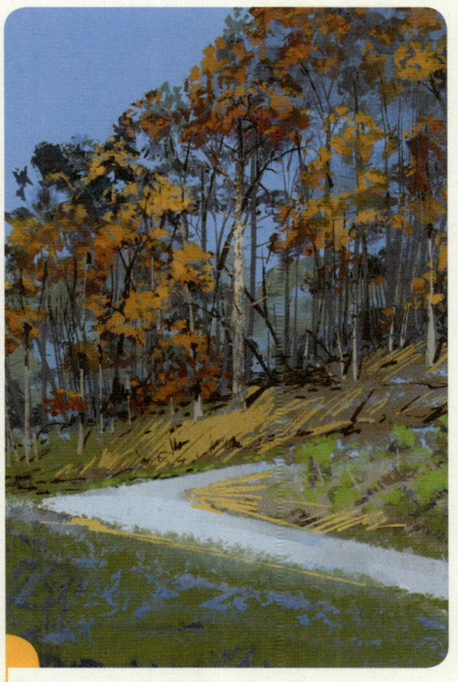

Paint in hard cast shadows to establish a sense of space and form

16

Now you need to ground your objects in space with shadows. Create a new layer called 'Shadows' above the Foreground layer; use **INKING > INKA** to establish hard brown shadows at contact points, such as the ground or where branches join a tree trunk. Shadows are such a powerful element for defining forms and establishing space. Paint in the cast shadows from the canopy and vary these from the lighter tree silhouettes that appear further back in space.

17

Once the hard-edged cast shadows are in place, use a softer brush such as **ARTISTIC > HARTZ** for diffuse shadows, which denote greater distance and the turn of rounded forms. Both these hard and soft shadows are an important indication of the lighting conditions and the turn of forms. In full sun, objects cast hard shadows that contort to the forms upon which they are cast. Shadows tend to soften as the distance increases between the object casting the shadow and the form upon which the shadow falls. With soft cast shadows in the foreground, you may allude to distant trees behind the viewer. For the soft shadows, you will not need to be as careful with shapes. Simply block them in and break them up using the Smudge tool set to **VINTAGE > RAD**.

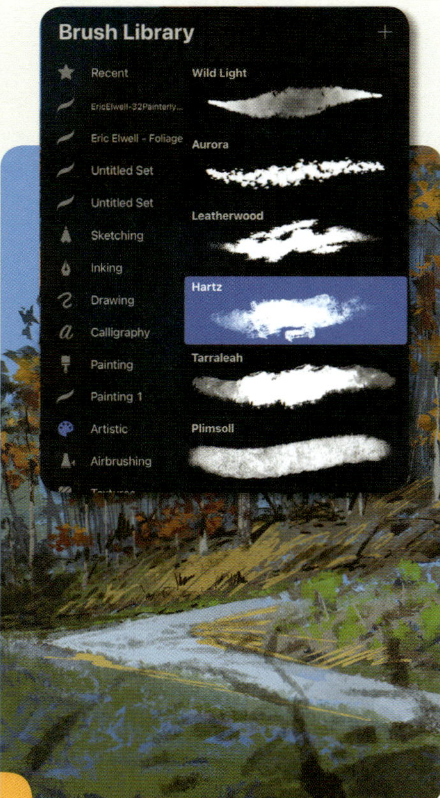

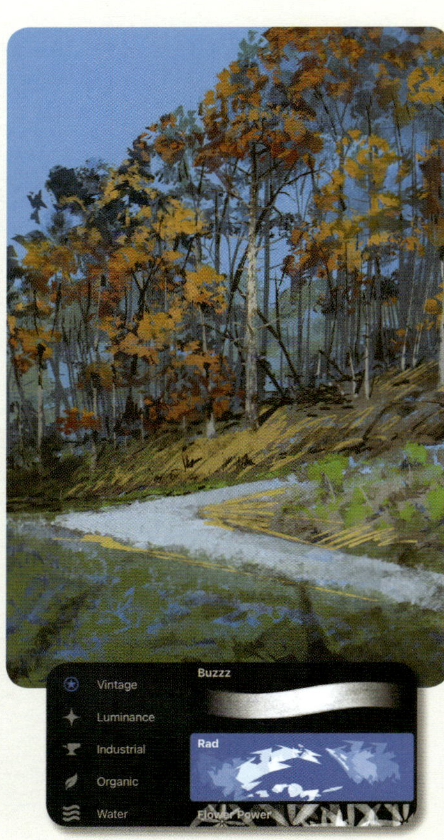

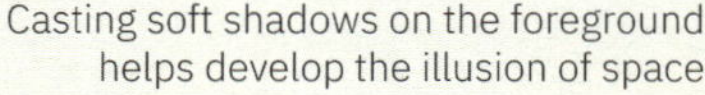
Casting soft shadows on the foreground helps develop the illusion of space

18

Do you recall saving your darkest and lightest values? Now it's time to use them. A simple, controlled way to manipulate contrast is with an Overlay layer. Create a new layer and tap the N (for Normal mode) in the Layers menu. Select Overlay from the blend mode options. With Overlay, values above middle grey will intensify in brightness, while values below middle grey will darken. If you are new to Overlay, start with grey, slowly working in extra hue and saturation. Give it a try now. You can go extreme at first and dial back the opacity later.

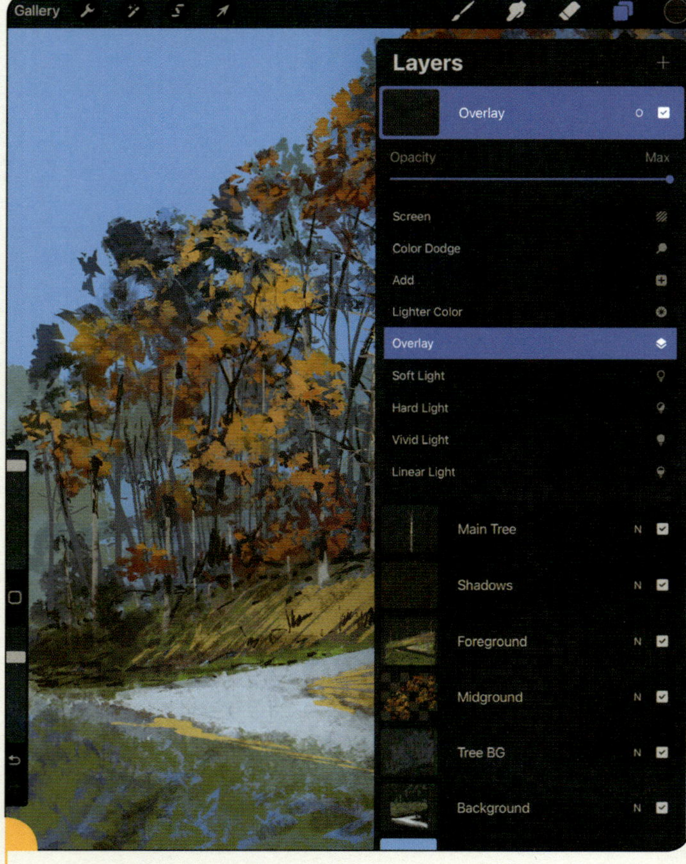
Add an Overlay layer to help give your values a boost

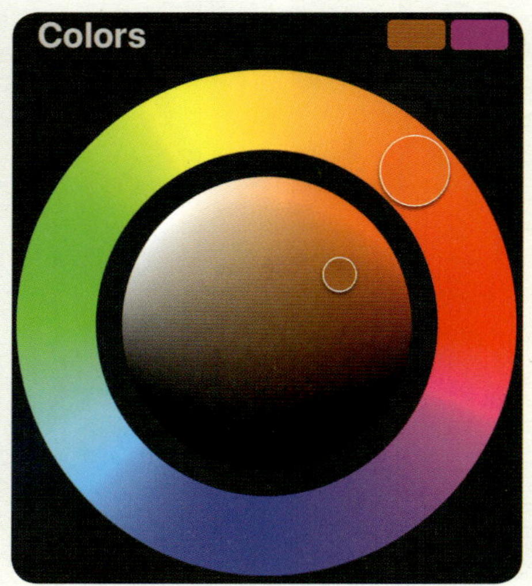

19

Have you gathered all the necessary information on location? You should have captured the major landmarks, areas of interest, lighting conditions, space, colours, and textures that produce the overall effect of autumn. Unless something else catches your interest, pause here until you have returned to the studio. With fresh eyes you may make adjustments to improve the image. For example, you could modify the background's shape to counterbalance the diagonal composition. Select **TRANSFORM > FREEFORM**, then tap and hold the corner of the 'Tree BG' layer until it moves independently, pulling the angle slightly upwards. Use **ADJUSTMENTS > HUE, SATURATION, BRIGHTNESS** to enhance the colour of the painted background layer. To mute the sky to a more realistic blue, try changing the 'Background Colour' fill.

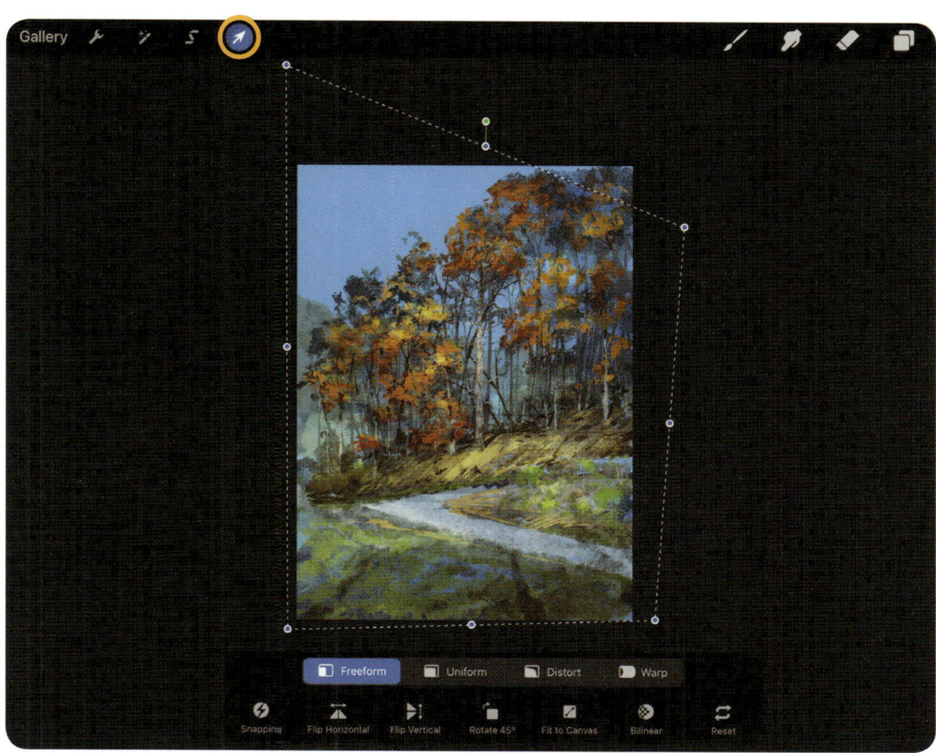

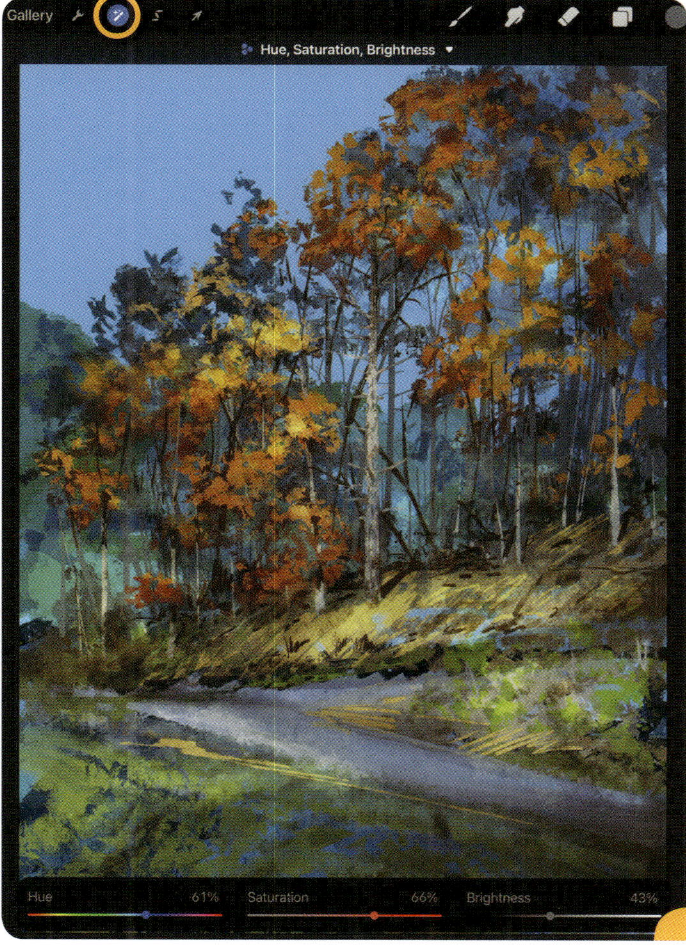

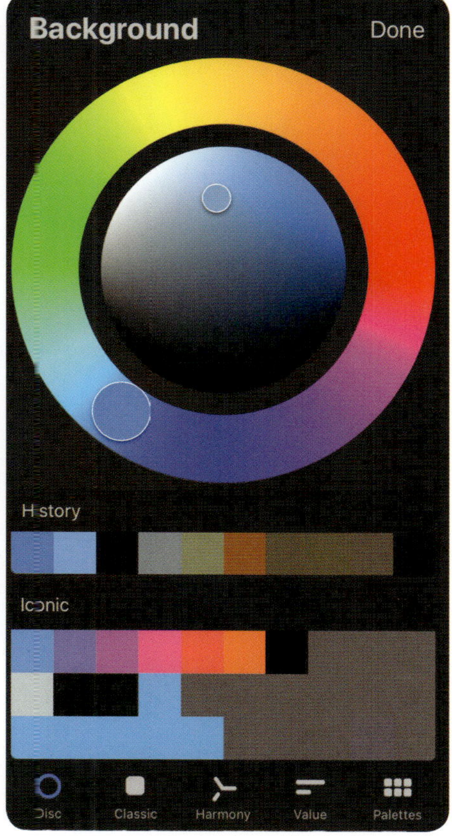

Adjust the image in-studio with the Transform tool and Hue, Saturation, Brightness adjustments

20

Continue with Hue, Saturation, Brightness (HSB) adjustments on the tree silhouette layer to rebalance the values with the new sky colour. For finer adjustments on the 'Midground' layer, use **ADJUSTMENTS > CURVES** – you can use the histogram to increase or decrease the intensity in select areas of the image. Switch from Gamma to the individual RGB colour channels to modify the colour mixture in select value ranges – this allows you to shift the colours as the values fade from light to dark. Utilize HSB and Curves to fine-tune your shadows, too, but be mindful that colour information can be compressed beyond the point of no return!

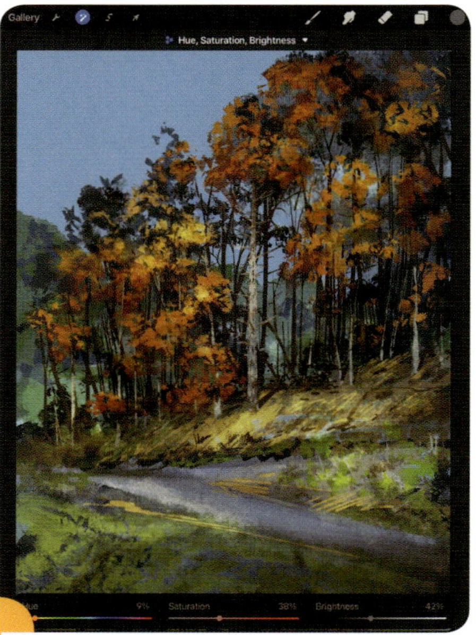
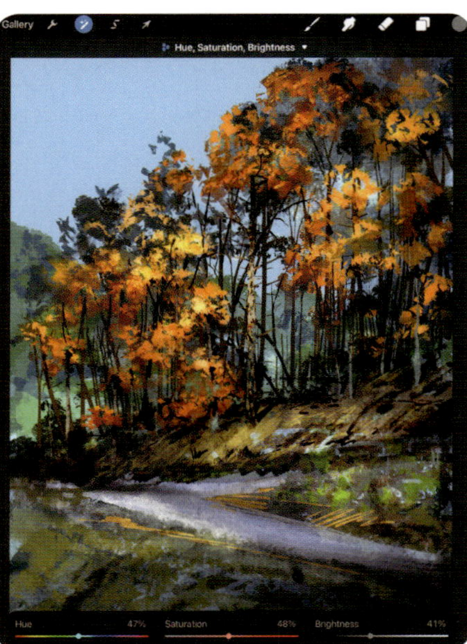

Refine your image and palette with HSB and Curves adjustments

21

You can experiment further with adjusting your colour palette to explore various impressions of the scene – for example, bringing a richer, deeper green to the forest floor to contrast with the autumnal orange canopy. With the 'Foreground' layer selected, create another Curves adjustment. Select the Blue channel and clamp the dark values to the bottom. This will remove all blue from your shadows, leaving only red and green. The result is a richer grass colour. Now select your Overlay layer and tap with two fingers to adjust the opacity to your liking. Apply a Hue, Saturation, Brightness adjustment to the Overlay layer to increase the overall brightness of the image, so the grass area isn't too dark.

Explore the variety of palette options by altering the colour channels with Curves adjustments

ERIC SAYS: *'In preparation for the focal point, you provided a neutral base with comparatively low contrast in the background and foreground. From there you were able to develop areas of interest with increased contrast of colour, value, and detail density. You created depth and space through thoughtful use of hard and soft shadows. The addition of an Overlay layer and a few adjustment effects allowed you to establish greater contrast and begin composing for the final image. You're almost there!'*

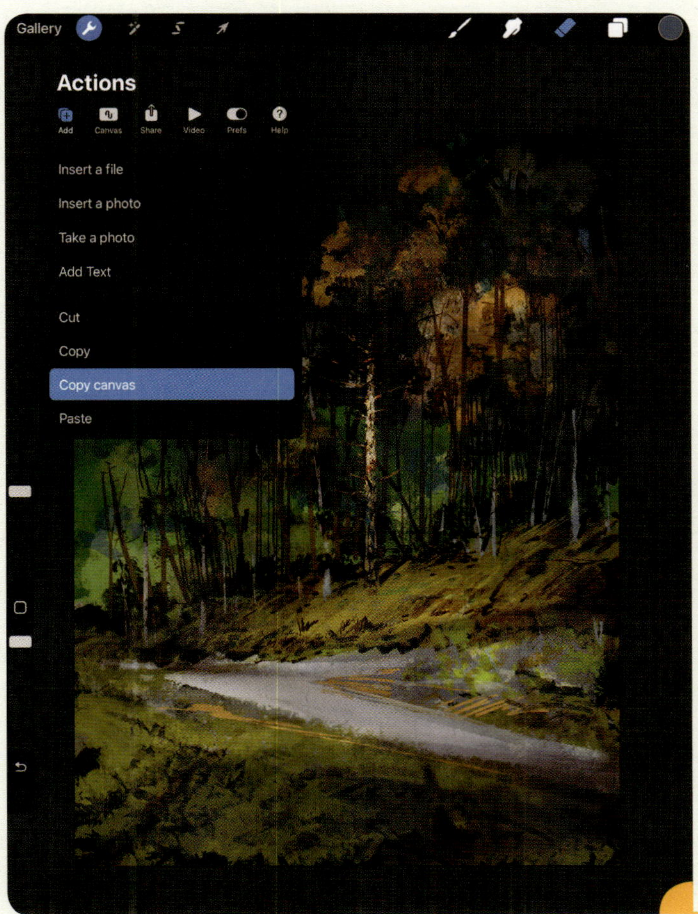

22

No: all adjustments can be done with sliders. You will need to use a brush to tie the final image together. Splash a bit of orange onto the 'Foreground' layer to create an association with the autumnal 'Midground' layer colours. Create a new layer below everything else and airbrush a light grey atmosphere in the sky. You may want to make a copy of the canvas prior to final adjustments. To do this, first hide the blue 'Background Colour' and 'Midground' layers, so you can manipulate them separately. Tap **ACTIONS > ADD > COPY CANVAS** and then **PASTE** to create an 'Inserted Image' duplicate layer that can live at the bottom of your stack as a backup.

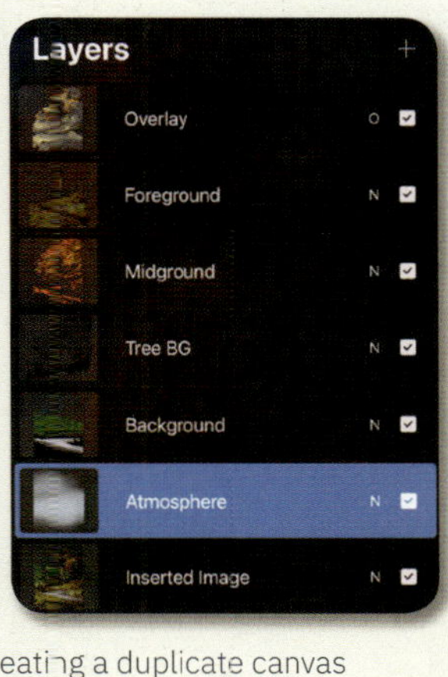

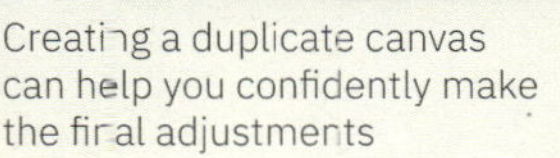

Creating a duplicate canvas can help you confidently make the final adjustments

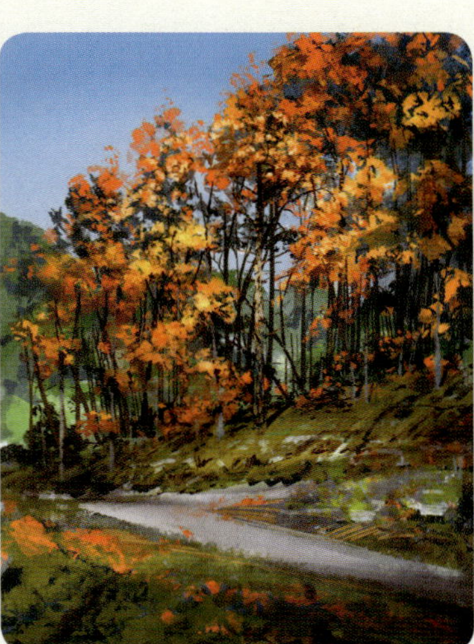

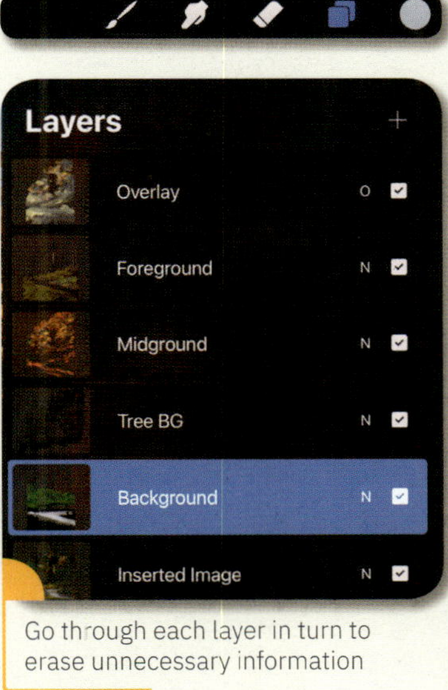

Go through each layer in turn to erase unnecessary information

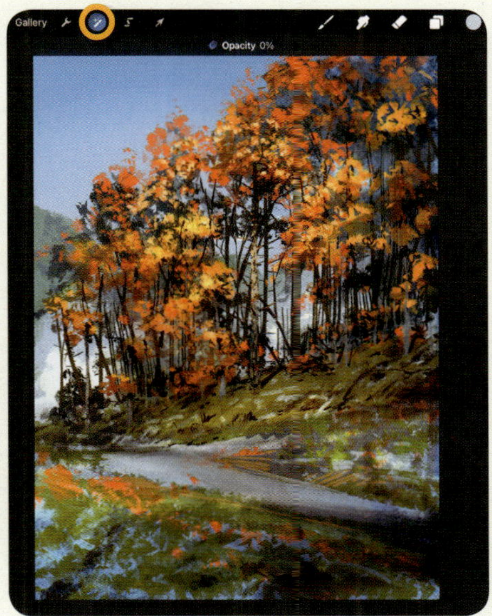

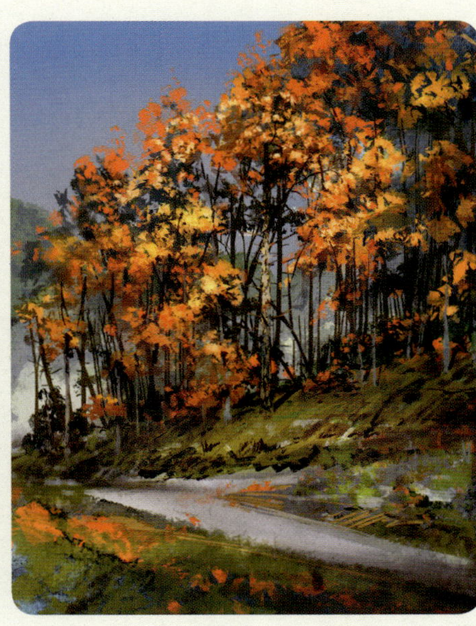

23

Scrub through each layer with the opacity slider to measure its effect on the overall image. You may notice that a layer presents trade-offs in some regions of the canvas. Take note of these and get a textured Eraser ready. If an area detracts from the image, cut away with the Eraser, brushing away the background to reveal the atmospheric fog layer behind it. Perhaps it wasn't a foggy morning on site, but the effect on canvas is pleasant. Continue to adjust the 'Background Colour' fill layer to explore different colour mixes. A slightly purplish sky could potentially enhance that warm autumn glow.

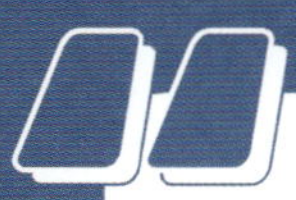

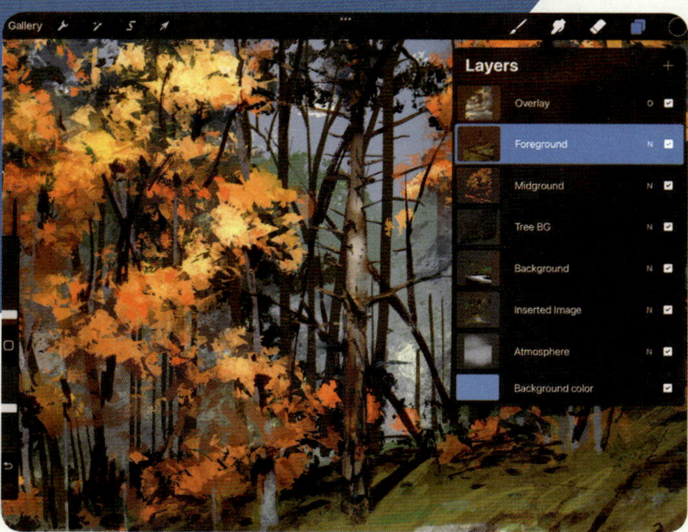

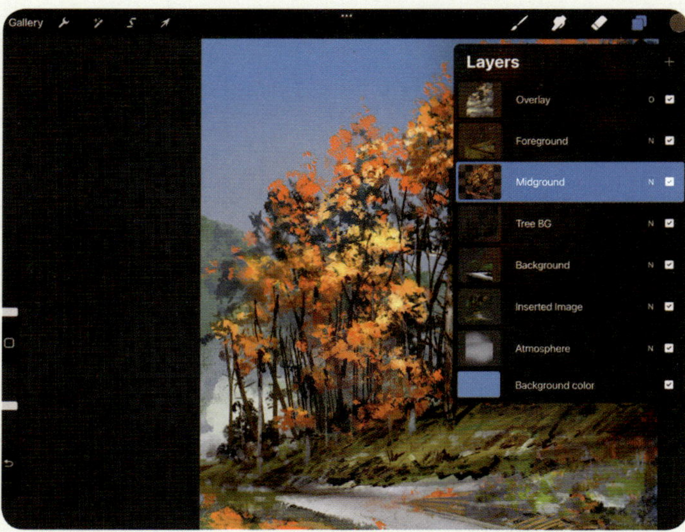

24

Zoom in close to the central tree. With Alpha Lock enabled on the 'Main Tree' layer, render a soft turn of the form on the outer edges using an airbrush. This gives the trunk a more cylindrical shape. Blend in softer gradations with the same brush. These soft shapes may be broken up by jagged shadows to create more interesting edges. Create contrast between the pale lightened shapes and the saturated browns of the bark. Returning the 'Background Colour' to a vivid, saturated, warmish blue gives the image its strongest finish.

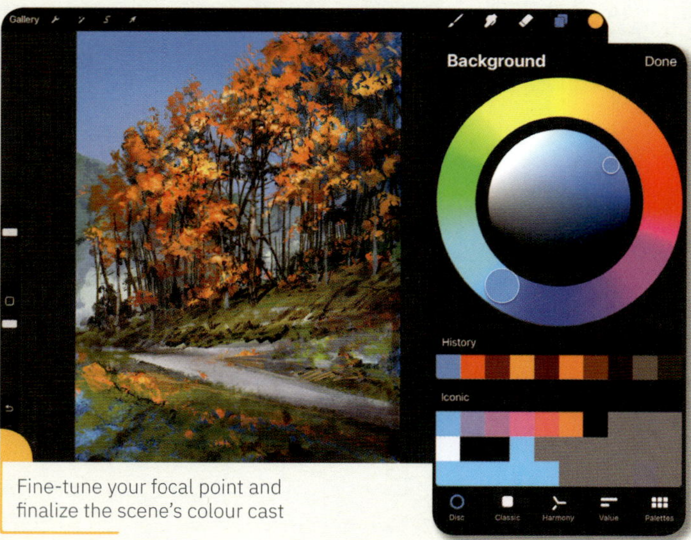

Fine-tune your focal point and finalize the scene's colour cast

CONCLUSION

This autumn scene captures the essence of a moment, a break in the canopy with one trunk standing out from the forest. A simple foundation is laid by dividing into background, middle ground, and foreground regions. The process is made efficient with textured brushes. A low-contrast block-in provided the base from which to push and pull contrast in areas of interest. Finally, a knowledge of adjustments allowed for flexibility in fine-tuning the final image.

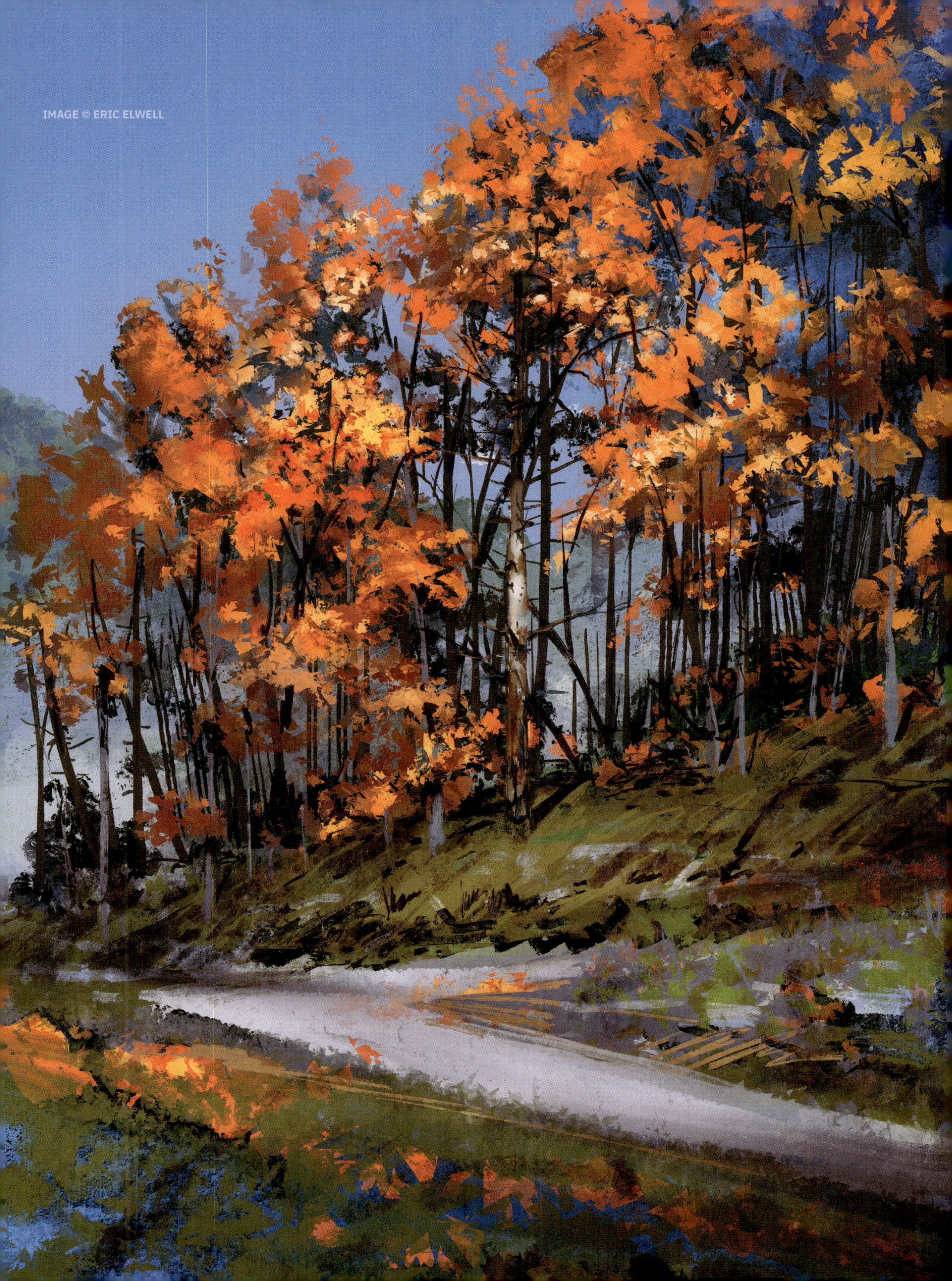
IMAGE © ERIC ELWELL

 Plein-air painting allows the time to enjoy a simple scene, such as a fallen tree
in an isolated pool – this log has been painted several times from different angles

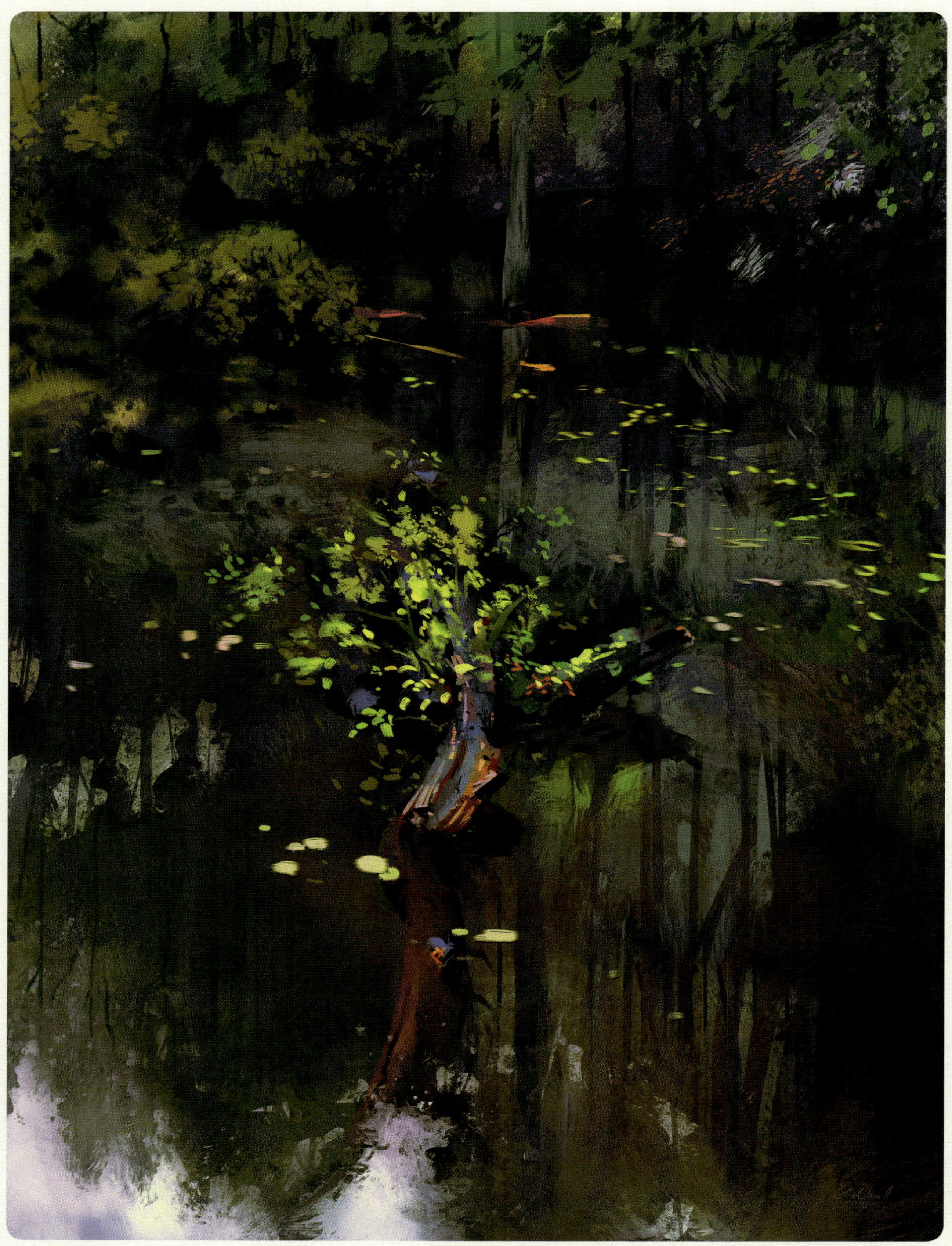

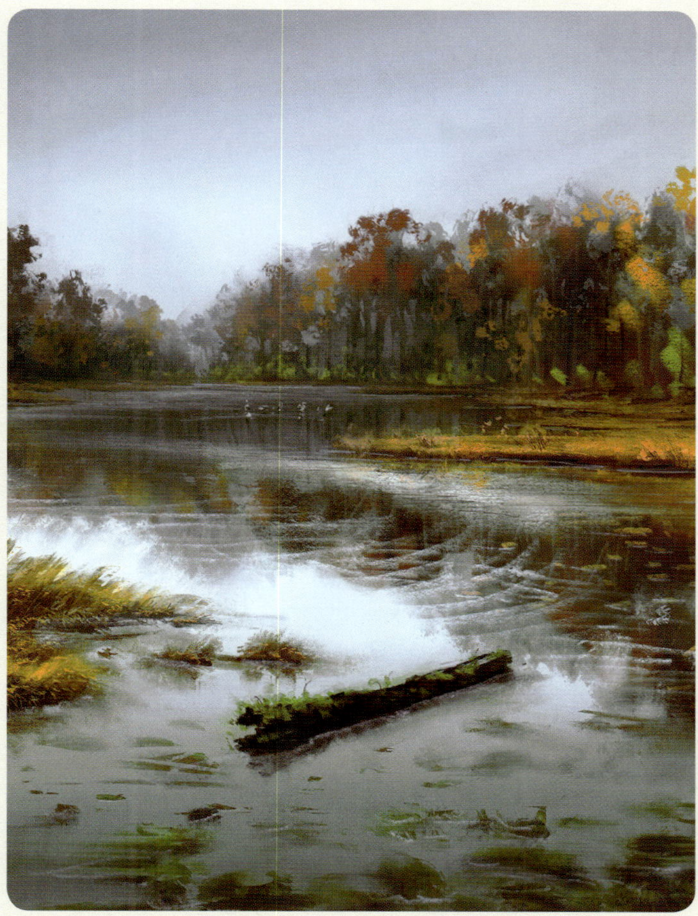

MOSS LAKE 2: Moss Lake is an easily accessible, well-shaded location; the woodland cover means minimal screen glare, making it ideal for plein-air painting

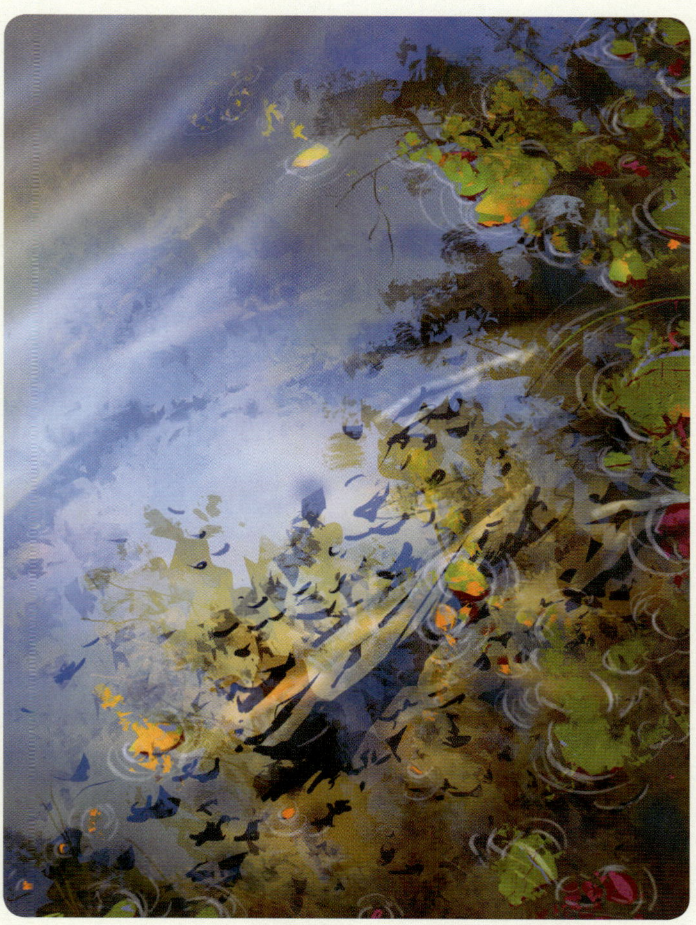

MOSS LAKE 3: Visits to the same location often present new and interesting subjects that escape notice upon earlier trips

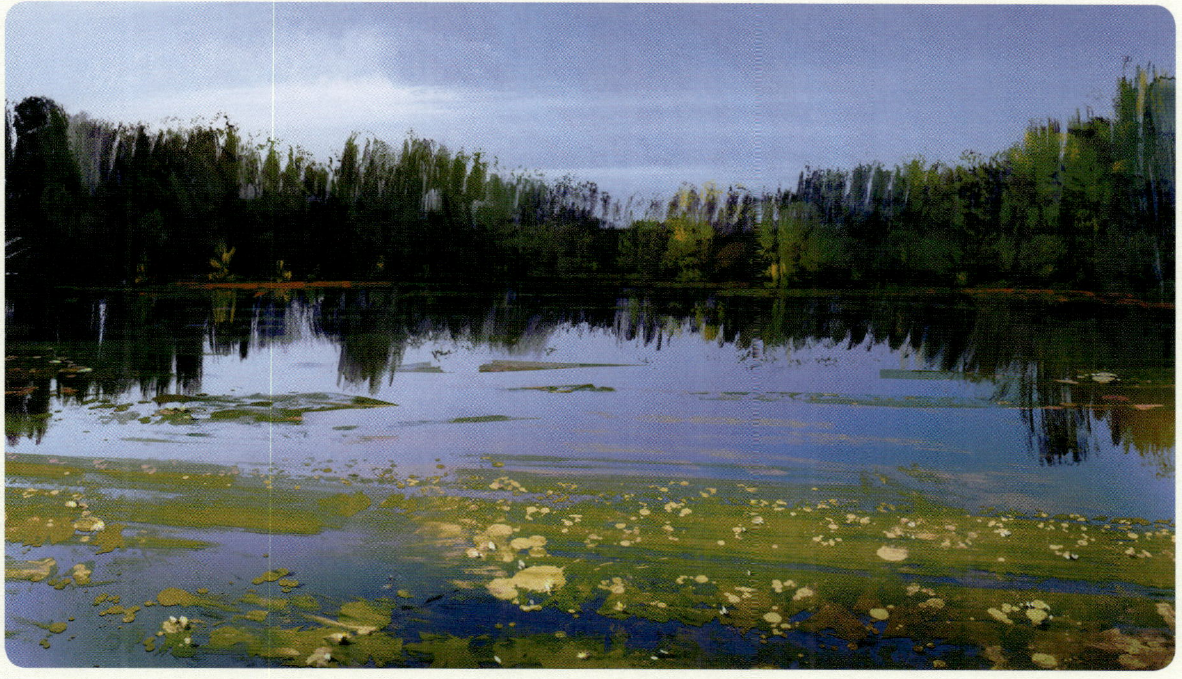

MOSS LAKE 4: As you can see, this lake has been a repeated painting subject; there is much to learn with repetition at the same location under varying conditions

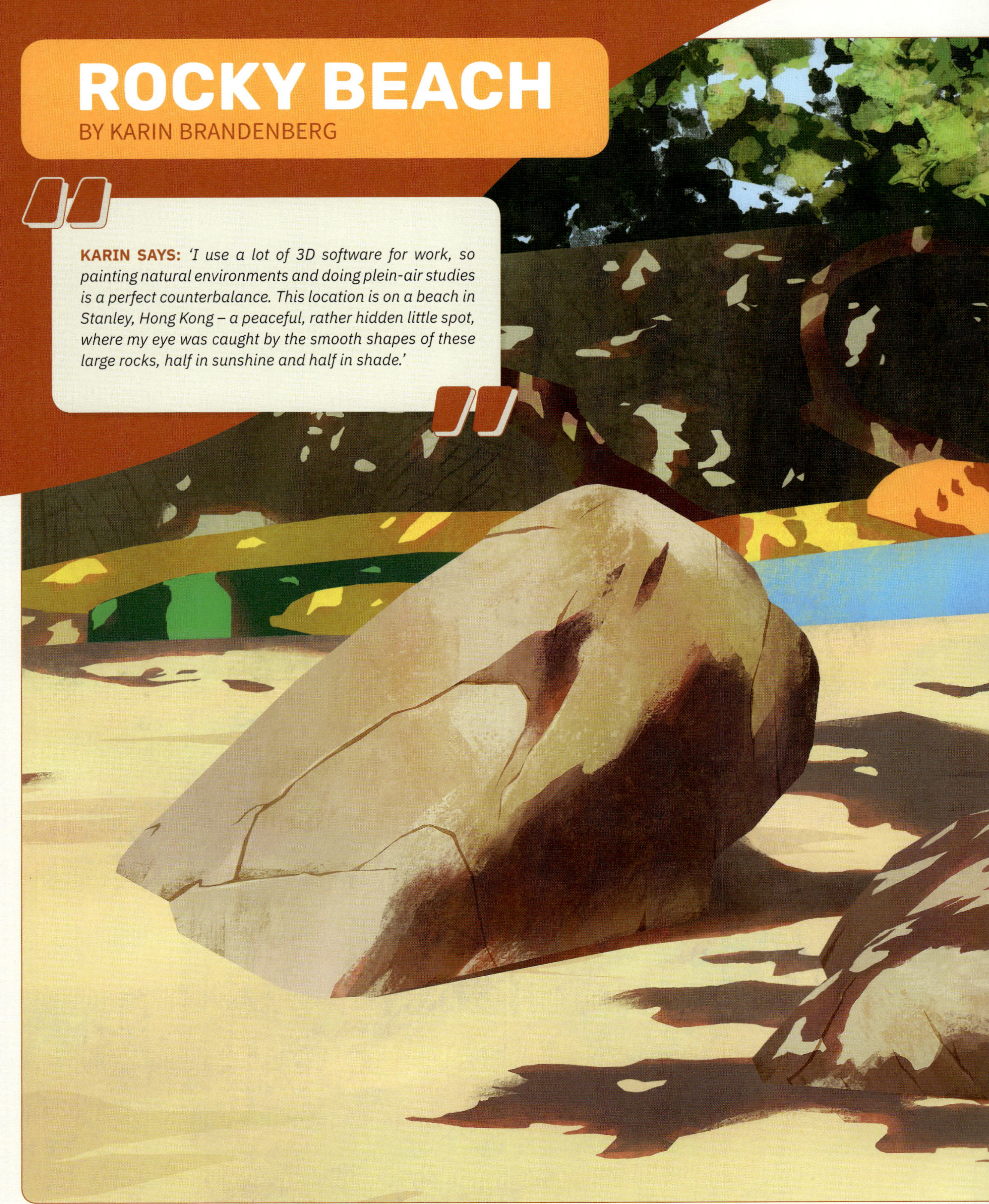

ROCKY BEACH

BY KARIN BRANDENBERG

KARIN SAYS: *'I use a lot of 3D software for work, so painting natural environments and doing plein-air studies is a perfect counterbalance. This location is on a beach in Stanley, Hong Kong – a peaceful, rather hidden little spot, where my eye was caught by the smooth shapes of these large rocks, half in sunshine and half in shade.'*

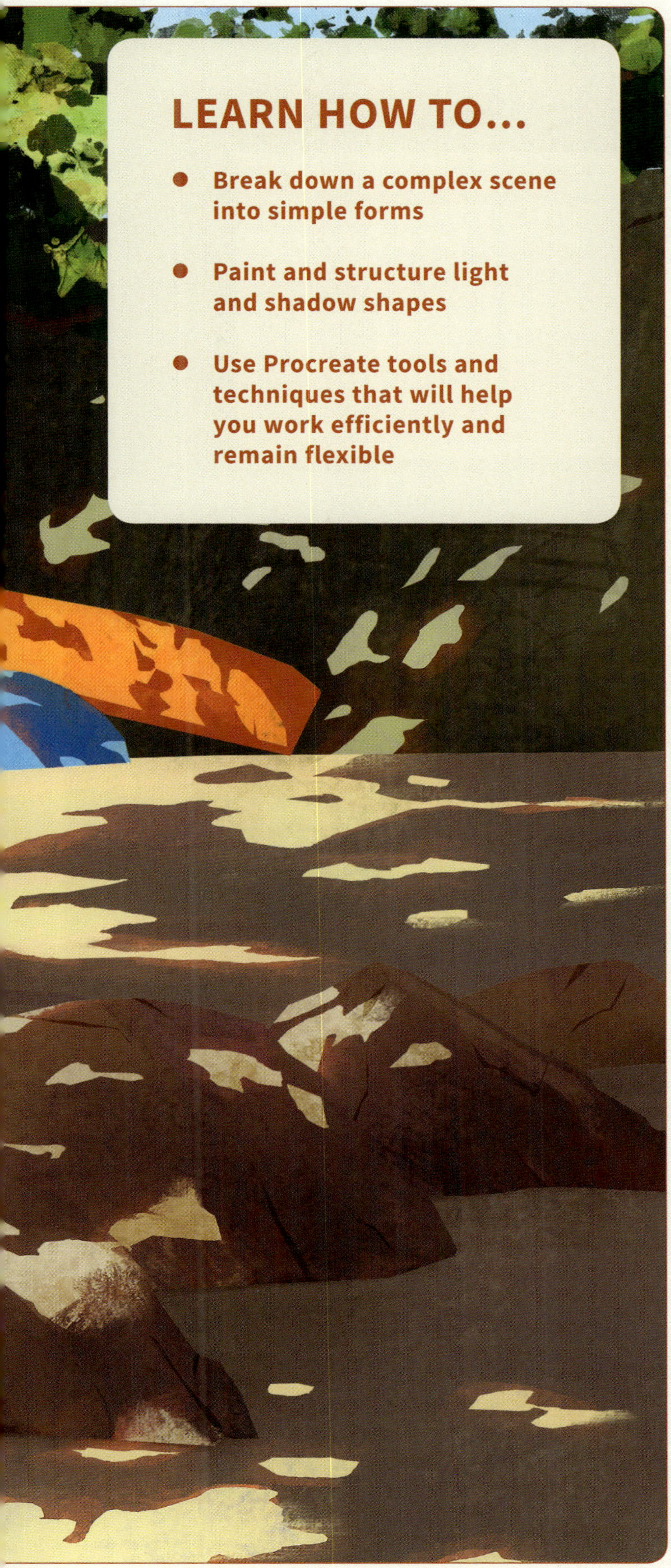

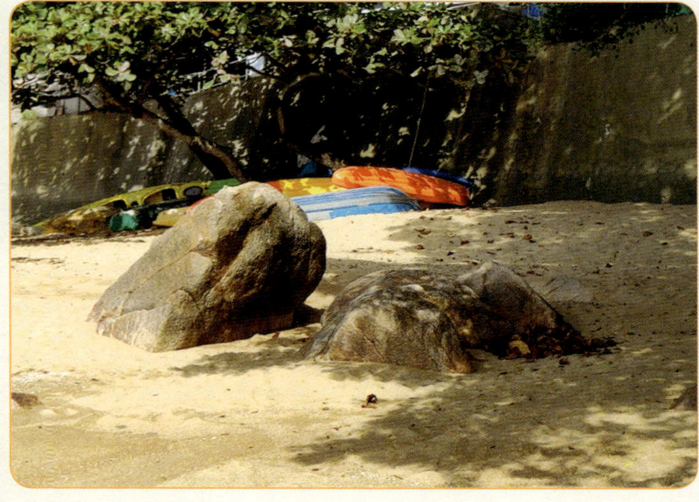

01

Begin by making a new canvas around 5,000 pixels wide by 3,300 pixels high. Select the **SKETCHING > 6B PENCIL** brush from the Brush Library and set the colour to black. Make sure the bottom slider on the vertical sidebar, which controls brush opacity, is set to the highest position. Use the top slider to set the brush's tip size to something that feels like a pencil.

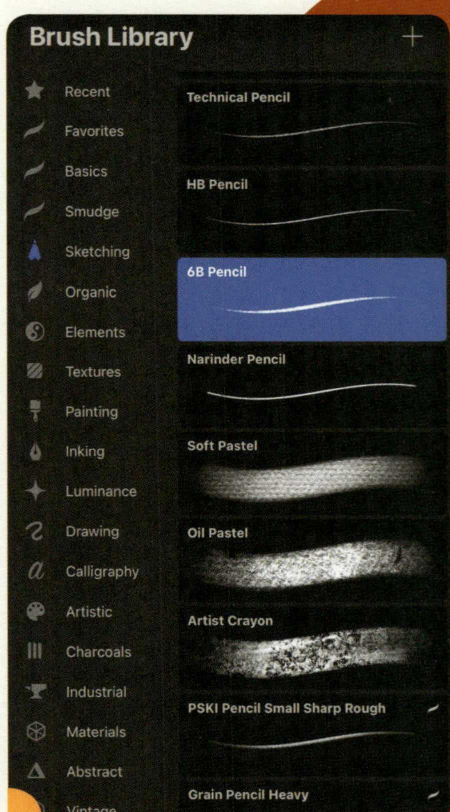

The Brush Library with the 6B Pencil brush selected

02

Using quick and loose brushstrokes, block out the main shapes of the objects in the scene with the 6B Pencil brush. Simplify the shapes as much as possible – it is not necessary to capture every single detail of the rocks and their silhouettes, only the most striking ones. Think about where you want your viewer to look. That will be the focal point. In this case, the focal point will be the group of rocks in the centre of the scene. Add more details in this area, so the viewer's eye will have an incentive to focus here. The next few steps will cover some tools and options that are especially useful during this early sketching stage.

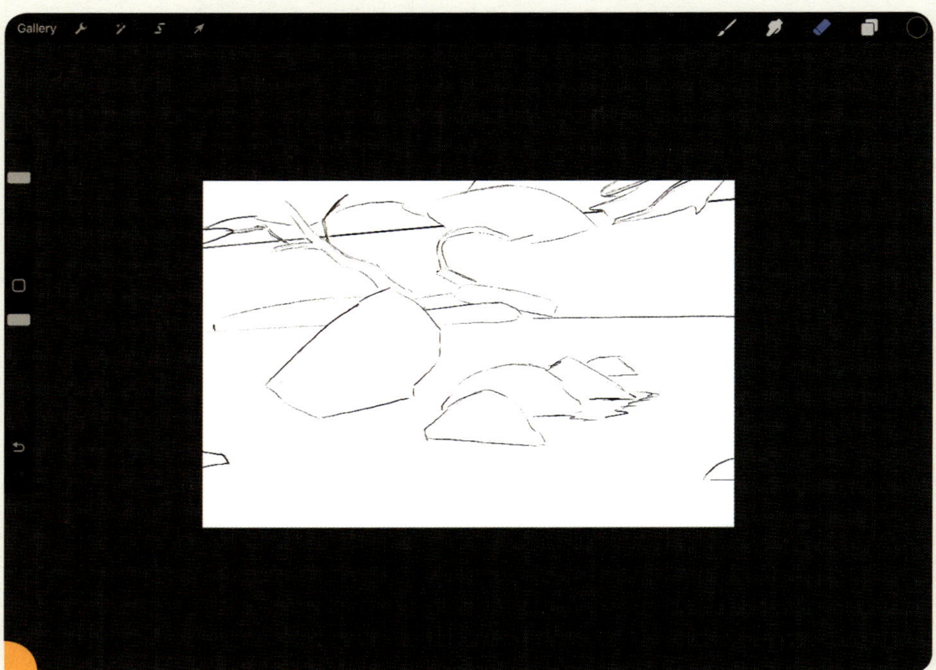

A simple sketch of basic shapes made with the 6B Pencil brush

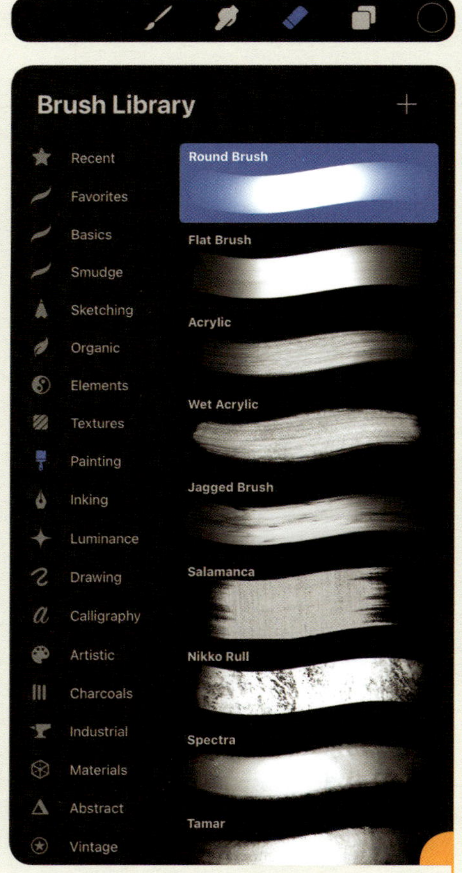

Using the Eraser and Selection tools to fix mistakes

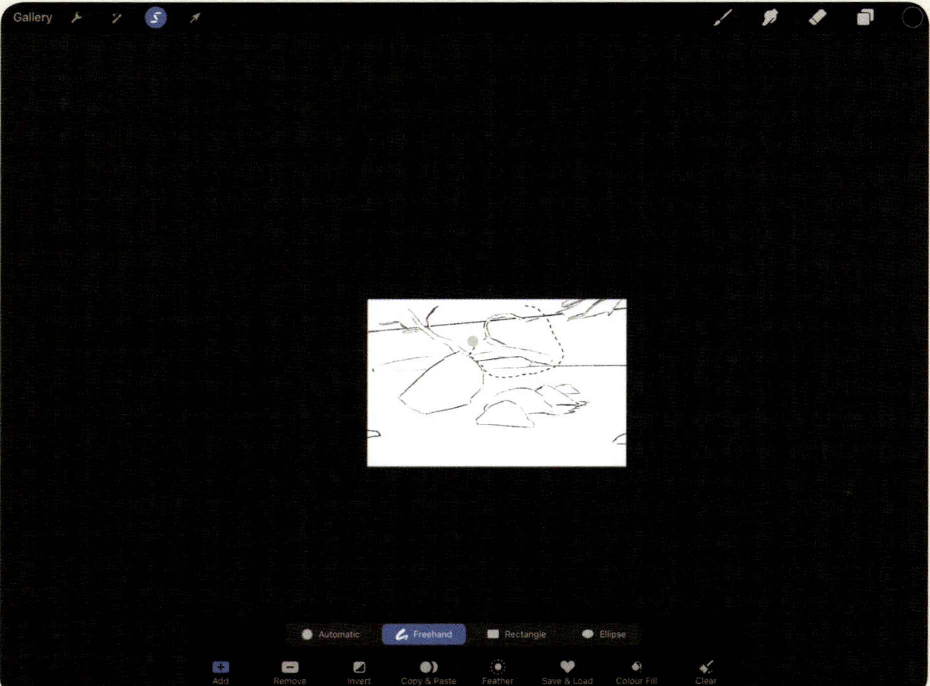

03

There are several ways to fix mistakes in your sketch if necessary. You can use the Eraser, set to **PAINTING > ROUND BRUSH** for a clean, solid stroke, or you can alter your drawing using the **SELECTION > FREEHAND** and **TRANSFORM** tools. These are useful for moving or scaling parts of your sketch that are almost right. Simply tap on the Selection symbol again to clear the selection once you're done.

04

If you need to draw a straight line, a perfect shape, or a smooth curve, draw the shape and keep your brush held on the canvas. Procreate will then snap it into a QuickShape for you. You can then edit that shape by clicking on the down arrow that appears at the top of the canvas next to the shape name. This will allow you to tap and drag the blue nodes to your desired positions.

However, don't worry too much about the sketch being clean, neat, or pretty. Try to keep it as rough as possible while staying accurate to your reference.

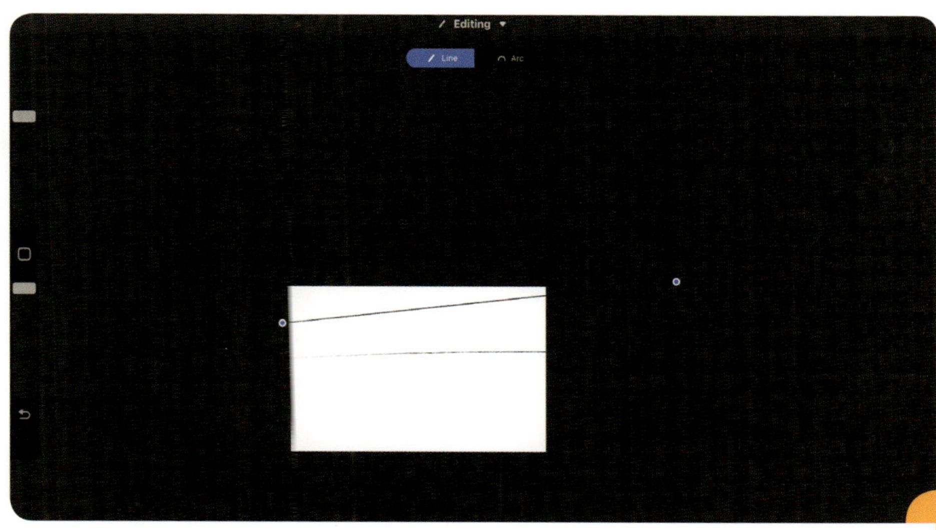

Drawing a straight line with QuickShape

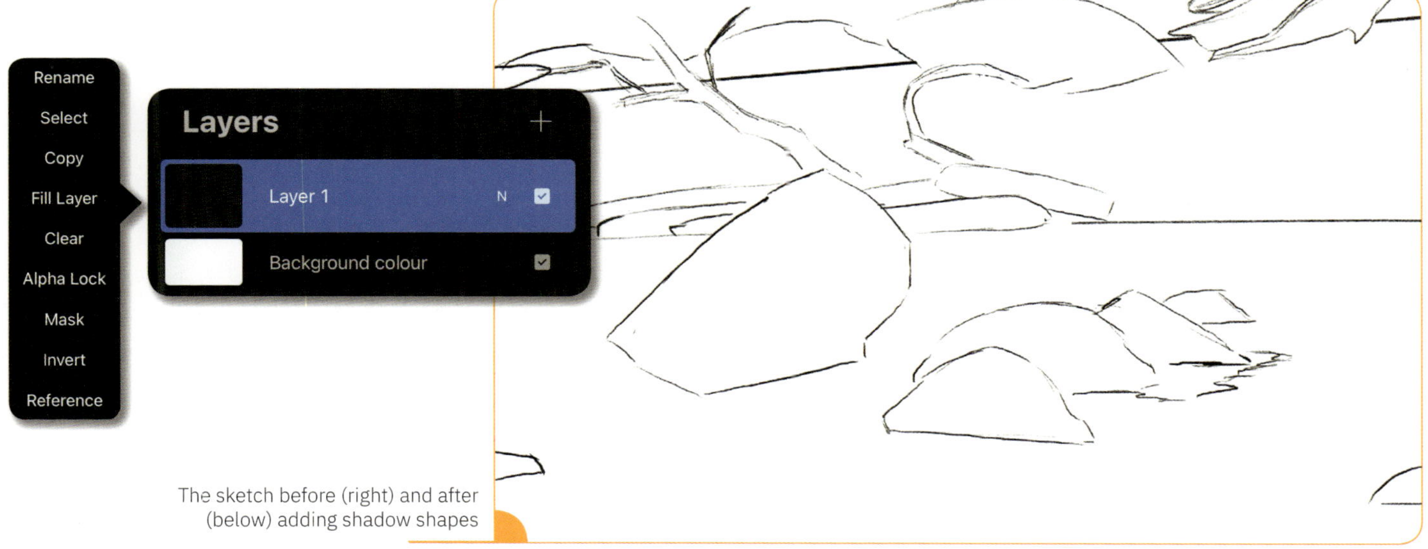

The sketch before (right) and after (below) adding shadow shapes

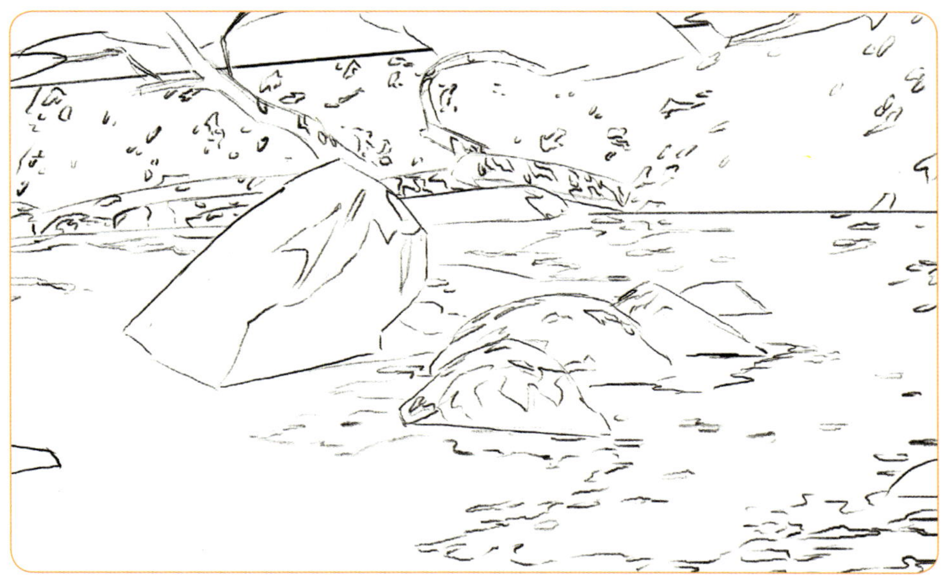

05

To help keep track of your layers, you can rename them as you go along. To do this, open the Layers menu, tap on 'Layer 1', and then tap on Rename in the options menu that appears. Type 'Sketch' to rename the layer, making it easier to find and manage later. Create a new layer and rename it 'Shadows'. Using the same techniques as before, analyse, simplify, and sketch the shadow shapes of the scene. Then open the Layers menu and tap the checkbox of the Shadows layer to hide it for now.

06

Create a new layer, hold and drag it to between the 'Background Colour' and 'Sketch' layers, and call it 'Underpainting'. Select the **ARTISTIC > AURORA** brush and choose a complementary colour to the overall warm scene, such as a cool, saturated blue. Zoom out of your canvas for the next stage, to avoid getting hung up on small details.

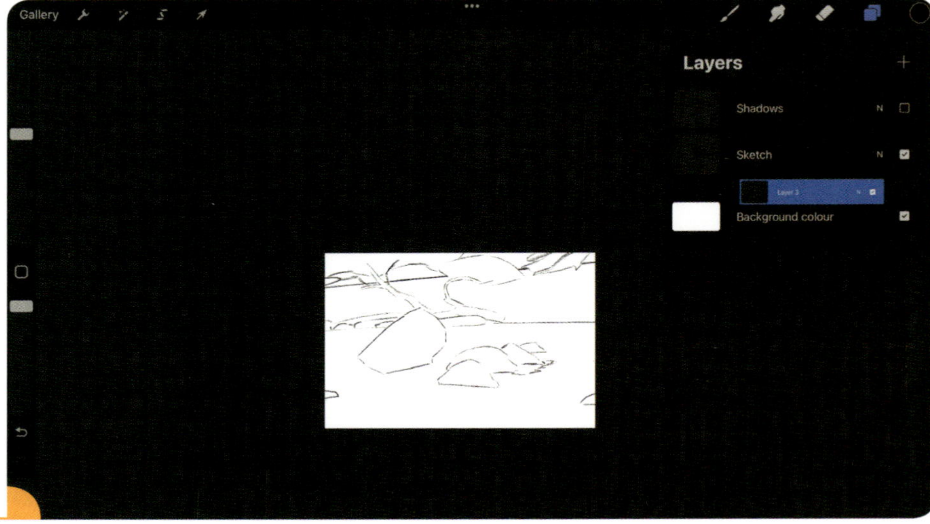

Change the layer order by dragging and dropping a layer within the Layers menu

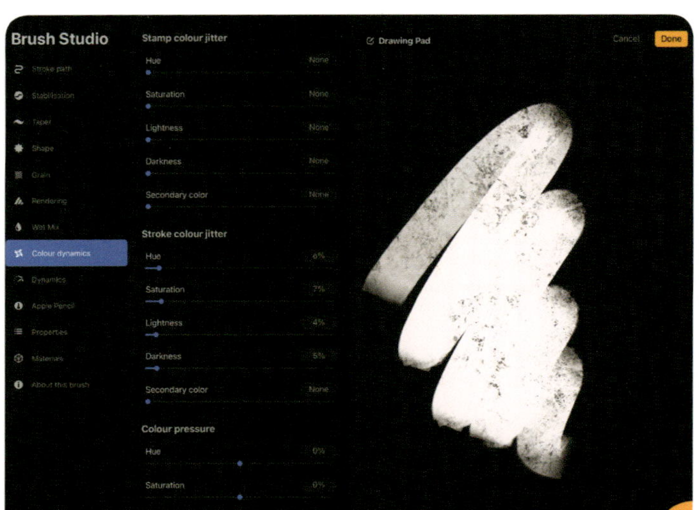

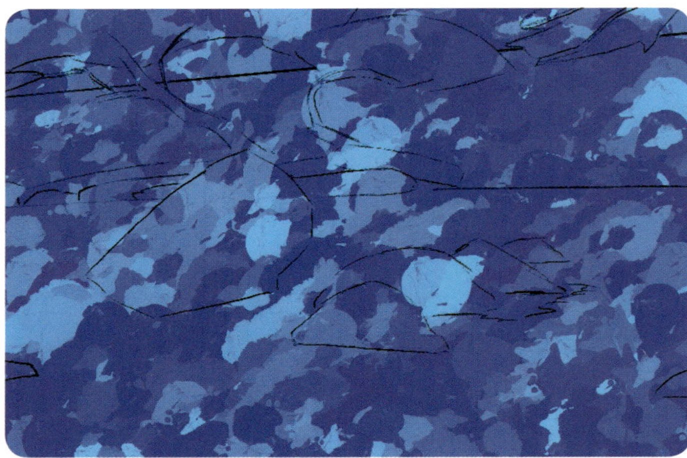

The Brush Studio settings for the Nikko Rull brush, and adding a new background layer

07

Drag the brush randomly across the canvas until it is filled with different blues. This will give the final painting vibrancy and you might feel more comfortable to start painting if your canvas is no longer white. Select the **PAINTING > NIKKO RULL** brush and tap on it to enter the Brush Studio again. Go to **COLOUR DYNAMICS > STROKE COLOUR JITTER** and set the Hue, Saturation, Lightness, and Darkness sliders to around 5% each. This will ensure that each individual stroke has some colour variation. Create a new layer above the 'Underpainting' layer and name it 'BG' for background. Pick a dark green colour and fill in the area behind the trees. Use several brushstrokes to get the most out of the brush's new colour jitter.

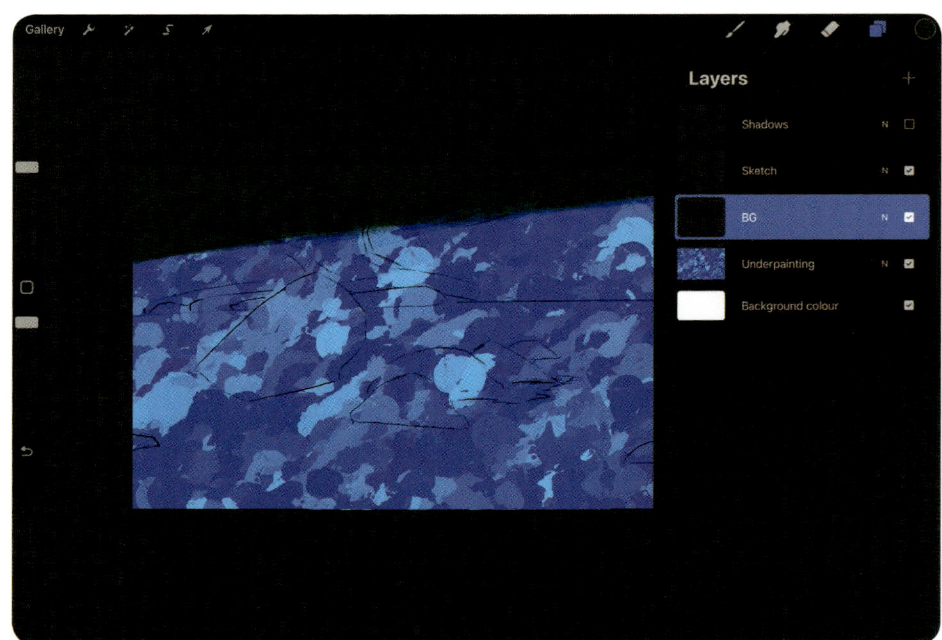

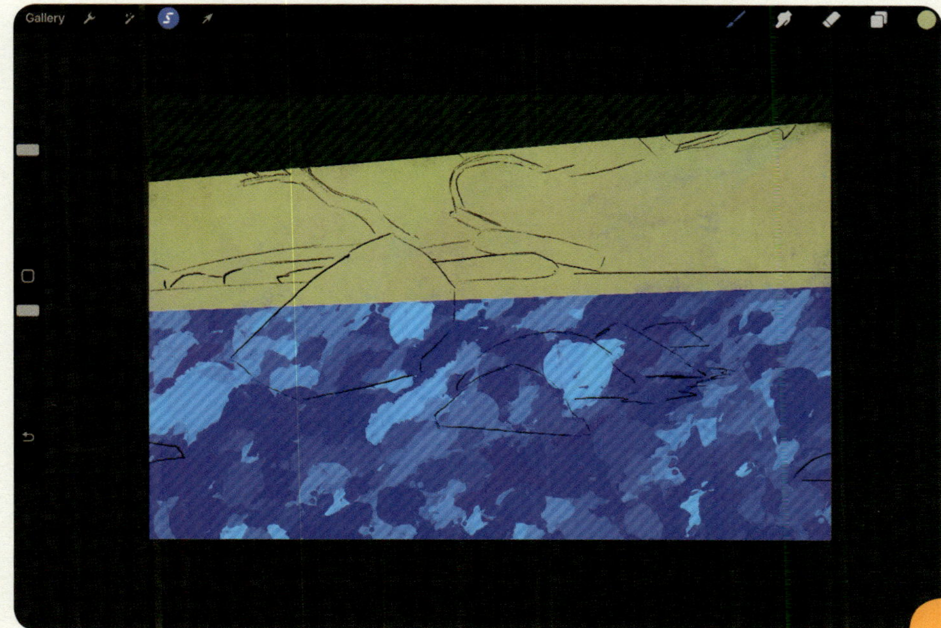

The filled selection and colour choice for the 'Wall' layer

08

Create another layer above the 'BG' layer and name it 'Wall'. Pick an unsaturated yellowish colour and use the **SELECTION > FREEHAND** tool to select the area that will become the wall, using your sketch as a guide. The lower part doesn't have to be exact, as the rocks and sand will overlap it anyway. Fill the selection, using a generously sized brush tip and several brushstrokes with light pressure, so the blue tones of the underpainting can shine through a little.

09

Repeat step 08 for the sand, foliage, trees, boats, and stones. Rename and layer them separately and in that order, from background to foreground. Fill in the objects' local colours – the colours as they would appear in flat, white light, rather than strong or coloured light. When you have blocked out flat colours for every element, hide the sketch. Enable Alpha Lock on all the layers by swiping right on each one with two fingers in the Layers menu. This will lock the layer's transparency, ensuring you will only paint inside the areas that are already painted. Unless you need to alter the overall shape of an object, leave the layers Alpha Locked for the rest of the tutorial.

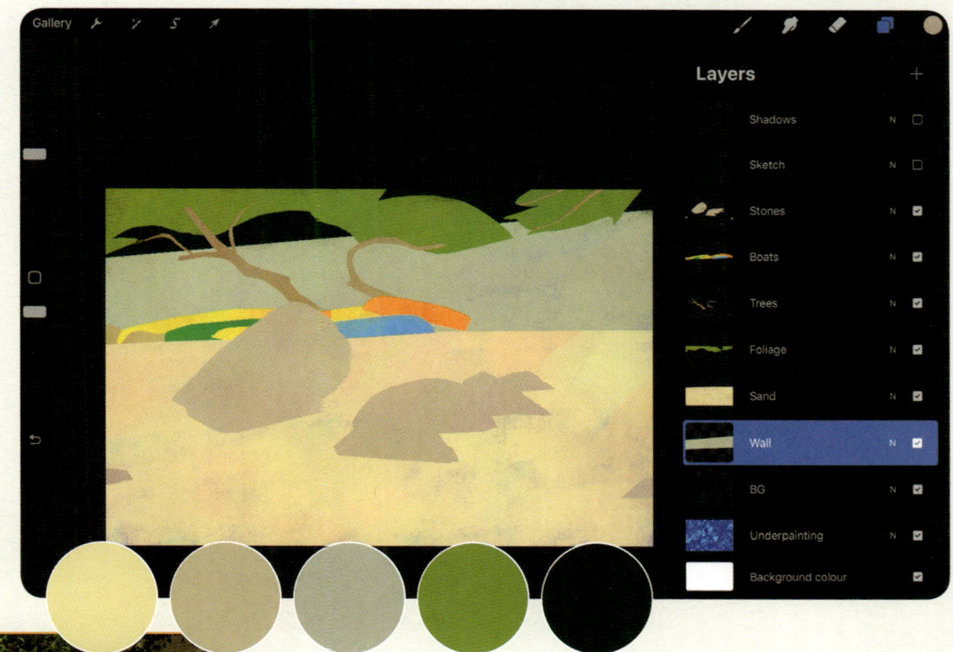

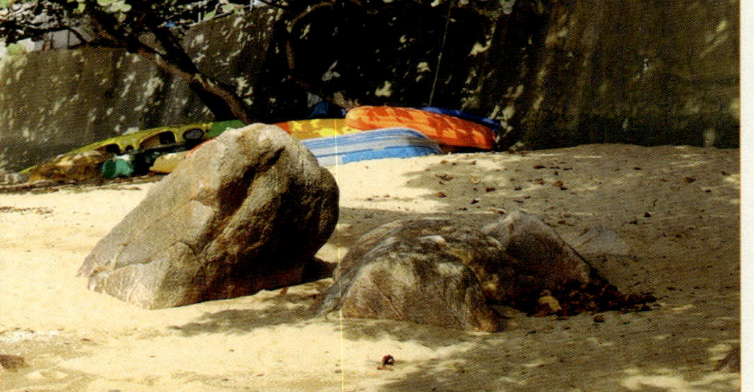

Fill out each shape according to the reference and Alpha Lock each layer

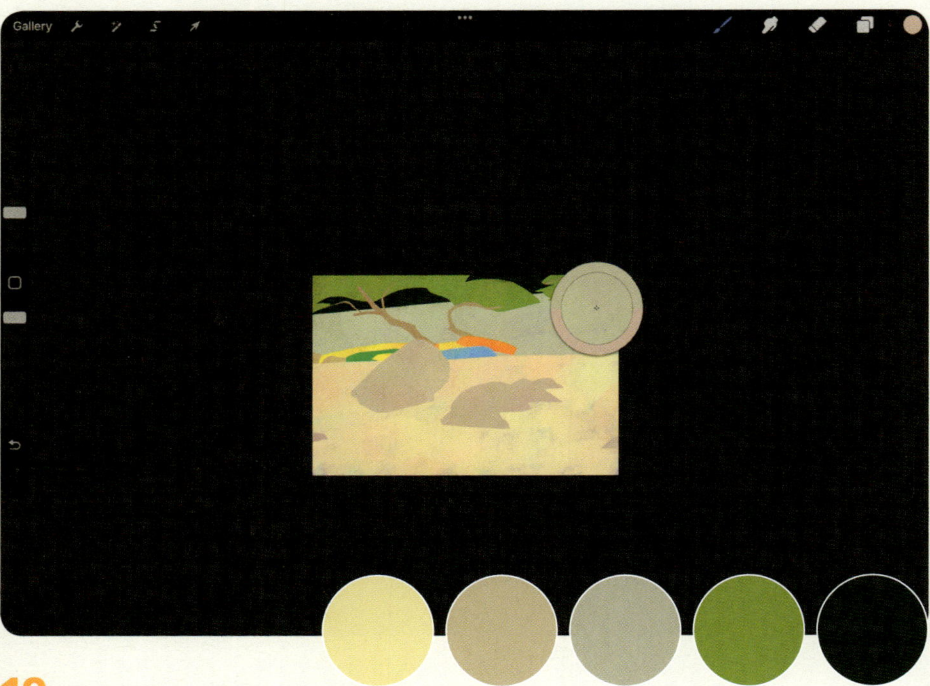

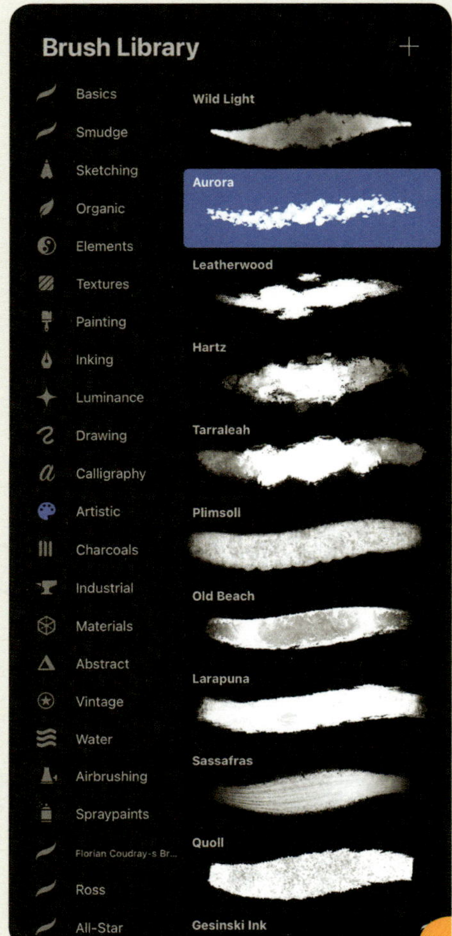

Colour-picking and adding colour variations and textures, then selecting the Aurora brush

10

Tap and hold on the canvas to activate the Eyedropper and colour-pick the wall colour. Select the 'Wall' layer, decrease your brush size with the slider on the left, and make some strokes to add colour variations. Repeat this with the layers for the boats, stones, and sand. With the Selection tool, select and paint the darker areas of the sand, according to the reference. Use the **ORGANIC > HESSIAN** brush and darken your colour slightly to add texture to the wall. Use the **ARTISTIC > AURORA** brush to paint the foliage and tree trunks to simulate leaves and a bark texture.

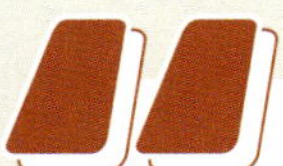

KARIN SAYS: *'As you are working on the painting, you might notice that colour choices you made early on start to look wrong at a later stage. Make it a habit to regularly reassess the colours and adjust them if necessary. To do so, select the layer in question and tap on the wand symbol in the upper-left menu bar to open the Adjustments menu. Use the Hue, Saturation, Brightness, Colour Balance, and Curves adjustments to tweak the colours to your liking. Tap the dropdown arrow in the middle to switch to Pencil mode if you want to use your brush to control where the adjustment affects your layer.'*

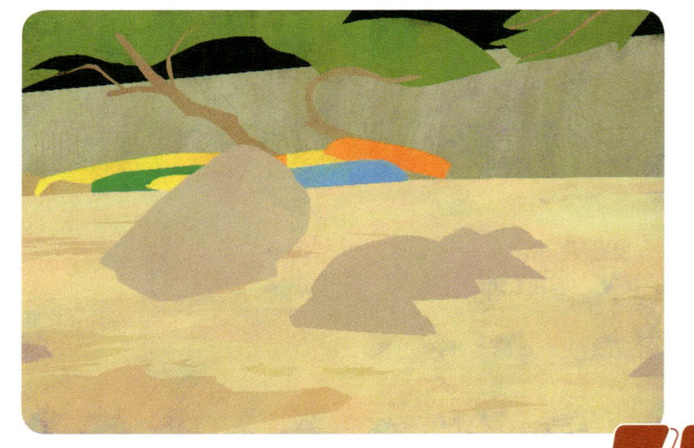

11

Tap the checkboxes of the Shadows and Sketch layers to unhide them. Then, using one finger, swipe left on the 'Wall' layer in the menu and tap Duplicate. Select that new layer and rename it 'Wall Shadow'. Using the sketch as a guide, select all the light patches on the wall with the **SELECTION > FREEHAND** tool. If you select an area by accident, you can cut out unwanted parts by switching the tool to Remove mode. Now tap the 'Wall Shadow' layer and select the Mask option. This will attach a layer mask to that layer based on the shapes of your selection.

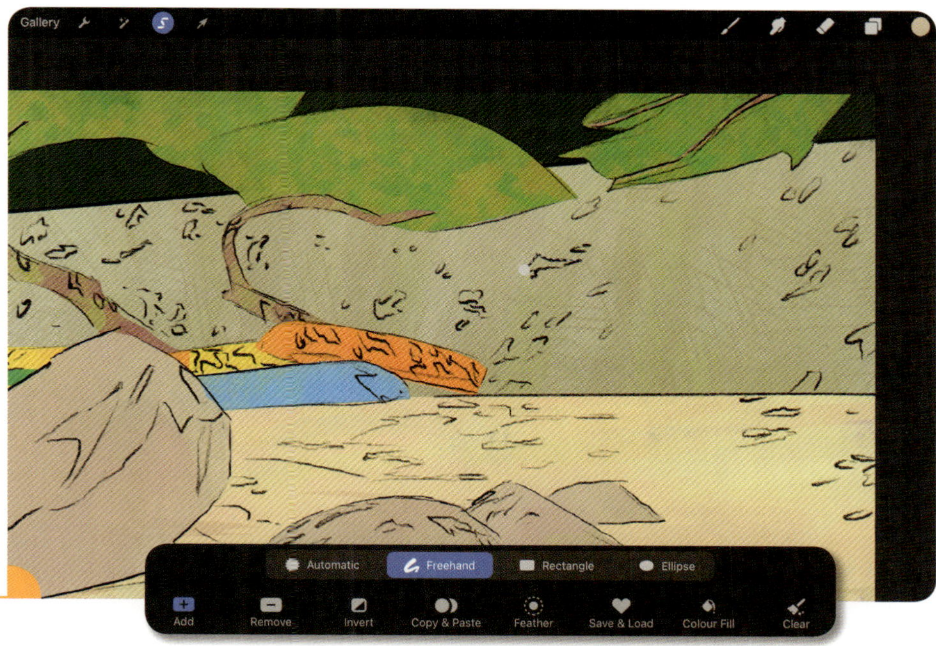

Using the shadow sketch to select the light shapes

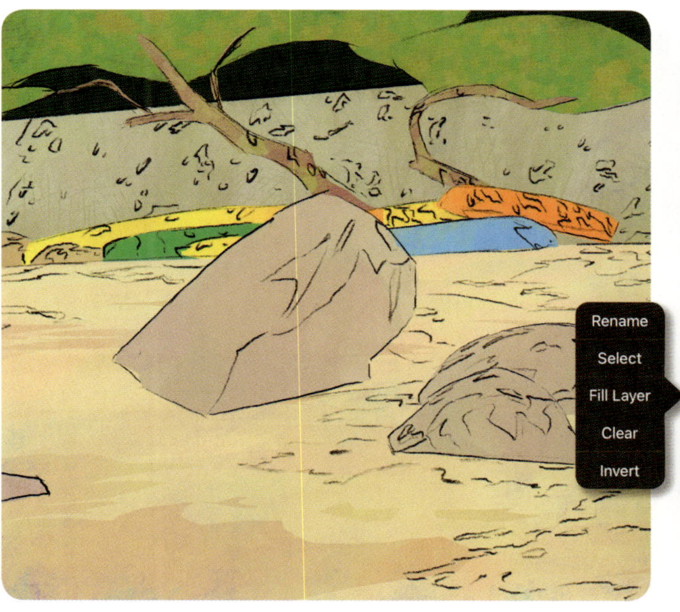

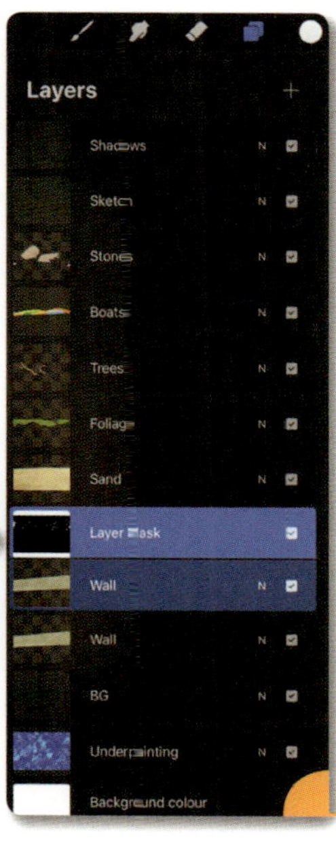

12

You can now modify the layer mask with your usual painting tools to hide or show any part of its parent layer. Painting with black will hide those areas of the original layer, while parts painted in white will be visible. You can also use shades of grey for anything in between. The light shapes are currently visible instead of the shadow shapes, as they were easier to select. To reverse this, tap the layer mask in the Layers menu and then select Invert. Since the two layers are still identical, you won't be able to see the difference just yet.

The completed layer mask and its layer mask menu with the Invert option

13

With the 'Wall Shadow' layer selected, open **ADJUSTMENTS > CURVES**. You can now change the brightness, contrast, and hue of the shadows. Darken the shadows considerably by dragging the upper-right node down about a quarter of the way, and then tap the centre of the curve to create a new node. Drag that node down slightly to create a curve that increases the contrast. Tap Blue and adjust the curve slightly to add a cool blue tone to the shadow.

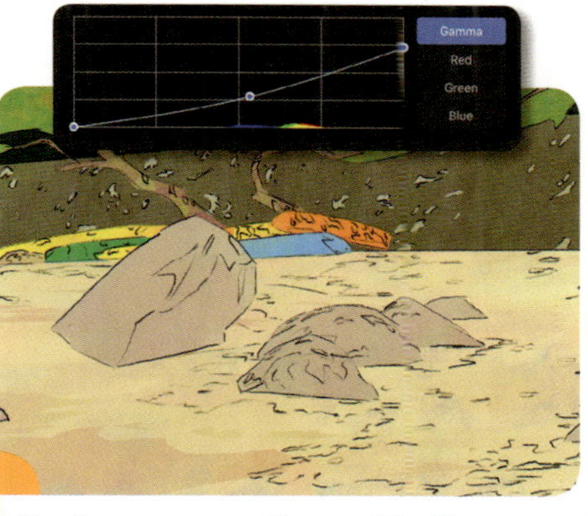

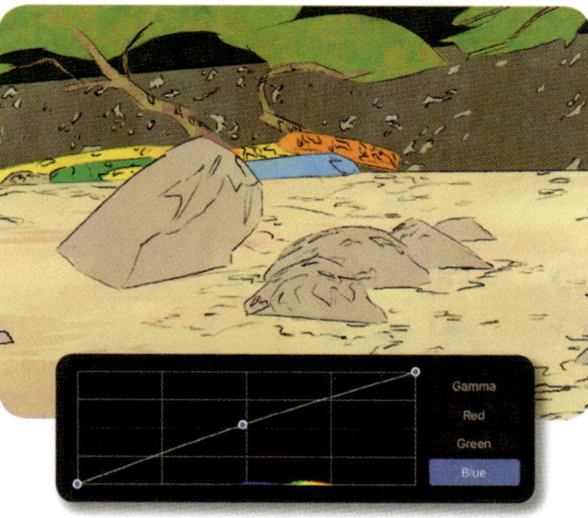

The Gamma curve settings and the Blue curve settings for the wall shadow

14

Repeat steps 11 to 13 for the sand, trees, boats, and stones. Then hide the sketch layers and create a new layer called 'Foliage Shadow' by duplicating the 'Foliage' layer. Adjust the curves to darken the layer and then create a layer mask. Without anything selected, it will just be filled with white. Make sure the layer mask is selected, set the brush colour to black, and then use the **ARTISTIC > AURORA** brush to paint in the light areas. If you paint too much light, change the brush colour to white and paint the shadows back in. You can go back and forth until you are happy with the shadow shapes.

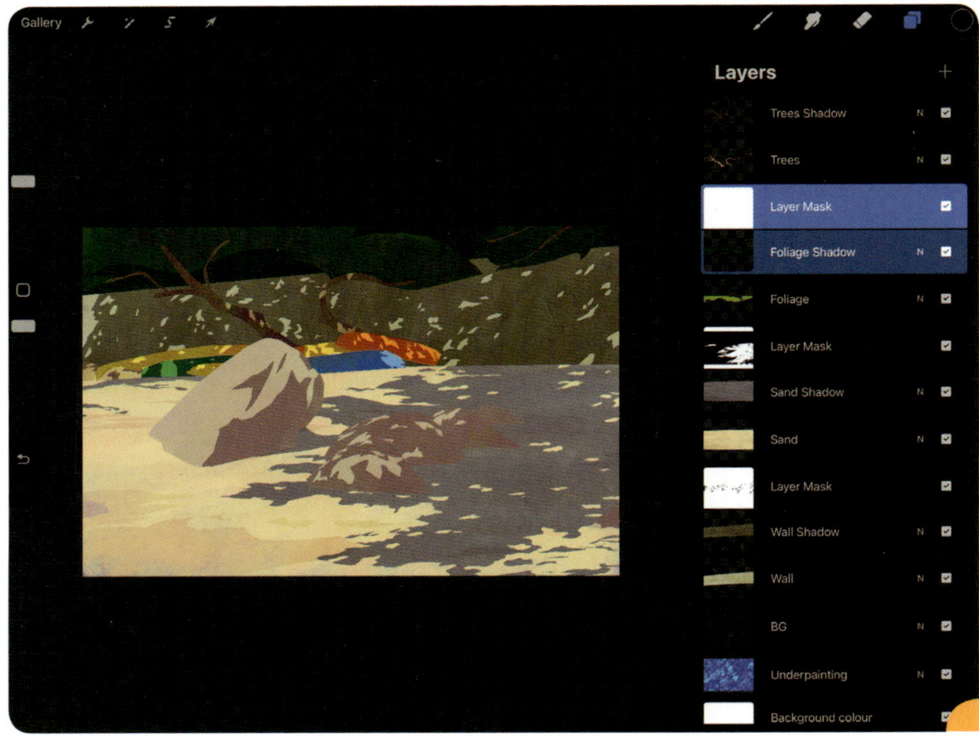

The completed shadow layers with the 'Foliage Shadow' layer mask selected

15

Tap the 'Foliage Shadow' layer and then Clipping Mask. The shadow layer (and its mask) will now be tied to the 'Foliage' layer's shape and visibility. Create a layer mask for 'Foliage' and invert it. 'Foliage Shadow' will now also be affected by this, temporarily vanishing. Use the **ARTISTIC > AURORA** brush to paint foliage back in, but leave some areas empty to break up the edges of the shapes for a more organic feel. Repeat steps 14 and 15 for the 'Trees' and 'Trees Shadow' layers to hide parts of the branches close to the foliage. The branches should look like they are being covered by leaves here and there.

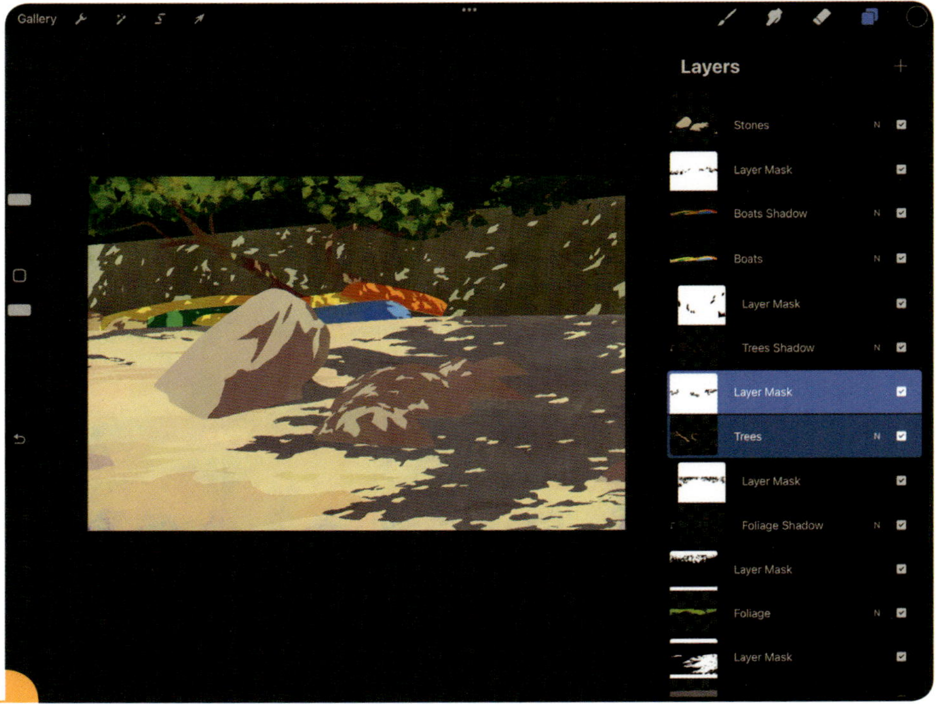

Breaking up the silhouettes of the foliage and branches using clipping and layer masks

16

Create a new layer named 'Contact Shadows' and clip it to the 'Wall Shadow' layer. Tap the N beside its name and select Multiply from the top of the list of blend modes. This mode will darken the areas you paint but will leave the textures of the underlying layer intact. The darkening depends on the colour you paint with.

To only add darkness without changing the hue, paint with the same colour as the underlying layer.

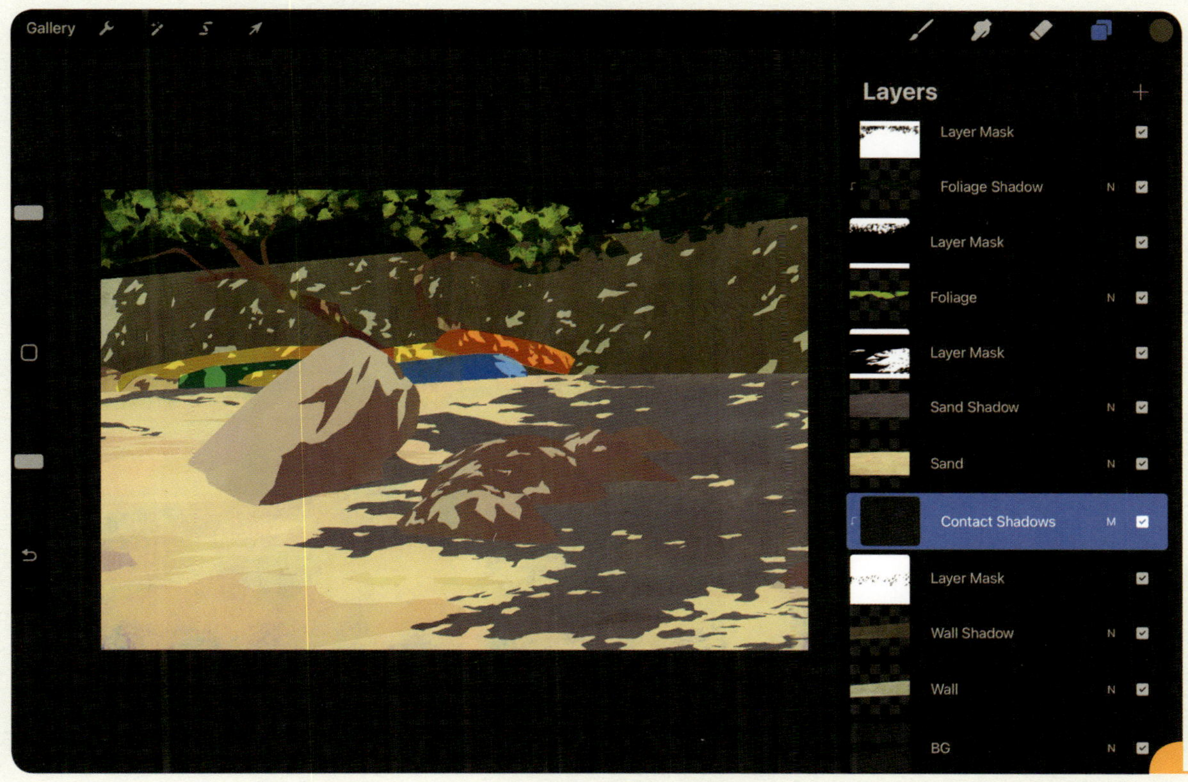

The 'Contact Shadows' layer clipped to 'Wall Shadow' and set to Multiply

17

Tap and hold one finger over the wall shadow to select its colour with the Eyedropper. Use the **PAINTING > NIKKO RULL** brush to add darkness where the tree is closest to the wall. Use less pressure as you move away from the area to create a smooth transition between the contact shadow and the overall shadow. Using the same method, add contact shadows to the sand, mainly where the rocks and sand meet. If the contact shadow seems too dark, simply lighten the colour you are painting with.

The finished wall contact shadows (and some corrections in the boat shadows)

18

Using the Nikko Rull brush, move between layers to add some darker and brighter tones to the stones and their shadows. Pay close attention to how the shadow behaves, especially where the sunlight bounces back on it from the sand. Select the **PAINTING > STUCCO** brush and use it to add crisp textures to the rocks by colour-picking from the colours already there. Select the 'Stones Shadow' layer mask and use the Stucco brush to break up some of the edges there too. Make sure to balance hard edges with soft edges.

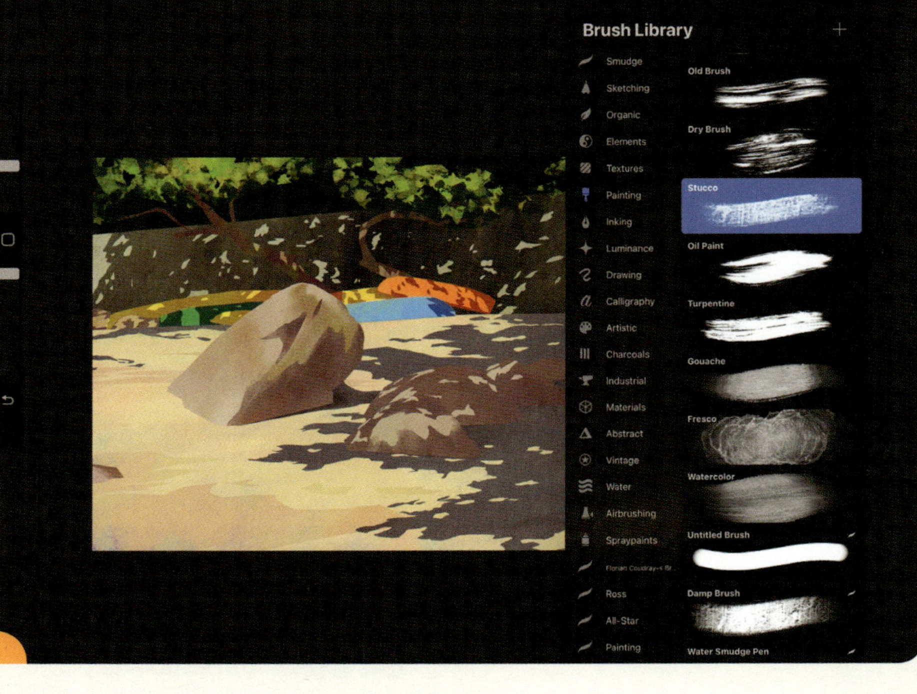

Selecting the Stucco brush after adding lighter and darker shades to the rocks with Nikko Rull

19

Create a new layer above the 'Stones Shadow' layer and clip both to the 'Stones' layer. Change the new layer's name to 'Contact Shadows' and its blend mode to Multiply. Use the Selection tool to create shapes for the cracks. Colour-pick the stone colour and use Nikko Rull to fill the area. Clear the selection and paint some contact shadows on the rocks right where they meet the ground. Add a core shadow to the stones' shadow by darkening the area that gets the least light. The core shadow is generally where the shadow meets the light, as it's furthest from the reflected light that often brightens other areas of the shadow.

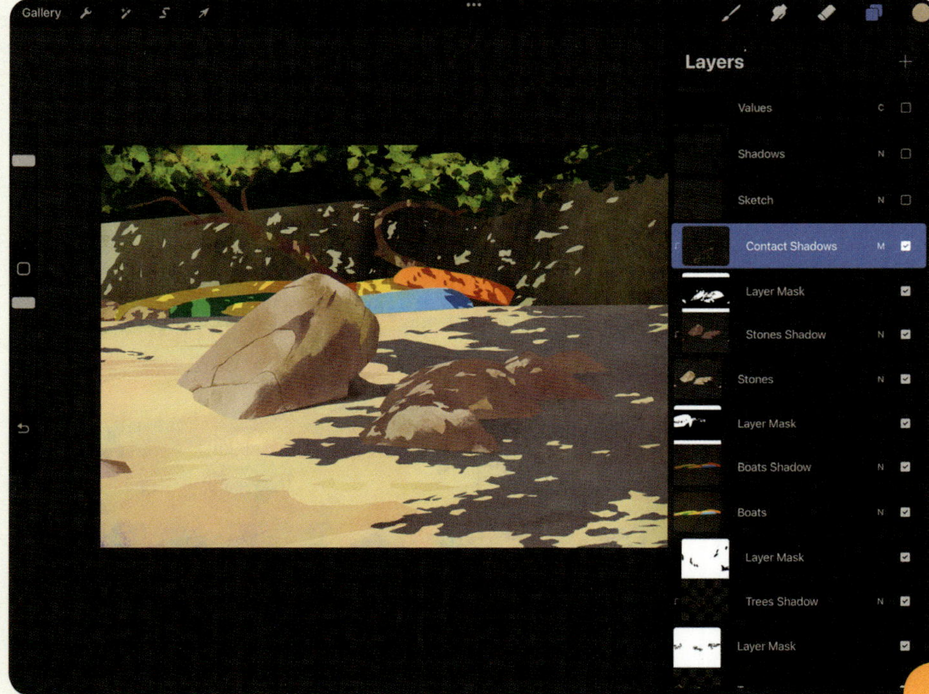

Adding cracks and core shadows to the rocks with a Multiply layer

20

As you saw in the reference on page 49, the background of this beach is very noisy, so this is where you get to exercise some creative freedom to improve the scene. Select the underpainting and use the Nikko Rull brush to paint in a light-blue sky. Tap on the 'BG' layer and colour-pick its green colour, then add a leaf texture to it with the **ARTISTIC > AURCRA** brush. With the 'BG' layer still selectec, create a layer mask and invert it. Paint in some areas to look like bushes, while leaving some negative spaces to show the sky. Try to match these negative spaces with the light shapes of the reference.

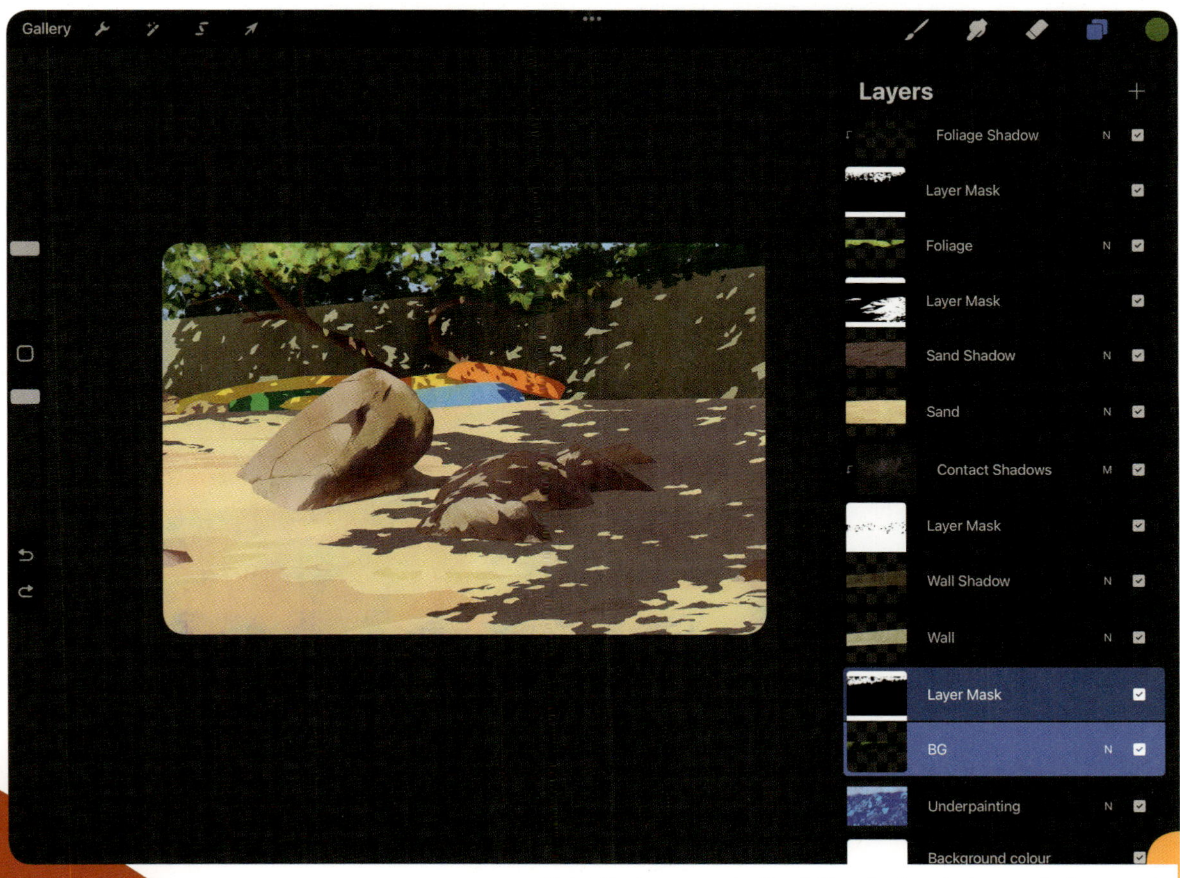

Fixing the background with additional colour, texture, and a layer mask

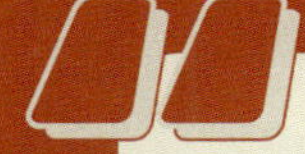

KARIN SAYS: *'Now that you have added shadows, your painting no longer consists of only flat colours and textures, so you'll have to pay attention to the values, too. Check your painting as a whole by zooming out often. Make it a habit to only zoom in when working on details. Check your values by adding a layer on top of everything, filling it with pure black, and setting the blend mode to Colour. This will show the painting in greyscale and help you evaluate which areas are too bright or too dark.'*

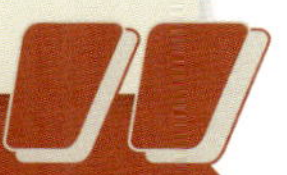

21

Select the 'Sand Shadow' layer and pick a saturated red-orange colour. Use the Nikko Rull and Stucco brushes to paint some redness along the shadow's edges. Repeat this process for the wall shadows, boat shadows, tree shadows, and stone shadows. Select the mask of each shadow layer and use the same brushes to break up the edges further, as you did with the stone shadows in step 18. Remember to use this sparingly and keep a good balance between the hard and soft edges.

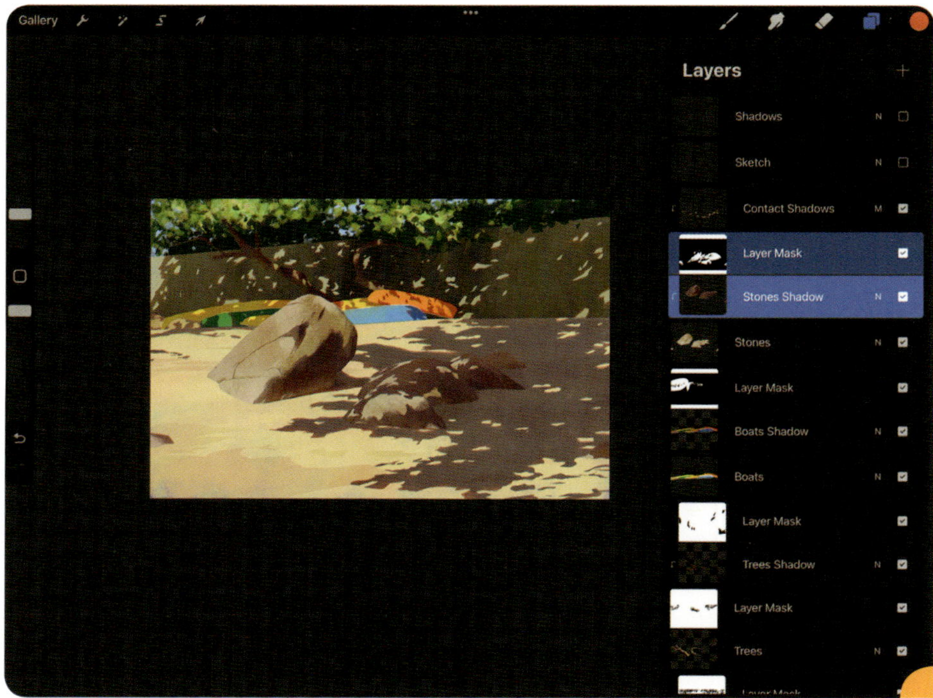

Adding a subtle, reddish fringe to the shadows using textured brushes

22

Select **AIRBRUSHING > SOFT BRUSH** and pick a brownish colour. Create a new layer on top of all the visible layers and set its blend mode to Colour Dodge. This mode will create a glowing effect based on the colour you pick. In this case, it will make the areas you paint appear brighter as well as slightly more saturated and orange, which helps convey the effect that sunlight has on bright and reflective yellow surfaces.

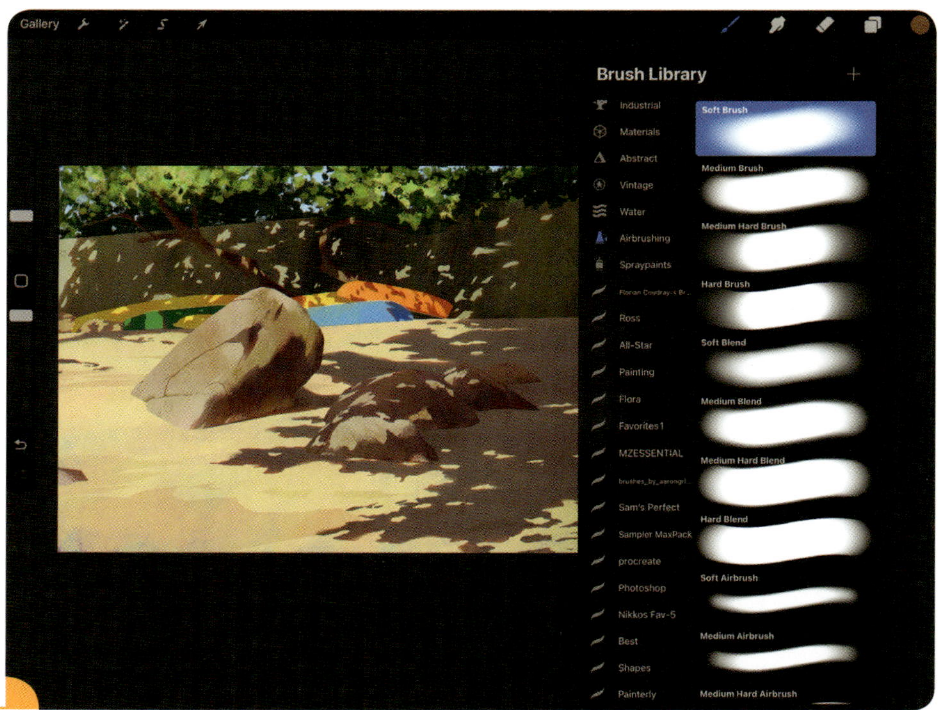

Selecting the Soft Brush and a brown colour for the Colour Dodge layer

23

Use the Soft Brush to paint where the sun hits the focal point – in this case, the large rock. Paint some of it on other bright areas, like the wall's or the other rocks' light spots, and on the foliage. Have the Soft Brush bleed over the edge of the shadow to soften it further, but make sure not to paint in the shadow areas exclusively.

You will notice that the glow is too intense when you first apply it. To soften it, tap the layer with two fingers to adjust its opacity, then slide one finger to the left to reduce the opacity to about 40%.

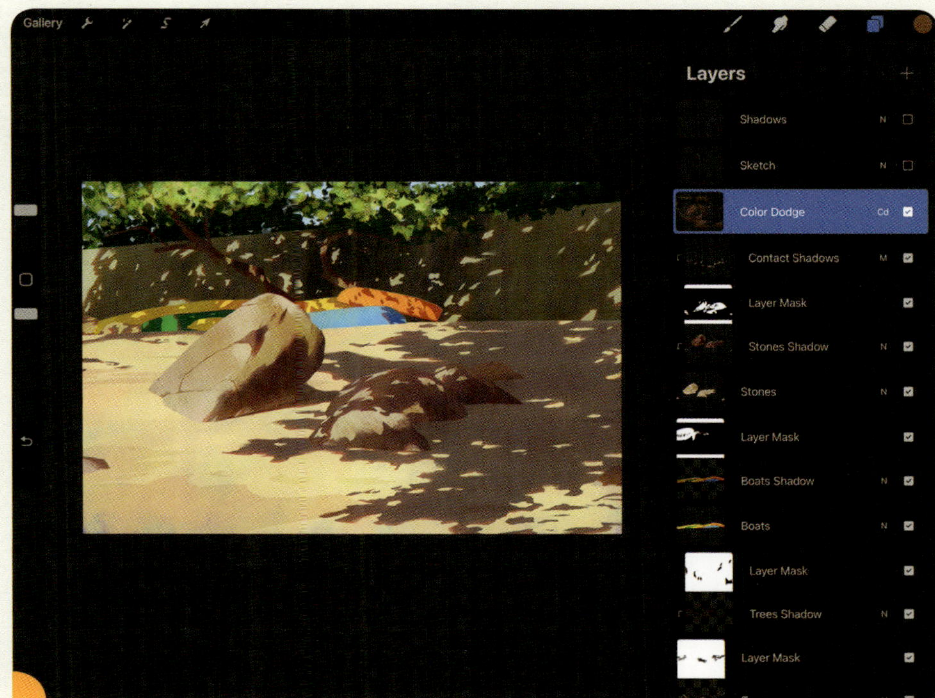

The finished Colour Dodge layer adds a slight glow to the sunlit areas

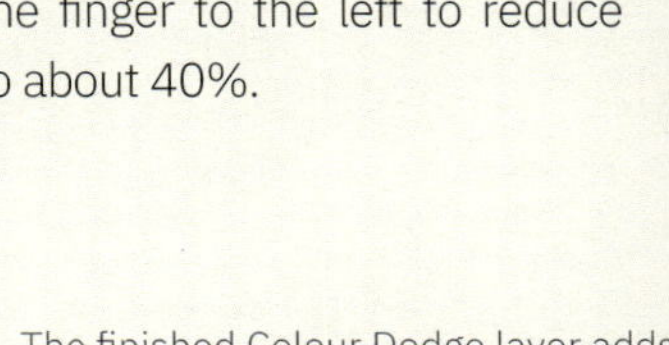

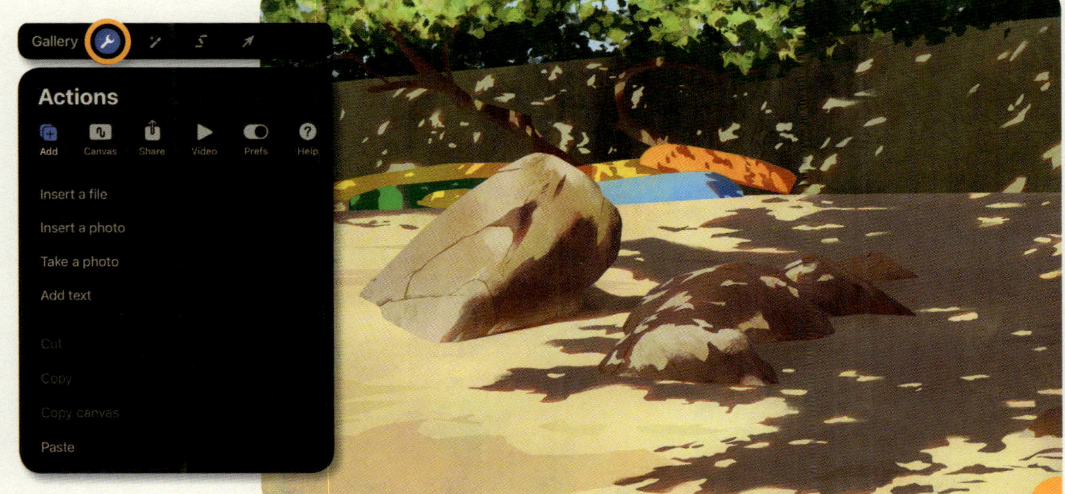

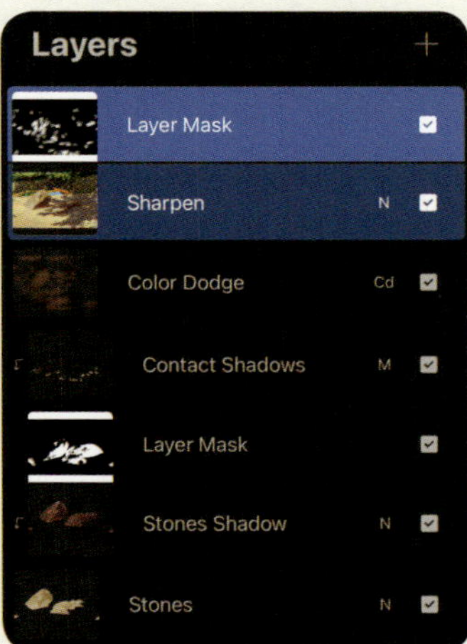

The Actions menu after tapping Copy canvas and the masked 'Sharpen' layer

24

Go to **ACTIONS > ADD > COPY CANVAS** and then **PASTE**. This copies and pastes the entire painting as a flattened image on a new layer. Rename it 'Sharpen', then go to **ADJUSTMENTS > SHARPEN** and slide your finger to the right to increase the effect to about 60%. Create a layer mask, invert it, and then use Nikko Rull to paint some of the sharpness back in. Focus on the textures and transitions between the light and shadow of the rocks and sand to make them pop.

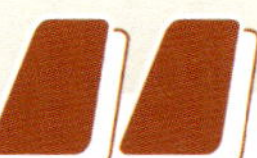

KARIN SAYS: *'When breaking up hard edges or softening a transition, the Smudge tool can be a better choice than the Paint tool. You will find it right next to the Paint icon, in the upper-right menu bar. Experiment with different brushes for different effects. Nikko Rull and Stucco work really well here. You can even use the Round Brush (with the Flow in the Apple Pencil settings set to 0% and the Smudge Pull in Properties set to Max) to easily refine the shapes of your objects by pushing and pulling the paint around on the canvas.'*

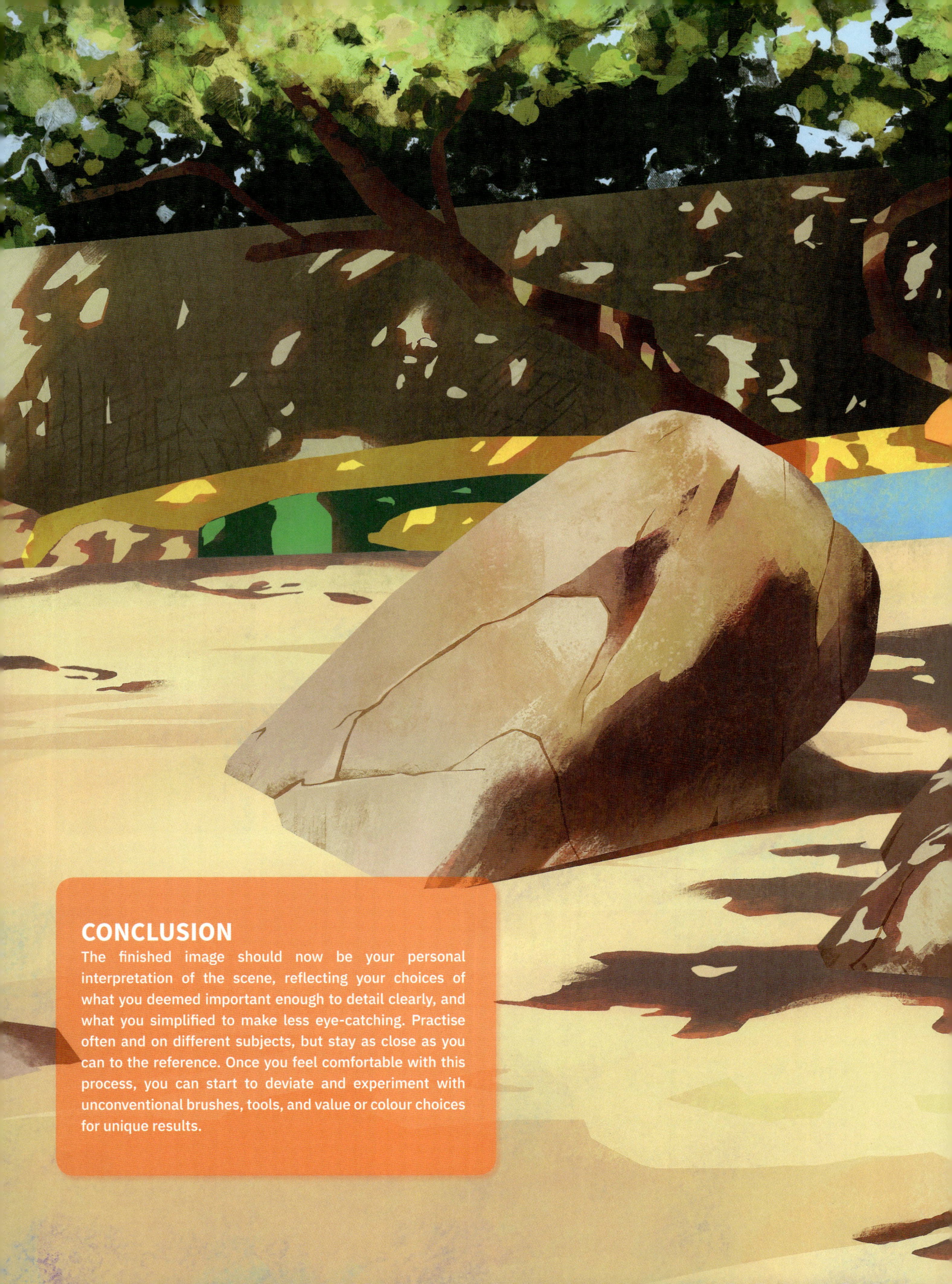

CONCLUSION

The finished image should now be your personal interpretation of the scene, reflecting your choices of what you deemed important enough to detail clearly, and what you simplified to make less eye-catching. Practise often and on different subjects, but stay as close as you can to the reference. Once you feel comfortable with this process, you can start to deviate and experiment with unconventional brushes, tools, and value or colour choices for unique results.

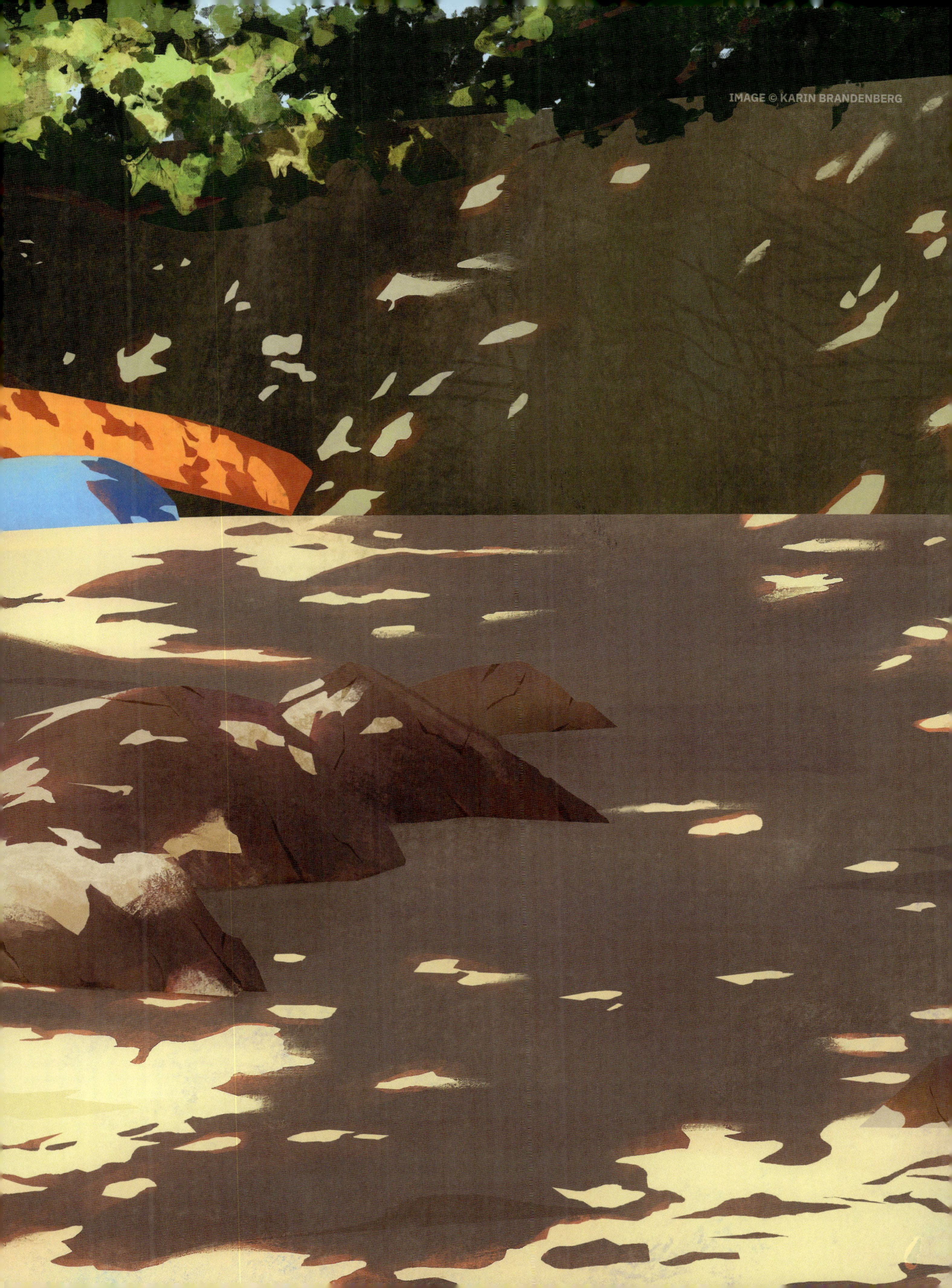

IMAGE © KARIN BRANDENBERG

LANDSCAPE ILLUSTRATION: This image was an attempt at a made-up and more stylized type of landscape meant for print

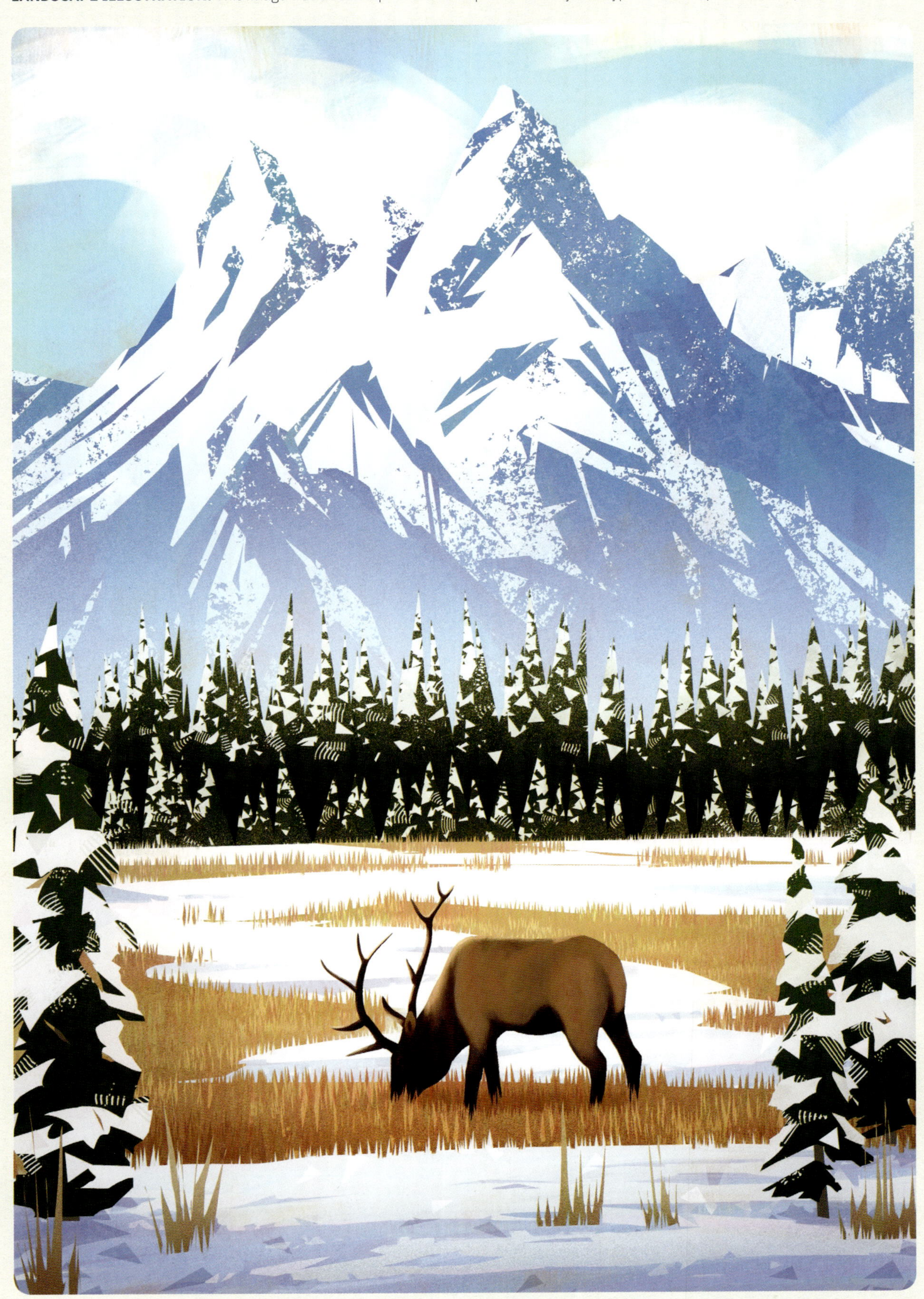

IMAGES © KARIN BRANDENBERG

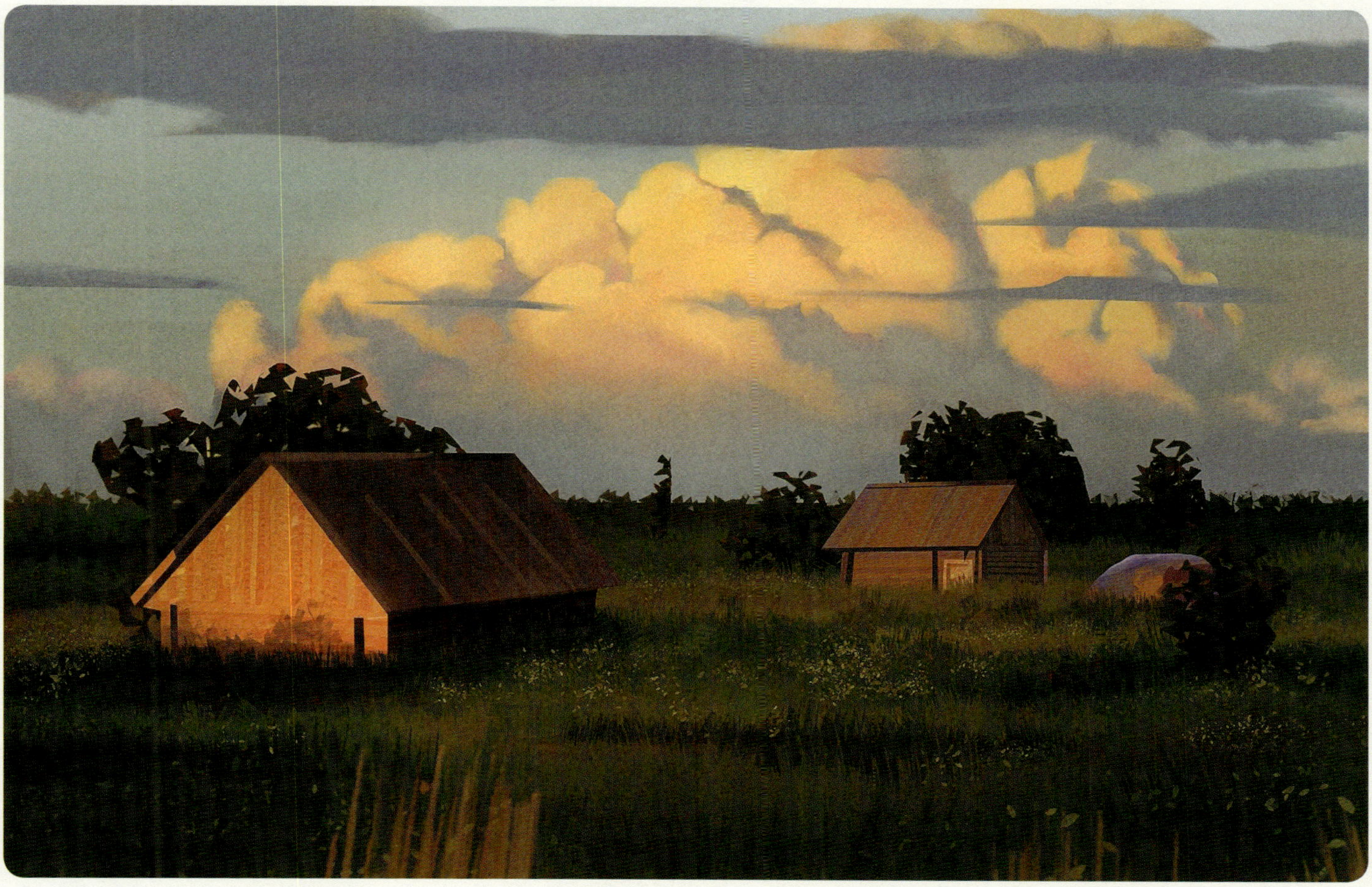

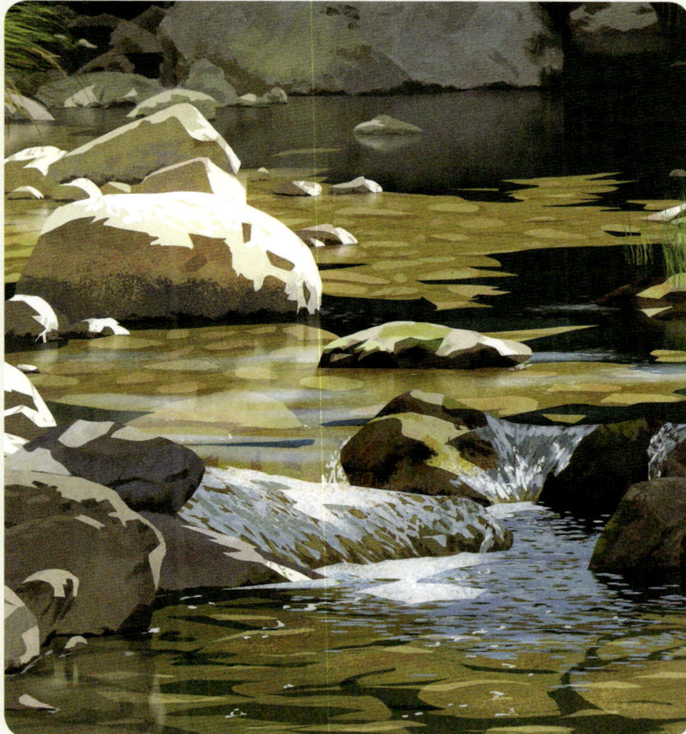

SUNSET SCENE: The main goal for this piece was to capture the atmosphere of the sunset and the towering clouds

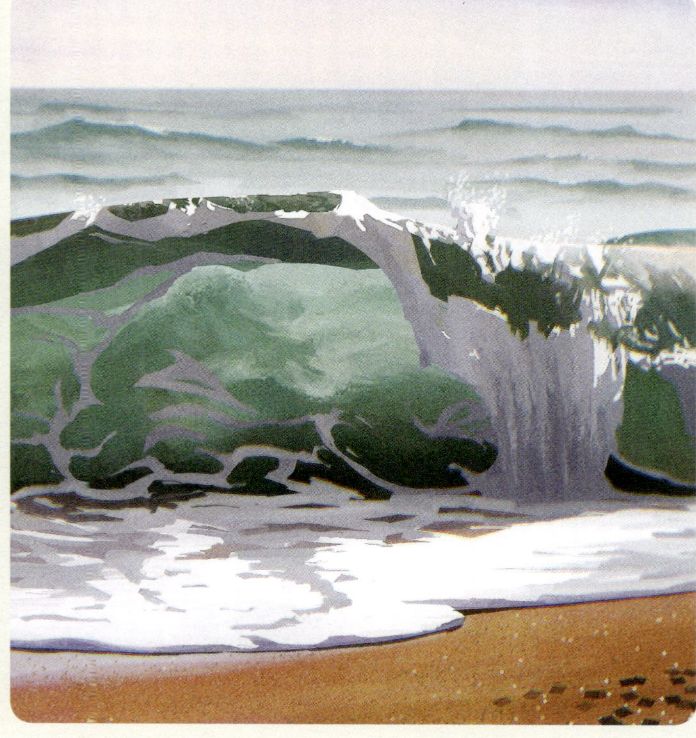

PLEIN AIR: A plein-air scene I painted
to study how light and colour behave

SEA STUDY: A study-turned-challenge where I limited myself to using
only a square brush that I tweaked slightly for each specific element

SYDNEY STREET CORNER

BY MOMO SUGIMOTO

MOMO SAYS: *'There are many different ways to approach a landscape or environment painting, depending on the scene, lighting, or objective of the painting. This tutorial uses a series of simple steps to light your scene with a workflow that can then be applied to similar types of environments, enabling you to retell what you see around you in your own style.'*

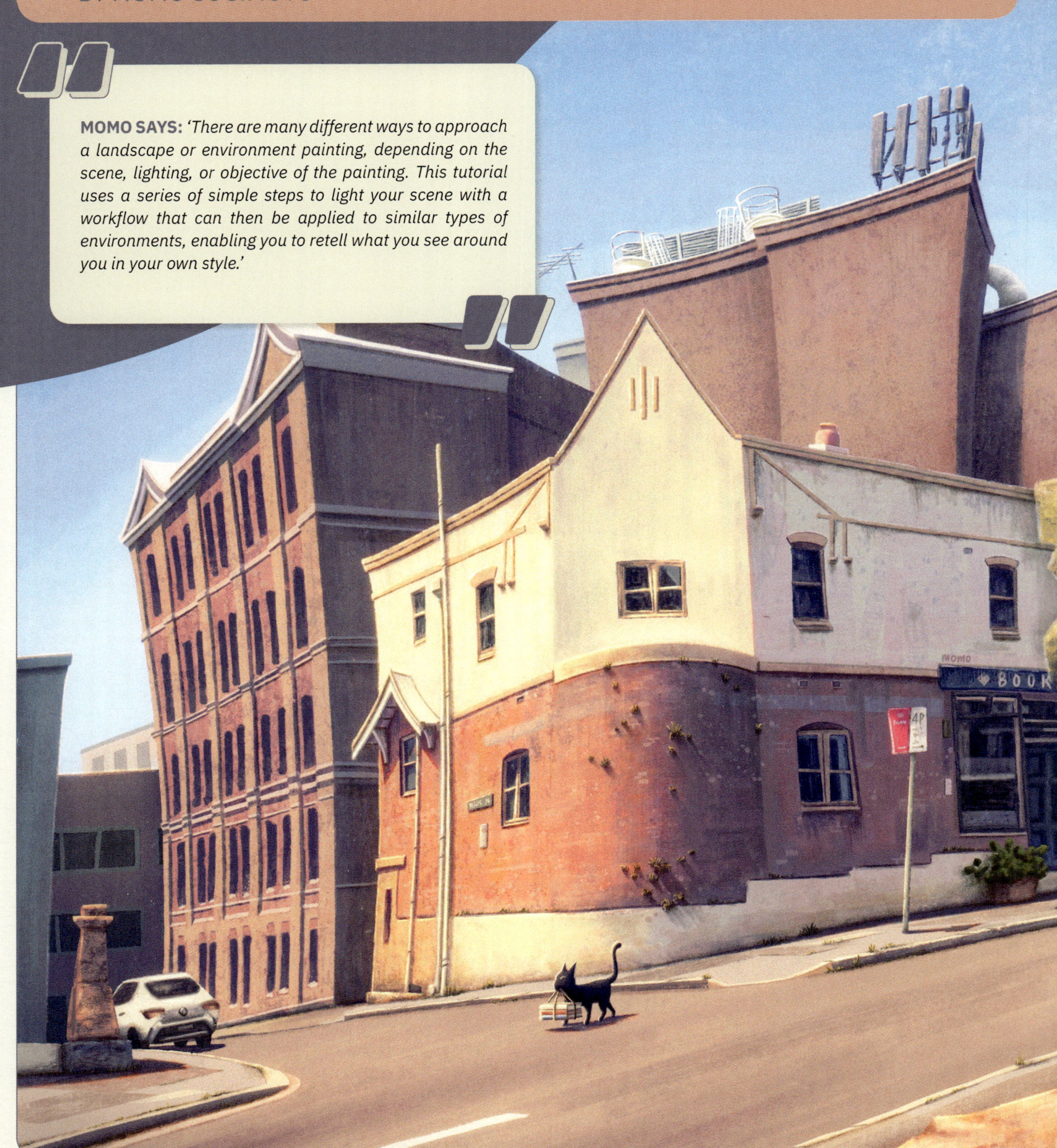

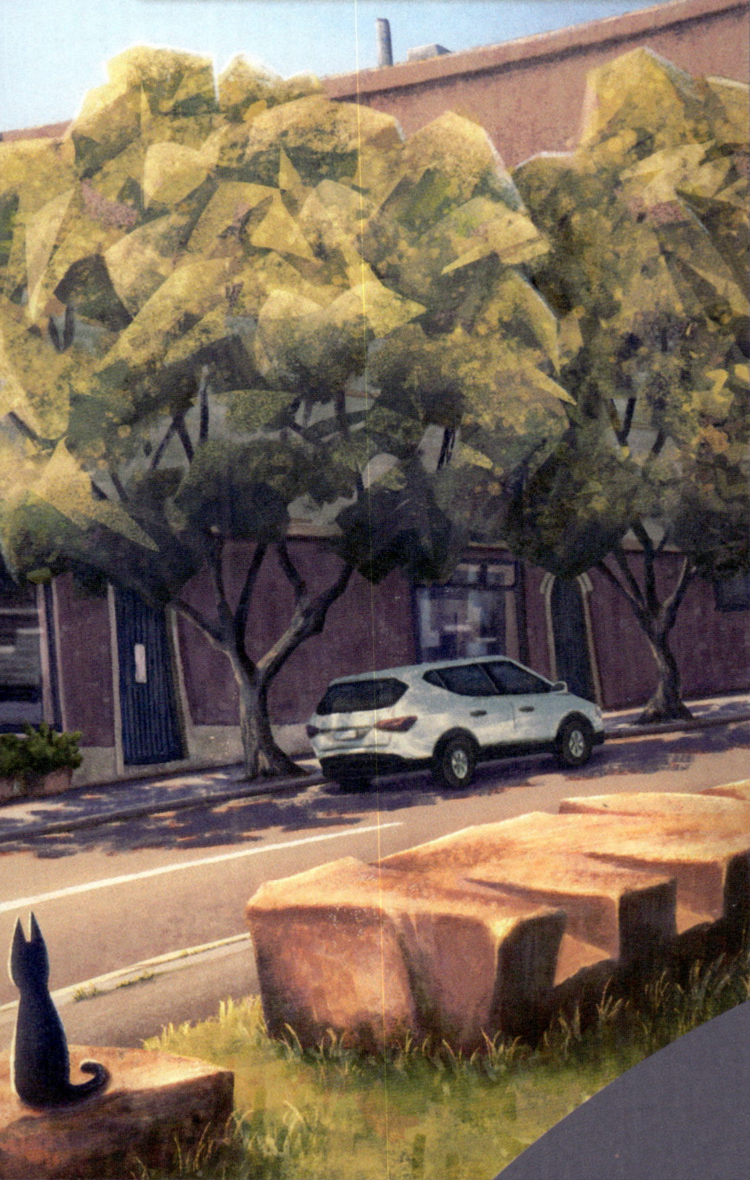

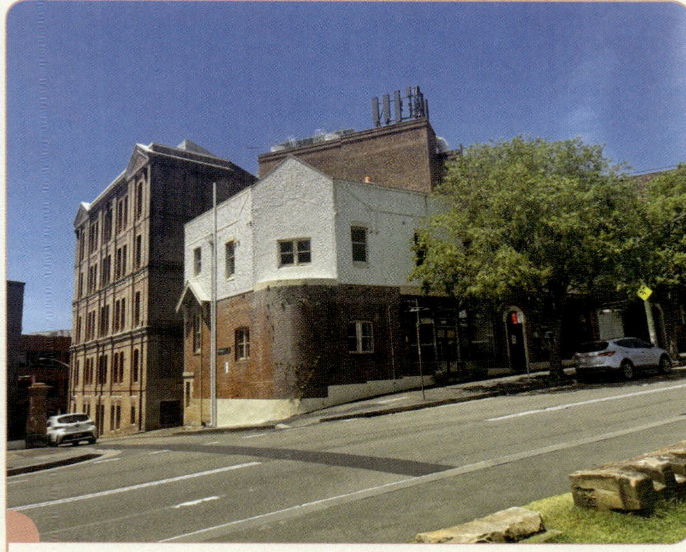

This reference photo was taken in Sydney, Australia

01

Let's start by finding a reference photo. The photo you choose does not have to be perfect – the aim instead is to find an ordinary moment in real life that contains potentially interesting elements that you can focus on in your painting. These elements might include interesting lighting or shadows, buildings that look appealing to you, strange angles, or unique flora and fauna. You can choose a photo from an outside source, such as the internet, but if you can, try taking your own photos – explore your own neighbourhood or city and see what catches your eye.

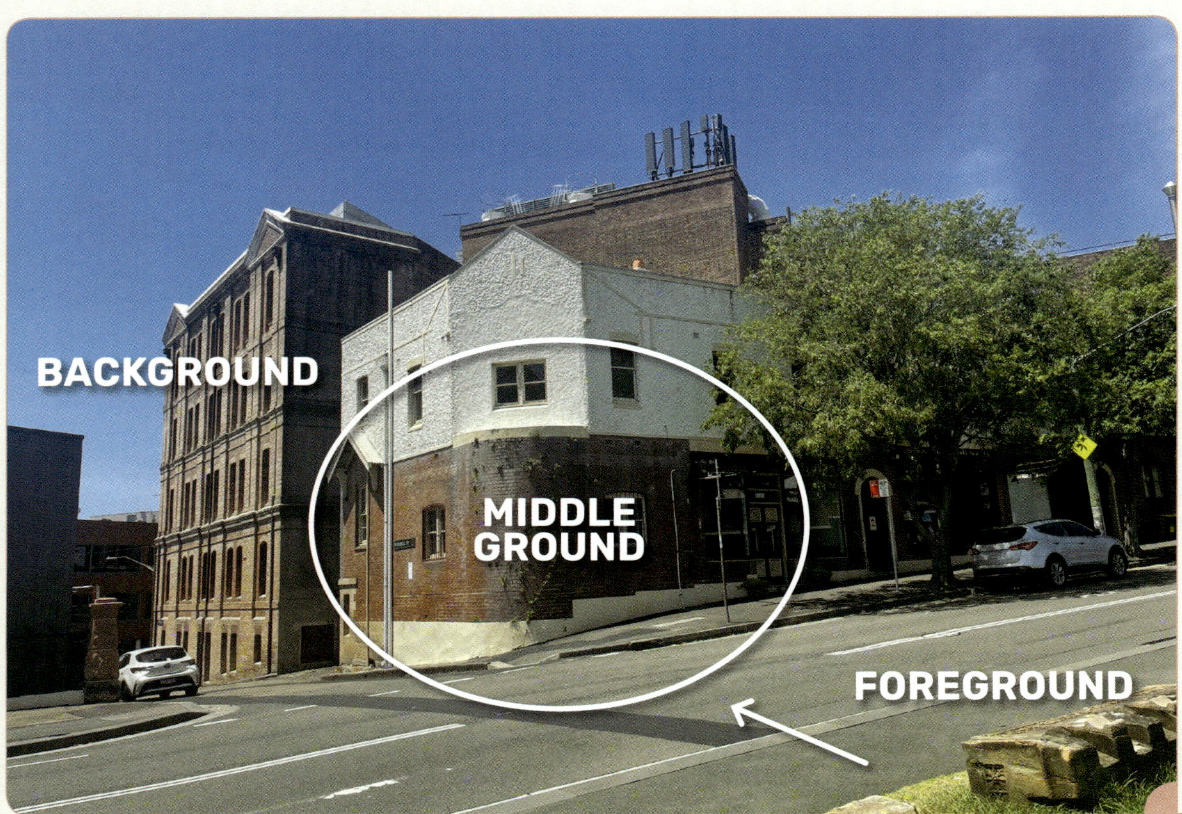

Analyse your reference photo to see how you can make it work for your painting

02

Consider the perspective and staging of your photo and be intentional about where the shapes draw the eye; use a grid if it helps. Avoid overly complex perspectives and scenes with excessive detail, as it will unnecessarily complicate the painting process while you're still learning. Try to choose a photo with a foreground, middle ground, and background, as this will also make it easier to create a painting with depth. That said, as mentioned before, the reference doesn't have to be perfect. You can always exaggerate and move things to make the composition work — it's your painting, after all.

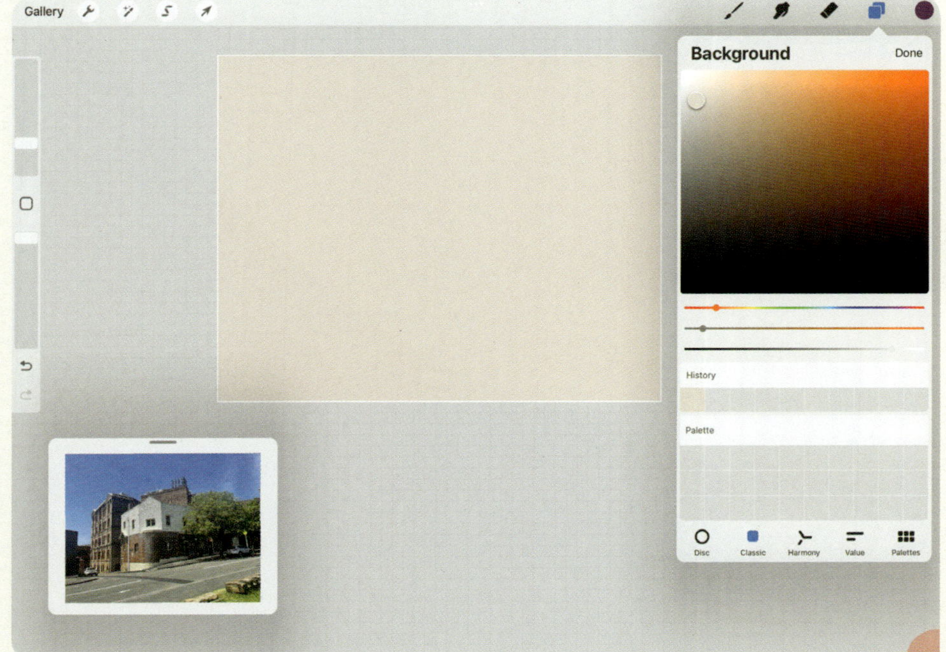

Stay zoomed out to start with, to prevent getting caught up in the details

03

Now you can get started with the sketch. Import your photo into your iPad and then create a new canvas in Procreate. For this painting, the canvas is in landscape format, around 3,300 pixels wide × 2,550 pixels high. Change the background colour to something pale, warm, and desaturated to set the tone for the painting. Bring your reference photo onto your canvas by going to **ACTIONS > CANVAS > REFERENCE**, and in the reference window that pops up, select **IMAGE > IMPORT**. Select your image from the iPad's Camera Roll. Keep the canvas zoomed relatively small and the reference photo even smaller at this stage.

04

Choose a pencil or pen brush with a textured edge, such as INKING > INK BLEED, and set it to a dark colour. On a new layer, start sketching in the main shapes – keep it loose and avoid adding small details. Don't be afraid to push shapes and exaggerate the perspective, and don't worry if the proportions are not perfect. The objective is not to create a hyperrealistic copy of the photo. Flip the canvas horizontally from time to time by tapping the screen to access the default QuickMenu or going to ACTIONS > CANVAS > FLIP HORIZONTAL. This will help you identify any elements that are out of balance or spatial ambiguities such as tangent lines. To emphasize shapes even further, use the Selection tool to make freehand or polygonal selections, then the Transform tool in Freeform, Distort, or Warp mode to transform the selection into your desired shape.

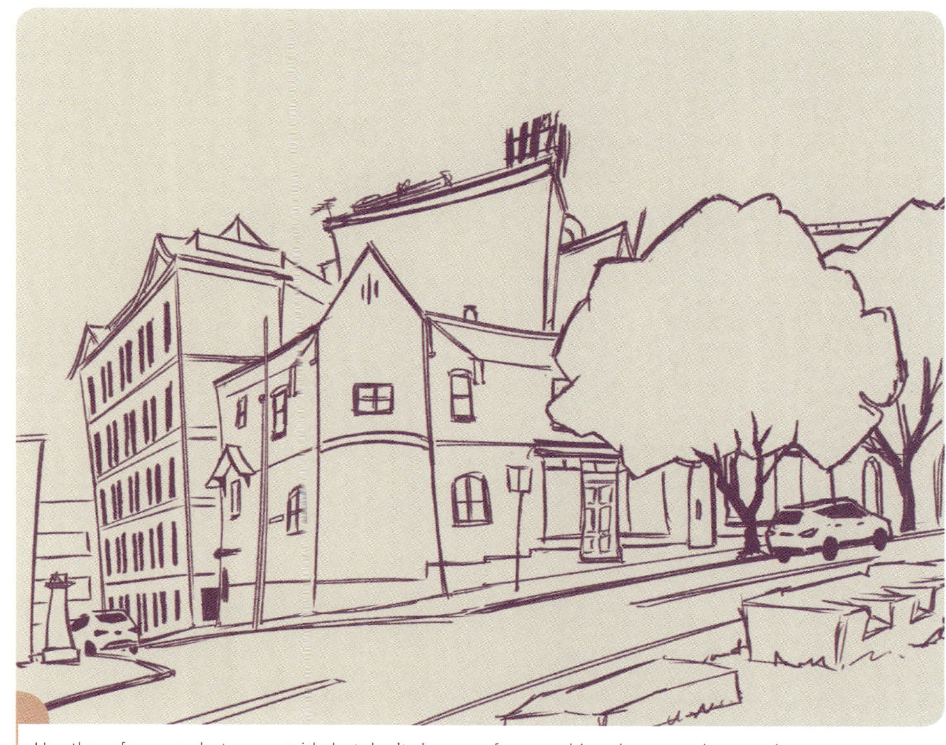

Use the reference photo as a guide but don't shy away from pushing shapes and proportions

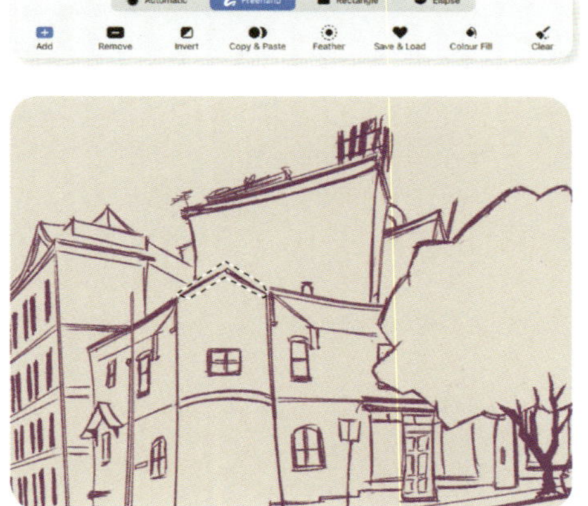

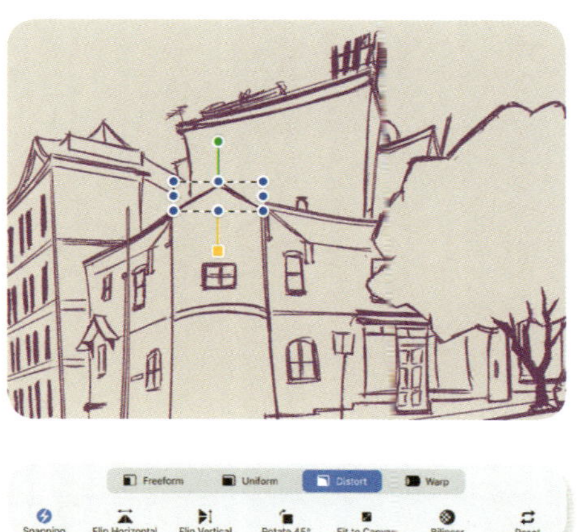

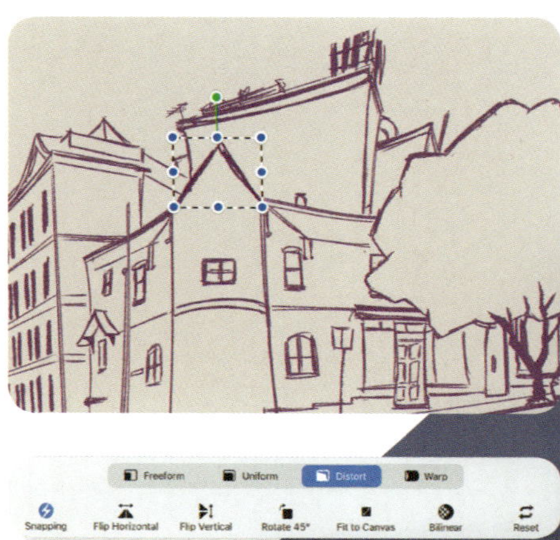

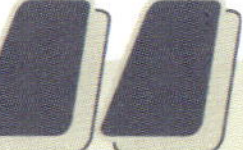

MOMO SAYS: *'This is your painting, so make changes to the scene as you see fit. While the aim is to interpret a scene from real life, if there are minor elements that bring unwanted focus to a certain area and may negatively affect the composition, feel free to leave them out or change them. For example, in this painting, some of the signposts have been moved and some elements on the right side of the painting have been simplified, as it was not an area of focus. The foreground was also made bigger, to better frame the image.'*

05

Rename each main layer as you go to keep things organized. Tap on the sketch layer in the Layers menu, select Rename from the pop-up menu, and name the layer 'Sketch'. Once you are happy with the sketch layer, set it to Multiply blend mode by tapping the N in the Layers menu and scrolling up until you get to Multiply. Once in Multiply mode, lower the layer's opacity to 30–50% by re-opening the blending mode options and adjusting the Opacity slider. Leave this layer at the top of the stack as you block in your colours.

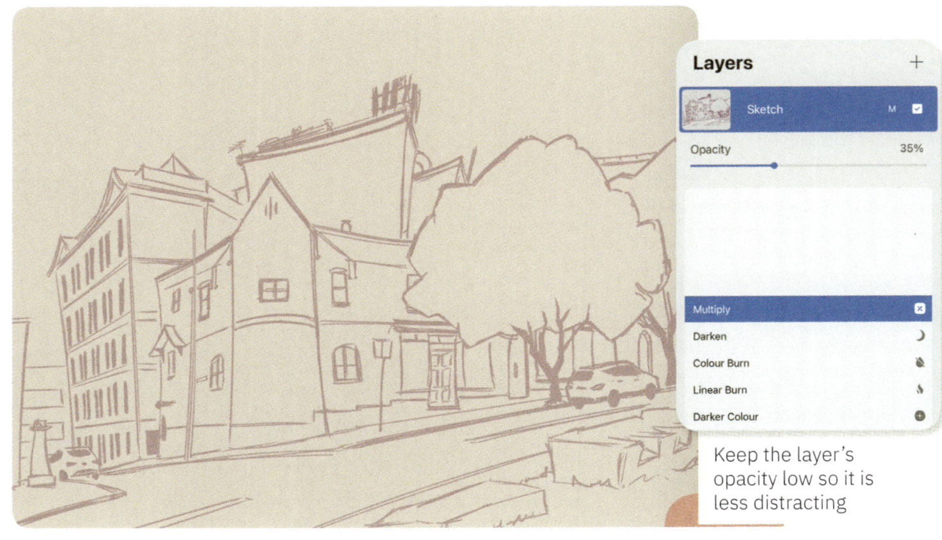

Keep the layer's opacity low so it is less distracting

06

Create a new layer below the Sketch layer for adding local colour. Local colour is the actual colour of a subject without external light affecting it (such as a red building or green grass). That said, the colours do not have to be completely accurate. You can exaggerate, create your own palette, or adjust as you go. Choose a versatile brush such as **PAINTING > NIKKO RULL** – your main brush from this point onwards – and fill in the sky and ground colours. Go to **ADJUSTMENTS > GAUSSIAN BLUR** and slide your finger to the right until the colours are blended. Rename the layer 'Sky & Ground'.

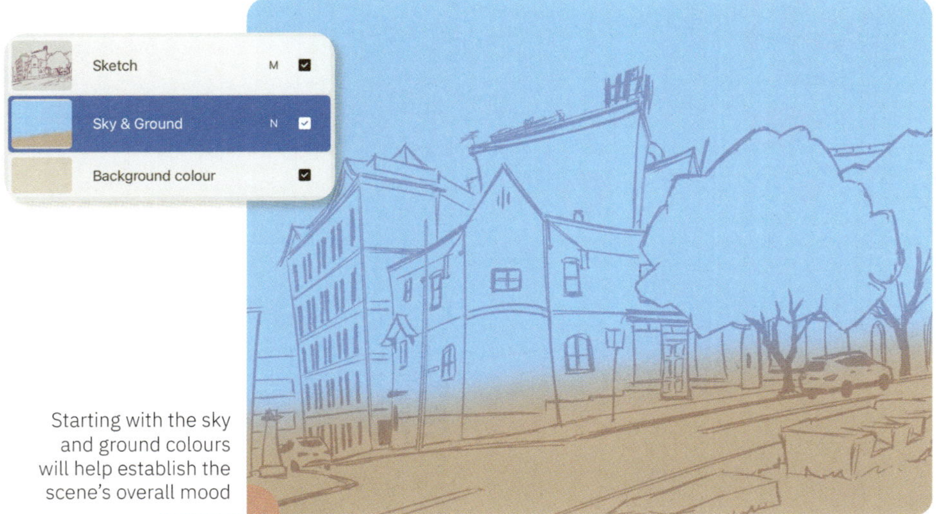

Starting with the sky and ground colours will help establish the scene's overall mood

07

Create a new layer above 'Sky & Ground' and start blocking in the local colours of the main element, which is the building in the middle of this scene. Note that you do not need to add volume yet. Colours that indicate volume and shadows will be added in the lighting phase. Repeat this step for each of the other foreground, middle ground, and background elements. Keep each of these main elements on separate layers as you go, to make it easier to work on them separately – though to save space, use the same layer for parts of the painting that are on the same plane but are not touching. Rename each layer as you go (for example, 'Main Building', 'BG', 'FG').

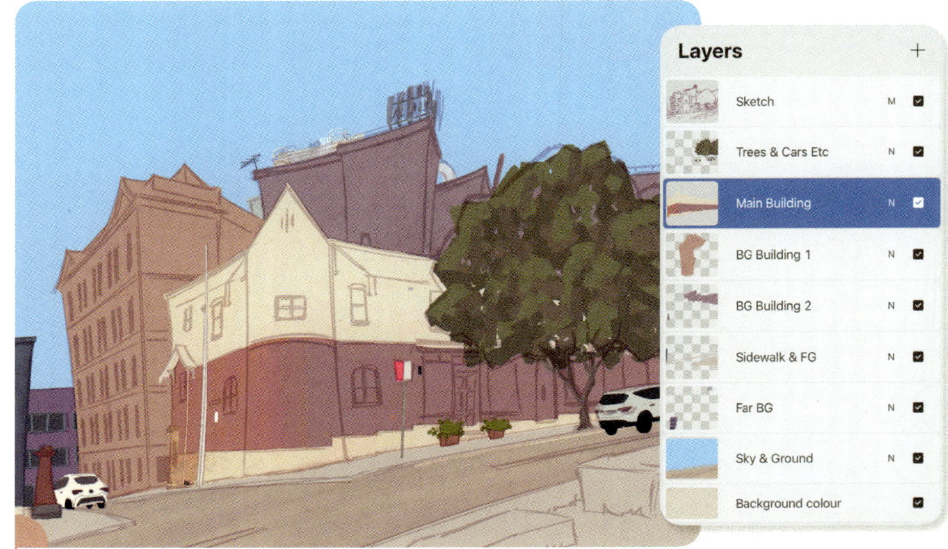

Keep the colours simple for now – they can be adjusted later

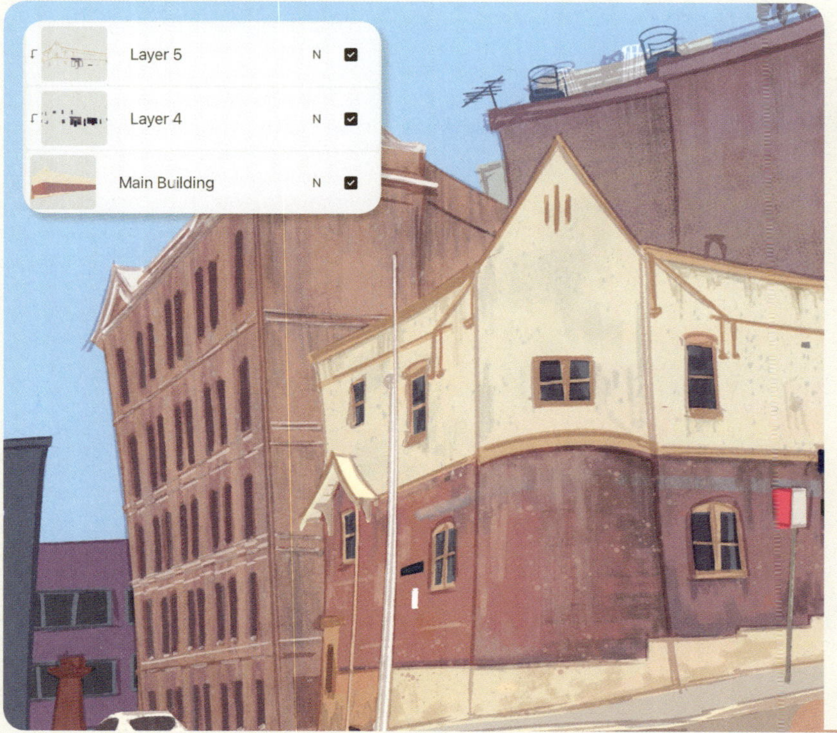

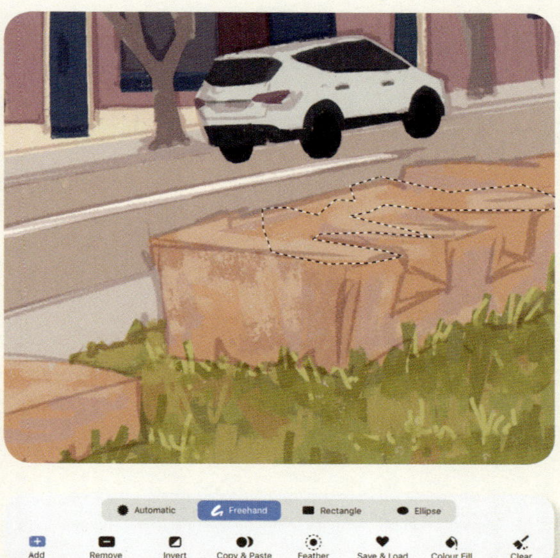

Add interesting shapes and textures to the
main elements by locking the pixels

08

Paint in the larger details of each element, such as windows and doors, using clipping masks and Alpha Lock (see below) to keep them attached to the building to which they belong. Once this is done, start adding texture and colour variation to each foreground, middle-ground, and background element – but still keeping the colours flat, without volume and shadows. Experiment with different hues and texture brushes at different opacity levels to get interesting results, but do not overdo it. You can also use the **SELECTION > FREEHAND** tool to section off a specific area, and lightly tap the brush to fill that area with texture.

MOMO SAYS: *'Alpha Lock lets you paint only within the existing areas of a layer, without worrying about painting outside that shape. To enable it, go the Layers menu and swipe left to right on the layer with two fingers, or tap on it and select Alpha Lock from the menu. Clipping masks allow you to do the same thing, but in a non-destructive way, using a separate layer. Create a clipping mask by adding a new layer above the layer you're working on, tapping on it, and then selecting Clipping Mask. This will "clip" the new layer to the existing*

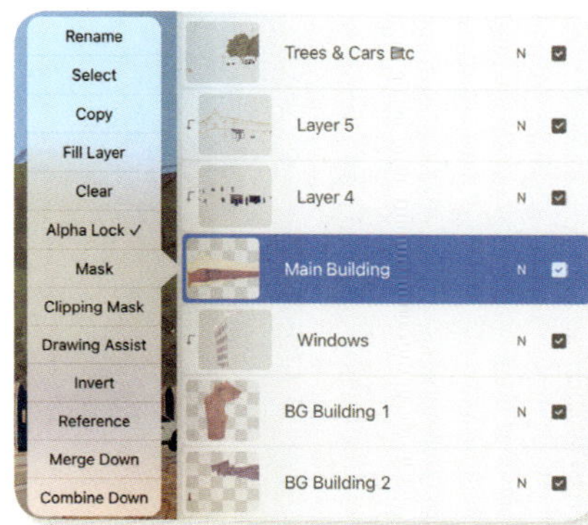

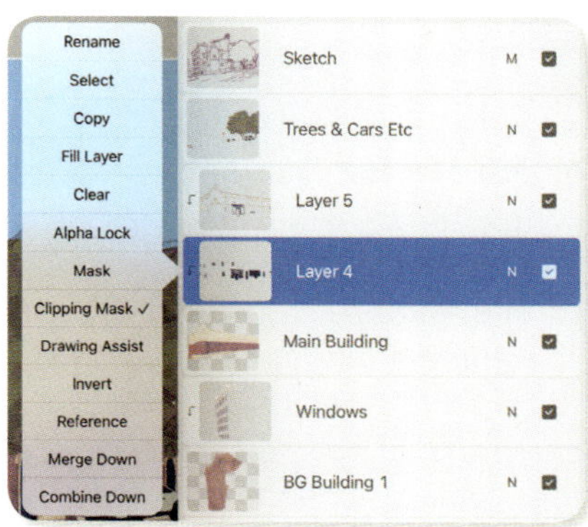

one, allowing you to paint something within its shape, while still having the freedom to transform or change it later. These techniques are perfect for adding elements such as windows and doors above the surface of a building.'

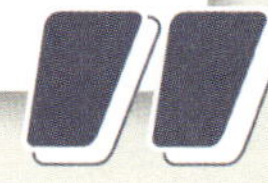

09

Do not worry about getting your lines perfect, as the sketch is only a guide, and you want to maintain an organic look and feel for this piece. Use the Smudge tool to blend colours and colour-pick in-between colours to create hue variation, but be careful not to overuse the Smudge tool in the actual painting. Do not be afraid of having some firm edges – you don't want the painting to look too smooth or over-blended. You can also use the Hue/Saturation tool (under **ADJUSTMENTS > HUE, SATURATION, BRIGHTNESS**) to adjust colours if necessary, until you achieve your desired look.

An example of how you can use the Smudge tool to find new colours

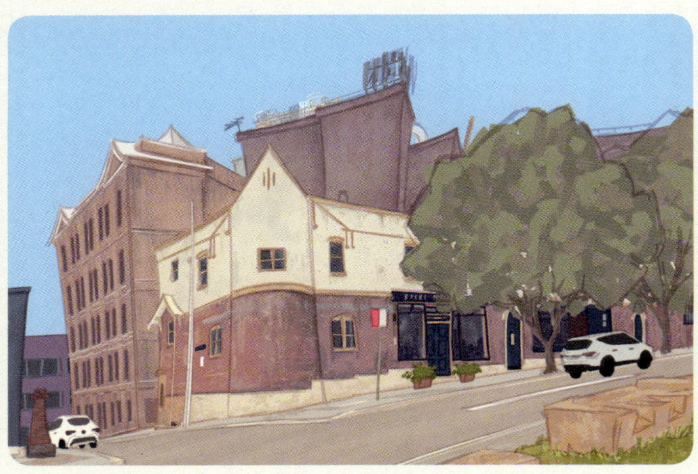

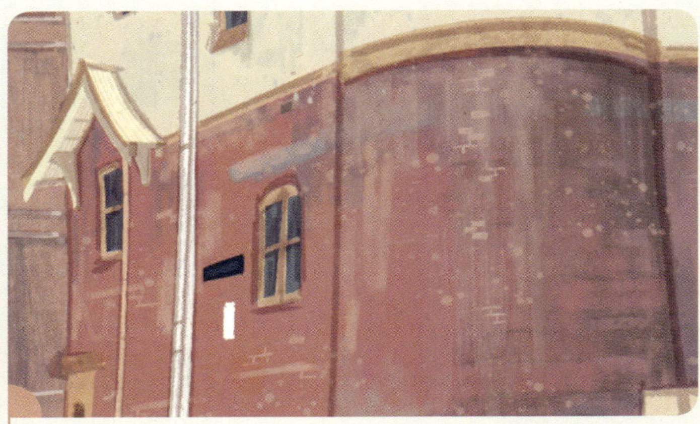

Just give an indication that the details are there and it will look believable

10

Begin adding finer details using the same Alpha Lock and clipping mask techniques as the previous steps. Don't worry about defining everything precisely – all you need to do is give the impression that something is there, and the viewer's brain will fill in the rest of the information. For example, do not draw every single brick or every blade of grass. For the building walls, experiment with different brushes and paint in a few individual bricks and mortar in a random fashion.

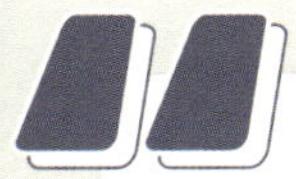

MOMO SAYS: *'Keep your layers organized by grouping them into their respective foreground, middle ground, and background layer groups. To create a group, select all the layers you want to group together by sliding each one to the right, then select the "Group" option that appears. Rename each group accordingly (for example, "Buildings") and keep creating new groups for each new element as required.'*

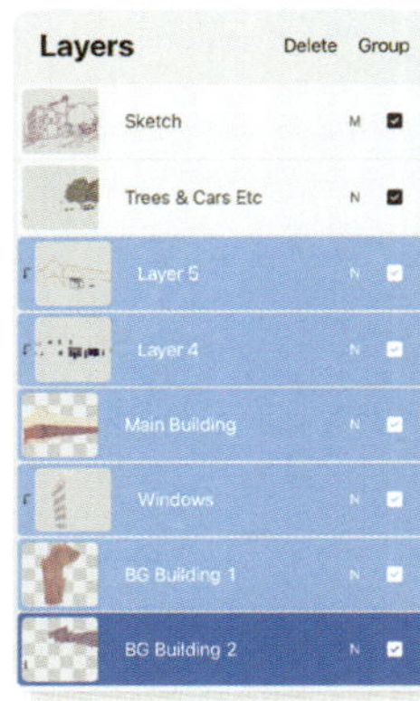

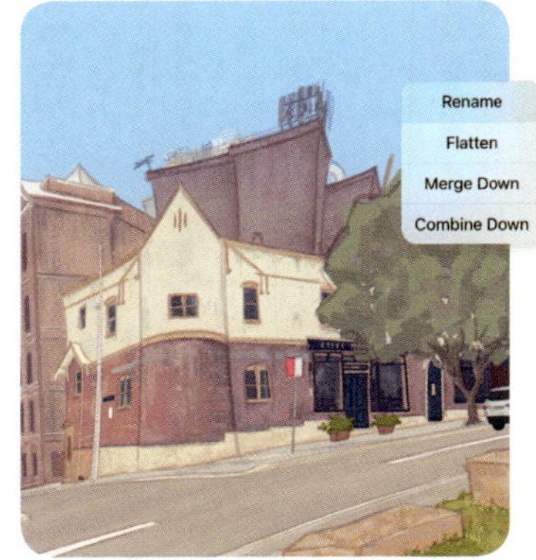

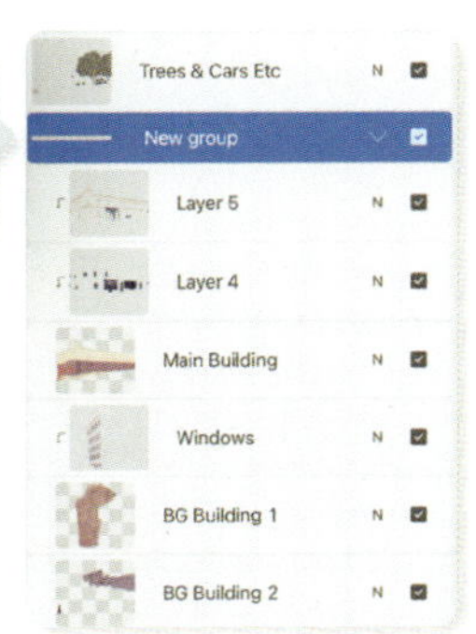

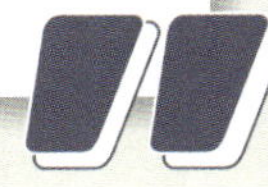

11

To start adding some lighting, look at your reference scene and observe which parts are in shadow. The main building is a good place to start. Create a clipping mask on top of your 'Main Building' layer and set it to Multiply mode. Use your main brush in a large size and start painting the shadowed areas with a light, desaturated blue. If you need to define sharper shadow edges, use the **SELECTION > FREEHAND** tool. If edges need softening, blend the colours or use a textured Smudge brush. You may notice that some surfaces have darker or more saturated shadows than others, as less light reaches them; adjust the shadow hue and value to reflect these shifts. Repeat this for the other buildings and elements.

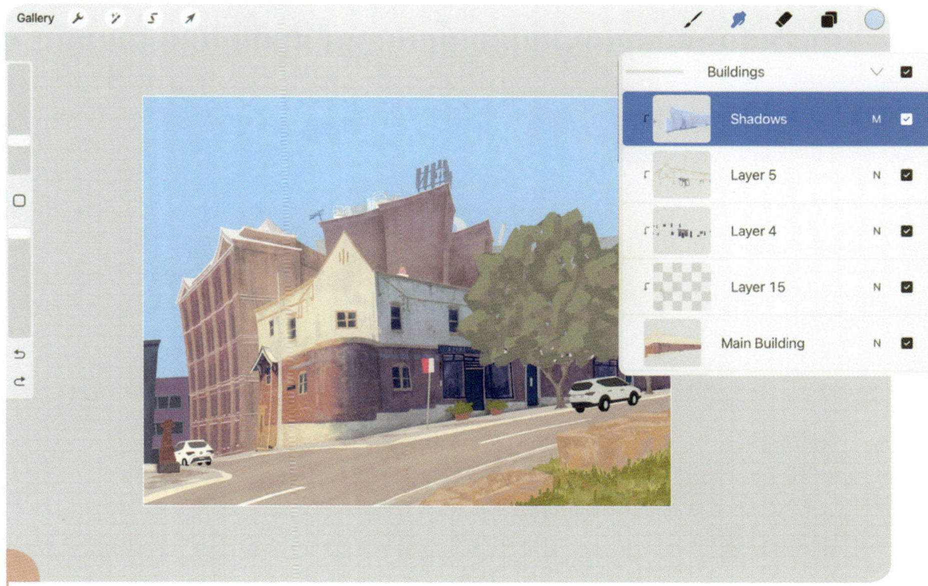

Establish where the light is coming from and paint shadows on Multiply layers

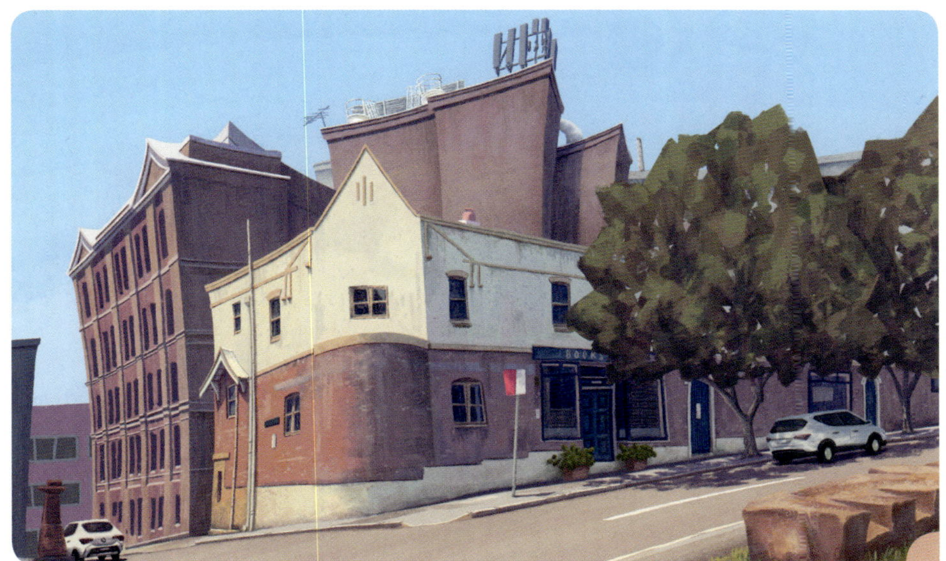

12

You can add volume to your surfaces on the same Multiply layers. Pay attention to the temperature of the atmospheric light in the shadows – although the shadows are generally quite cool, add a bit of warmth to create volume in areas where the light struggles to reach the most (such as under windowsills or where objects meet the ground). Adjust the brush size as necessary. If you haven't already, you can now turn off the 'Sketch' layer – you can always toggle it on again if needed.

Now that lighting has been added, the scene is beginning to come together

13

There are many different types of light affecting every surface, so look at your photo and adjust the colours as you go. You might notice in the photo that there is some 'bounce light' reflecting a different colour onto a surface, such as orange brick reflecting onto a nearby wall. Paint in the bounce light using your main brush at a lower opacity, onto the same Multiply shadow layer if it's in shadow; if it's not in shadow, attach a clipping mask to the layer it is affecting and set it to Overlay mode.

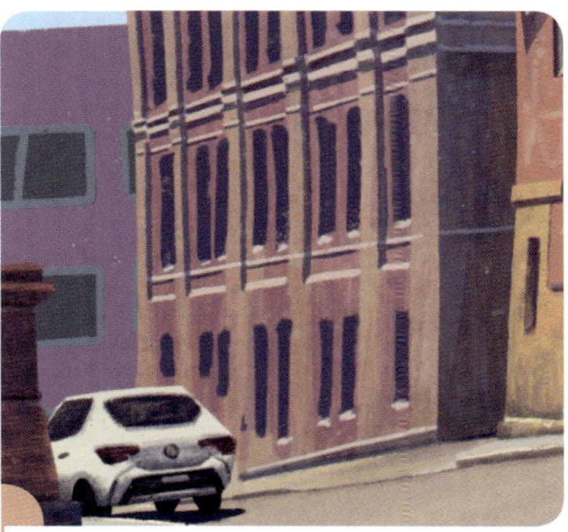
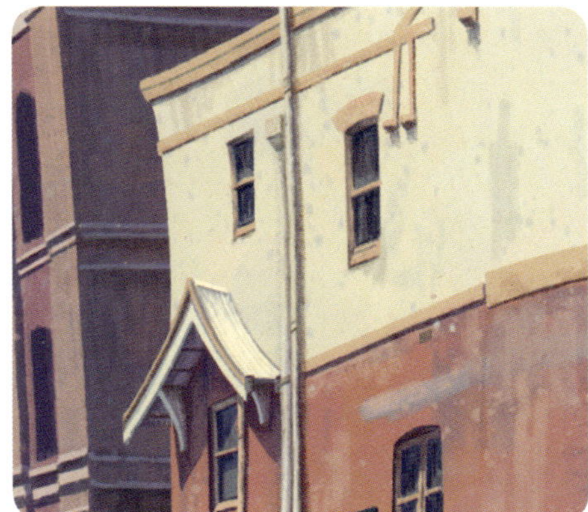

Bounce light in the shadows adds subtle colour variation

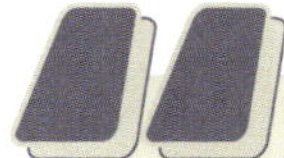

MOMO SAYS: *'When adding different types of light, play around with the layer blend modes to see how the light reacts with the surface through each blend mode. You might find that you want to use different blend modes (such as Overlay, Linear Light, or Screen) for different surfaces, depending on the combination of colours you are using. Use the Hue, Saturation, Brightness tool or Curves, both found under Adjustments, to make overall colour tweaks to any of your layers if necessary.'*

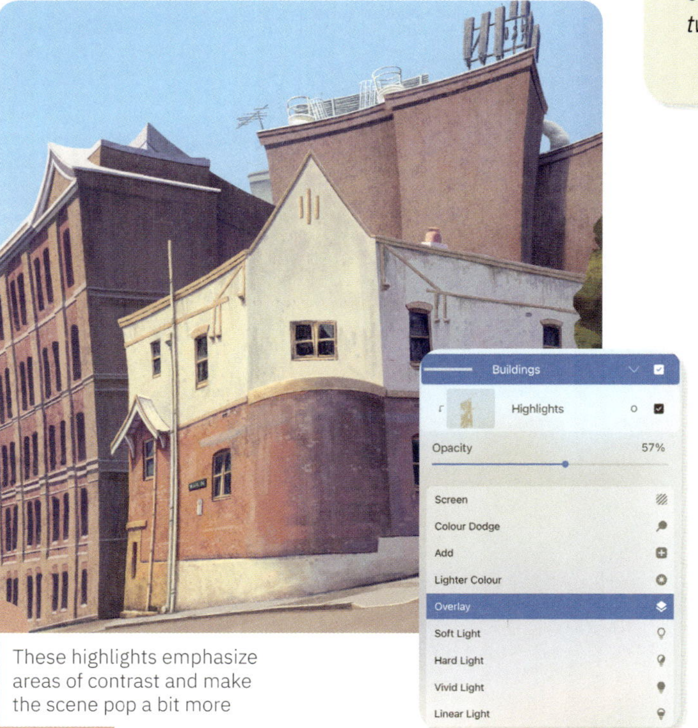

These highlights emphasize areas of contrast and make the scene pop a bit more

14

Now you can begin to add some highlights. Add a new clipping mask to the top of your 'Main Building' layers and set the blend mode to Overlay (or experiment and find a different blend mode that works for you). Using your main brush, choose a desaturated orange/yellow colour and add light to areas that are getting hit with the most light. Lower the layer or brush opacity if the effect is too intense. Repeat with the other buildings and elements.

15

Now is a good time to check your values if you haven't already. Create a new layer at the very top of the painting, set its blend mode to Colour, and rename it 'Values'. Fill the layer with black. Now you should be able to see your painting in black and white. Toggle this layer on and off to check your values as you continue with your painting. The areas of strongest contrast should be the main focus of the painting, with less contrast the further back you go. Look at any buildings that are set back and adjust the values if necessary, using the **ADJUSTMENTS > HUE, SATURATION, BRIGHTNESS** or **ADJUSTMENTS > CURVES** options.

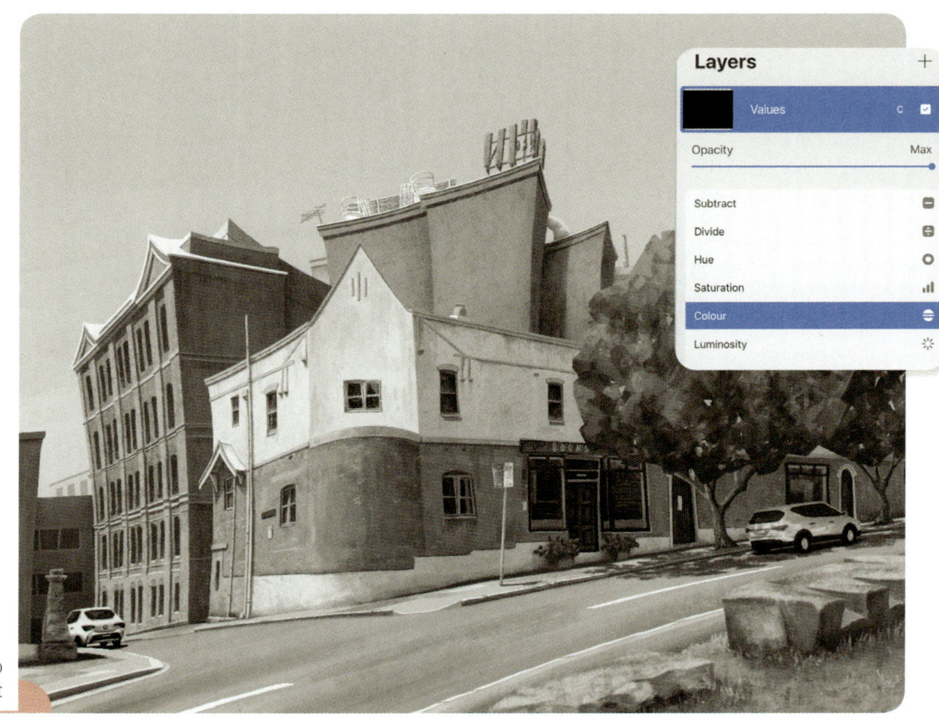

Check your values in black and white to see which areas have too much contrast

 'As you work on your painting, you might come across some stylistic roadblocks, where the shape or texture is just not working as planned and slight colour and value adjustments don't seem to be fixing the problem. In such cases, like the trees in this painting, don't be afraid to go back and redo the element. This is when the use of separate layers is advantageous, as you can change and revise specific areas and follow the same steps to add light and shadow again.'

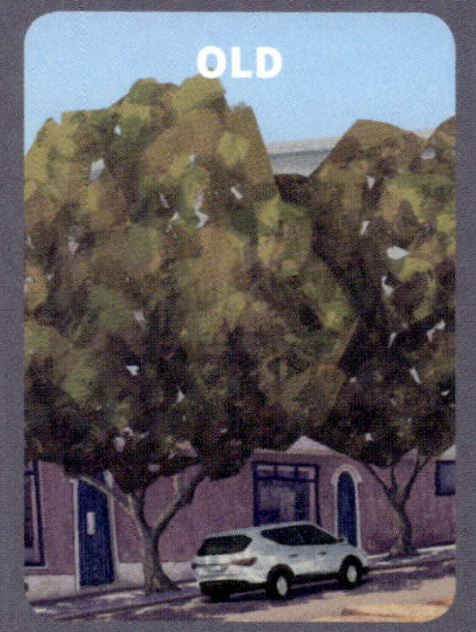

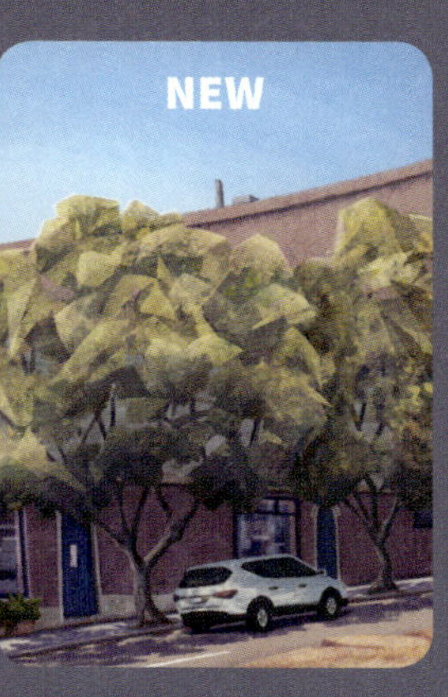

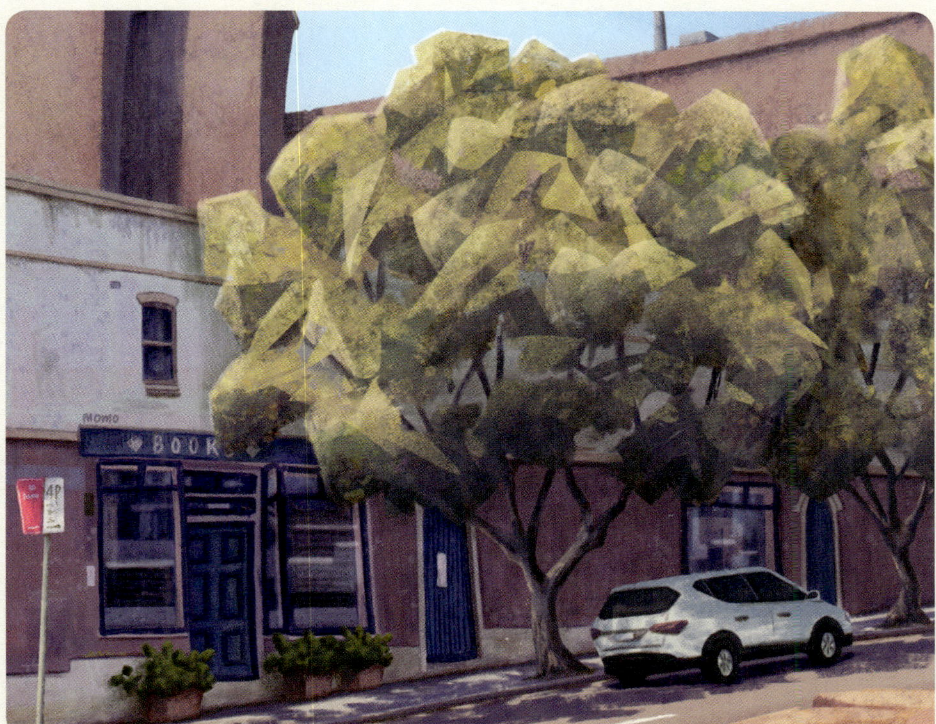

16

Your painting should be taking shape now. Refer to your photo and look for any details you may have missed. Remember, however, that you do not have to include every single detail – just those that you think will add character and vibrancy to your painting. Using a soft brush, for example, you can paint some reflections onto the windows of the main building. Adding random bits of grass to the pavement can also make it look more real and weathered. These details can be painted onto a new layer, on the original layers, or added with clipping masks – and again, experiment with different blend modes to see what works for you.

The window reflections are painted using a soft brush on a low-opacity clipping mask set to Screen mode

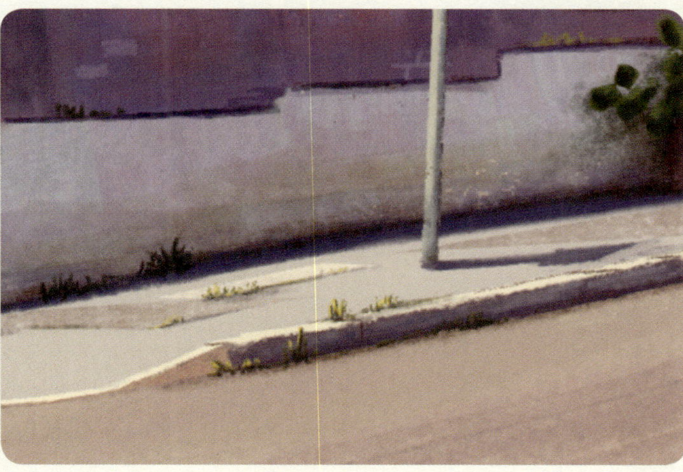

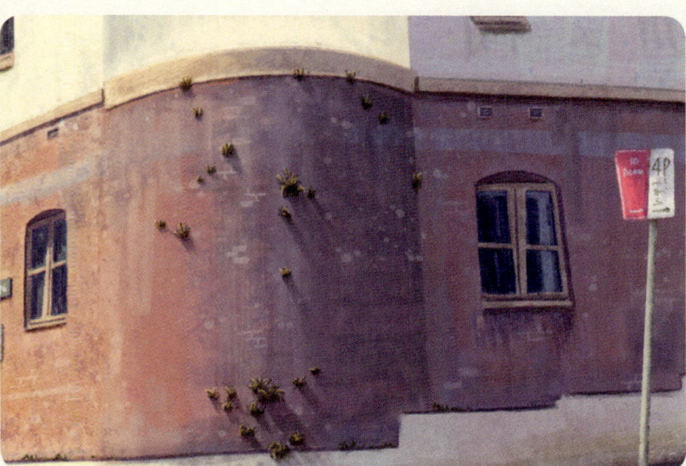

17

Now that the environment is nearing completion, you can add some characters. This step is optional, but a good idea for those who want to add a story element to the painting. As you can see in the original reference, there were no people or animals on the street at that moment, but adding some would help add life and scale to the location. This painting will include some simple cat characters, but feel free to create your own – be as creative as you want! Add a new layer on top of everything (but still underneath the Values layer), rename it 'Characters', and block in your character/s with a flat colour using your main brush.

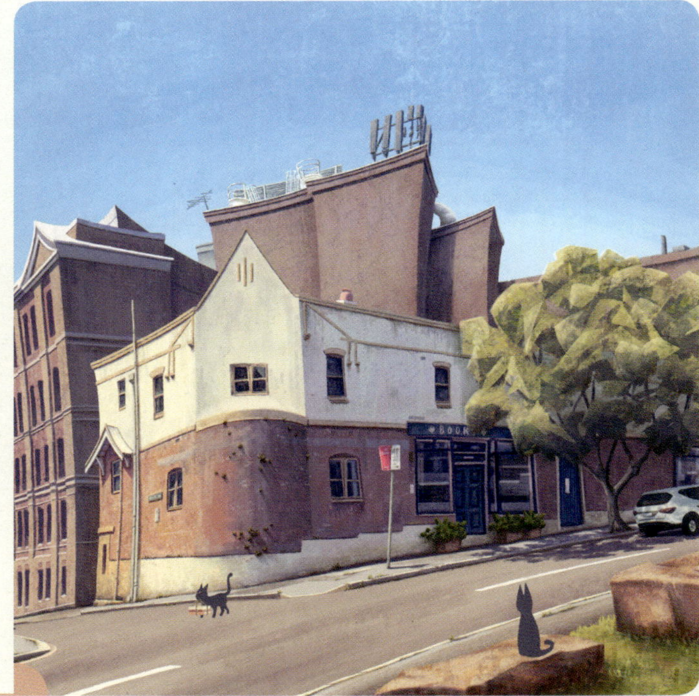

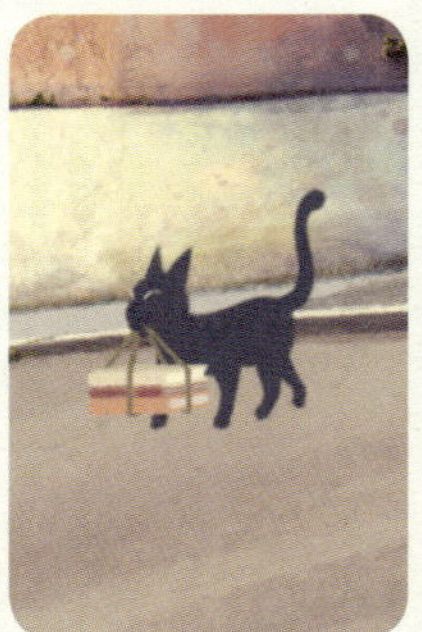

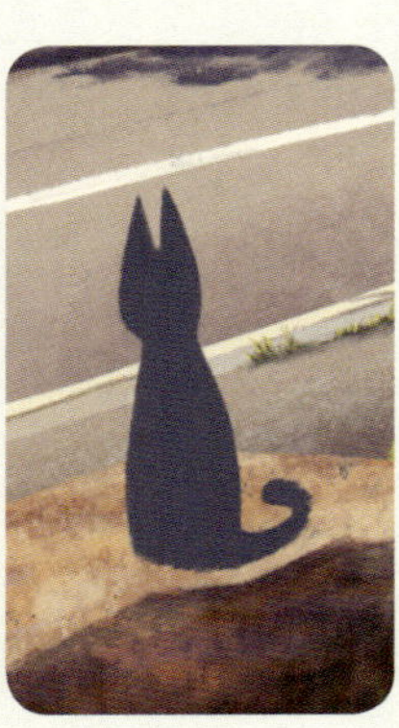

Establishing the silhouettes first will help you to see if the characters read well against the rest of the image

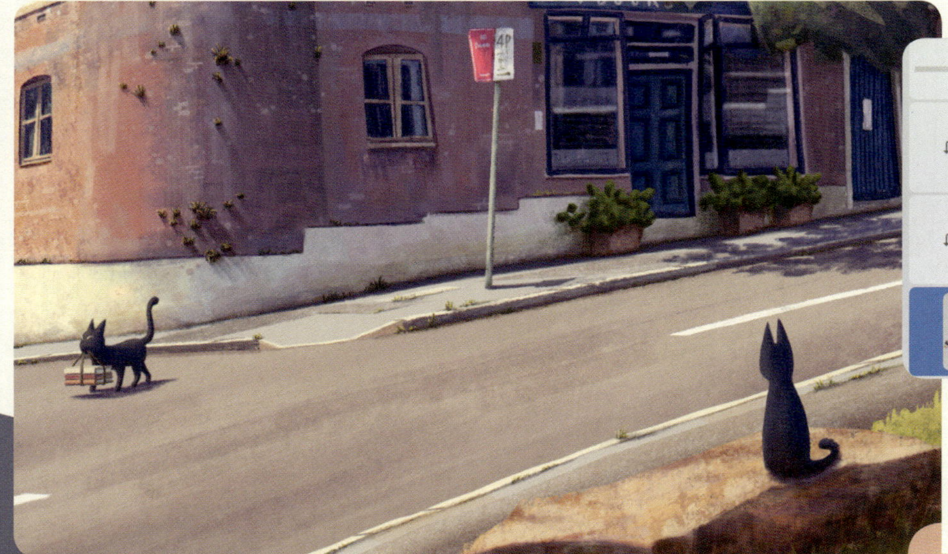

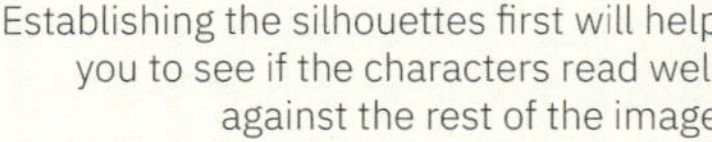

Characters help direct the viewer's eye and frame the scene

18

Follow the same steps as you used for the buildings and other elements to bring your character to life – using Alpha Lock and clipping masks in different blend modes to add shadow and light. Add cast shadows underneath the characters so they feel grounded in the environment. For organization, keep the character layers in a group as mentioned on page 72. Keep flipping the canvas to check that the characters are also looking balanced.

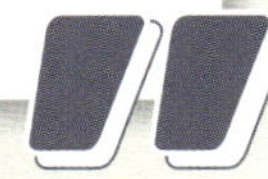

MOMO SAYS: *'Try not to zoom in too much while painting. If you are zoomed right in, it's easy to get carried away and it often results in unnecessary detail that may affect the painting's overall cohesiveness. When you are focused closely on one specific part of your painting, remember to regularly zoom out and look at the painting as a whole. This applies throughout the whole painting process.'*

19

Create a new layer above the 'Characters' group and set it to Screen mode. Make your main brush small, around 2–3%. With a warm orange/yellow colour, paint some rim light around the sunlit edges of elements that you want to emphasize. Lightly add cooler rim light on some edges that are facing away from the light, using a less saturated blue colour. Keep zoomed out and don't overdo this effect – not every object will need it. Add even more vivid highlights to the important areas by creating another layer on top of the Screen layer and setting it to Add mode. Using the same brush, paint some highlights to bring extra vibrancy to the main areas of focus.

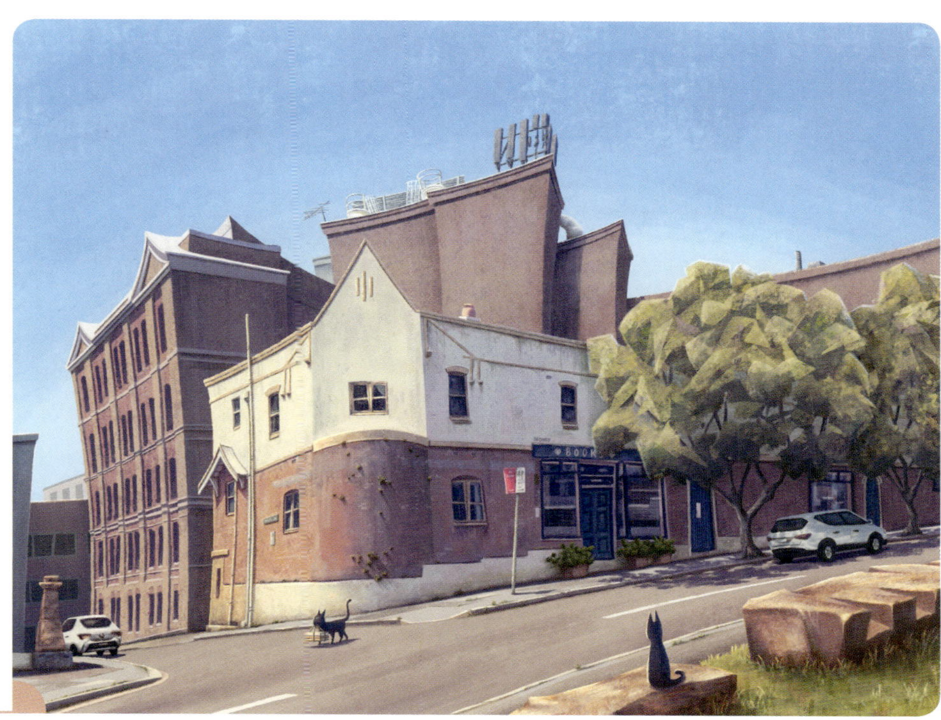

Add extra highlights to the edges that catch the most light

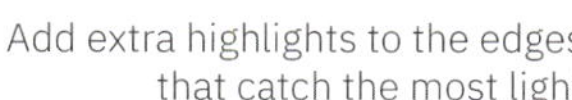

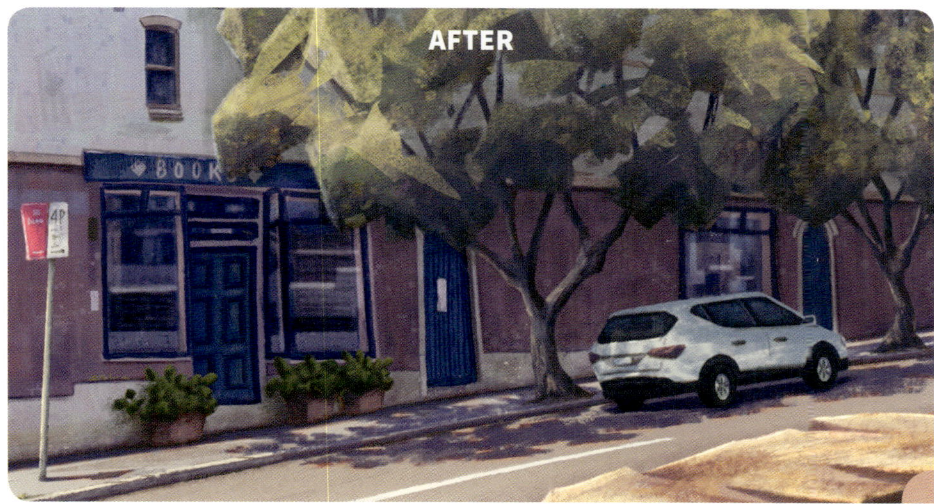

20

Create a new layer on top and set it to Overlay mode. Using the same brush, but this time with a bright, saturated orange colour, paint along shadow transitions in key areas, as well as around the edges of the dappled shadows underneath the trees. Go to **ADJUSTMENTS > GAUSSIAN BLUR** and slide your finger to the right to apply a blur of about 10%. Lower the opacity of the layer until the colour is less intense, so it just gives the shadow edges a bit of chromatic aberration.

Add a fringe of colour to the shadows and lower the opacity so the effect is subtle

21

Zoom out to make your painting small and check how it looks at thumbnail size. It needs to read well, now that the painting is almost complete. Don't forget to check the values again by toggling the 'Values' layer on and off. Make final adjustments and see if any elements need retouching or any extra highlights need adding. This can be done on a new layer on top or just by editing the original layer(s).

Does your painting read well at this size? In this case, the values still need adjusting

22

Create a new layer on top of the layer stack and set it to Multiply mode. Using a desaturated light blue-purple and a large, soft brush such as **AIRBRUSHING > SOFT BRUSH**, lightly sweep some colour around the corners and edges of the painting to create a slight vignette feel. Lower the opacity of the layer and apply **ADJUSTMENTS > GAUSSIAN BLUR** to make it less intense.

Although a vignette can sometimes be a little cheesy, it can help to bring an image together

23

Swipe down with three fingers to call up the **COPY & PASTE** menu. Select Copy All. Repeat the swipe gesture and select Paste. View the image zoomed out to do your final checks. Use the Curves, Colour Balance, and Hue, Saturation, Brightness adjustments to make any final colour tweaks. If you want to test out different looks, duplicate the layer by swiping left on it in the Layers menu and selecting 'Duplicate'. You can create a new layer on top of those if you feel the need to add anything else.

The colours can be pushed quite a bit further using adjustments such as Curves

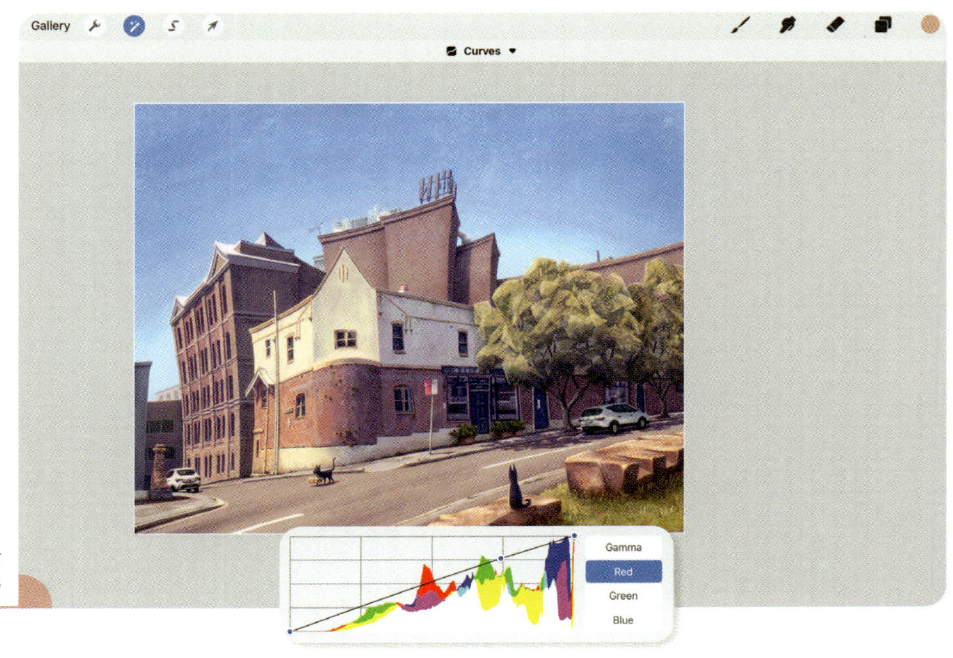

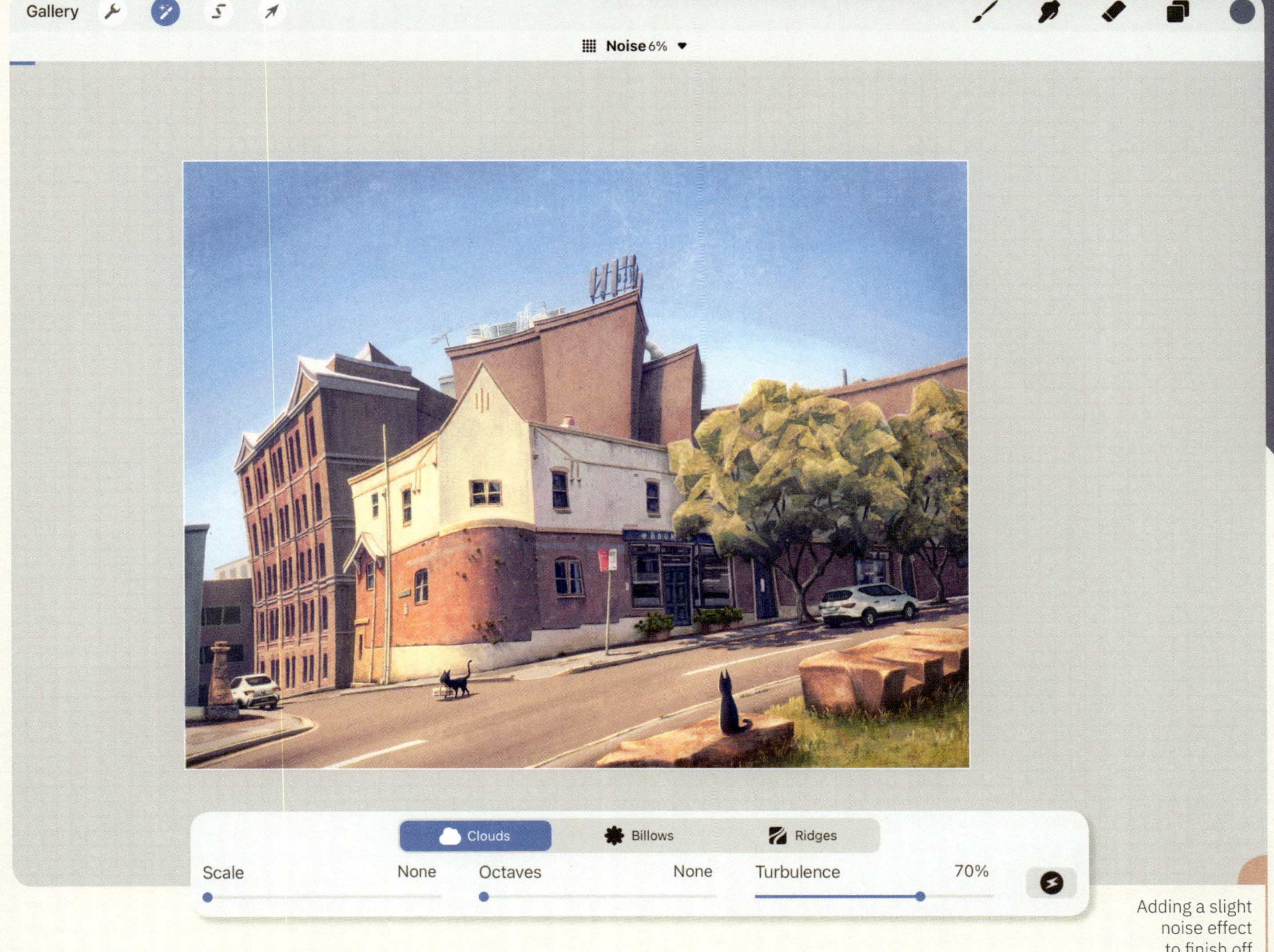

Adding a slight noise effect to finish off the scene

24

As an optional finishing touch, you can add some noise to your painting to create a more vibrant and textured, grainy feel. Copy and paste the canvas using the three-finger swiping gesture again. Rename this layer 'Noise'. Go to **ADJUSTMENTS > NOISE** and drag your finger across the screen to the right to adjust the noise to your desired level (aim for around 5–8% for a subtle effect).

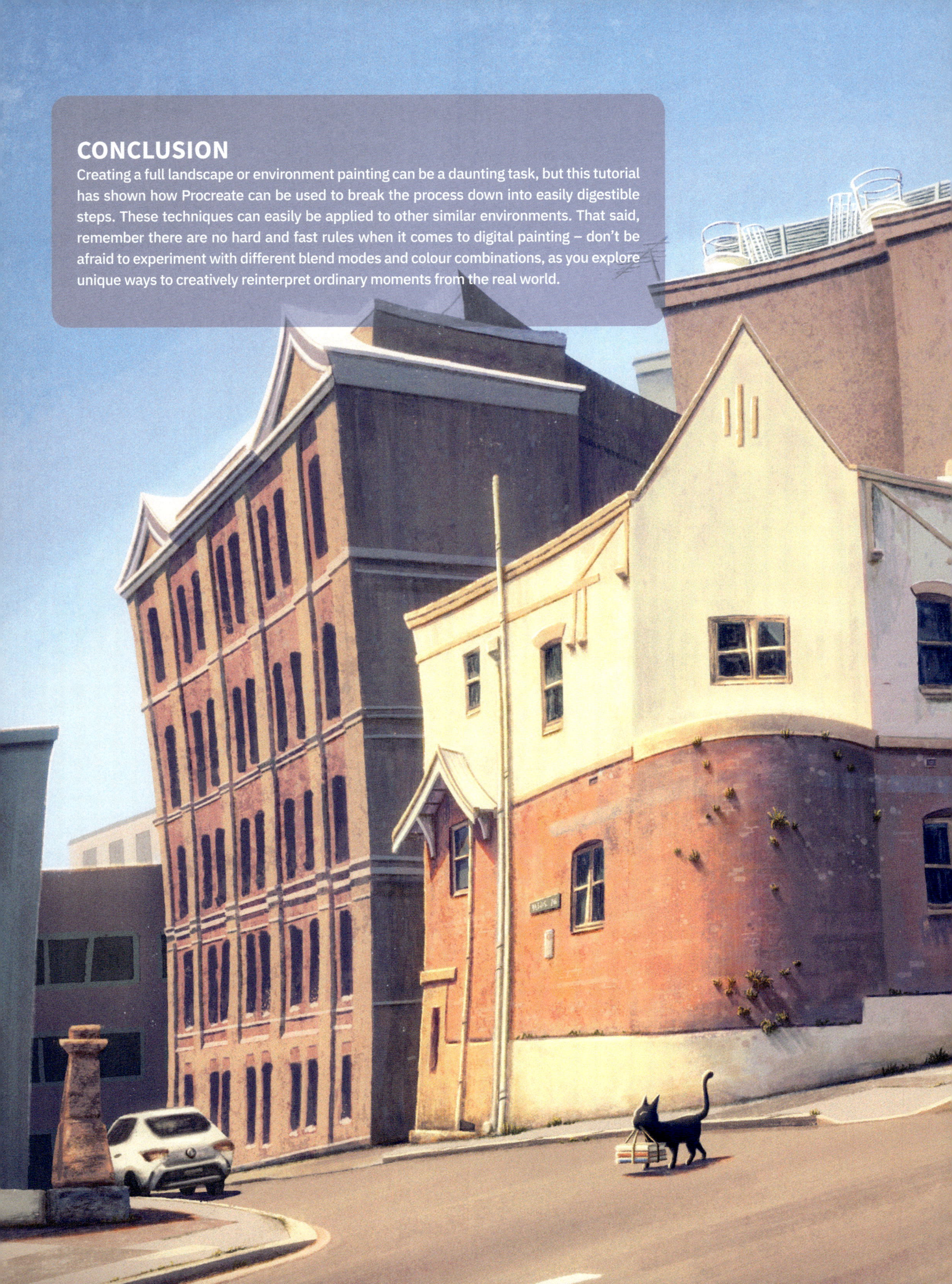

CONCLUSION

Creating a full landscape or environment painting can be a daunting task, but this tutorial has shown how Procreate can be used to break the process down into easily digestible steps. These techniques can easily be applied to other similar environments. That said, remember there are no hard and fast rules when it comes to digital painting – don't be afraid to experiment with different blend modes and colour combinations, as you explore unique ways to creatively reinterpret ordinary moments from the real world.

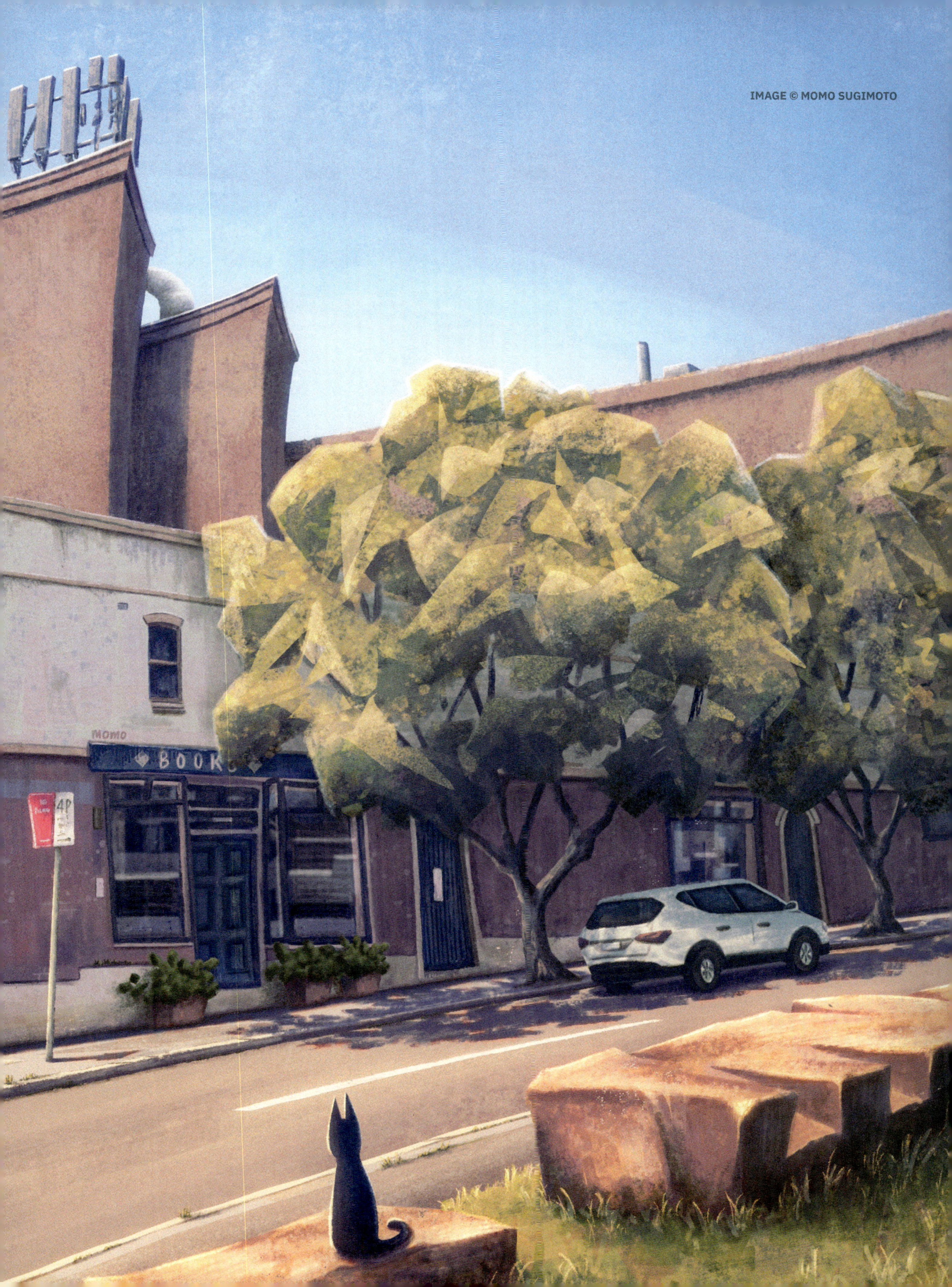

IMAGE © MOMO SUGIMOTO

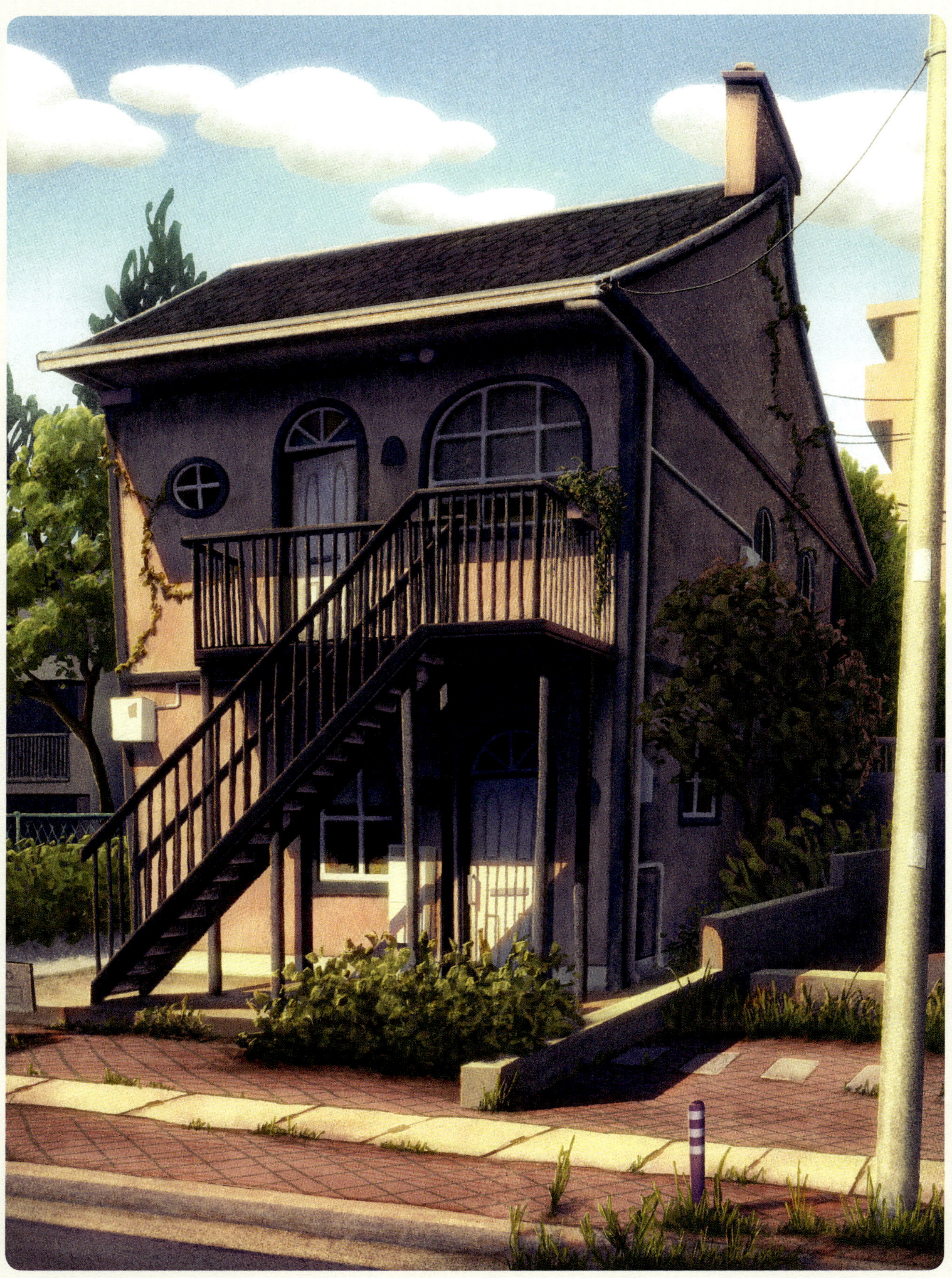

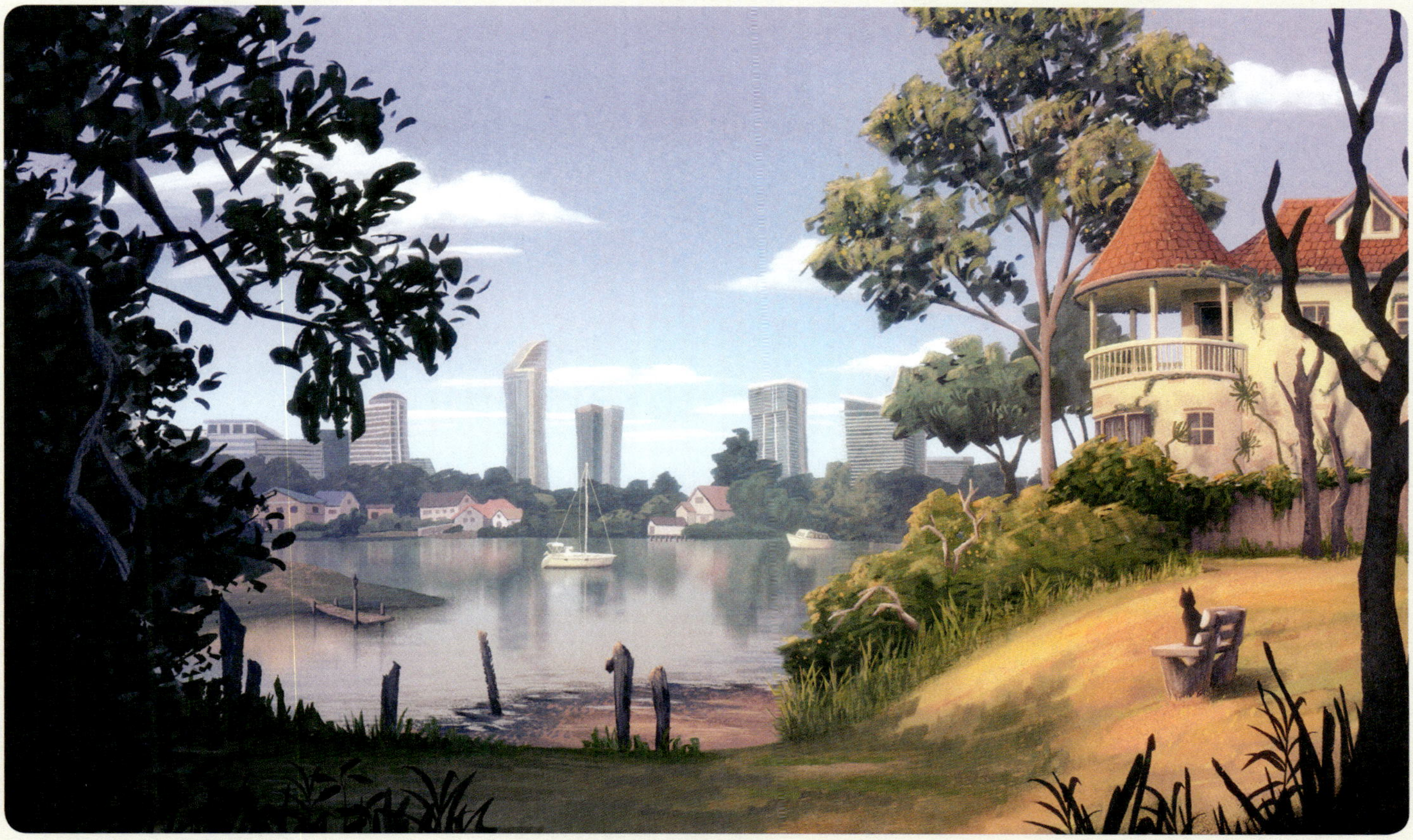

DOWN BY THE RIVER: This is a loose reinterpretation of a real, local place, with background and foreground elements changed and added to create a story

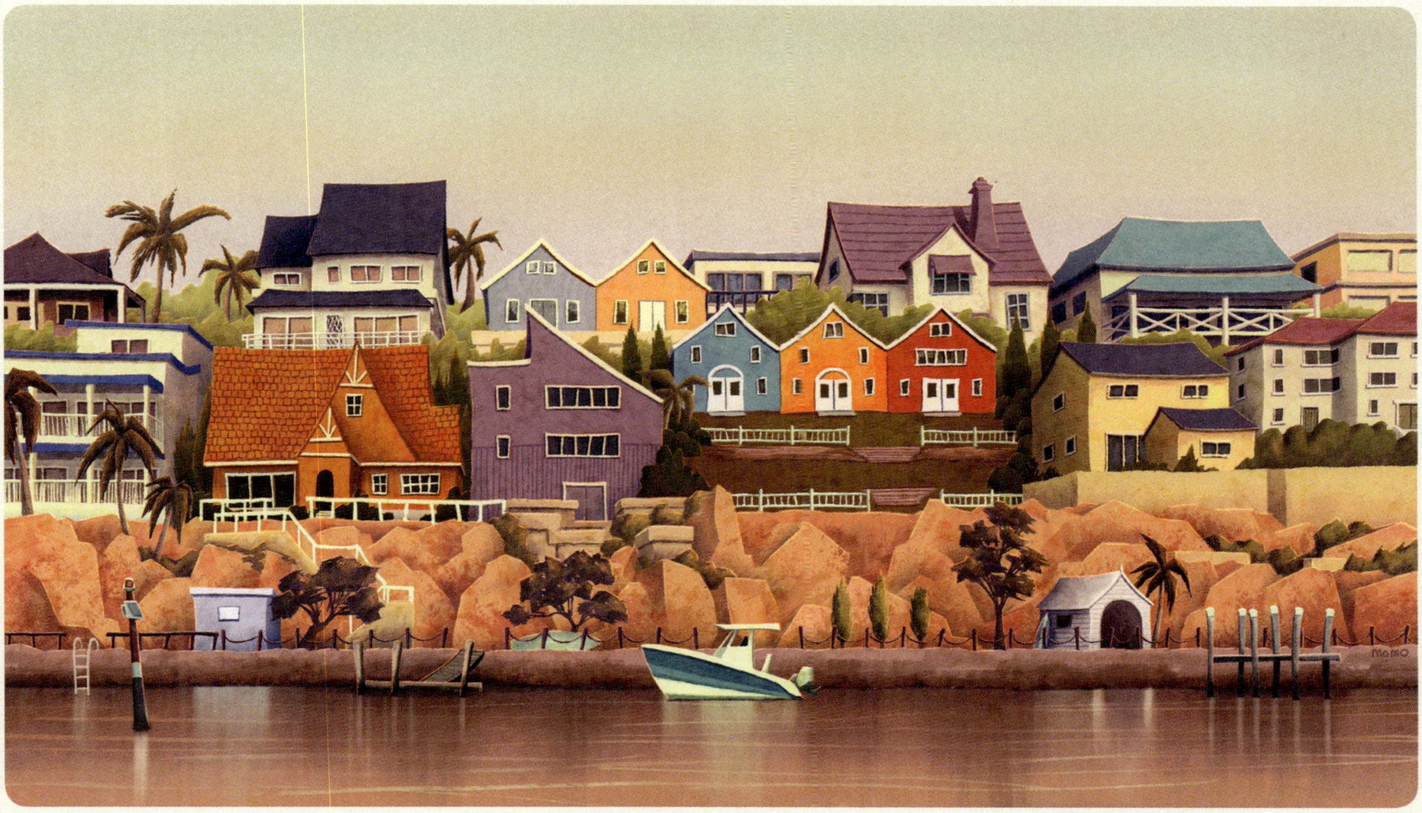

RIVER SUNSET: This was painted in a more graphic style, with an emphasis on shape and colour, and was inspired by the houses perched along the river near where I live

NOVA SCOTIA DOCKS

BY TREVOR CLARE

TREVOR SAYS: *'This painting will be of a fishing boat scene that I photographed while on vacation in Nova Scotia. This specific location intrigued me because the tide was out, leaving the boats resting on the ocean floor. Because the tide was coming back in, painting directly on location proved to be risky, so I quickly snapped some reference photos to work from!'*

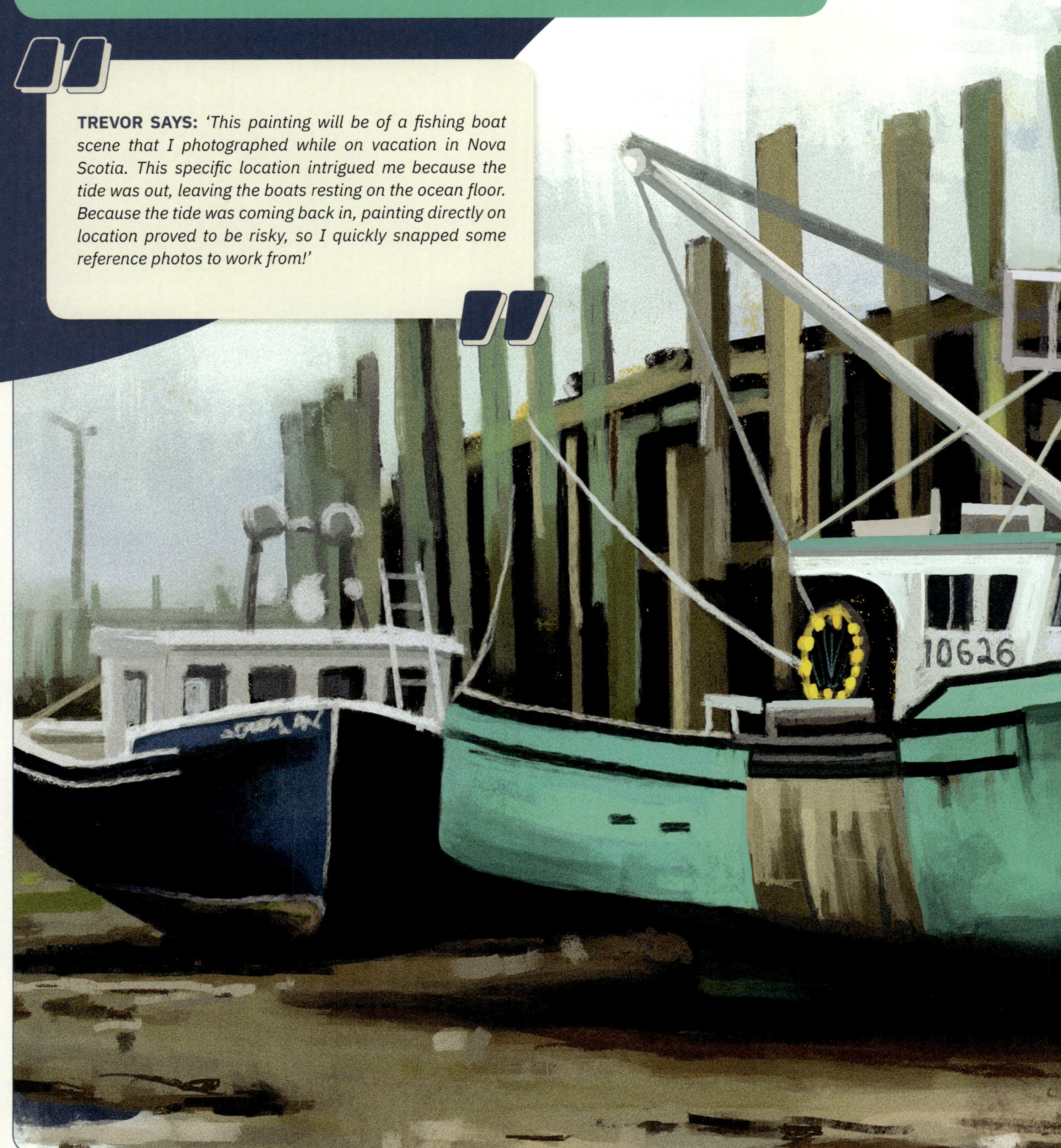

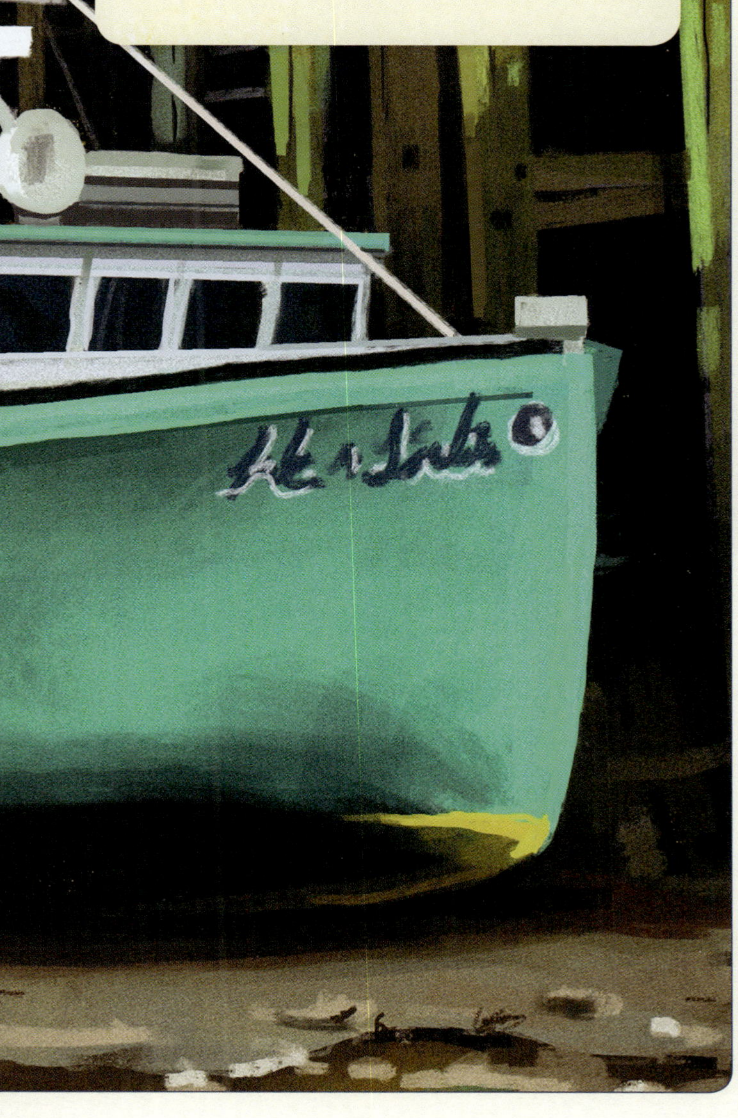

LEARN HOW TO...

- **Analyse a scene for excess details to remove**

- **Build on a strong foundation of shapes and values**

- **Achieve a painterly finish with few brushes and layers**

- **Save colour swatches for later with Palette options**

- **Use Selection tools to create clean edges**

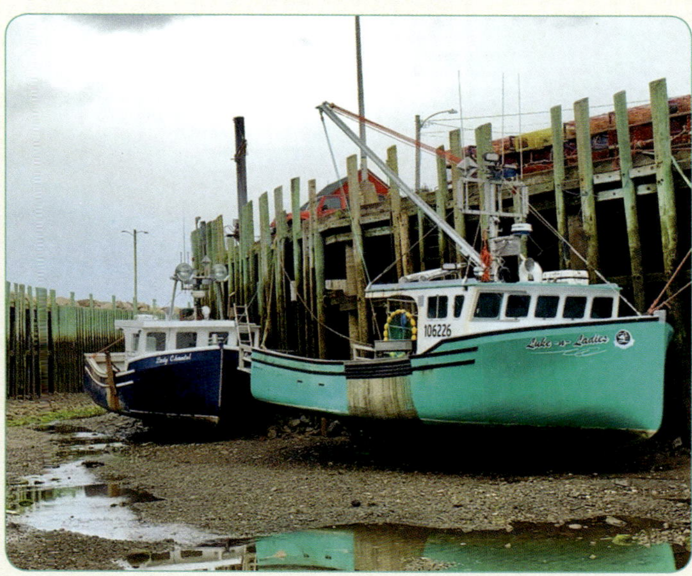

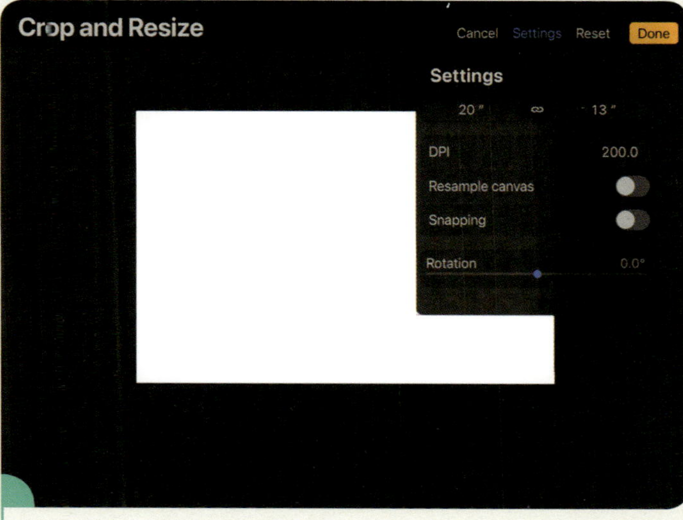

Set up your canvas and define your preferred resolution

01

This scene will be in landscape orientation to capture the view across the dockland, so begin by creating a canvas that is 20 inches wide × 13 inches high, with a resolution of 200 dpi. This will ensure high-quality prints, if you choose to print the final illustration.

02

Even if you can't stay on location for long – safety comes first! – you have the advantage of being able to take your time deconstructing the photo references in front of you. Review the reference photo and analyse the scene. What is the primary focal point? In this example, the eye is naturally led from left to right in an arc, landing on the primary focal point, which is the large teal-coloured boat. A successful landscape painting will typically have an entrance and an exit. You just need to figure out what to feature and what can be stripped away.

In this case, you can remove the distant red building and the red lobster traps on the dock because they are simply too distracting and compete for the viewer's attention. You can also remove the boat tail on the far right and the hydro pole in the centre of the scene.

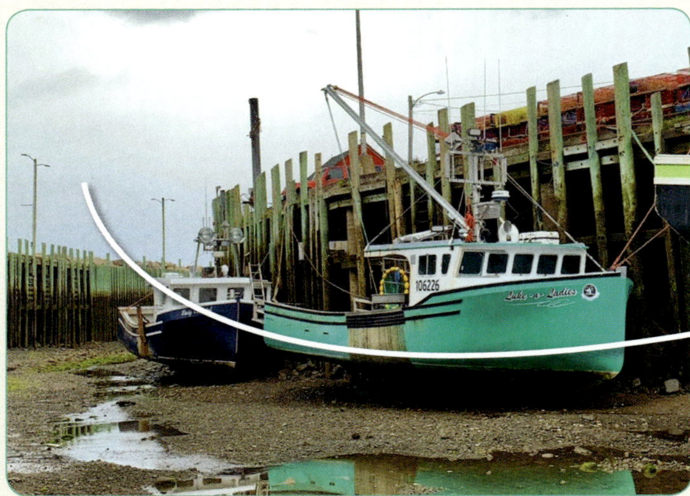

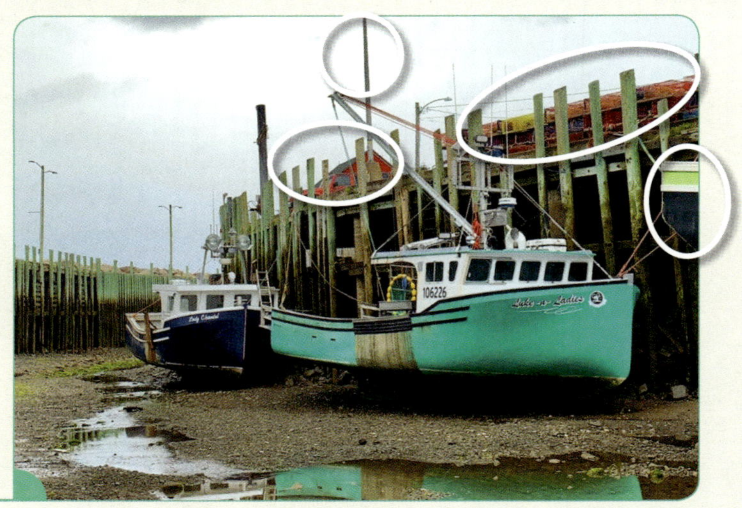

Determine the primary focal point and analyse which elements to remove

03

Next, you need to set up a grid. This tool can be activated and edited by going to **ACTIONS > CANVAS > DRAWING GUIDE**. A grid is helpful for arranging objects better while referencing the photo. Set the grid to be 6 columns wide × 4 columns tall. Drag along the coloured bar to make the lines a bright colour, such as magenta, to provide plenty of contrast so you can see the grid.

Establish a grid to help guide the sketching process

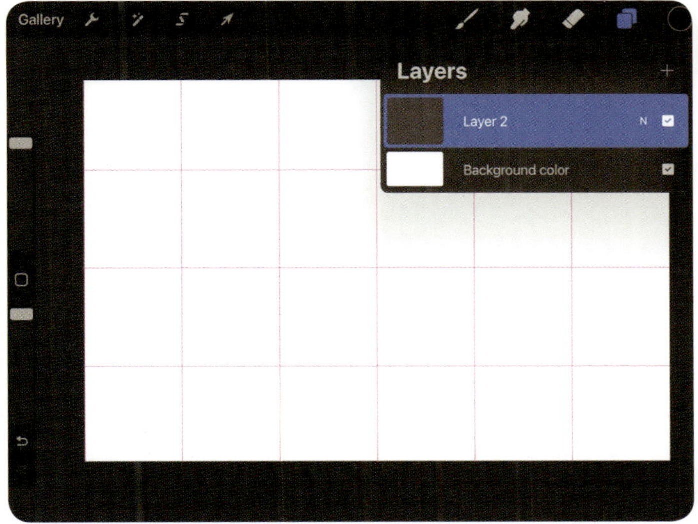

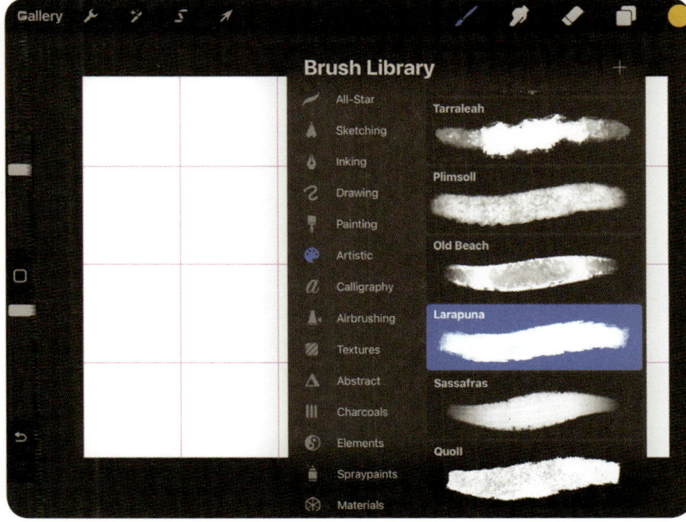

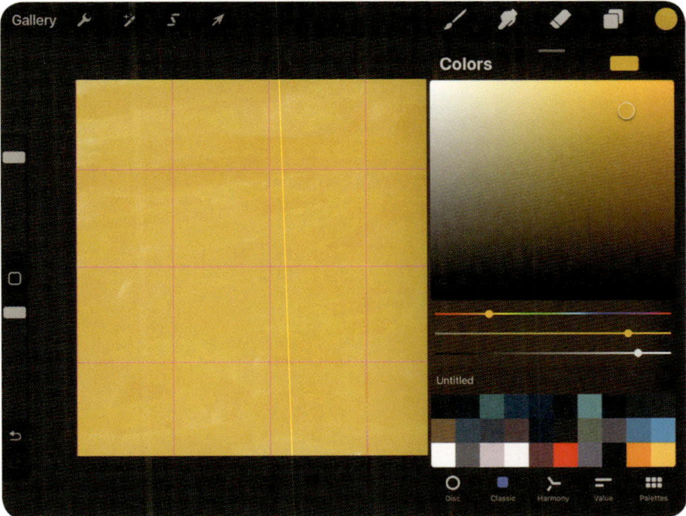

Make a new layer and prime the canvas using a large textured brush and a warm yellow base colour

04

Now you can build a foundation and 'prime' the canvas the way you would if you were painting on an actual canvas with real paint. Make a new layer and set the tone with a base colour, such as a yellow-ochre or burnt-umber hue. Having a base colour, rather than a stark white canvas, makes the process feel much less intimidating and adds cohesiveness to the resulting painting. It does not matter which brush you use at this point, but the **ARTISTIC > LARAPUNA** brush is a good choice.

The primed undertone layer

05

Begin the sketching process, working from the photo reference to establish a composition. Pick a dark colour and the **SKETCHING > PROCREATE PENCIL** brush, which works well for quick, loose sketching. Start by creating a new layer, then establish a horizon line, build in the background, and sketch the foreground boats last. Do not get too detailed at this stage, or you will not be able to make your own decisions and add your own personal flair as you journey through the painting process, creating a more 'paint by numbers' result.

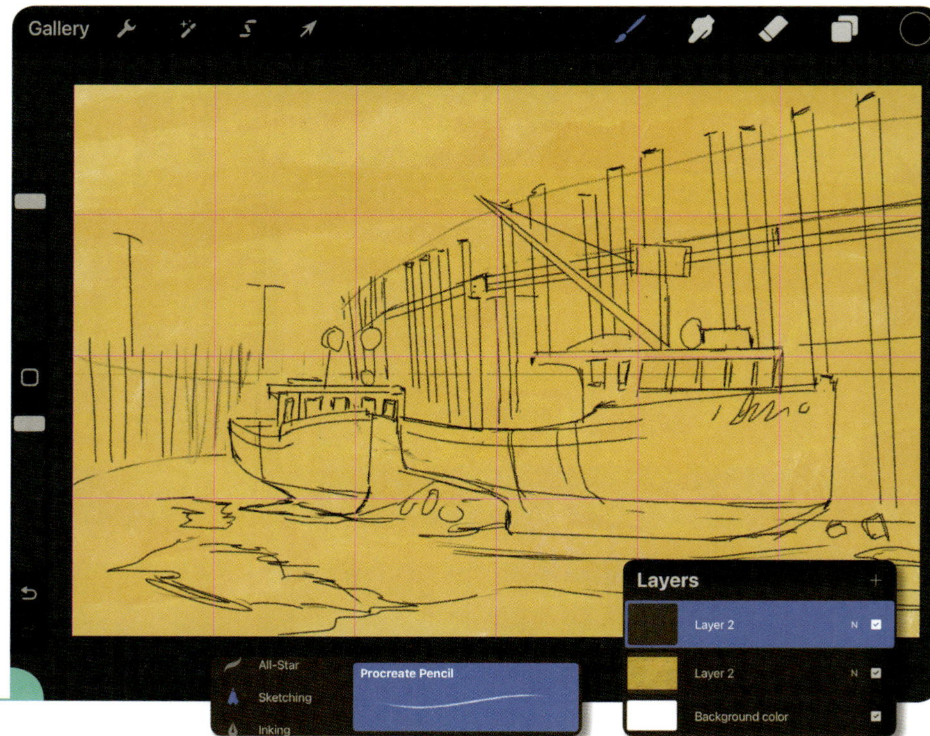

Sketch out the composition and elements of your scene

06

Now you can create a colour palette based on the core colours you observe and are drawn to in the scene. Open the Palettes menu, hit + and select Create New Palette. Now return to the Disc view (or your Palettes view of choice), select your colours, and save them as swatches by tapping the empty palette squares. You can delete or replace a saved swatch by holding down on it and releasing. Keep in mind that this palette will simply be a base for your painting – you can deviate and explore additional colours as you go. Do not be afraid to try new things and add your own unique twists along the way. You can always redo any section – natural imperfections give personality to a painting.

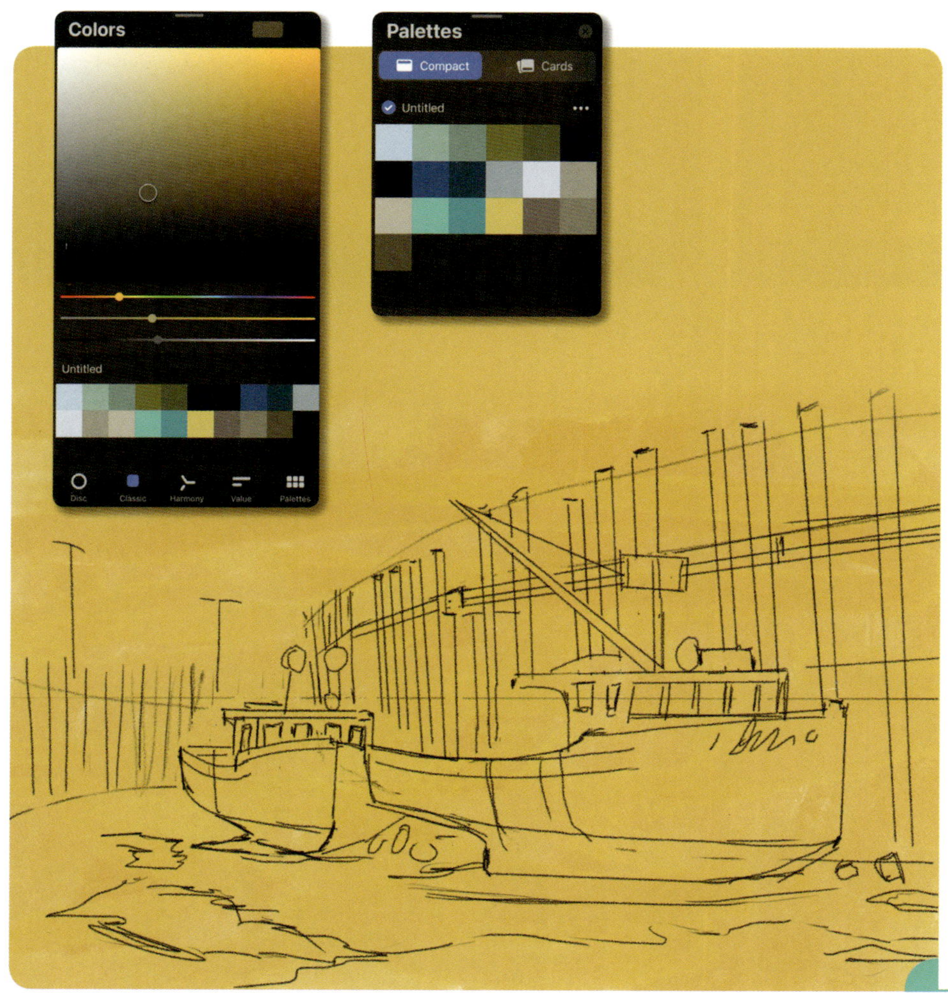

Create a core colour palette from which you can derive additional colours

07

Now that you have established your colour palette and sketched out the composition, you can get to the fun stuff: value blocking. Start by creating a fresh layer for the sky and placing it behind your sketch layer. Select the **PAINTING > NIKKO RULL** brush, which is good for blocking out large, rough areas, and loosely paint a pale blue sky. Keep zoomed out to the full canvas and use a large brush so you aren't tempted to get carried away with unnecessary details. A large brush will also allow you to make more confident brushstrokes as you build up the main masses and shapes. Keeping the sky separate for now allows for quick changes without having to work around the details of the dock in front of it.

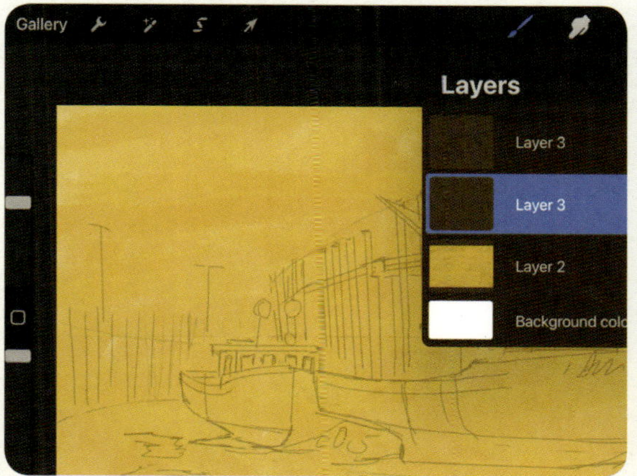

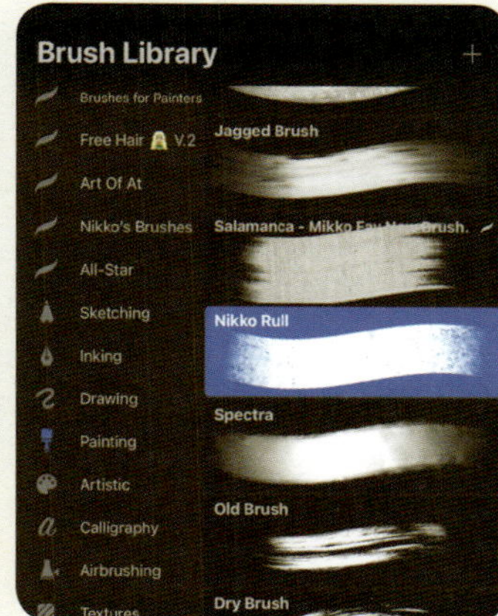

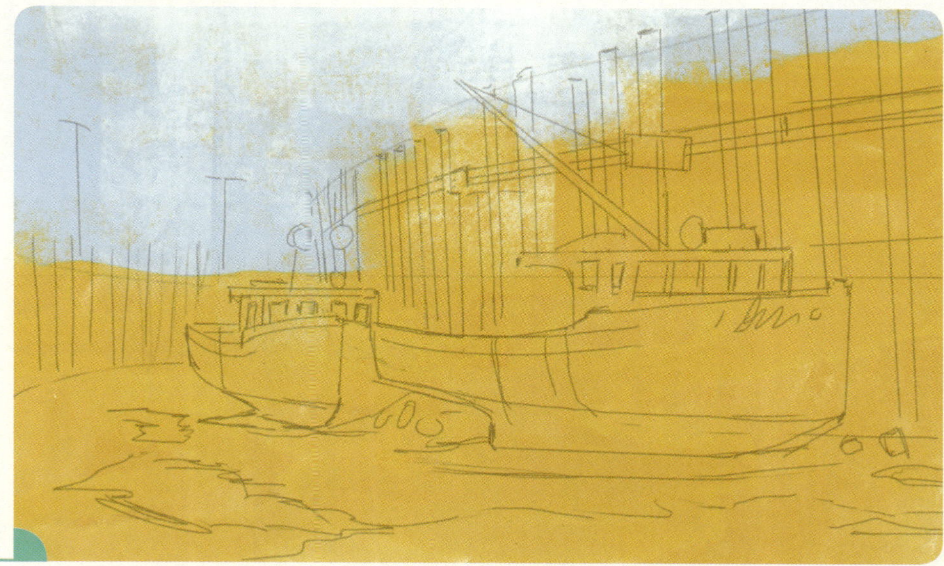

Begin blocking in the sky with large, loose brushstrokes

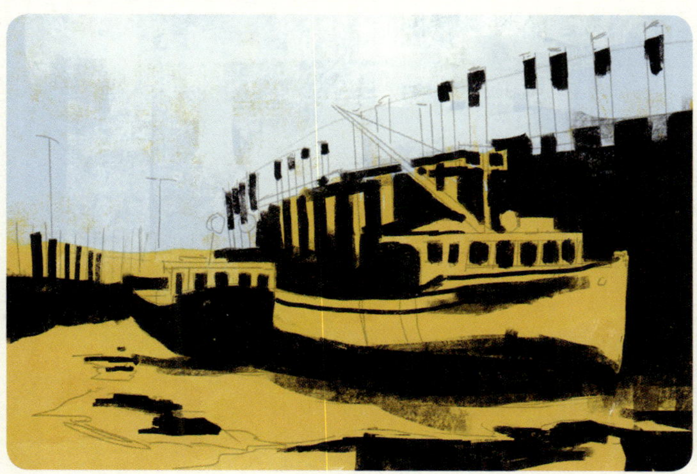

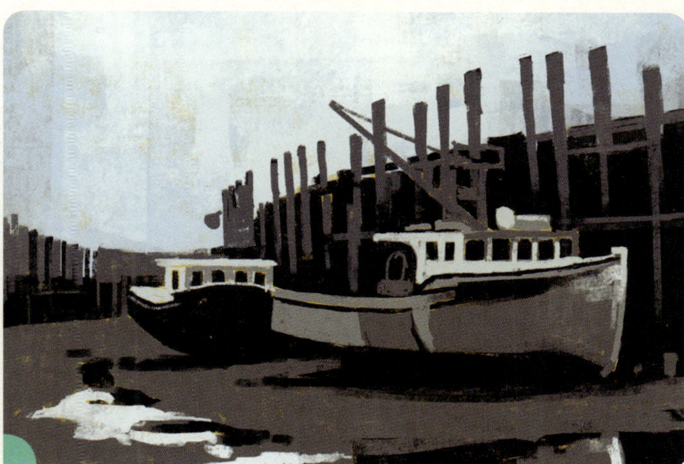

Begin to distil the scene's darker values into masses and shapes

08

It's time to begin the important work of shaping masses and identifying values. Getting the values correct upfront is critical. Your colours can be inadequate, but if your values are on point, the painting will still look great! Make a new layer for everything in front of the sky and grab a dark grey-blue colour. Continue using the Niko Rull brush at full opacity and a fairly large size. Start filling in the darker masses and shadow areas, and you will see shapes and depth begin to form.

09

After you have identified the darkest values, stay on the same layer and begin blocking in the medium values in the same way you did the shadows. Use a medium grey-blue for this. The goal is to work fast and loose at this preliminary stage, so do not worry about refinement yet. Next, use a light grey-blue to paint the brighter value shapes that represent the highlights in the scene. Notice how some bits of yellow from the undertone layer are still peeking through – this is a good way to have some texture and cohesion throughout.

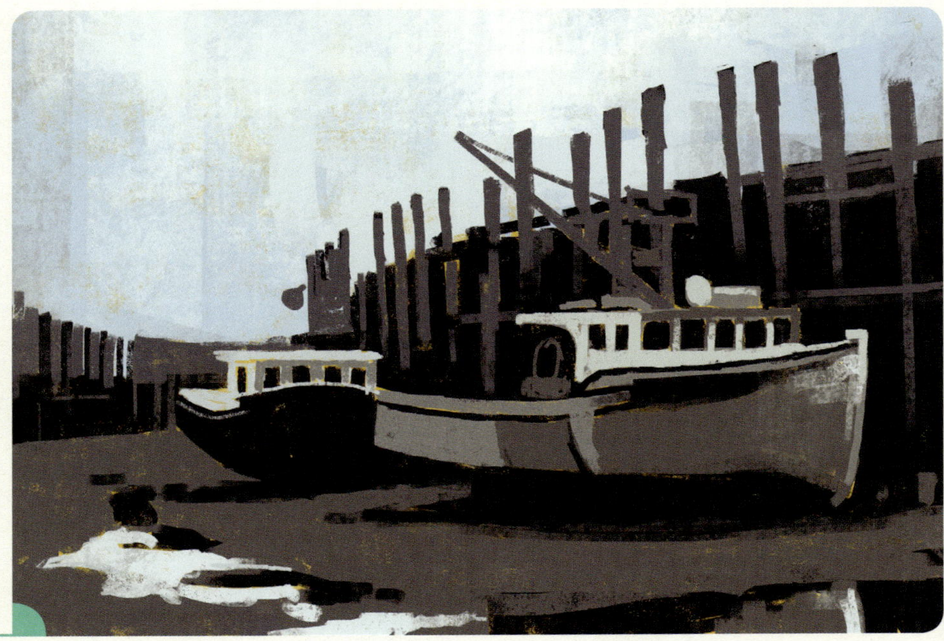

Distil the medium and lighter values of the scene into masses and shapes

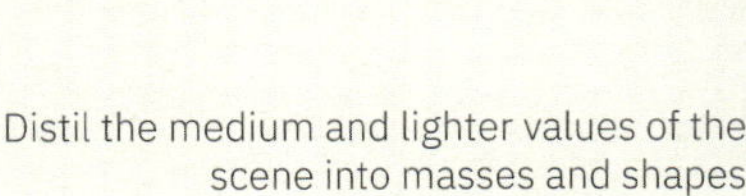

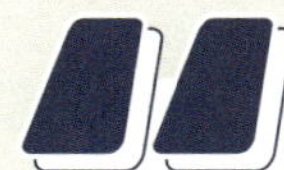

10

Now that you have blocked in the values, turn off the sketch layer and create a new layer on top, where you will start adding colour. Pick a brush or two of your choice that conveys the mood and style you wish to portray – the brushes used throughout this project are the **PAINTING > JAGGED** and **PAINTING > NIKKO RULL** brushes, since they have an attractive painterly quality. Stick to a very small selection of brushes at full opacity, as this will force you to work within consistent parameters and create cohesion throughout the painting.

Select a few large, painterly brushes for colour blocking

TREVOR SAYS: *'Be careful of relying on too many layers. My approach is quite traditional – I want to find that sweet spot where traditional techniques collide with contemporary/ digital techniques. Layers can be very helpful, but I try to use them sparingly so that the work has an organic, painterly vibe. If I do use multiple layers, I will keep combining them as I work, fixing mistakes and reworking a piece the way I would on a canvas. Those natural imperfections create character. This is just my approach. If I were doing a more illustrative style for a complex project, I would make use of a lot more of Procreate's bells and whistles.'*

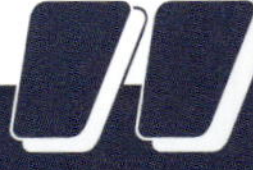

11

Working on the new layer, fill in the sky with lighter blues, greys, and perhaps even some soft yellows to portray an overcast scene with the sun trying to push through. Try to work loosely and move quickly. Since the background naturally recedes into the distance, consciously choose to use lighter values and hues in the distance. This will allow the foreground to be the centre of attention, which is the way the human eye observes reality.

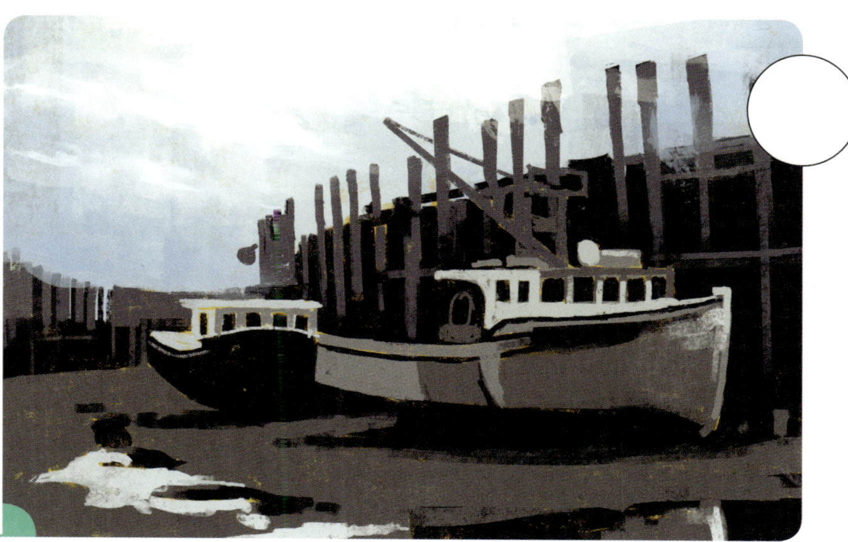
Start to paint in the colour for the sky and most-distant elements

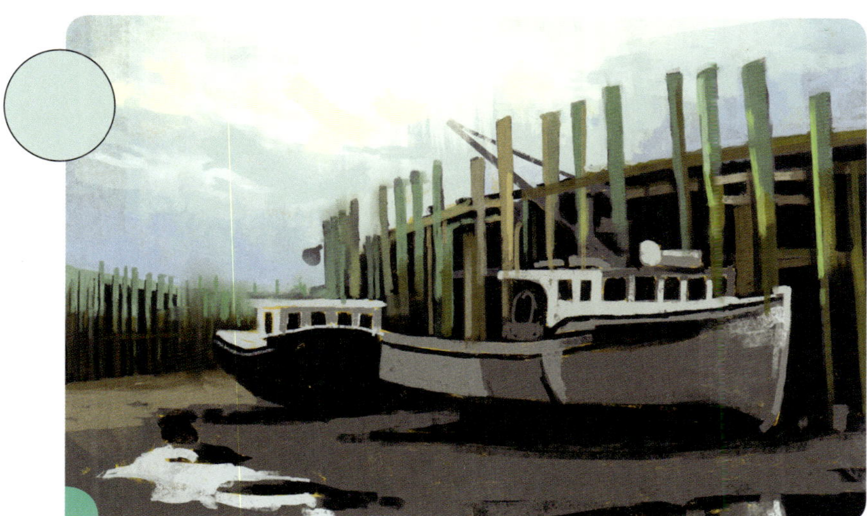
Begin to add colour to the dock structures

12

Staying on the same layer, start adding colour to the dock posts while keeping in mind the values you originally planned beneath. Try to keep the distant posts less detailed, but add more detail and more saturated colours as you begin to define the posts in the foreground. By moving around the canvas and using similar colours throughout, you will create a natural harmony and cohesion. Try to keep your brushstrokes simple and loose. Using broader brushstrokes and looser edges in the distance will allow the foreground to have more contrast and stand out.

13

Now you can start to add some colour to the ocean floor and rough in some basic colour for the puddles. Keep working on the same layer for these colouring stages – it will create a more organic look reminiscent of real paints. There's a handy technique you can use later to finesse the puddles and define some of the reflections and edges of the water, but keep things rough for now. Leaving elements such as reflections until closer to the end will allow you to reflect the natural surroundings more accurately.

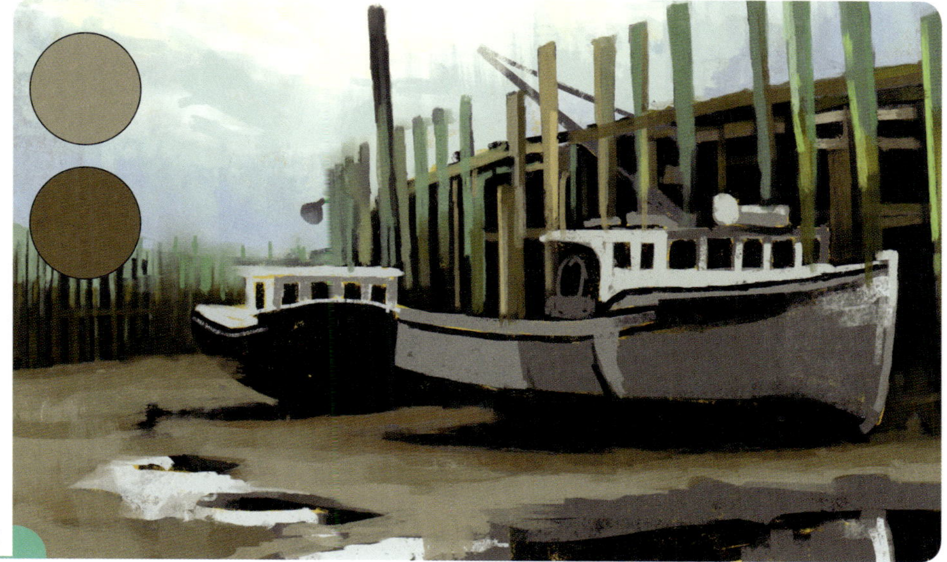
Establish the ocean floor with some basic colour-blocking

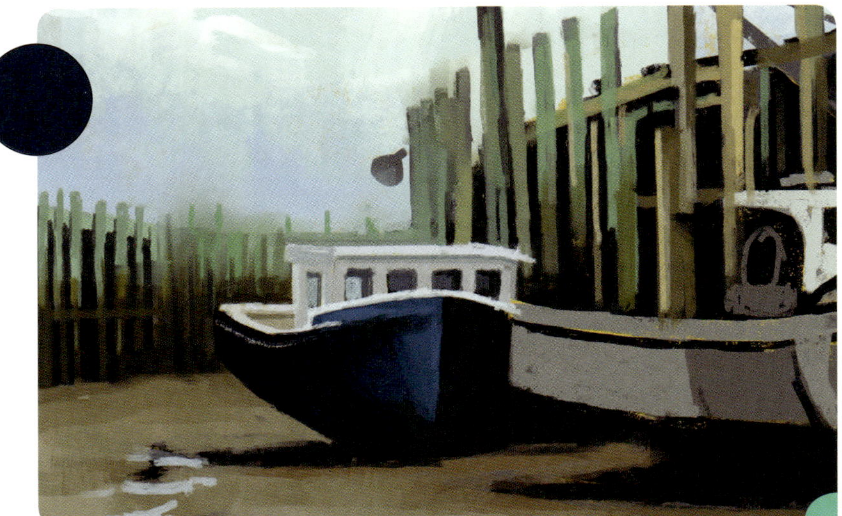

14

Now you can progress further on the boats. Focus on the distant one first, without getting overly detailed – just start defining windows and sculpting the outline of the boat a little more. A slightly smaller brush will begin to yield more defined shapes, bring clarity to the boats, and offset the boats from the background you have established.

Begin to define the shape of the most distant boat

15

You can now focus on blocking in the foreground boat (which is the primary focal point, so you need to work a little tighter). Continue to be intentional with laying down your brushstrokes. Avoid using the Smudge tool for this style of painting; changing the tones and values yourself is much more interesting and creates a shimmering, harmonious effect that brings life and character to a painting.

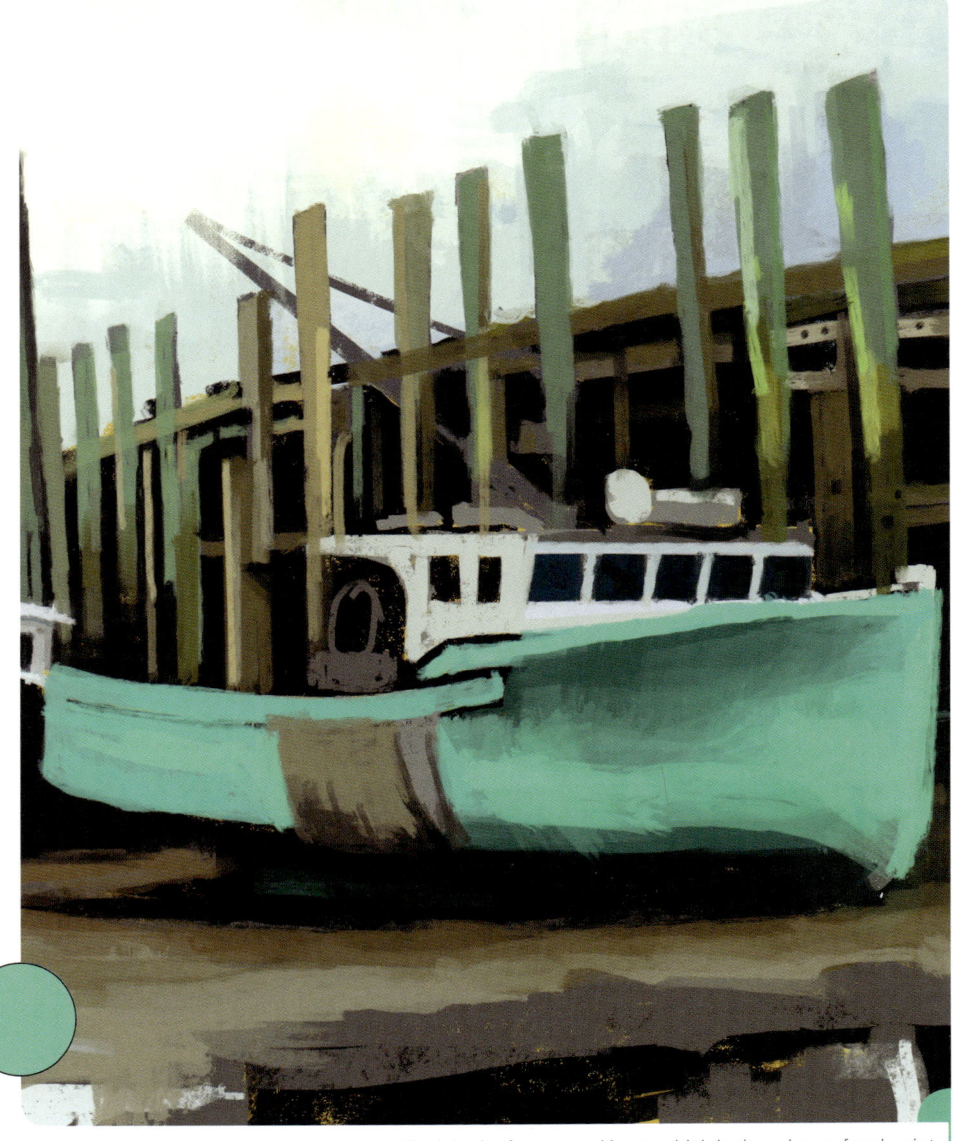

Block in the foreground boat, which is the primary focal point

16

Now that you have blocked in the colours, you can begin working on some more of the detailed elements of the foreground boat. Focus on the intermediate, medium-sized details and save the finer ones for later. It is important to note that these secondary details can be 'implied' by working loosely. You can also begin adding some sharper edges where you want to draw the viewer's attention. You will also notice that once you start adding small pops of colour, the painting really starts to come to life.

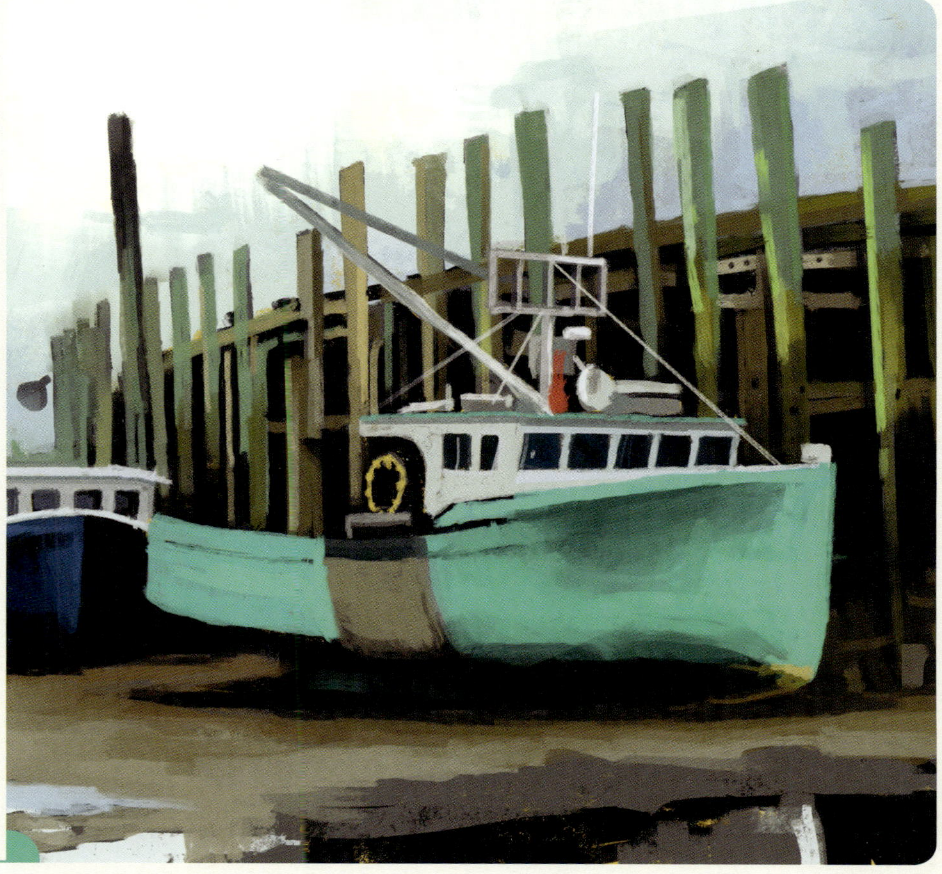

Build up the foreground boat with intermediate details

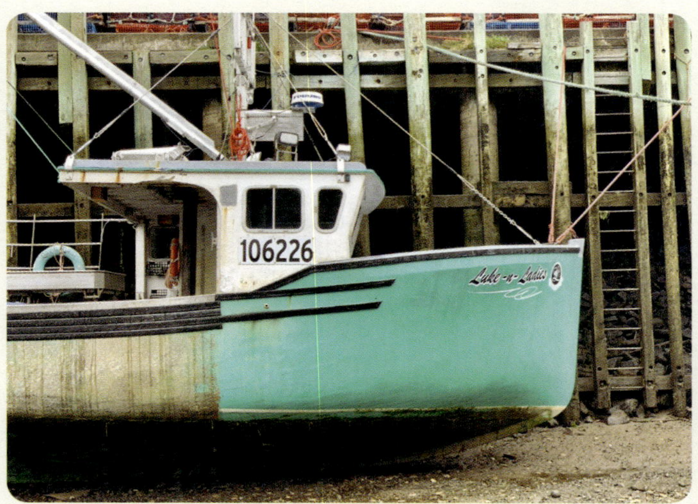

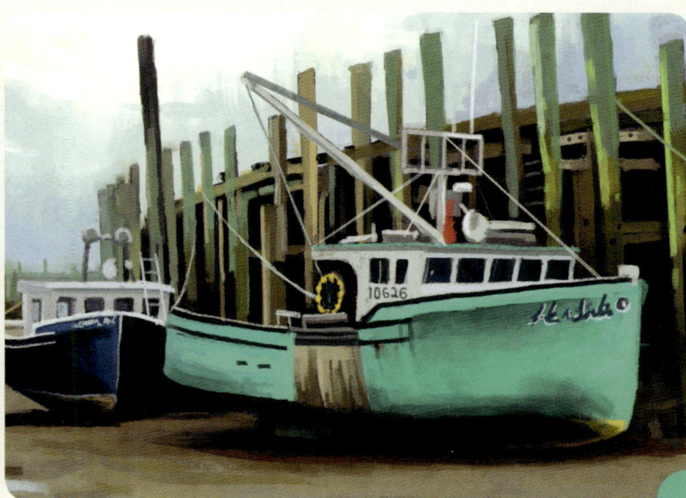

Add some texture and further details to the foreground boat

17

Now you can start adding some textures and smaller details to the boats. If you take a closer look at the real boat, it features details such as a name on the side, a number, and other elements that can either be implied or accurately written out. Details can be simplified, compressed, or minimized to fit the desired complexity of your final painting – for example, shortening the number and loosely suggesting the text rather than replicating each ornate letter. At this point you can also begin refining the shadows under the boats. Focusing on light and shadows will start to generate a more believable environment.

18

Shift your focus to the details on the ocean floor. Add some green seaweed sparingly on the left side. The addition of a green hue will not only contribute some interesting textures, but also tie in with colours that are already present elsewhere in the painting, such as on certain sections of the dock posts.

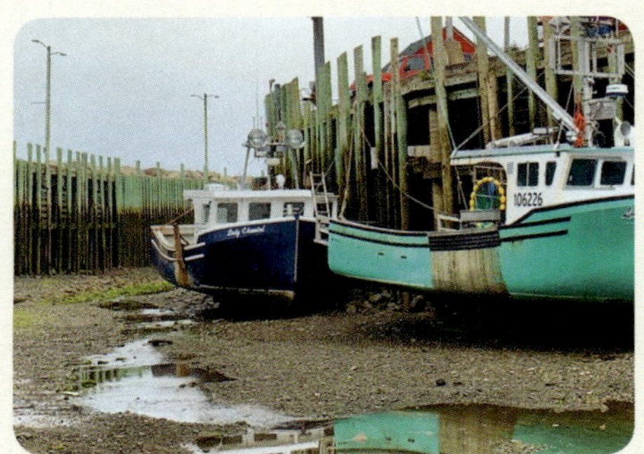

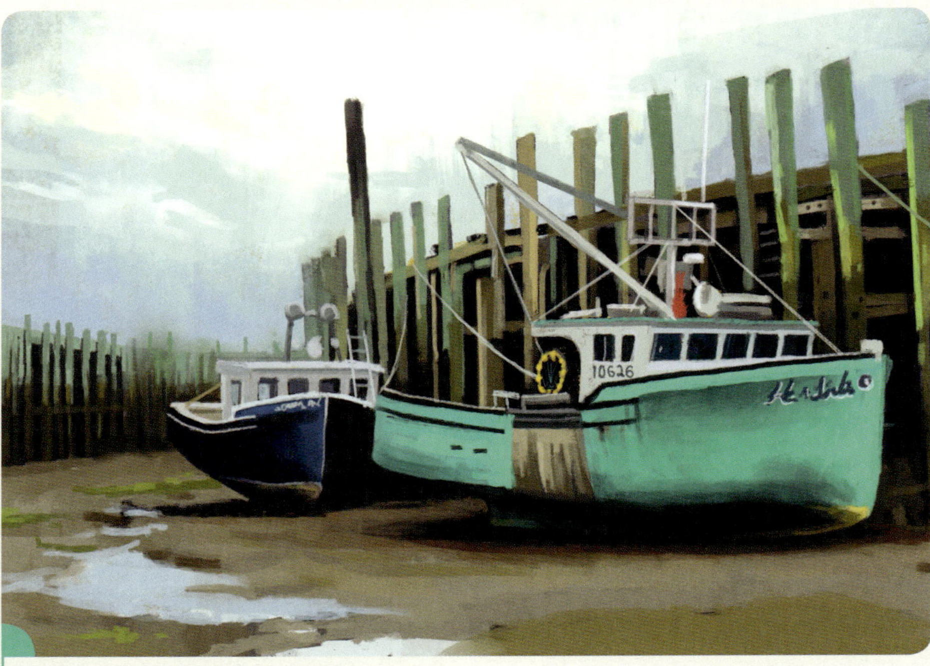

Focus on the details of the ocean floor

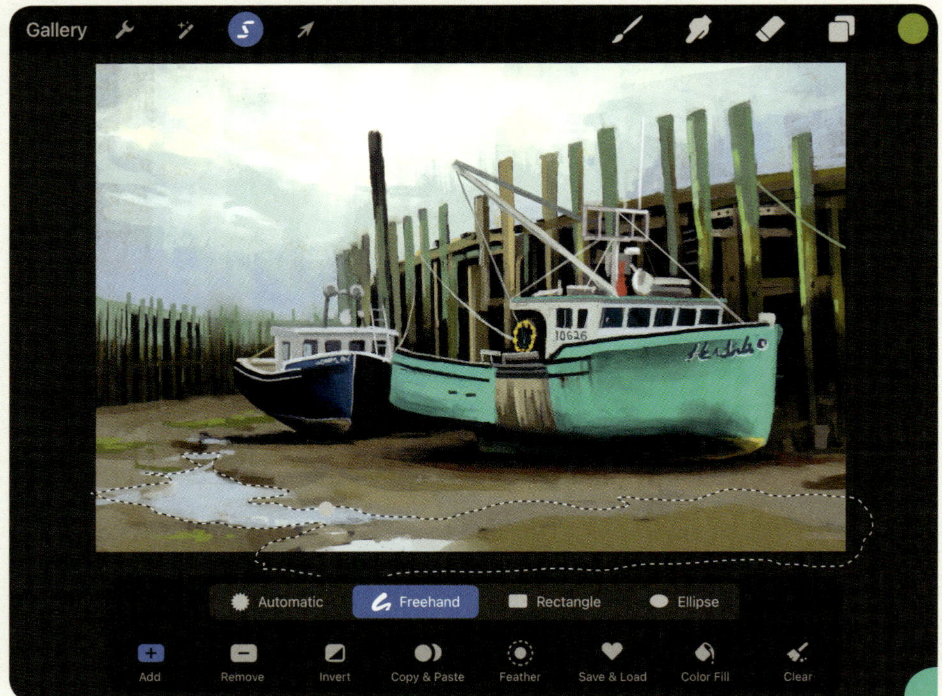

19

Create a new layer and draw a lasso around the puddles using the **SELECTION > FREEHAND** tool found in the main toolbar. This shape will be used for the reflections, and since it's independent of your painting, it will allow you to control the reflections and tweak the puddles however you wish as you progress through the image.

You can turn the selection off by tapping the Selection icon, and turn it back on when needed by holding down on the Selection icon. To make sure you don't lose useful selections, you can save and reload them with the **SELECTION > SAVE & LOAD** option.

Create a selection on a new layer for the puddles

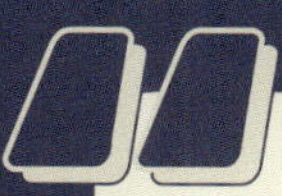

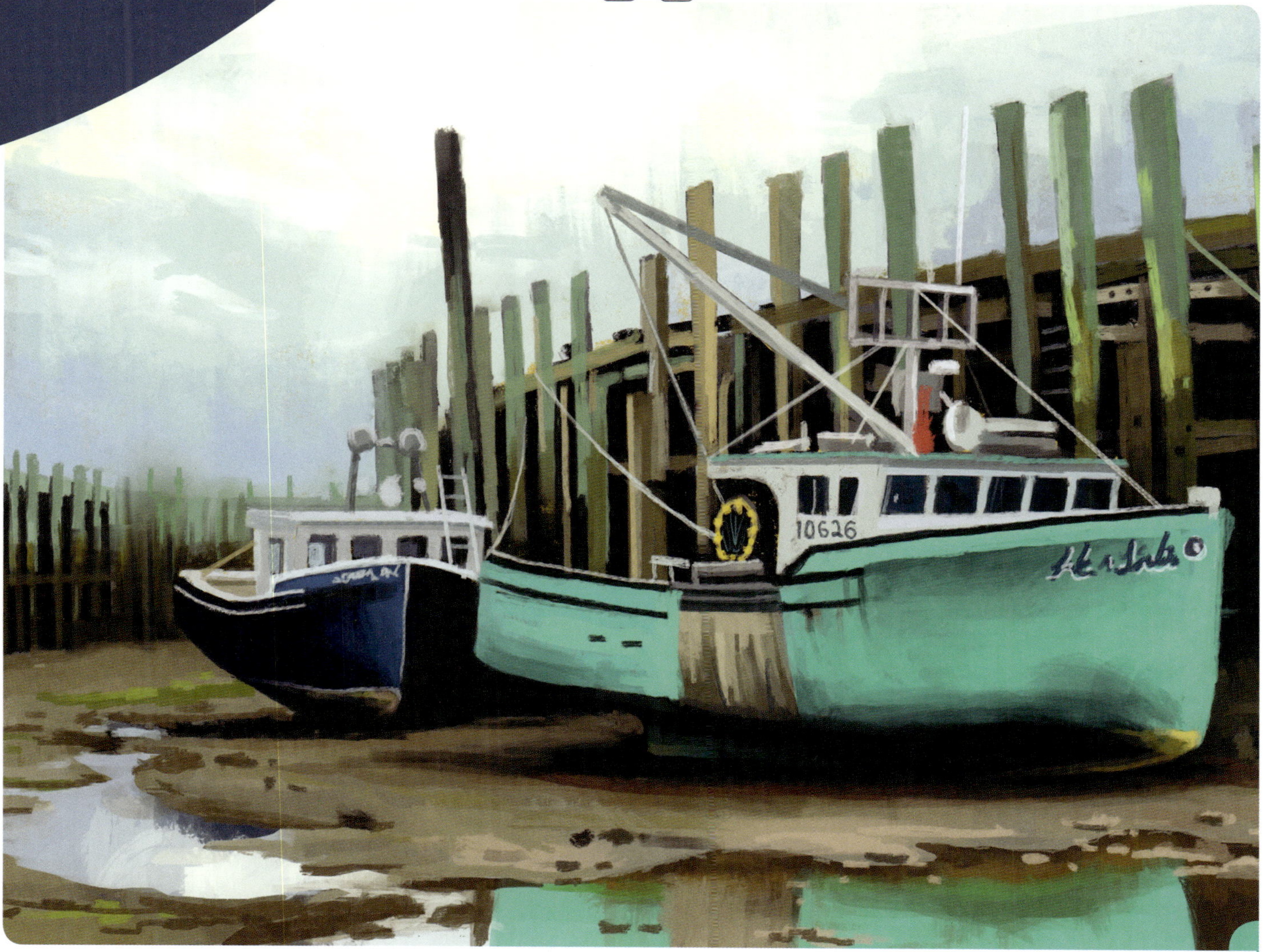

Fill in the puddle selection with painterly reflections of the sky and boats

20

With your selection active on that new layer, you can now paint the reflections in the puddle. Try to keep them quite loose. Note how the water is dark brown where the ground is more visible at the shallow edges, then changes colour to reflect the sky and boats. If you wish, you can select the Smudge tool and a brush of your choice, and use a mixture of smudging and brushstrokes to create a reflection. However, it is good practice to not use the Smudge tool at all, instead keeping your brush at full opacity and using the Eyedropper to grab colours from the boat. Overusing the Smudge tool might diverge too much from the painterly qualities you have established throughout the rest of the painting.

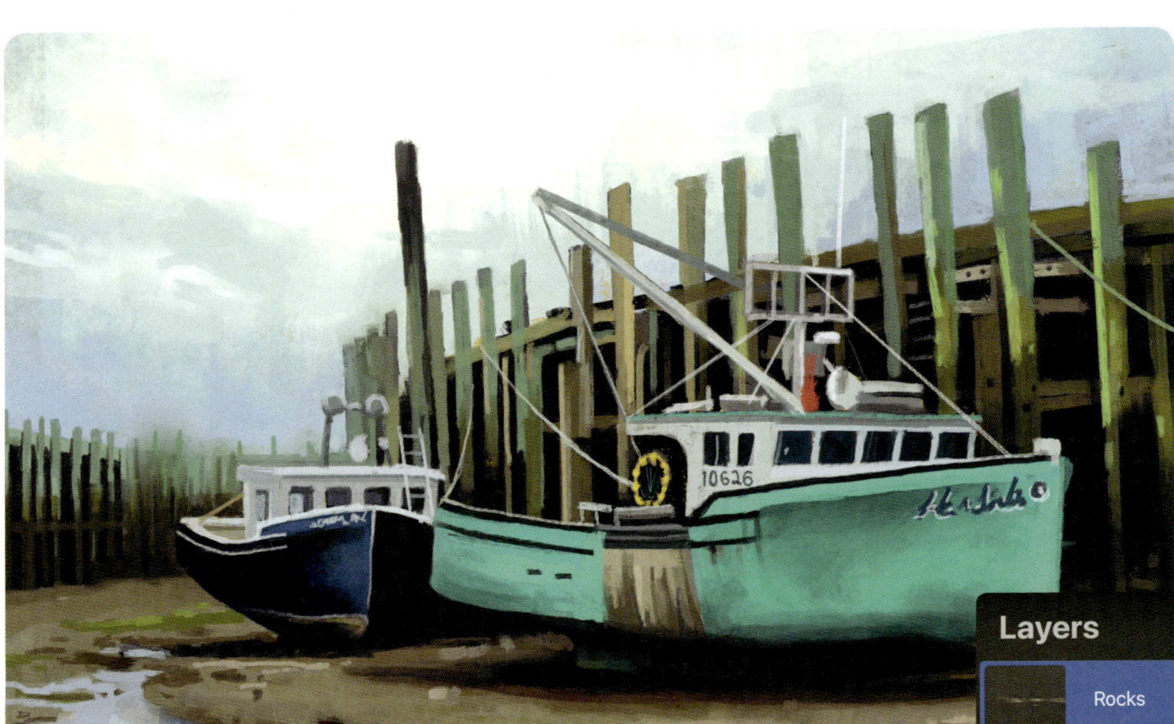

21

The ocean floor looks quite flat right now, so create a new layer above the puddle layer and focus on adding some rocks and pebbles in the water and on the ground to add some texture. Using a separate layer will allow you to make any revisions you wish without damaging your puddles. You can also use the rocks layer to add details and roughness to the edges of the puddles to make them appear more realistic and not quite as 'perfect'.

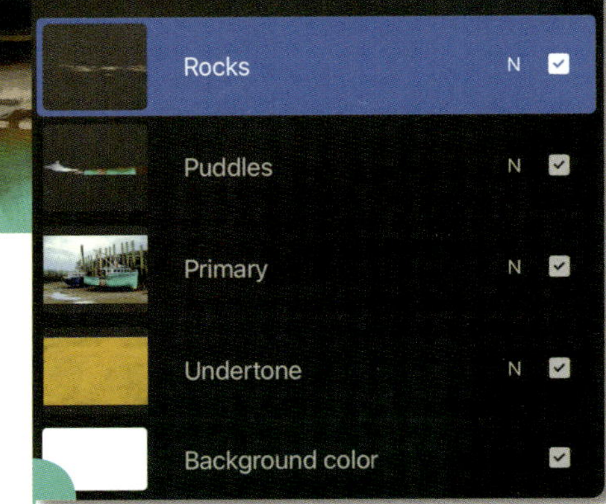

Add some details to the ground, such as rocks and pebbles

22

Sometimes the smallest details can add life and bring personality to a painting. In this case, the scene doesn't really show any signs of life, so try adding a pair of birds in the distant sky. You can also add the light posts that are depicted in the reference photo, which will balance the painting a little more and help fill the void on the left side. It is important to note that maintaining more emphasis on the right side is still crucial and ultimately creates a destination for the eye to move towards.

Finesse the painting by adding subtle details in the distance

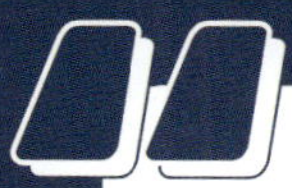

TREVOR SAYS: *'Try to work loosely in the distance with softer edges and broader brushstrokes. As you move into the foreground, paint with crisper edges and more detail. This keeps the foreground focal point as the centre of attention – the viewer's eyes are automatically guided to it without distractions.'*

23

Now you can once more move around the canvas, reworking any sections that need improvement, and adding highlights, details, and subtle textures. A few vertical strokes in the sky add to the rainy, overcast feel; some brown strokes add weathering to the ground and dock posts. At this stage, it's easy to overdo the details, so be careful not to overwork the image; you can even remove details if needed. Focus primarily on the foreground subjects and ocean floor, breathing life and personality into the image as you see fit.

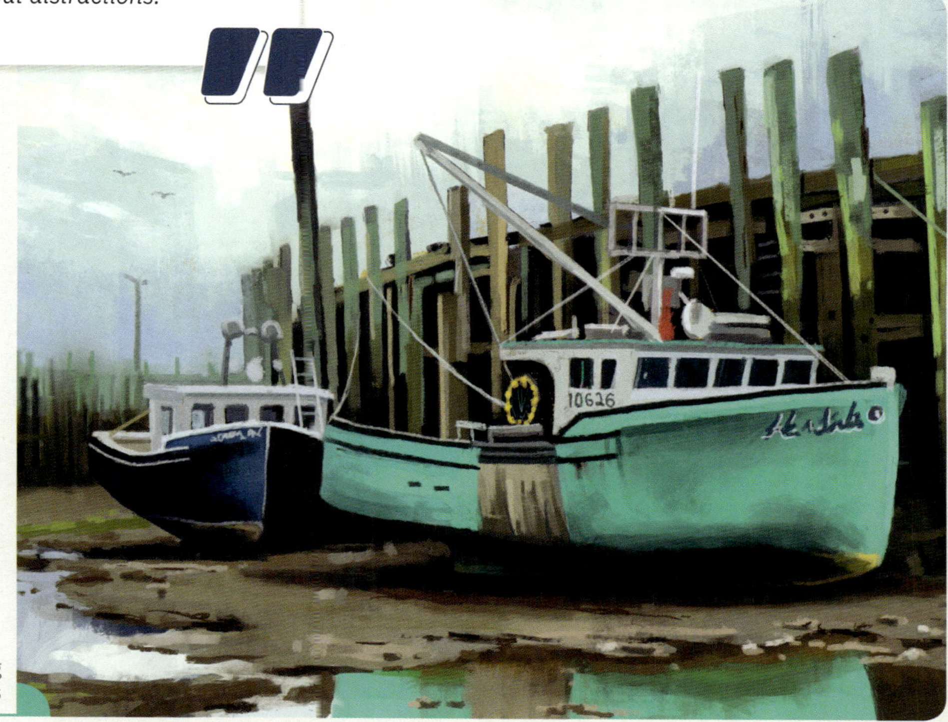

Make final adjustments to the scene by adding highlights, details, and subtle textures

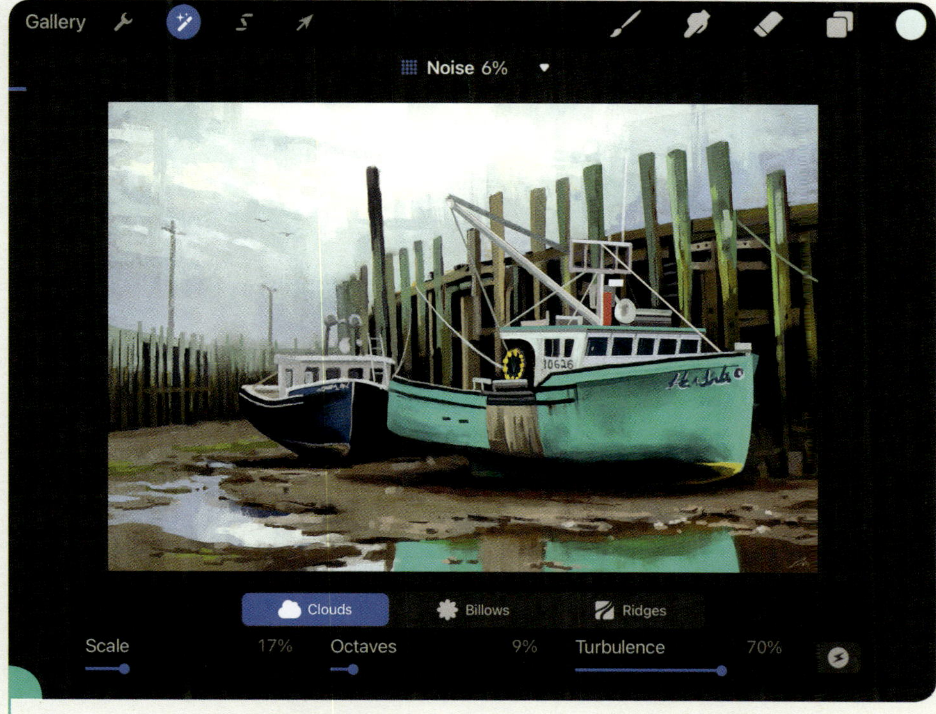

Fine-tune the entire painting by adjusting the vibrancy and contrast and adding some grain

24

Go over the teal boat one last time to give it crisper, cleaner edges, tidying up finer details such as the lines and windows. Use light grey-blue to push back the wooden posts in the background, giving them more distance from the foreground. Once you are happy with everything, collapse all the layers and go to the Adjustments menu to make some final overall tweaks. Try increasing the image's vibrancy and contrast or tweaking the colour options a little to make the piece more dynamic.

A good finishing touch is grain or 'noise', which gives digital paintings some grit and a more organic texture, but be careful to use it sparingly. Go to **ADJUSTMENTS > NOISE**. Set Noise to 6% by sliding your finger across the screen, then select Clouds and set it to 17% Scale, 9% Octaves, and 70% Turbulence.

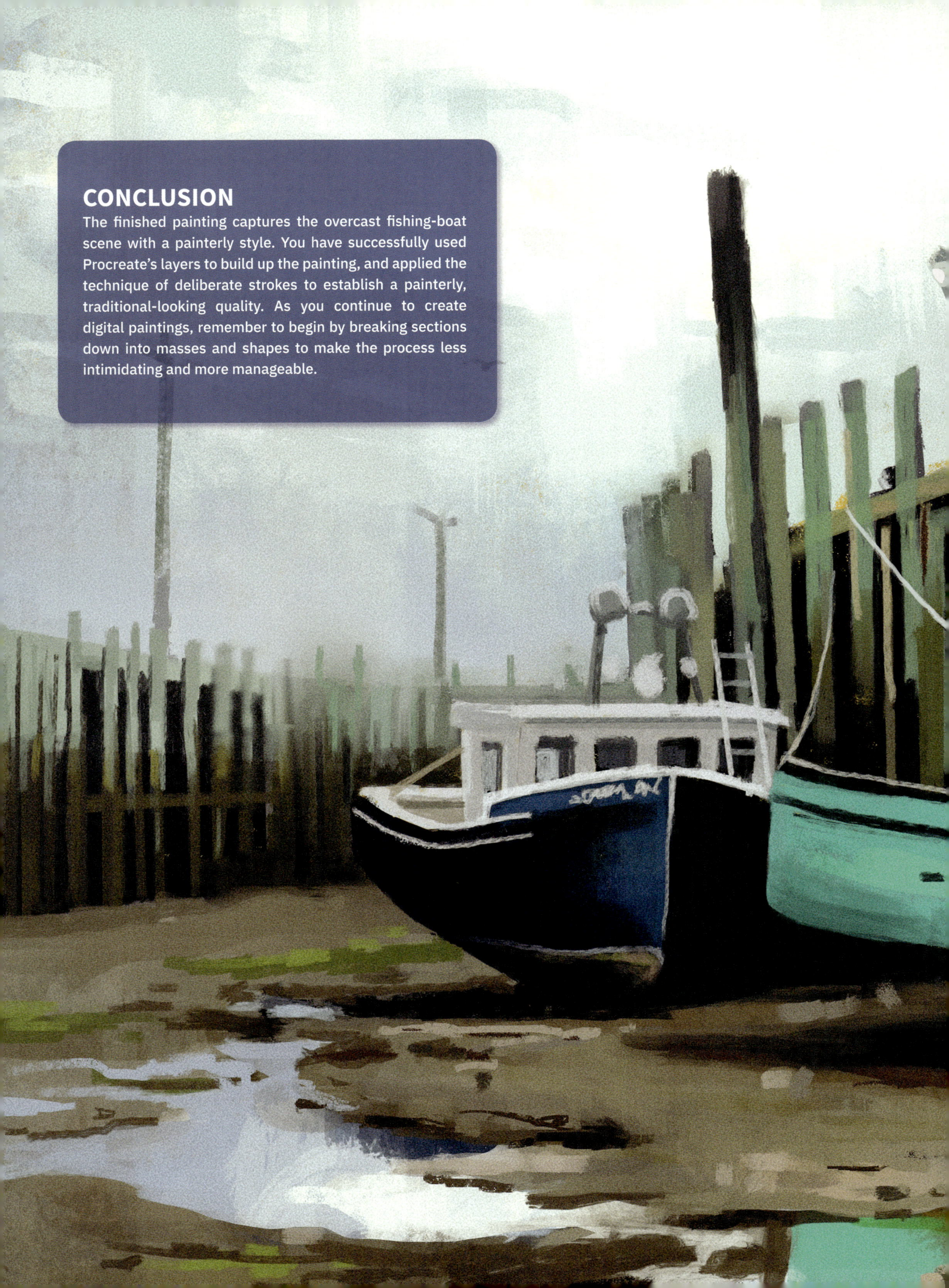

CONCLUSION

The finished painting captures the overcast fishing-boat scene with a painterly style. You have successfully used Procreate's layers to build up the painting, and applied the technique of deliberate strokes to establish a painterly, traditional-looking quality. As you continue to create digital paintings, remember to begin by breaking sections down into masses and shapes to make the process less intimidating and more manageable.

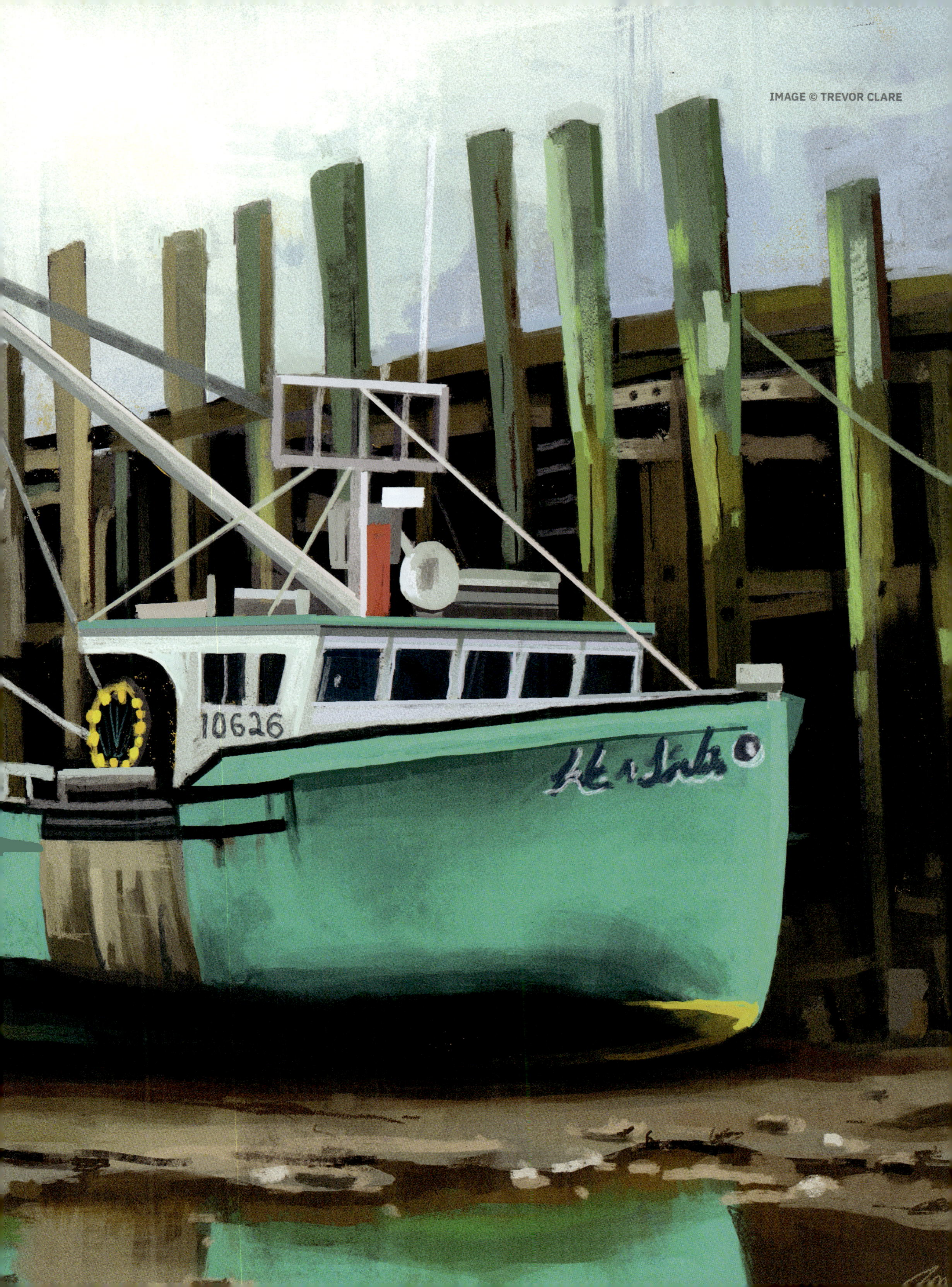

10626

ECHOES: After reviewing my photos from a day excursion to Niagara-on-the-Lake, I knew I needed to capture this desolate house that was standing alone in a field while a foreboding storm approached

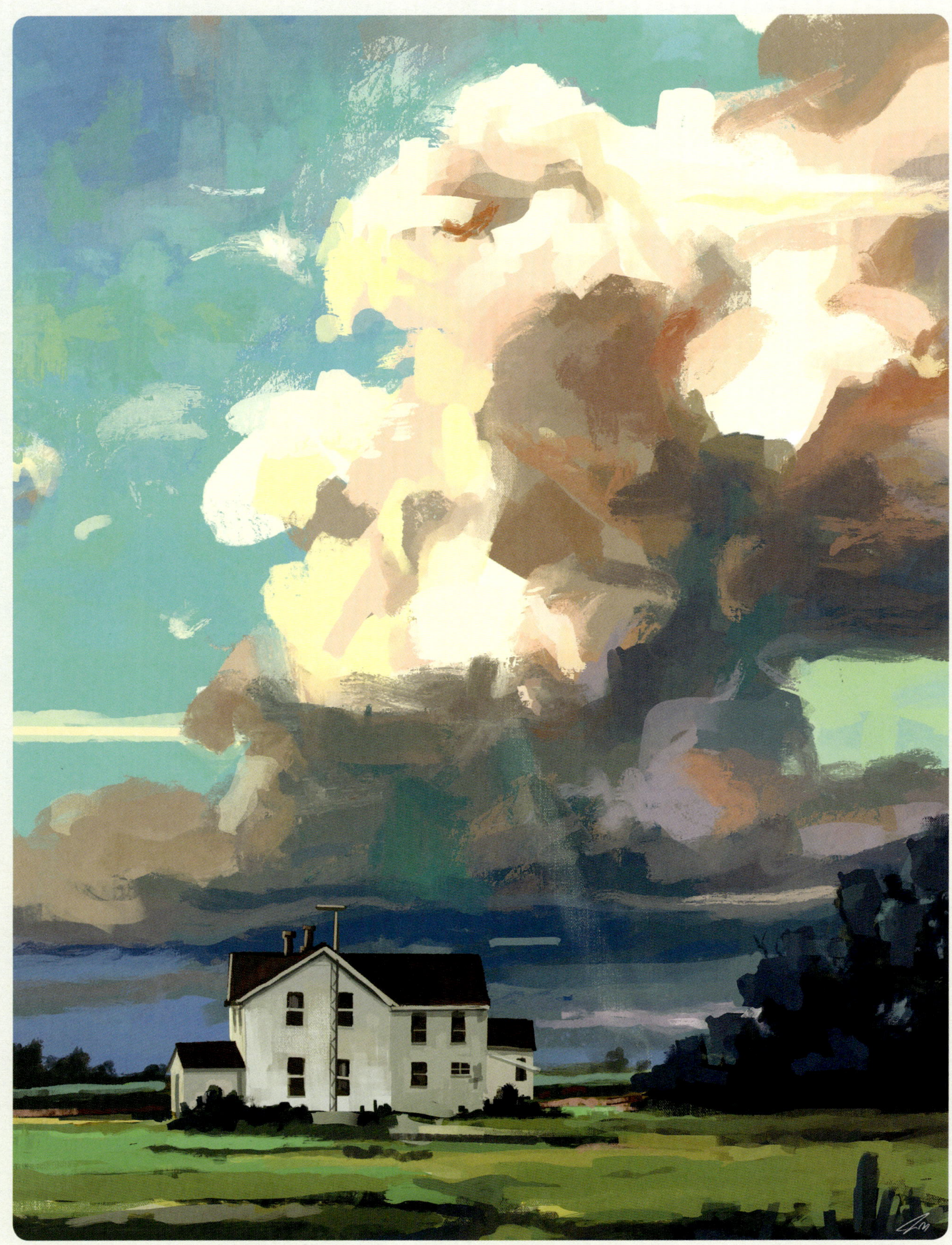

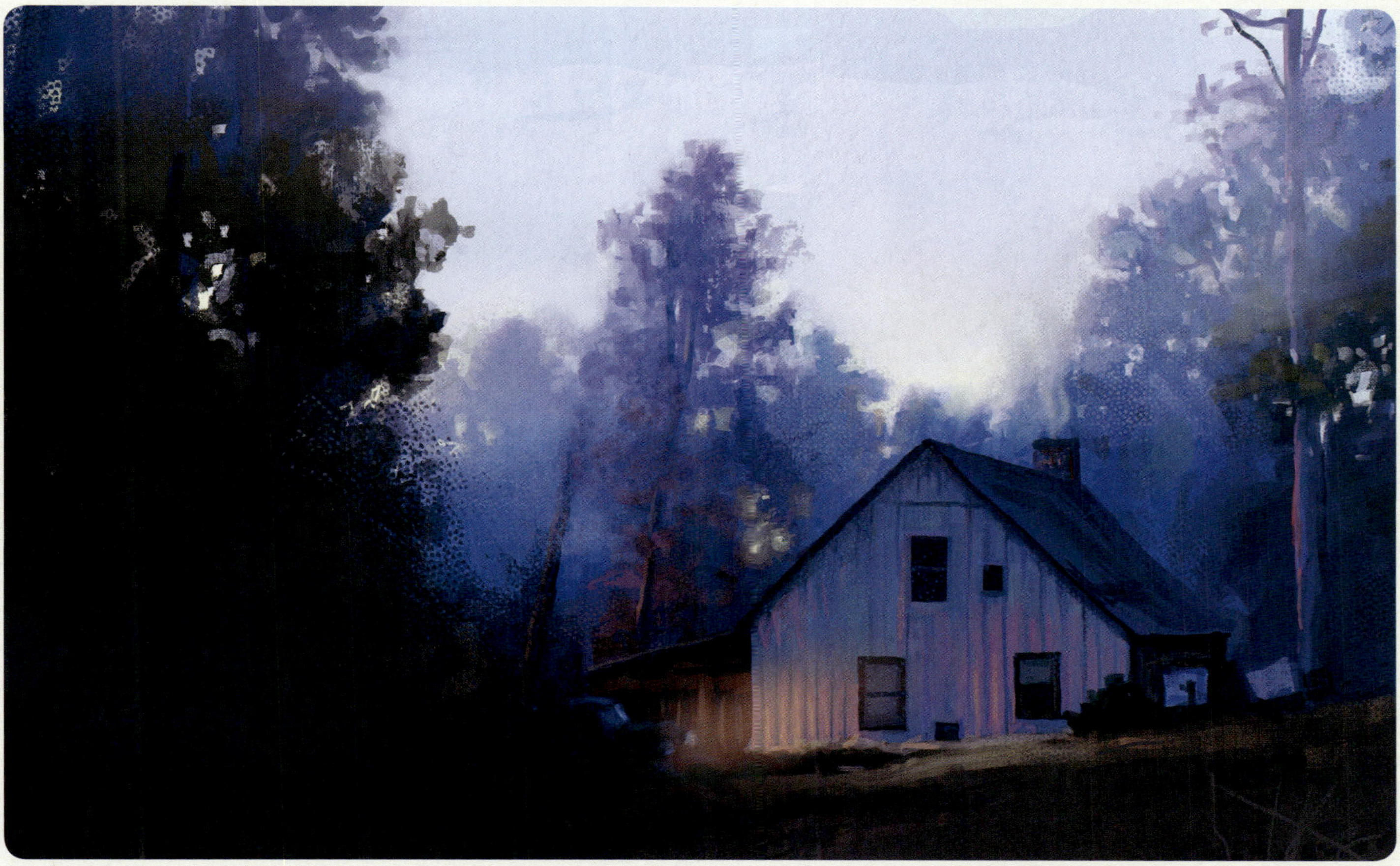

THE VISITOR: Inspired by a film with exceptional cinematography, I tried to capture the mood of an unfolding mystery narrative in this painting

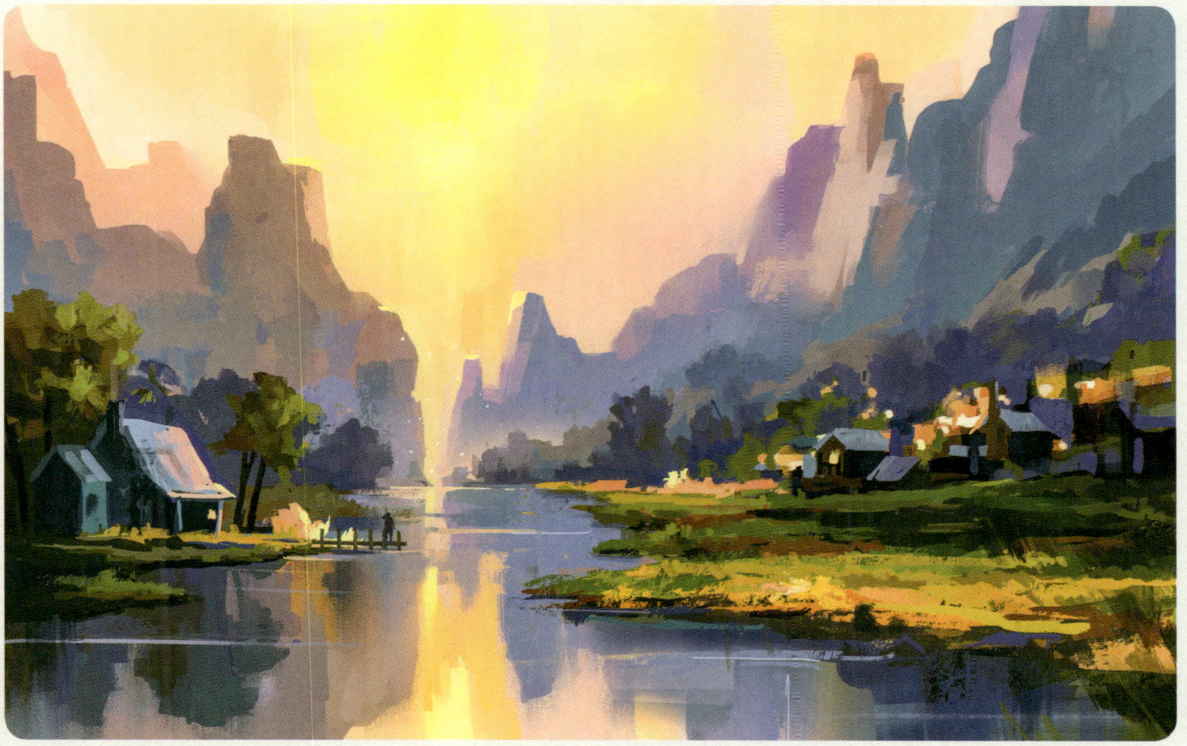

FLIGHT OF MOMENT: Drawing from examples of gorgeous terrain found in South-Asian countries,
I created this fantasy-like utopia by focusing on the use of warm light and a vibrant colour palette

STUDIO CITY AT NIGHT

BY JOJO LU

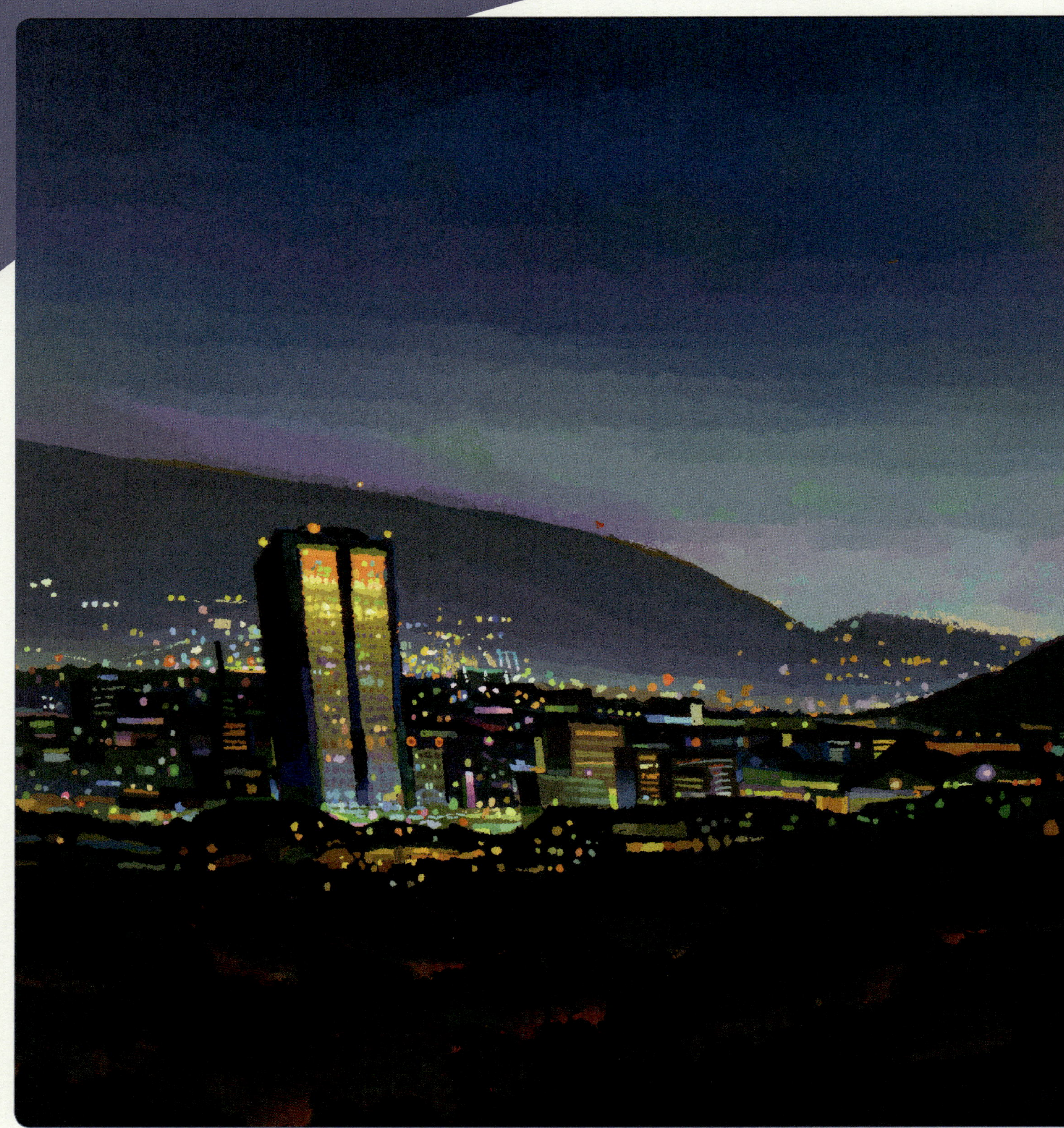

- **Create a stylized composition based on what you see**

- **Pick colours that feel realistic yet vibrant**

- **Manage the visual complexity of a cityscape**

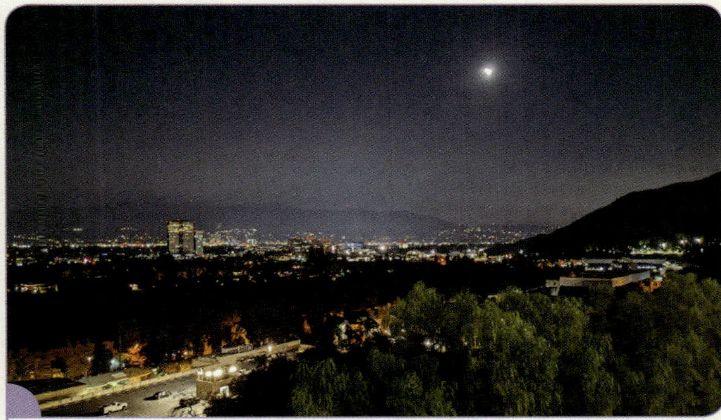

This nocturnal cityscape is full of details to break down and simplify

01

Cityscapes are tricky, but by breaking the process down into smaller steps they become more manageable. The environment here is filled with city lights, buildings, hills, cars, and trees – you will have to be selective in what to capture. Start by creating a new canvas set to 96 cm wide × 72 cm high and 72 dpi (or a higher dpi if you plan to make large prints). For the initial sketching stage, select a plain, quite solid brush, such as **PAINTING > ROUND BRUSH**.

JOJO SAYS: *'Before you start a painting, always ask yourself what you're interested in. Everyone finds different things interesting, and this is what creates an artist's style and unique voice. Here I painted Studio City in Los Angeles at night. I really liked the contrast between the city and the moon, as well as the under-glow of orange from the parking lot in the foreground. Think about what you like and keep it in mind while you paint to make sure it's expressed.'*

02

Before you start painting, make sure you have a good composition. Sketch a few quick thumbnails with just two or three colours to get a better idea of how the painting will read from a distance. Try to keep it simple – the aim of this step is to get the overall statement and not focus on the small details. To make a composition more interesting, vary the use of big, medium, and small shapes. A good painting should be able to be read clearly from far away. The top-right example here achieves a good balance of legible shapes in a variety of sizes, and contrasting values.

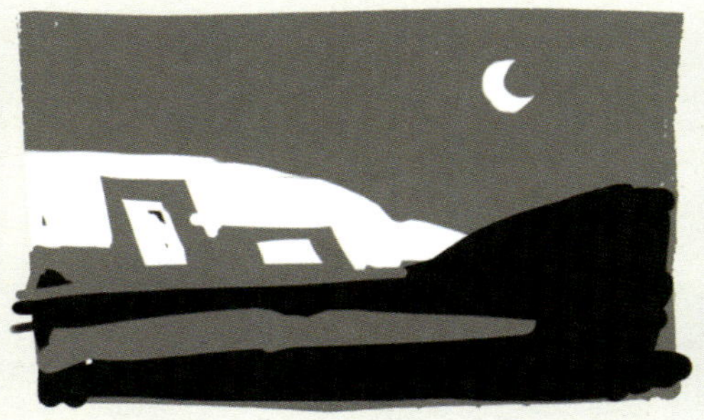
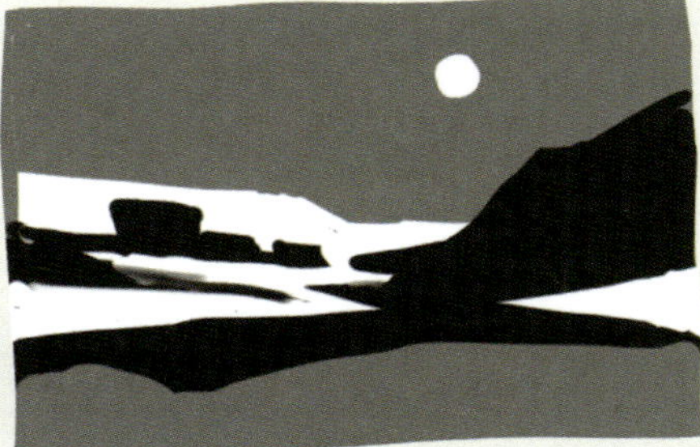
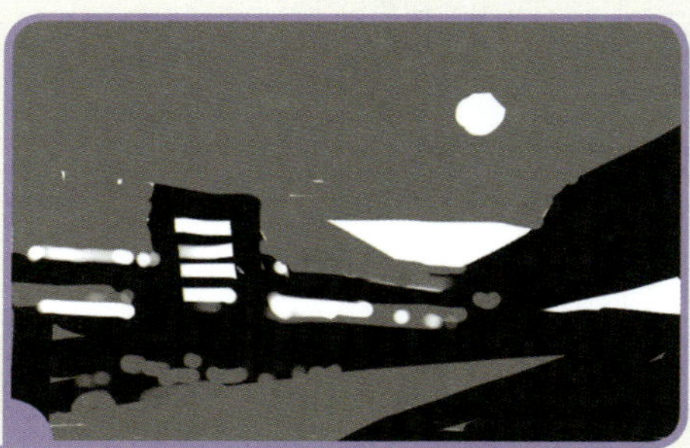
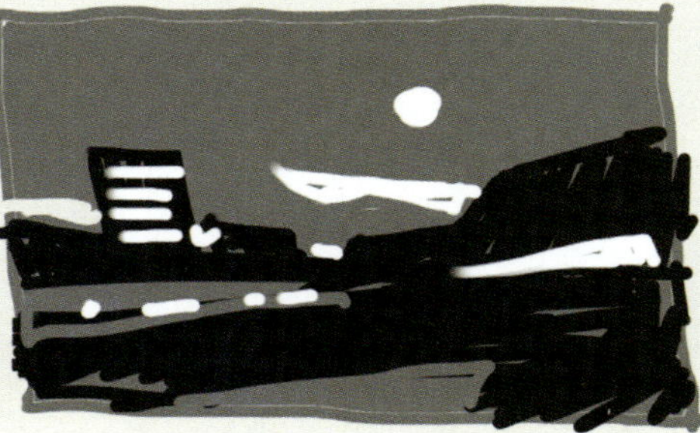

Try to make around three to five compositions before picking a final one

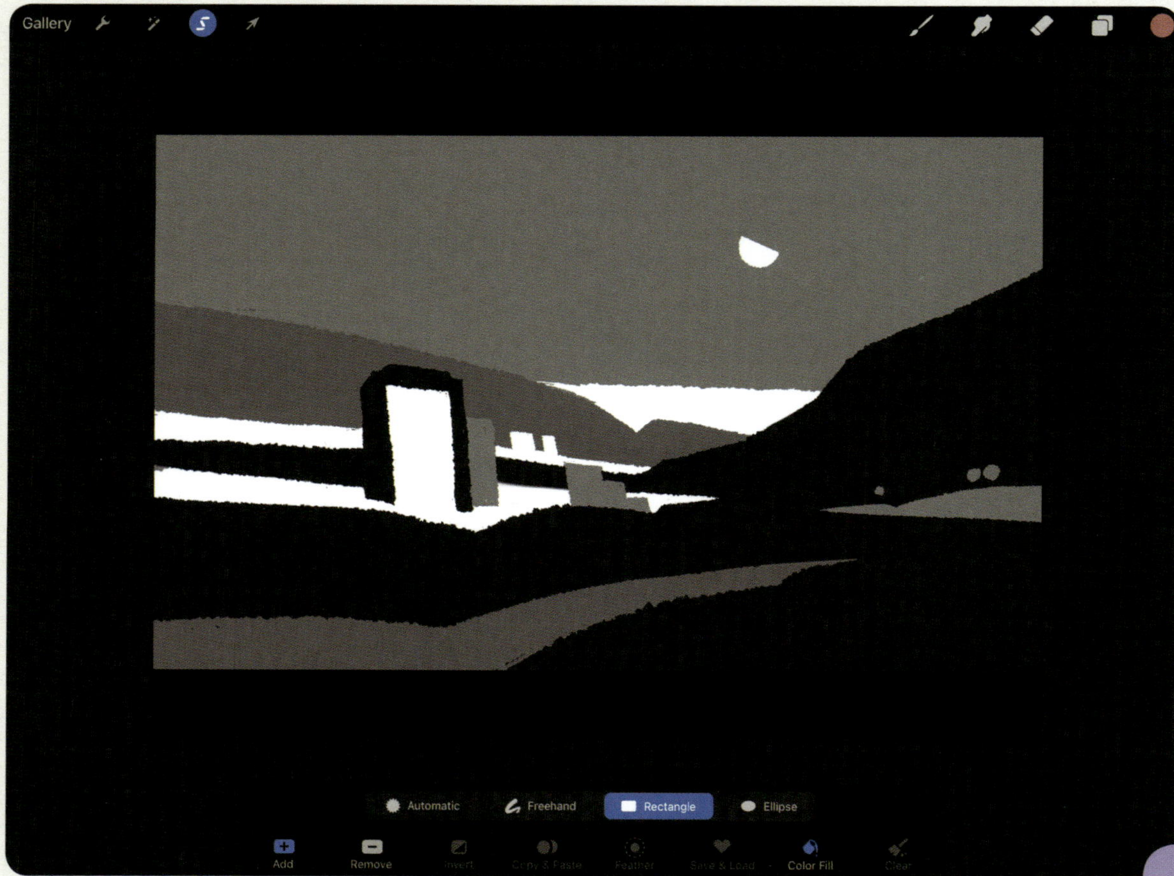

Keep the values and shapes simple and easy to read at a first glance

03

Select your chosen thumbnail with the Selection tool and expand it to fill the whole canvas with Transform. Refine the shapes some more, using an opaque, textured brush such as **DRAWING > EVOLVE.** Keep in mind your original statement from step 02 and make sure all the big shape ideas are still there. Make a new layer on top of this and add black 'letterboxing' bars on the top and bottom of the canvas to give the scene a cinematic look. Do this using **SELECTIONS > RECTANGLE** with Colour Fill set to black.

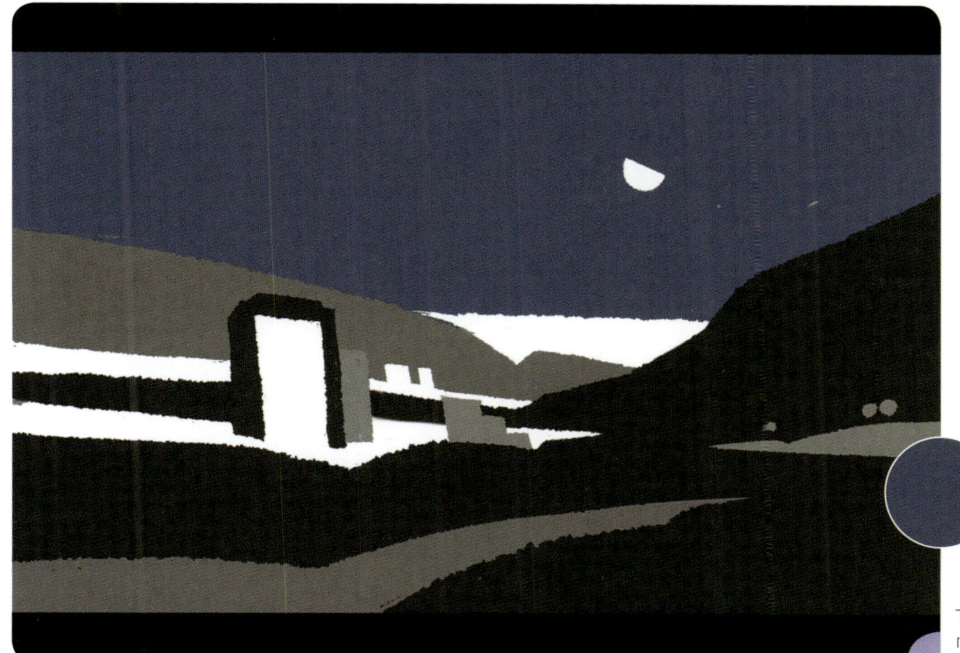

The ColourDrop feature is very useful for recolouring different parts of a painting

04

Duplicate the layer with the refined composition on it. You can now use ColourDrop to fill in the base colours for each area of the composition. To use ColourDrop, quickly drag the colour icon from the top-right of the screen onto the area you want to recolour. Still holding down, you can slide left and right to adjust the threshold if too little or too much colour is being filled in. Start by ColourDropping a blue-grey colour onto the sky.

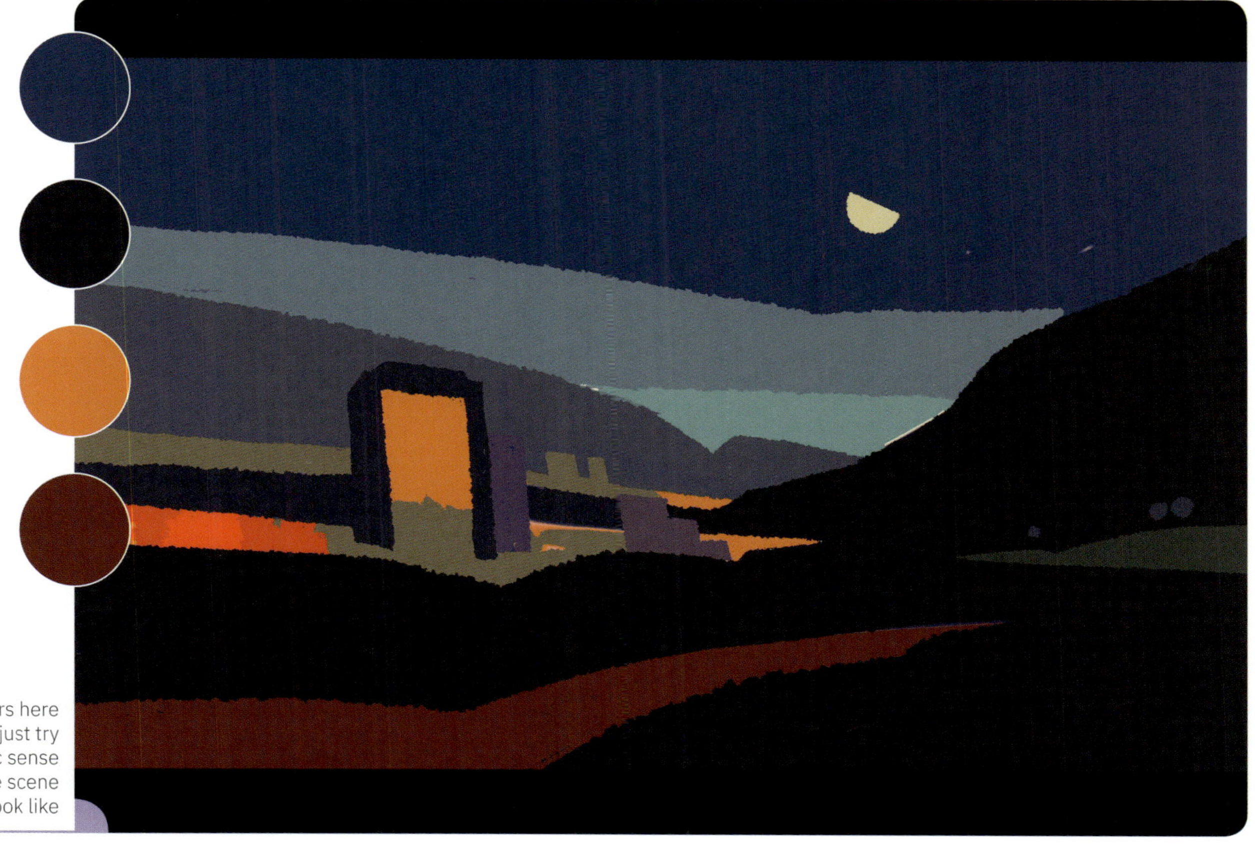

The colours here are not final – just try to get a basic sense of what the scene might look like

05

When picking base colours, try to think about their value and temperature. Value is the range of how light or how dark a colour is and the temperature is how warm or cool it is. You can pick any colours you want as long as you keep their relationships consistent. Colours are perceived relative to what's next to them – for example, here you can use a warmer (more purple) blue for the top of the sky and a cooler (more green) blue for the bottom to create a sense of depth.

06

When you have finished picking all the base colours, you can move on to refining the painting and adding details. Continue using the **DRAWING > EVOLVE** brush for this part. This painting will be built up from back to front, so start with the sky and begin to add in-between shades and subtle colour variations. This night is very smoggy, so add some greys at the bottom of the sky as well.

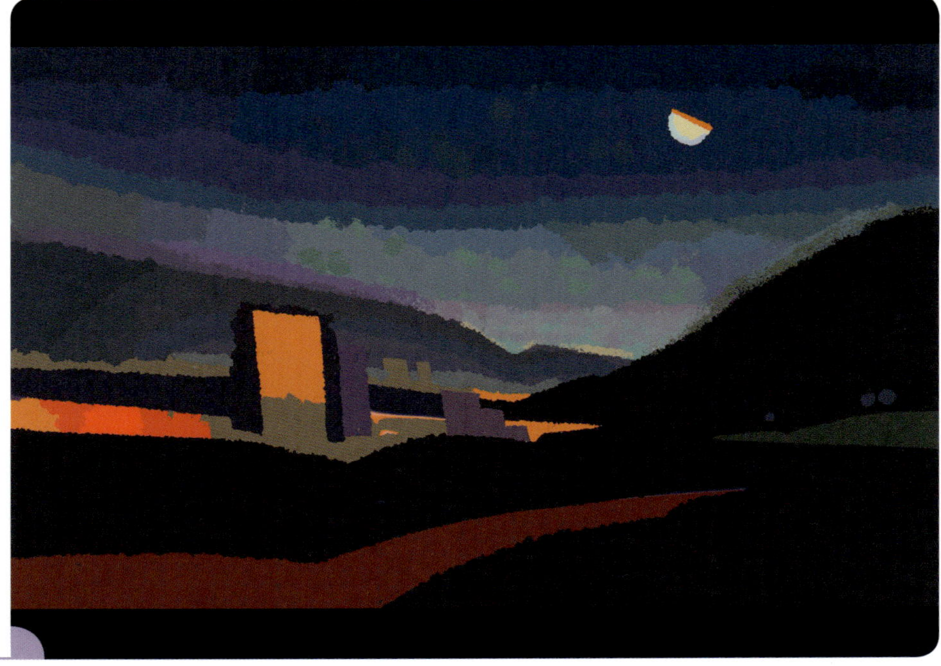

Don't worry about blending yet – you will do that in a later step

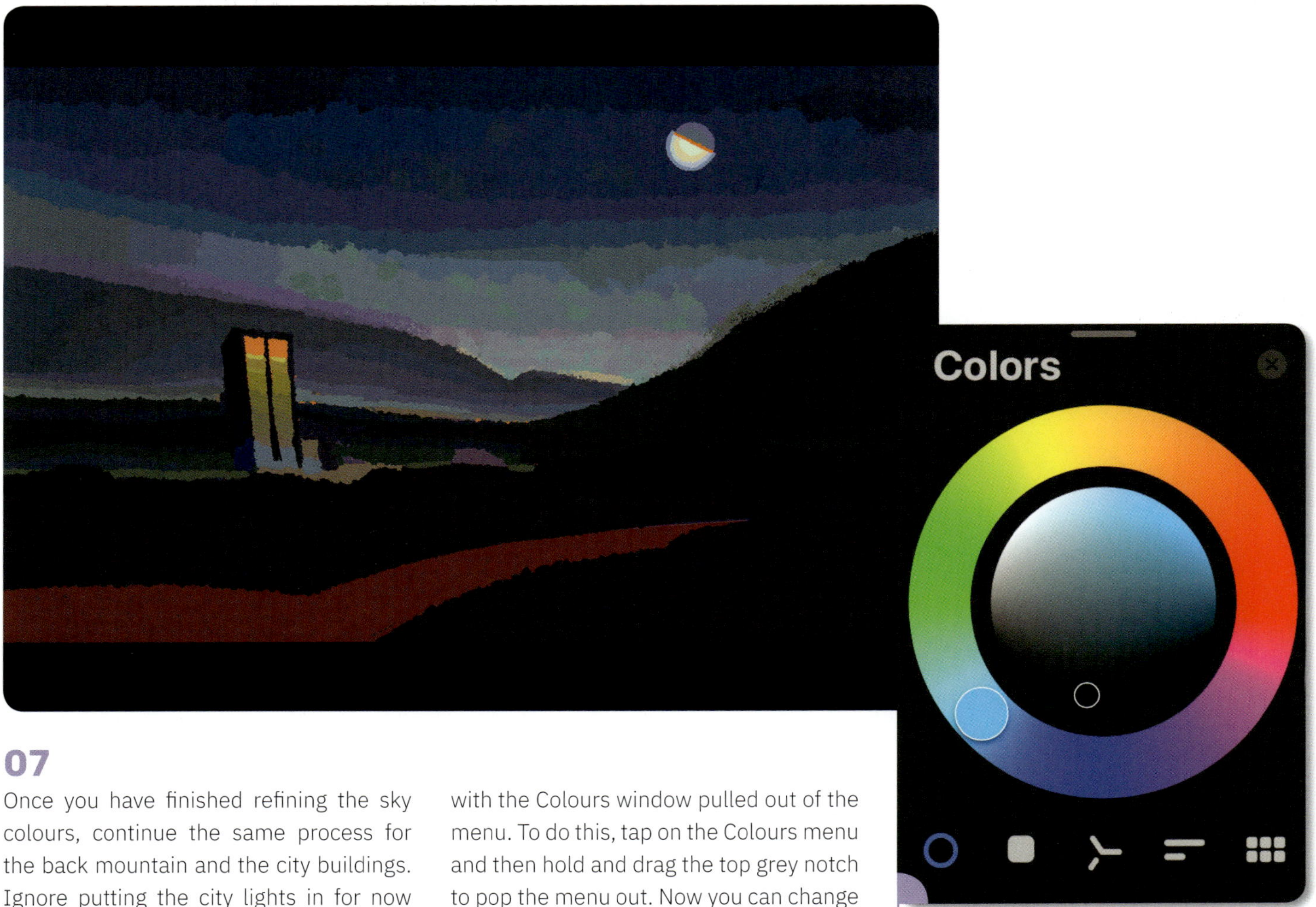

07

Once you have finished refining the sky colours, continue the same process for the back mountain and the city buildings. Ignore putting the city lights in for now – those will be put in later. For ease of changing colours frequently, try to work with the Colours window pulled out of the menu. To do this, tap on the Colours menu and then hold and drag the top grey notch to pop the menu out. Now you can change colours without having to open the menu every time.

The Colours window is handy to always have pulled out so you can change colour easily

08

Finish refining the colours for the foreground trees and mountains. Take a moment to pause and evaluate your colour choices so far. Try alternate layering of cool and warm colours to create a feeling of depth and atmosphere in the painting. If your colours are feeling muddy, check your colour temperatures. If your painting is feeling flat, check your values. Think about what statements you wanted to make in step 02 and see if your painting reflects that. So far, this painting captures the changing hues of the smoggy night sky, the warm glow of the street lights, and the varying colours of the shadowy foliage.

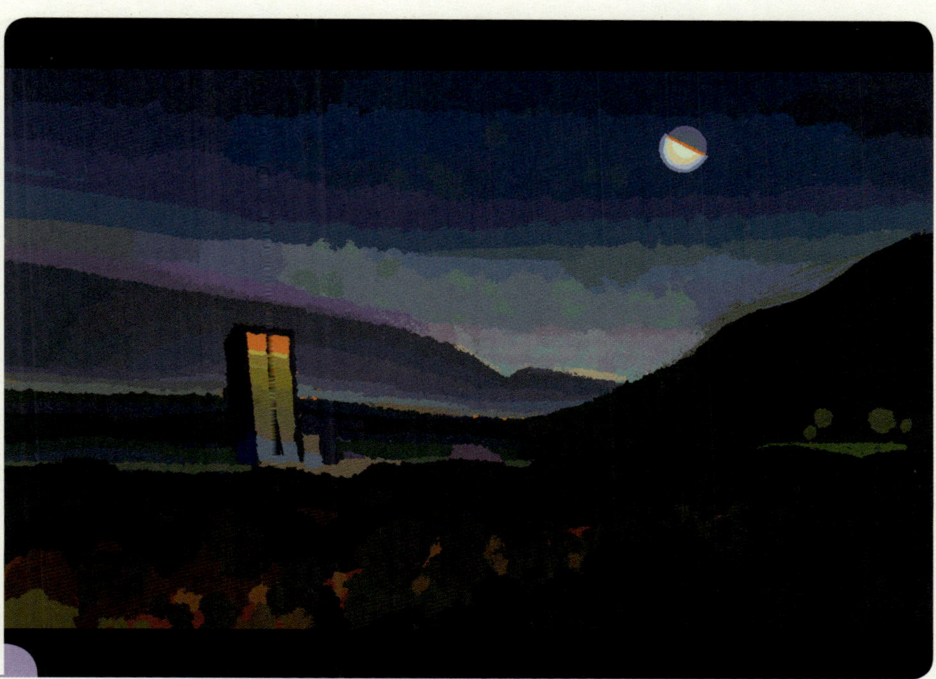

Colour is always relative, so think about the surroundings of your chosen colour

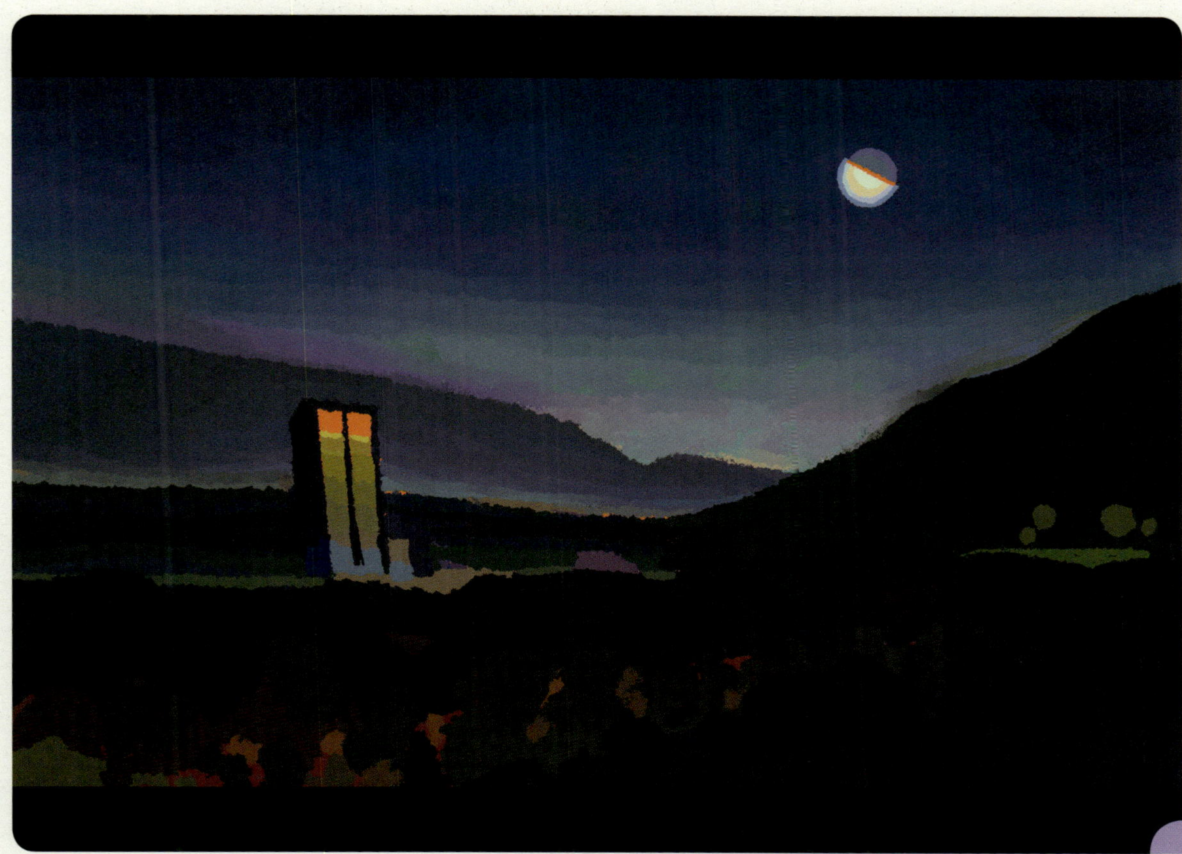

Getting the balance of blending and not blending is tricky

09

Next, you can begin to blend some of the colours in the sky and furthest mountain together using the Smudge tool. Tap the hand icon on the tool bar to select Smudge, then set it to the same **DRAWING > EVOLVE** brush that you used for painting. The goal is to have a good balance of soft (blended) edges and hard (unblended) edges to make the painting interesting. Drag your brush along the edges of colours, going back over as needed until the scene is blended well.

10

Once you have finished blending, you can start to add in the shapes of the smaller cityscape buildings. Rather than trying to replicate all the building shapes there, try instead to get the rhythm of the buildings. Your aim here should be to convey the feeling of many buildings, rather than drawing each one exactly, so try to simplify and group the shapes together. You want the main building to stand out, so try to arrange the other shapes in a way that leads the eye towards it to create a focal point. You can create the rhythm of the buildings by stacking horizontal lines and rectangles, using a darker hue to suggest the shadowed sides.

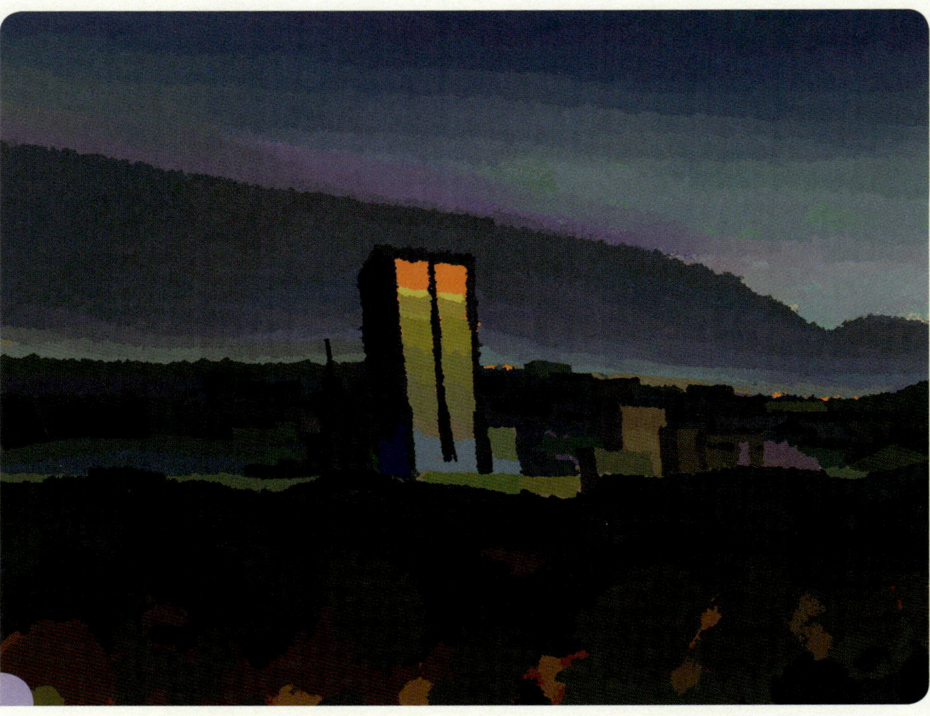

Don't try to paint every building – instead, try to capture an overall impression

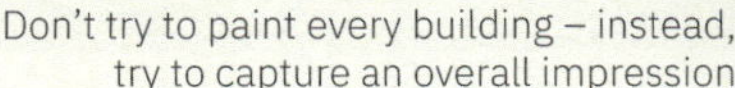

You can just dab and draw dots to indicate city lights – it doesn't need to be very complicated

11

Now that you have all the buildings blocked in, you can move on to the most fun part: lights. Start with the lights on the furthest mountain in the background. When you look at the scene in reality, you can see lights are clumping towards the main building, so you can use this to guide the viewer towards your focal point. You can also draw the eye there by reserving the temperature contrast for lights in that area. Do this by keeping most of the lights orange and reserving a few blue highlights for near the main building.

JOJO SAYS: *'Check your composition by pinching in to zoom out to make your canvas smaller. Does it still read similarly to your initial compositions from steps 02 and 03? Remember it's important for a painting to still be recognizable even as a small thumbnail. If you feel like it is not reading well, check back in with the composition you made earlier to help guide you. Breaking the process down into smaller steps makes it easier, so you do not have to juggle all the parts of a painting at once. Instead you can think about it in chunks that are easier to manage.'*

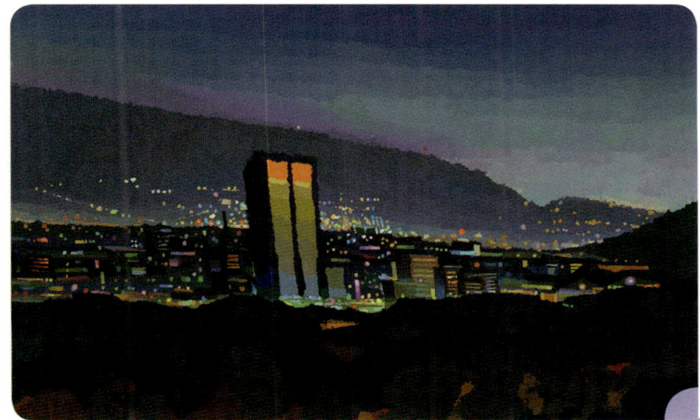

12

Once you have finished adding the lights at the back, move on to the lights in the middle. Notice that there are mostly orange, yellow, and green tones being under-lit in the front area, and lots of cooler blue lights near the main building. Try to organize the lights in a way that implies that there are buildings there. For example, you can draw several horizontal lines to imply the light coming from an office-building window. You can draw a variety of light shapes to make it more interesting.

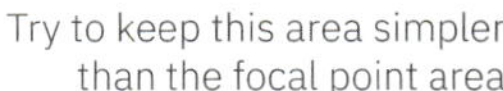

Try varying the shapes and colours of the lights within the same hue to create interest

13

Next, you are going to paint in the lights on the right side in front of the mountain. There are not as many colours on this side and it mostly looks green. You can still add a few different colours for interest, but keep most of them to a green hue. You should also keep the lights darker than they are in reality, so you do not draw attention away from the focal point of the main building. As you move from right to left, transition the green into orange to connect it back to the main lights in the centre of the scene.

Try to keep this area simpler than the focal point area

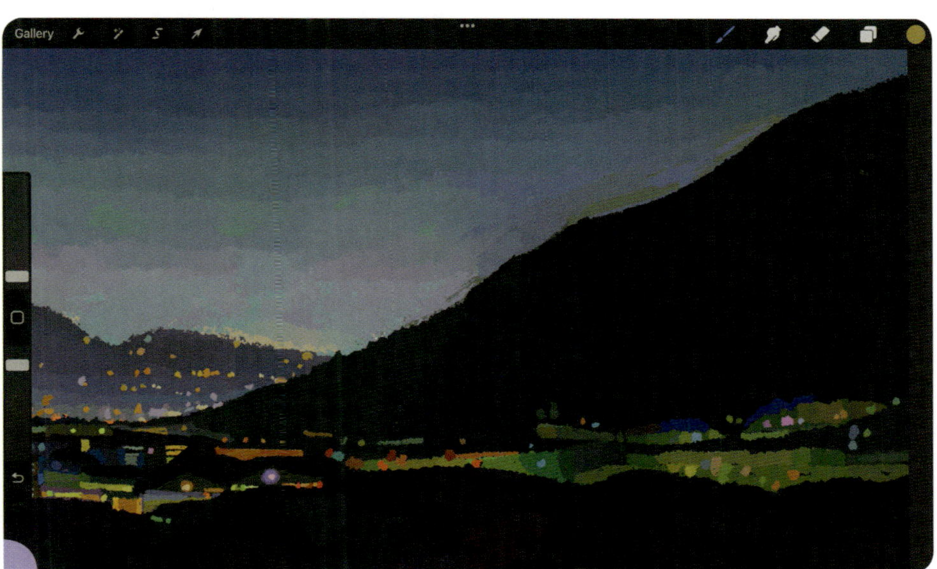

14

With most of the lights done, you can move on to detailing the main building. Draw a few dots to represent the lights on top, and then also a few bright dots to represent individual office lights turned on. You can also add some darker dots for darkened windows, to represent offices where people aren't working late. You do not have to follow the colours exactly as you see them – do what feels best for your painting. It is important not to be too beholden to what you see in real life or in your reference, but instead make a choice that fits your painting.

Even though these do not look like window lights close up, they do from further away

15

Next, you can add the under-lighting in the trees below the main building. Keep these in the yellow/orange hue range to maintain the most colour variation in the main area. Again, you should not go too bright with these or they will conflict with the main focal point. Try to group most of the lights under the main focal building while keeping other areas as dark tree silhouettes.

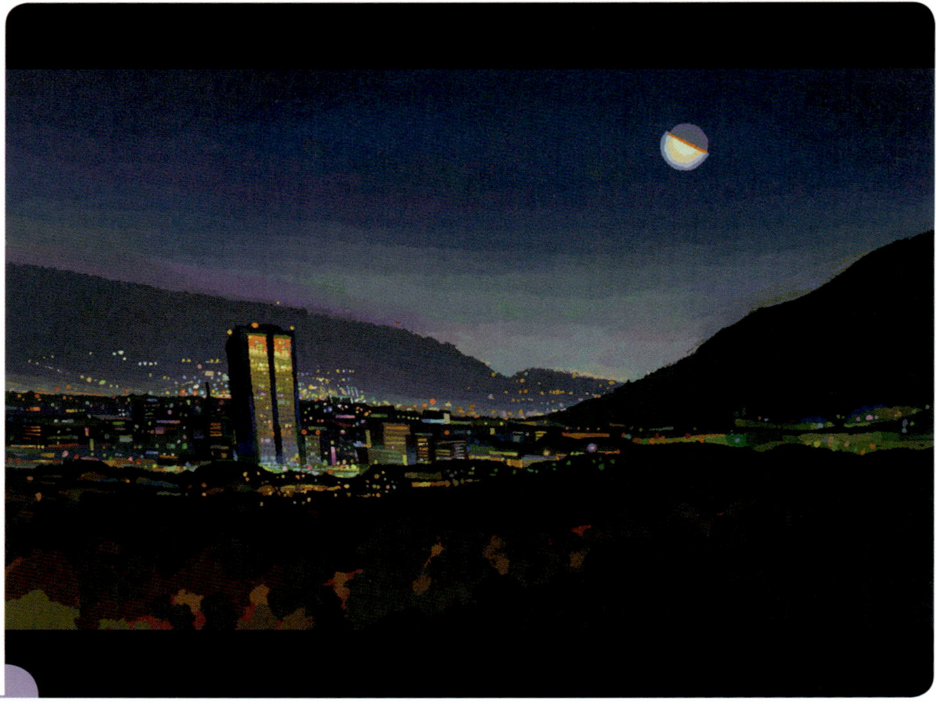

The viewer will infer that these simple dots and lines are the lights of some buildings

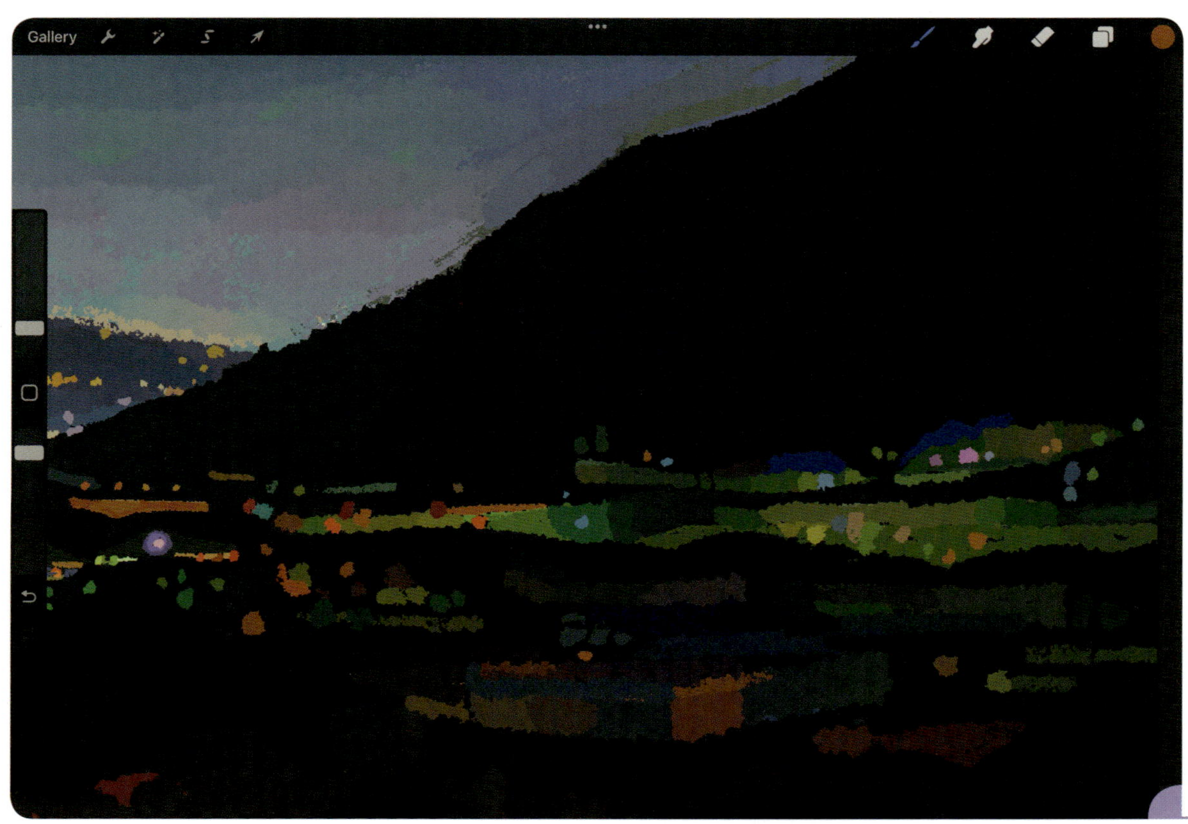

The key is to imply that something is there – the viewer will fill in the rest

16

To balance out the main area, you can loosely indicate the foreground buildings on the right. These should be darker so they do not compete with the focal point.

As with the previous steps, you don't need to make them very detailed – just a few lines to imply that there are buildings in the front. If you are having trouble simplifying

shapes, try squinting to blur the details and then paint the big shapes you can still see. Remember that the bigger composition is more important than the smaller details.

17

You are now almost done detailing the painting. The last part you have to refine are the trees in the front. Once again, we want to make the under-lit areas follow up towards the focal building. This is a good time to take a break and step away from the painting to rest. It's important to take mental and physical breaks from painting so you can refresh your mind and body. You will also be able to see the image with fresh eyes – there might be things you missed that you didn't notice while painting.

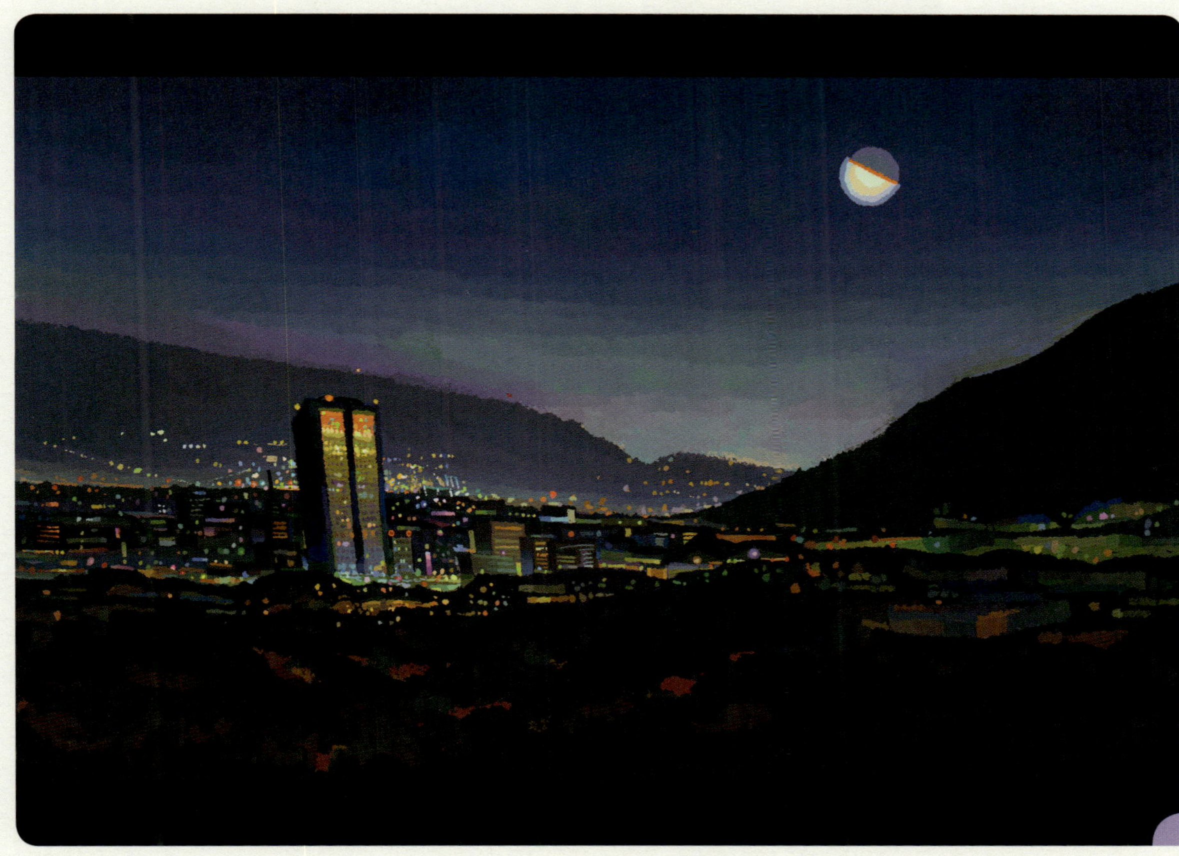

Try to place the under-lights in a way that leads up to the focal point

18

Do you notice anything you want to fix in your painting after taking a break? One thing that could be improved is the blending of the orange under-lighting. As you did in step 09, use the Smudge tool set to **DRAWING > EVOLVE** for this. Keep the parts where the underlighting touches the trees unblended, and blend the light going upwards into shadow. This gives the trees a more believable gradient, as the light sources would be brighter nearer to the ground. Be careful again to not over-blend and let the edges of the tree silhouettes still have form.

Blend the under-lights upwards and then side to side

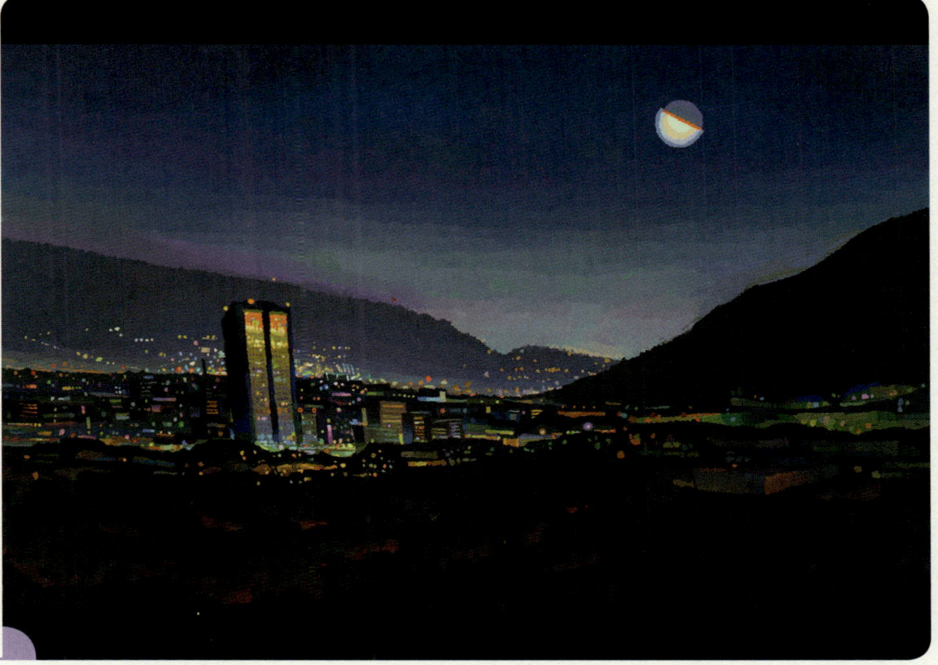

19

To make the palette pop, you can edge some colours with their complementary or 'opposite' colour. The main complementary pairs are red/green, yellow/purple, and blue/orange. You can look at Procreate's colour wheel and find the colour diagonally opposite your chosen one. Try lining part of the back mountain with a pale orange to help the blue stand out. Do this throughout the painting in areas that you want to pop a little more, but don't overdo it.

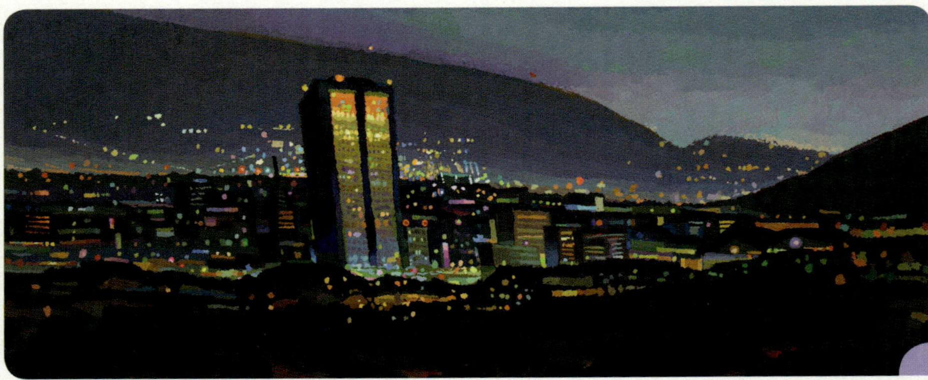

Adding touches of complementary colour is a very subtle detail, but it makes the colours look richer

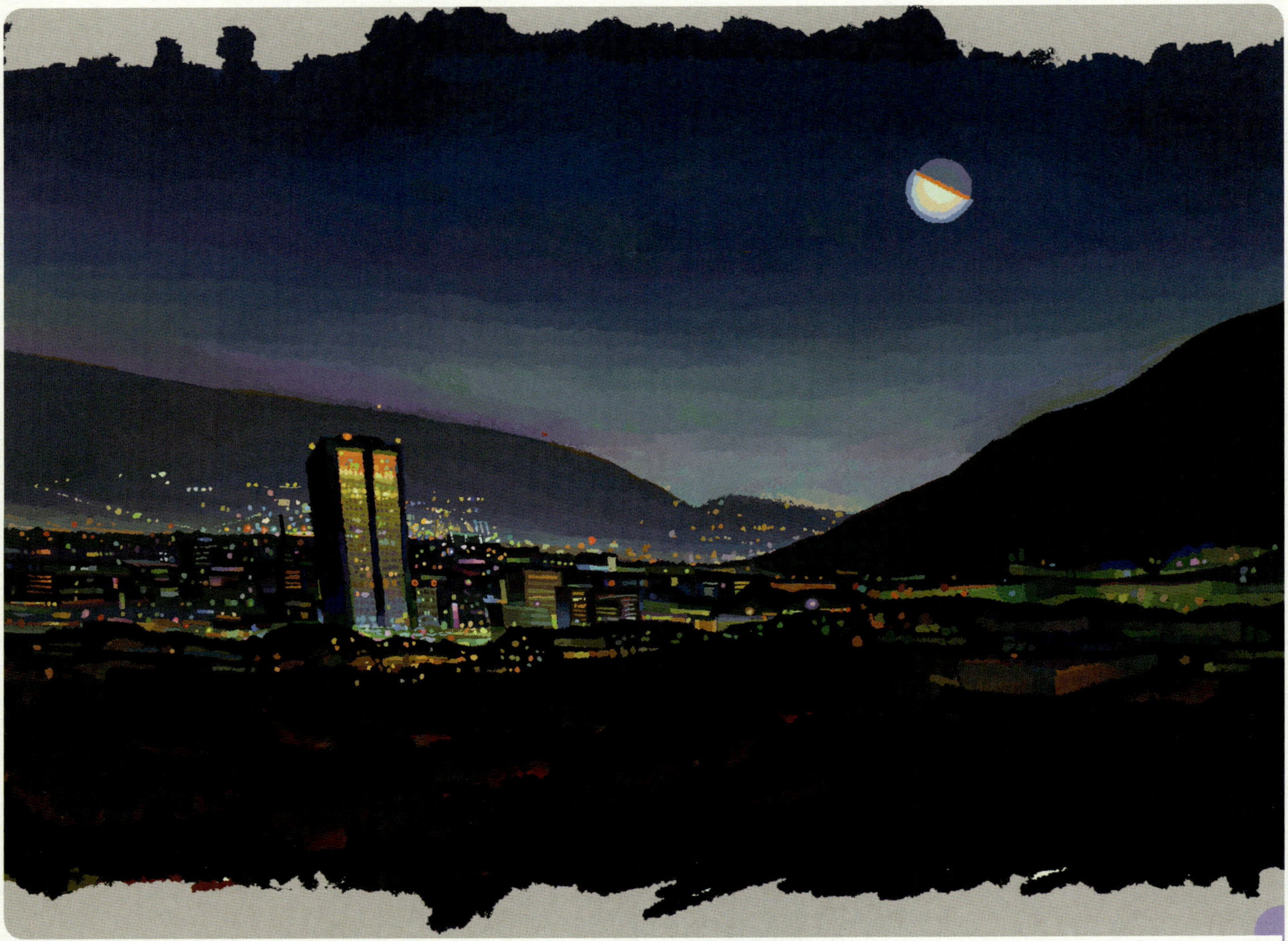

Painting all on one layer will help teach you planning and discipline; here is the painting with the black letterboxing removed

20

You may have noticed that you have been working on this painting from back to front. Even though digital paintings allow you to work with multiple layers, it is a good exercise to paint everything on one layer, so the process is similar to a traditional painting. Since you have been painting mostly on one layer, building up the painting from back to front allows you to layer up the details without having to repaint parts. It forces you think about the painting more thoroughly, since you have to plan out what you are going to do in advance. Take stock of your layers so far and see if any can be merged or deleted.

21

To add some glow, you can use a Soft Light layer. Make a new layer and change it to Soft Light mode by tapping the N in the Layers menu. Scroll down until you reach Soft Light and select it. Using **AIRBRUSHING > SOFT BRUSH**, gently add some light-orange glow to the moon. Brush a bit of light orange at the top of the main building and a tiny bit of light blue at the bottom.

> **JOJO SAYS:** *'We can create interest with colours by using contrast. Colours are seen relatively, so choosing a suitable colour depends on what colour you can put next to it to make it pop. For example, the same shade of yellow will look brighter next to a dull blue than a bright blue. Try contrasting saturation by putting a bright colour next to a dull colour, contrasting hue by putting a colour next to its complementary "opposite" colour, or contrasting value by putting a light colour next to a dark colour.'*

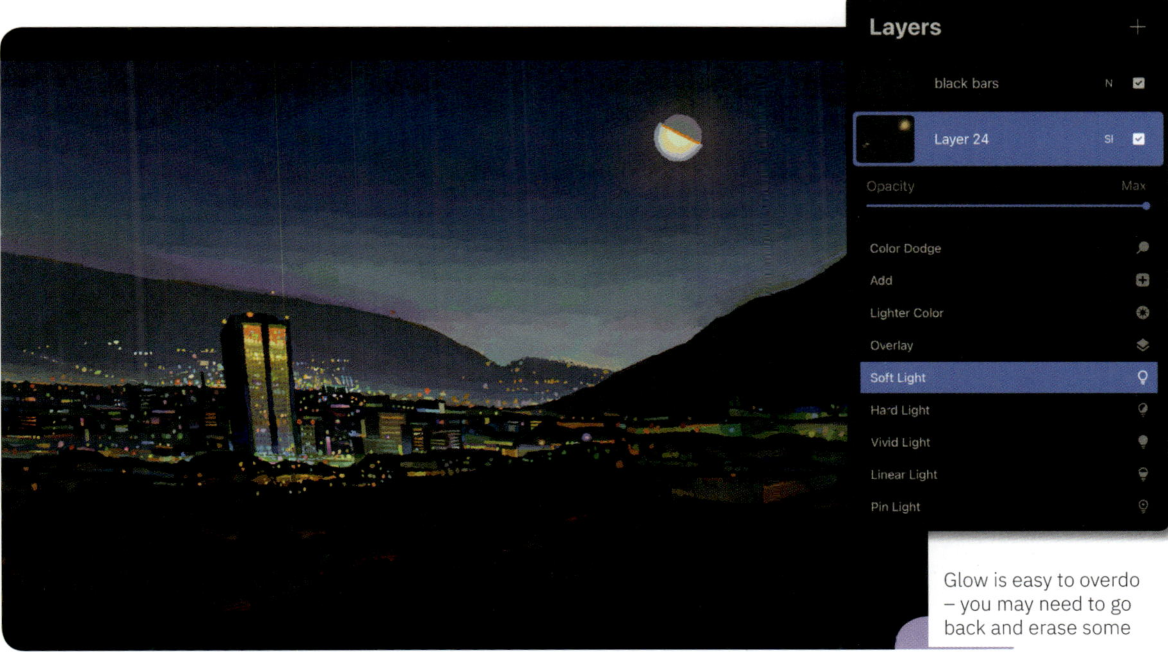

Glow is easy to overdo – you may need to go back and erase some

22

You are now ready to add some final adjustments to the entire painting. To do this, you first need to make a layer of all the layers merged. Go to **ACTIONS > ADD > COPY CANVAS** and **ACTIONS > ADD > PASTE**. This will insert a new layer of all the others merged into one. It is a duplicate, so don't worry about losing your existing layers. This new layer is useful for applying adjustments to your entire scene once you are happy that the painting process is complete. You can also find these options in the **COPY & PASTE** menu, which can be accessed by swiping down with three fingers.

Copy and paste a duplicate of the whole canvas for easy editing

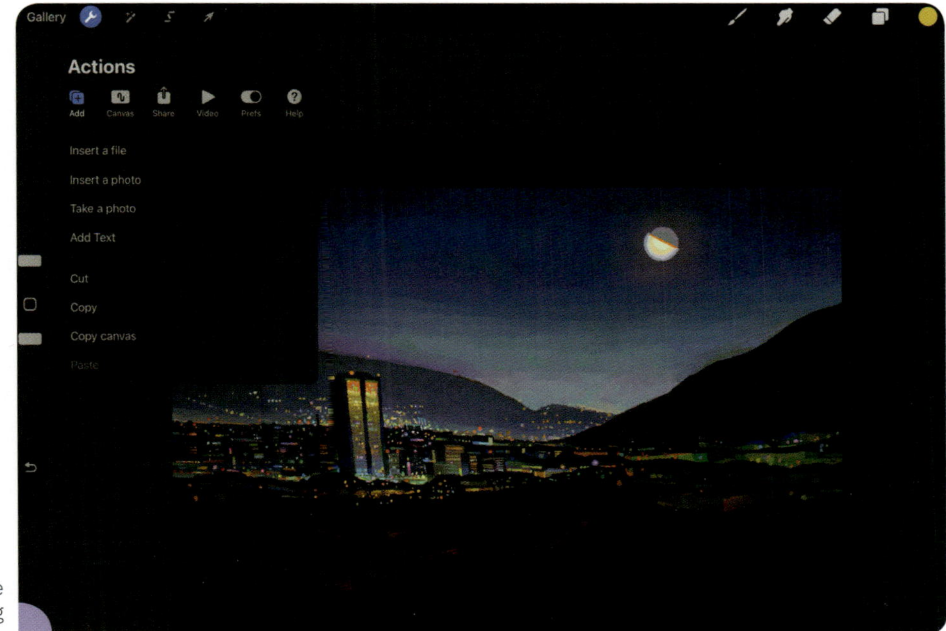

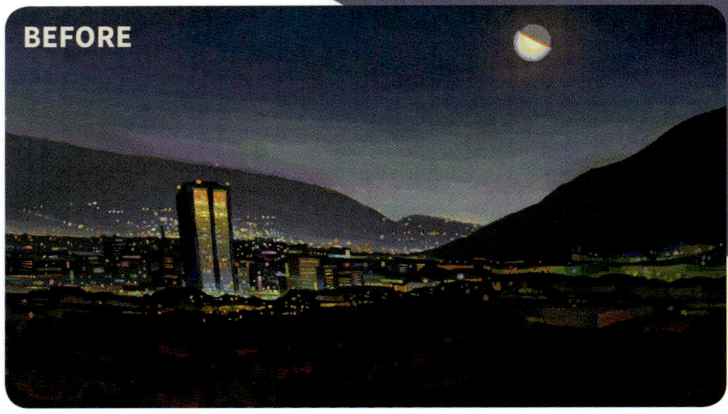

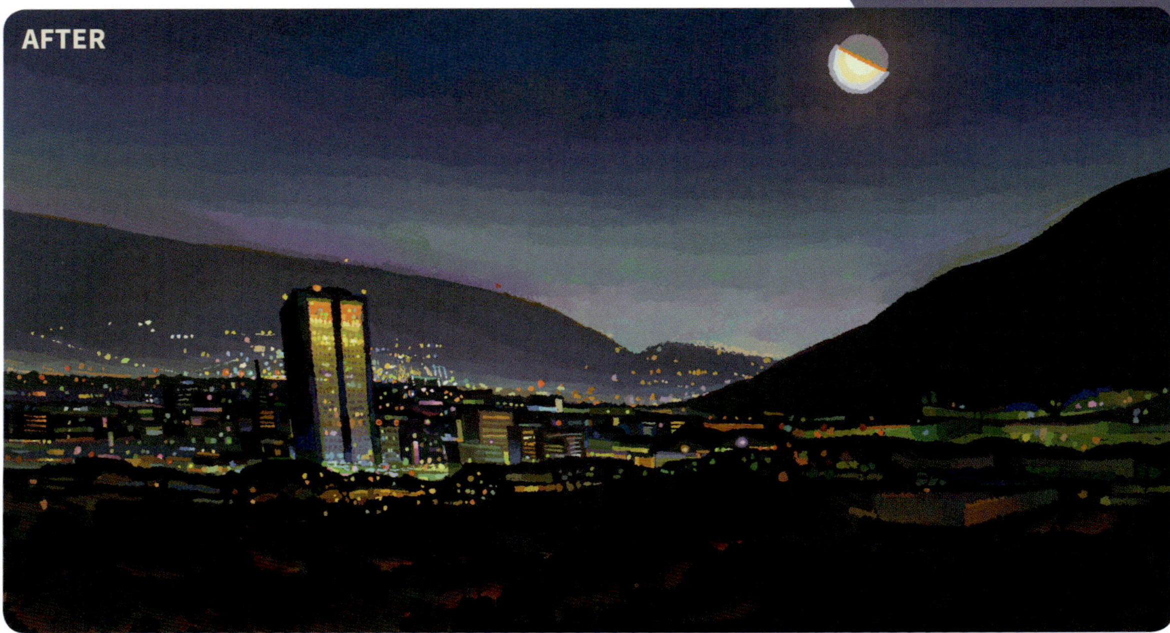

23

To adjust the values a little bit, you can make a Curves adjustment. To do this, go to **ADJUSTMENTS > CURVES**. The leftmost side adjusts the darker values and the rightmost side adjusts the lighter values. You can make the highlights a little brighter and the shadows a little darker by dragging the curve into the position shown on the right, or just try playing around with the tool until you find something you like.

Play around with the Curves tool to get a better understanding of what it does

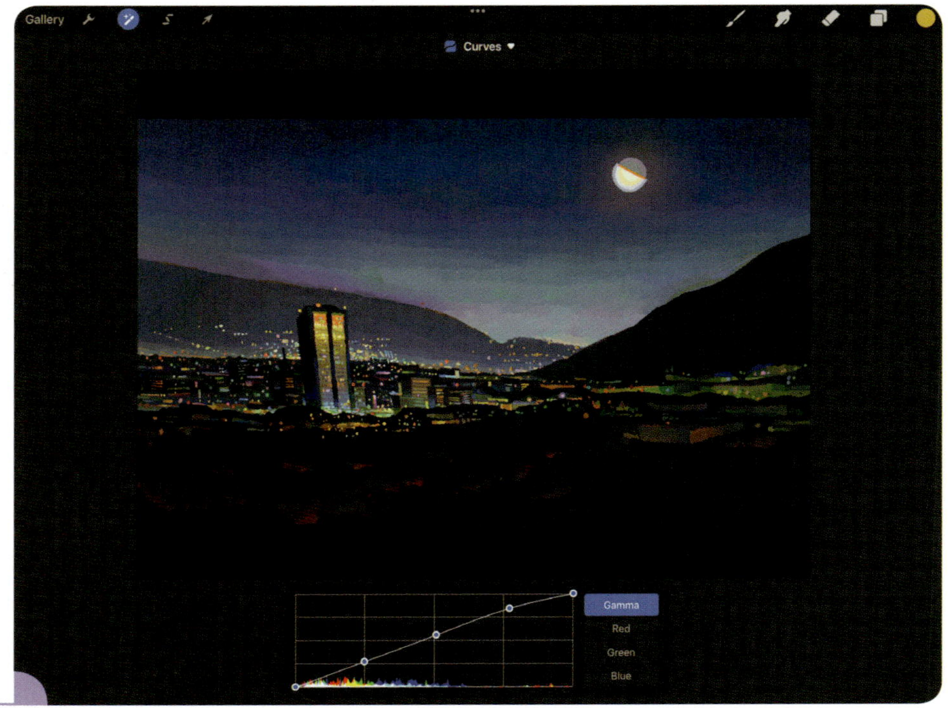

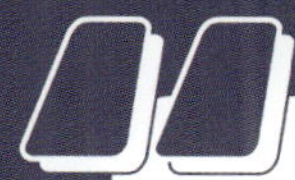

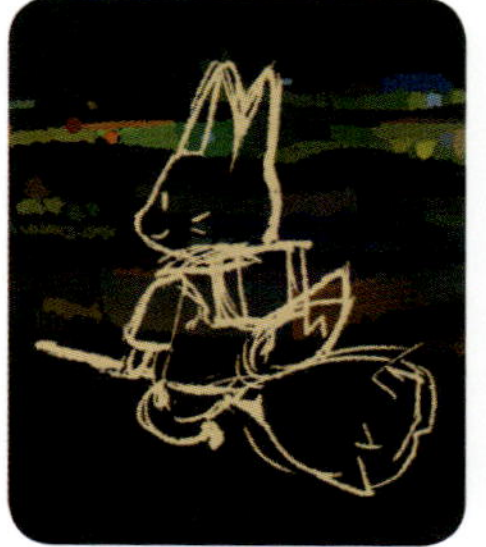
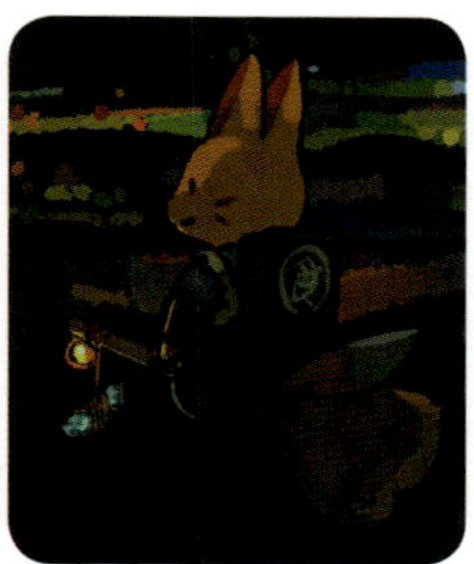

BEFORE

AFTER

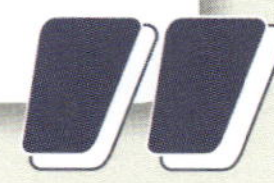

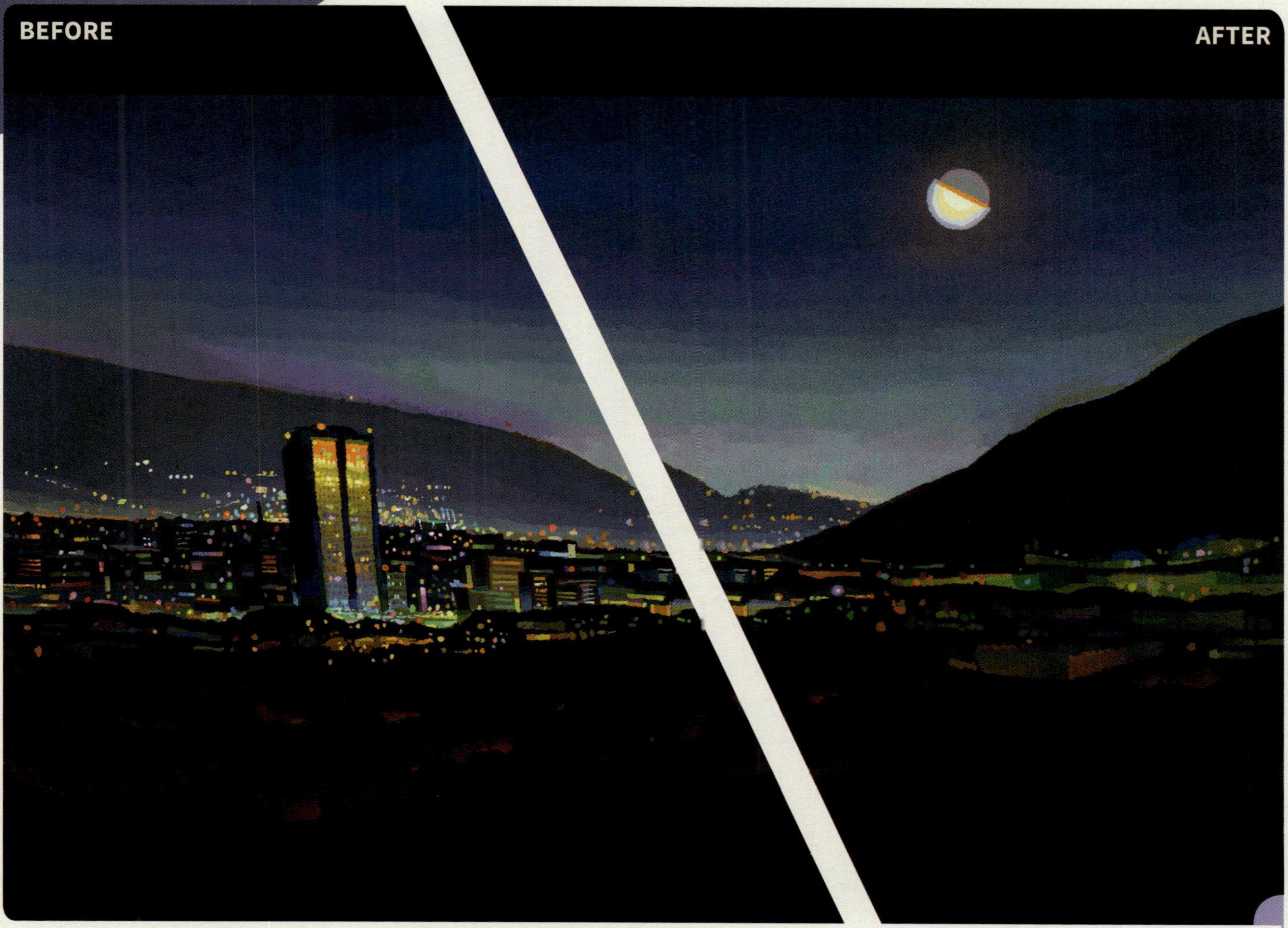

Add a few subtle effects to enhance the final painting's presentation

24

To add a few more final touches, go to **ADJUSTMENTS > NOISE** to add a grain effect to the image. Duplicate the layer, return to Adjustments to add a bit of Gaussian Blur and Chromatic Aberration, and lower the opacity of that layer to soften the results. This makes the effects feel more subtle and a little less digital.

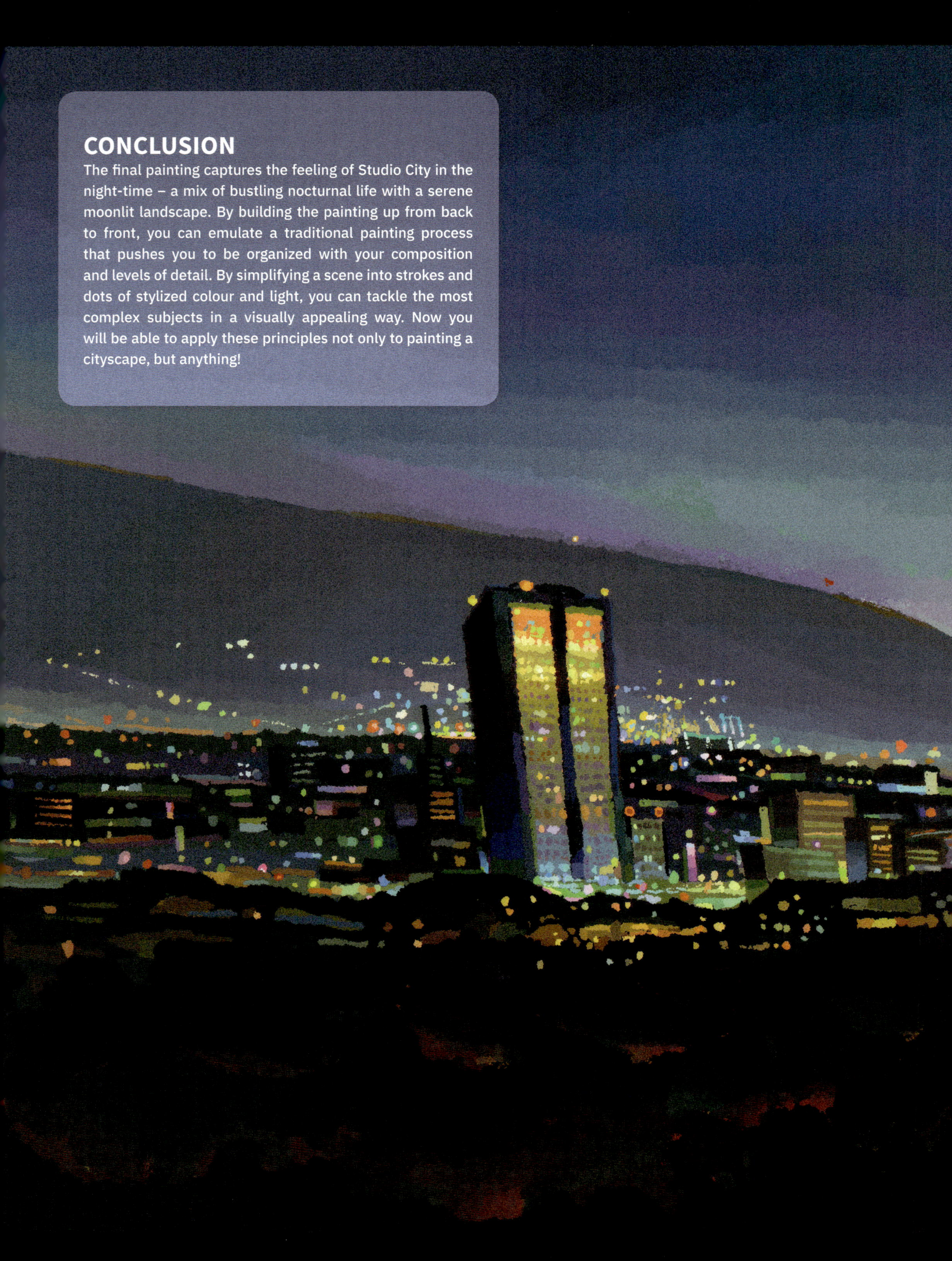

CONCLUSION

The final painting captures the feeling of Studio City in the night-time – a mix of bustling nocturnal life with a serene moonlit landscape. By building the painting up from back to front, you can emulate a traditional painting process that pushes you to be organized with your composition and levels of detail. By simplifying a scene into strokes and dots of stylized colour and light, you can tackle the most complex subjects in a visually appealing way. Now you will be able to apply these principles not only to painting a cityscape, but anything!

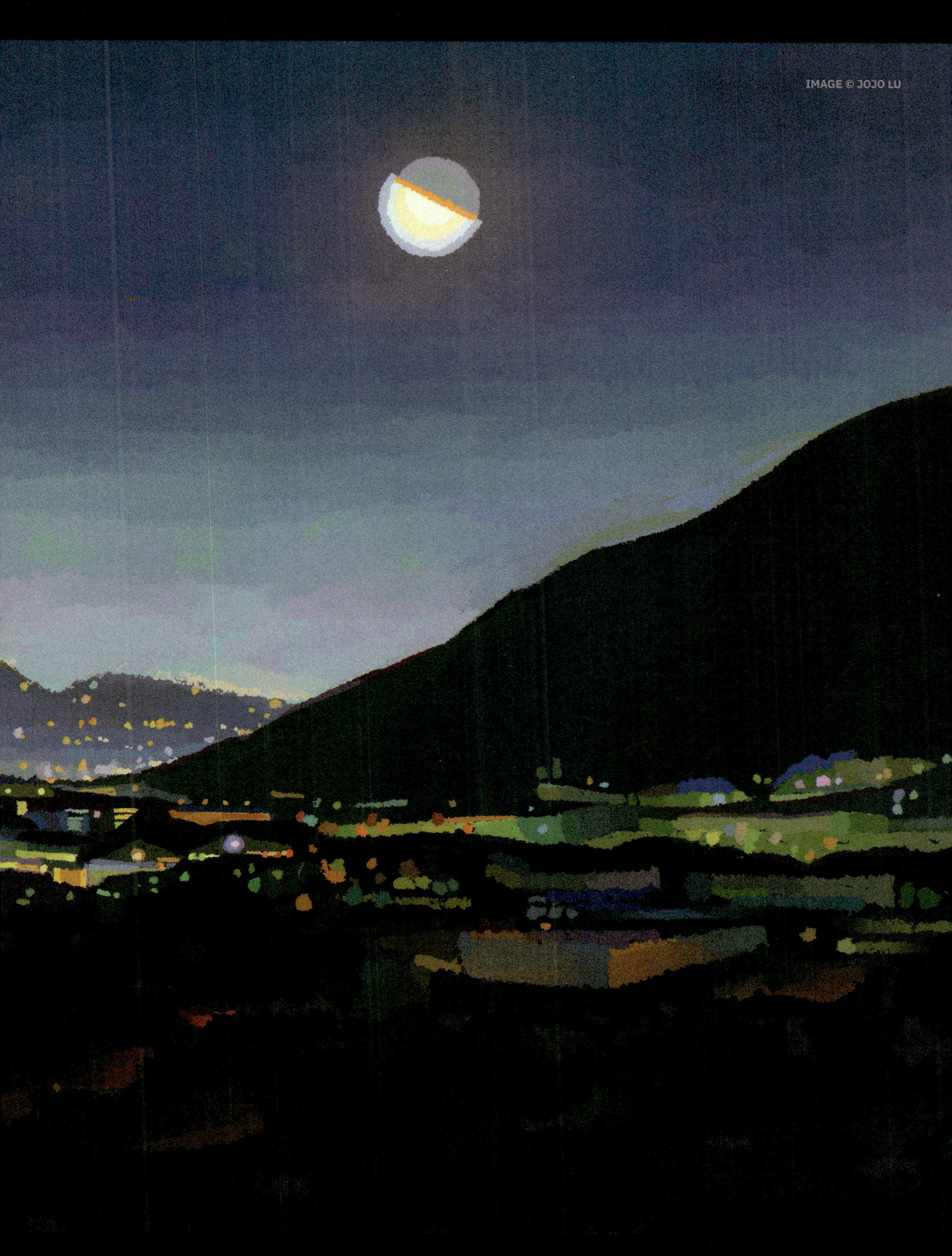
IMAGE © JOJO LU

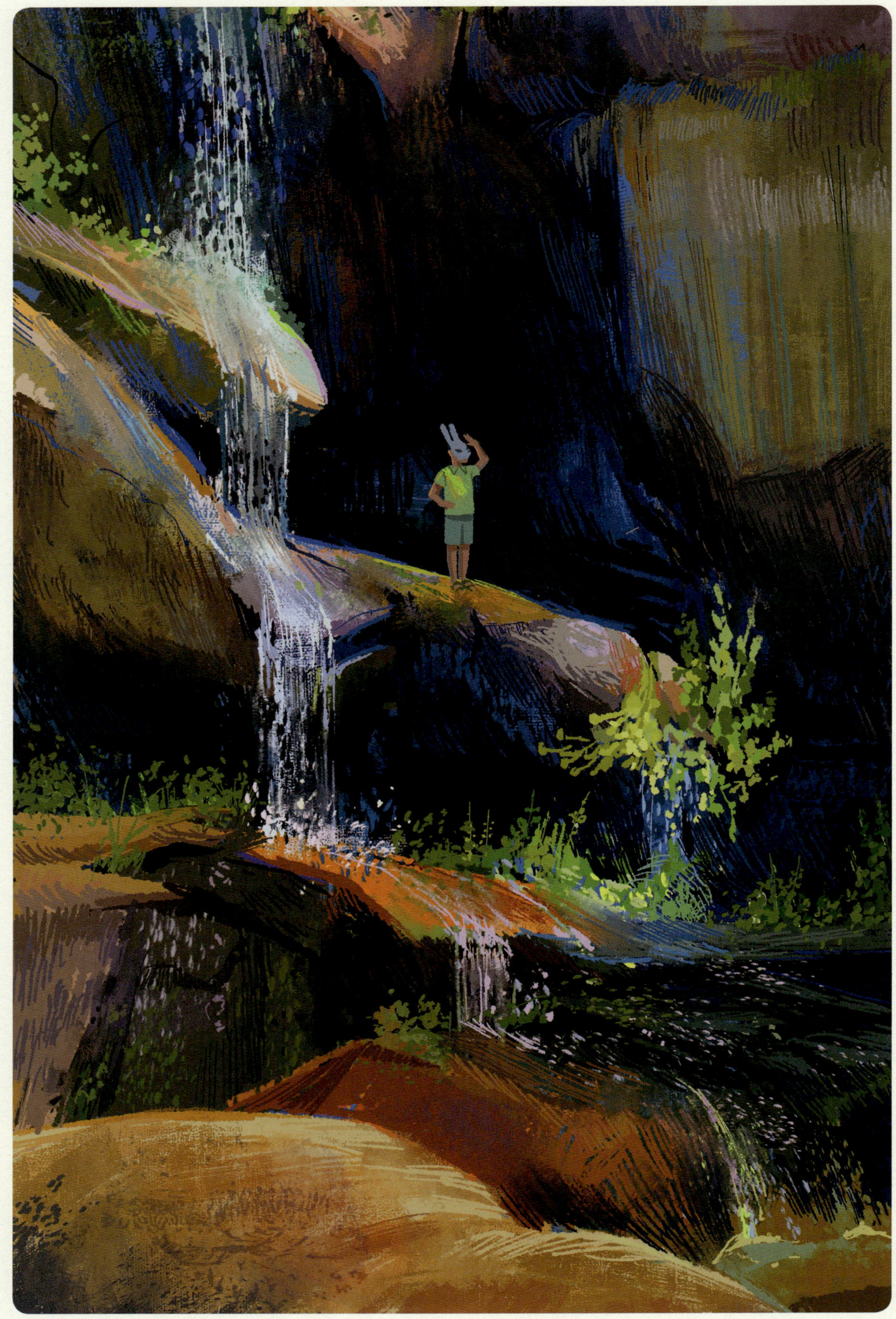

NOBE YOUNG FALLS: I went under the waterfall at Nobe Yong Falls – it was very cold!

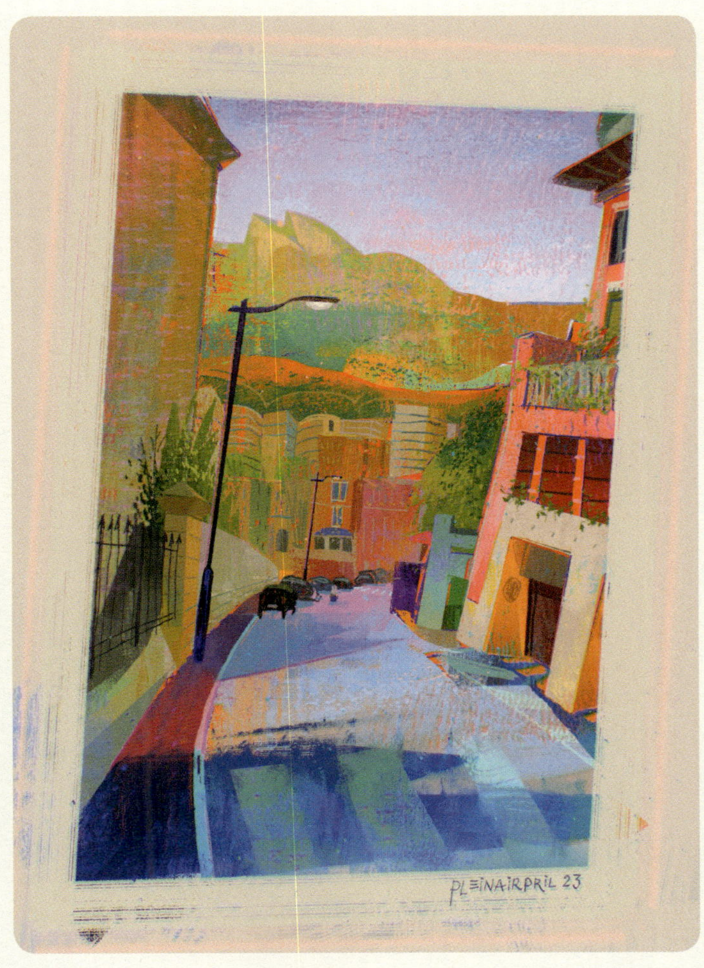

MONACO: A study from reference; I would like to go to Monaco one day

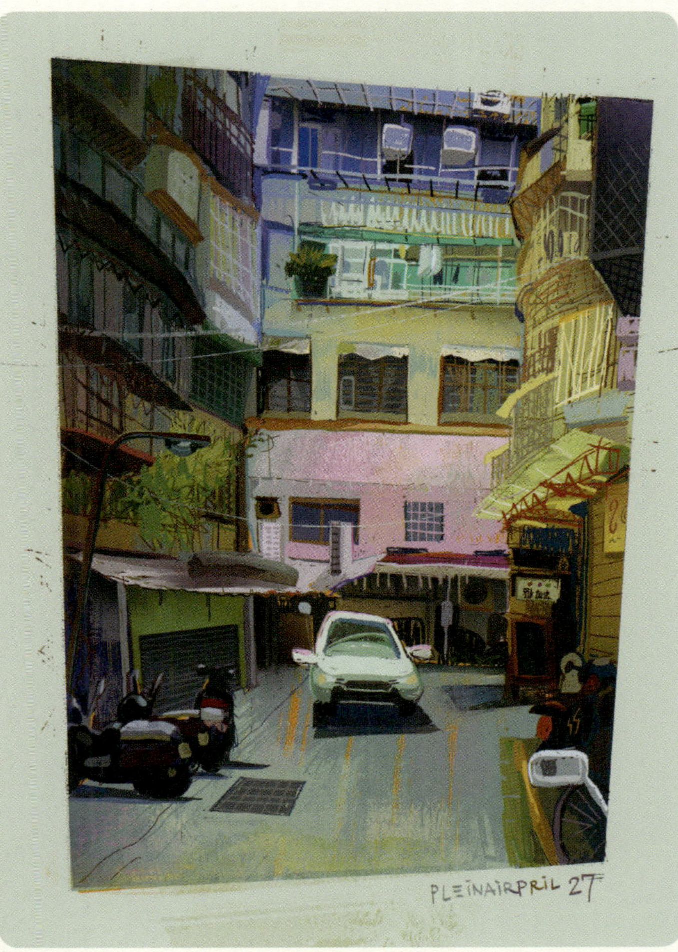

TAIWAN: Taiwan is another of my dream destinations

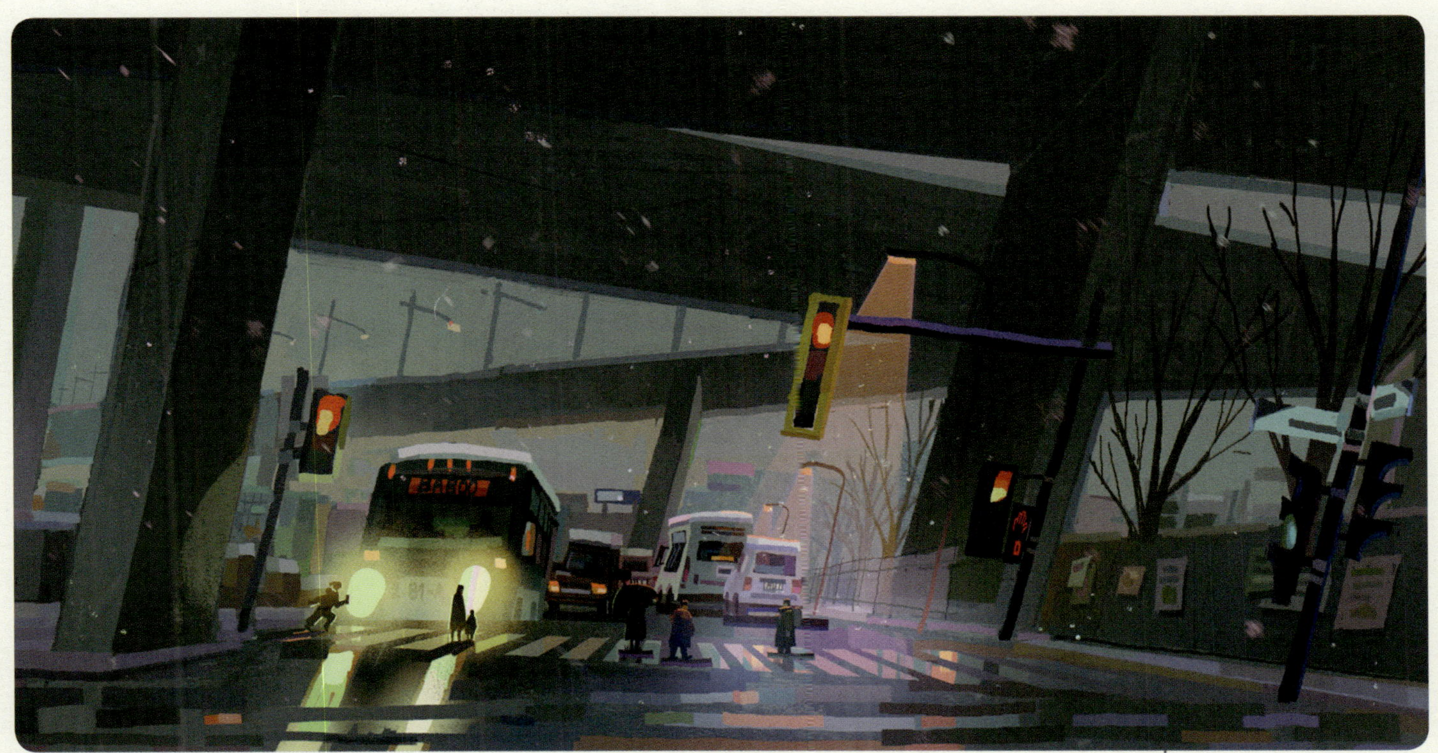

MONTREAL: I painted this scene after visiting Montreal; I wanted to capture the feeling of the end of winter in a city

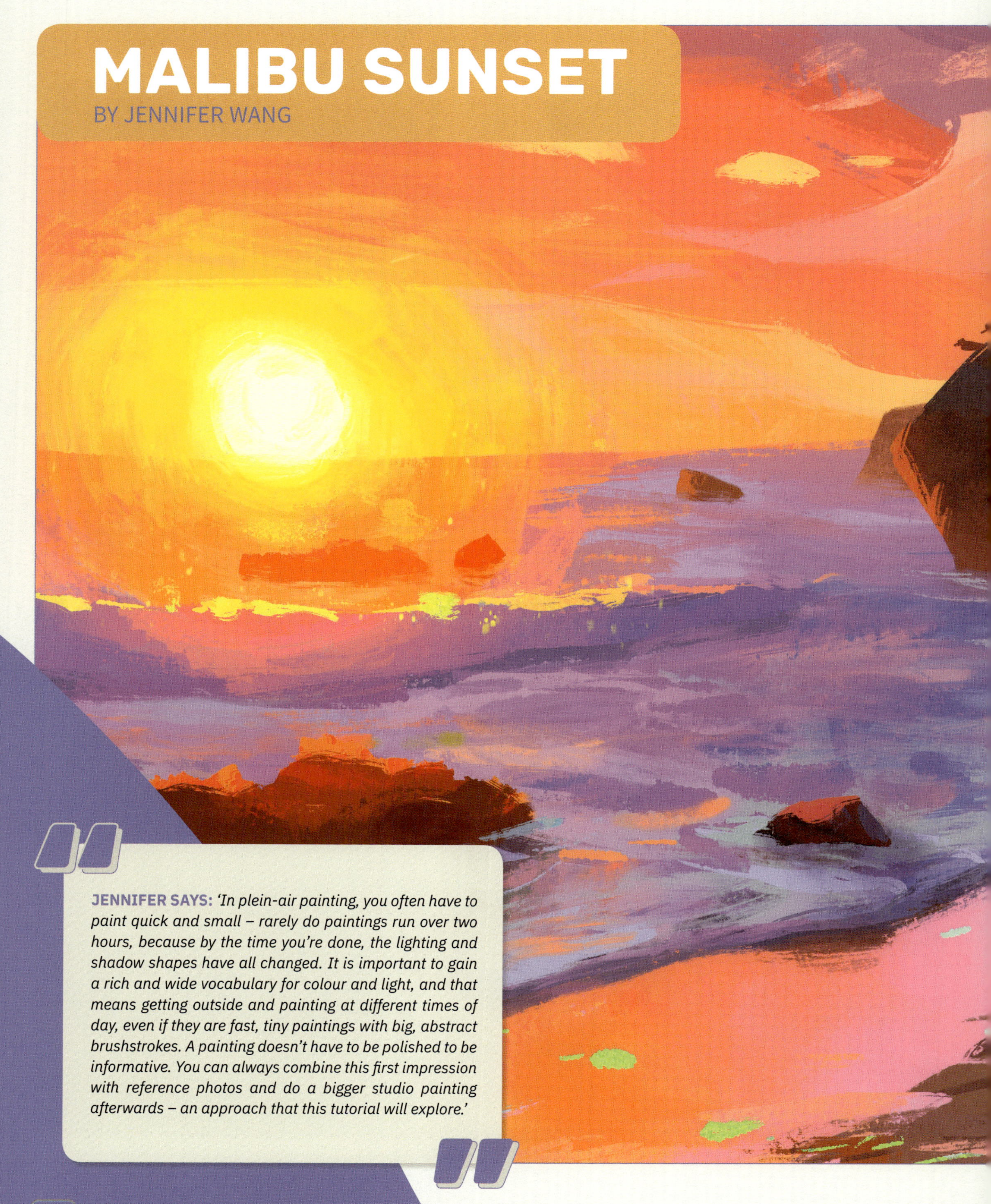

JENNIFER SAYS: '*In plein-air painting, you often have to paint quick and small – rarely do paintings run over two hours, because by the time you're done, the lighting and shadow shapes have all changed. It is important to gain a rich and wide vocabulary for colour and light, and that means getting outside and painting at different times of day, even if they are fast, tiny paintings with big, abstract brushstrokes. A painting doesn't have to be polished to be informative. You can always combine this first impression with reference photos and do a bigger studio painting afterwards – an approach that this tutorial will explore.*'

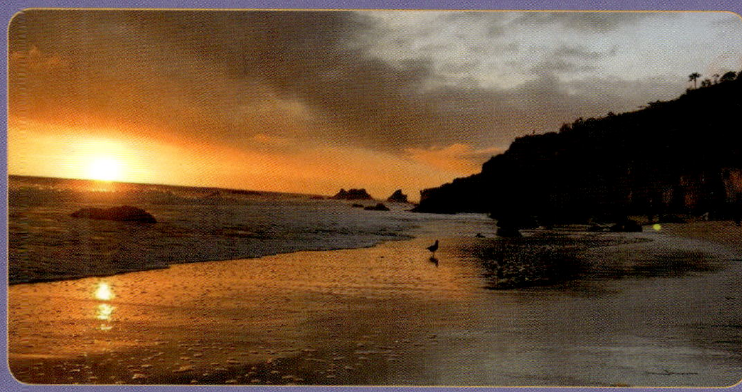

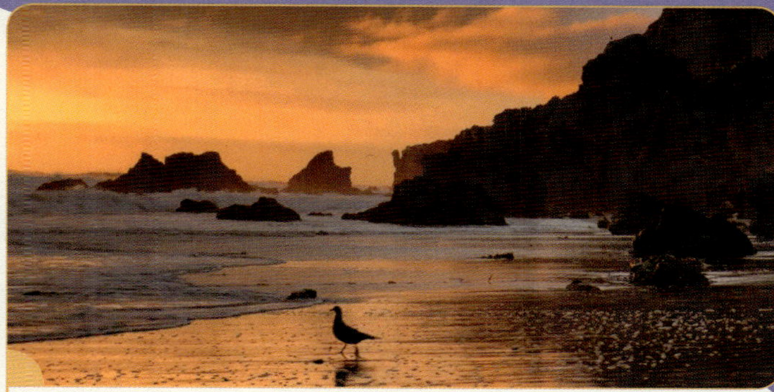

Capture the view with an initial sketch (below), quick and observational, on a standalone layer

LEARN HOW TO...

- **Digitally paint a Malibu beach scene based on a plein-air study**

- **Design shape, value, and colour to convey the story and mood of an environment**

- **Create dynamic colour using multiple tools, modes, and options in Procreate**

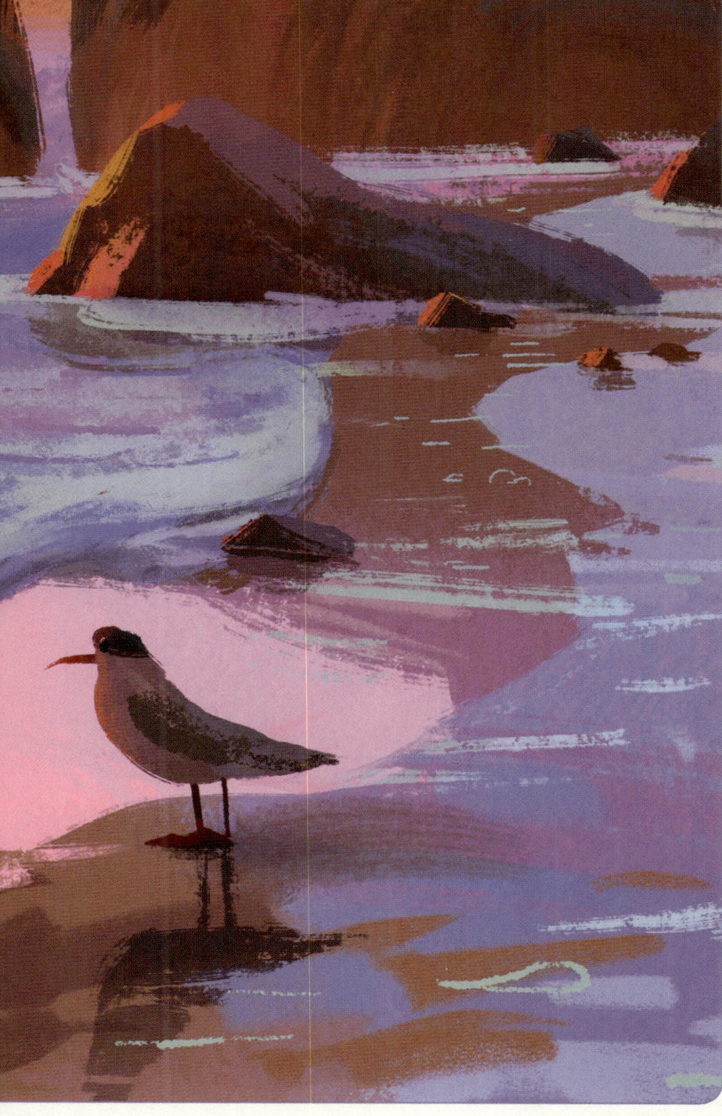

01

Begin by taking your plein-air setup – your iPad – to your location. In this case, the scene is a beach in Malibu, California. Quickly lay in a background colour with a large brush. For a sunset environment like this, a good base colour is warm and midtone, like a slightly desaturated pink or orange that will give the colours a warmer overall tone to relate to as you paint layers on top. Add a new layer on top and begin your sketch with the **SKETCHING > 6B PENCIL** brush in a dark brown. The sketch doesn't have to be perfect – it just needs to lay a foundation for your shapes and colours. Place in the cliffs, the rocks, and the shoreline – the main big shapes of the scene.

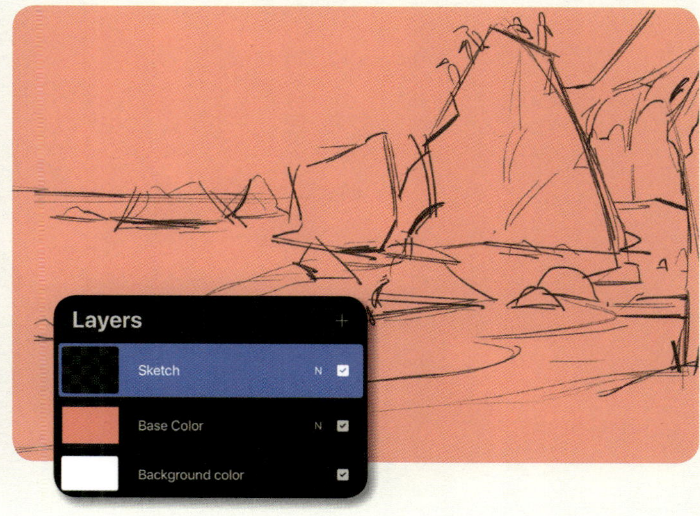

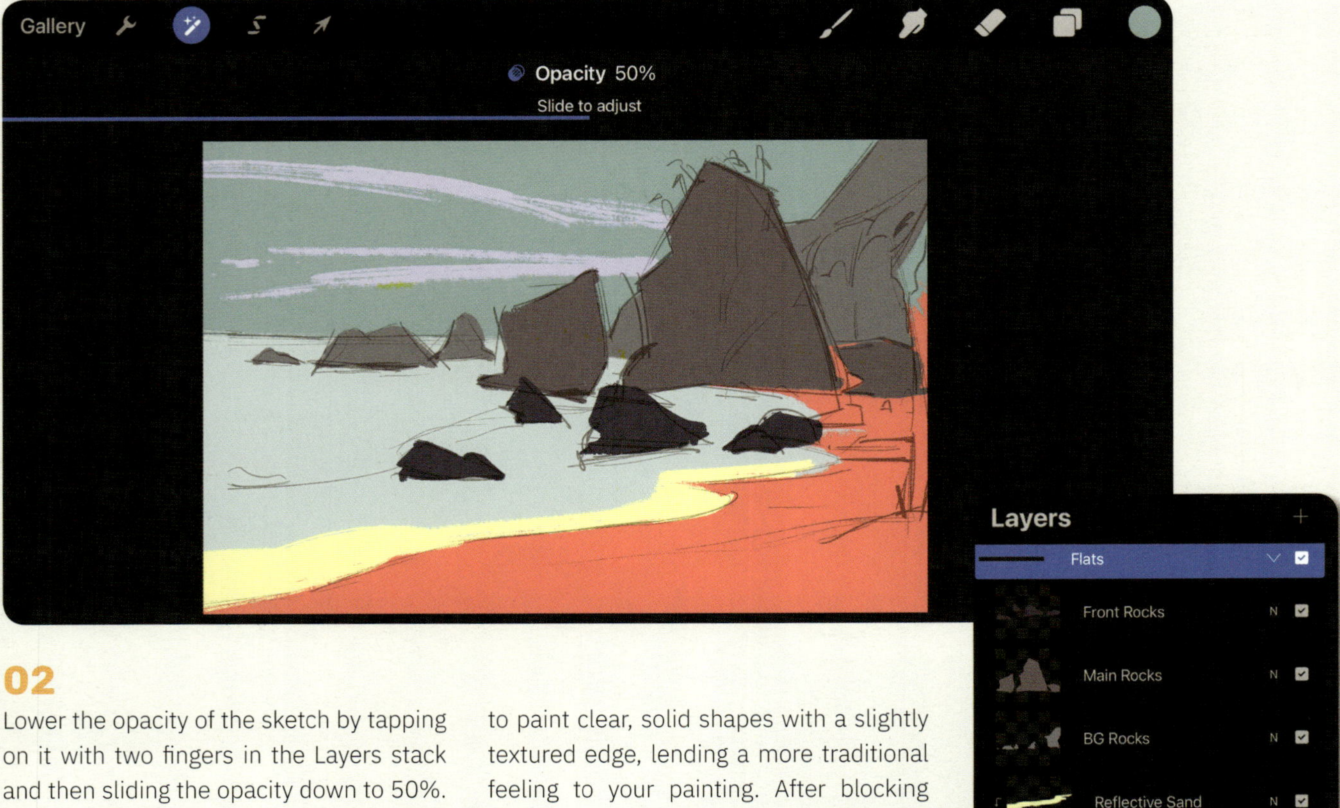

02

Lower the opacity of the sketch by tapping on it with two fingers in the Layers stack and then sliding the opacity down to 50%. Below the sketch layer, place each shape into your study on a different layer, going from the back-most element to the front-most element. In this case, the layers are 'Base Colour', 'Sky', 'Clouds', 'Ocean', 'Reflective Sand' (for the bright sand near the water), and three layers of rocks. Using the **DRAWING > BLACKBURN** brush enables you to paint clear, solid shapes with a slightly textured edge, lending a more traditional feeling to your painting. After blocking out an element, use two fingers to swipe right on the layer in the Layers stack. This enables Alpha Lock, which means that you can't paint outside of the object you have already painted on that layer.

Painting the shapes on different layers allows more flexibility later on

03

Procreate has several colour-selection options. The Classic view allows you to rapidly transition between different hues, saturations, and values depending on which corners and sides of the rectangular panel you move your picker to. You can also use the hue slider beneath it to hop over to other colours on the spectrum. Choosing colours that gravitate closer to the greyscale side of the panel, rather than the fully saturated side, will generally allow your colours to harmonize more with each other. Keep this in mind as you block out each object and fill the scene.

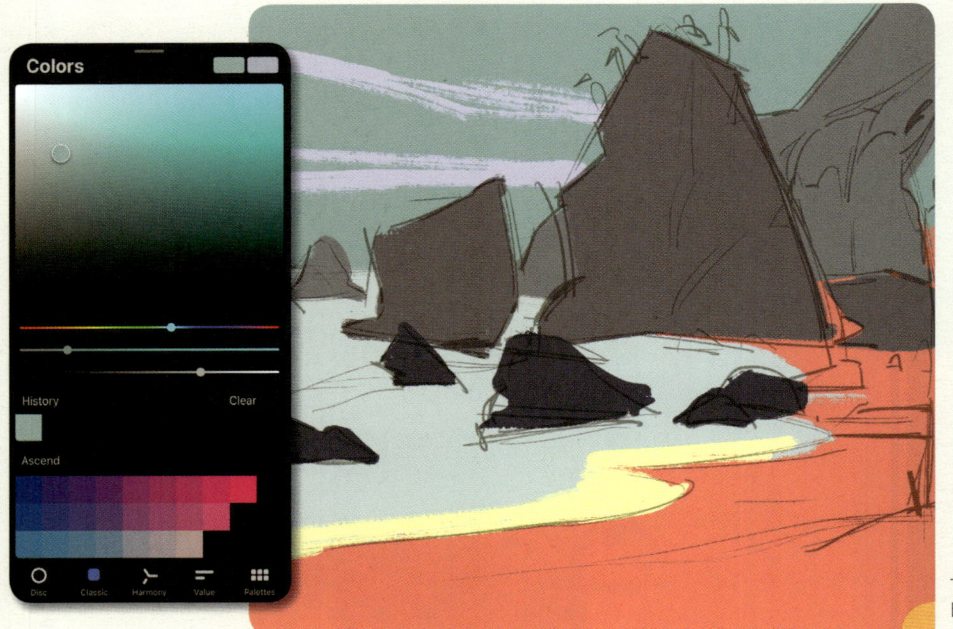

The canvas and Colours panel are side by side to allow for a quicker workflow

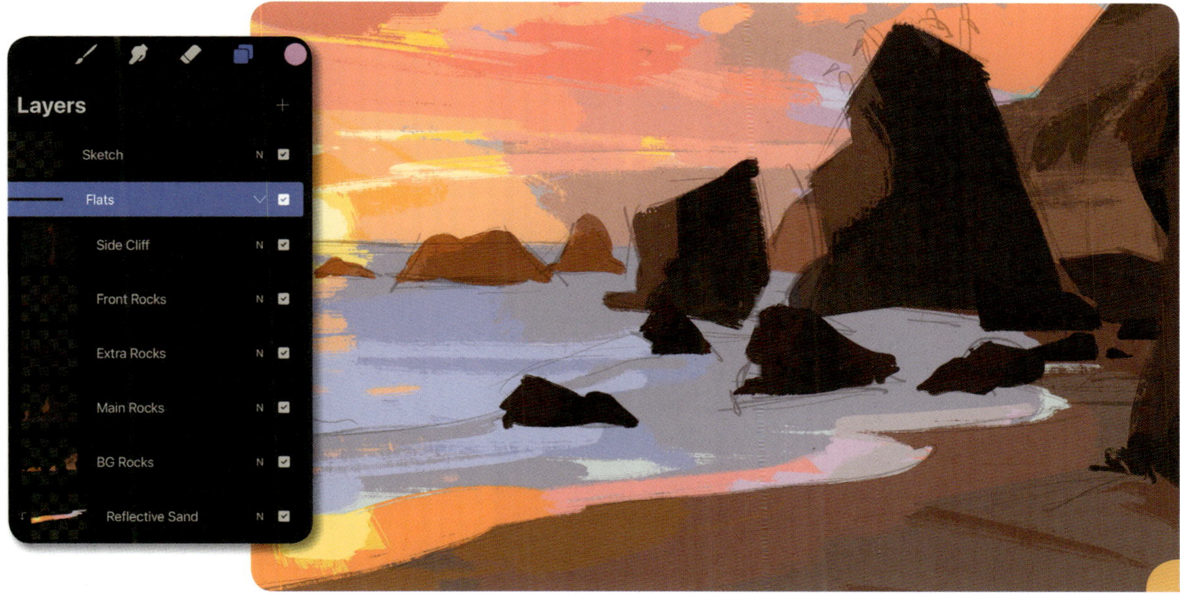

The shapes remain unchanged, but the colours are now vibrant and impressionistic

04

Now that you have Alpha Locked each layer, you can paint into each one with the colours that you see on the beach in front of you. Speed is of the essence, as the setting sun accelerates the changing of colours around you. Start painting in the elements that are likely to change their colours most drastically first – the ocean, the sky, and of course the sun itself. Once those main colours have been blocked in, you can paint in the surrounding land as well – the sand, rocks, and cliffs.

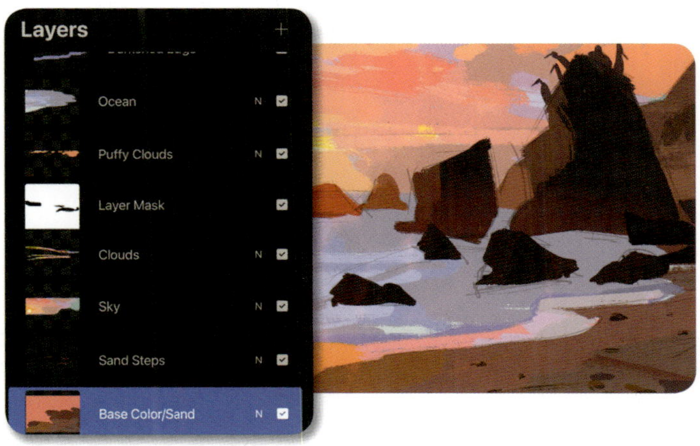

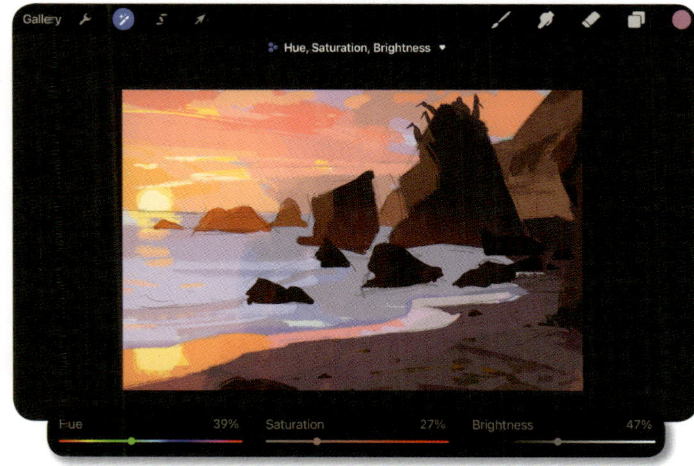

05

The sand darkens and becomes cooler – more purple-toned than red – the further away from the sun it gets. There is a way to darken it without changing all the brushstrokes you have added. Duplicate the 'Base Colour/Sand' layer and go to **ADJUSTMENTS > HUE, SATURATION, BRIGHTNESS**. Change the hue towards purple, and desaturate and darken with the other sliders. Add a mask to the layer and paint black into it to brush some of the darker sand out. Using a mask allows you to preserve the layer beneath.

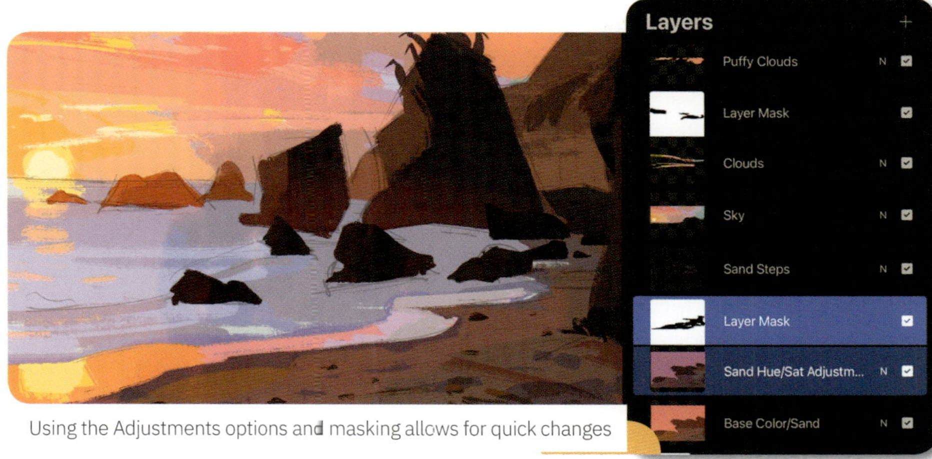

Using the Adjustments options and masking allows for quick changes

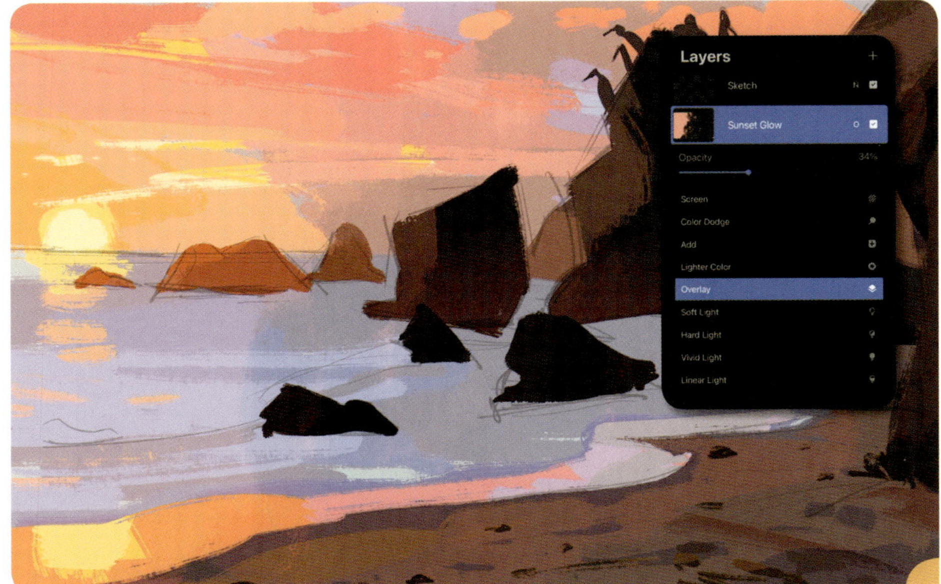

06

Lastly, to convey the glow of the sun, brush a peach tone onto a new layer. Open the Layers panel, tap on the letter next to that layer, and select Overlay mode from the list. It will create a really strong glow, so you will need to reduce its opacity for a subtler feel. When plein-air painting, you can observe more colour complexity, warmth, depth, movement, and wildlife. It is most important in plein air to capture the fresh impression of the sunset you have just witnessed – the way it radiated and transformed its surroundings.

The final plein-air study is complete; by now, the sun has set!

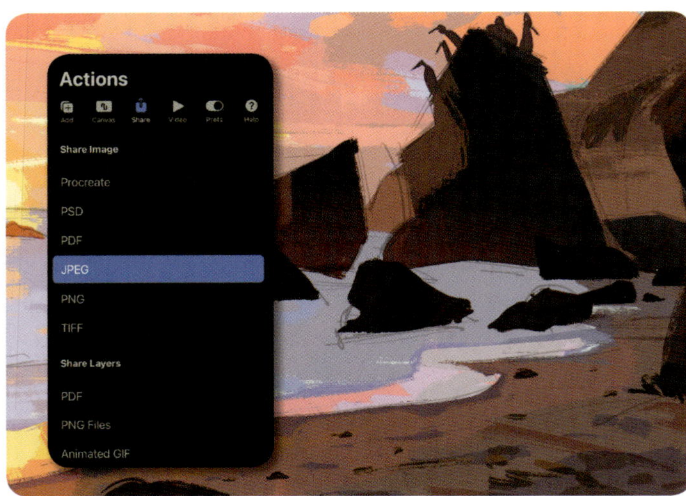

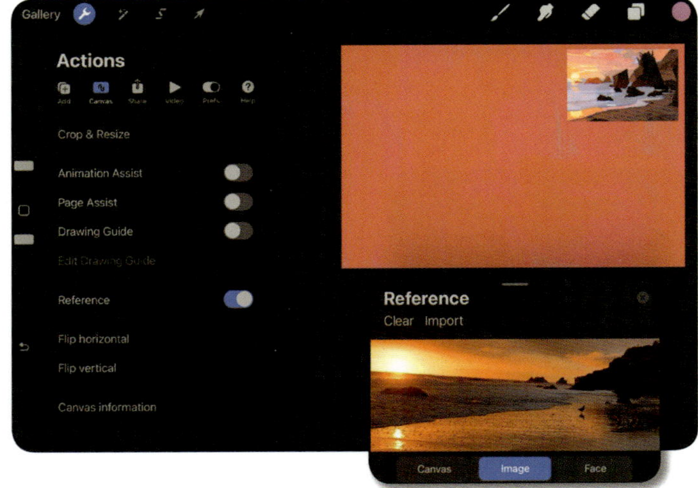

07

Once your plein-air study is complete, you can begin to refine everything towards a final studio painting. Go to **ACTIONS > SHARE IMAGE > JPEG > COPY** to export your study as a JPEG. Create a new Procreate file called 'Linework' and use **ACTIONS > ADD > PASTE** to insert the plein-air study copy as a layer. If you took any photo references, go to **ACTIONS > CANVAS > REFERENCE**, and import one. Start to rework your drawing on layers over a rough orange underpainting. Think about what story and mood you want to emphasize, and how you want the viewer's eye to travel through the painting – across the rocks, shore, and sky – to arrive at the focal point of the setting sun.

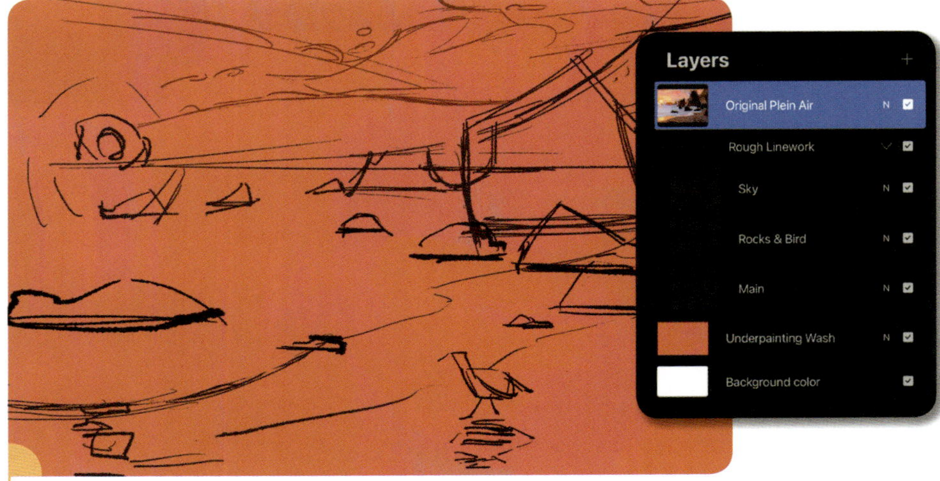

Use your plein-air study and photo references to redesign the drawing and stylize it

08

Add 'tracing paper' on top of the first drawing by filling a new layer above with white and lowering its opacity to 50%. In another new layer on top, continue refining your composition, redrawing it in more detail. The original plein-air sketch was a much more representational portrayal of the beach. Here, as you refine your line work, you can choose to stylize the painting by simplifying the shapes and amplifying their gestures, making the elements gravitate towards the sun. Afterwards, you can refine smaller details and decide their placement. This step saves you from having to rework your composition drastically later, once you have started painting.

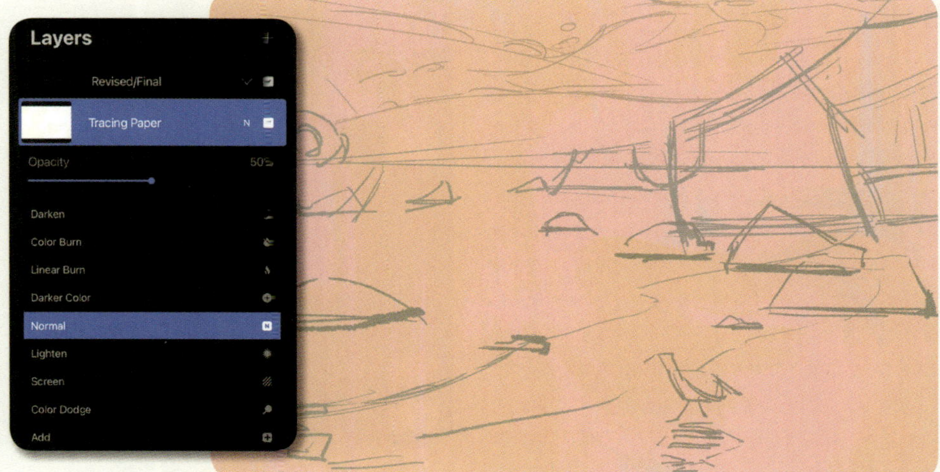

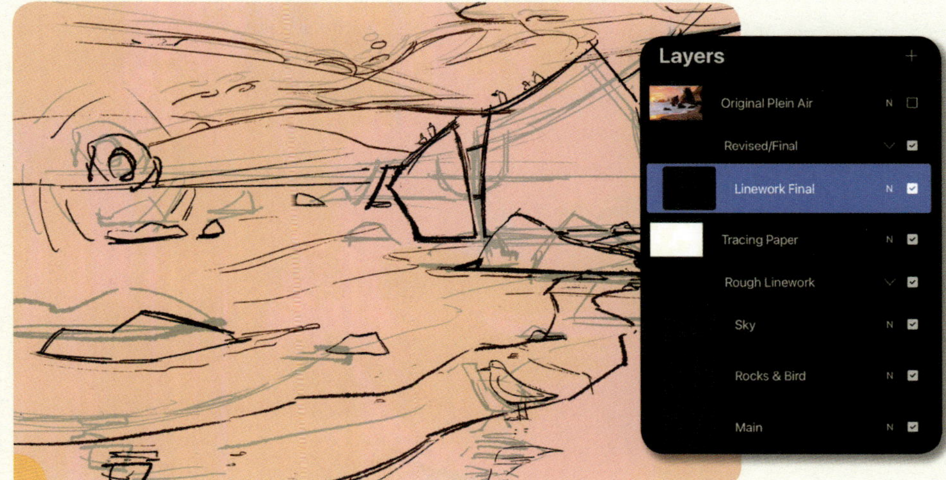

Drawing above your first sketch allows you to refine while referring back to it

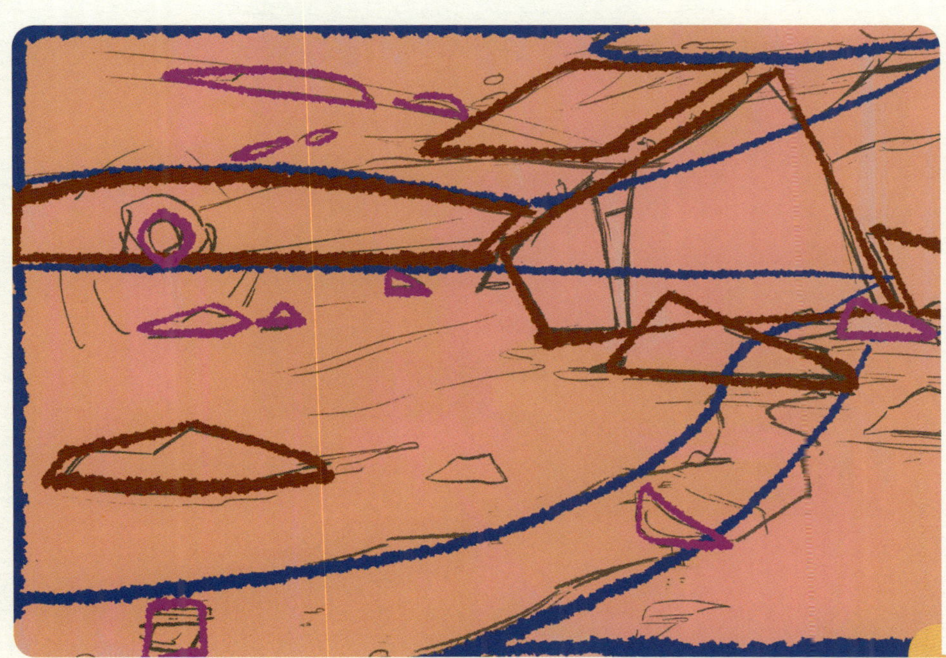

09

The relationships between big, medium, and small shapes are crucial to any composition. The rhythm of their placement directly affects how the composition will be interpreted and felt by the viewer. You can draw shapes on new layers over your line work as a method of checking the design of your composition and seeing what's working, or for checking whether there are too many repeating, evenly spaced shapes that interfere with the image's flow. Here, the rock groupings become tighter the further into the distance you go, emphasizing the long stretch of the shoreline.

The final line work and its shape breakdown

10

Continuing to use your plein-air study and photographs as reference, create a new Procreate document called '4-Value Study', where you will decide the light and shadow groupings in your landscape. Transfer the line art you drew in previous steps into this new document using **ACTIONS > ADD > COPY** to copy the layer, then **ACTIONS > ADD > PASTE** to insert it into the new file. Below this line-work layer, block in your value groupings – dark, medium-dark, medium-light, and light. A good value study creates a solid and clear foundation for your colours and the lighting scheme of the environment. It reinforces the strong and simplified graphic statement of your painting, so that it remains cohesive and unified by value groupings as you move forward.

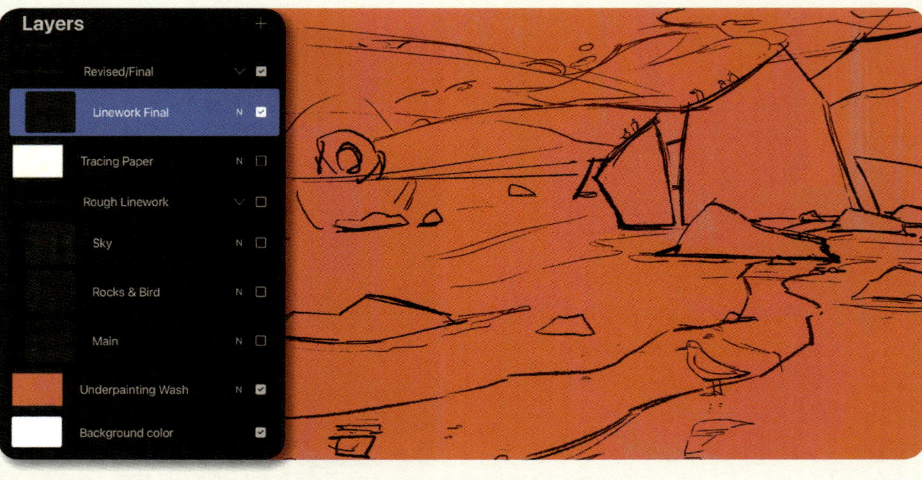

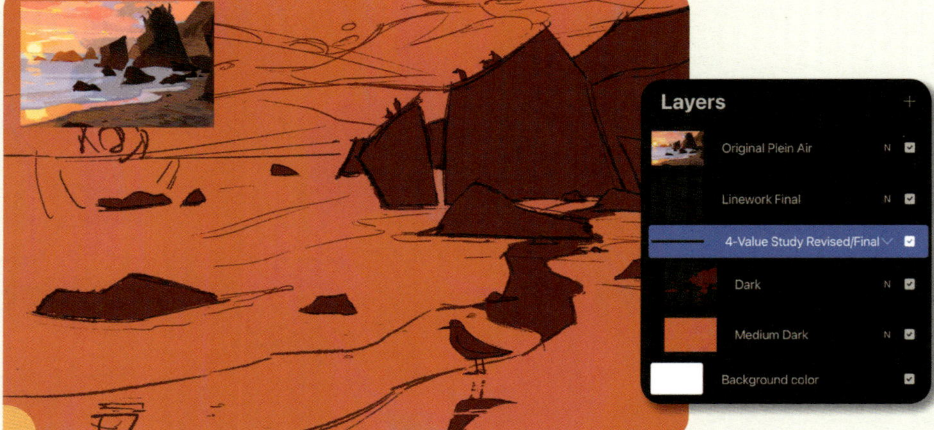

Having plein-air and value study references will allow you creative flexibility and range in deciding what to include

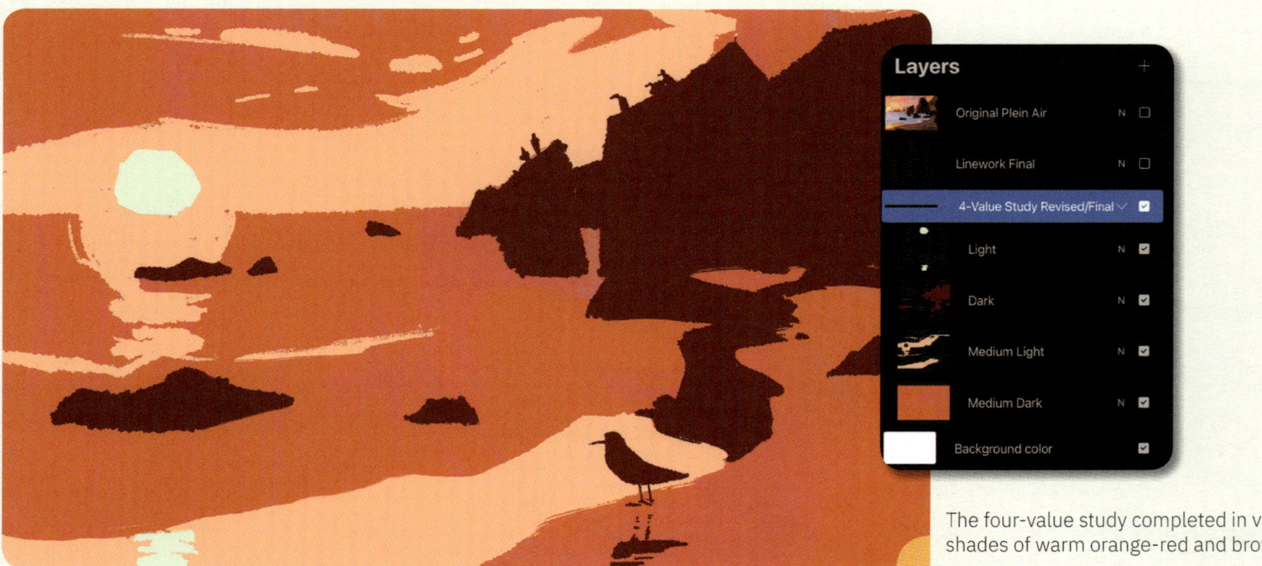

The four-value study completed in various shades of warm orange-red and brown

11

After completion, you can turn off your line-work layer to see your final four-value study as shapes only. In terms of value, the ocean had previously been grouped with the sky, around the medium-light range, which created a dreamier look. However, in this new value study, the ocean is rearranged into the medium-dark value group, its lower value allowing the reflection of the sun to contrast against the water more brightly.

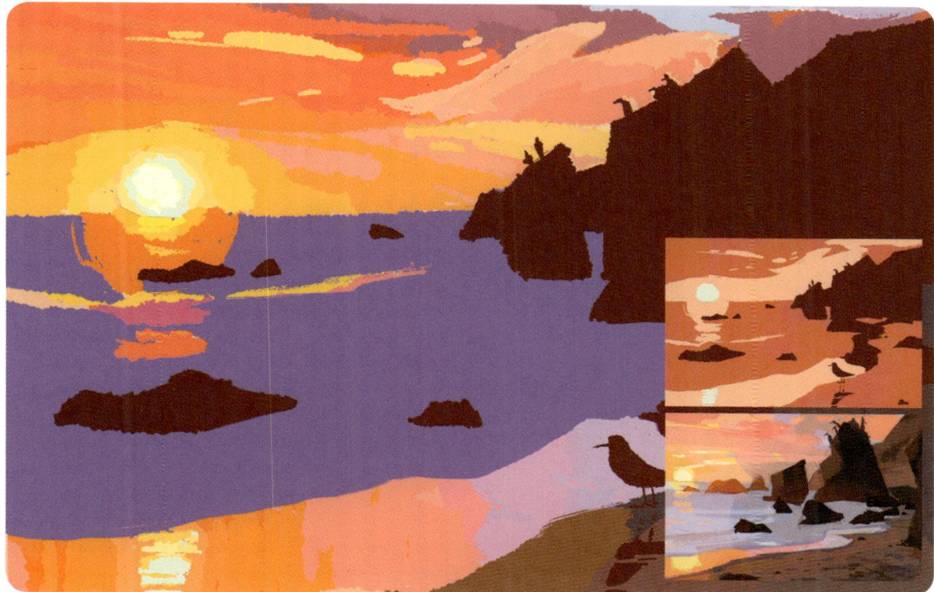

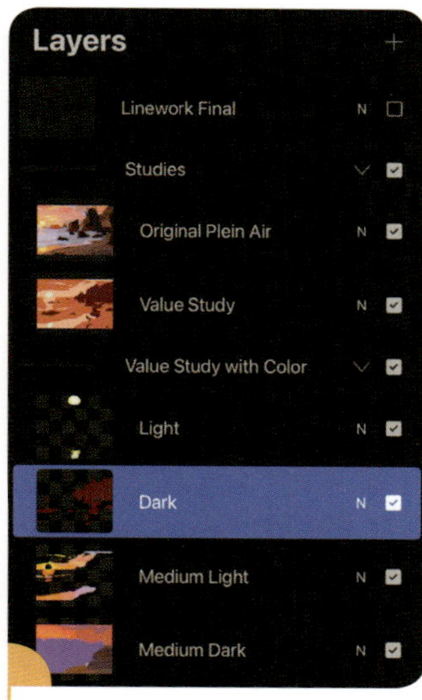

The value layers are Alpha Locked before the colours are painted in

12

Duplicate the value study layers and merge them into a flat copy that you can scale down and keep to one side for reference, alongside your plein-air reference. Looking at the resources you have now gathered, there are certain colour ideas to keep and others to leave behind.

Working from the original four-value study layers you have created, you can begin to fill in the shapes. Use the Eyedropper tool to sample colours from the original plein-air study, then adjust to make them darker, lighter, brighter, or more muted as you paint a new, more stylized colour study.

Using the value layers as your base allows you to maintain the big value relationships as you translate them into full colour. Use a solid brush such as **DRAWING > EVOLVE** for fully opaque painting.

13

In this colour study, it's crucial to capture the colour relationships and various light sources present in the environment. Any details or more nuanced colour variations can be saved for the final painting. Brush in the strong, vibrant, glaring light of the sun – the way it warms everything around it in a radiating circular glow and gently lights the edges of the cooler, darker rocks with a warm, deep orange. Include the secondary light source, too – the purple-blue sky light behind our scene, softly brushing on the top planes of the rocks and reflecting in the wet sand. The ocean in the plein-air study had the right colour temperatures, accurately conveying the water's warm pink-to-purple hues and blue sky-light reflections.

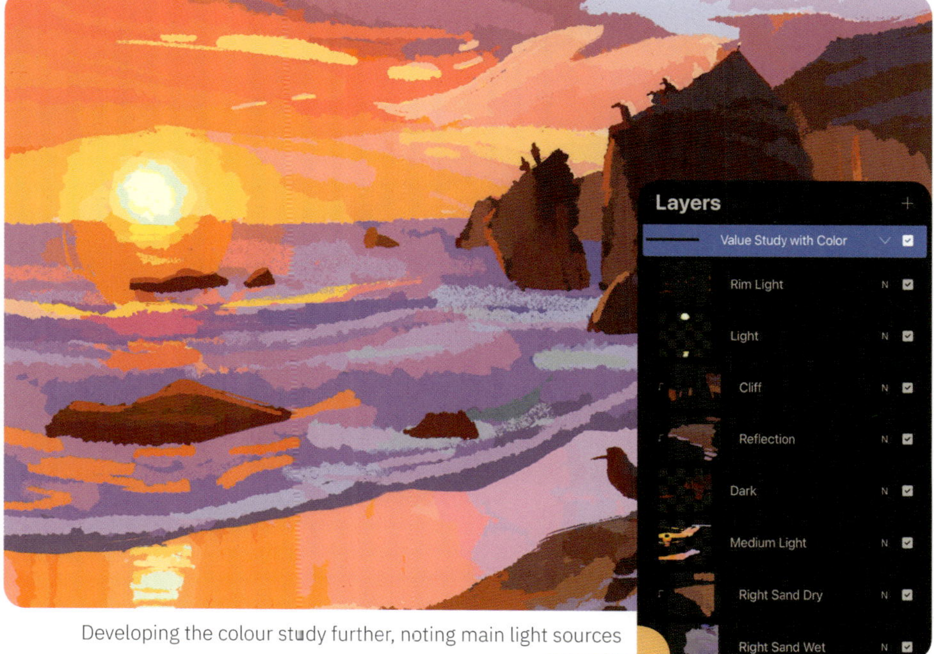

Developing the colour study further, noting main light sources

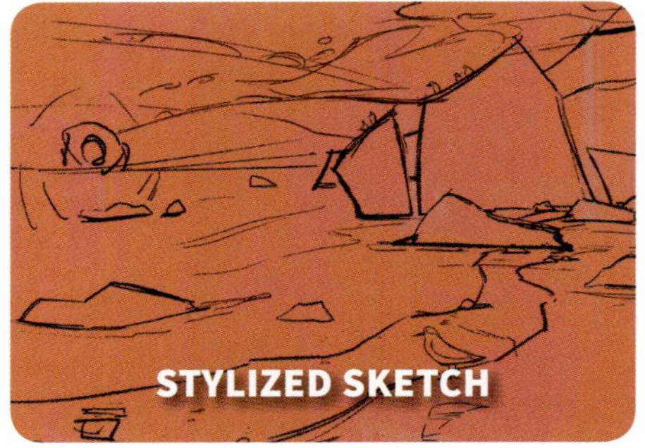

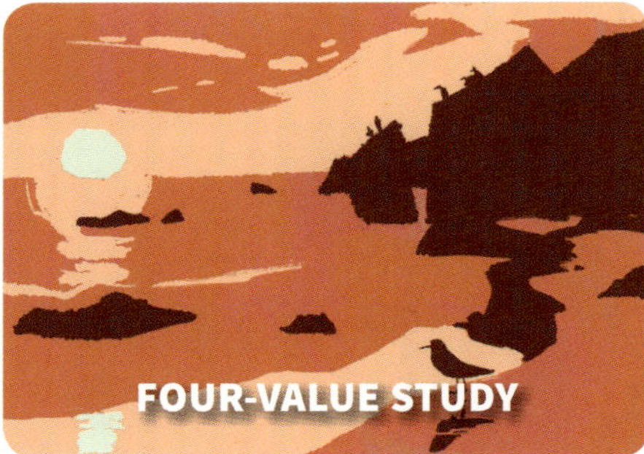

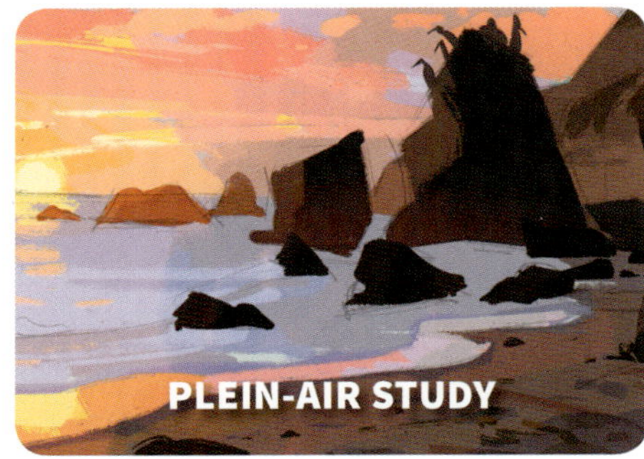

14

You can amplify harmonies and contrasts using blend modes. On a new layer in Overlay mode, fill in a solid red-purple midtone to unify all the colours towards pink. Use a Darken layer to paint a cool purple vignette on the right-hand edges of the painting to convey light fall-off. Use a Colour Dodge layer to add general glow and warmth throughout, and use Overlay again to create a strong glow from the sun and its reflection. Place a peach-toned Normal layer on top and brush into it with a mask to further unify the colour scheme. Vary the opacities of every blend mode so they don't overpower your colour study.

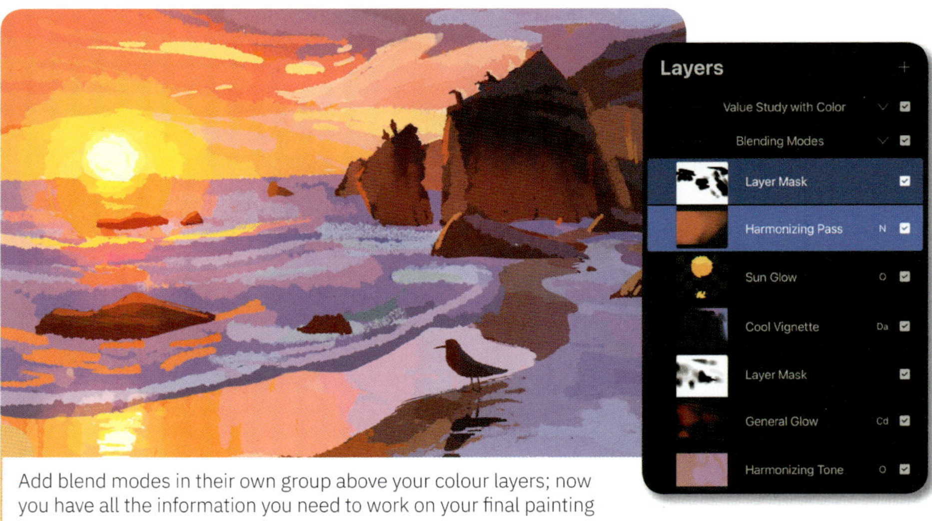

Add blend modes in their own group above your colour layers; now you have all the information you need to work on your final painting

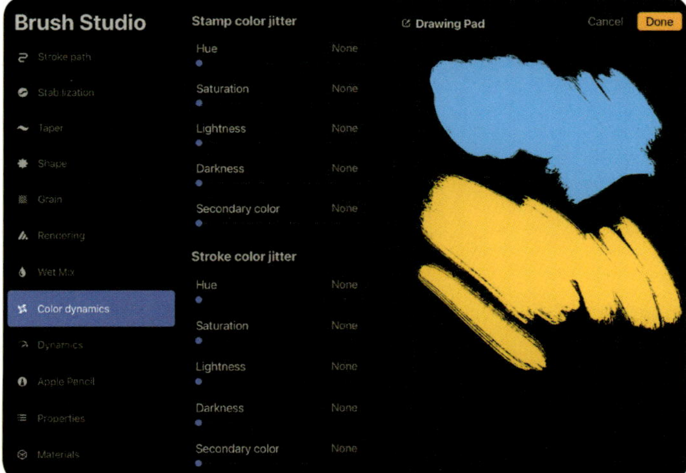

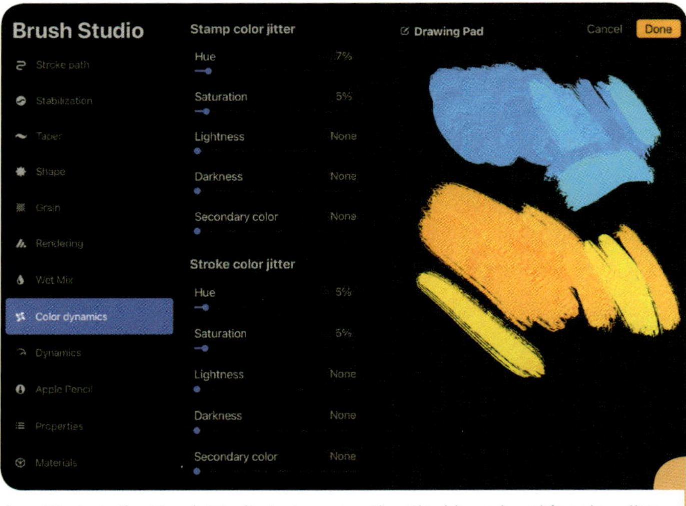

Adjust brush settings in the Brush Studio to increase the Blackburn brush's colour jitter

15

You can tailor a brush to your liking by tapping on it in the Brush Library to reveal the Brush Studio. For this painting, swipe left on the default **DRAWING > BLACKBURN** brush to duplicate it. Open the copy in the Brush Studio, go to the Colour Dynamics tab. Under the Stamp Colour Jitter and Stroke Colour Jitter sections, slightly increase the Hue and Saturation sliders. The Stamp Colour Jitter affects the colour of your stroke every time you make a new one. Adding this slight colour variation to your brushstrokes can quickly add colour complexity to your painting, emulating colour vibrations in real life. Lastly, go to the 'About this brush' tab, where you can tap the brush name and rename it 'Blackburn Colour Jitter'.

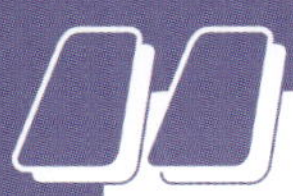

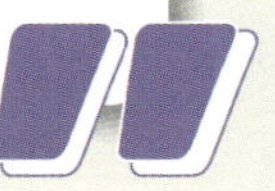

JENNIFER SAYS: *'Sometimes you can feel like there are too many brushes to choose from. You can end up only using a single brush for the entire painting, or using so many brushes that you lose any cohesive sense of mark-making. Experiment with different brushes as you paint to find the ones that feel right for you, then narrow them down to a handful. You can duplicate and move some of your favourites into your own folder. The brushes in "Jennifer's Default Pack" (provided as a download, page 215) were selected for their painterly effect, which is to say many of them emulate the tactility and natural feel of traditional mediums like gouache, oil, and pastel.'*

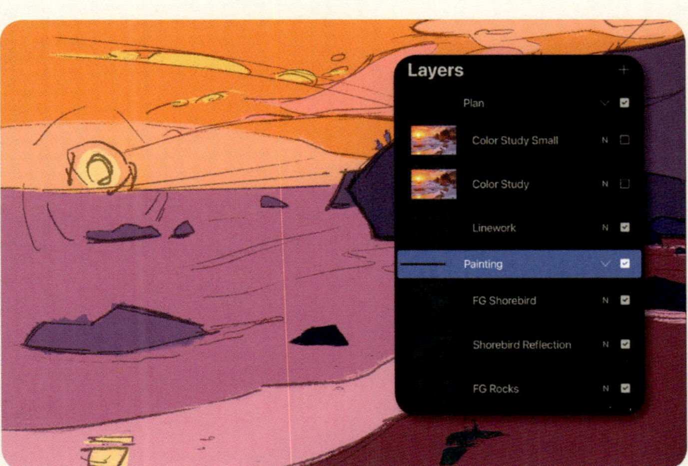

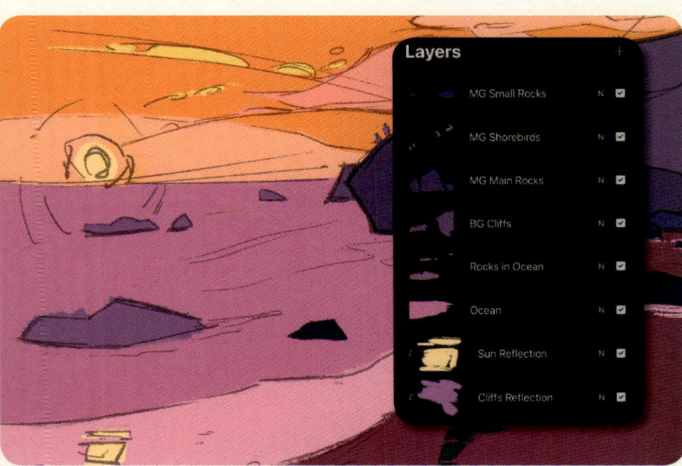

16

Transfer your line work and final colour study into a new file called 'Final Painting'. Have a full-size and small colour study available to toggle on and off and to sample from, respectively. Much like the original plein-air study, start by brushing in the shapes on individual layers beneath your line-work layer, but this time adhere more closely to the line work. To indicate depth with the edge quality of the silhouettes, use a softer, fuzzier brush such as CALLIGRAPHY > CHALK for faraway shapes and DRAWING > BLACKBURN for closer shapes. Using different colours for each shape group helps keep them visually separate.

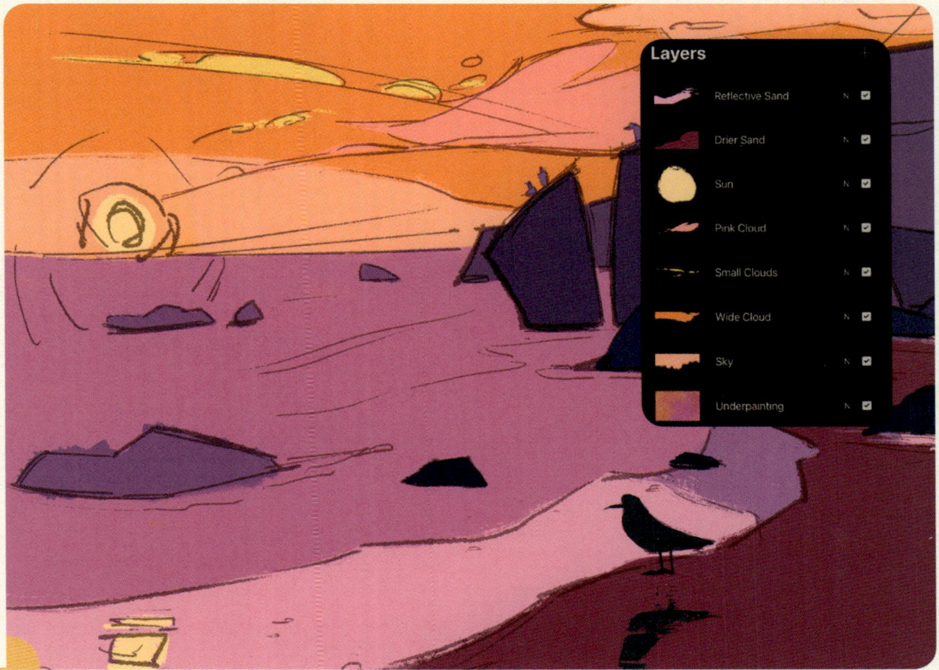

Layer organization of all the shape groupings in the painting

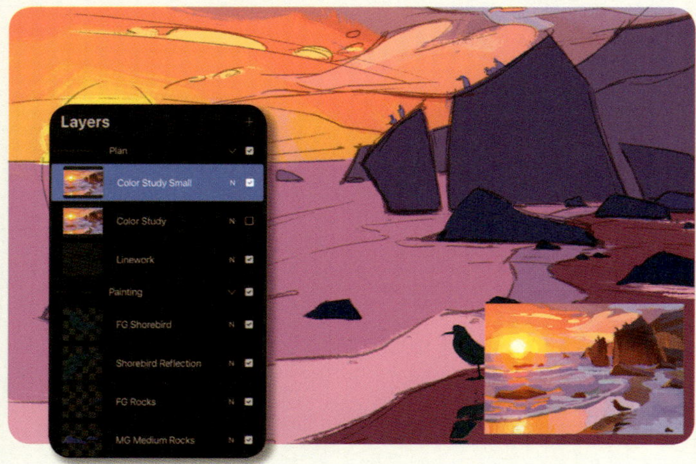

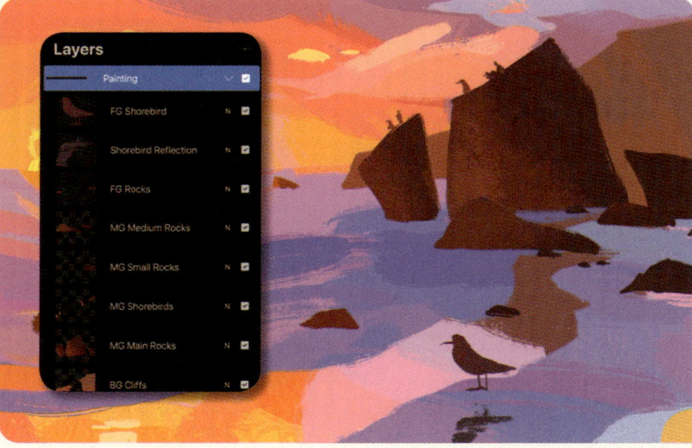

Prepare all the major colour block-ins and begin to render them

17

Alpha Lock your layers once again and begin painting in the general colours of each element. Keep your brush size quite large and use the Eyedropper tool to sample from the colour study at the corner of your canvas. In general, you should start with big, broad brushstrokes and gradually work up to smaller and smaller marks. This helps you capture the main mood, colour, and feel of your environment quickly at the beginning, without getting bogged down by nuance and detail. Starting with detail can be a slippery slope that diverts you from making a cohesive overall statement.

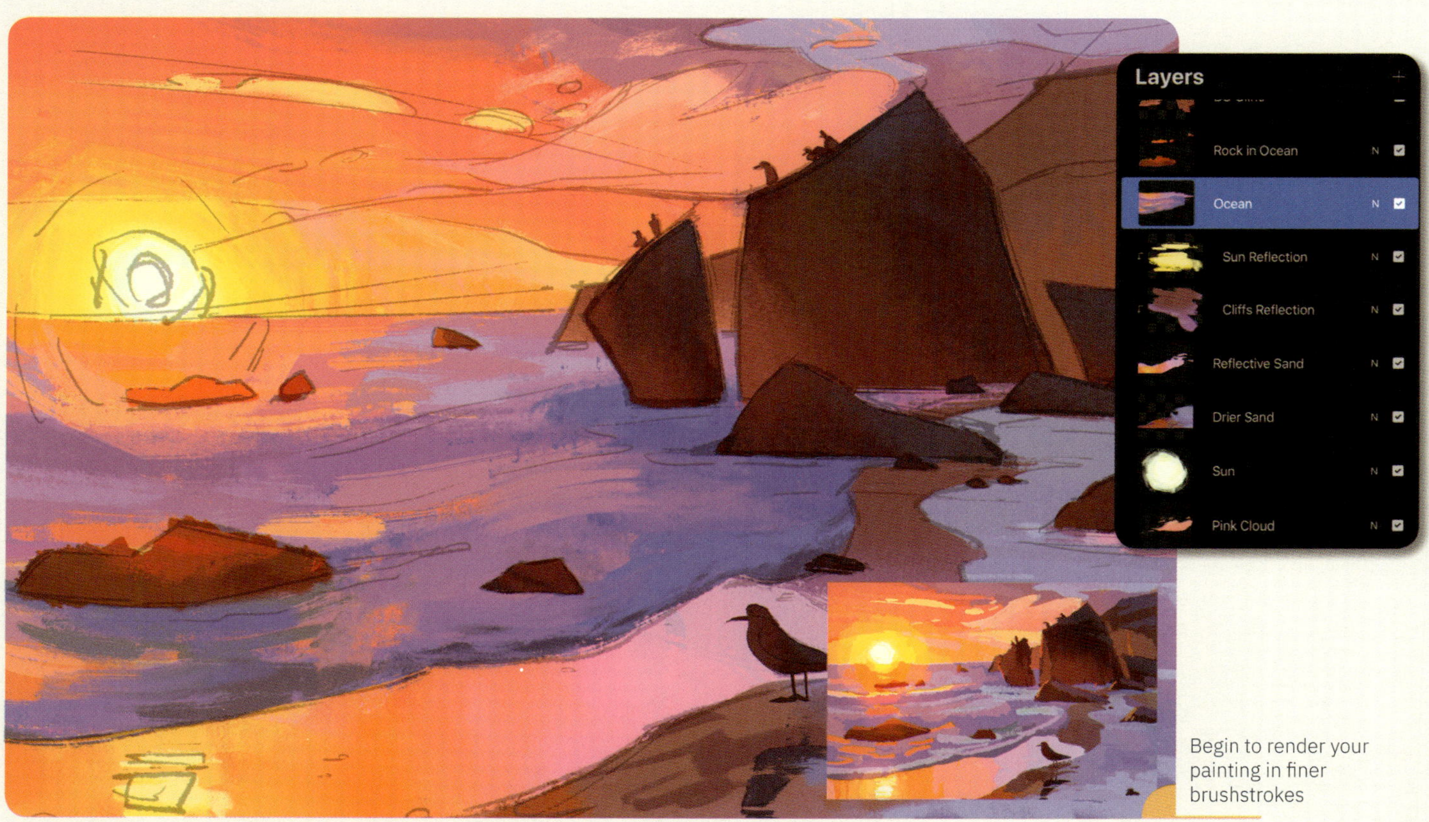

Begin to render your painting in finer brushstrokes

18

Keeping your layers Alpha Locked, start to paint in all the gradations and finer details of the sky, ocean, and land. Using a combination of sharper brushes like Blackburn and softer ones like **SKETCHING > SOFT PASTEL** and **PAINTING > TURPENTINE**, paint in these elements by continuing to sample from your colour study. Keep in mind here to also increase the size of your brushstrokes as the elements you are painting come forward in space and appear bigger.

19

Brush in the sunlight hitting the rocks and the sky light filling in from the right. Be sure to darken the rocks on the shadow side, on planes where light falls off. During sunset, the light is more orange-pink and the shadows tend to be cooler violet. Add the distant wave on a new layer, clipped to the ocean layer so it adheres to the existing ocean shape. Trim the shape of the pink cloud, and add rock reflections on the water. Paint in the saturated orange of the sun reflecting on the water.

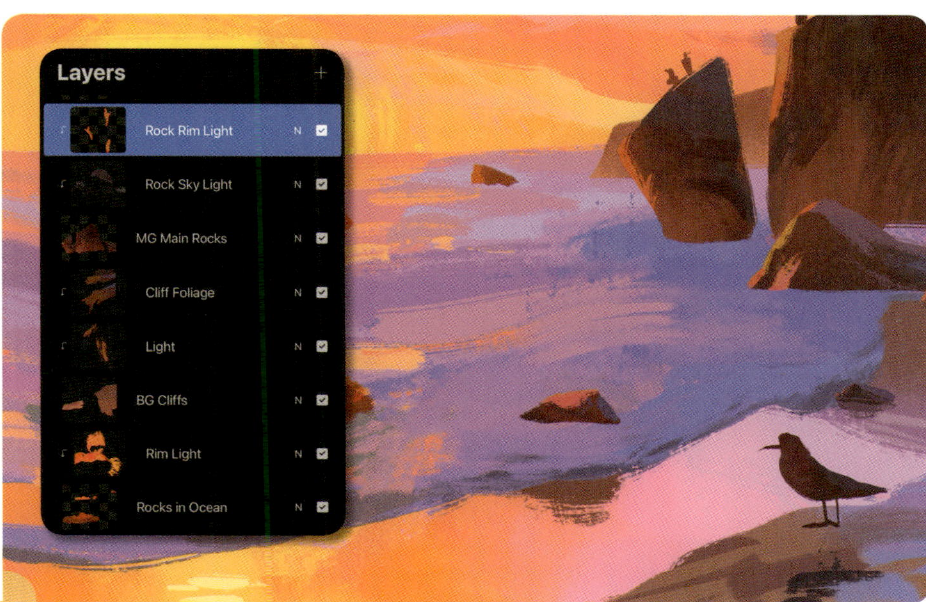

Continue to refine with the light sources in mind, considering how different surfaces reflect light

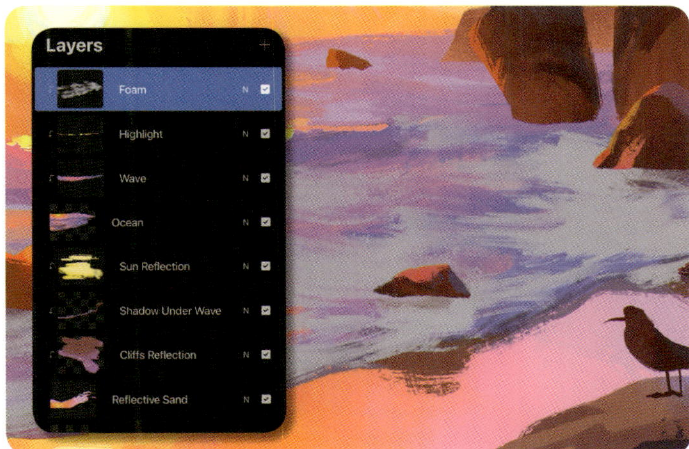

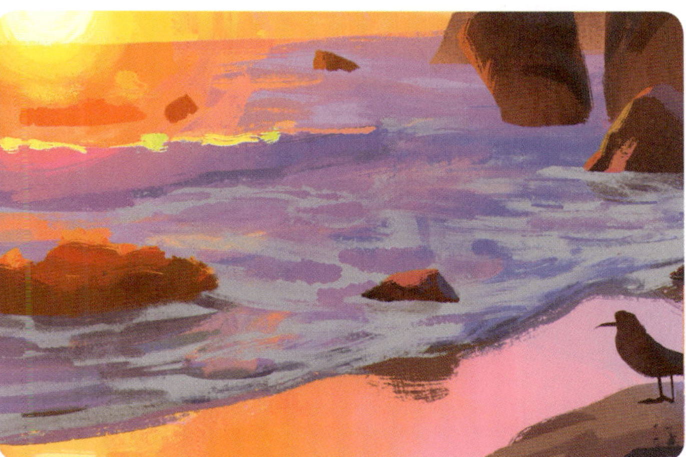

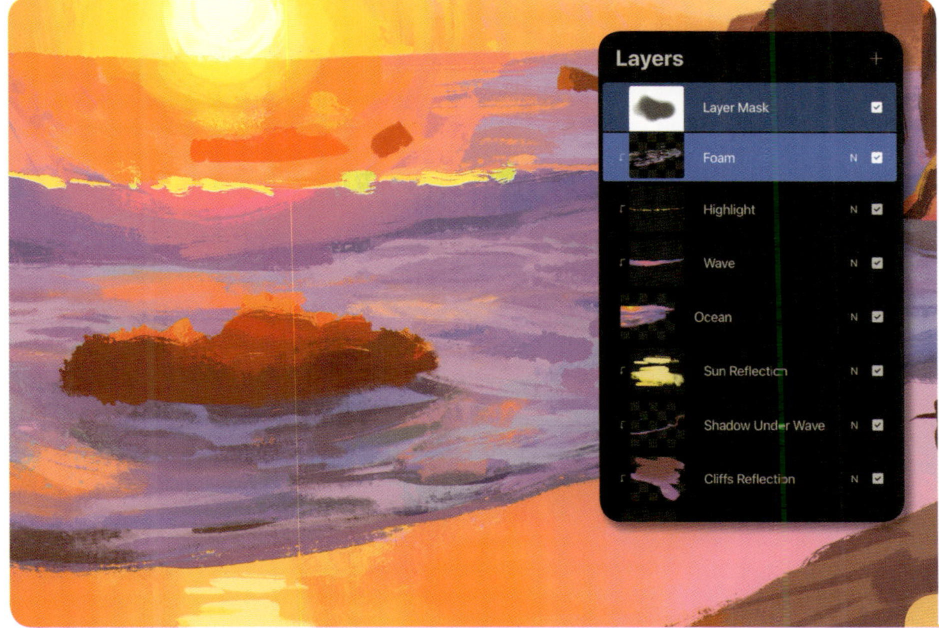

20

Layer the sea foam on a separate layer above the ocean. Add foam with **PAINTING > OLD BRUSH**, brushing in the same directions in which the water is moving. Old Brush's rough texture is perfectly suited to represent wispy foaminess. Afterwards, you can erase the negative shapes with a sharper brush, such as **DRAWING > EVOLVE**, to allow the ocean underneath to show through and create some appealing shapes in the process. Add a mask to the Foam layer and brush in some grey with **SKETCHING > SOFT PASTEL**, which will make the foam fade into the distance.

Keeping the ocean and foam layers separate grants more flexibility to revise both of them

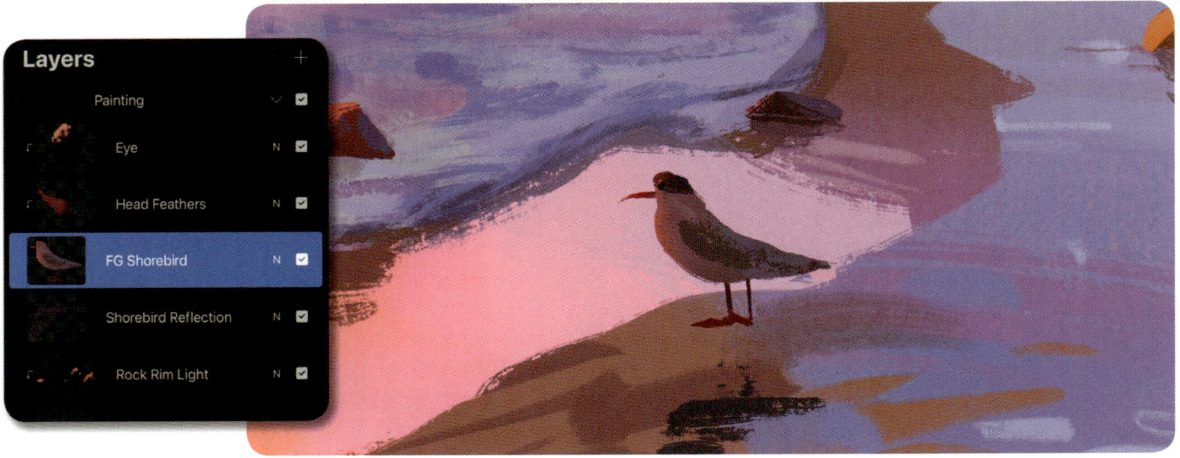

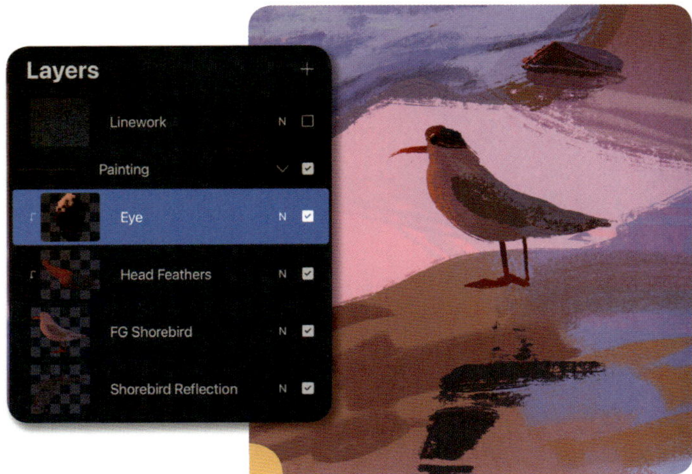

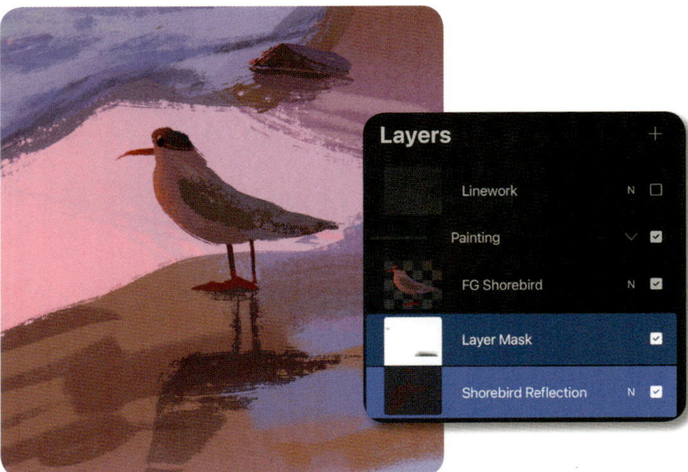

Save zooming into your canvas until the end – for small, refined details such as the birds

21

Paint the foreground bird with sharper brushstrokes and more detail, since it is the element closest to the viewer. You can paint each element on a separate layer clipped to the bird's silhouette, and merge into one when you are happy with the elements. You can create the bird's reflection by painting a rough silhouette on a layer below and fading it out slightly with a mask.

Revising the distant birds from the initial line work, shrink them down even more, and brush them in only with the loosest of strokes. The shorebird in the foreground and the ones in the distance add an element of aliveness to the landscape painting. They also accentuate the sense of depth and scale – just how far those big rocks in the distance are, and how big and heavy those rocks are in relation to the tiny, soft birds.

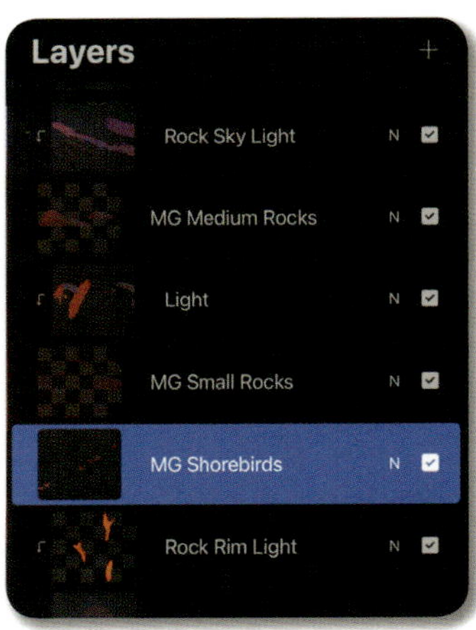

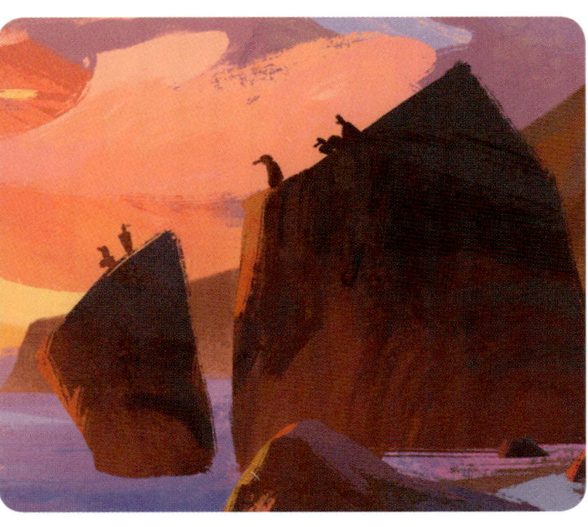

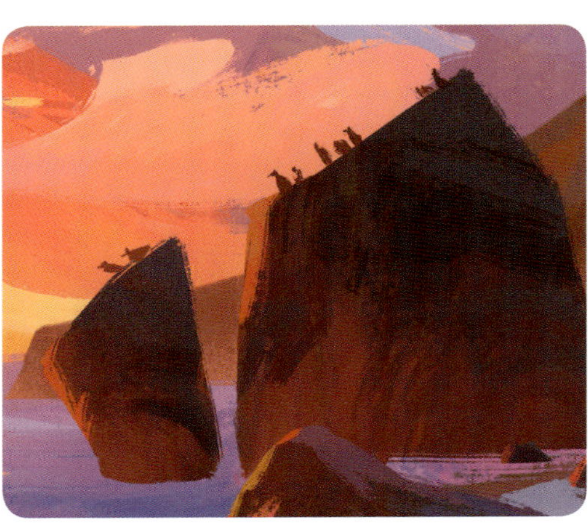

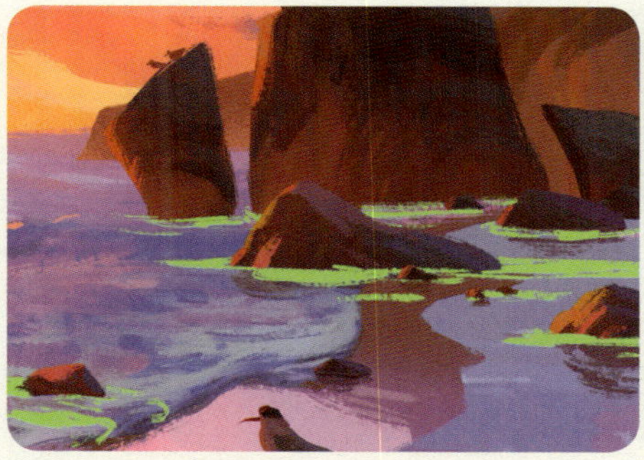

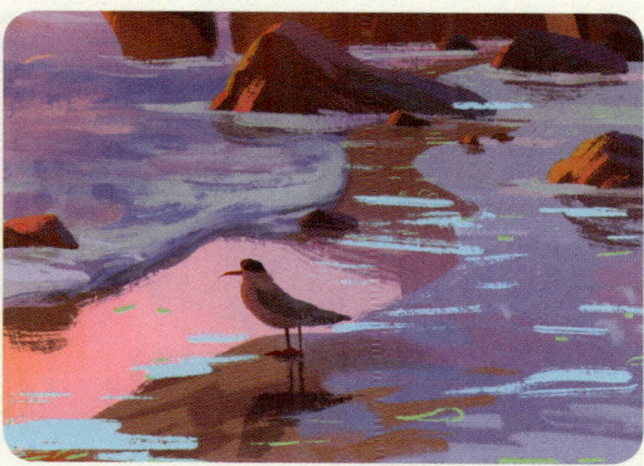

22

Now that all the major shapes and details have been finished, you can add in smaller details on layers above the rest of the painting: foamy waves around the rocks, bubbles created as the waves recede back, and the streaks in the sand that blend the various parts of the shore together. As always, begin by brushing in flat shapes in an easily distinguishable hue, before Alpha Locking them and painting more colours in, allowing you to focus on the shapes' gesture and design before choosing their colours. This detailing adds more nuance and visual complexity to the scene, bringing it near to completion.

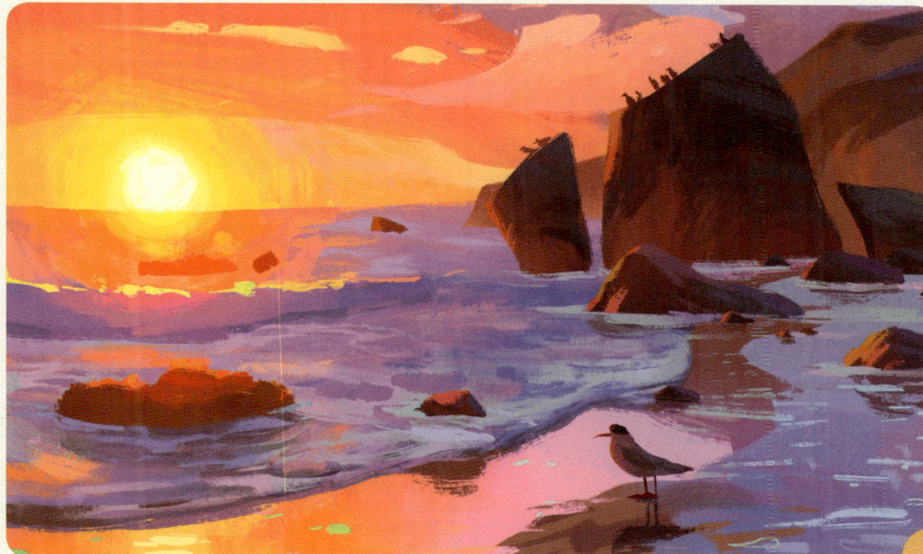

The last refinements to bring the painting together – add more details closer to the viewer

23

Make a copy of your painting file and go through the layers to merge all the clipped layers to their target layers by pinching them together with two fingers. The flattened layers make it easier to sort through everything while wrapping up the painting process. Some of the elements, such as the sky and rocks, still feel sharp where they meet the water, so add layers above them and use **PAINTING > OLD BRUSH** to sample the nearby colours and soften the edges. Then add some other finishing details as needed, including colourful splashes of water to further enhance the splendid effects of the sun.

A combination of hard- and soft-edged brushstrokes adds a more complex painterly effect

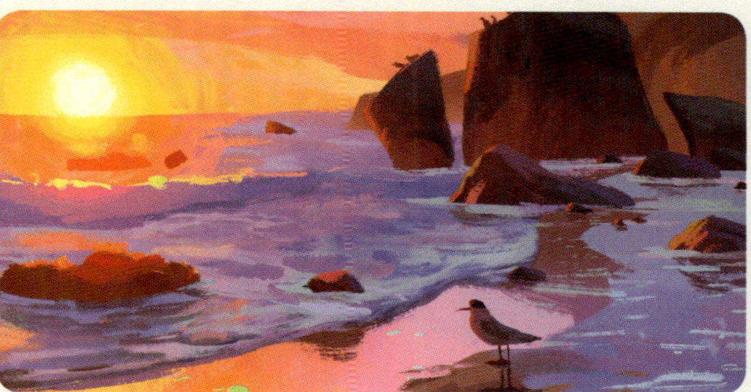

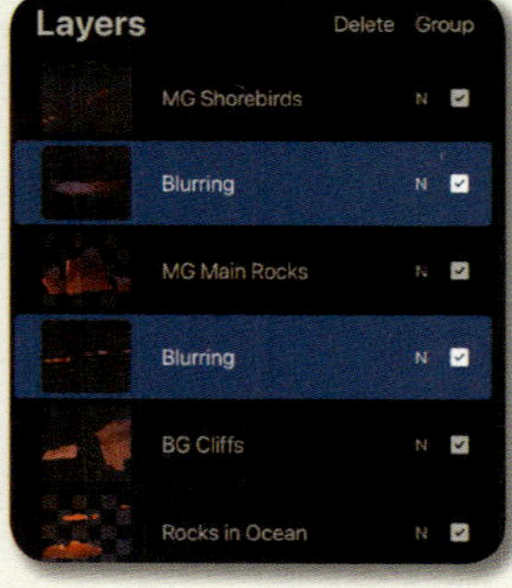

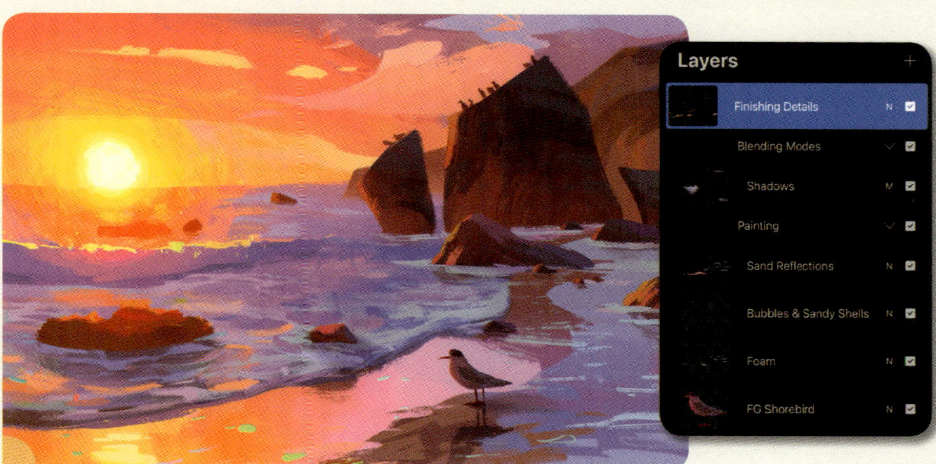

24

You can enhance the scene's depth by adding more atmospheric effects. Duplicate the distant cliffs and use **ADJUSTMENTS > HUE, SATURATION, BRIGHTNESS** to lower their saturation and lift their brightness to indicate 'atmospheric perspective' – the effect of distant objects being relatively pale and faint. Reduce the opacity of the duplicate layer to 50% so it harmonizes with the original cliffs layer. On another new layer, add a glow around the sun and its reflection with a bright yellow. Change its blend mode to Overlay and lower the opacity to around 40%; then smudge the edges with the Smudge tool set to **PAINTING > OLD BRUSH**. Add a cooler vignette towards the right side, in Multiply mode, to indicate light fall-off as elements retreat from the sun.

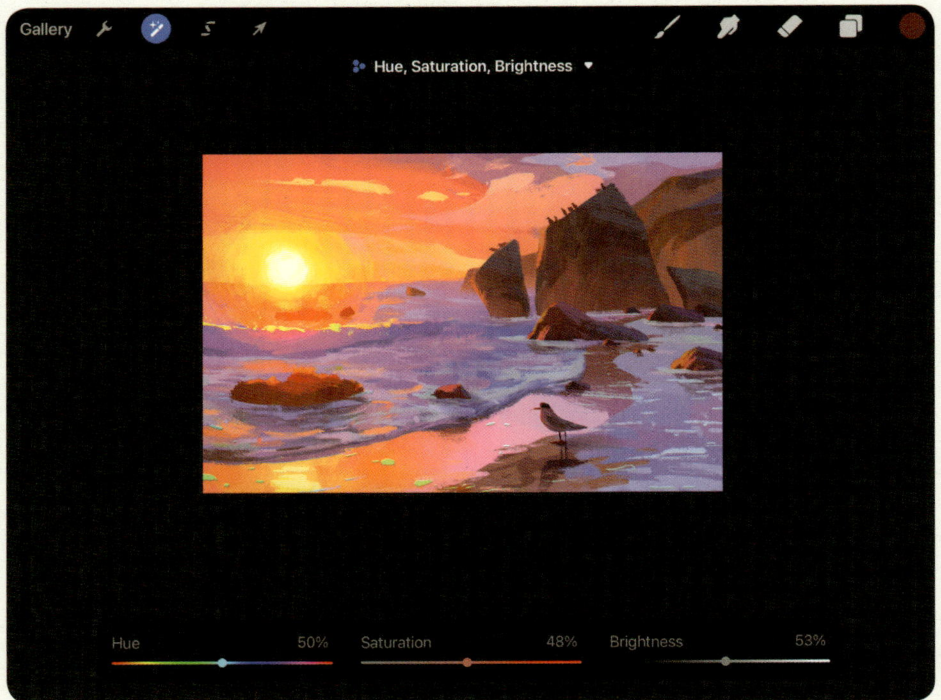

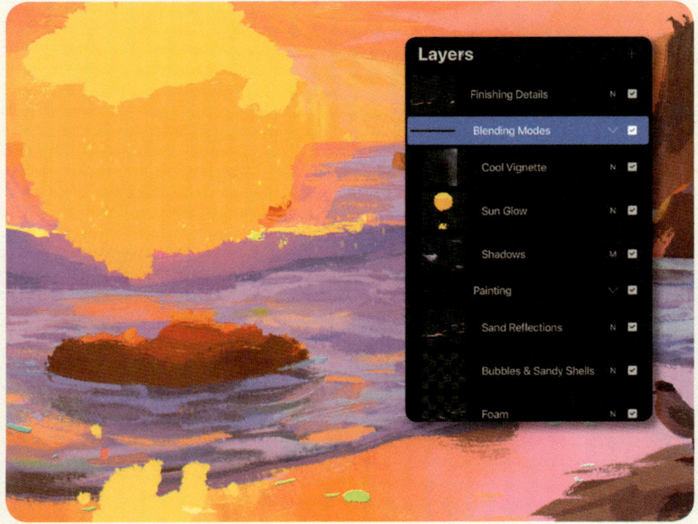

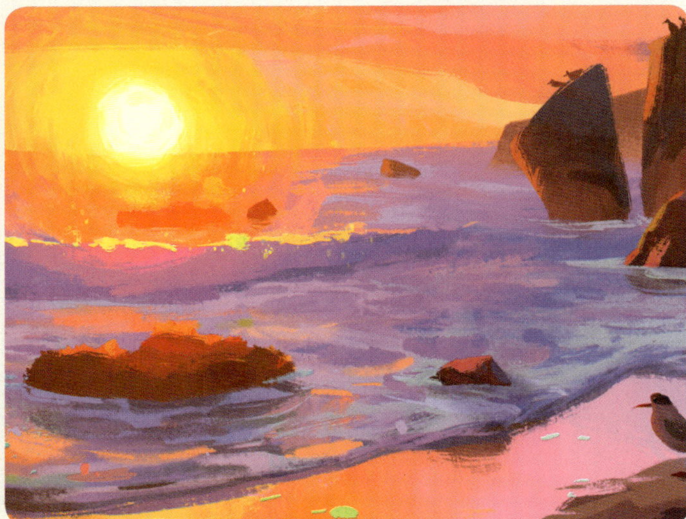

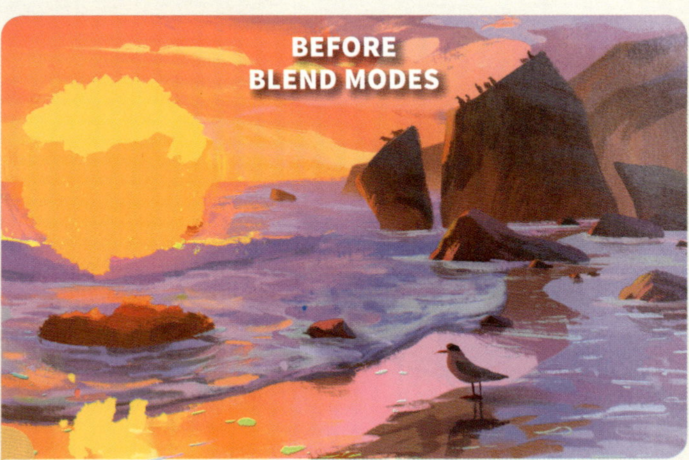

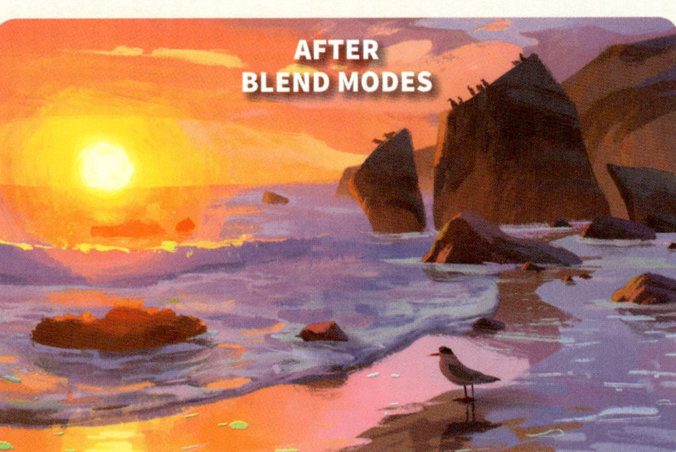

Use blend modes to create finishing effects: sun glow, vignette, and extra shadows

25

If you can, step away from your painting for a day or two and come back to it with fresh eyes. You may notice some potential changes or revisions that wouldn't have occurred to you while you were deep in the painting process. In this case, perhaps the distance and perspective of the shoreline could be captured a little better if the water had a stronger diagonal on the lower left. The water there could be more blue and foamy, too, giving it more form. After testing the new composition with a quick drawover, these changes can easily be made by using **SELECTION > FREEHAND** and **TRANSFORM > WARP** to lasso and reshape the water, then painting over it on a new layer to seamlessly blend in the changes.

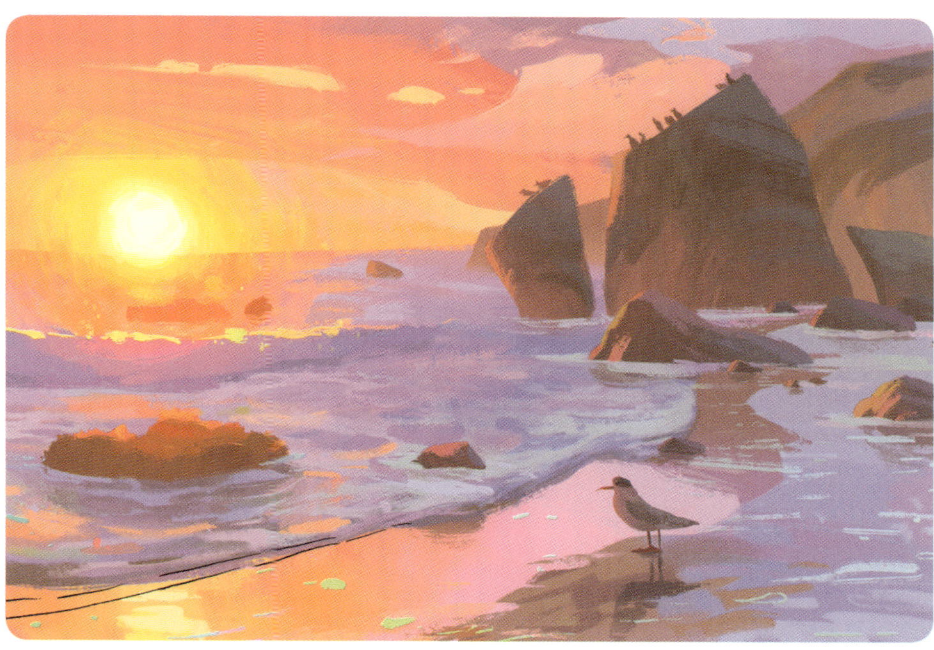

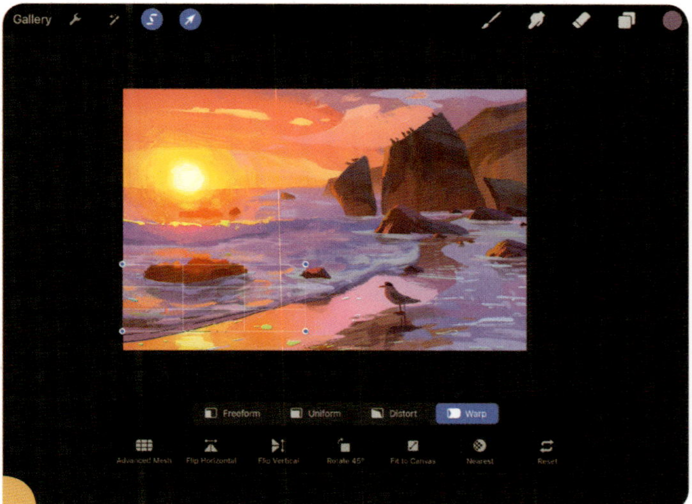

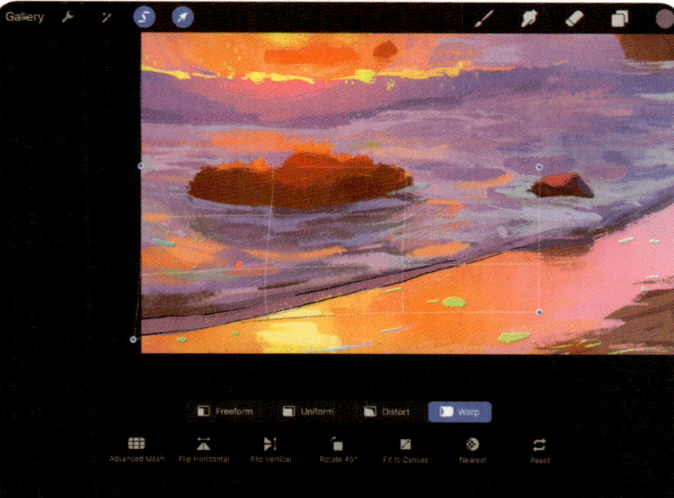

Before calling a painting finished, try to give yourself a break from it – you might notice new things to change!

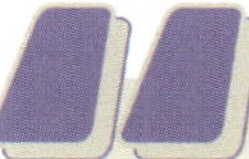

JENNIFER SAYS: '*Experiment with the boundless options and versatility that digital painting provides you. Try painting with intentional limitations – paint with only the Selection tool, paint with a single hard round brush, paint with a blendy oil brush, paint in greyscale, play around with gradient mapping and accidental colour schemes. Break out of plein-air methods and be more unconventional and inventive. Keep your colour study file, duplicate it, and go back to the location you visit and paint the same scene in different weather conditions and at new times of day. Use your Procreate file as a field journal for colour and light.*'

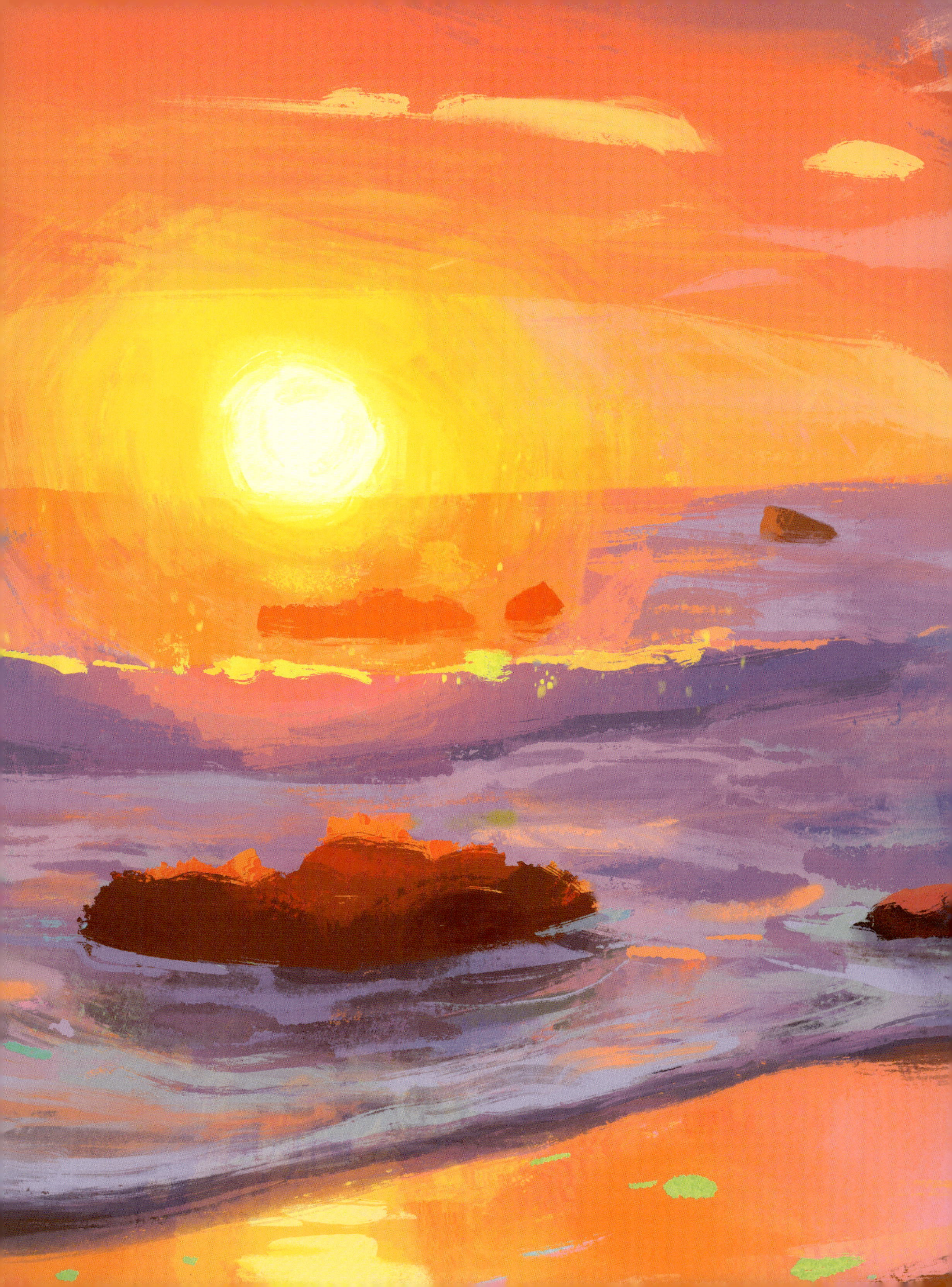

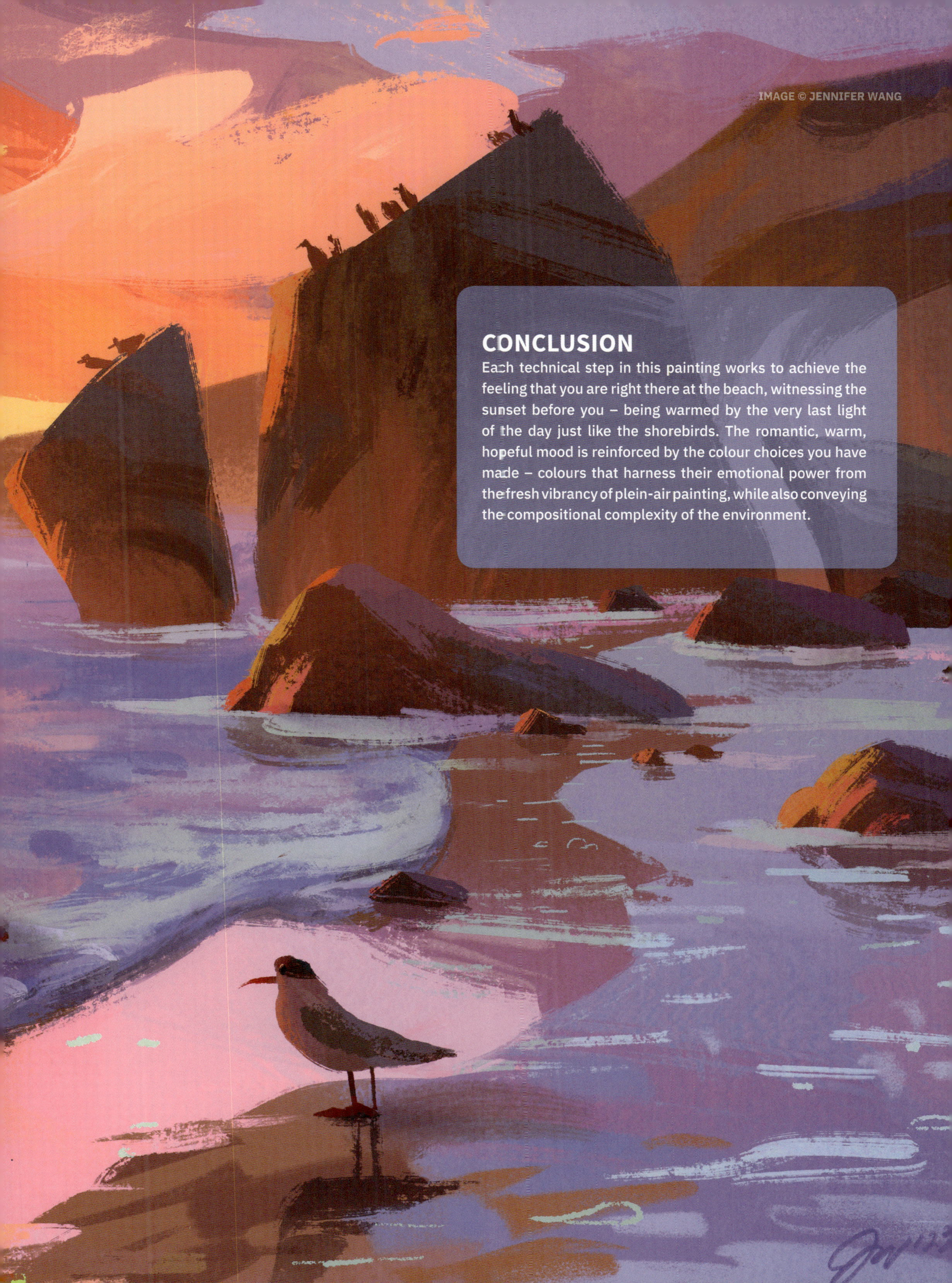

CONCLUSION

Each technical step in this painting works to achieve the feeling that you are right there at the beach, witnessing the sunset before you – being warmed by the very last light of the day just like the shorebirds. The romantic, warm, hopeful mood is reinforced by the colour choices you have made – colours that harness their emotional power from the fresh vibrancy of plein-air painting, while also conveying the compositional complexity of the environment.

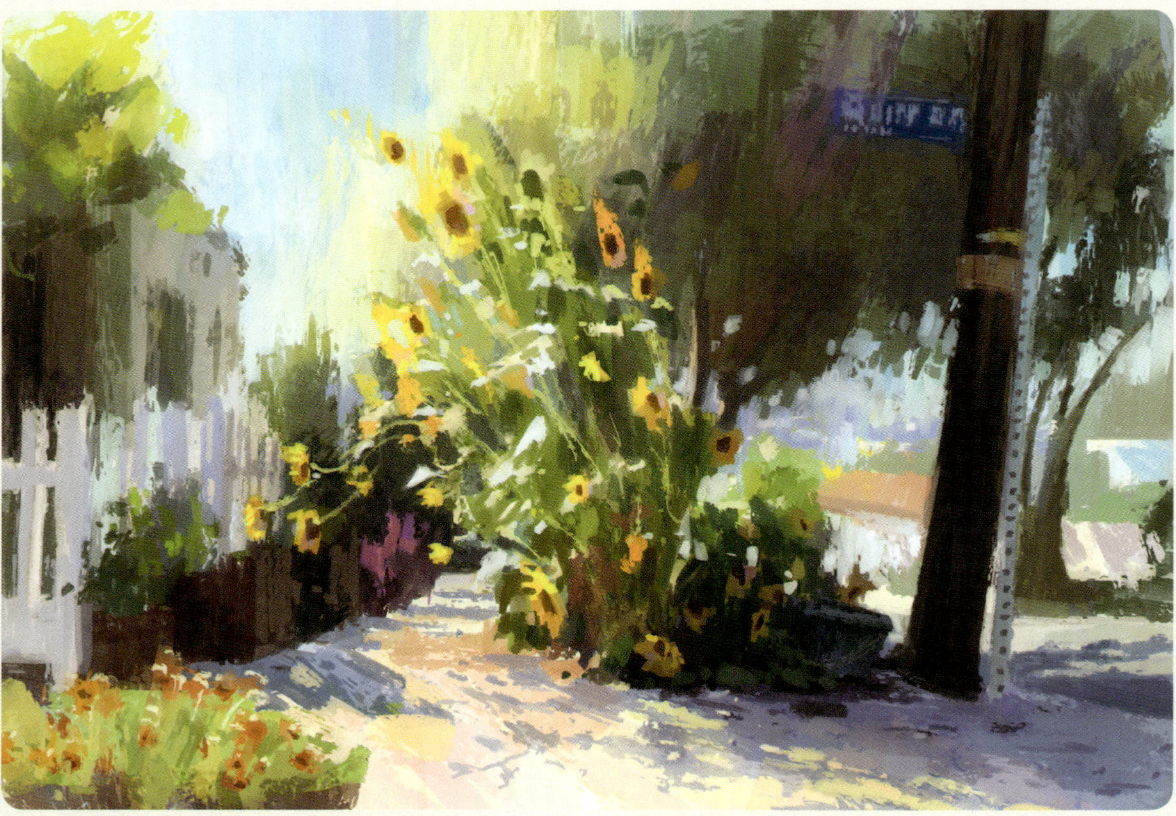

SPRING IN ECHO PARK: A big motivation here was to explore how to make digital painting in Procreate feel more like traditional painting, and also to capture the towering gesture of these radiant sunflowers

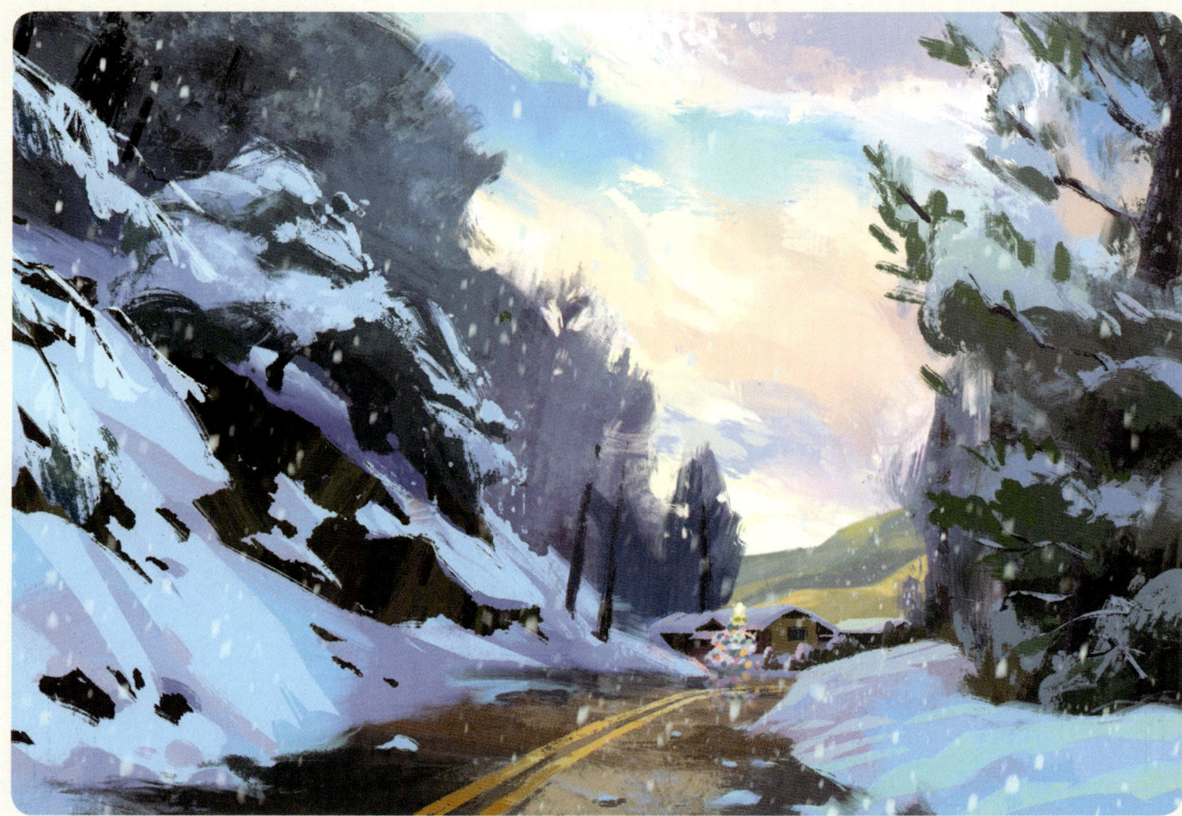

CALIFORNIA SNOW: Mid-December, I drove to Angeles National Forest, near Los Angeles, and was surprised by a generous snowfall; I was captivated by the contrast between the California sky and the wintry trees

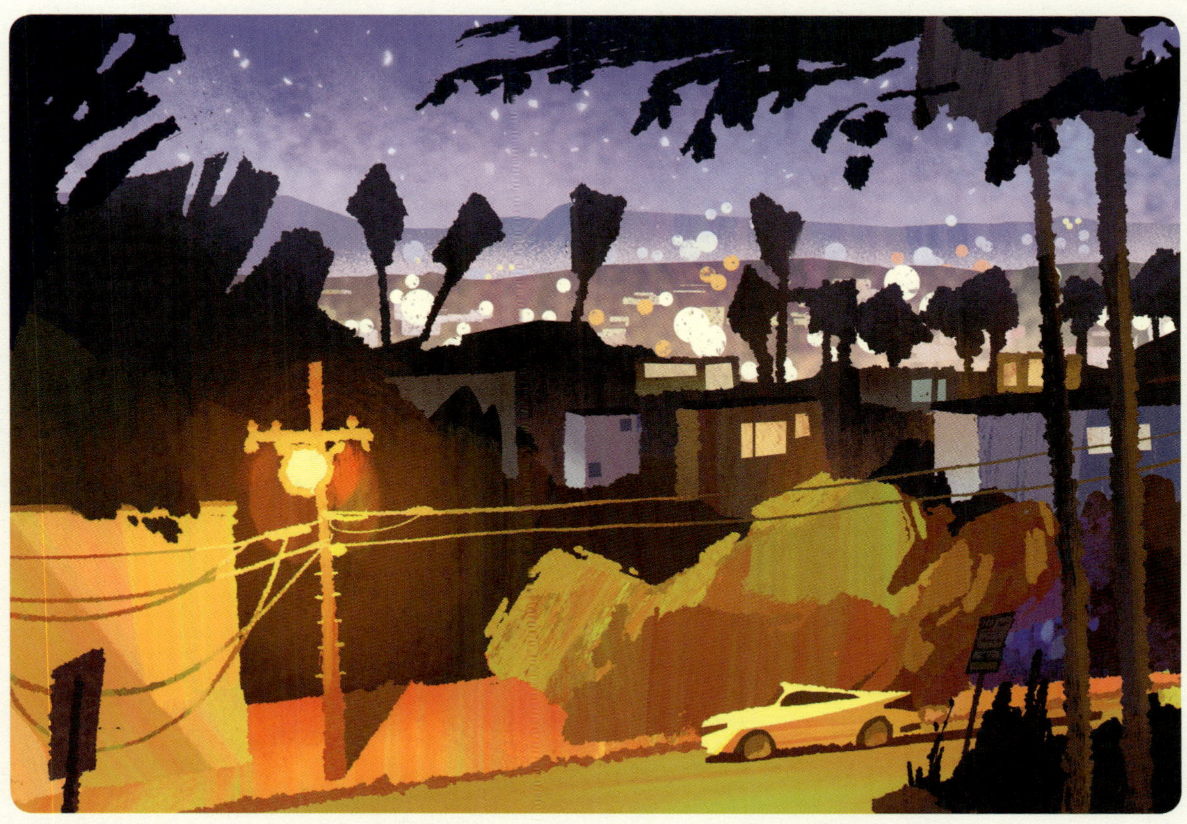

HILLY NOCTURNE: From an Echo Park hilltop, this view always stood out to me because of the stark temperature contrast between the orange street lights, the sparkling city lights far away, and the night sky

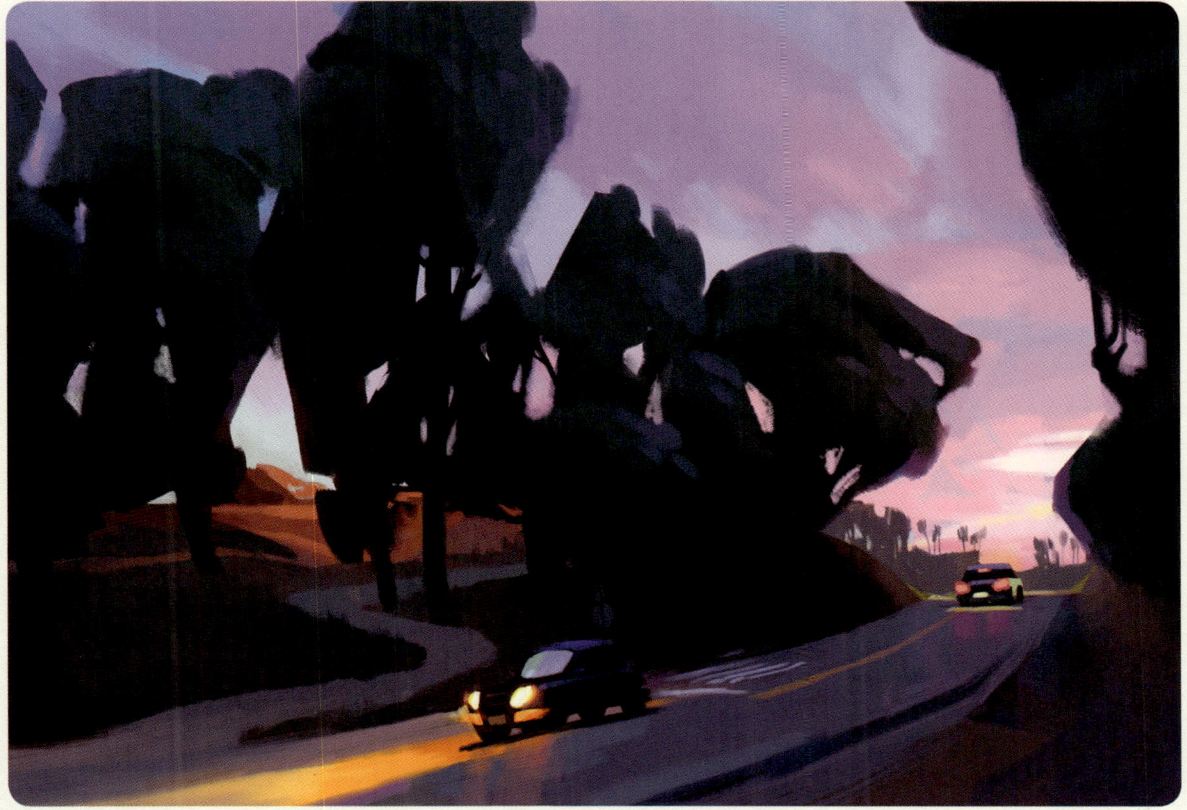

ELYSIAN WALK: In Elysian Park, there's a street interrupting one of the trails; I wanted to convey how much I love specific corners of Los Angeles, and how vivid the sunsets are here

ENGLISH MODEL VILLAGE

BY NEVENA NIKOLCHEVA

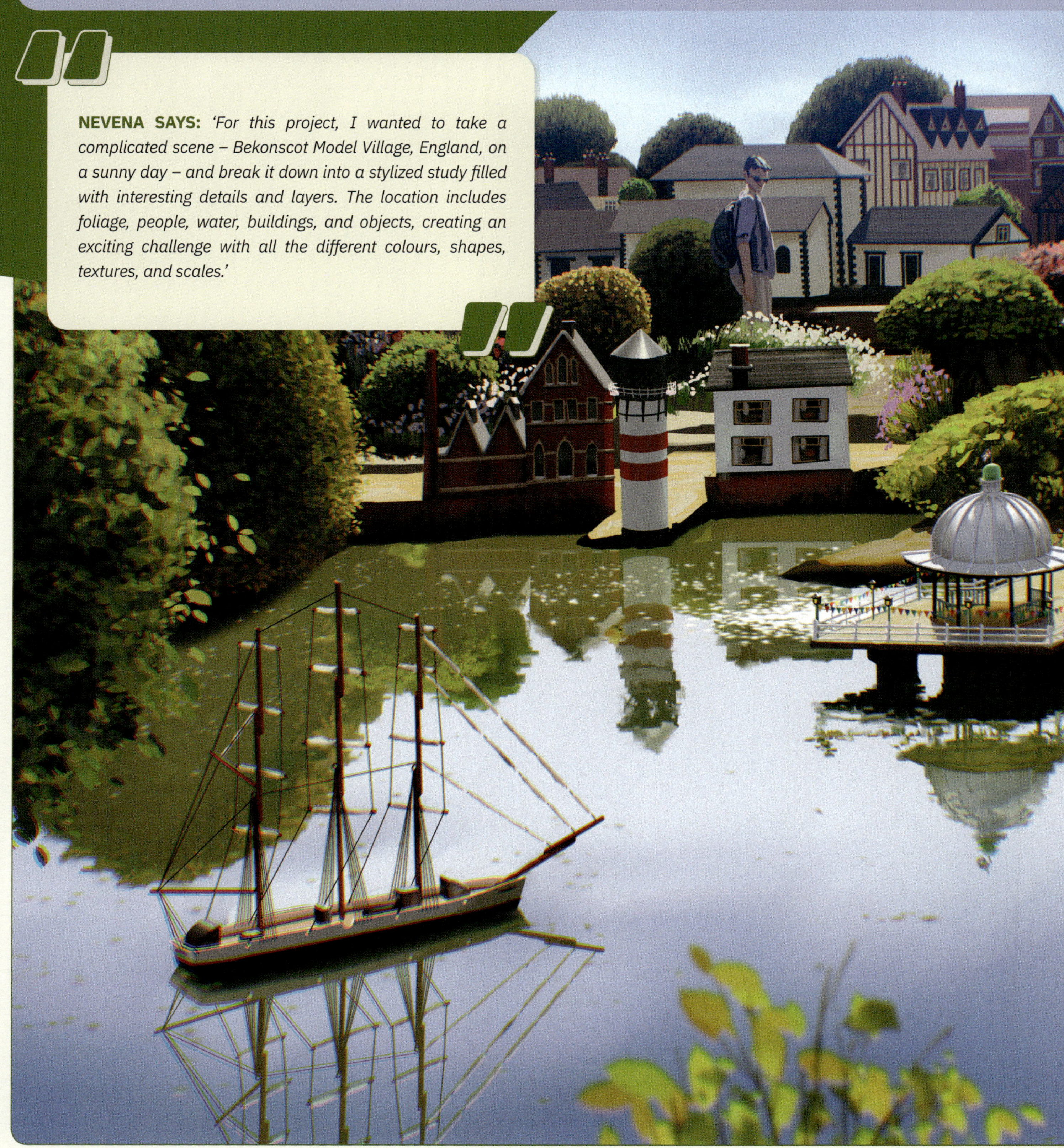

NEVENA SAYS: *'For this project, I wanted to take a complicated scene – Bekonscot Model Village, England, on a sunny day – and break it down into a stylized study filled with interesting details and layers. The location includes foliage, people, water, buildings, and objects, creating an exciting challenge with all the different colours, shapes, textures, and scales.'*

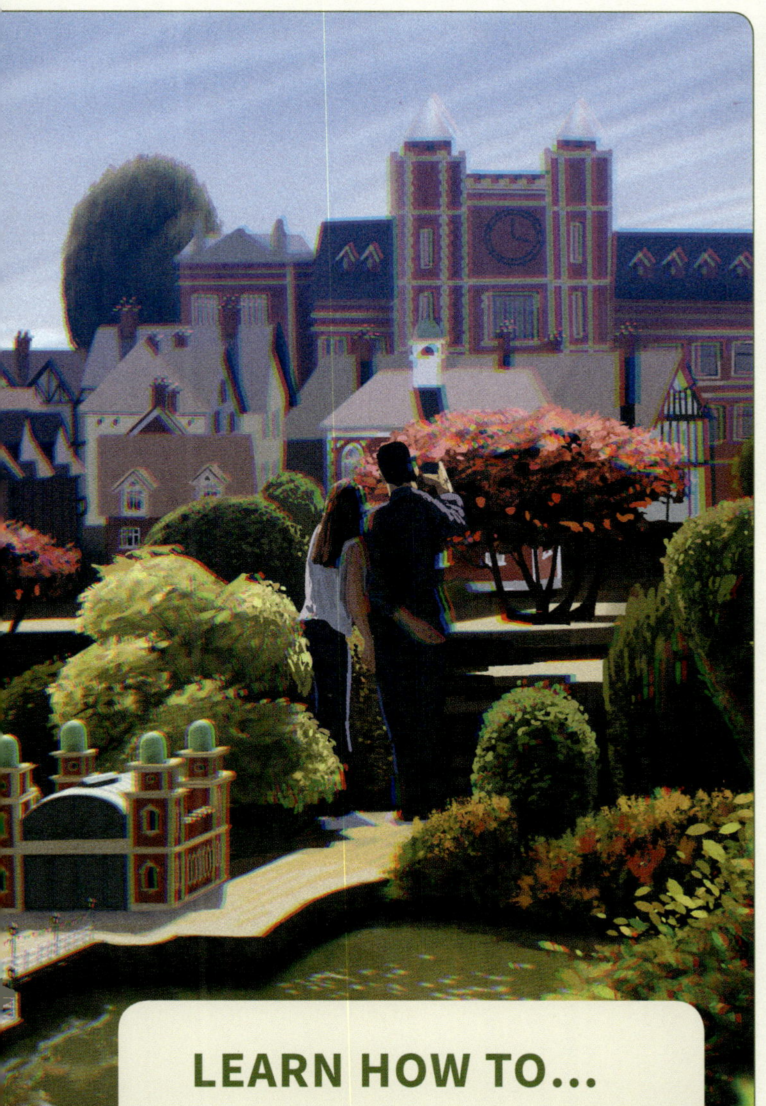

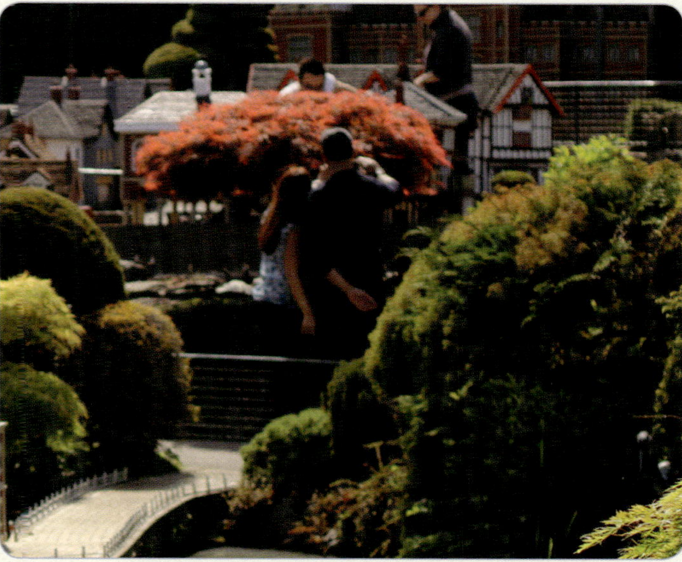

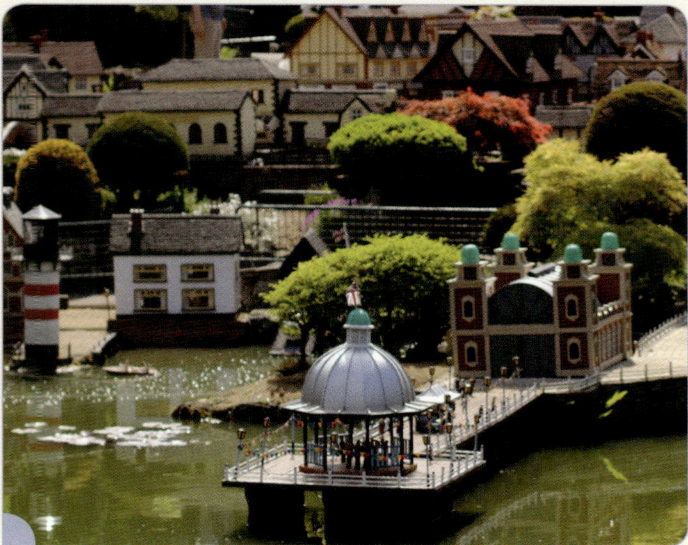

If your time on location is limited, capture as much reference material and soak up as much atmosphere as you can

LEARN HOW TO...

- **Break down a complex scene into an illustration with multiple interesting layers**

- **Have a critical eye for your reference and manipulate it in your image's favour**

- **Balance clean, graphical style with soft, blended edges**

- **Experiment with Procreate brushes to create different textures**

01

First, find a place that you want to paint. This model village would be a great scene to paint, but the narrow paths make it difficult to settle down for a plein-air study without getting in people's way. However, with plenty of reference photos, it will still be possible to capture a strong scene. As you take photos, think of the overall composition of the images to make sure you capture all the information you need.

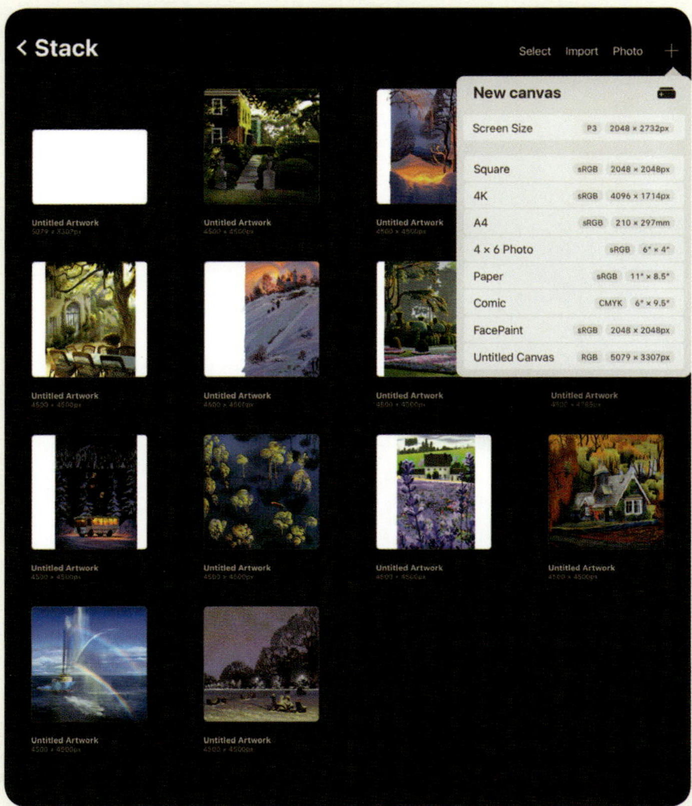

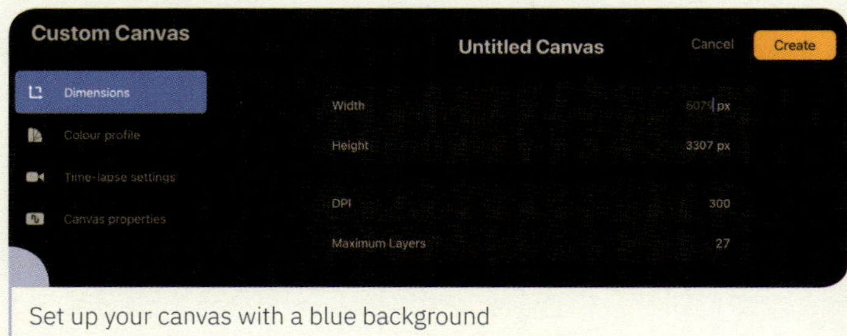

Set up your canvas with a blue background

02

When you are free to start painting, open Procreate and create a canvas around 5,000 pixels wide and 3,300 pixels high, with up to 300 dpi resolution (if possible – the greater the size and dpi of your canvas, the fewer layers you will be able to make). This will create a wide canvas ready for sketching your scene. Change the white background to a sky colour by tapping on the 'Background Colour' layer in the Layers menu and selecting a light blue. In reality the sky is blocked from this low angle by dark foliage, but you can omit that and opt for a clear blue sky to emphasize the bright, sunny day.

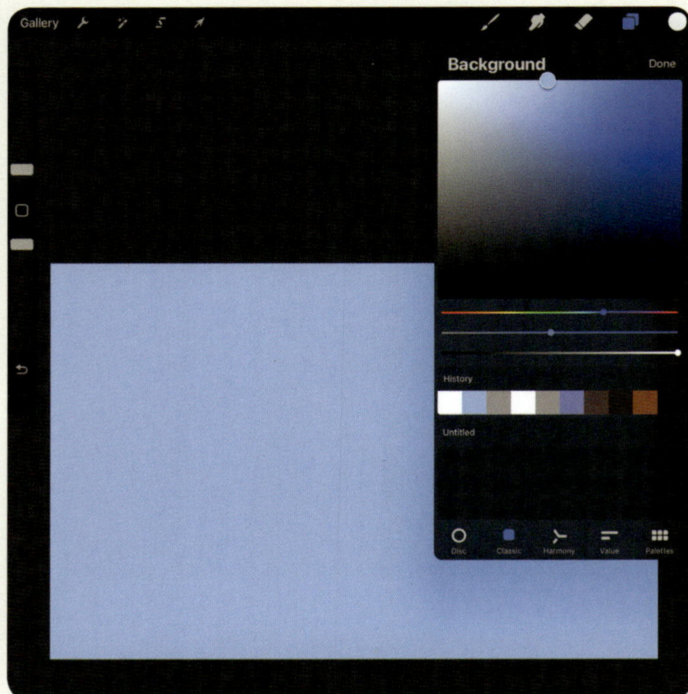

03

To load one of the reference photos you took, go to **ACTIONS > CANVAS** and turn on the Reference option. In the box that appears, tap **IMAGE > IMPORT IMAGE** and find your photos in the gallery. Once the image is imported, you can reposition, resize, and zoom the Reference window just like your canvas. You can close the window by tapping the × in the corner, then reopen it as needed by toggling Reference back on.

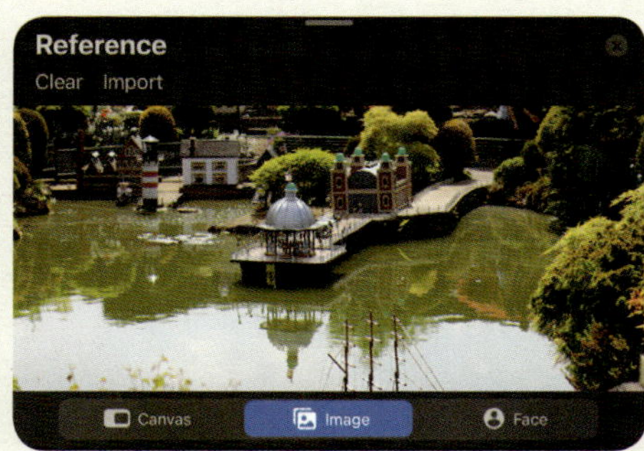

Set up your reference ready for sketching

04

Select a dark colour to sketch with – black will do for now. Open the Brush Library and select **SKETCHING > 6B PENCIL**. Begin loosely sketching the objects you want to include in your scene. As you don't have to rush on location, you can take your time sketching and getting everything in the right place. It helps to keep some elements on different layers, such as the boat, so you can move them around the scene until you are happy with the composition. You can use the Transform options to adjust and resize elements, too.

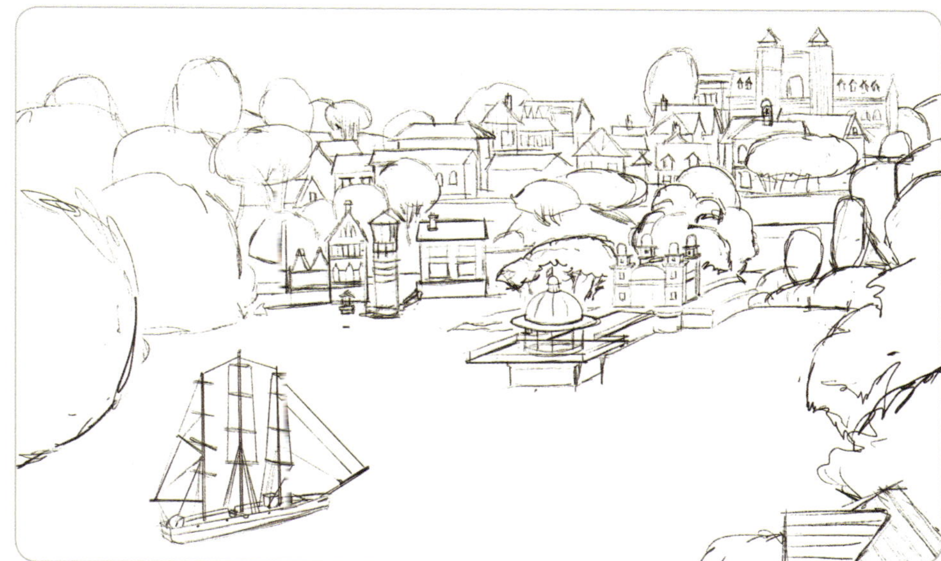

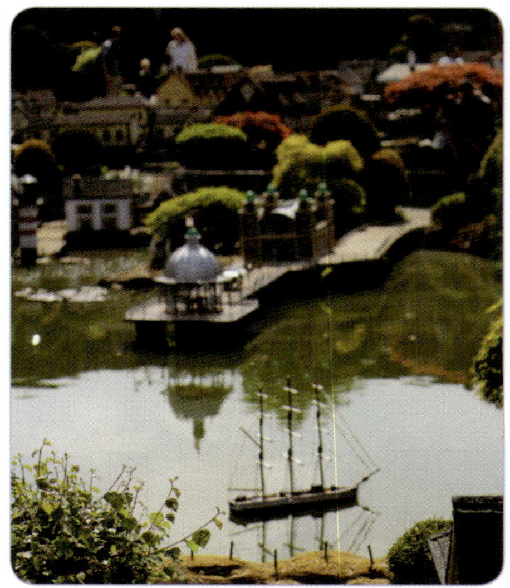

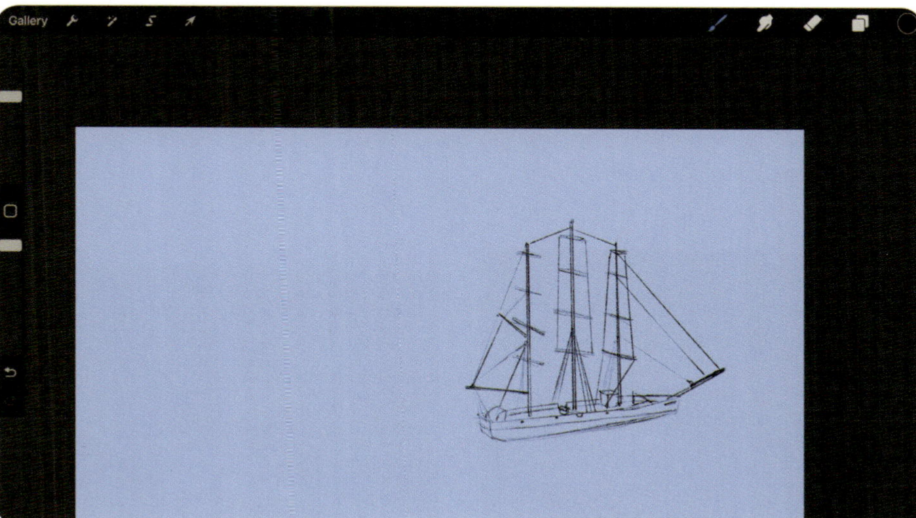

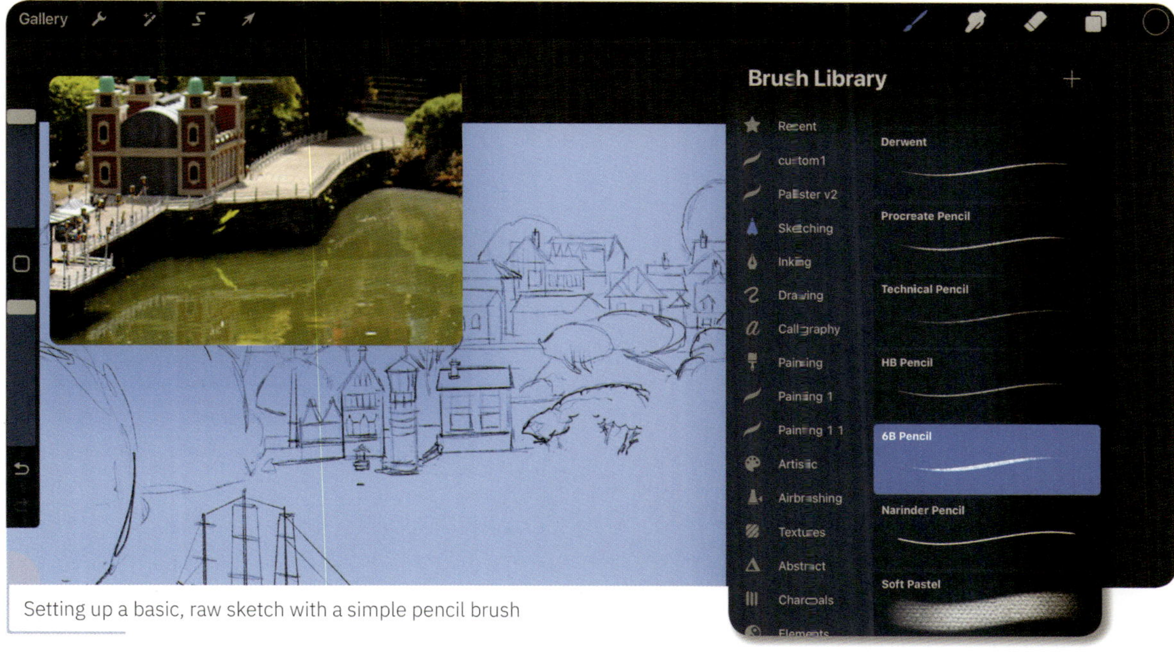

Setting up a basic, raw sketch with a simple pencil brush

05

Tap on the sketch layer in the Layers menu and lower its opacity with the slider, giving you a better view of where you are painting. On a new layer under the sketch, use PAINTING > ROUND BRUSH to begin setting up the basic colours of the sky and pond, as these will help you orientate yourself when choosing other colours later. Add some light cloud textures to the sky and use solid greens and blue-greens to indicate the sky and scenery reflected in the pond below.

You can make your brush even more flat and opaque by tapping on it to open the Brush Studio, going to the Stroke Path tab and lowering the Spacing. You can also go to the Rendering tab and select the Uniformed Glaze option. If you want to revert a brush to default settings, swipe left on it in the Brush Library and tap Reset.

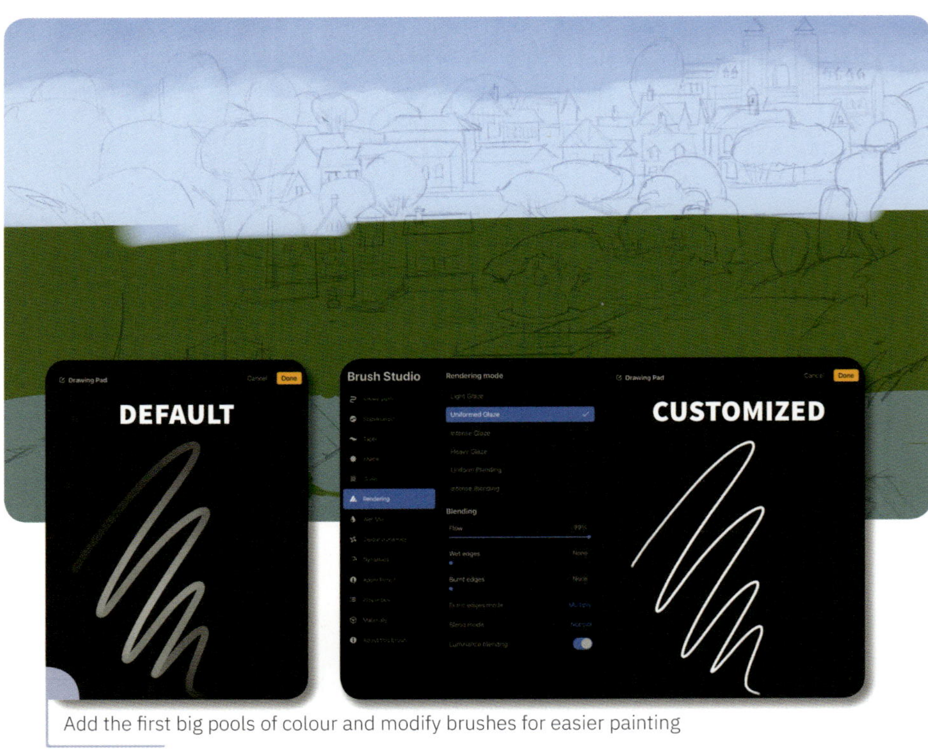

Add the first big pools of colour and modify brushes for easier painting

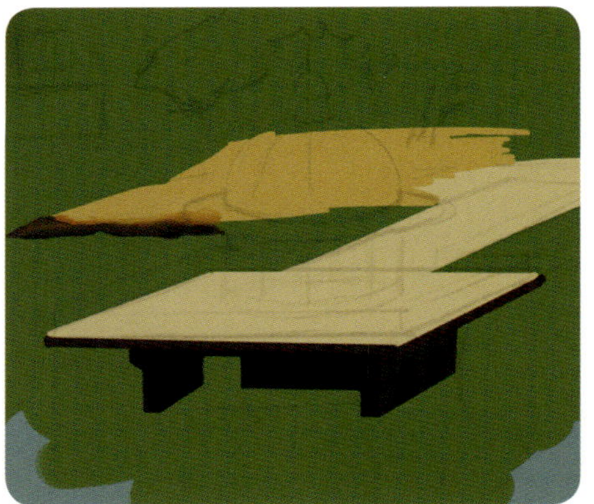

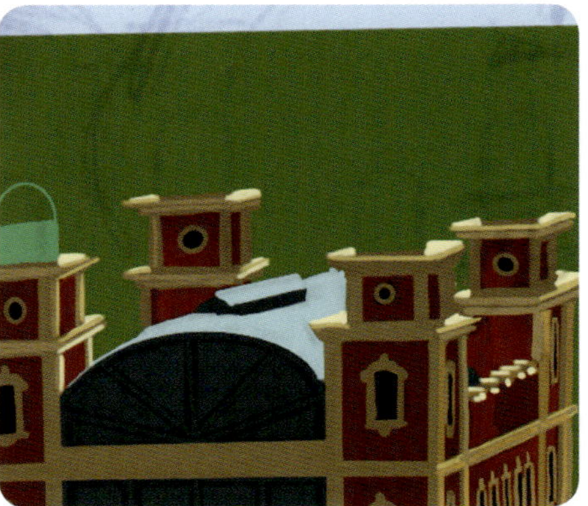

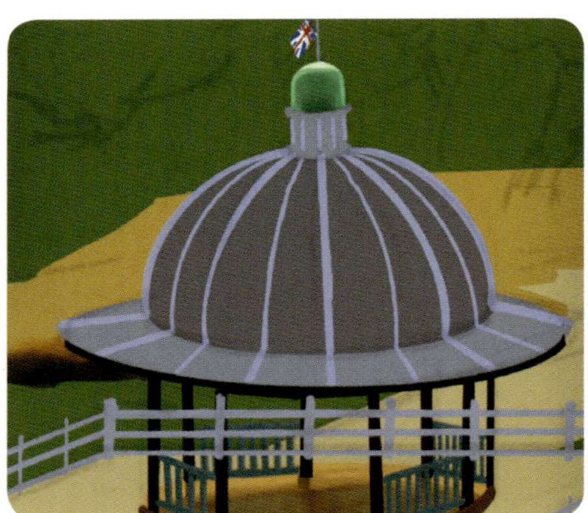

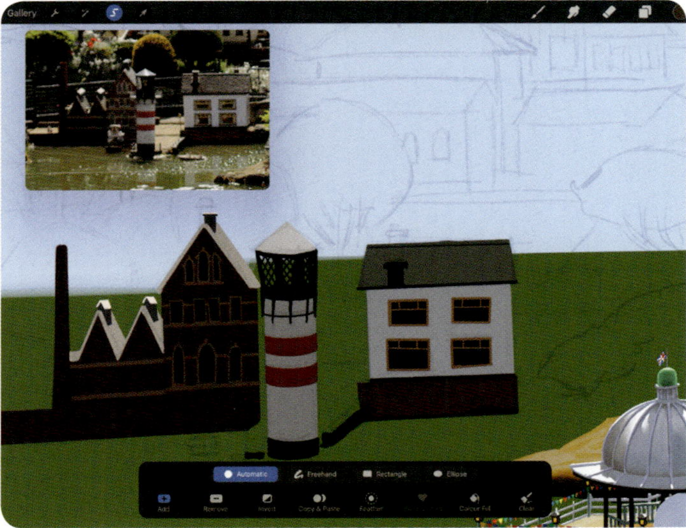

06

Start your painting with the detailed elements in the foreground. You can do this by making flat-colour shapes on new layers, which you can paint over later. Start by outlining and filling in the shapes of the pier and waterside buildings, using basic colours with one or two darker steps of shadow for depth. To make a straight line, draw a stroke, hold your pencil down at the end, and Procreate will straighten it out. You can make smooth ovals and circles using the same method, drawing the rough shape and holding your pen down. This function will help you paint out all of the buildings and small human-made elements in the scene. For now, put each different element on a separate layer.

Block out foreground structures using Procreate's auto-straightening and Transform tools

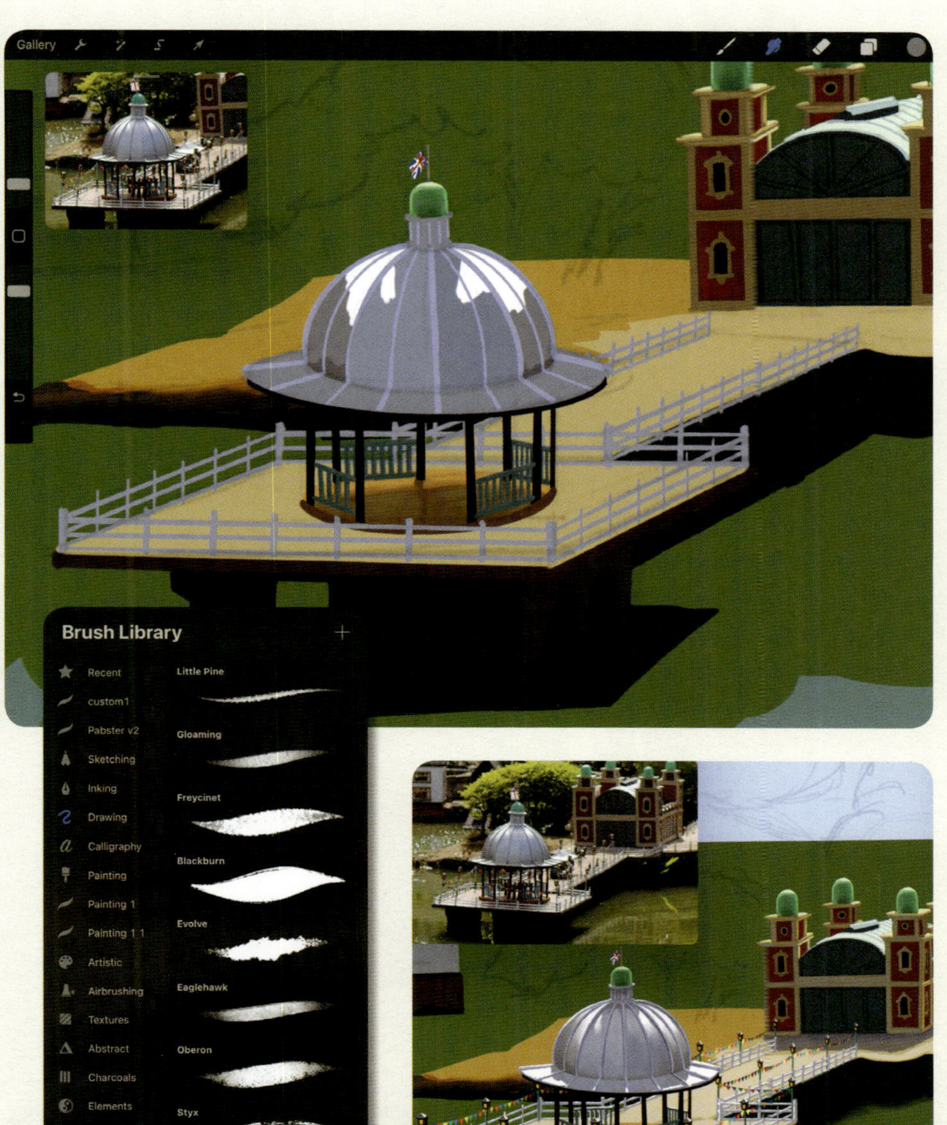

07

Now that you have made some building shapes, lock their opacity by tapping on each layer thumbnail and selecting Alpha Lock. This will enable you to shade each element without colouring outside their shapes. If you have too many layers, start merging the finished ones by pressing a finger on the top and bottom layers and pinching them together in the Layers stack. But be careful which ones you merge! For example, don't merge all the fence and bandstand layers together or you will no longer have independent control over those overlapping elements. Instead, you could merge the front fences into one layer and the back fences into another, keeping the merged bandstand separate in between. If you do need to paint a trickier section within a locked shape, you can use the Selection tool to cordon it off from the rest first.

Start adding a bit more texture to the rooftops, exploring different brushes to see how they work with different objects. Try painting a solid highlight on the bandstand roof and blending it with the Smudge tool set to **DRAWING > MOORILLA** for texture. For the small house in the background, use the **ELEMENTS > DRIVEN SNOW** brush to create a mottled effect, then the **MATERIALS > FINE HAIR** brush to make long strokes that suggest rows of tiles.

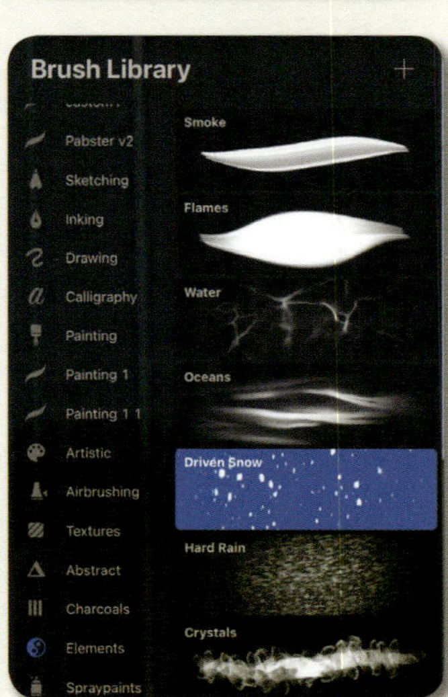

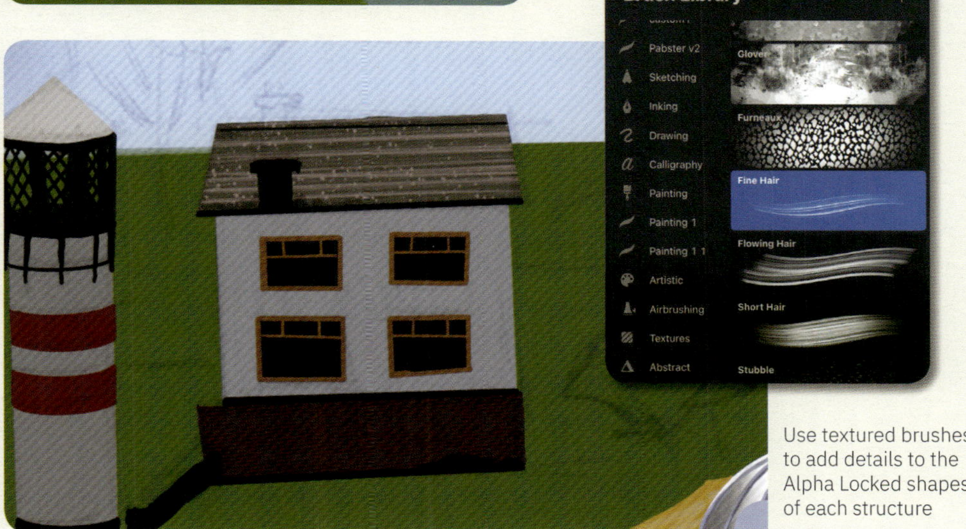

Use textured brushes to add details to the Alpha Locked shapes of each structure

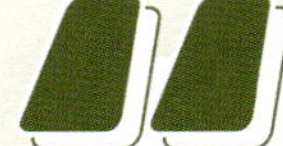

08

Continue using the same opaque brushes and automatic straightening you used in steps 05 and 06 to block out the foreground boat. Keep the colours close to what you can observe in the reference, but clean and simple, with just a bit of Smudge for texture. Keep the elements on separate layers for now, so that it's easy to adjust or correct overlapping parts, such as the masts and ropes.

Once you have done all the boat layers, make a copy of each one and merge them together to create a copy of the whole boat. Use TRANSFORM > FLIP VERTICAL to flip the duplicate boat upside down, creating the reflection below. This flipped version will need some extra painting, since the water should be reflecting a bottom view of the objects. So, on a new layer between the mirrored boats, repaint the reflection's hull to make it more believable. Keep these reflection elements on separate layers with no colour modification for now.

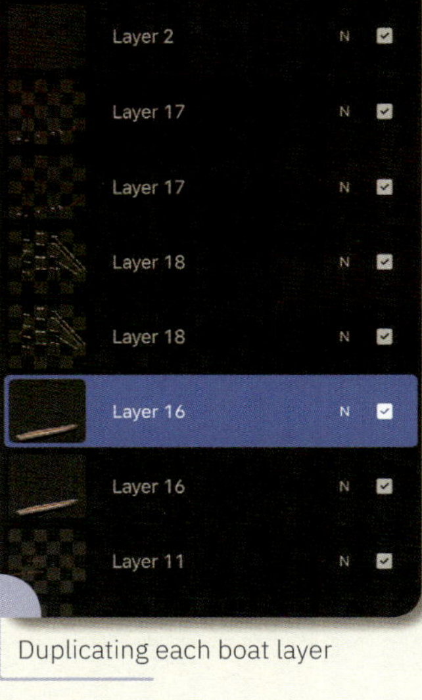

Duplicating each boat layer

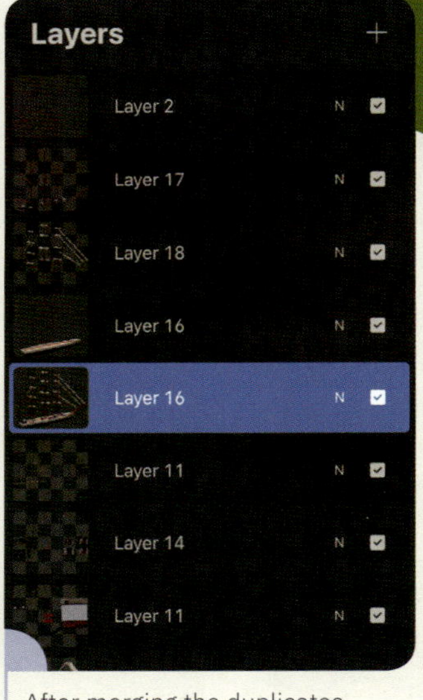

After merging the duplicates

Block out the boat and mirror a duplicate to create a reflection

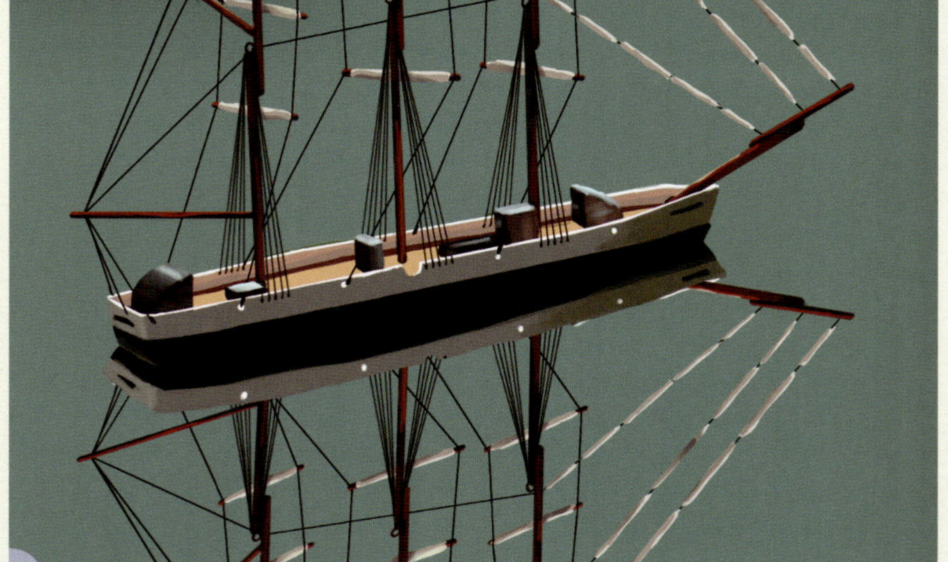

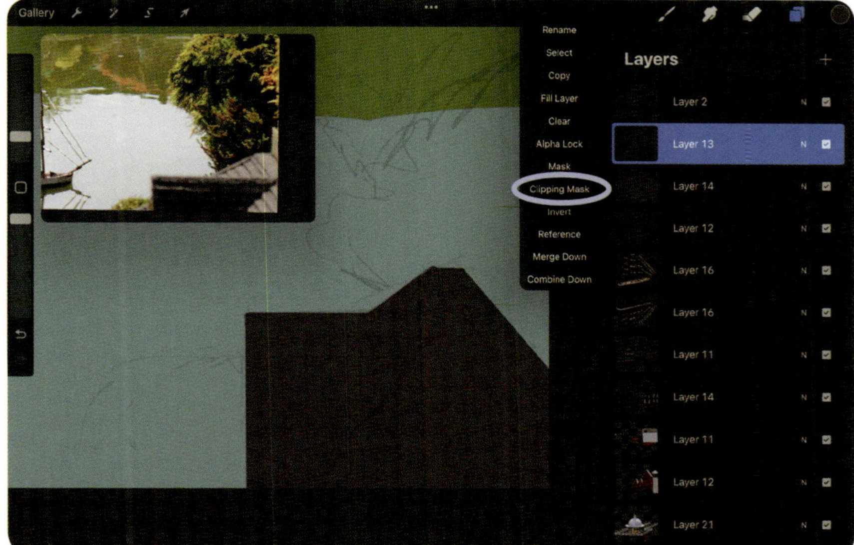

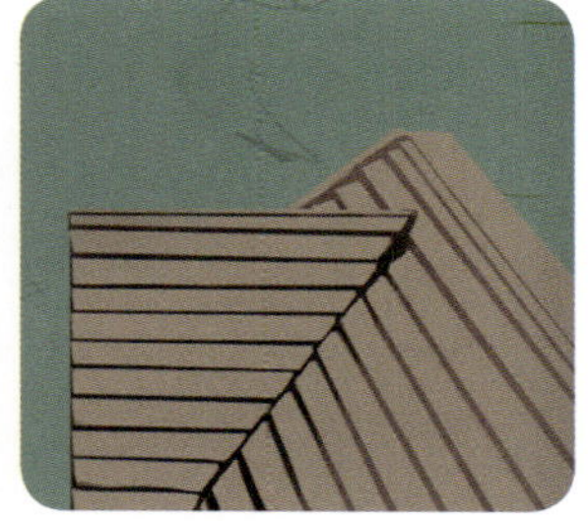

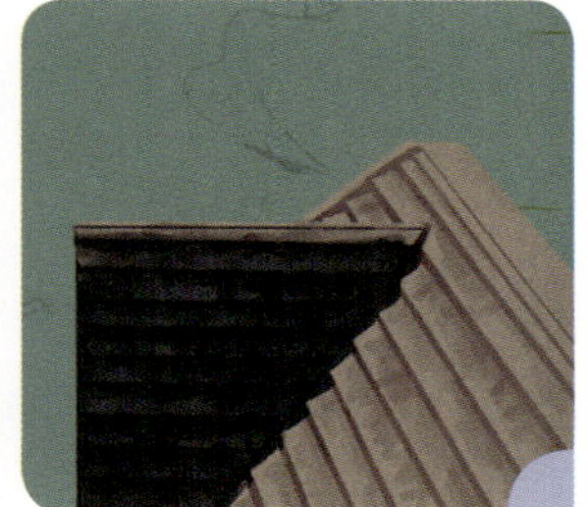

Paint the closest roof using a clipping mask above its base shape, then merge when complete

09

When you have finished roughly painting the main foreground buildings and boat, you can start painting the base shapes for all the other elements, such as trees, building walls, and roofs. Do this with the same technique used so far: create a flat base, use Alpha Lock or Clipping Mask to colour inside that shape, and merge the finished results to save layer capacity.

Fill all your shapes with an approximate raw colour for now. Some elements can have two colours, such as the roofs and walls, but for now keep the elements flat and focus on layer arrangement and building up the scene as a whole. Naming the layers will help as the scene becomes more complex; do this by tapping on them in the Layers menu and selecting Rename.

At this stage, aim to have the three finished foreground buildings merged into their own layers. The roof of the closest building (above) can also be merged into a single layer once it is sufficiently lit and detailed. The walls and roofs of the background buildings, a few different groups of trees, the boat, and the boat's reflection are intact on their own layers.

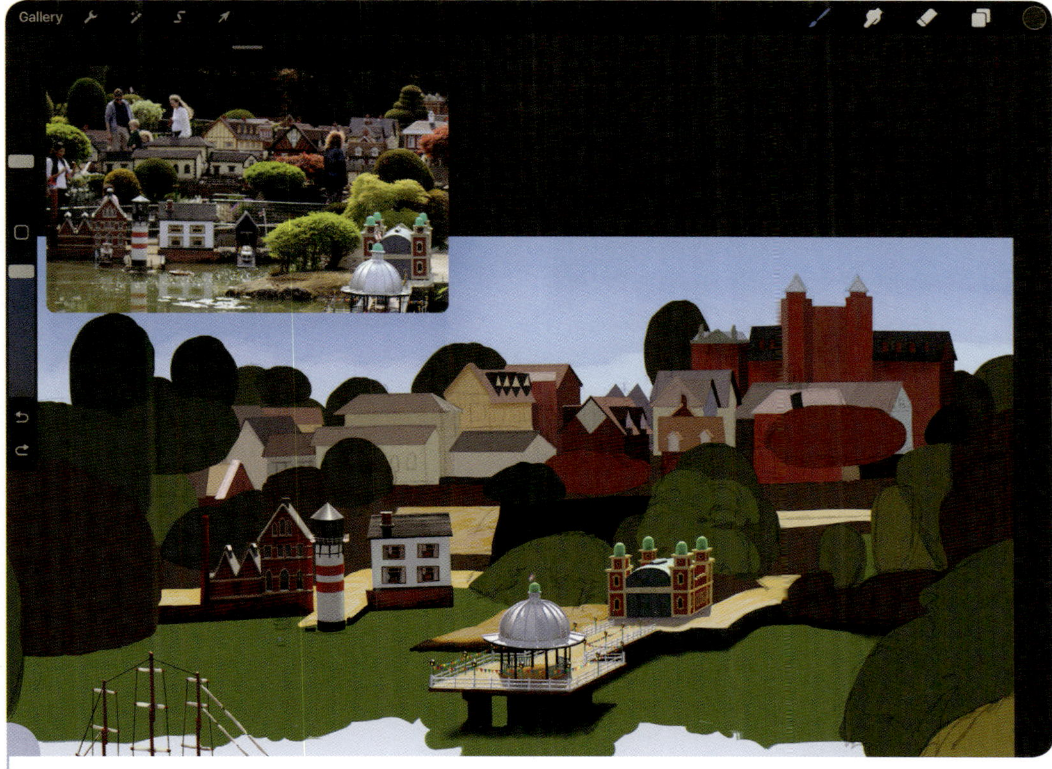

Build up the rest of the scene as a whole, including blocking out the trees and background town

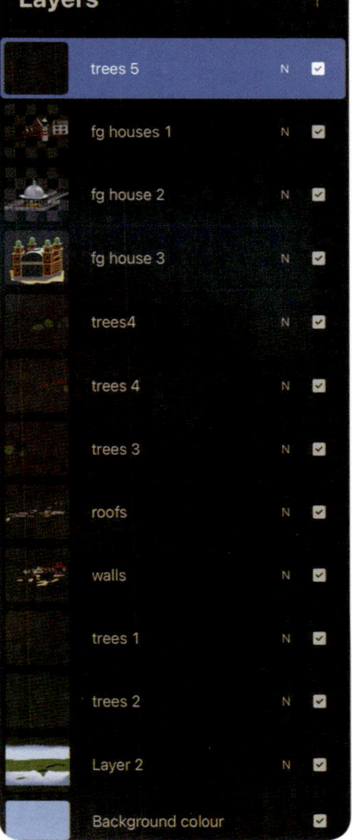

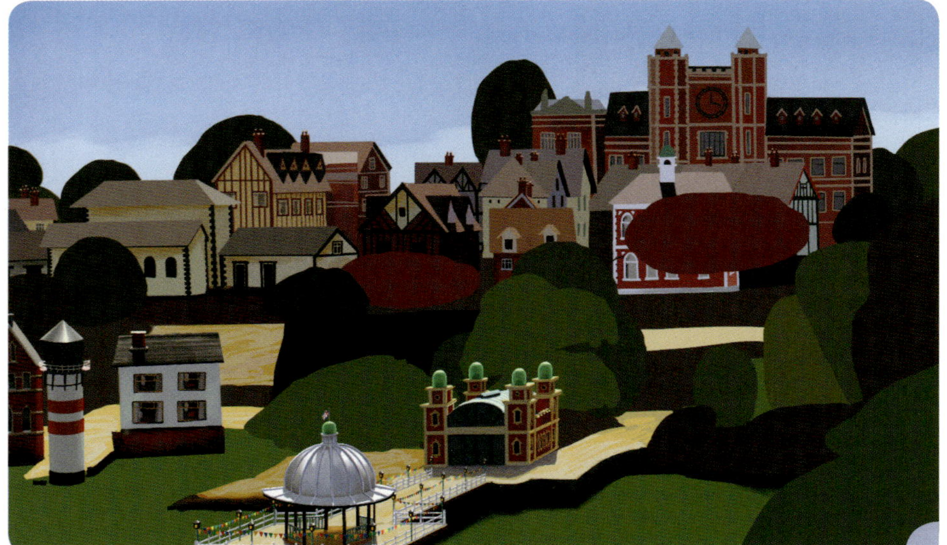
Detail the background buildings

10

Make new layers for details on the walls (windows, trims, and pillars) and details on the roofs (chimneys, trims, and lines) separately. Draw those details in with a small opaque brush. Some elements may have to be on the same layer even if they are not in the same category or area, such as some of the background trees, just to keep a manageable file without too many layers. However, always try to think ahead to how you will select and shade elements, so that silhouettes are separate where you need them to be.

11

Explore the Brush Library and experiment with different textured brushes on the tree shapes in order to add basic shadow and light colours. ORGANIC > SNOW GUM and ARTISTIC > AURORA are good options to use here. Alpha Lock the tree layers beforehand and start painting leaves on them with different shades to suggest shadows and sunny highlights, following the colours and hues in the reference. The foreground trees should have more leaves poking out of their main shapes, which you can do by turning off Alpha Lock. Shade the background trees with smaller leaves and the foreground ones with larger, chunkier leaves, until all the trees are shaded.

When you find a brush you like, go to the Recent tab in the Brush Library, swipe left on the brush, and tap Pin. This will add a star icon to the brush and pin it to the top of your Recent tab, which helps you switch quickly between different favourite brushes when making variations in the trees and other surfaces.

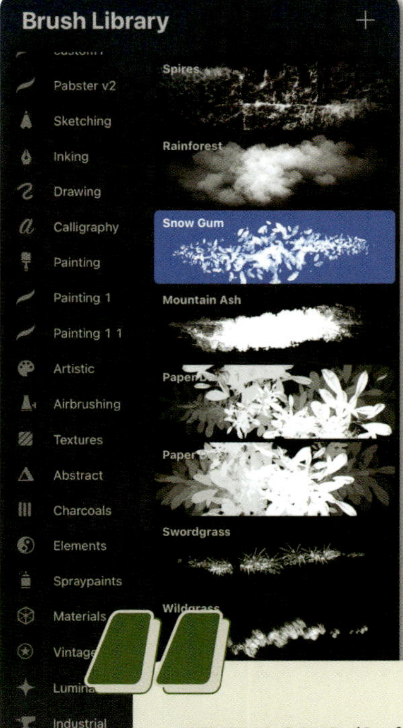

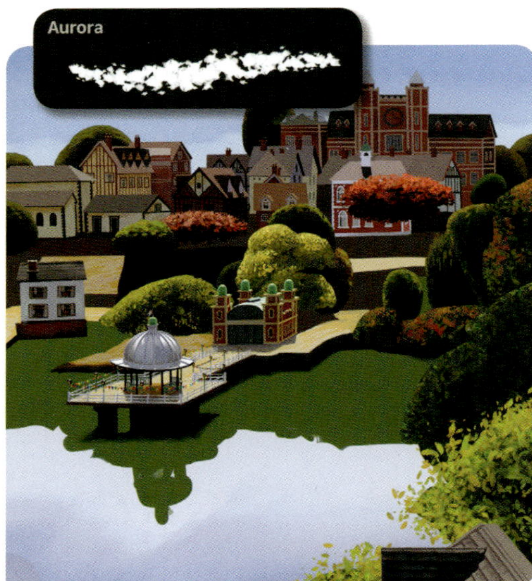

Add leafy textures to the trees

NEVENA SAYS: *'So far you have used the basic but most important tools that you need to create any image. Mastering the usage and order of these tools takes practice. An image like this one, with lots of repeated elements, is a great opportunity for that. Even if the steps are simple, building the basic light in a scene can be difficult. If you don't like your progress, you don't have to delete or undo everything you have done. You can simply duplicate the file you are working on and try painting over the layers, so that you can easily compare techniques and outcomes. Do this by tapping Select on the top right of Procreate's file gallery view, selecting the file you want to copy, and tapping Duplicate to make a spare.'*

12

Make your way across the scene, making a duplicate of each element above the water and mirroring it with **TRANSFORM > FLIP VERTICAL**. Just as it did with the boat, the water is reflecting these from below – you can't just flip the layers to create a realistic reflection. Use the Selection and Transform tools to adjust the reflections until they match the reference better, and use brushes to paint elements that are not visible from above, like the undersides of floating objects. Do this for all the buildings, trees, and other objects reflected along the waterside.

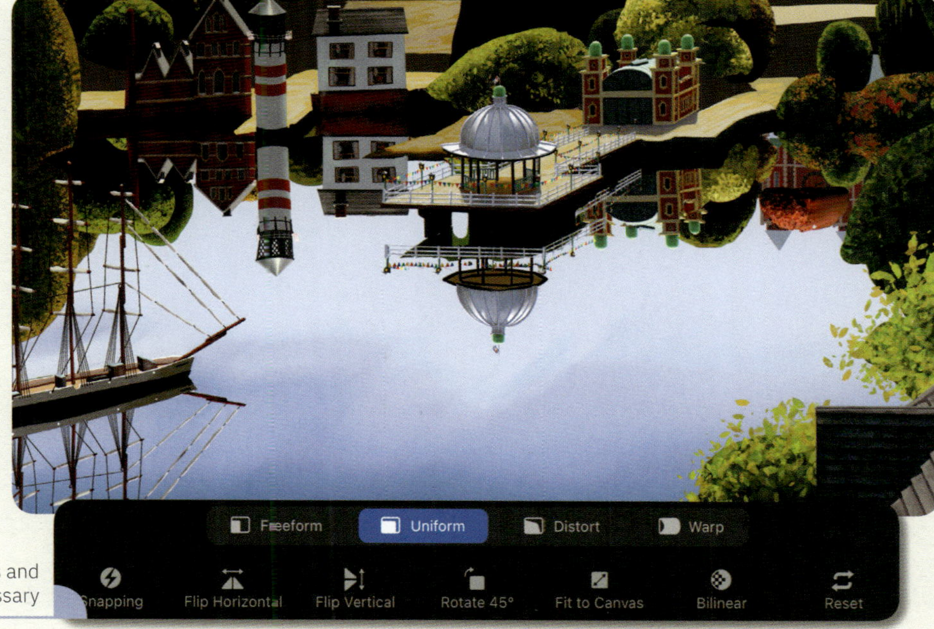

Mirror the other waterside objects and repaint them where necessary

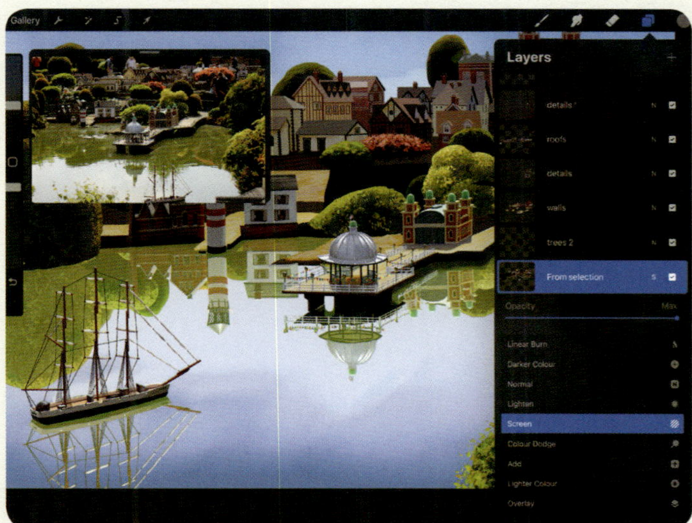

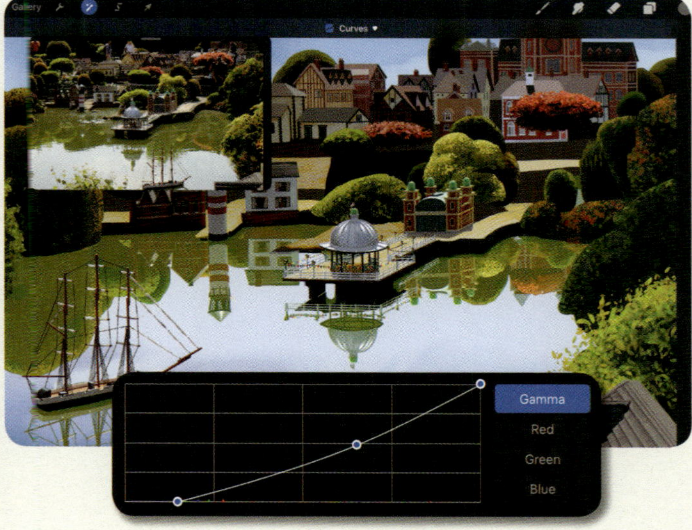

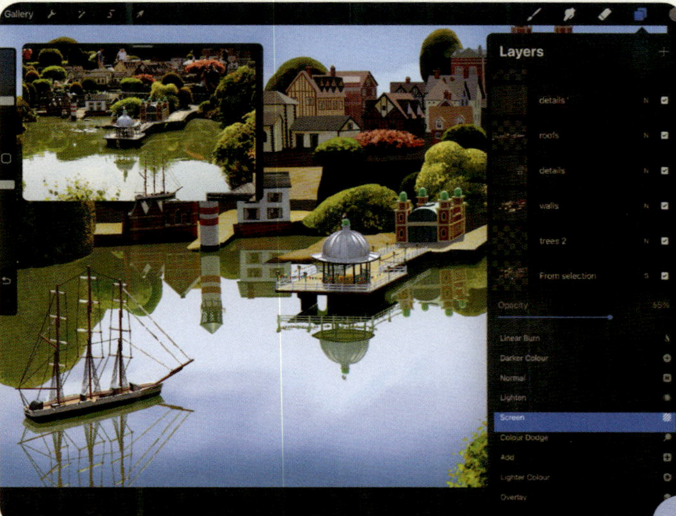

Colour-correcting the reflection for a more realistic look

13

Merge all the reflected objects into one layer and make a selection of them by tapping on the layer icon and tapping Select. Invert that selection by tapping Invert in the Selection menu at the bottom, so that everything around the reflection is active instead. Now go to the pond layer and paint in the reflected sky with a soft airbrush – keep the water green but create some variation. Return to the reflection layer in the Layers menu and set it to Screen mode to make the reflection lighter and translucent. Next, use **ADJUSTMENTS > CURVES** and **ADJUSTMENTS > HUE, SATURATION, BRIGHTNESS** to reduce the layer's gamma and saturation. Finally, lower the layer's opacity to around 65% in the Layers menu.

14

Make a selection of your reflection again by tapping in the layer stack and choosing Select. Go to the water layer and tap ACTIONS > ADD > COPY and then PASTE to make a new layer in the shape of your original selection. If you hide the reflected buildings, you will see the new pasted layer is a water-coloured silhouette of them. Make this new layer darker and desaturated using ADJUSTMENTS > HUE, SATURATION, BRIGHTNESS, and play with the opacity until the main colours and values are close to the ones in the reference. When you are happy with them, merge all your reflections and water into one layer, then swipe left in the Layers menu to make a duplicate of that layer.

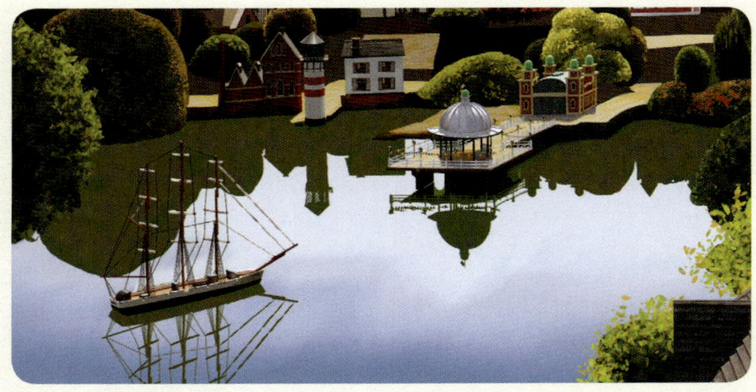

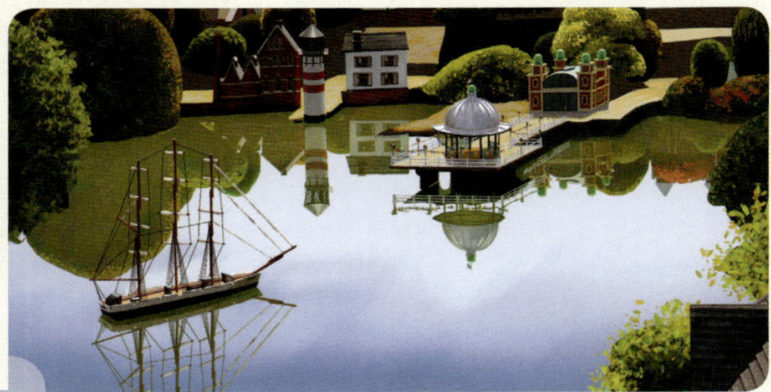

Create a silhouette of the reflected scenery for easy colour adjustment

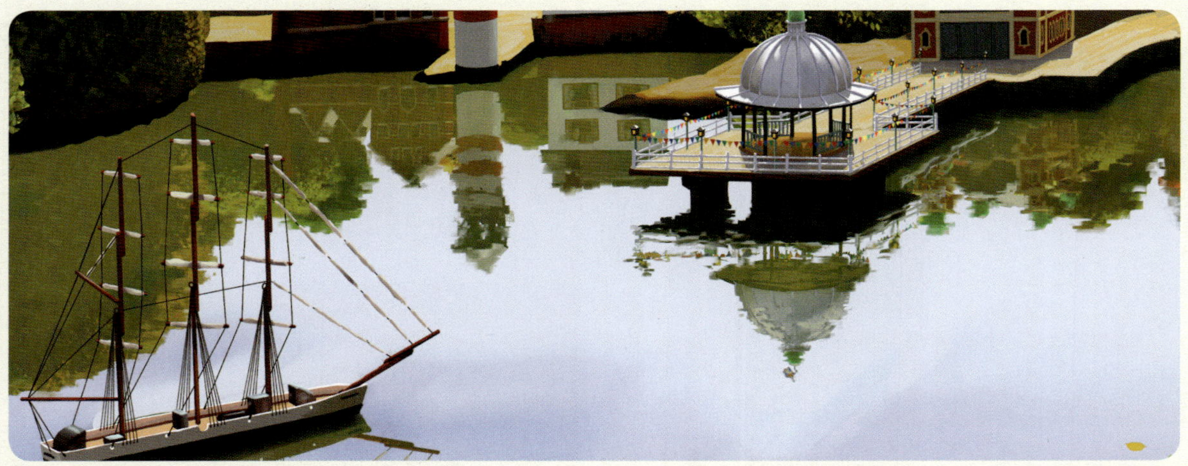

15

Select the Smudge tool at the upper right of your screen. Set it to PAINTING > FLAT BRUSH and tap on the brush to modify it in the Brush Studio. Under the Shape tab, lower the rotation of the brush to 0%, then hit Done. This angular brush will help you make the reflection more realistic by smudging horizontally across the merged layer you just made. The duplicate you created is a backup, since smudging requires a lot of experimentation – you need to keep a spare copy! Carefully smudge the reflected scene, but do not overdo it. You can see in the reference that the reflections are quite clear the closer they are to their source object, but they become more distorted the further they go into the pond.

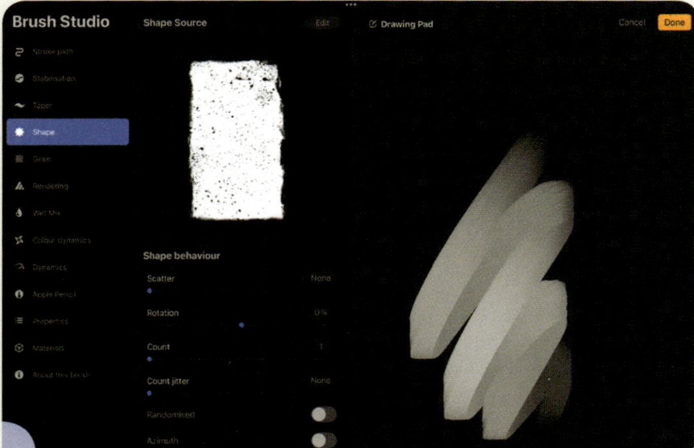

Use a customized Smudge tool to create distorted reflections

16

After smudging your reflected scene where needed, make a new layer above it, and select the LUMINANCE > GLIMMER brush. Tap on it to open the Brush Studio and select the Shape tab again. Grab one of the blue nodes on the Brush Roundness diagram and drag it closer to the centre, until the results in the drawing pad on the right become more flattened. Click Done and choose a very light yellow-white colour to paint with. Paint with your edited brush on the new layer to create the small blooming reflections in the water, where tiny ripples are catching the light near the central pier.

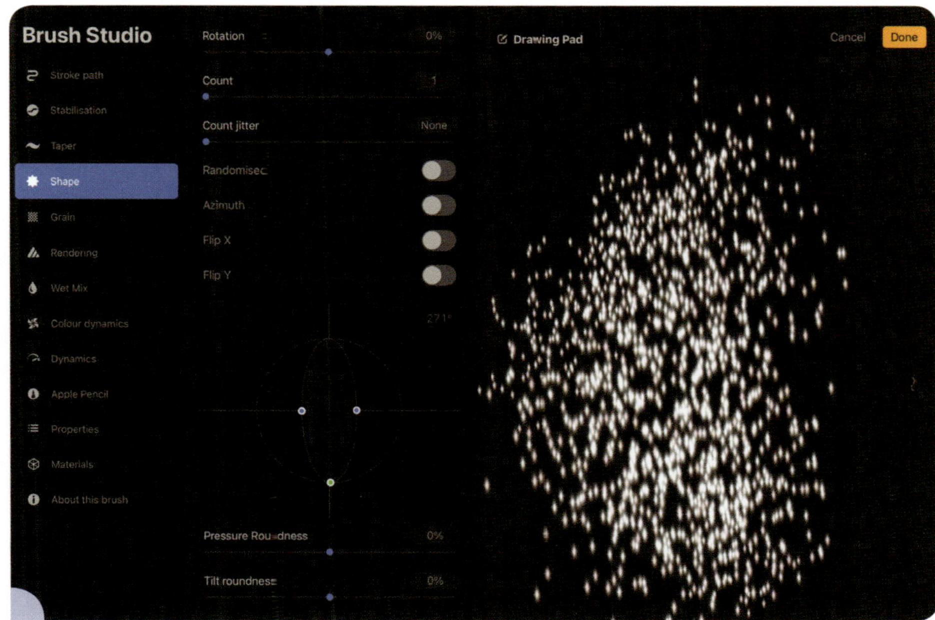

Use a customized Glimmer brush to capture tiny glints of light on the water

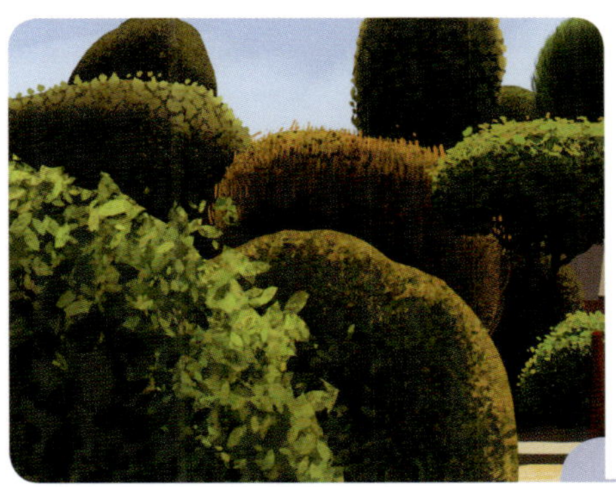

Experiment with different brushes for detailing the trees

17

Go to the Brush Library and start exploring the Materials, Inking, and Drawing tabs for brushes that will help define your trees. Brushes such as MATERIALS > FURNEAUX, INKING > SYRUP, and DRAWING > STYX are good choices for making your trees more interesting. Use them to create texture variation that will separate your trees and make them look richer, but explore other options, too. Exploration and experimentation are key in having fun and developing your skills, and subjects such as trees are perfect for this.

18

Without the tourists for comparison, the buildings currently resemble a full-sized picturesque town. You can heighten this feeling of depth and scale by adding perspective fog to suggest greater distance. Make a new layer at the top of the stack and use a soft brush to paint a dark blue gradient over the tops of the background elements. Move that layer behind the foreground buildings. It will cover the sky, so cut the sky out again by selecting the different layers at the back, inverting the selection to highlight outside the objects instead, and erasing around them to uncover the sky. Finally, set the gradient layer to Screen mode.

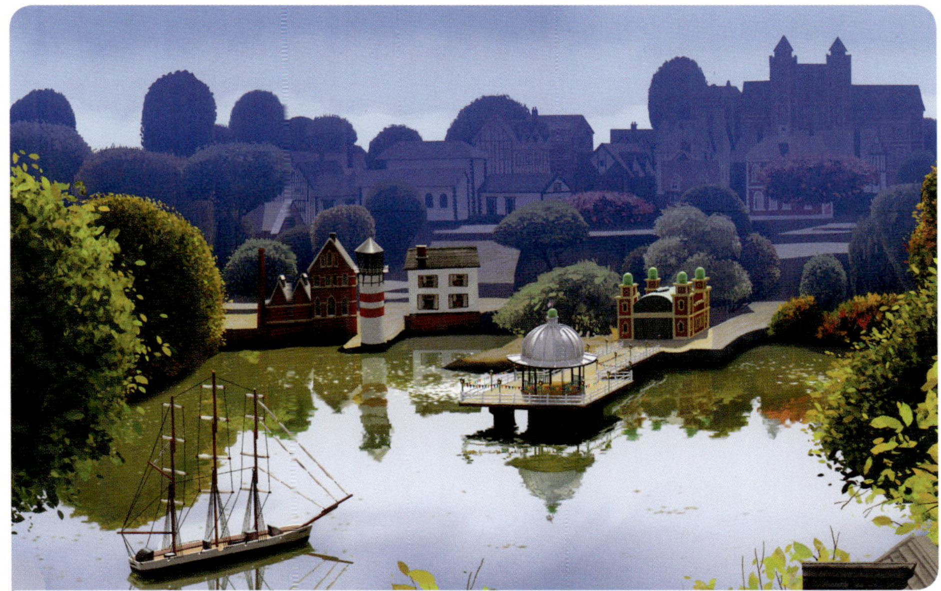

Add perspective fog to modify the image into something more than a study

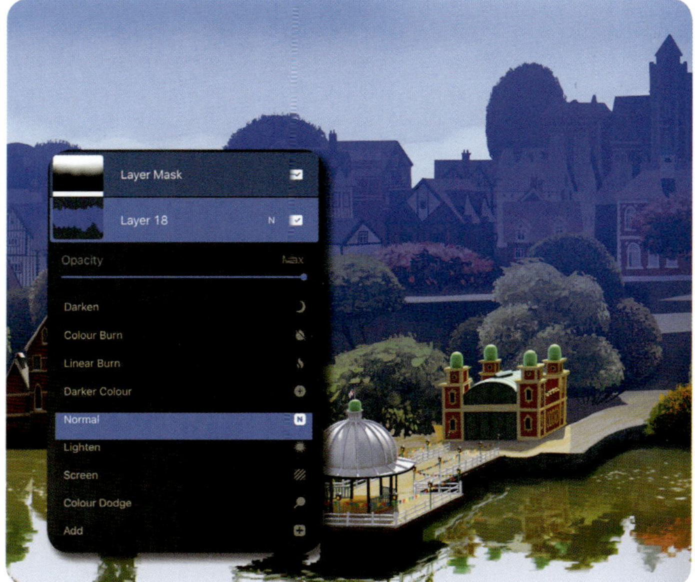

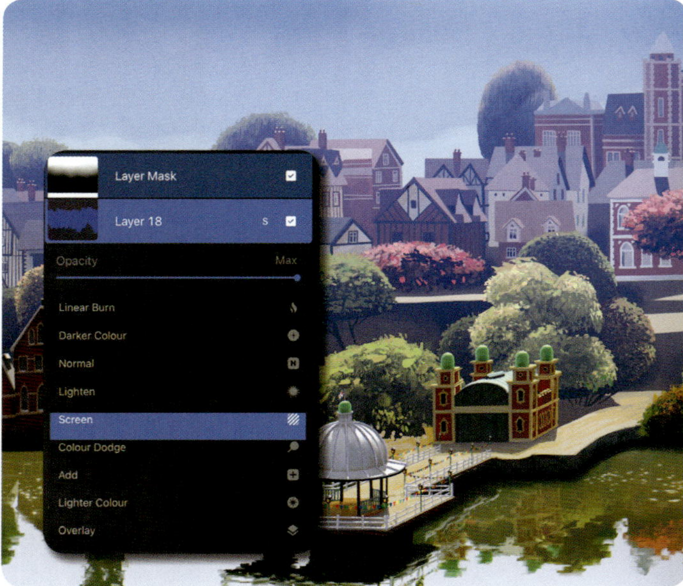

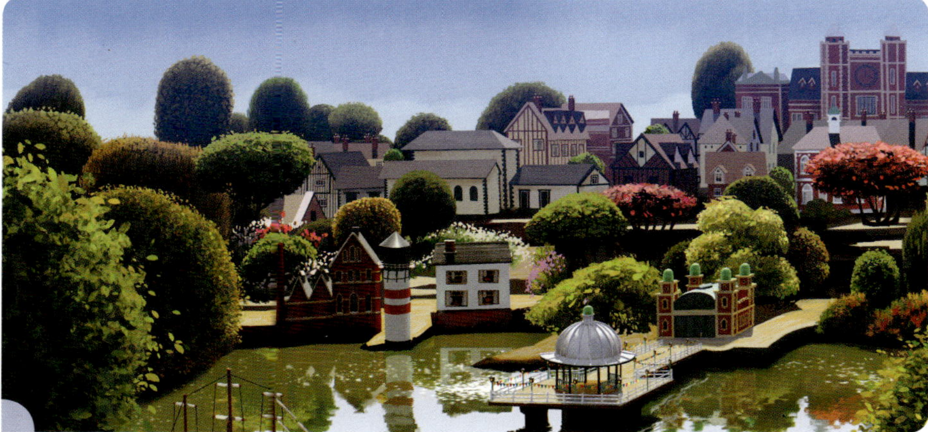

Adjust the fog with a mask to make it more subtle and realistic

19

Tap the gradient layer's icon in the Layers menu and select Mask. This will help you make better transitions and cut out areas where you don't want the gradient to affect the scene. Paint in the mask with black to non-destructively 'erase' the gradient, or with white to reveal it again, so the nearer trees and buildings emerge from the fog more naturally. Lower the gradient layer's opacity and even try experimenting with the shade of blue to make a more natural fog. The result should be subtle but slightly heightened compared to reality.

20

At the very front of the foreground, you can add big, exaggerated leaves to emphasize the perspective even more. Even if this is not totally realistic, it will enhance the scene's depth and create more variation in the image. To do this, add a new layer on top and paint some larger leaf shapes on the closest trees. You can continue using the large brushes you have used for foliage, such as **INKING > SYRUP**; using a mix of different brushes will make the results more interesting. You can also make freehand selections with the Selection tool and fill them with colour. Use the **SKETCHING > 6B PENCIL** brush to add a few branches connecting the leaves.

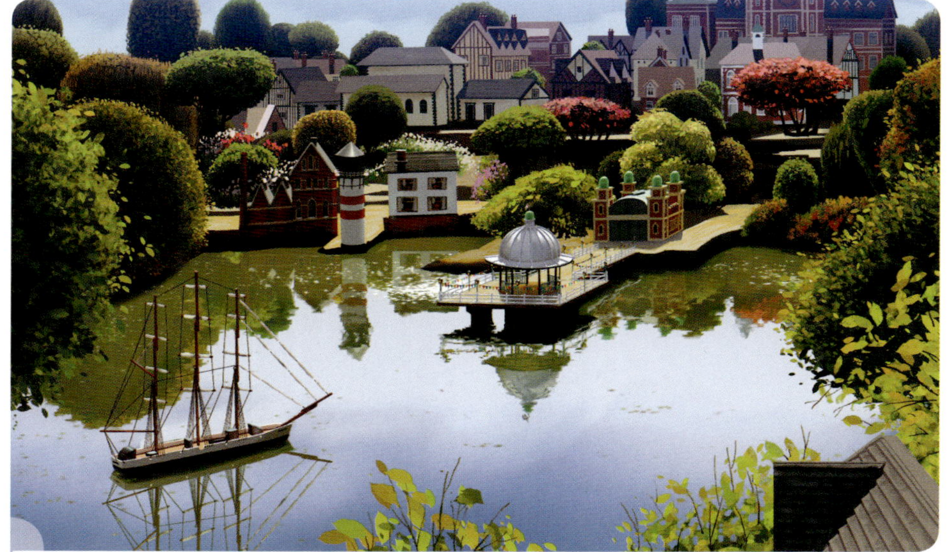

Enhance the depth and composition with some oversized foreground leaves

21

So far you haven't added any new details to the sky. Creating some light clouds and contrails will make it much more believable. Make a new layer and select a very light blue colour, almost white. Paint some vertical and diagonal lines in the sky with a soft brush, then go to ADJUSTMENTS > MOTION BLUR and drag across the canvas to modify the slider until you have a smudged, cloudy effect. You may need to erase parts of the lines with a soft brush to create variation and give them a more realistic look. Use TRANSFORM > DISTORT to stretch and squash the lines into believable contrail shapes.

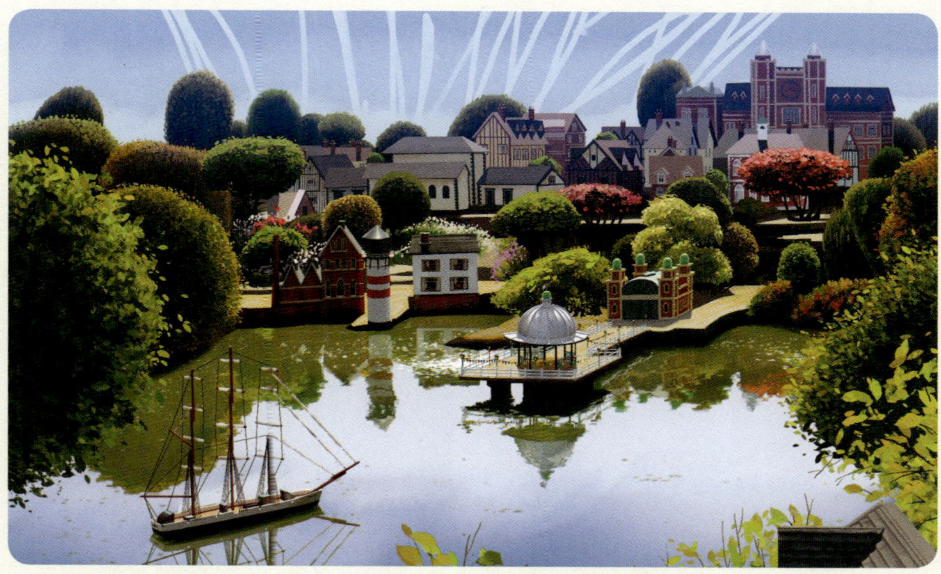

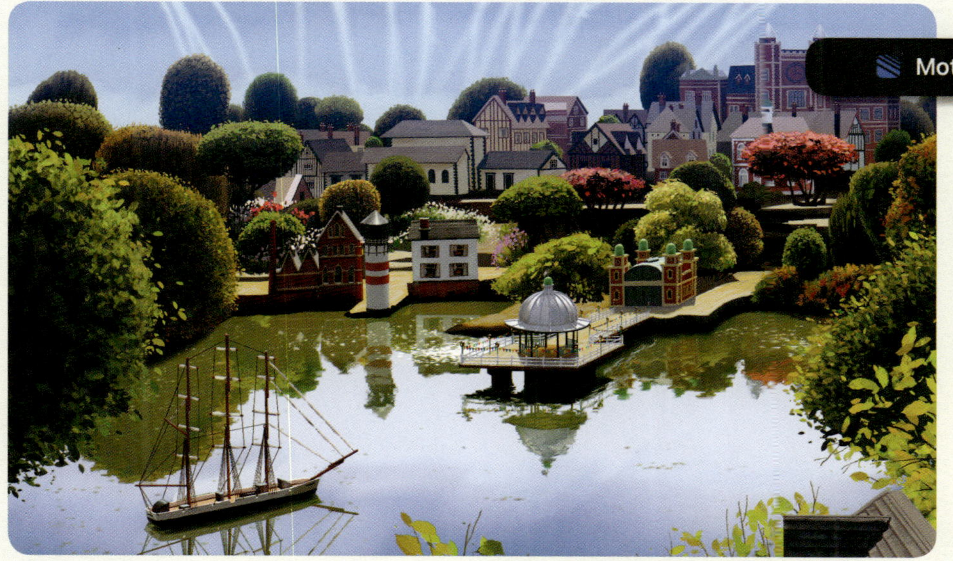

NEVENA SAYS: *'This image is now at a very developed stage. Some details have been kept deliberately unpainted, such as some of the fences, so they don't clutter the scene. Building a reflection can be complicated and take many steps, but it gives the image a very special, immersive feeling. Exploring more brushes and tools has enabled you to create different textures and materials that you can use as a skill in any project you work on. Experimentation is so important when painting, so don't let any mistake get your spirits down – count those as experiments!'*

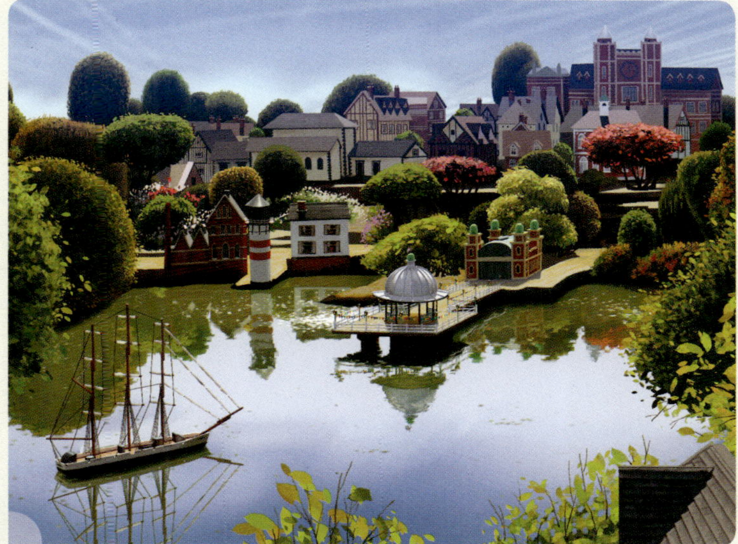

Add realism to the sky by adding cloudy plane trails

22

Use **ORGANIC > TWIG BRUSH** to add some flowers and small bushes around the pathways between the houses. Switching to the **INKING > SYRUP** brush will add more colour variation in the flowers, since it has a colour jitter element. To clean up the paths next, tap on the Syrup brush to open the Brush Studio. Go the Shape tab so you can edit the Shape Source. Import 'Calligraphy 1' from the Source Library as the new Shape Source, then use this new Syrup brush to shape up the pathways and add stems to the trees where needed.

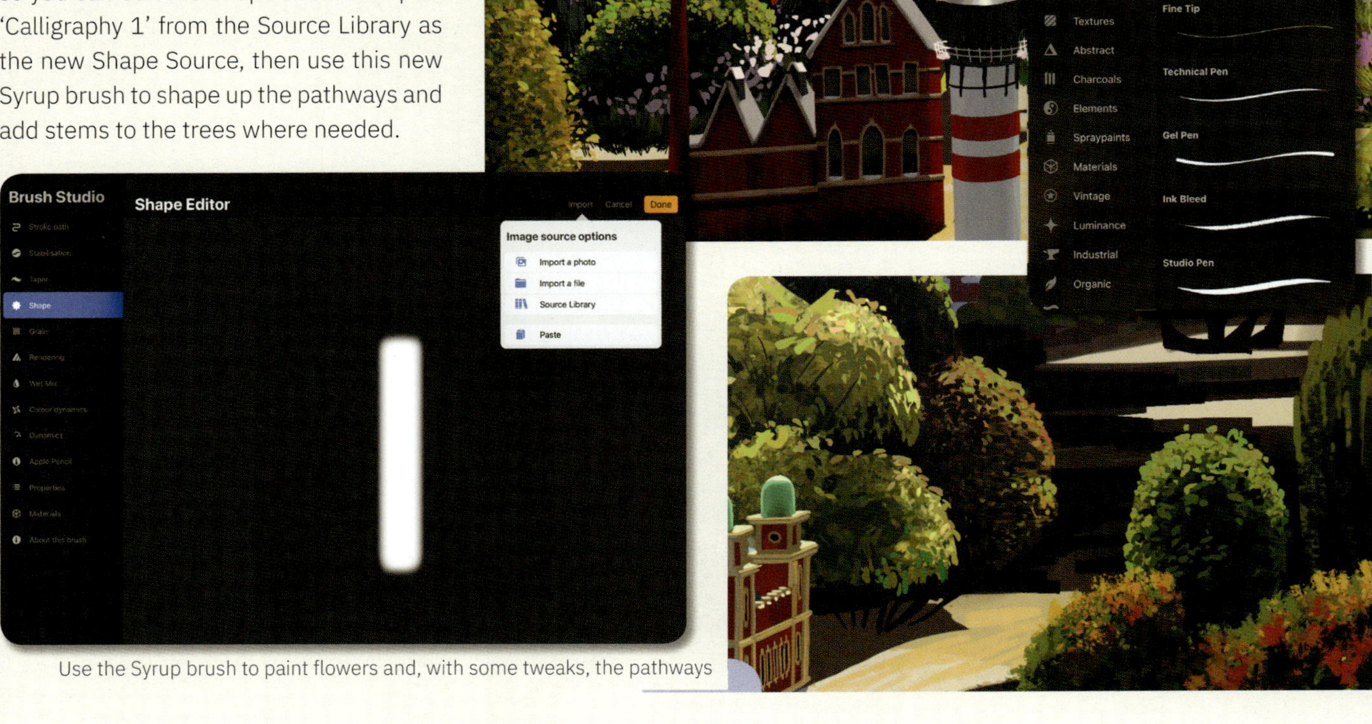

Use the Syrup brush to paint flowers and, with some tweaks, the pathways

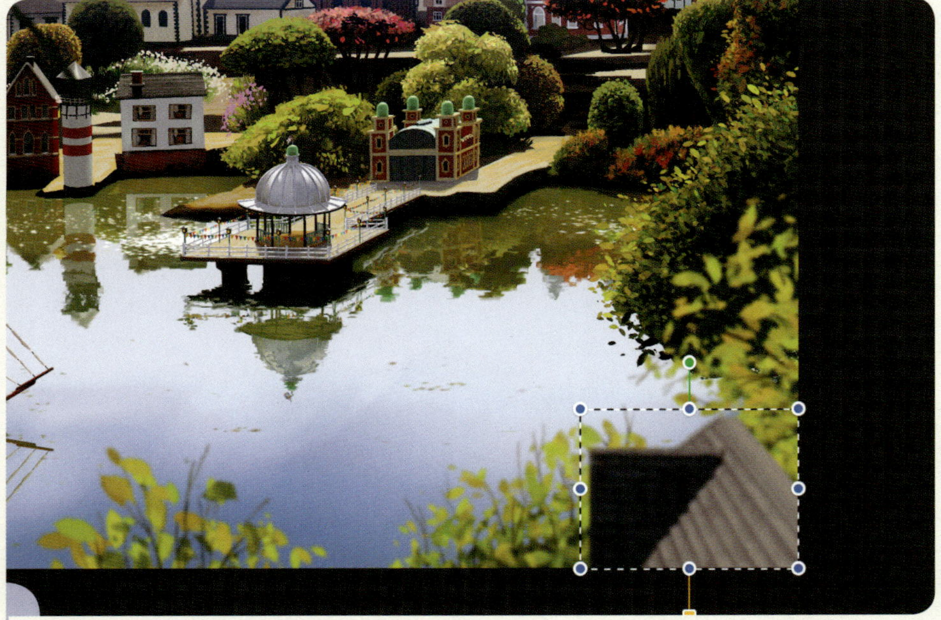

Push the image's depth with Gaussian Blur

23

Select the layer with the foreground trees and apply **ADJUSTMENTS > GAUSSIAN BLUR**. In the Layers menu, go to the layer containing the foreground roof, tap it, and choose Select. Apply Gaussian Blur to this layer as well – though make sure Alpha Lock is off, or the blur won't work properly. If you also make the roof slightly bigger with Transform, this enhances the scene's perspective even more.

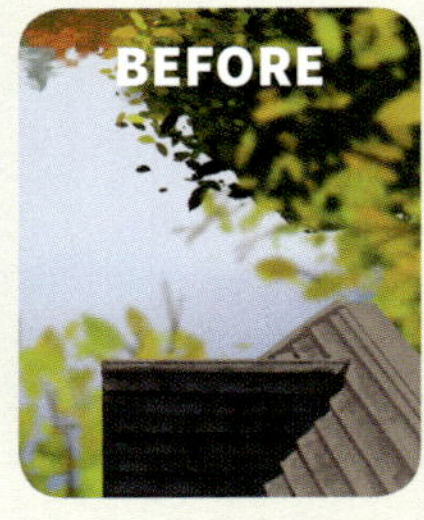

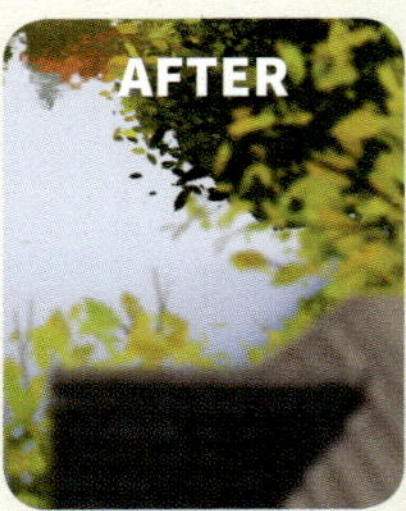

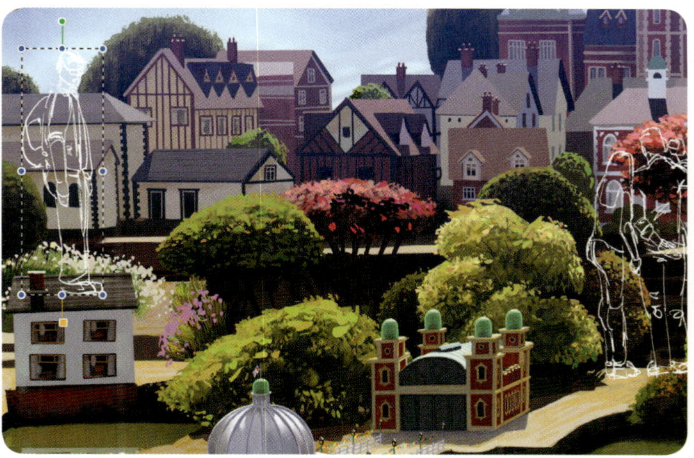
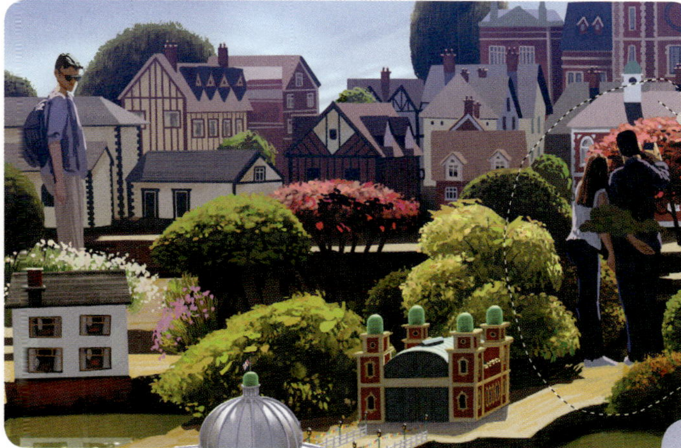

Adding people between the buildings as a layer of detail

24

You can now bring in a few tourists from the reference, but only in a few select areas. You don't want to overcrowd the scene, so just three people will do to add a layer of story. Sketch them on a new layer, using black or white for visibility against the scenery. On a layer under the sketch, colour and shade the figures simply using an opaque brush – they do not have to be very detailed. Delete the sketches afterwards. You can use the Selection and Transform tools to lasso and move the figures until you find the best placement and scale for them, overlapped by the houses or foliage to maintain depth.

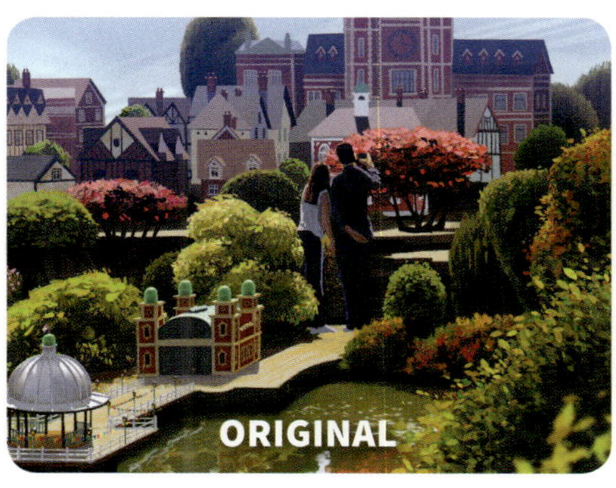

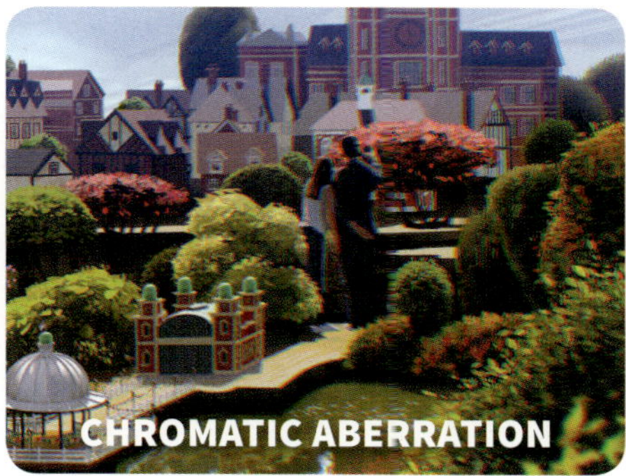

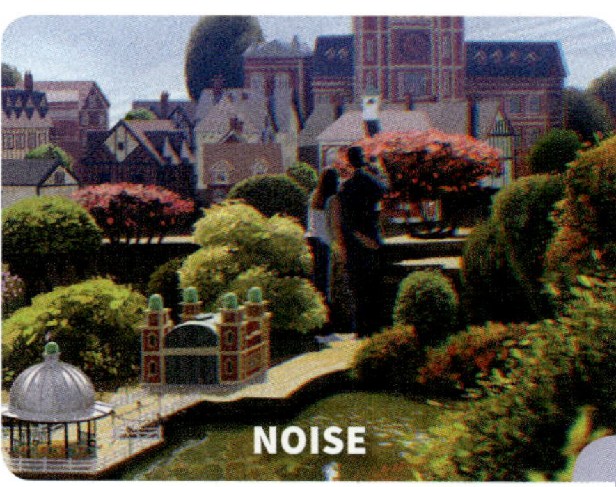

Final adjustments to wrap up the finished study

25

Tap Gallery in the top-left corner of your screen to return to an overview of your files. Tap Select, choose the artwork file, and select Duplicate to make a copy of your image. You will use this to add some finishing effects while keeping a copy as backup – you can even make more than one copy to try a few different versions.

In the new copy, merge all the layers into one by pinching together all layers in the stack. Make a few duplicates of this layer so you can test out different effects. Go to ADJUSTMENTS > CHROMATIC ABERRATION and drag across your screen until the slider is around 6% – just enough aberration to be visible. Go to ADJUSTMENTS > NOISE and add a little of that to give your final image a film-grain effect. Be careful not to overdo these effects, as too much of either of them can kill any picture. If the grain is too much in some areas, you can use a mask to erase the layer and reveal one of the original versions below.

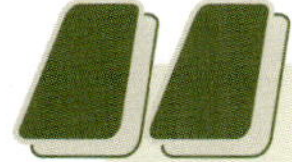

NEVENA SAYS: *'Building light slowly in your scene by working on individual elements, as well as on the whole image in general, is a key skill for any project. Now you know how to do that step by step. Never stop having fun with experimentation when painting. I encourage you to always take reference photos with your phone or camera and keep them in a special folder. I guarantee that one day they will be needed in one form or another.'*

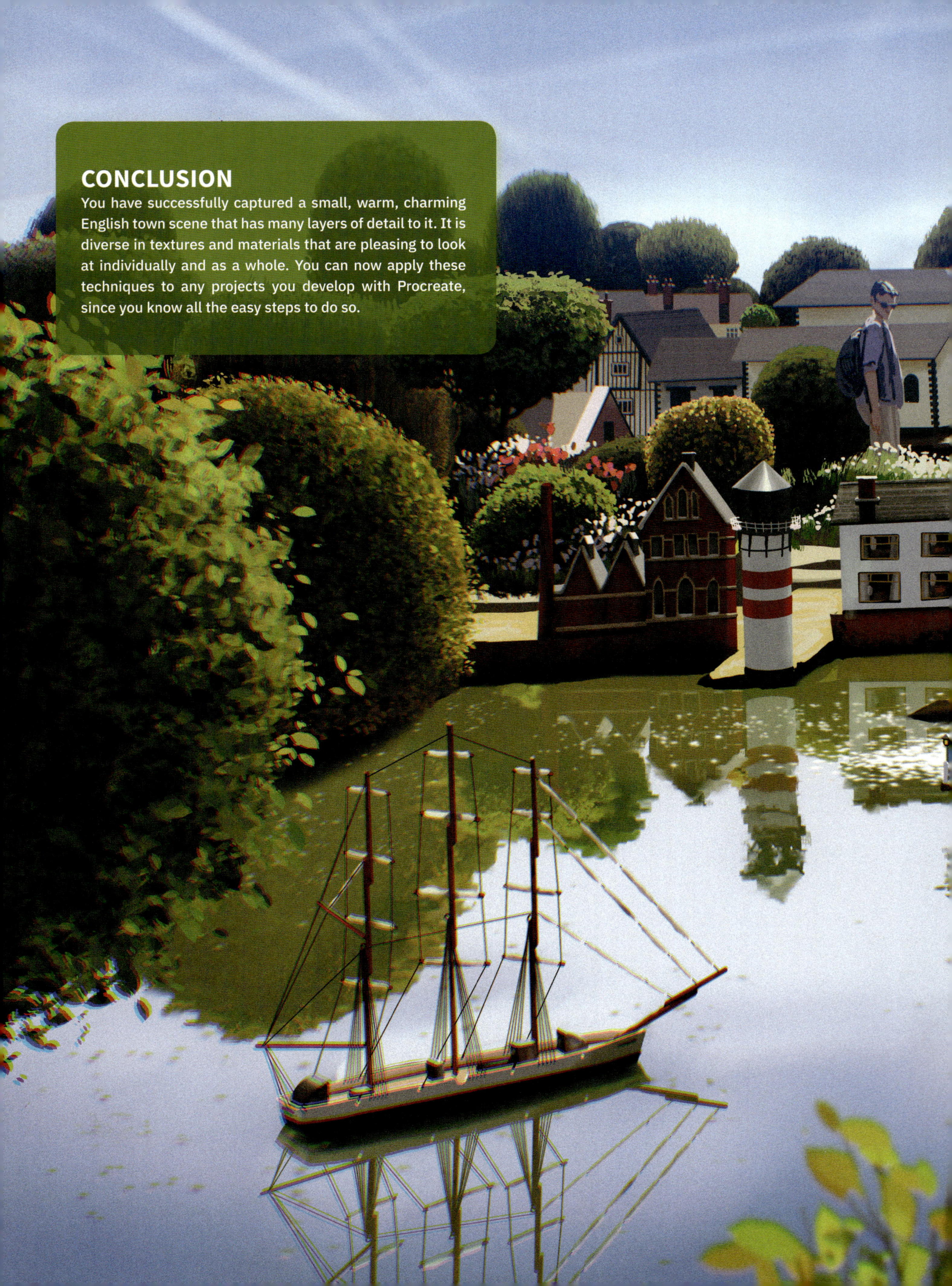

CONCLUSION
You have successfully captured a small, warm, charming English town scene that has many layers of detail to it. It is diverse in textures and materials that are pleasing to look at individually and as a whole. You can now apply these techniques to any projects you develop with Procreate, since you know all the easy steps to do so.

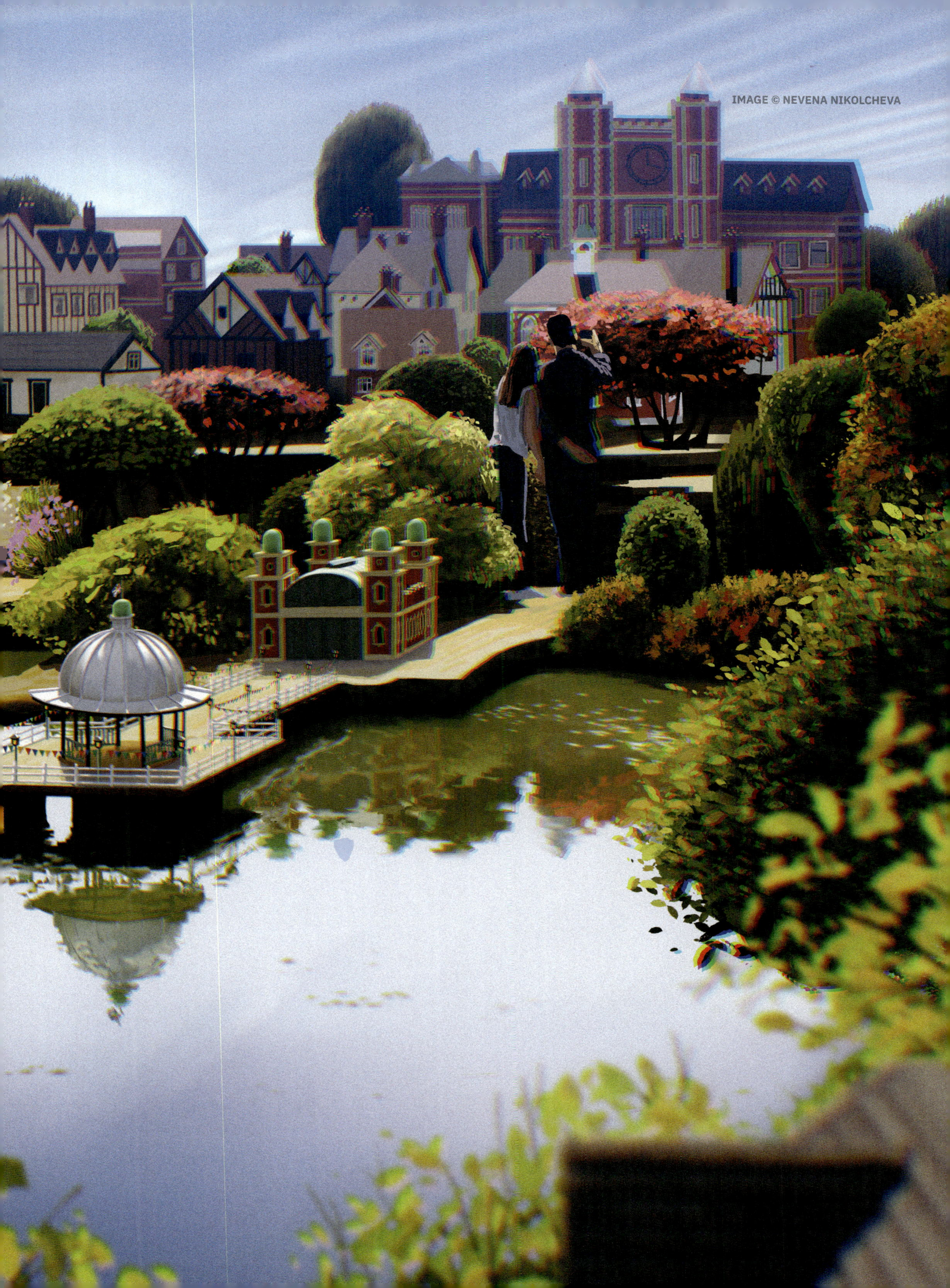

IMAGE © NEVENA NIKOLCHEVA

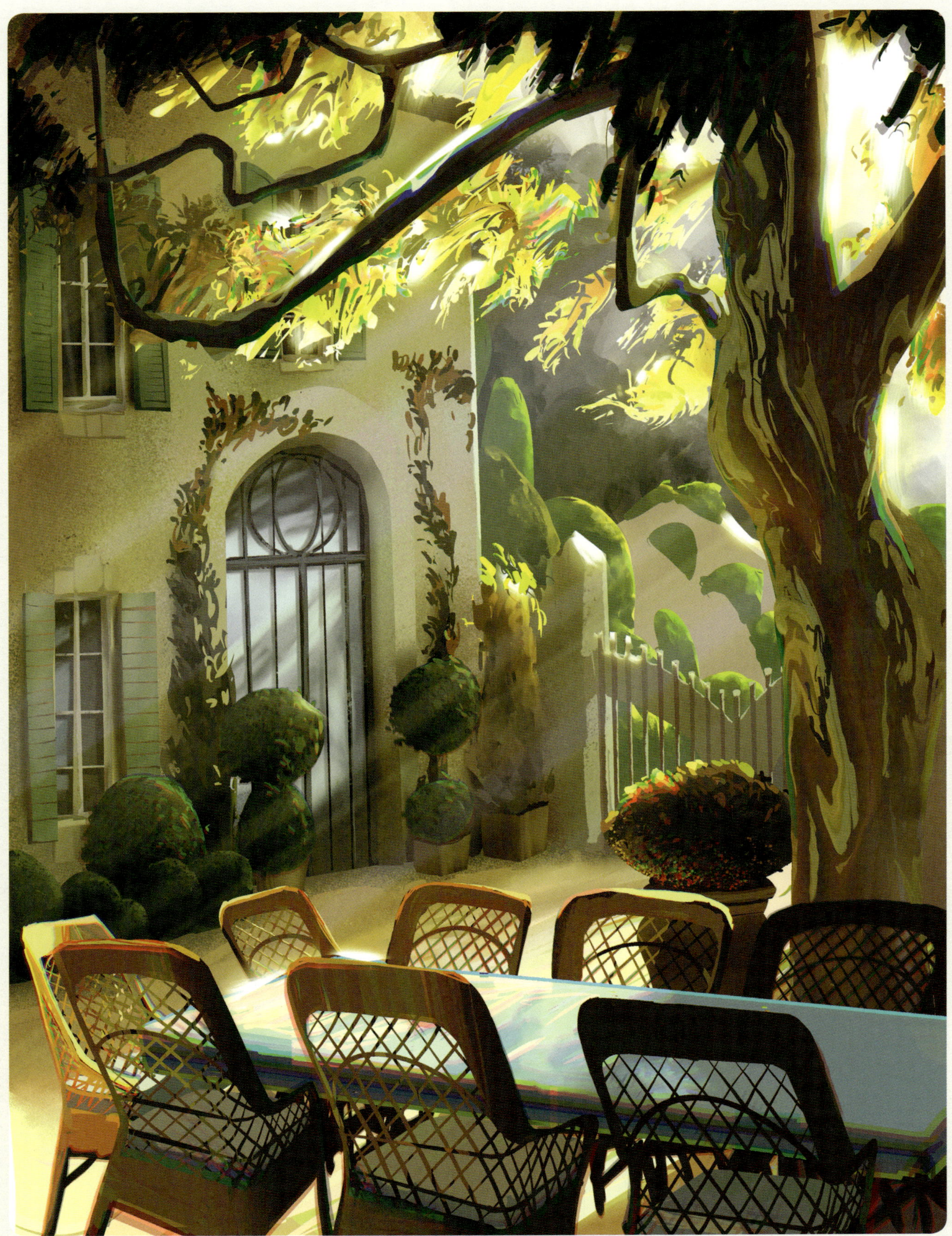

GARDEN STUDY: I wanted to capture the warm light in the scene and also explore the use of subtle, contrasting colours in the textures and materials that vibrate in the light

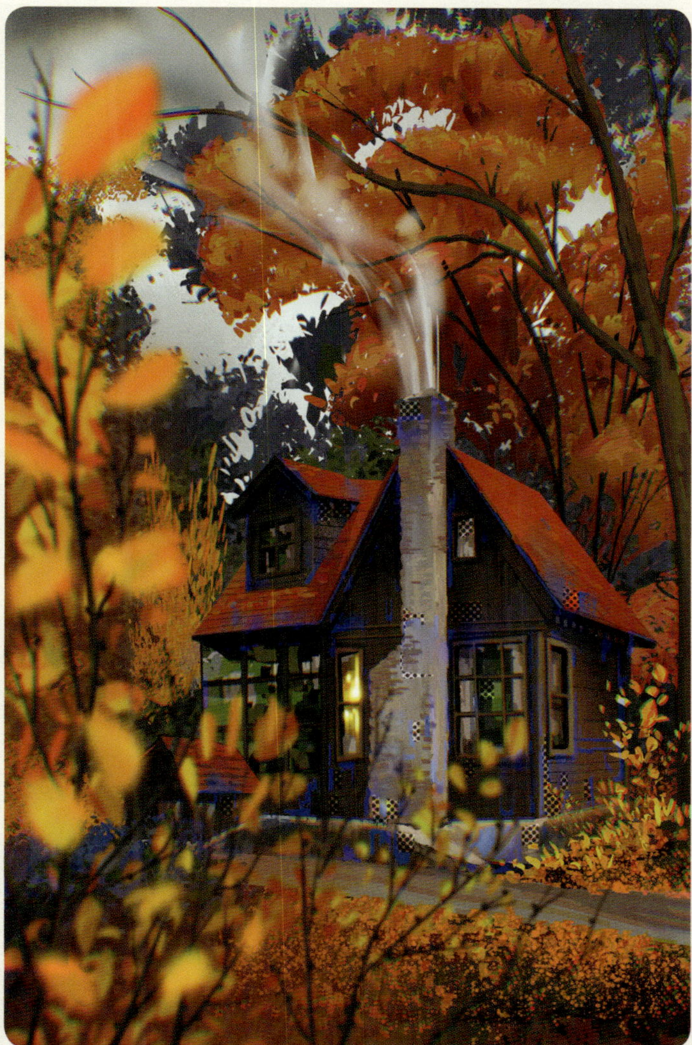

AUTUMN STUDY: I wanted to experiment with a limited (here mostly two-colour) palette of colours that I don't use often; I tried adding detail in an unconventional way by using small bursts of filters

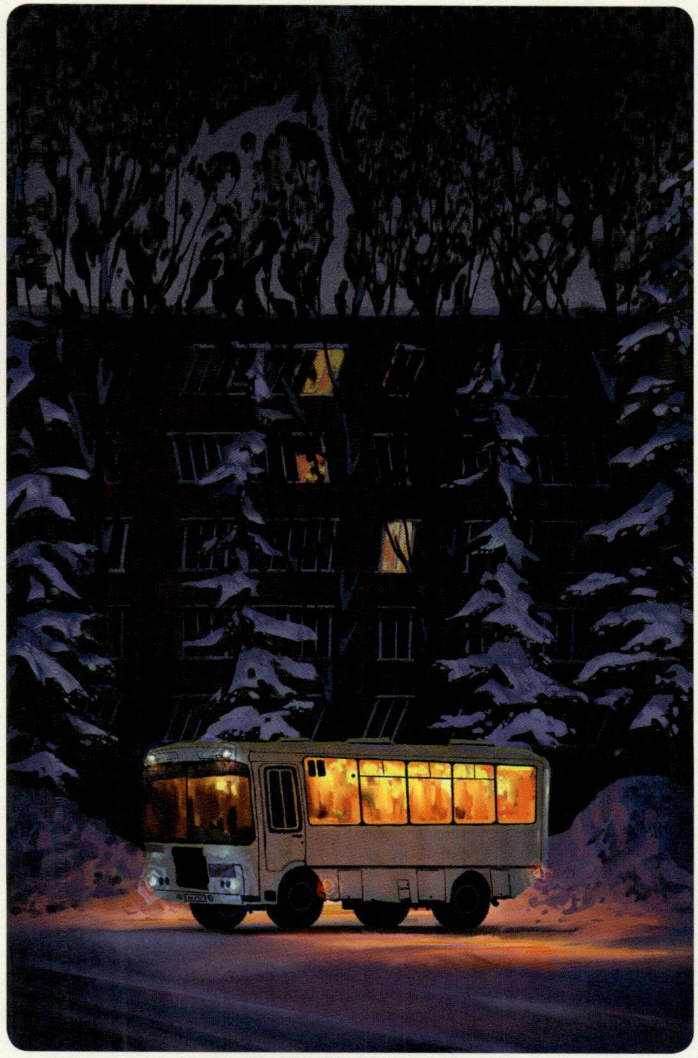

BUS STUDY: I really liked the contrast and mood created by the combination of the light, season, and composition here; I tried to stylize a lot of the elements in a way that was new to me at the time

MORNING FOG IN PUSHKAR

BY AYAN NAG

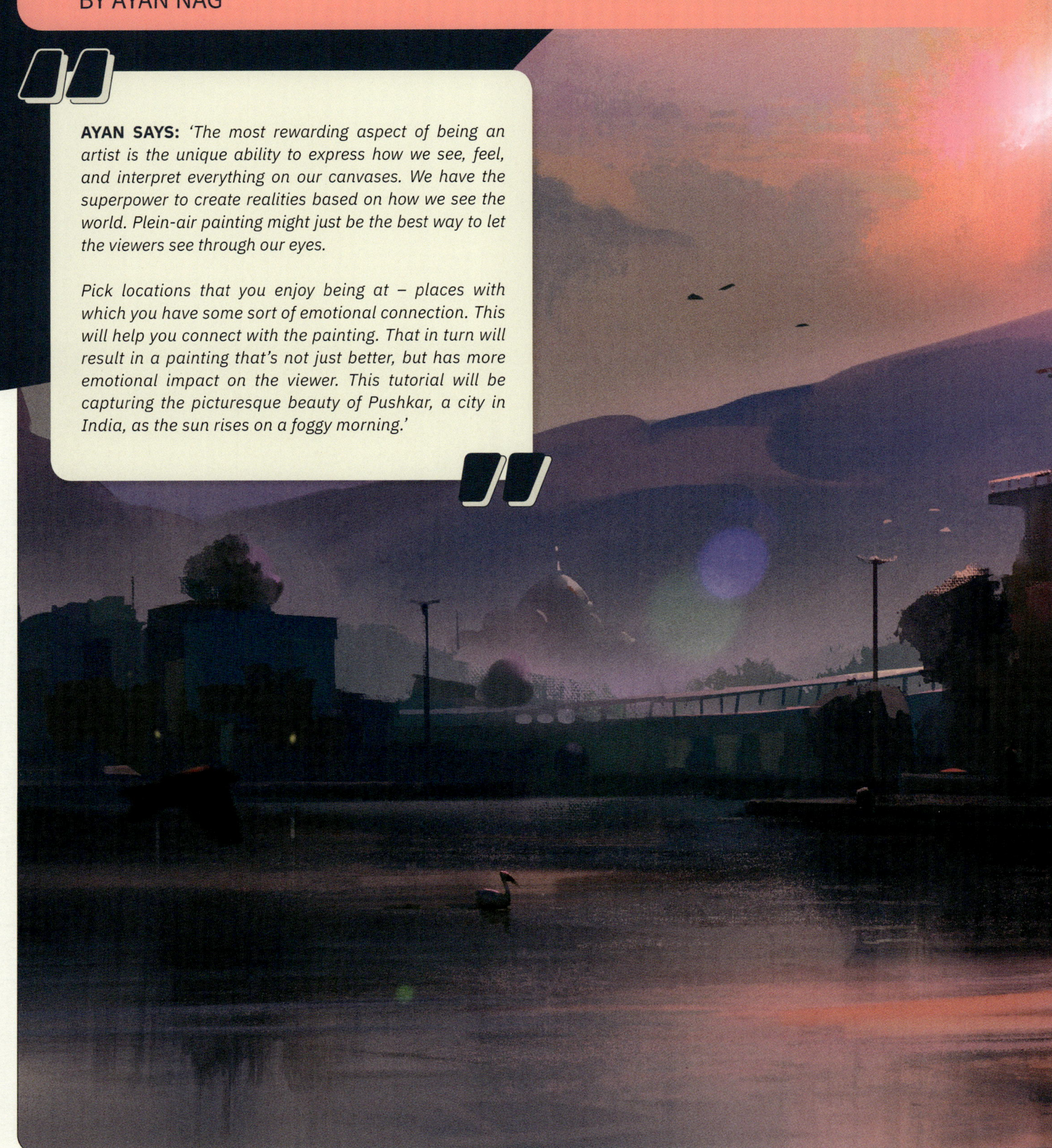

AYAN SAYS: *'The most rewarding aspect of being an artist is the unique ability to express how we see, feel, and interpret everything on our canvases. We have the superpower to create realities based on how we see the world. Plein-air painting might just be the best way to let the viewers see through our eyes.*

Pick locations that you enjoy being at – places with which you have some sort of emotional connection. This will help you connect with the painting. That in turn will result in a painting that's not just better, but has more emotional impact on the viewer. This tutorial will be capturing the picturesque beauty of Pushkar, a city in India, as the sun rises on a foggy morning.'

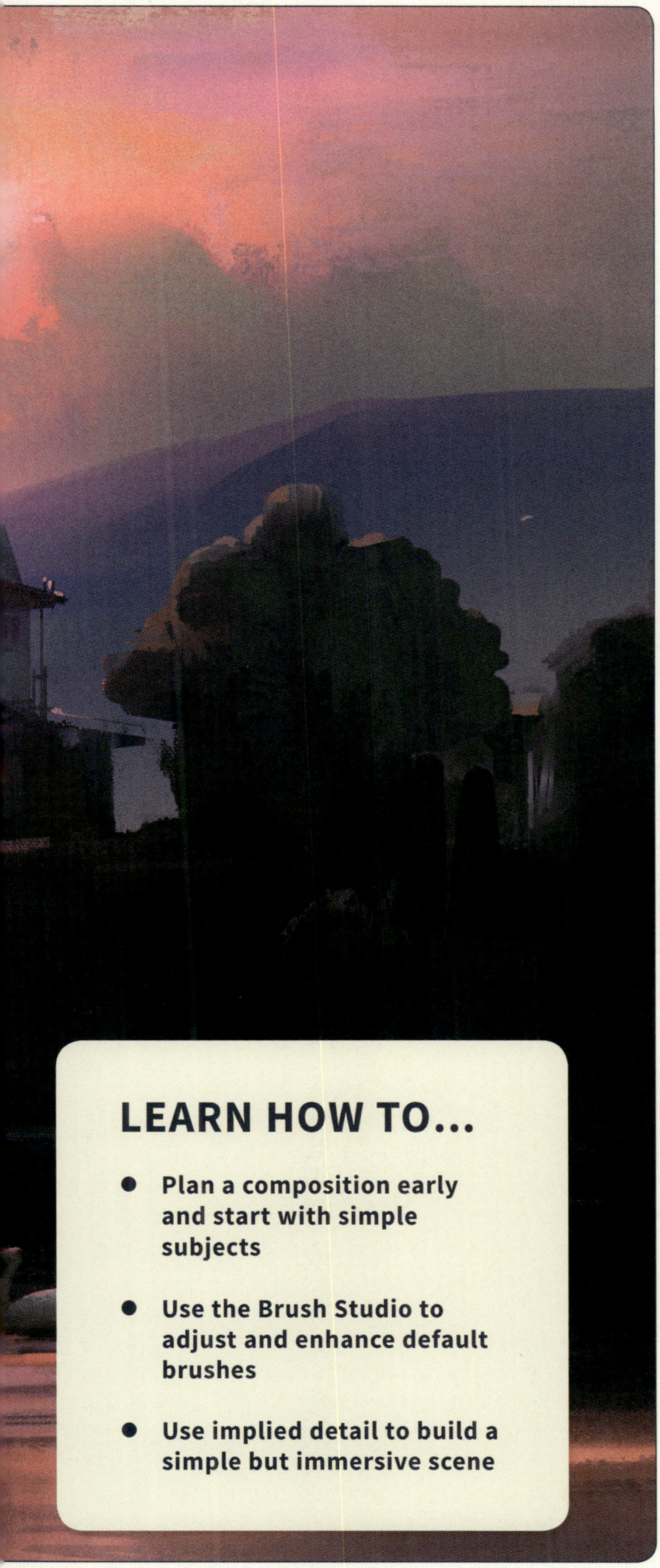

01

It is always a good idea to quickly snap a few photos before starting the painting. Depending on the weather and other external factors, light can change very quickly outdoors. If you have to leave the location and finish your image another time, having some references will help you bridge the gaps between your painting and reality. This particular location is seen early in the morning. It is hazy and blue, with a pale sun, light clouds, and distant mountains in silhouette. Various birds fly around or float on the water. When the sun is lower, it casts warmer light and more dramatic shadows.

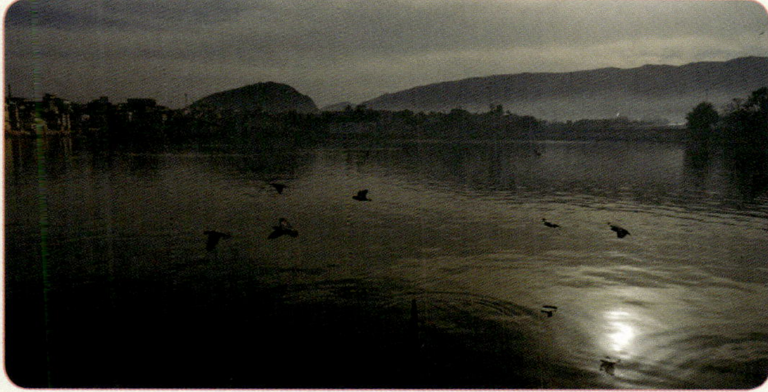

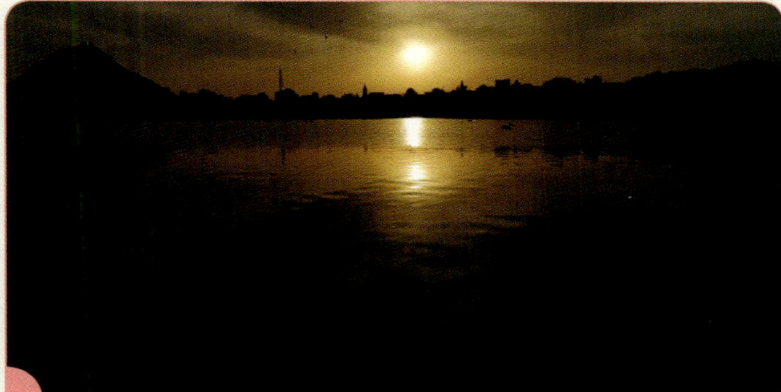

Choose a location – somewhere personal to you is always a good choice

LEARN HOW TO...

- Plan a composition early and start with simple subjects

- Use the Brush Studio to adjust and enhance default brushes

- Use implied detail to build a simple but immersive scene

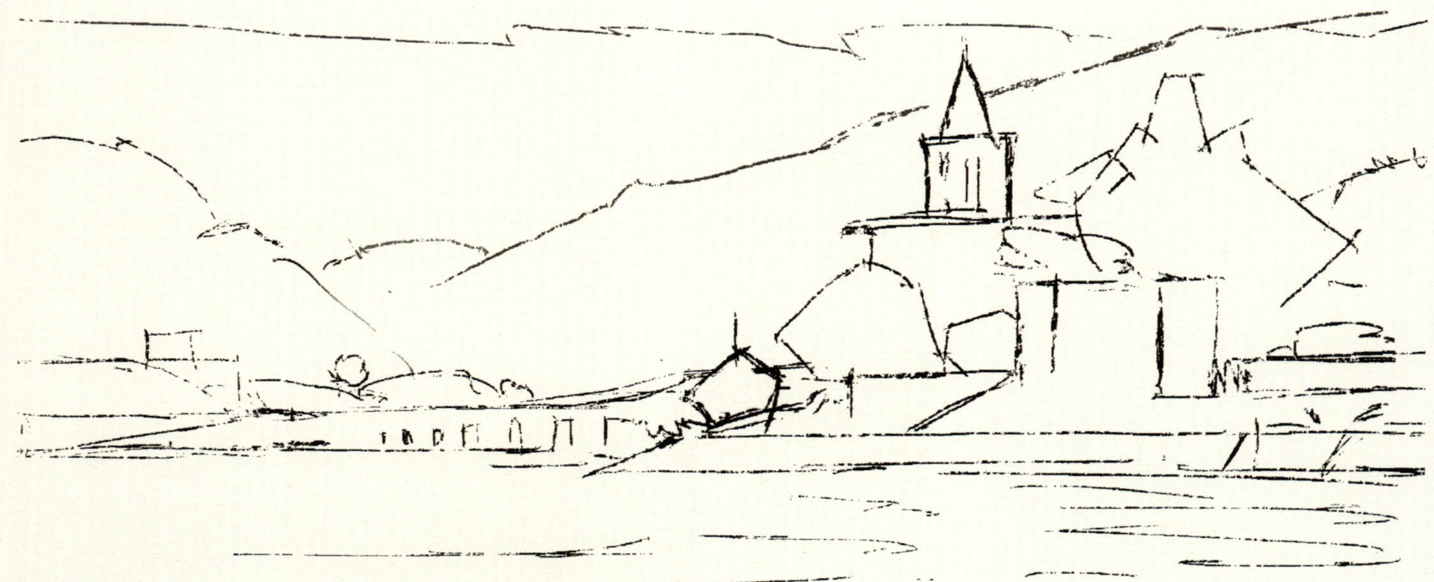

02

It is possible to just start painting right away, but it's helpful to start with a basic sketch of your composition. Starting an unplanned, spontaneous painting is fun, but spending 10–15 minutes figuring out the direction of your scene will save you a lot of time later. Start by creating a new canvas around 3,200 pixels wide × 2,140 pixels high. Tap on the Background layer and set it to a medium grey, then start sketching on an empty layer with your brush of choice. This stage is very rough and simple, just outlining the key features of the landscape and skyline. If you are comfortable with going straight into colour with paintbrushes, you can skip this step, but a line sketch enables you to arrange your subjects early on for a better composition.

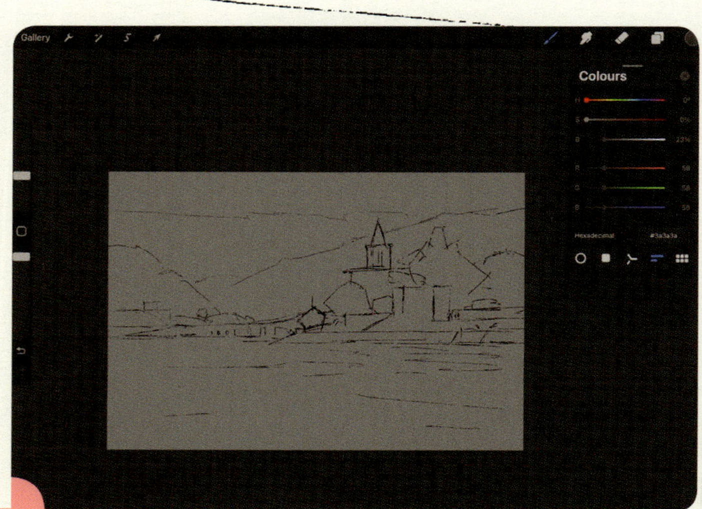

Sketch out the composition

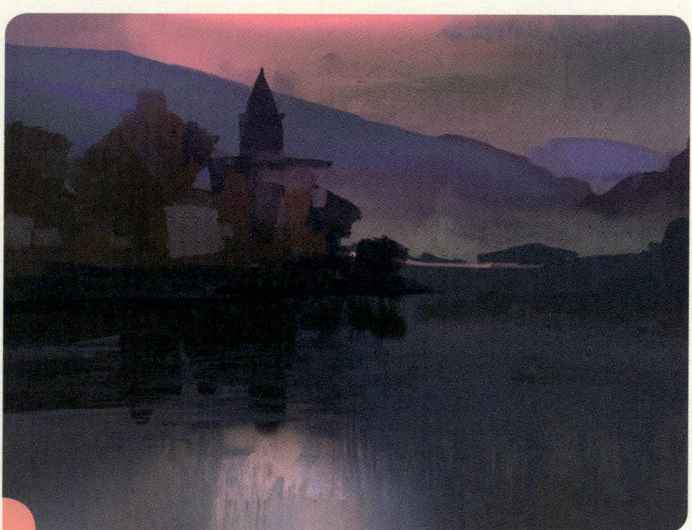

Roughly paint base colours, toggling the sketch layer off as needed

03

Create four new layers below the sketch (for the sky, background mountains, middle-ground buildings, and water) and start painting rough colours, using the sketch as a guide. Stay zoomed out as far as possible and use large, simple strokes to help you focus on the big picture. The goal is to fill the canvas quickly and establish the overall mood.

Use warm pinks and purples for the sky, and cooler blues and purples for the mountains. Use a soft airbrush to add a pale fog on a layer between the mountains and buildings. For the buildings, use darker, desaturated blues, purples, and browns. Don't forget to bring some of the environment colours into the water, to create a reflective effect. Once you have blocked out the main reflections, add a new layer above them, paint thinner horizontal scribbles, and then blend them with the Smudge tool to create ripples.

04

These base-painting stages are the most important part of the process. All the big decisions and changes take place during this phase. As you are working with a big brush, it is very easy to change the large shapes and overall readability of the scene. When the canvas is filled and you feel you've blocked out all the elements you need, try zooming right out to view the image at thumbnail size. This tiny version should read very similarly to the final painting, so take your time and make adjustments if it doesn't look quite right.

Keep thinking about how the location makes you feel. What story would you like to tell your audience with the image? This early-morning twilight scene feels quiet and serene, almost otherworldly, which the cool blues and purples help to emphasize.

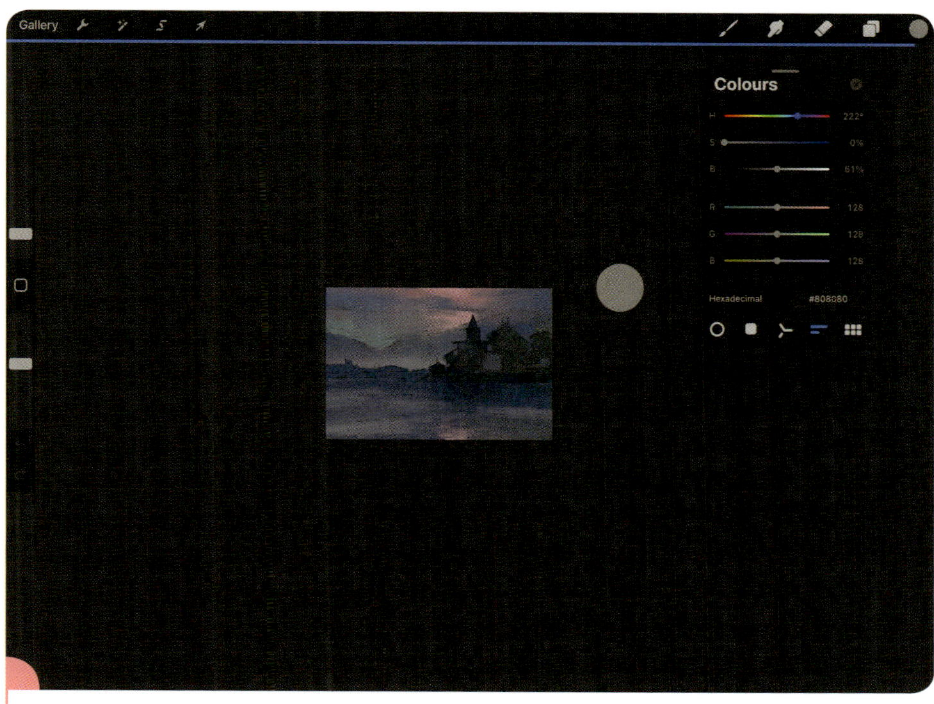

Zoom out to check how the image reads

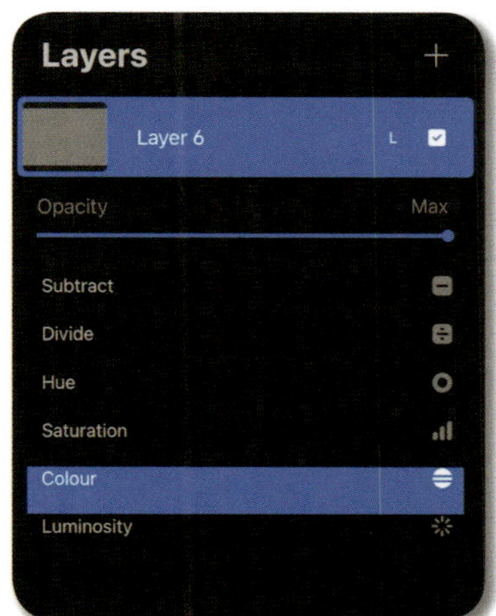

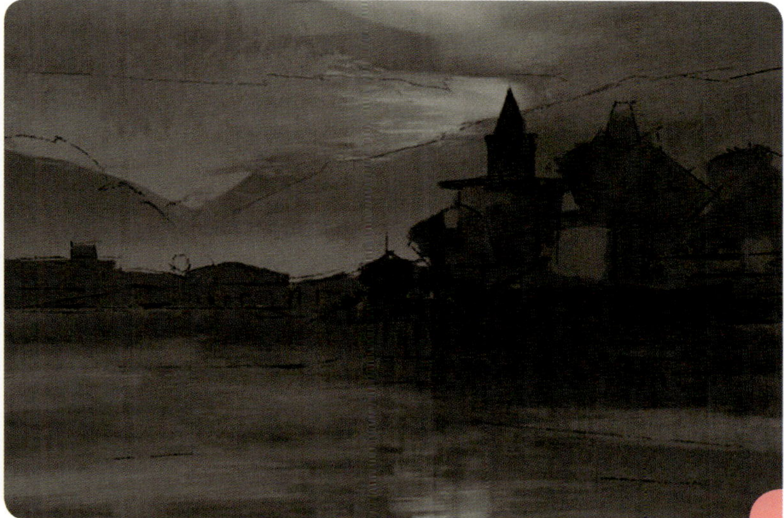

Make a greyscale adjustment layer that you can toggle on and off

05

Before going any further, it will be helpful to check the painting's values and see if any adjustments are needed. You can do this by creating a new layer on top of the image, filling it up with any shade of grey with zero saturation, and setting the layer mode to Colour. You can keep this 'zero saturation' layer as a guide for your values throughout the painting process, simply toggling its visibility on and off as needed. Try to group your values well using this layer as a guide – the painting's focal points should have the most contrast to help guide your viewer's eyes.

Another helpful technique is to regularly flip the canvas as you go along (**ACTIONS > CANVAS > FLIP CANVAS HORIZONTALLY**) to check the scene's balance. While the goal is to capture the scene in front of you, the painting must also work well as a composition in its own right.

06

Layers can quickly get out of hand. You need to manage them early on and keep them as simple as possible. Ideally, your Layers stack should resemble something like this, from bottom to top:

- Sky layer
- Background layer (distant mountains, forests, and so on)
- Middle-ground layer (main subject and bigger shapes)
- Foreground layer (nearby subjects)
- Sketch layer (to toggle on and off)

Try to keep to 2–4 layers for the early stages of an image, building up the sky and landscape elements on their respective layers. You can always add extra layers later on for adjustments, details, and finishing touches.

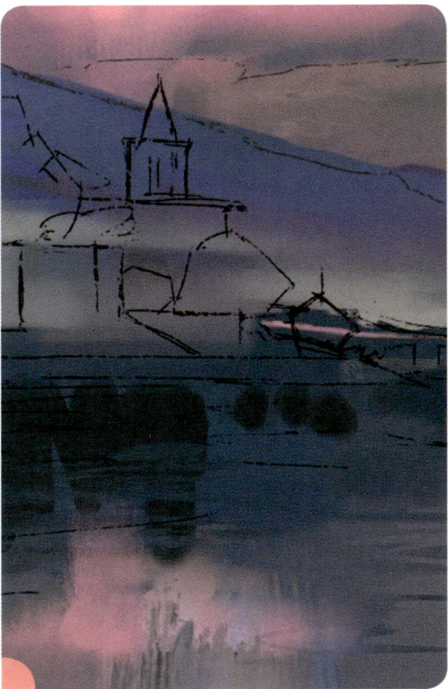

Keep your layers simple for now – here's the scene with the middle-ground layer toggled on and off

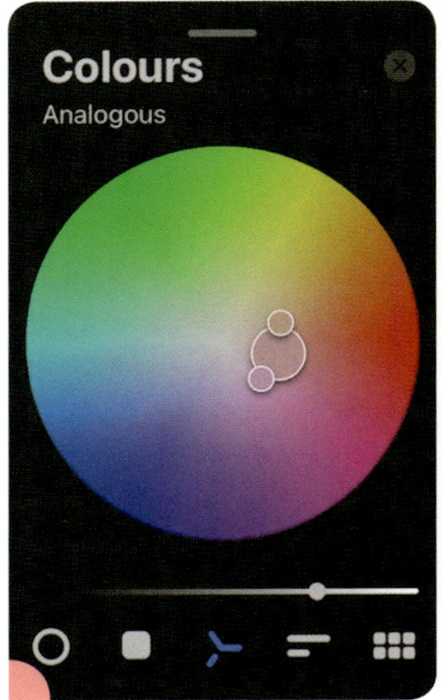

Try different colour interface options to see which is most comfortable for you

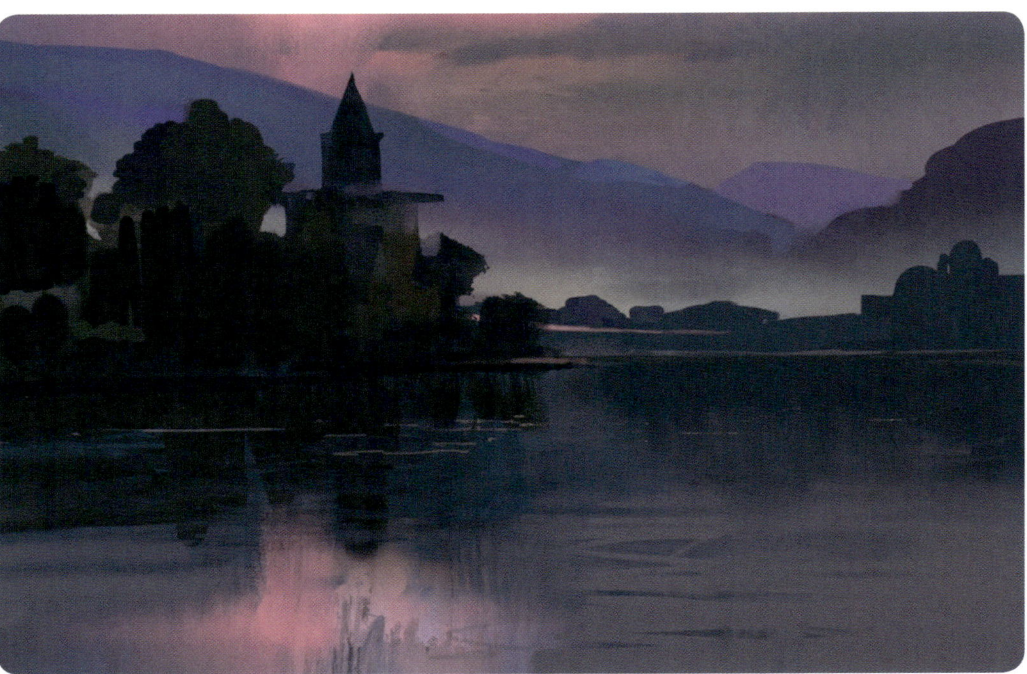

07

Continue blocking out the middle and distant buildings with cool, opaque colours. The colour interface you use is up to you; the Disc view is a common choice, but the Values sliders offer benefits, too. The sliders for HSB (Hue, Saturation, Brightness) and RGB (Red, Green, Blue) give you precise control over a colour's saturation and brightness. Play around with the different options to see if they can make your process more streamlined, and try switching between them from time to time. Using the HSB sliders, you can contain the dynamic range of the scene at this early stage. For now, do not use anything darker than 15 or brighter than 90 on the Brightness slider. They can be bumped up later in the process!

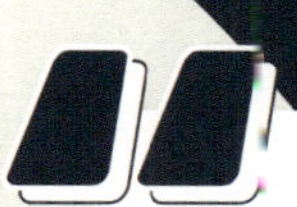

> **AYAN SAYS:** *'Outdoor painting can be challenging: finding new places, discovering something new in a familiar place, trying to capture those moments, and failing a lot in the process. It is a journey of its own. Embrace those failures and learn from them. The process shown here is something I have learned over many years of learning and plein-air painting, but as you pursue your own journey into art, you will discover your own ways of doing things, too.'*

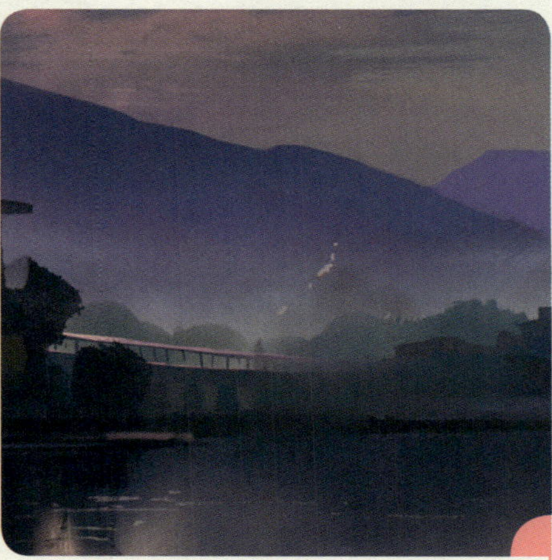

Choose a colour palette that enhances what you see and feel in reality

08

When trying to choose the 'right' colour, remember that there are no right or wrong colour choices, as each of us perceives colour in a different way. Even when you start paying attention to the subtle colour shifts in nature, that perception changes over time. Your primary reference for colour should be what you are seeing in nature; however, rather than simply replicating that, try to combine what you see with how the location makes you *feel*.

In this case, it's a sunny morning, slightly foggy. The temperature is comfortable but there is an early-morning coolness to the atmosphere, which you can see in the photographs on page 161. This particular colour palette is focused on warm purples and pinks, so complement them with some cool teal elements in the distant trees. Block out and build up the background bridge, adding a warm highlight where the top catches the light, and then push one end into the distance by covering it with fog. Add a bright, pale highlight to the water as if a bit of early sun is coming through the clouds above.

09

You can set up a perspective grid to help as the painting progresses. Eyeballing most of your perspective works well in the early stages, as it helps you innately understand how perspective functions; but if you tend to hyperfocus on small details and errors early in the process, using a grid from the beginning will only exacerbate this and waste a lot of your time. Those early sketching phases are all about how efficiently you can express your ideas on the canvas – readability, not perfection, is key. That is why staying zoomed all the way out is so useful – it helps you ignore small issues and focus on the overall scene!

However, now that the scene is advancing, a perspective guide will help make it feel more concrete and believable. Enable the grid by going to **ACTIONS > CANVAS > DRAWING GUIDE**. To edit the grid's angle and shape, go to **ACTIONS > CANVAS > EDIT DRAWING GUIDE > PERSPECTIVE**. Tap near the right edge of the horizon to place a horizon line, then outside the left side of the canvas to place a vanishing point. Drag the vanishing point to resemble the shape shown, then hit Done to confirm. You can toggle the grid's visibility on and off again with **ACTIONS > DRAWING GUIDE**.

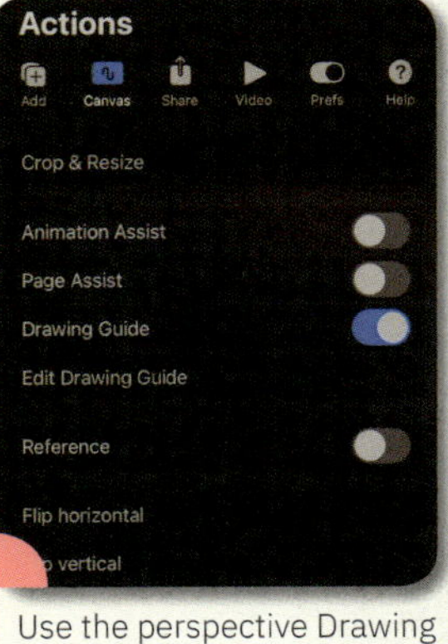

Use the perspective Drawing Guide tools to help build up more realistic depth

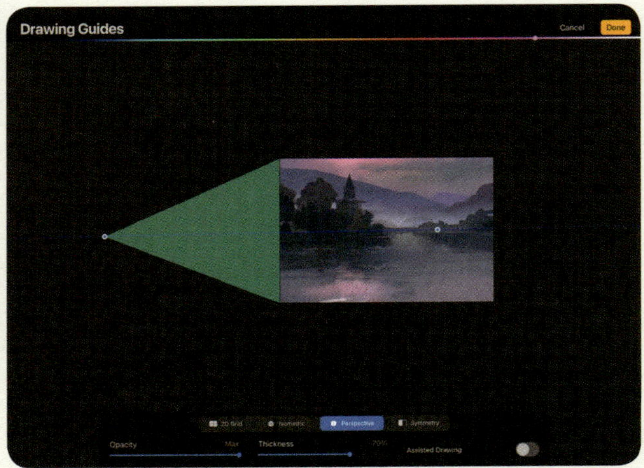

10

Procreate has a very intricate and advanced brush engine. Its Brush Studio options are detailed, powerful, and worth exploring if you haven't already done so. Try this now by tapping on **PAINTING > DRY BRUSH** to open Brush Studio. Go to Shape, and under Shape Source, tap Edit and go to **IMPORT > SOURCE LIBRARY**. Search or scroll down to 'Brick' as the new Shape Source, then hit Done. Test the results by doodling in the Drawing Pad area on the right.

Under Shape Behaviour, scroll down to Flip X and Flip Y, and toggle them both on. The result should be a textured, organic brush with a chunkier stroke than the original Dry Brush. Under the Colour Dynamics tab, go to Stamp Colour Jitter and set the Hue and Saturation sliders to 2%. Do the same for the Hue and Saturation sliders under Stroke Colour Jitter, then tap Done.

Test the results by painting in the sky area. Instead of a flat colour, you will see your strokes have shifts in hue and saturation, without having to manually change the colour! This creates a lot of interest and organic variety even within flat shapes.

Try changing the source and behaviour of your brush's shape

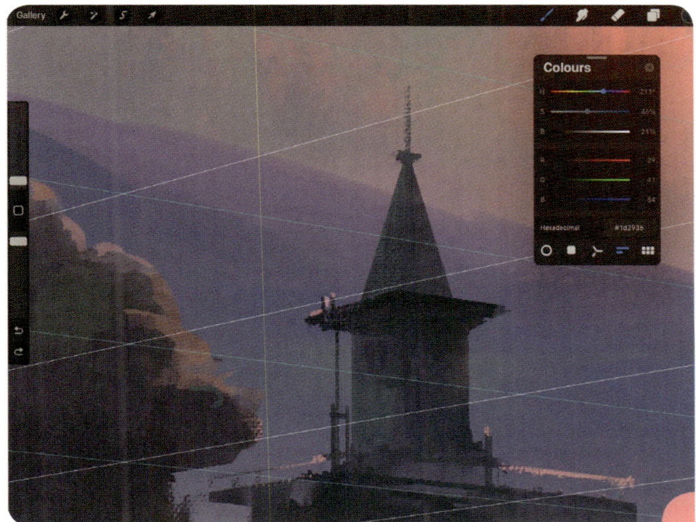

11

You can now start adding smaller details and finer textures to the composition. Start by picking a square brush, such as **FAINTING > NIKO RULL**, and open the Grain settings in the Brush Studio. For the Grain Source, select the Canvas option, and lower the Scale slider for a finer texture. Use this brush to paint grainy strokes on areas such as the rooftop, adding rough texture that implies bricks or tiles. The perspective grid will help you line up finer details such as roof edges and railings.

Create a grainy brush for detailing the buildings

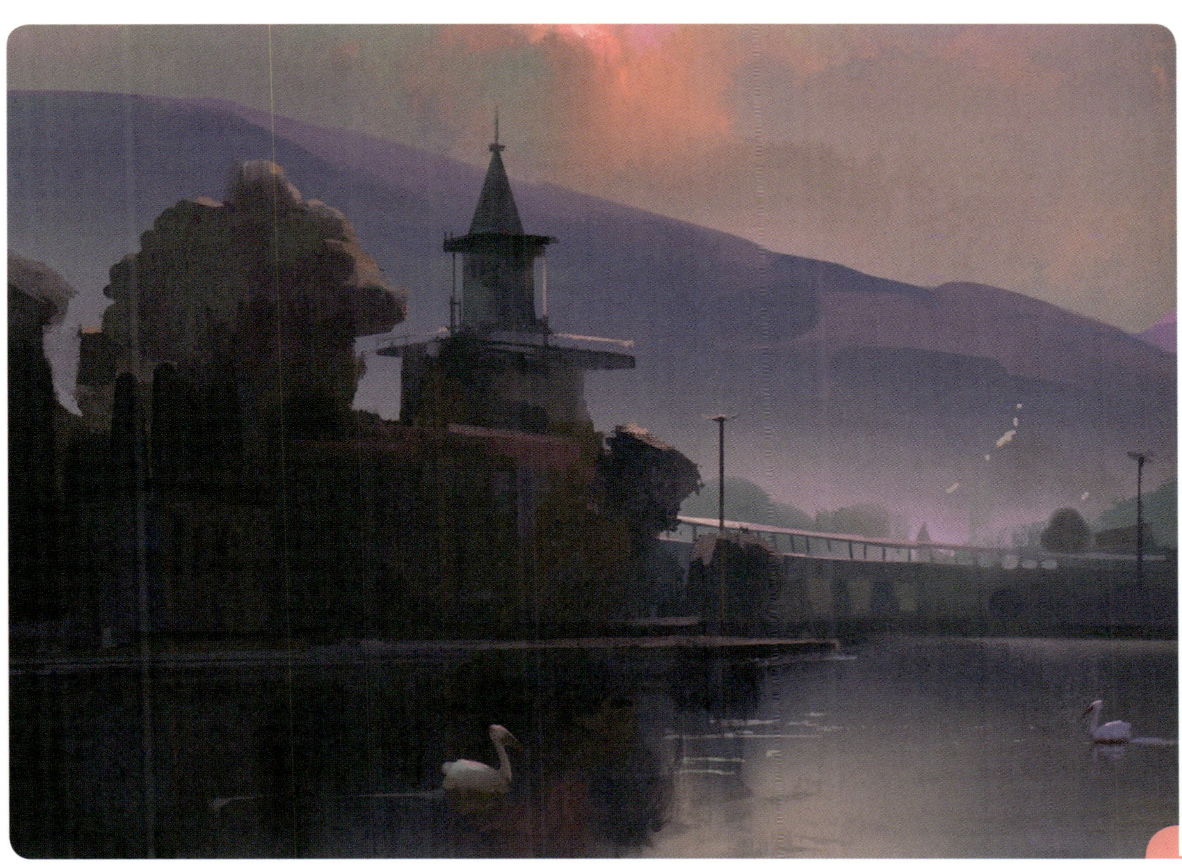

Paint birds in the water with a simple round brush

12

Storytelling elements can be anything from human figures to clothes hanging on a balcony. These are the details that can breathe life into a seemingly desolate composition. On a new layer, loosely paint the two floating birds using a hard-edged round brush. Don't forget to include their reflections and the ripples in their wake.

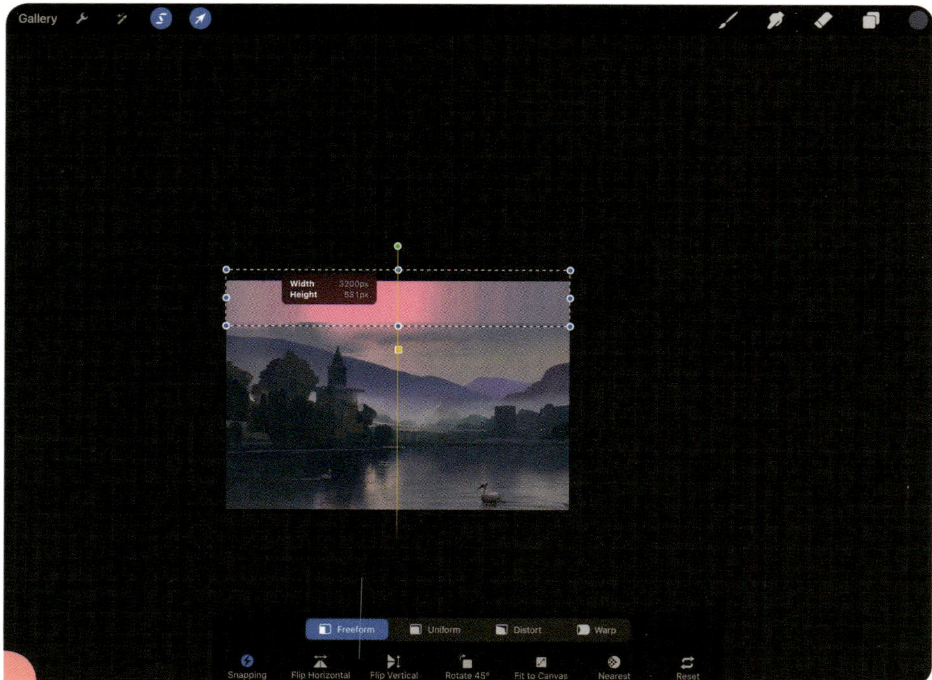
Reframing the composition gives the sky more room to breathe

13

The sky could be emphasized even more to really capture the warm glow of the sunrise. However, this requires reframing the scene to give the sky more space. To do this, swipe right on each layer in the Layers stack to highlight them all, then tap Group to group them into a folder together. With this main group folder selected, go to **TRANSFORM > FREEFORM** and move the whole scene down a little, losing a bit of water in favor of increasing the sky space. This will create a blank strip at the top of the canvas. Tap the sky layer, use **SELECTIONS > RECTANGLE** to select the uppermost section of the sky, then use Transform again to stretch it up and fill the gap. Give the stretched section a paintover with your textured brushes to blend it in. Toggle your greyscale layer on to check that the sky still works well.

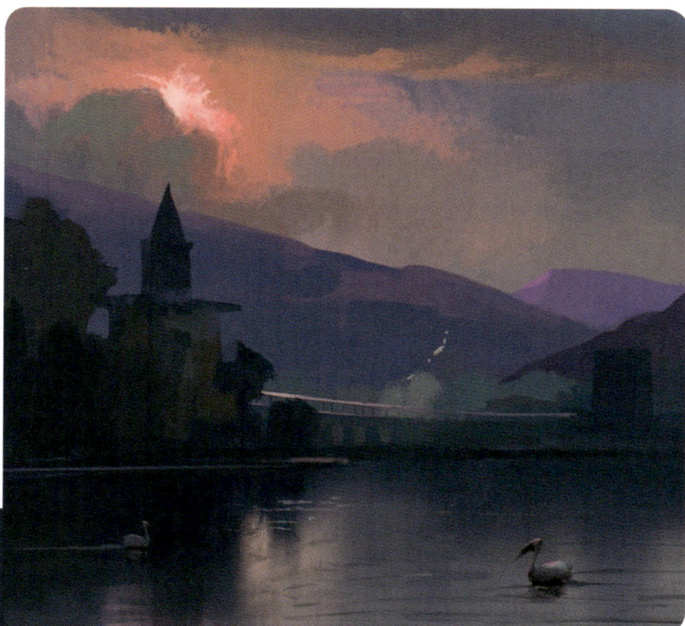

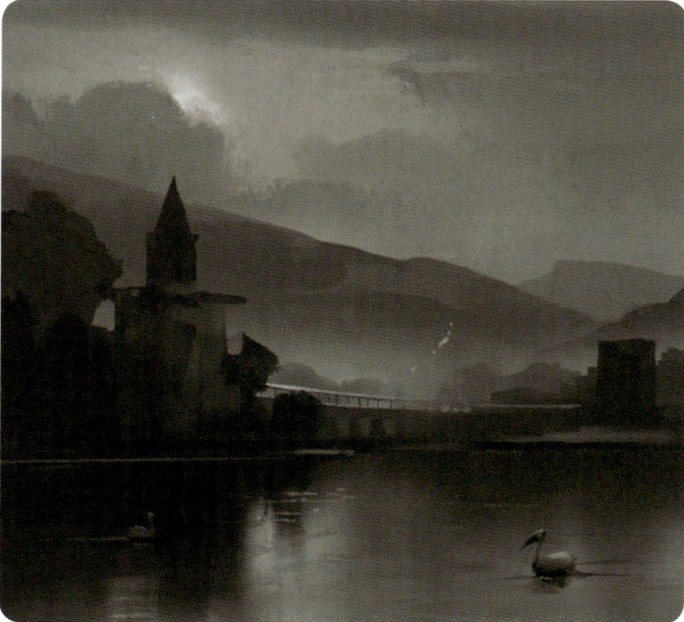

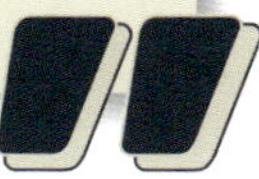

AYAN SAYS: '*These migratory birds were one of the highlights of my trip to Pushkar, Rajasthan. They were huge and were always shooing other birds away from their territory. I watched them do this for hours on end, every day, so naturally I had to include them in my painting! Moments like these take place almost daily in our lives and are forgotten about. If you include them in your paintings, especially plein-air paintings, they will enhance your composition and help create something precious that is unique to you.*'

14

To enhance the composition and give the image an appealing presentation, even at this unfinished stage, you can add a letterboxing effect on top. This is a great device for fine-tuning an image's framing, especially with a square composition – you can start with a square canvas and reframe it later as a widescreen image, which keeps your process very flexible. Add a new layer at the very top of your Layers stack, open the Selection tool, and activate the Fill option at the bottom of the screen. This will automatically fill any selection you make with your currently selected colour. Use it to add a black bar to the top and bottom of your canvas.

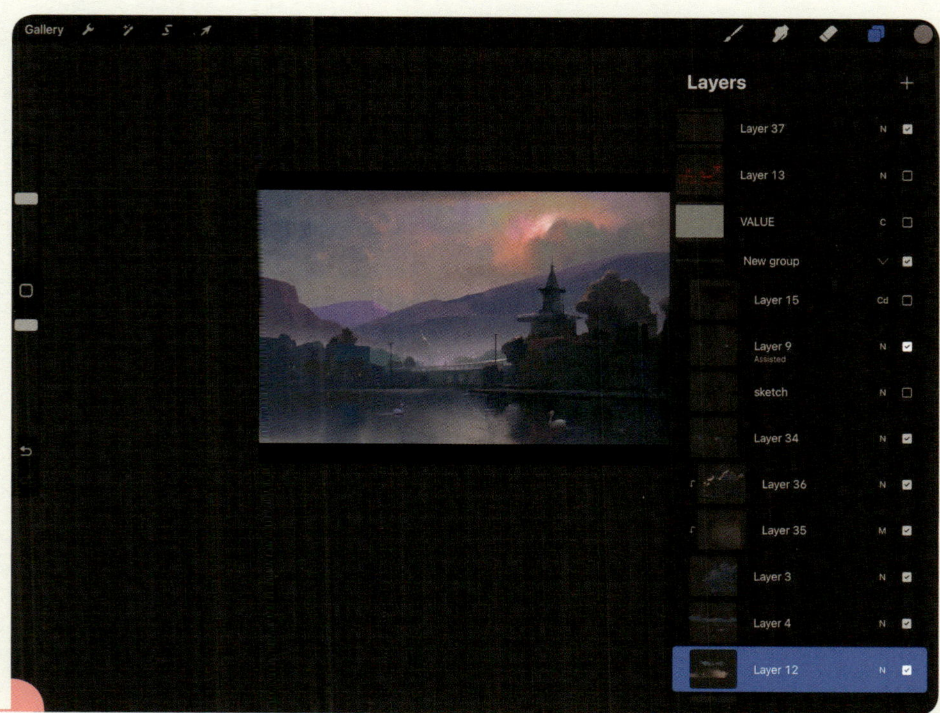

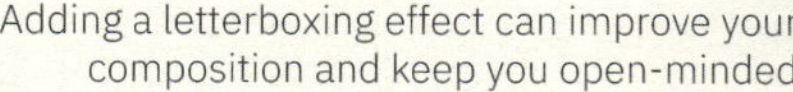
Adding a letterboxing effect can improve your composition and keep you open-minded

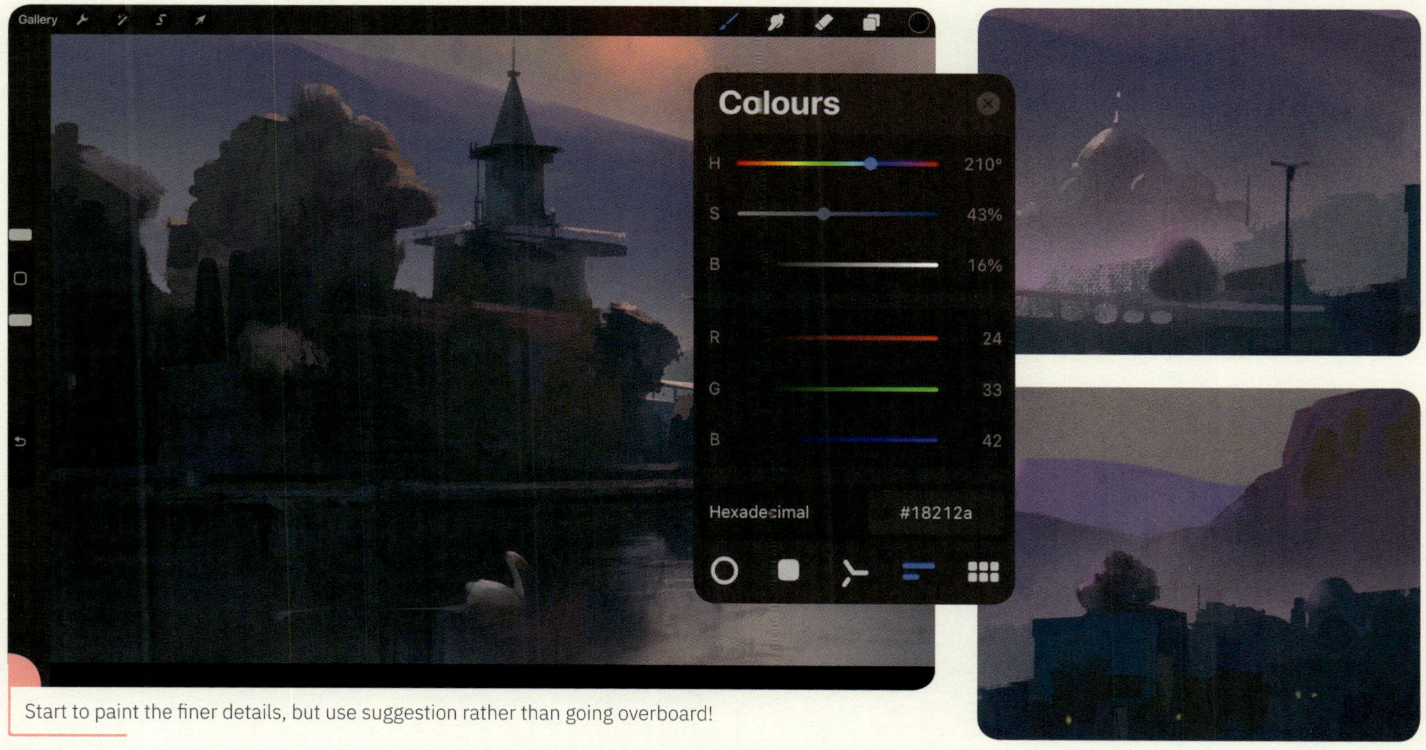
Start to paint the finer details, but use suggestion rather than going overboard!

15

Now you can begin zooming closer in to fine-tune the medium-sized and smaller shapes. Do not overdo the details – just render enough that the scene reads as you intend it. For example, with the architecture, this could just be a matter of tweaking the perspective with Transform to match the grid, or lighting the surfaces properly to match the environment with a few simple strokes of colour Try to capture details such as distant railings and steps with as few strokes as possible.

For organic shapes such as trees and bushes, adding some extra texture and brushwork may be all the refinement you need. You can see here how slight daubs of green and single strokes from a roughly textured brush are all that the trees need.

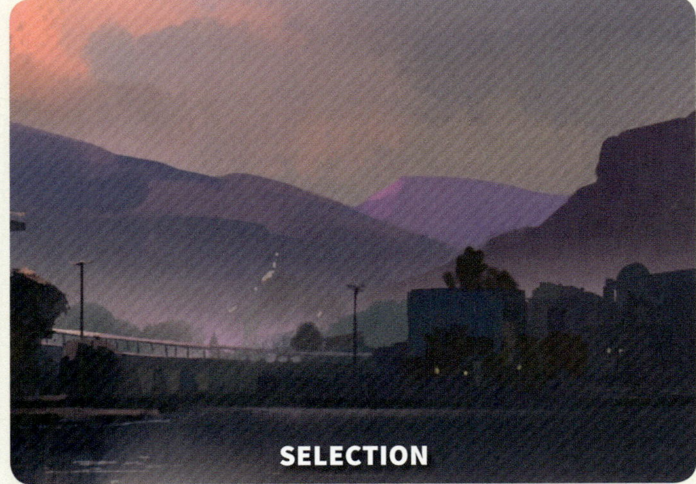

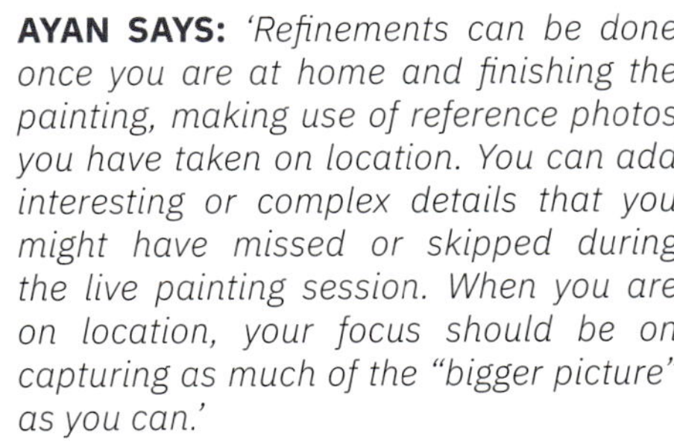

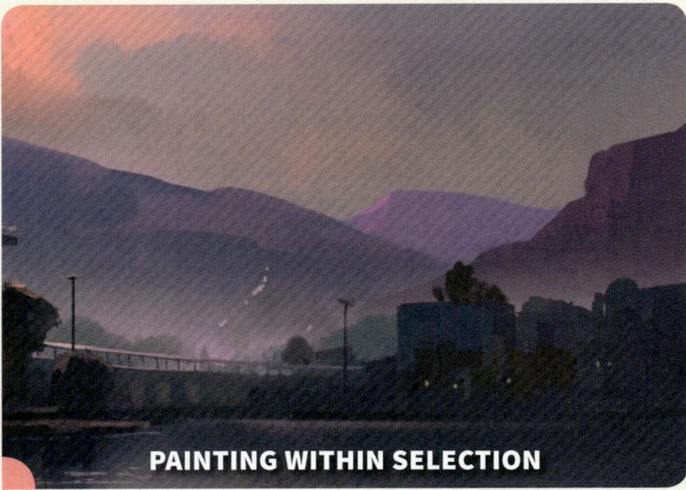

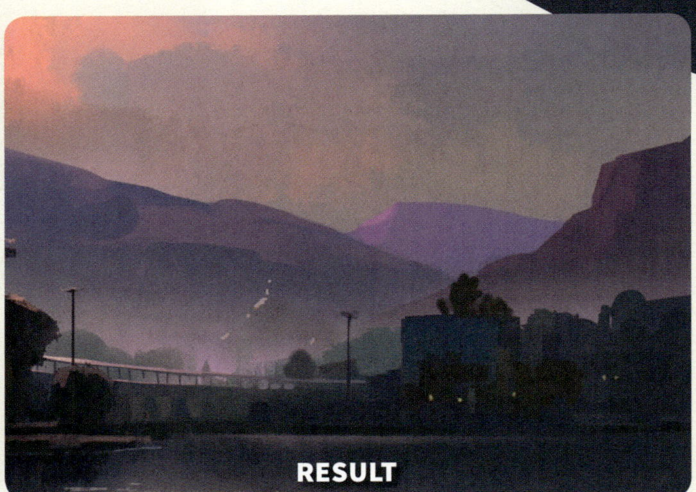

Try painting within a selection to achieve hard, clean edges ar

16

Managing your edges can really improve the overall read of an image. Knowing where to use hard or soft edges will further enhance your composition and make your painting more interesting to look at. To paint crisp edges on a distant hill, lasso it with Selection first. Try to blend in some edges that feel too obvious, in areas like the building, to make the structure less predictable. Let your viewers work for it a little – it's much more engaging! If you look closely at the waterside, there is actually very little edge detail inside the shape – it's all soft and implied with similar hues of brown, grey, and purple. In contrast, the silhouette is strong, with distinct shapes of the trees and the lamp post. The viewer knows what they are looking at without seeing every detail.

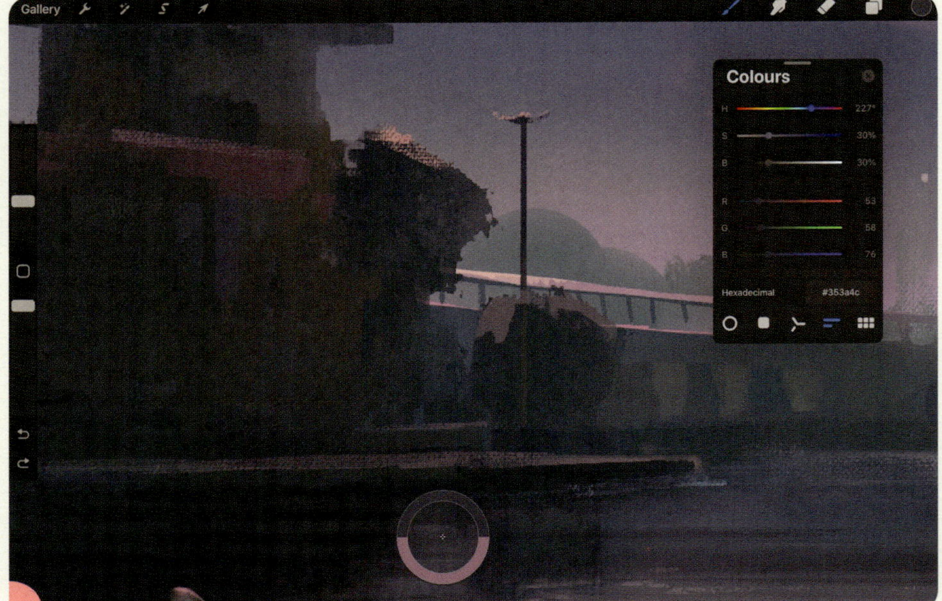

Be conscious of the balance between hard and soft edges

17

When you have a painting you are happy with, you can enhance it with some quick colour and value adjustments. Remember how you restricted the dynamic range during the early stages? This is where you can push it to enhance the contrast and lighting of the final scene. Use Colour Dodge layers to add bloom effects and lift the overall brightness, and use Darken or Multiply layers to deepen the shadowed areas. Making these changes towards the very end of your plein-air painting gives you more flexibility. If you end up taking extra time at home to finish the painting, or if the lighting quality changes, you can fill the gaps using these adjustments.

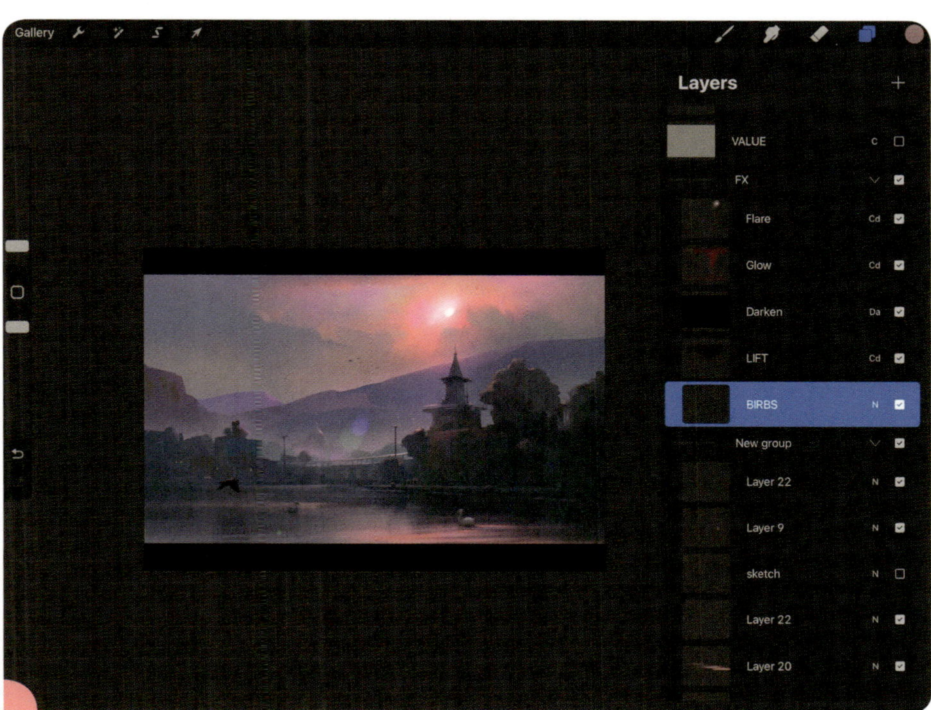
Use blend modes in moderation to boost the scene's lighting

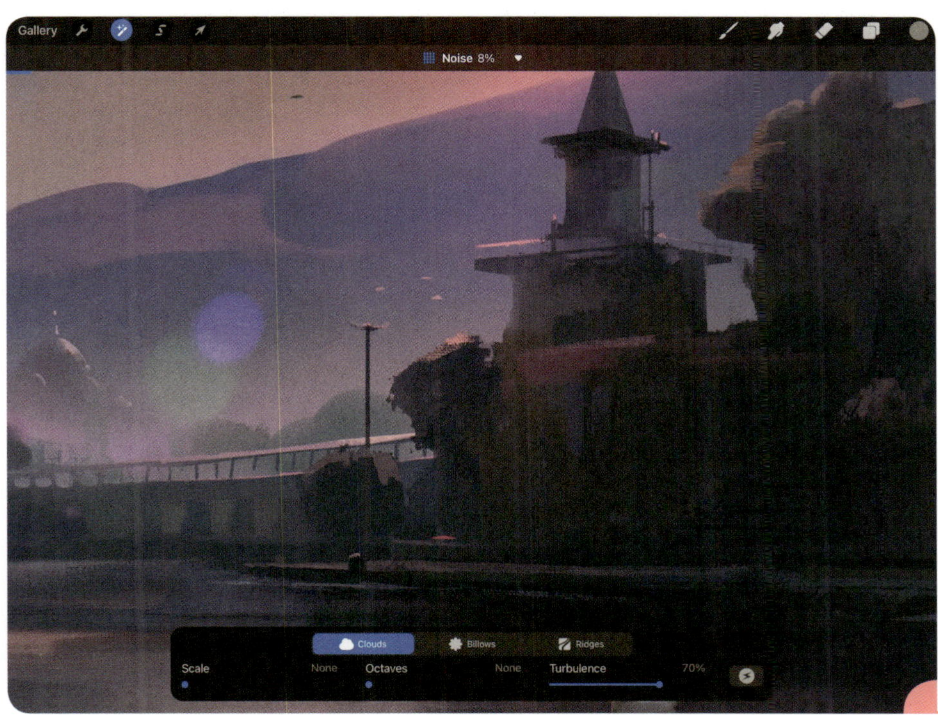
Wrapping up the final painting with a subtle grain layer

18

To finish off the painting, you can add a layer of grain and mild sharpening on top of everything. This will add a lot of perceived detail to the image. To do this, create a new layer, fill it with 50% grey, and set its blend mode to Overlay. Then go to **ADJUSTMENTS > NOISE** and use the slider to increase or decrease the amount of noise. Try to mimic how a camera would work in natural conditions – daylight scenes would have low ISO (a camera's light sensitivity), hence a lower amount of grain, while a darker scene would need higher ISO to capture the details, resulting in a grainier photo. Depending on your preferences, you could even merge the whole image and apply the sharpening and noise then.

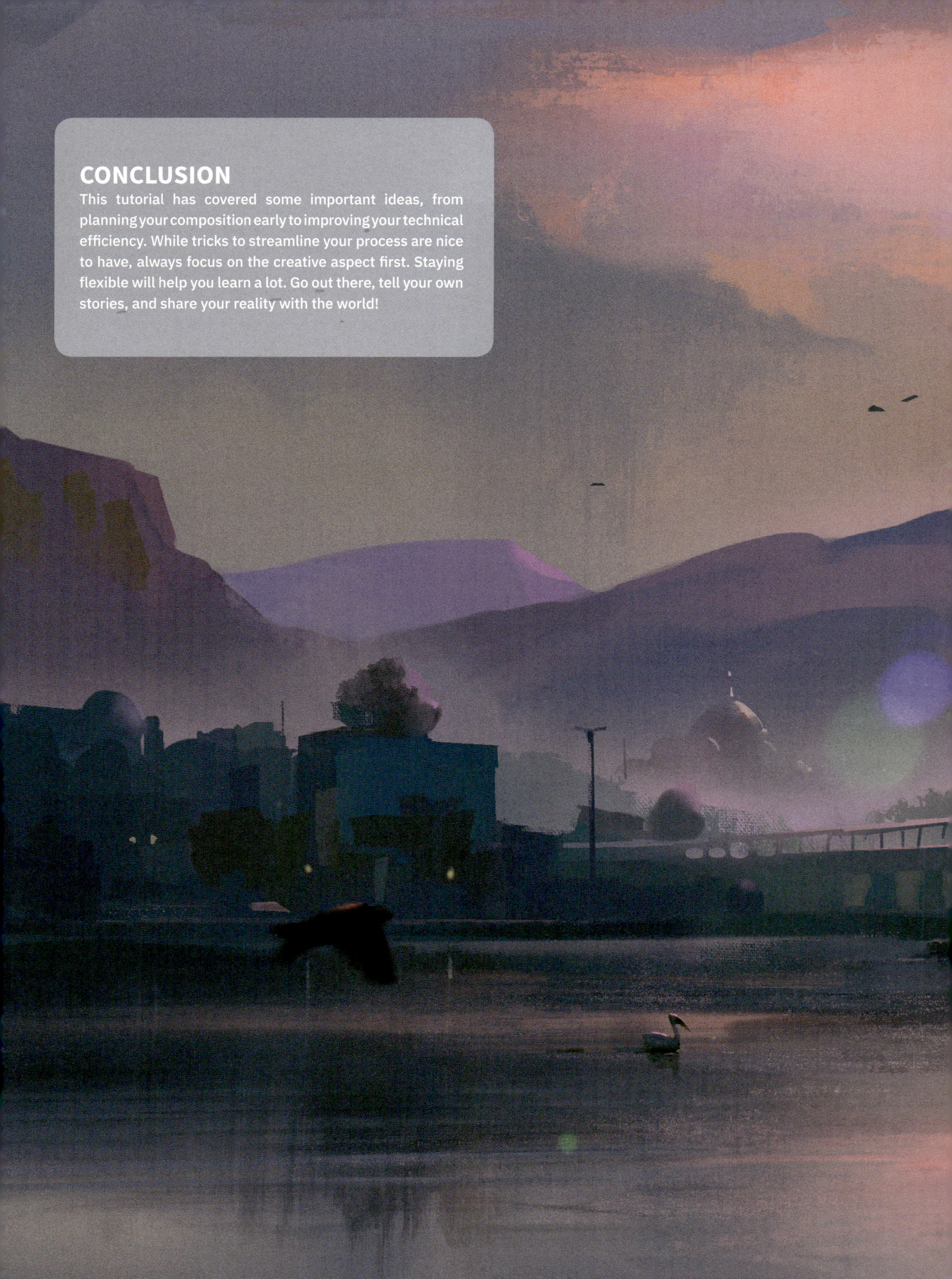

CONCLUSION
This tutorial has covered some important ideas, from planning your composition early to improving your technical efficiency. While tricks to streamline your process are nice to have, always focus on the creative aspect first. Staying flexible will help you learn a lot. Go out there, tell your own stories, and share your reality with the world!

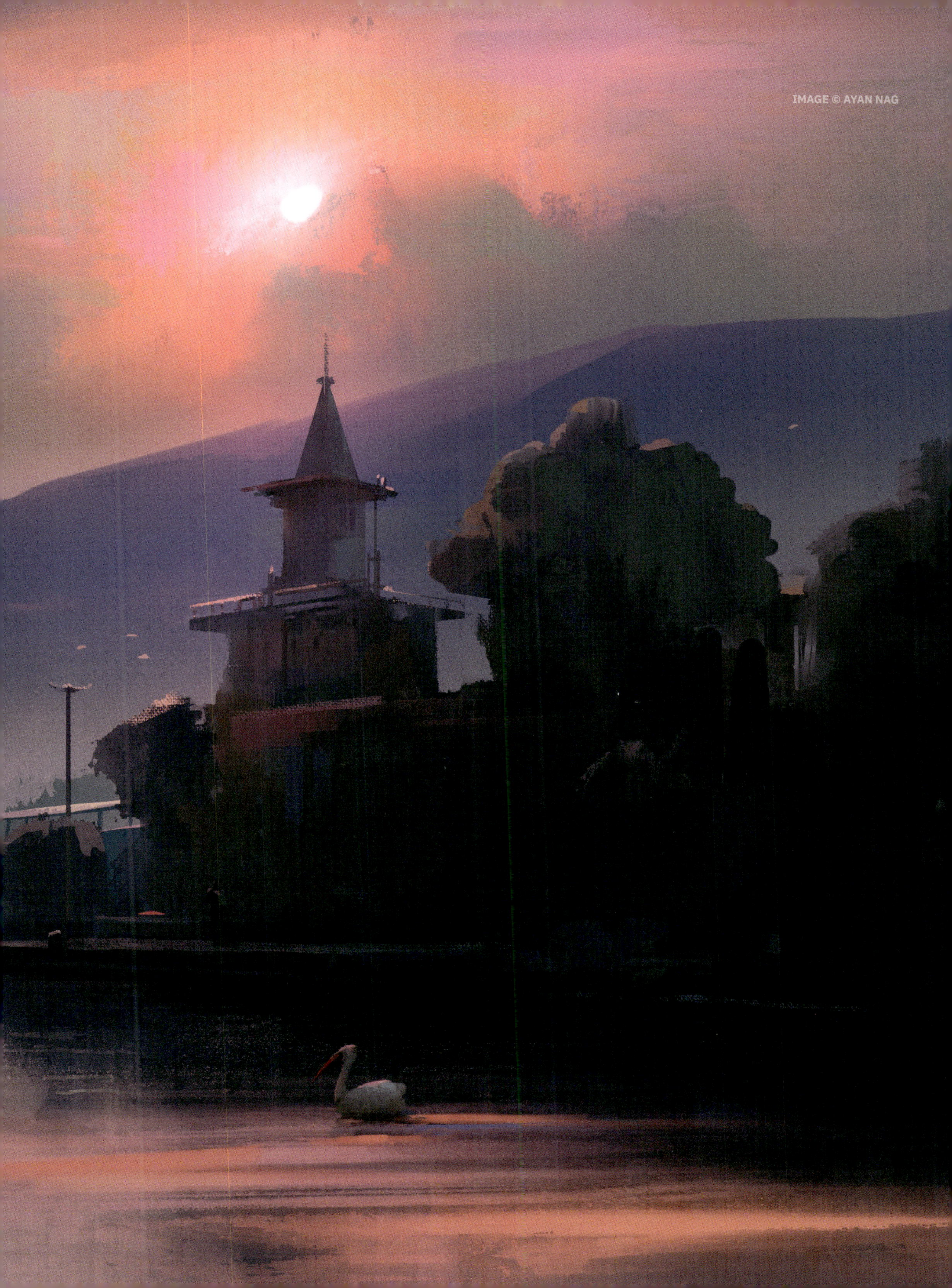
IMAGE © AYAN NAG

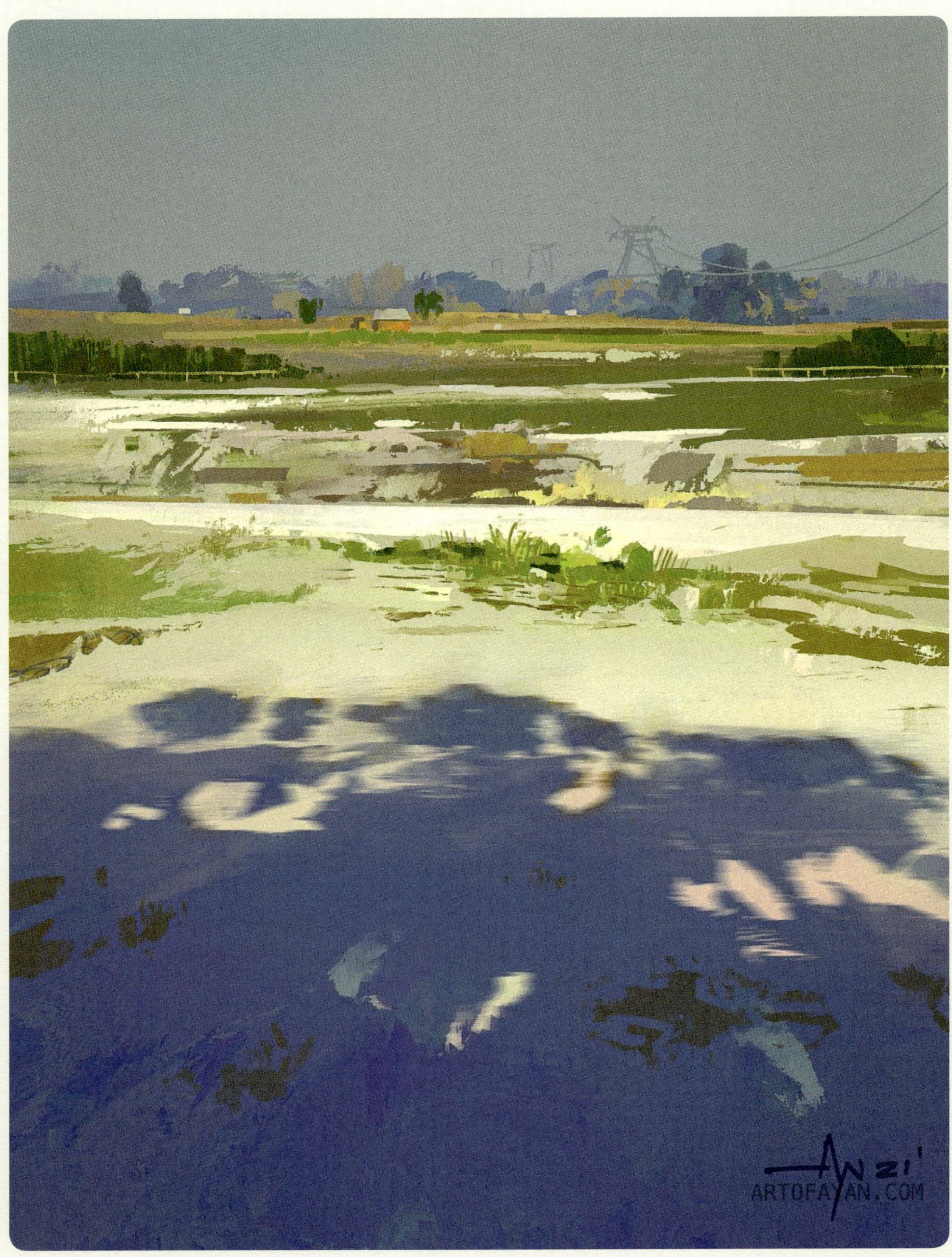

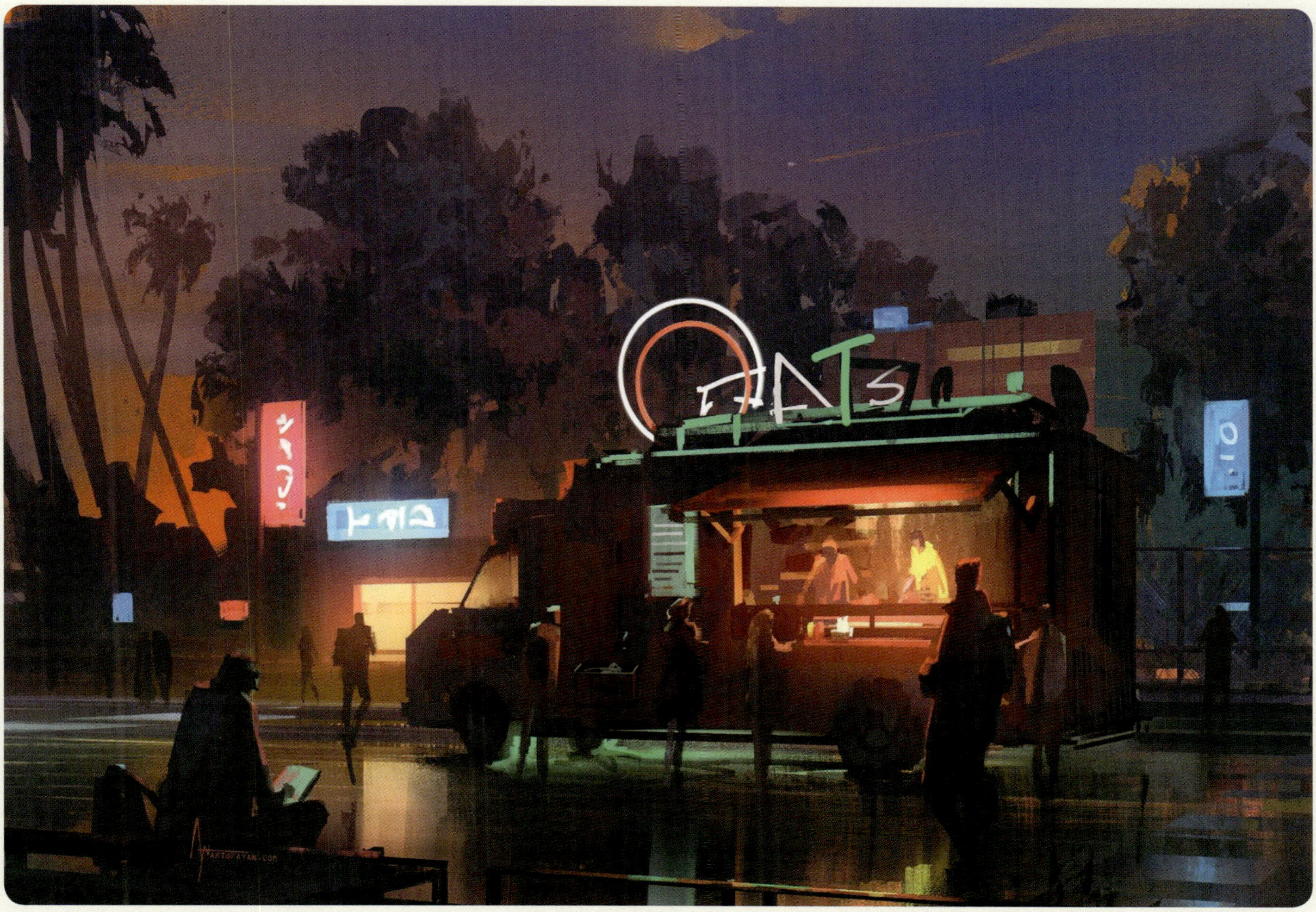

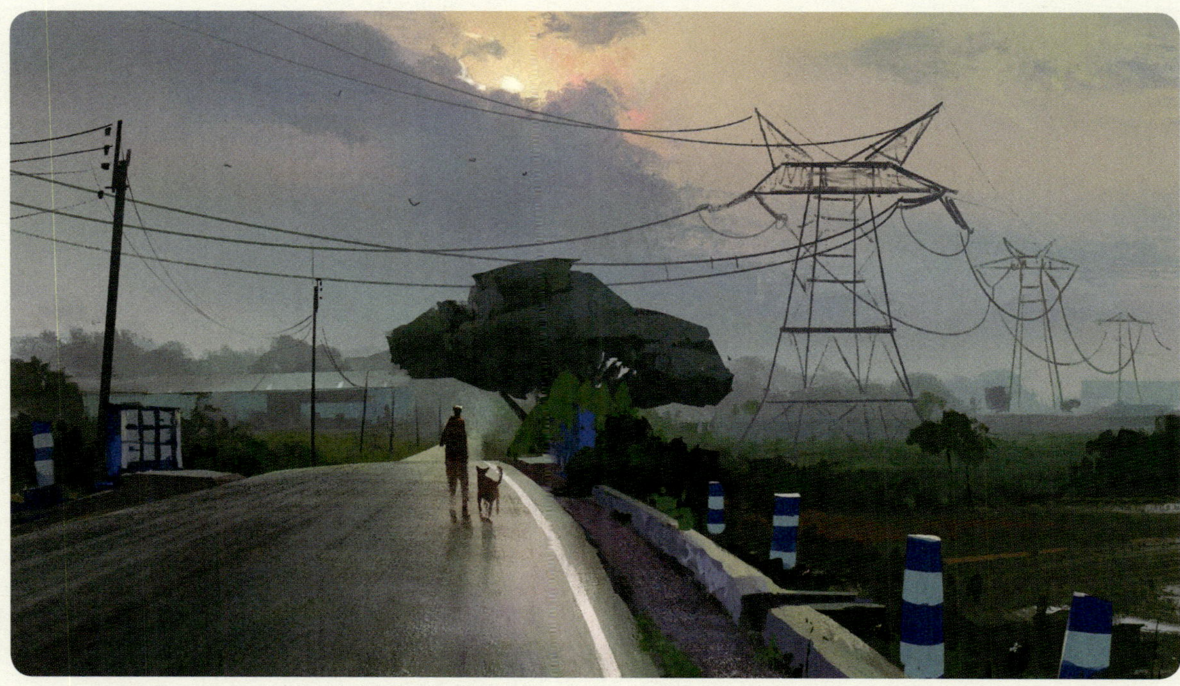

FOOD TRUCK: I went through a phase of watching cooking documentaries and obsessing over food trucks!

PLEINAIRPRIL: Another of my daily environment paintings from PleinAirpril

EVENING IN BAGUIO

BY GILLIAN GALANG

> **GILLIAN SAYS:** *'Painting a night scene can sometimes be intimidating. The darkness makes it harder to judge colours and light, identify shapes, and capture reference photos. This scene of an illuminated waterside in Baguio, in the Philippines, is a perfect challenge for stylizing light, colour, texture, and shape while maintaining a nocturnal atmosphere.'*

LEARN HOW TO...

- **Block out and design a scene with strong shapes**

- **Use different brushes and Colour Dynamics to create a graphic art style**

- **Maximize Procreate's layers and blend modes to create vibrant light and texture**

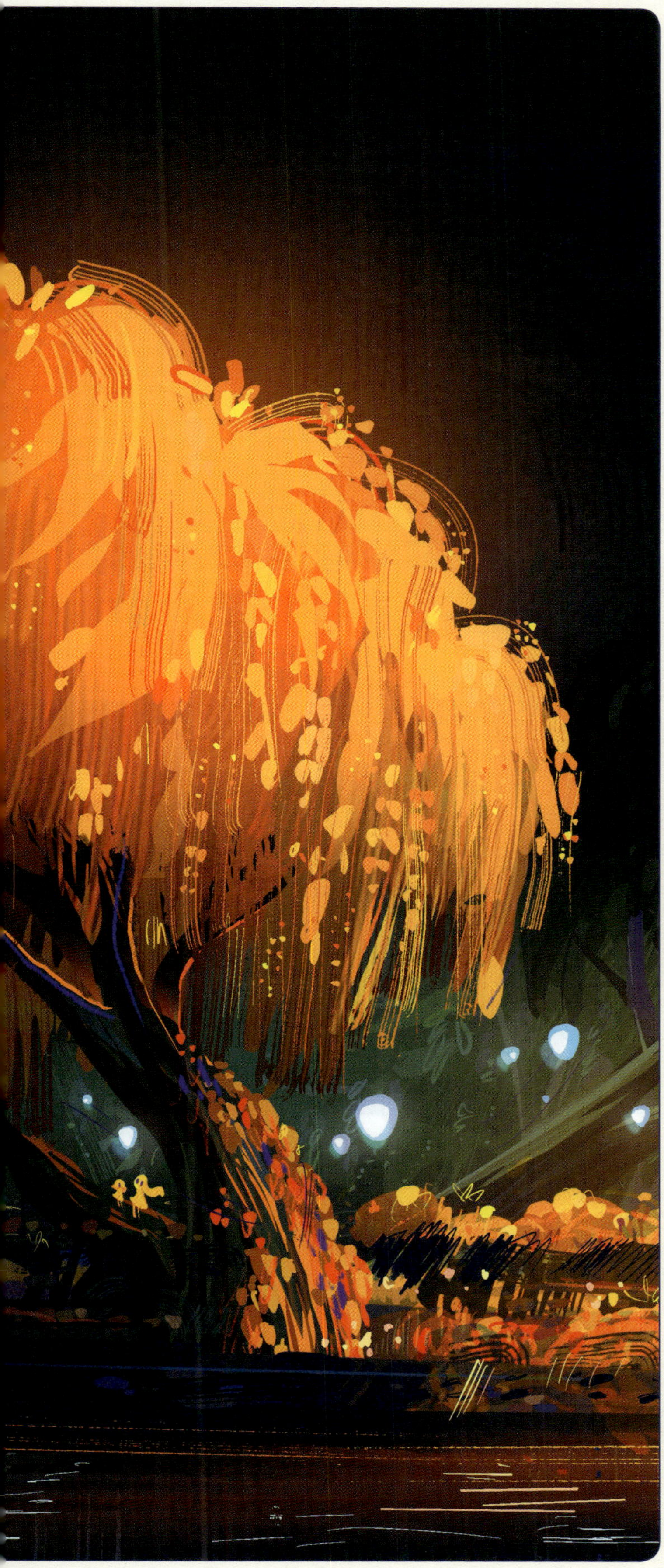

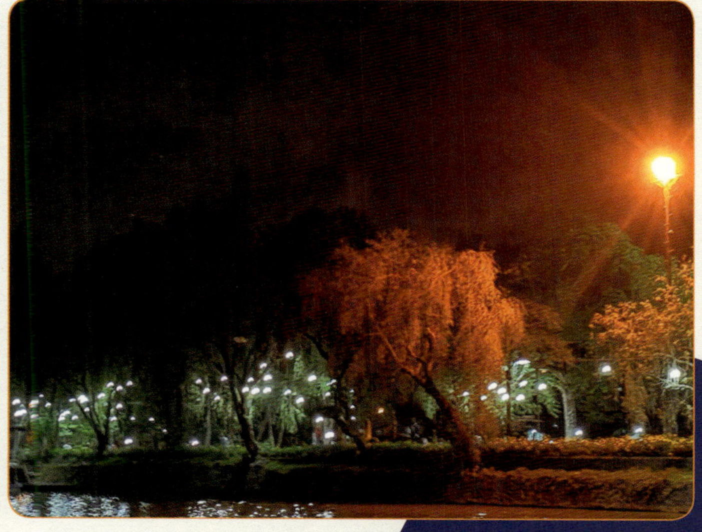

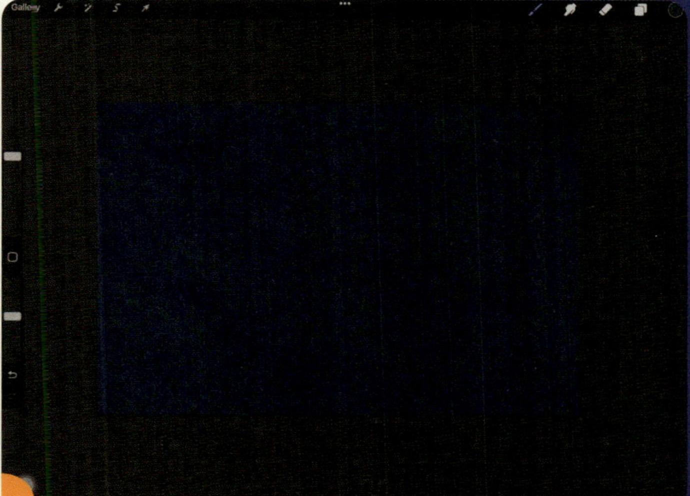

The canvas is now filled with a starting background colour with subtle variations

01

Create a landscape canvas, ideally 5,000 pixels wide by 3,300 pixels high, or a similar proportion that will allow you to create up to 50 layers if needed. Choose the **PAINTING > NIKKO RULL** brush and double-tap it to open the Brush Studio. Under its Colour Dynamics tab, raise the Hue slider under Stamp Colour Jitter to 12% and the Hue slider under Stroke Colour Jitter to 2%. Hit Done to confirm. Raise your brush's size to maximum, pick a dark blue-grey colour, and drag your brush diagonally across the canvas until you have filled the whole area.

02

Now you can block in the first shapes of the environment. Add a new layer and then pick the **DRAWING > EVOLVE** brush and set its size to around 40%. Pick a darker green colour and draw half-ellipse shapes that will form the tree-line. Then pick a lighter green colour, not as light as the background colour, and start layering the shapes to add depth to the trees. Add a dark rectangular shape below the trees, using a very deep navy or purplish hue, as a backdrop for the waterside.

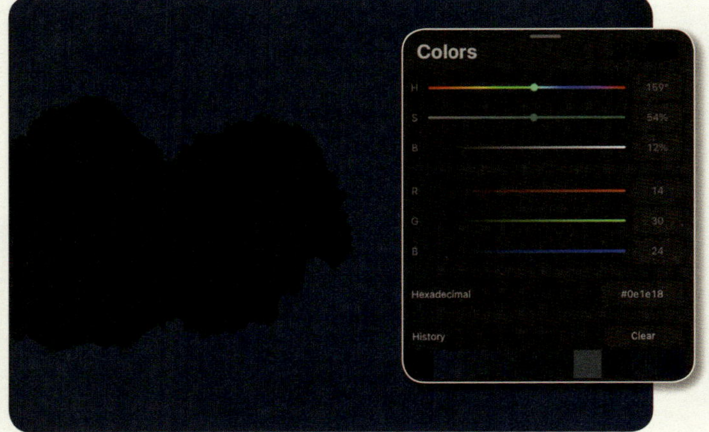

The first block-in is made by drawing simple shapes for the trees

03

Add a new layer below the trees block-in layer, pick a darker indigo shade, and set your brush size to around 25%. Block in more background trees peeking through the darker green shapes. Next, pick a grey-toned indigo colour. Add a new layer below all the tree layers and start to block in the clouds with stylized crescent shapes – an exaggeration inspired by some of the curves visible in the real clouds. Add a new layer above all the trees and pick a cool light-green shade. Set the **PAINTING > NIKKO RULL** brush to a large size and paint short vertical strokes to create a glow effect along the waterside.

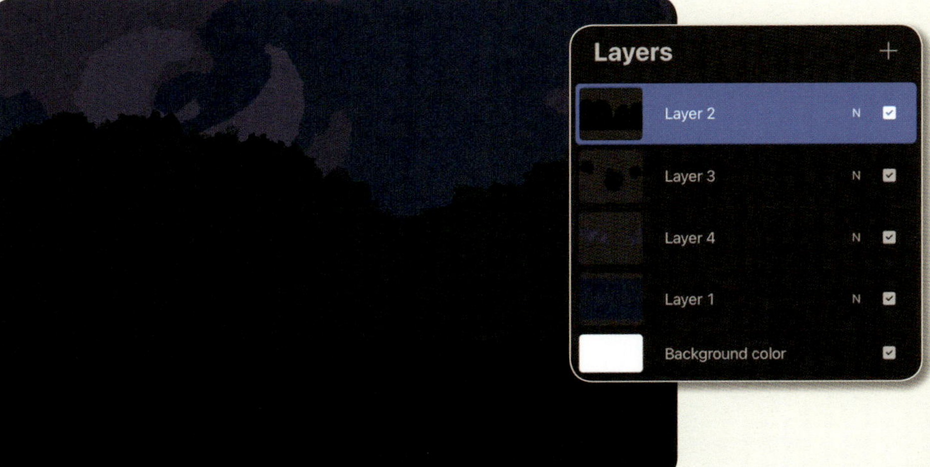

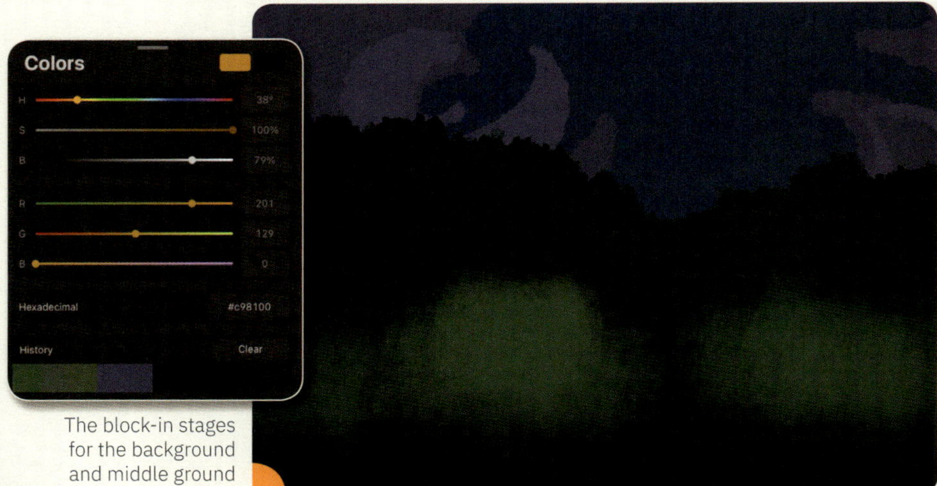

The block-in stages for the background and middle ground

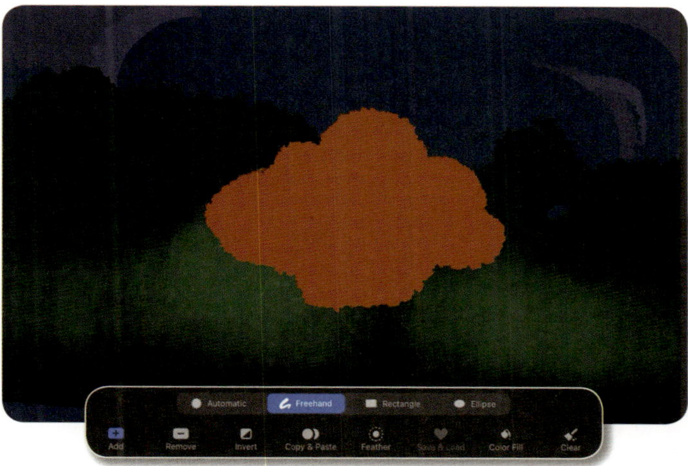

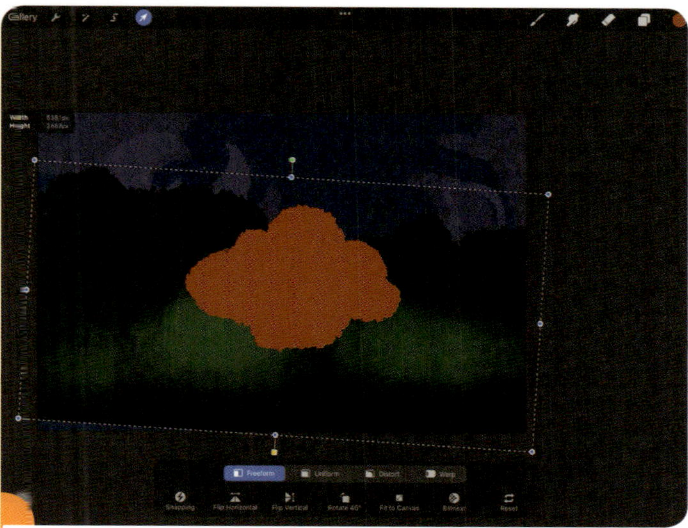

Add the beginnings of the foreground tree to the painting

04

Add a new layer on top and select the **DRAWING > EVOLVE** brush. Paint a cloud-like orange shape to block in the foreground tree. Tap the Transform tool and rotate your layers slightly using the green node, so that the tree layers and ground plane aren't perfectly flat. You may need to use the Eraser to remove some parts of the clouds, ensuring they frame the foreground tree.

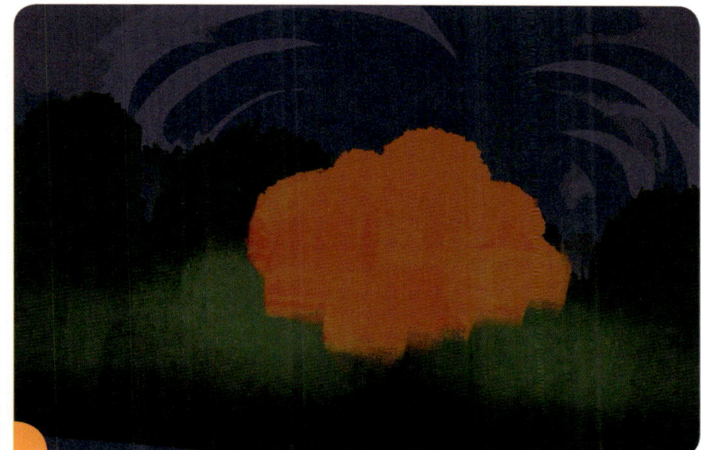

Add texture and colour variations to the foreground tree and the clouds framing it

05

Continue cleaning up and developing the clouds, using the Selection tool to lasso crescent shapes and fill them with a lighter violet-grey. Select **AIRBRUSHING > SOFT BRUSH** and go to the dark indigo trees layer. Colour-pick that light violet-grey cloud colour and drag it up over the bases of the trees, without touching their tops, to create the impression of the furthest trees fading into the atmosphere.

06

Go to the light-green glow layer and paint three dark, round bumps below it using **PAINTING > NIKKO RULL**, roughly blocking out where some bushes will be. Add a new layer on top of the foreground tree and draw its trunk, using the **INKING > SYRUP** brush in any colour for now. Switch back to Nikko Rull and add a new layer on top. Here, paint a diagonal plane across the foreground using a light mustard yellow, holding down to automatically snap it into a QuickShape. This is where there's a walkway along the waterside. On a new layer above that, paint another line of light orange to add depth to the foreground.

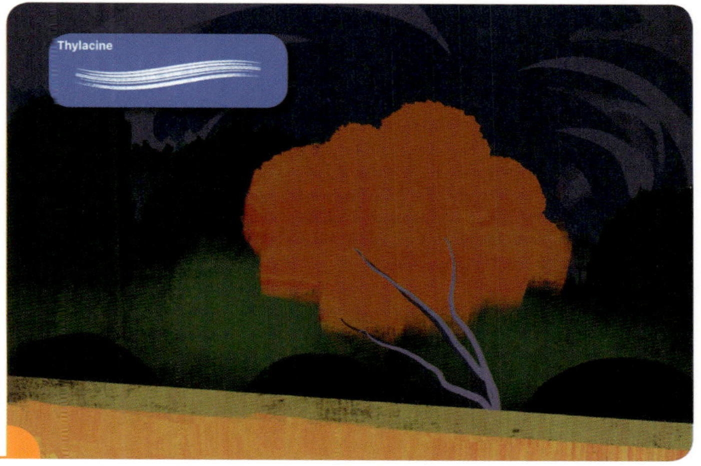

Finish the medium-sized shapes by adding tree trunks and a foreground

07

Add a new layer on top of the clouds and background fill, and colour-pick from the clouds again. Still using the Nikko Rull brush, lightly drag upwards to add more texture to the sky, switching the colour as you go to introduce a bit of blue. Change to the **INKING > THYLACINE** brush to add more texture to the clouds by following their curves. Merge the results and go to **ADJUSTMENTS > HUE, SATURATION, BRIGHTNESS**, then lower the background's saturation to about 25% to deepen the nocturnal atmosphere. Use the Thylacine brush on the background trees layer to give them some vertical texture, too.

Open the **INKING > DRY INK** brush in the Brush Studio. Set the **STAMP COLOUR JITTER > HUE** slider to 5% and **STROKE COLOUR JITTER > HUE** slider to 10%. Use this on the bushes layer to flesh out their shapes with dark blue-green. You can even add some branches and twigs, picking colours from the sky and yellow foreground. Finally, create a new layer between the bushes and foreground planes, and add some large grey-blue tree trunks that curve around to frame the main orange tree.

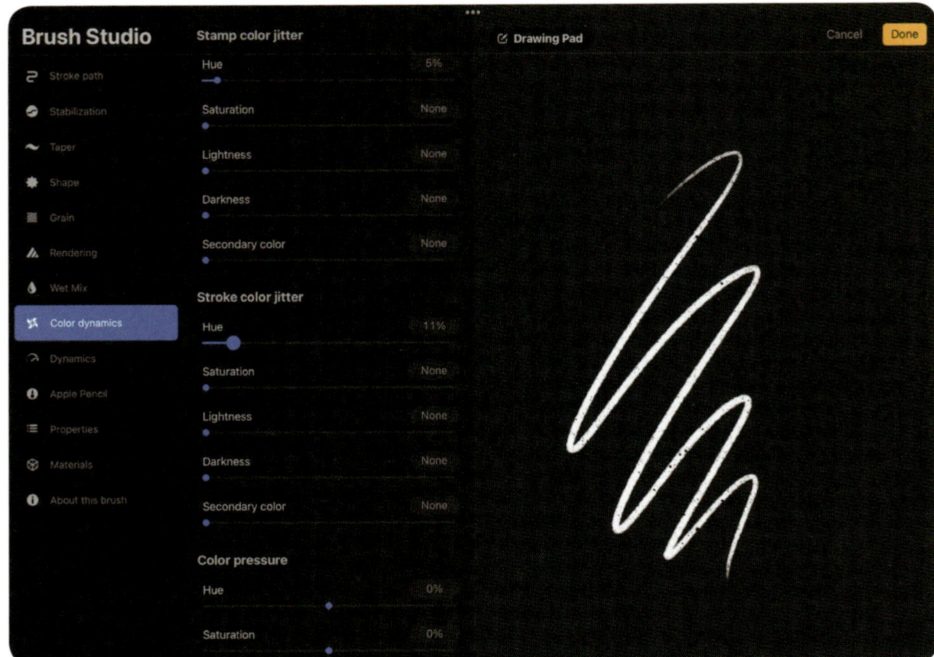

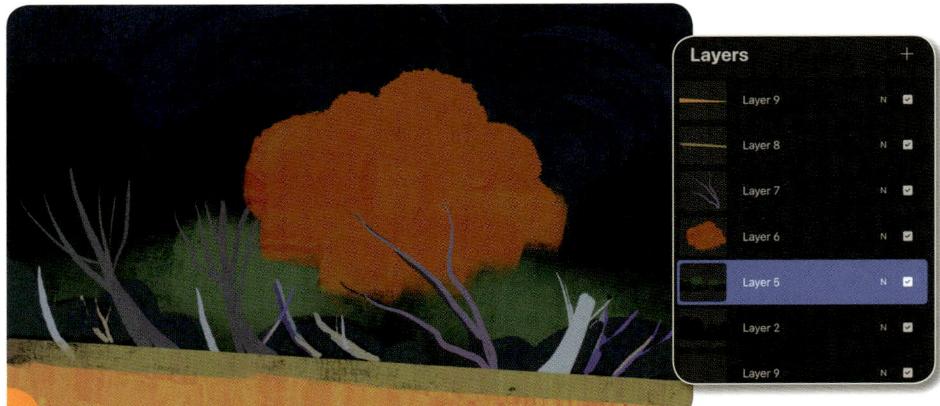

Add the smaller shape block-ins and a bit more texture painting

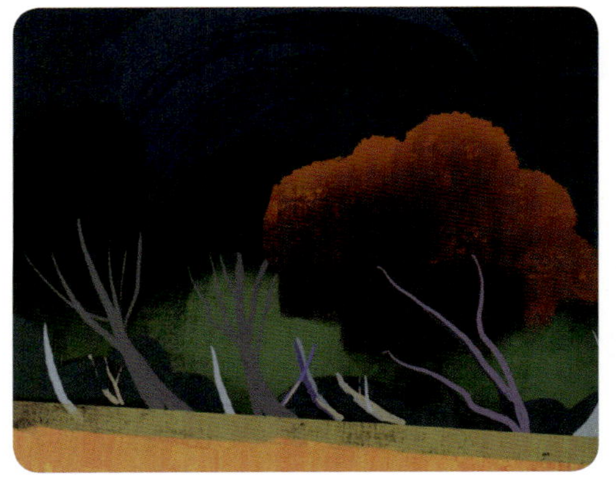

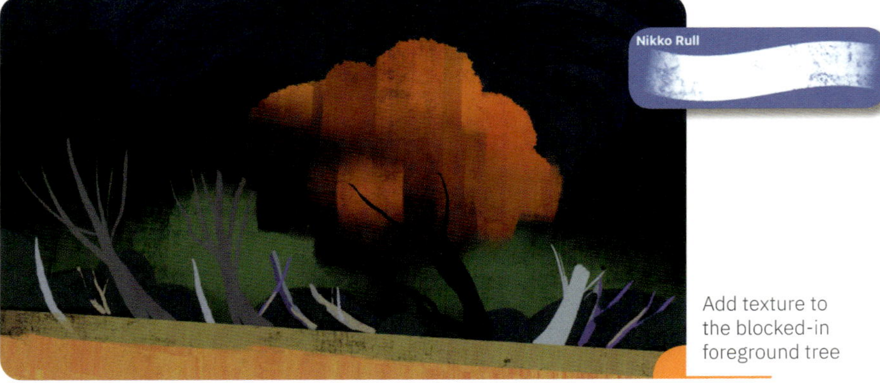

Add texture to the blocked-in foreground tree

08

In the Layers menu, tap on the thumbnail of the orange tree layer and enable Alpha Lock. With the Nikko Rull brush and a dark magenta colour, paint short vertical strokes to darken the underside of the tree without touching the top parts. Colour-pick the bright orange from the treetop and make more downward strokes over the shadowed areas, creating big, chunky groups of leaves. Next, go to the separate tree trunk layer, Alpha Lock it, and fill it with dark blue.

09

Now you can go through each layer to build up every element a little more. Go to the mustard-yellow walkway layer, Alpha Lock it, and use Nikko Rull to paint variations of blue and violet onto it. Alpha Lock the lower orange foreground layer next and paint it with a solid violet stripe. Move the main tree-trunk layer on top of the foreground layers (or toggle off the foreground layers' visibility) so you can refine the trunk more easily, adding some extra branches and definition. Go to the background layer and add a new layer above it. Use Nikko Rull and Thylacine to paint the top of the sky with a dark blue; set the layer to Multiply mode and lower its opacity to around 48%. This will give the sky a deeper, cooler tone with layered textures. Finally, paint more detail into the middle-ground layer, using Nikko Rull in dark blues close in tone to the original tree colours. Try using **SELECTION > FREEHAND** to lasso irregular shapes and curves, creating dark, crisp shades and leaf groups with the **INKING > SYRUP** brush.

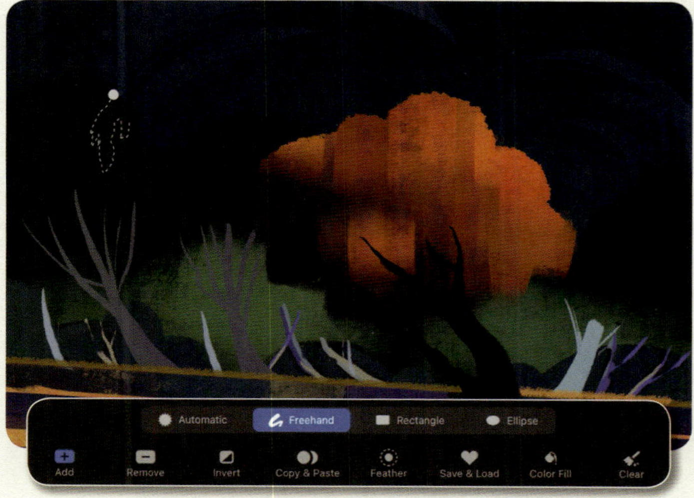

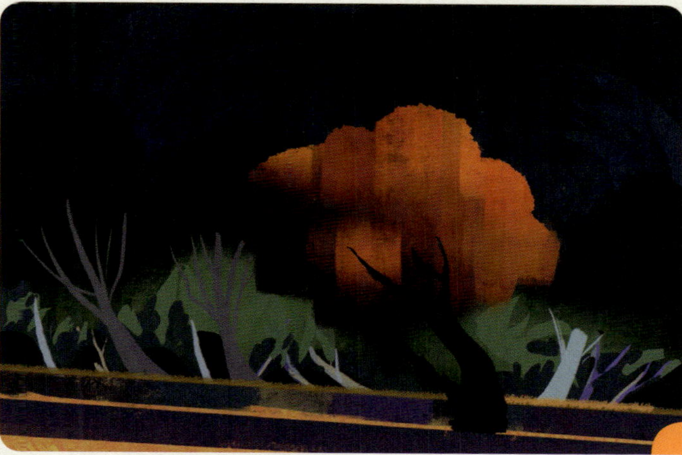

The background now has depth, the trees are textured evenly, and the foreground elements are more readable

10

With **INKING > SYRUP** still selected, open the Brush Studio and go to the Colour Dynamics tab. Set the **STAMP COLOUR JITTER > HUE** slider to 20% and **STROKE COLOUR JITTER > HUE** slider to 2%. Paint smaller trunks into the middle-ground undergrowth layer using shades of light beige, green, and purple, and add another larger, dark trunk on the right side.

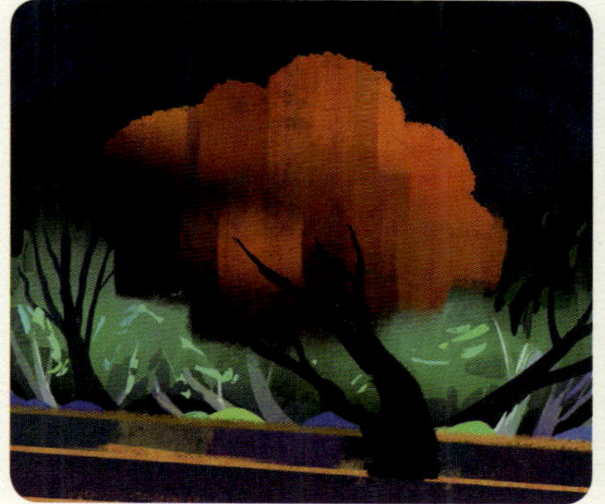

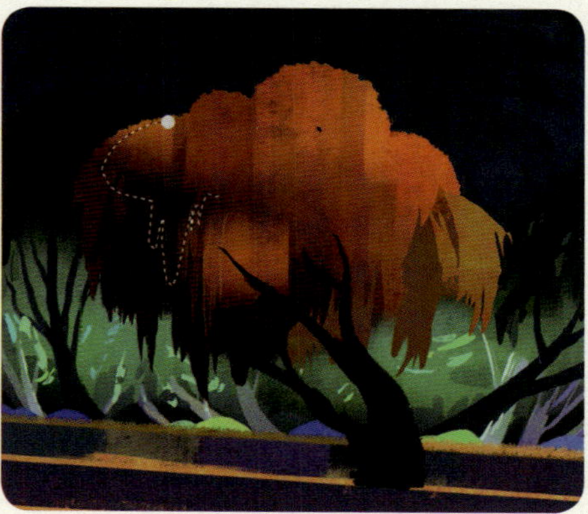

Switch back to the Nikko Rull brush, choose a light green, and lightly brush the undersides of the middle-ground trees to capture the glow of the lights beneath them. Add a mix of dark- and light-green leaf details by drawing them with the Syrup brush, or by using the Selection tool to lasso and fill several leaf shapes at once, erasing parts afterwards if needed. Below the trees, block out some more small bushes in shades of blue and green. Go to the orange tree layer, turn off Alpha Lock, and use the Selection tool to lasso some hanging leaf groups on the lower-left side, painting them with shades of burgundy and red-brown. Use the Thylacine brush to add strokes of texture in red, yellow, and orange, and break the tree's silhouette with some looser lines. On the main trunk layer, enable Alpha Lock and use Thylacine to create texture, dragging turquoise and orange strokes down along the tree's curved form.

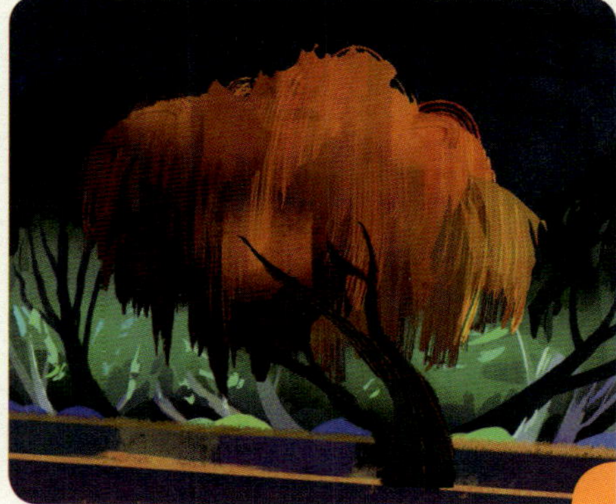

Developing the main tree

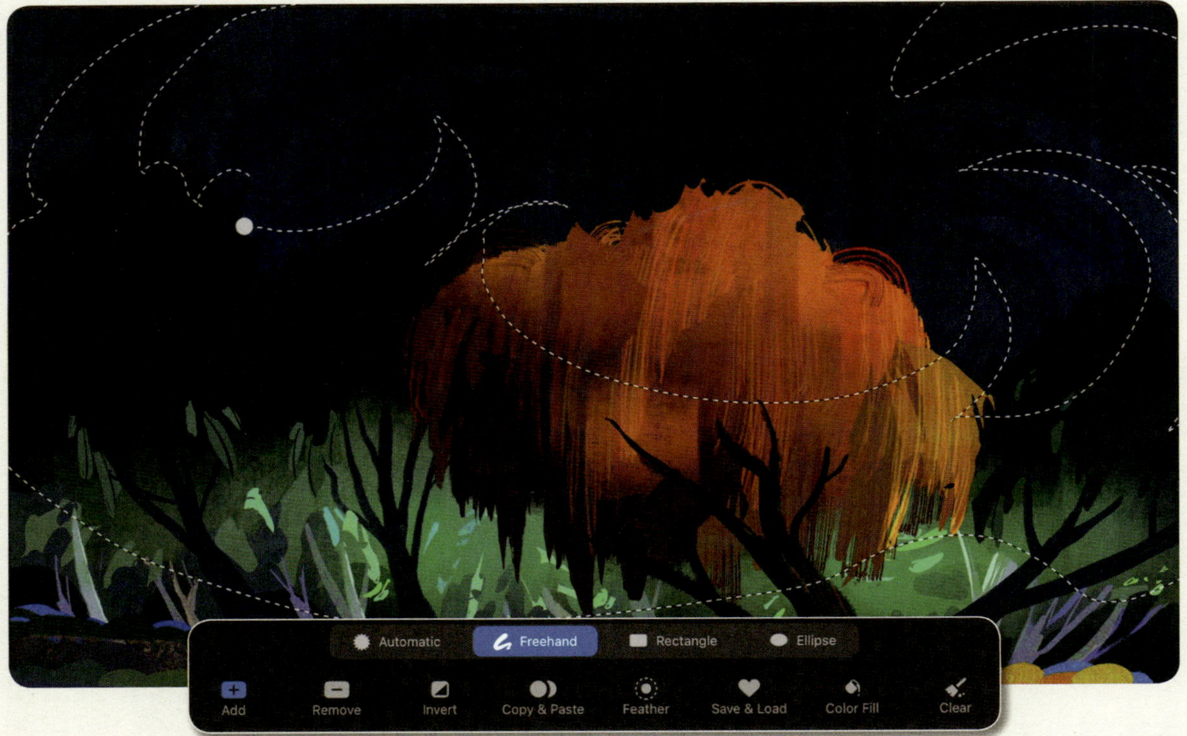

11

Still on the foreground tree-trunk layer, use the Selection tool to lasso the left side of the trunk, where the shadow would be cast from the light source on the upper right. Paint in those shadows with the Nikko Rull brush and a dark turquoise colour.

After all this tree detailing, it's a good time to revisit the background and foreground. Add a new layer behind all the trees and use the Selection tool to confidently draw big, curving shapes in the sky area. Fill them with light blue-purple, then set the layer mode to Colour Dodge and lower the opacity to 10%. Colour-pick the darkest blue from the background and add some curved and straight strokes to the sky for extra texture. If you lose the subtle gradient effect in the sky, you can use **ADJUSTMENTS > HUE, SATURATION, BRIGHTNESS** to bring some blue gradation back.

On the lighter foreground layer, use the Syrup brush to block out rows of simple bushes in different shades of green and orange, balancing out the colours of the foreground and middle ground.

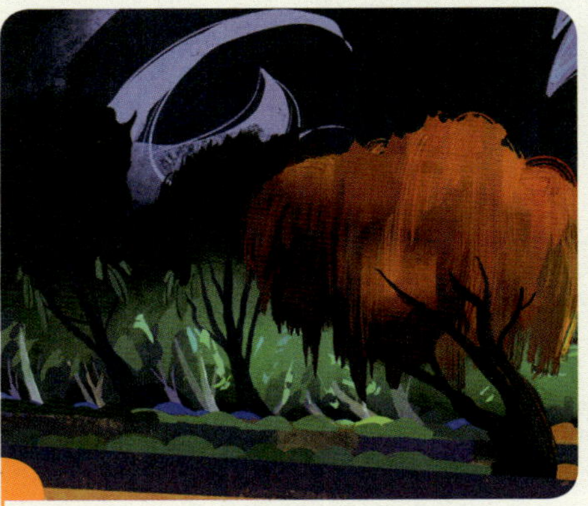
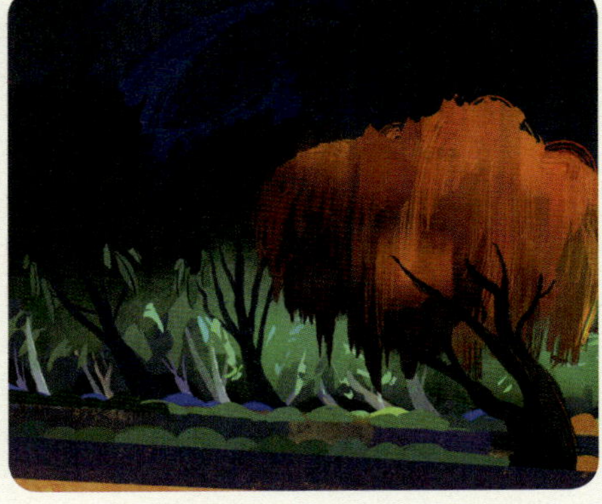

The sky now looks more lively with its texture variety, curved forms, and gradient effect

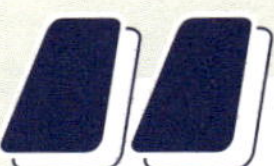

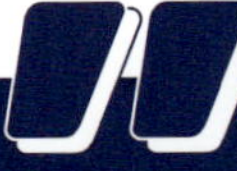

GILLIAN SAYS: *'So far you have blocked in the shapes of the background, middle ground, and foreground. You have used the Nikko Rull, Syrup, Dry Ink, Soft Brush, and Thylacine brushes, changing their Colour Dynamics settings to add hue variety. Importantly, you started painting from big to small shapes. This makes the painting process faster by blocking out the skeleton of the whole painting. To develop this process in your future paintings, do it consistently and analyse your reference first. Look for the biggest shapes first, then the medium ones, and the smaller shapes last.'*

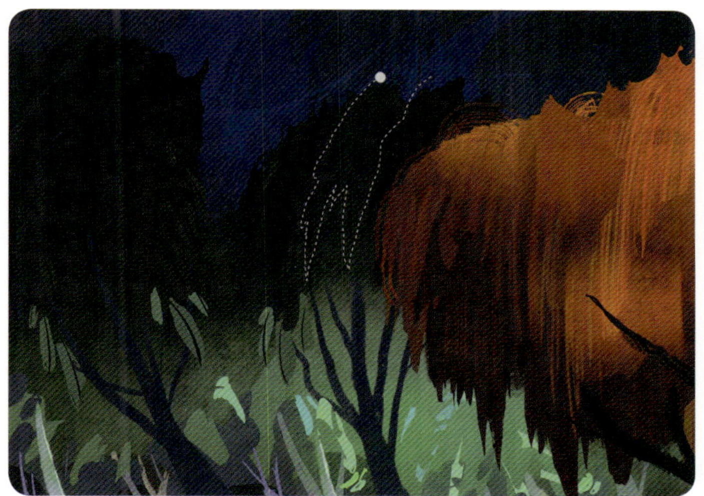

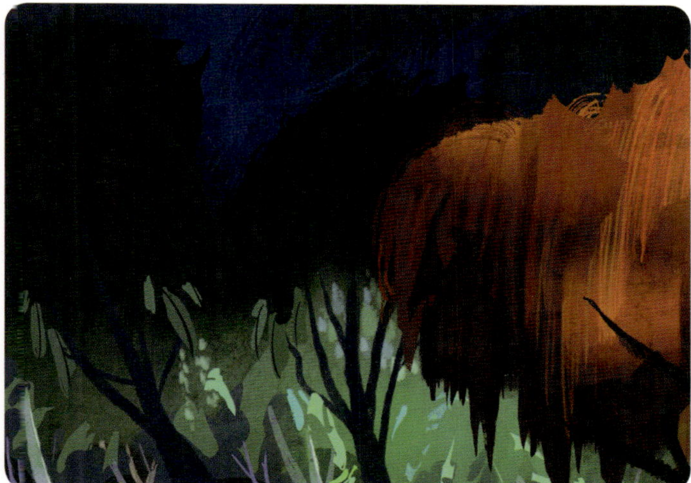

12

Continue using **SELECTION > FREEHAND** as a way to easily create shape and colour variety in the scene. In the middle-ground layer, use it to lasso the tops of the trees and paint in shades of deeper blue-green. Add tints of red for the light reflection from the main tree and use the Syrup and Nikko Rull brushes to draw more small shapes. The second middle-ground tree trunk could have a curvier shape, to better frame the orange tree, so select it and use **TRANSFORM > DISTORT** to adjust it.

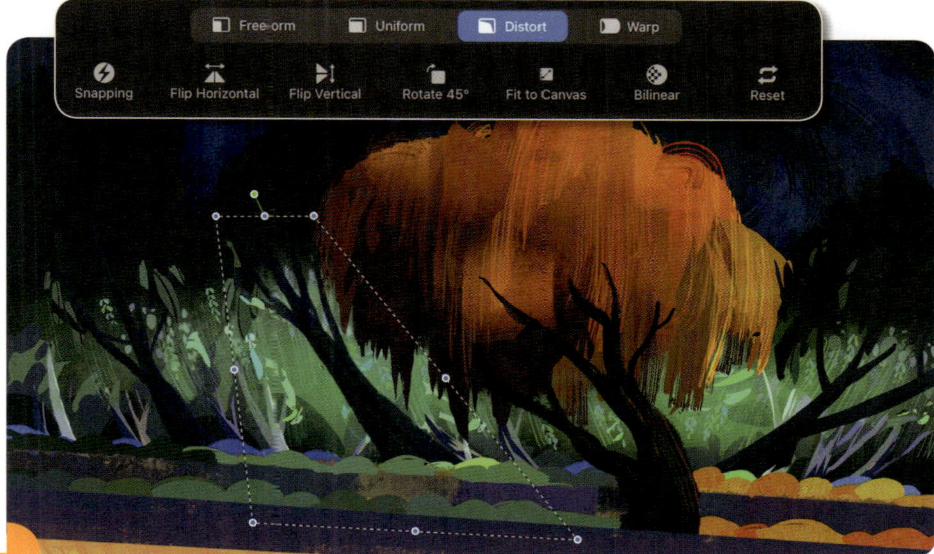

The middle-ground trees are becoming more recognizable with their leaf details and textures

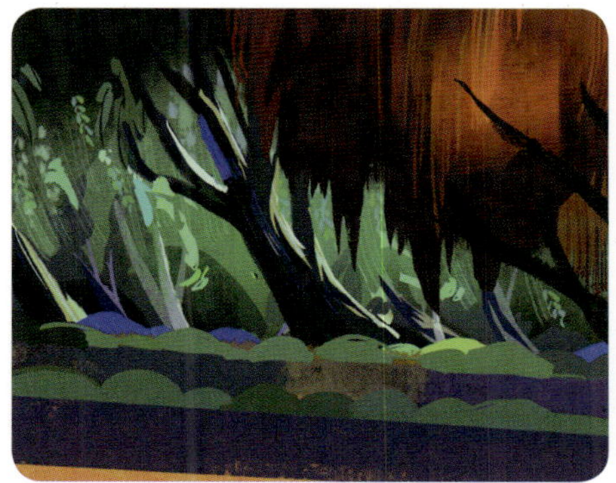

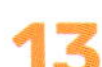

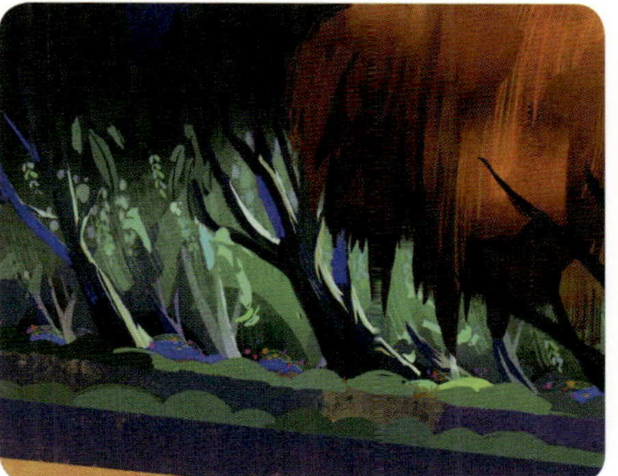

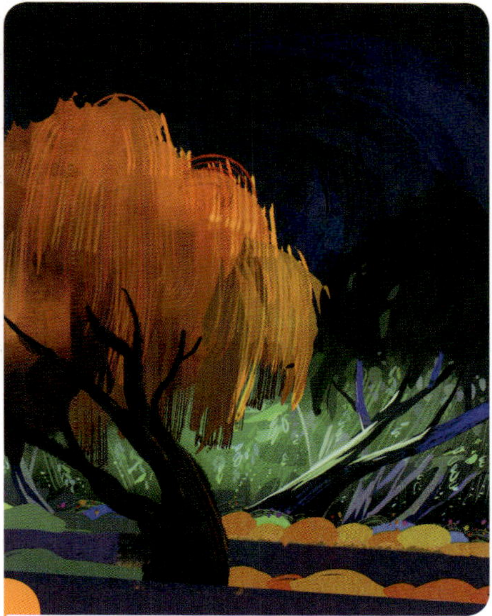

Introduce more vibrant colour and lighting into the middle-ground elements

13

To develop the middle-ground trees even more, paint more shape and definition into their trunks with the Syrup brush, and Alpha Lock the layer afterwards. Use the Selection tool to lasso areas on the right-hand edges of the trunks, where highlights would be, and paint them with light green shades. For texture, use Nikko Rull and Thylacine to add a few strokes of vibrant blue and purple per tree. Use Thylacine and Syrup to paint in some small flowers and leaf details in a mix of colours.

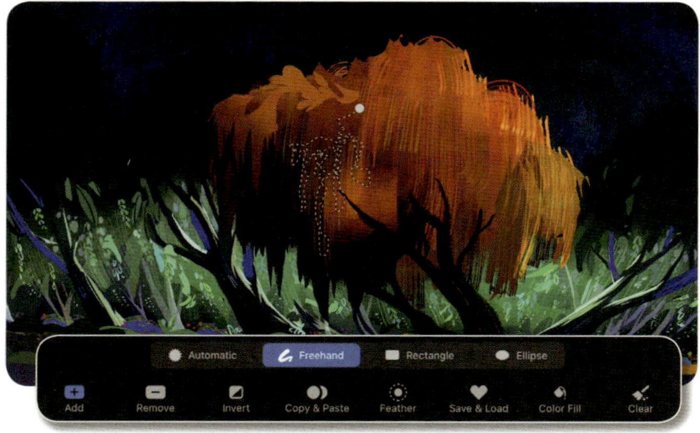

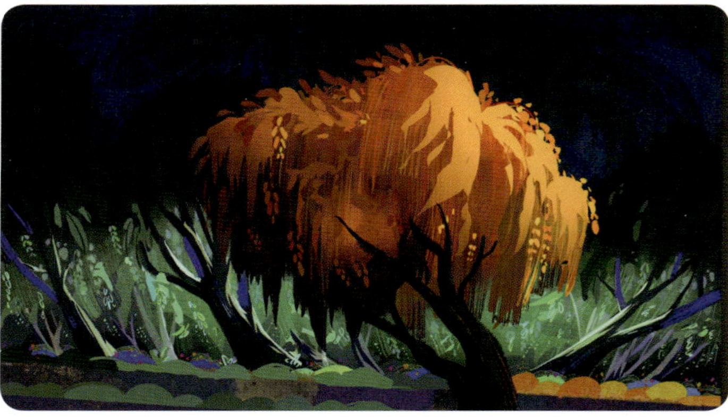

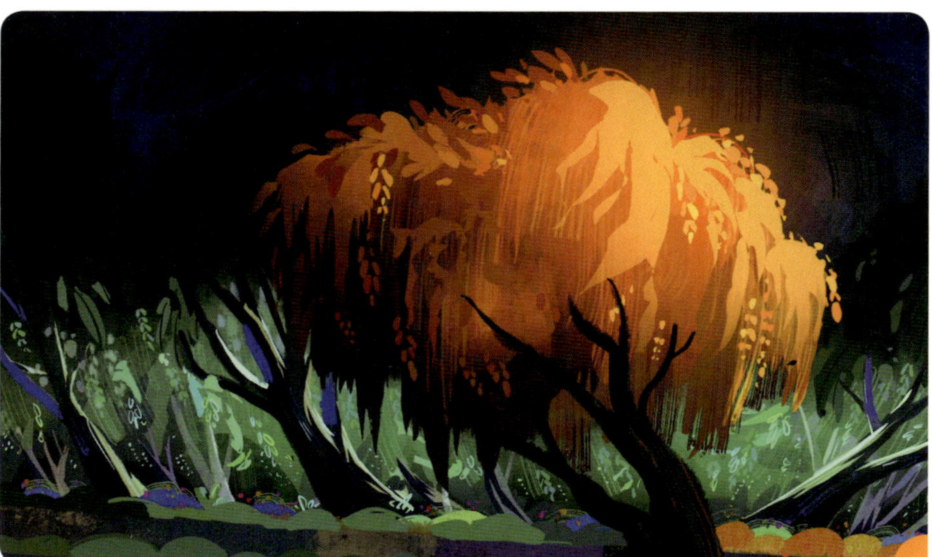

The foreground tree will start glowing at this stage

14

The bright lamp post in the real-life scene creates the impression that the main tree is glowing orange, which is something you can really exaggerate and stylize here. On the main tree layer, lasso willow-like leaf groups and paint them with the Syrup brush according to the light source – darker orange shapes on the left side and brighter golden shapes on the right. Set the brush to a smaller size to paint in random leaf patterns. Add a new layer, set it to Overlay mode, and use Soft Brush at a large size to dab a warm orange glow on the upper-right side of the tree.

15

As you did for the middle-ground trunks, use the Selection tool on the main tree's trunk layer to lasso areas to highlight. Paint these with yellow and orange tones colour-picked from the leaves. Use the Dry Ink brush to paint some extra branches touching the light, adding depth to the tree's structure. Use the Syrup brush and colour-picked orange hues to add more details to the foreground layer bushes.

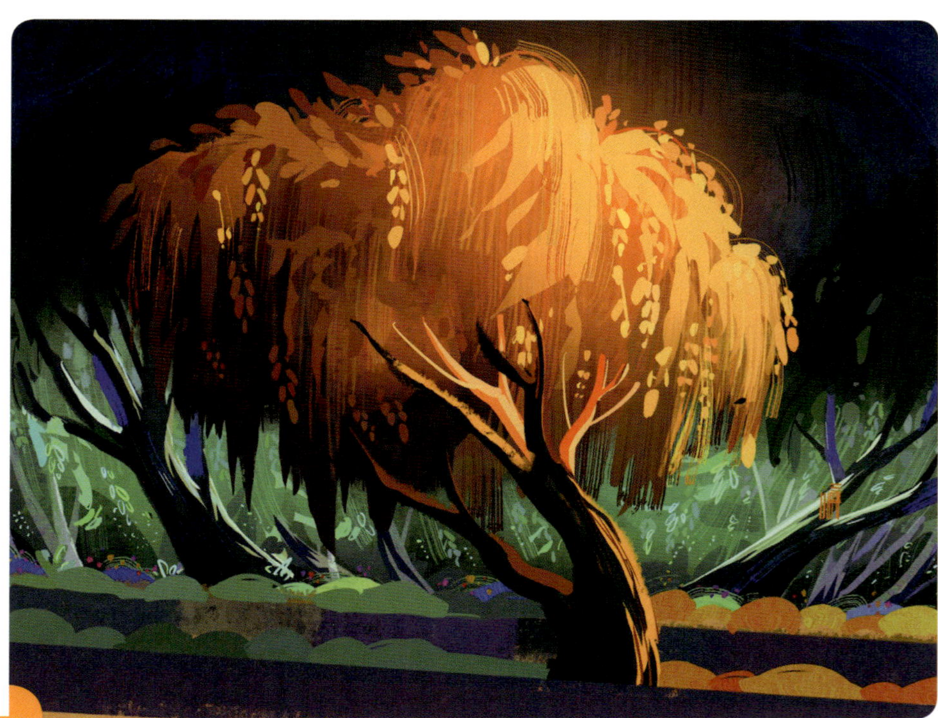

Add detail in and around the foreground tree, making it the centre of attention

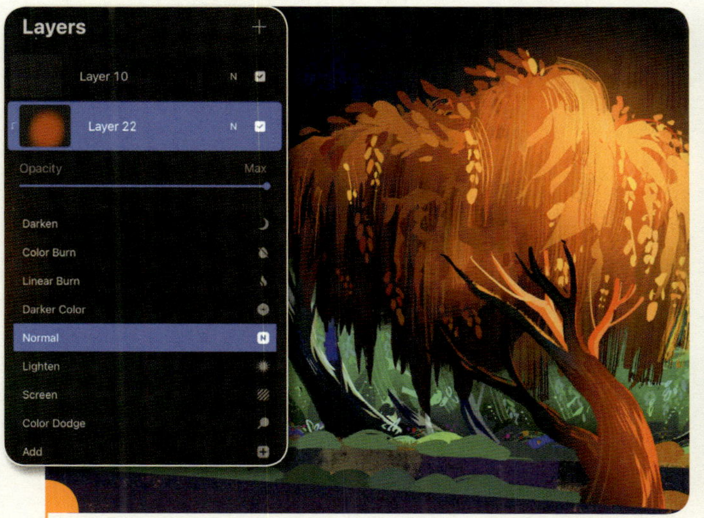

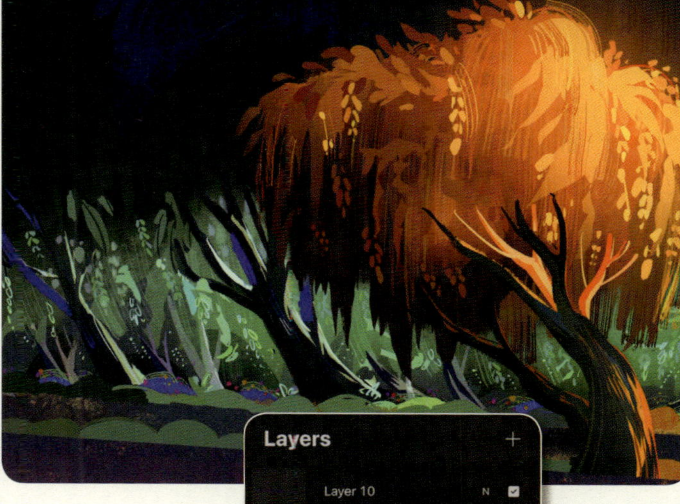

Paint more tree-trunk details to balance it against the leaves

16

Add a new layer on top of the foreground tree's trunk, tap on its thumbnail in the Layers menu, and select Clipping Mask to clip it to the trunk layer. Use Soft Brush to paint a vibrant orange glow on the lower right of the trunk. Set the layer's mode to Luminosity and lower its opacity to around 45%. Use the Selection tool to lasso parts of the tree trunk – aim for flowing, streaky shapes resembling tree bark. Make another clipping mask layer and fill those selections with a dark red-brown shadow.

Finally, create another new layer and paint dabs of orange and yellow on the tree trunk with the Syrup brush, suggesting soft mosses growing on it. In the Colours menu, you can use the HSB sliders in the Classic or Value views to switch colours and quickly create variety between each bit of moss and flora.

Use Syrup and Thylacine with shades of pink, purple, orange, yellow, and teal to add flowers, leaves, and grasses along the foreground. Use multiple layers if you want to, so you can easily undo details, and keep the most warmth and detail in the area nearest the light source.

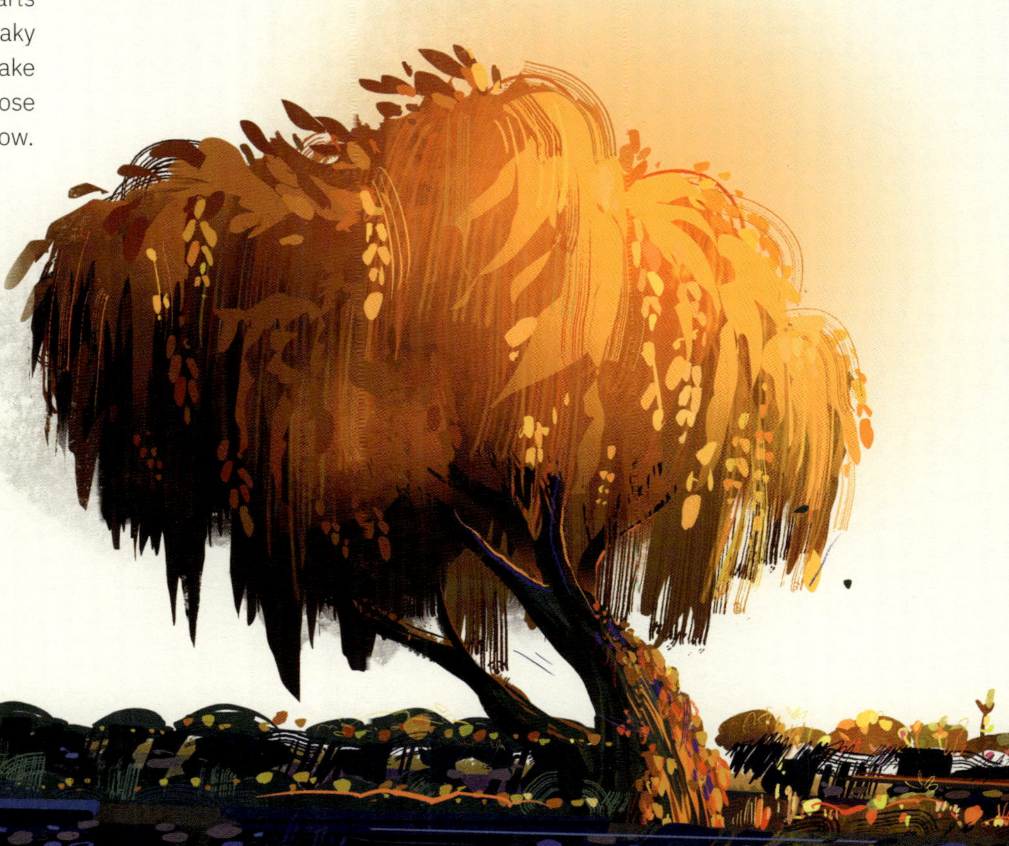

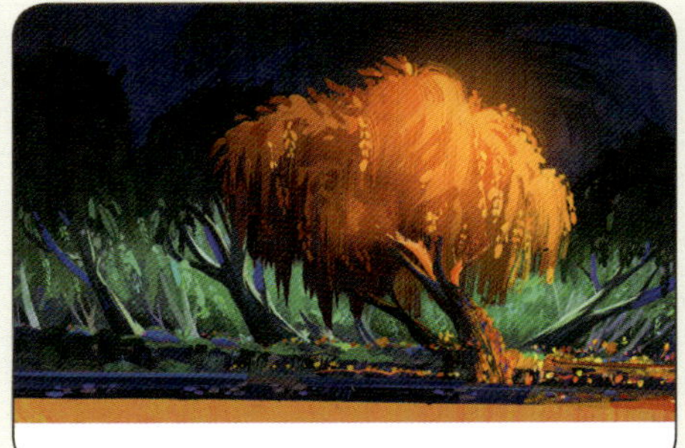

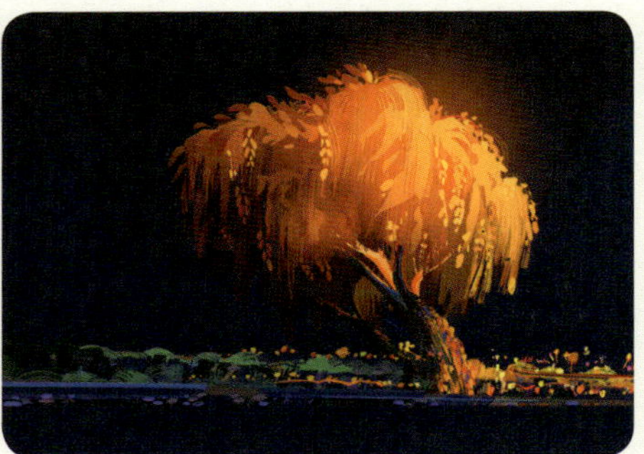

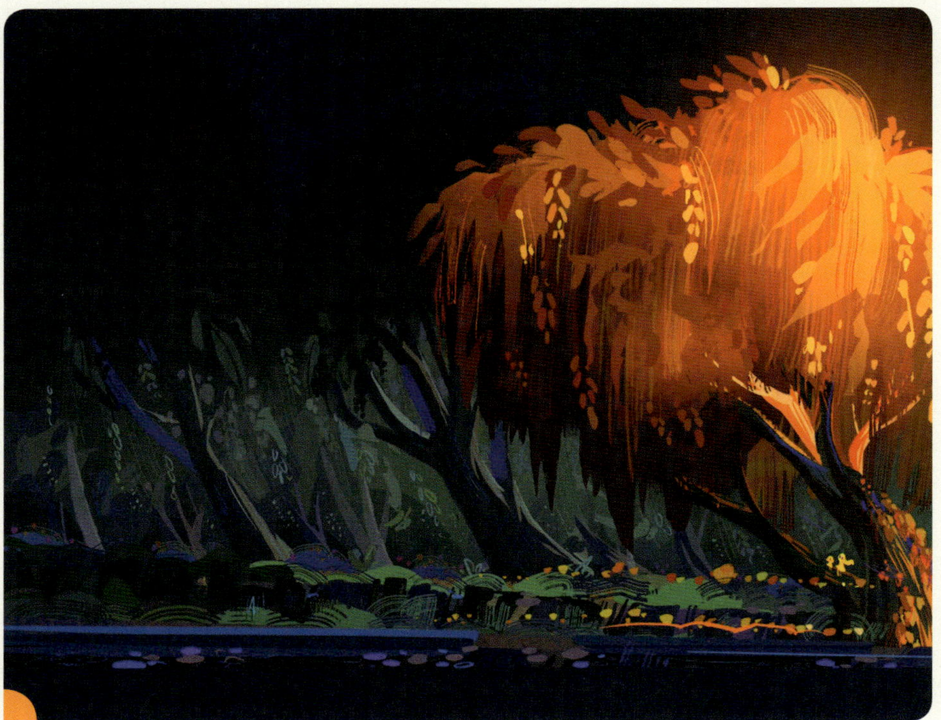

You can even add some little creatures to your scene to emphasize the fantastical mood

17

Stepping back from the painting, the composition feels a little off. With the details added to the trees and bushes, the canvas is feeling slightly too bottom-heavy, and the vibrant green glow draws attention away from the orange tree. Moving everything up a little and refocusing the values would balance the scene back out. To do this, group all your layers together by going to the Layers menu, swiping right on each layer in turn, and selecting Group. Tap on the group's name to select the overall folder, then tap Transform and drag everything upwards a little, creating more negative space for the water. Go to the foreground bushes layer and use **TRANSFORM > DISTORT** to straighten it up a little to support this new space.

On the closest foreground layer, use Nikko Rull to fill the gap at the bottom of the canvas with a straight stroke of dark blue. This is where the new waterline will be. Between the middle-ground trees and the orange tree, create another new layer, and fill this with dark blue as well. Lower this layer's opacity to around 57% — you will see that this harmonizes the middle ground with the dark water, and helps showcase the vivid orange tree without other light sources creating a distraction.

18

Now it's time to start painting the water. On a new layer, use **SELECTION > RECTANGLE** to draw long, thin, horizontal rectangles on the water. Create a variety of them, making some longer, thicker, thinner, or smaller. Use Nikko Rull to paint these a dark blue, even darker than the current water shade. Use **TRANSFORM > DISTORT** to stretch and flatten the rectangles outwards, then lower their opacity to around 55%.

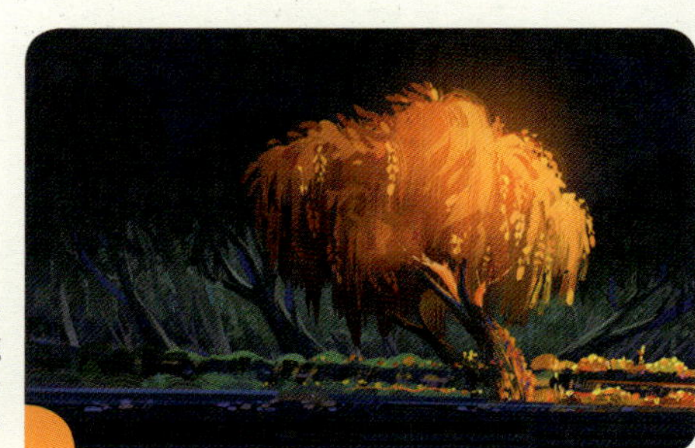

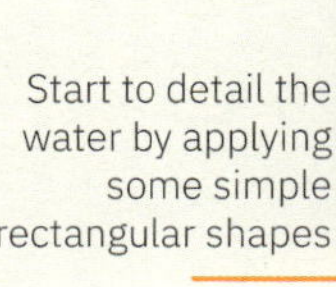

Start to detail the water by applying some simple rectangular shapes

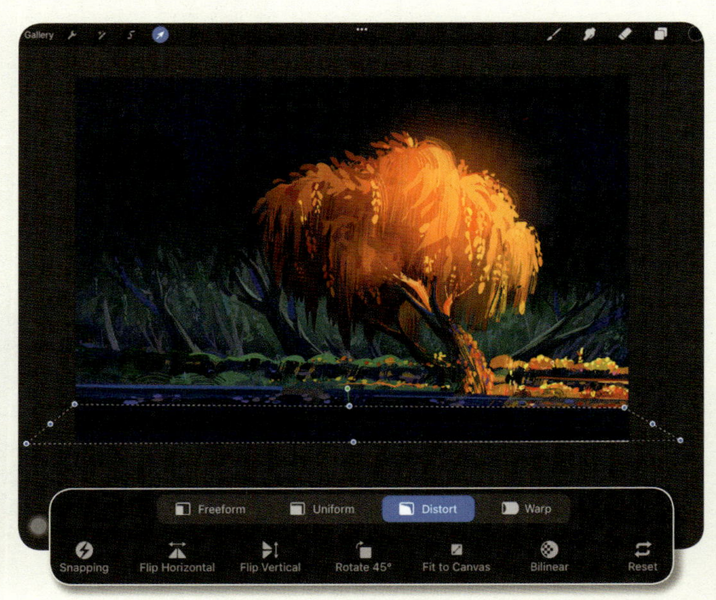

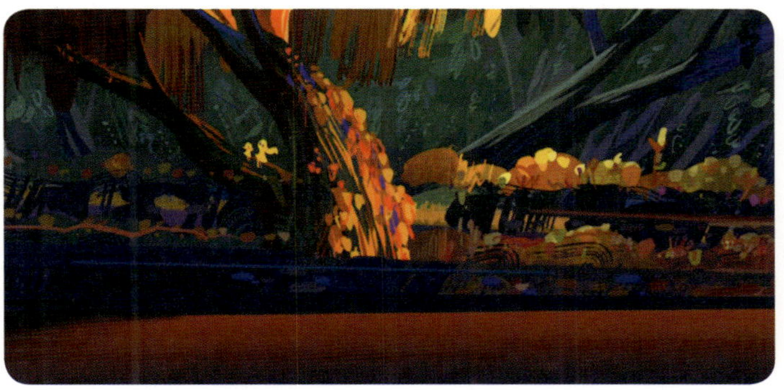
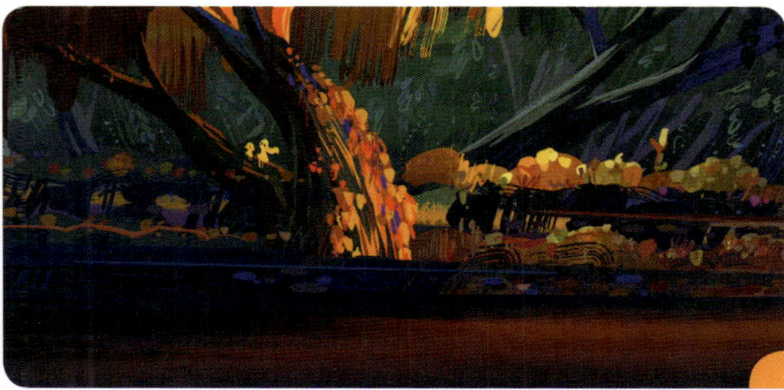

Use the Selection tool, Soft Brush, and Smudge tool to paint reflections in the water

19

Add a new layer on top and use **SELECTION > FREEHAND** to lasso an angled rectangle on the right side of the water – simply tap to place each point and make a straight-edged selection. Colour-pick an orange hue from the top of the tree and use Soft Brush to paint a warm gradient inside the selection, as if orange light is shining on the water's surface. Select the Smudge tool, set it to the Thylacine brush, and drag a few times horizontally to soften the reflection.

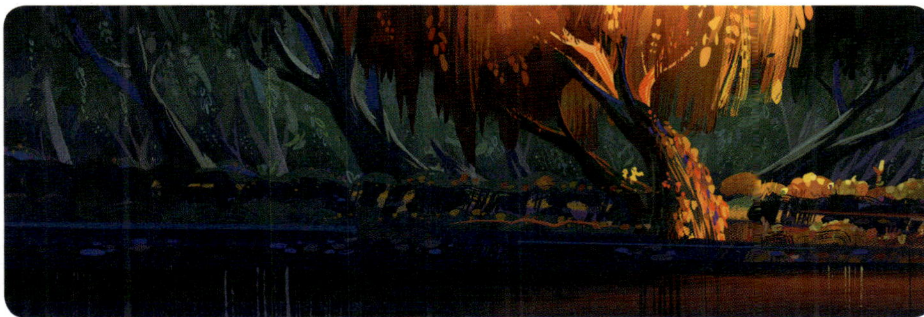

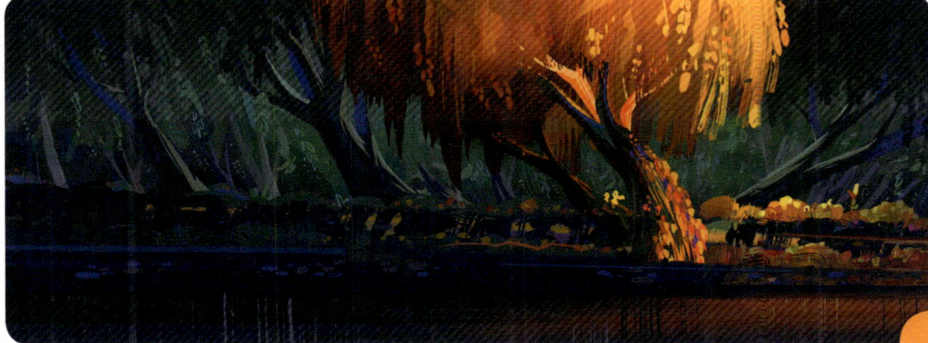

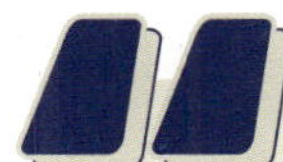

20

You will also need to add some vertical shapes in the water, suggesting the reflections of the trees and plants without going into too much detail. To do this, add a new layer on top of the water reflection and select a dark blue colour. Drag the Thylacine brush downwards to create some sketchy vertical strokes here and there. Switch up the colours by using light blue in cool areas of the water and yellow in the orange parts. Some rough ends of the strokes might encroach above the waterline, so use **SELECTION > RECTANGLE** to select and delete where they overlap. Finally, set the layer's mode to Screen and lower the opacity to around 70%.

Use the Thylacine brush to create water reflection textures and lighting

GILLIAN SAYS: *'Now that you have added textures using different brushes and colours, the painting is almost finished. You have used the Selection tool to make selections for neater edges and shape-painting. In future paintings, I recommend exploring how to paint different textures using the Selection tool with different brushes, and practising how to use the Selection tool to make Quick Shapes. Finally, remember not to overwhelm your painting with smaller details. They give a lot of personality, but you should intentionally plan where to put them – for example, the flowers add colour and texture to the bushes here. Simplifying the form of these details makes them more supportive of the overall painting.'*

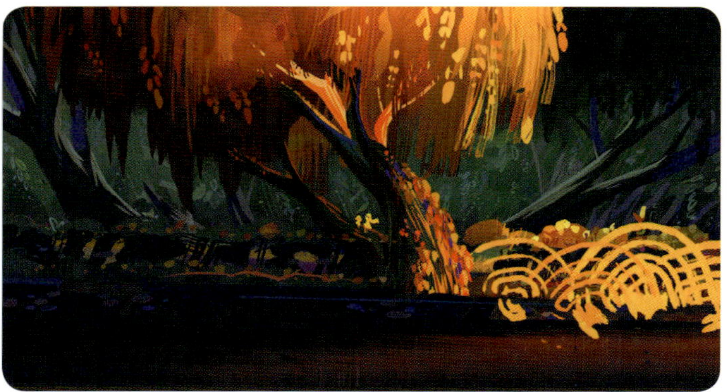

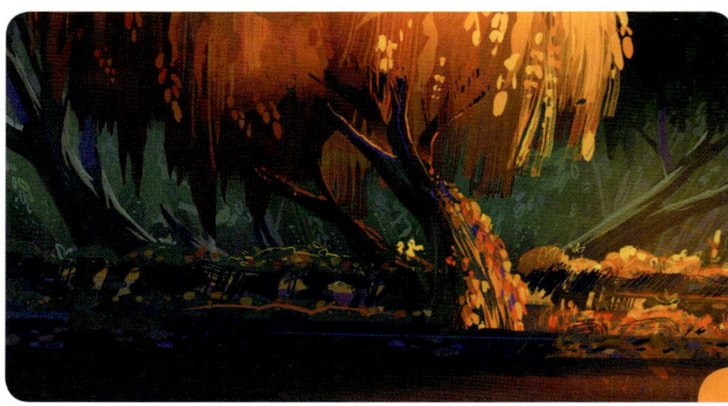

Making a few adjustments and beginning the final touches of the painting

21

Create a new layer on top and use the Thylacine brush to add circular yellow and orange strokes around the right-hand bushes and flowers. Set the layer's blend mode to Overlay. On another new layer, use Soft Brush to add a warm glow to the same area, unifying the plants' colours; use the Syrup brush to scribble dark blue strokes of texture along the walkway area. The scene's orange glow is now a little too strong, so use Alpha Lock and Soft Brush to revise the main tree-trunk layer, darkening the branches to a brownish hue. This brings back a little more definition and shadow to the bright focal area.

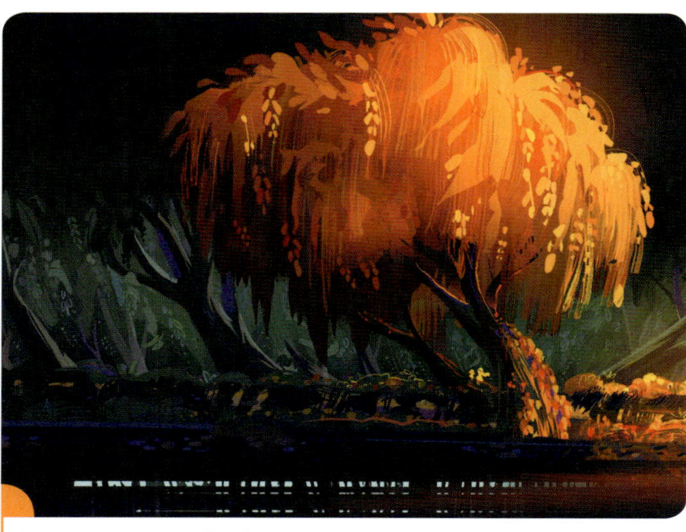

Create more water reflections using the Selection and Transform tools

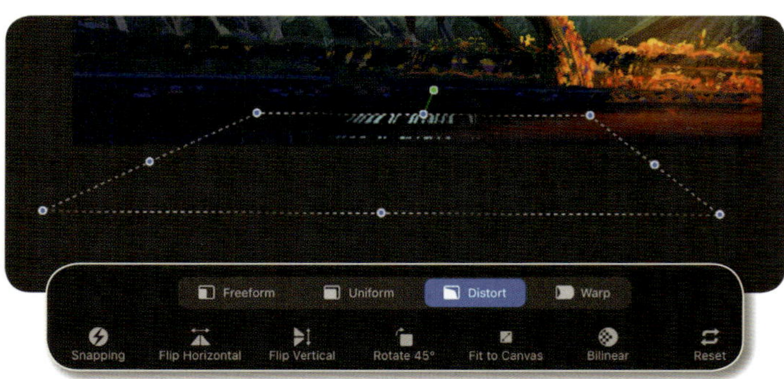

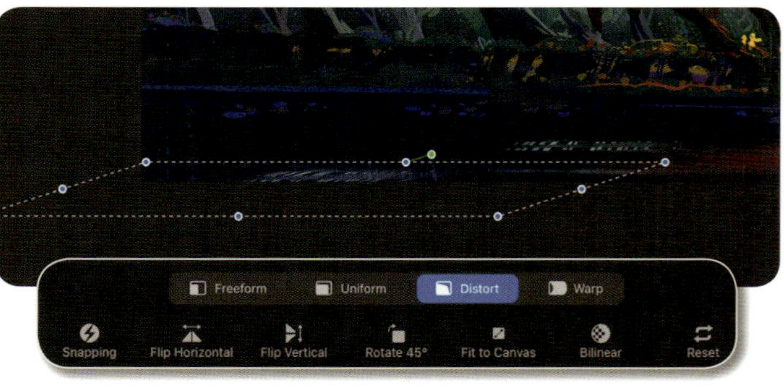

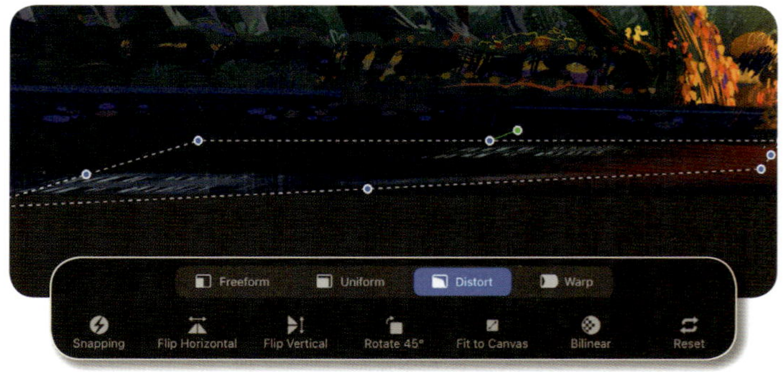

22

You can build up the water reflections a little more, adding some blue to indicate the other lights that will be in the scene. Using **SELECTION > RECTANGLE**, select at least three long rectangles of different thicknesses, as you did in step 18. Use Syrup to paint a light blue colour inside each, then set the Eraser to Soft Brush and scribble some of it away. Use **TRANSFORM > DISTORT** to stretch out the reflection, set the layer's blend mode to Colour Dodge, and lower its opacity to around 50%. Create a duplicate and place it further along in the water. Distort both reflections to match the scene's perspective, and merge both reflections afterwards.

23

On a new layer, use a small Syrup brush to scribble some sharper cool reflections, and Thylacine to lightly add horizontal reflections on the right. On the foreground bushes layer, use Thylacine to add some long, dark blue horizontal strokes to support the ground there. Open the Nikko Rull brush in the Brush Studio, go to Colour Dynamics, and set the **STAMP COLOUR JITTER > HUE** slider to 6% and the **STROKE COLOUR JITTER > HUE** slider to 14%. Use this to add a little more variation and round shapes to the bushes, using a new layer if needed.

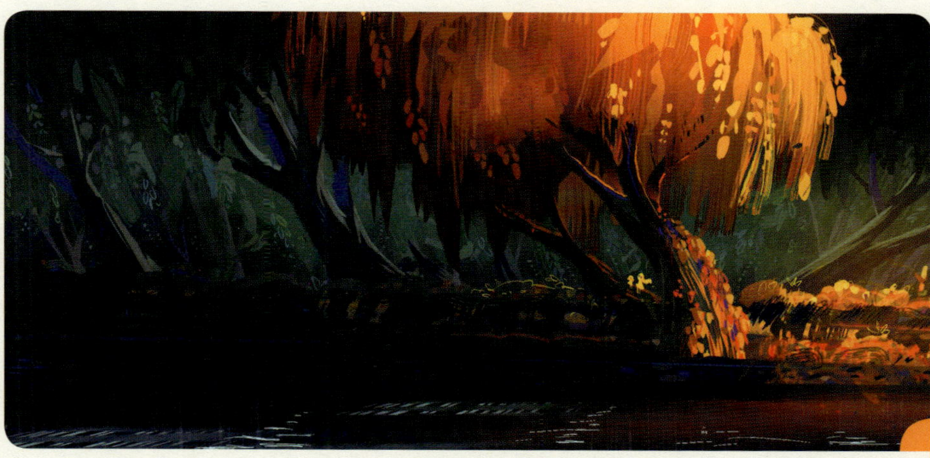

Adding more details to the water and foreground area using different brushes

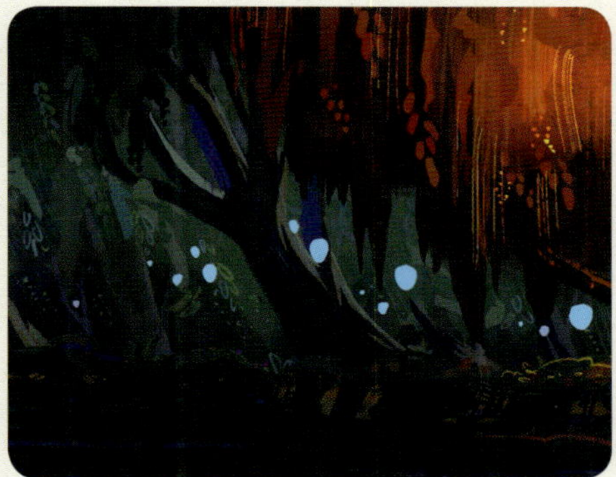
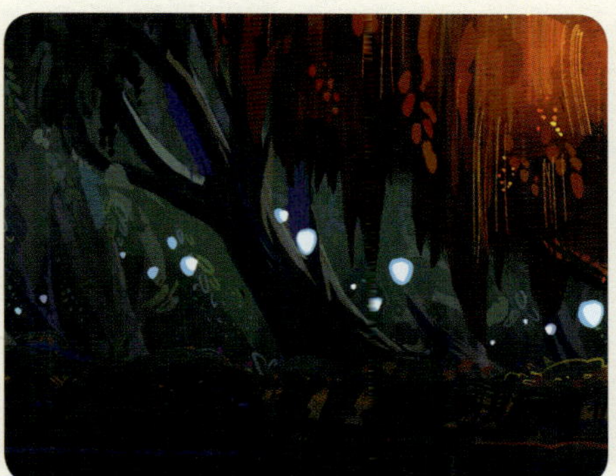
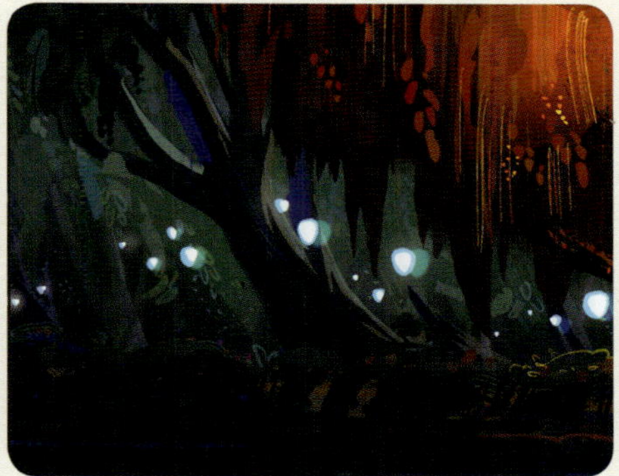

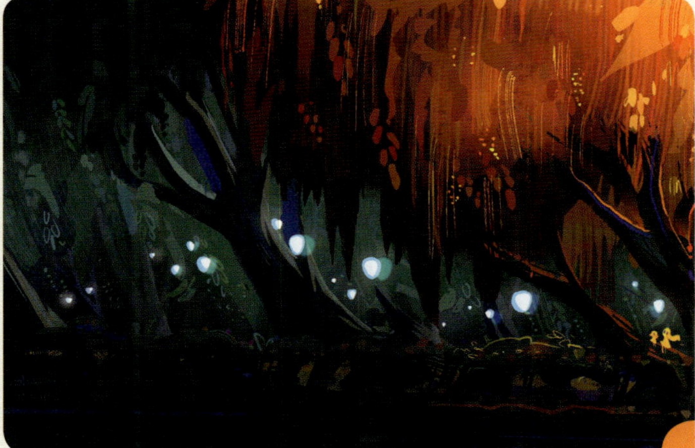

24

Last of all, you can add the small, cool lights of the lamps under the trees. Add a new layer and use the Syrup brush to paint a few small, irregular dots among the tree trunks, using light, saturated blues. Paint some white inside each circle, where the glow would be brightest. On a new layer set to Colour Dodge, paint more blue blobs on top of each light. Lower its opacity to around 40%, then apply **ADJUSTMENTS > GAUSSIAN BLUR** with an intensity of 3%. On a new layer above that, use the Soft Brush to paint a bit of white over each light, then set the layer mode to Overlay to finish off the scene with a little extra glow.

Finish the painting with bokeh-like lights surrounding the foreground tree

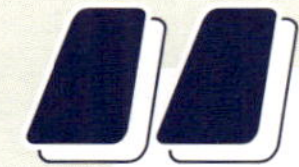

GILLIAN SAYS: *'The final touches and adjustments are important when finishing a painting. When you're close to completion, you will likely notice many adjustments that you want to make. If those adjustments can really make the painting better, try your best to do them, but avoid zooming up close on small details too much. You might end up focusing on one small aspect for too long, losing sight of its impact on the rest of the image. Always try to keep plenty of the canvas in view.'*

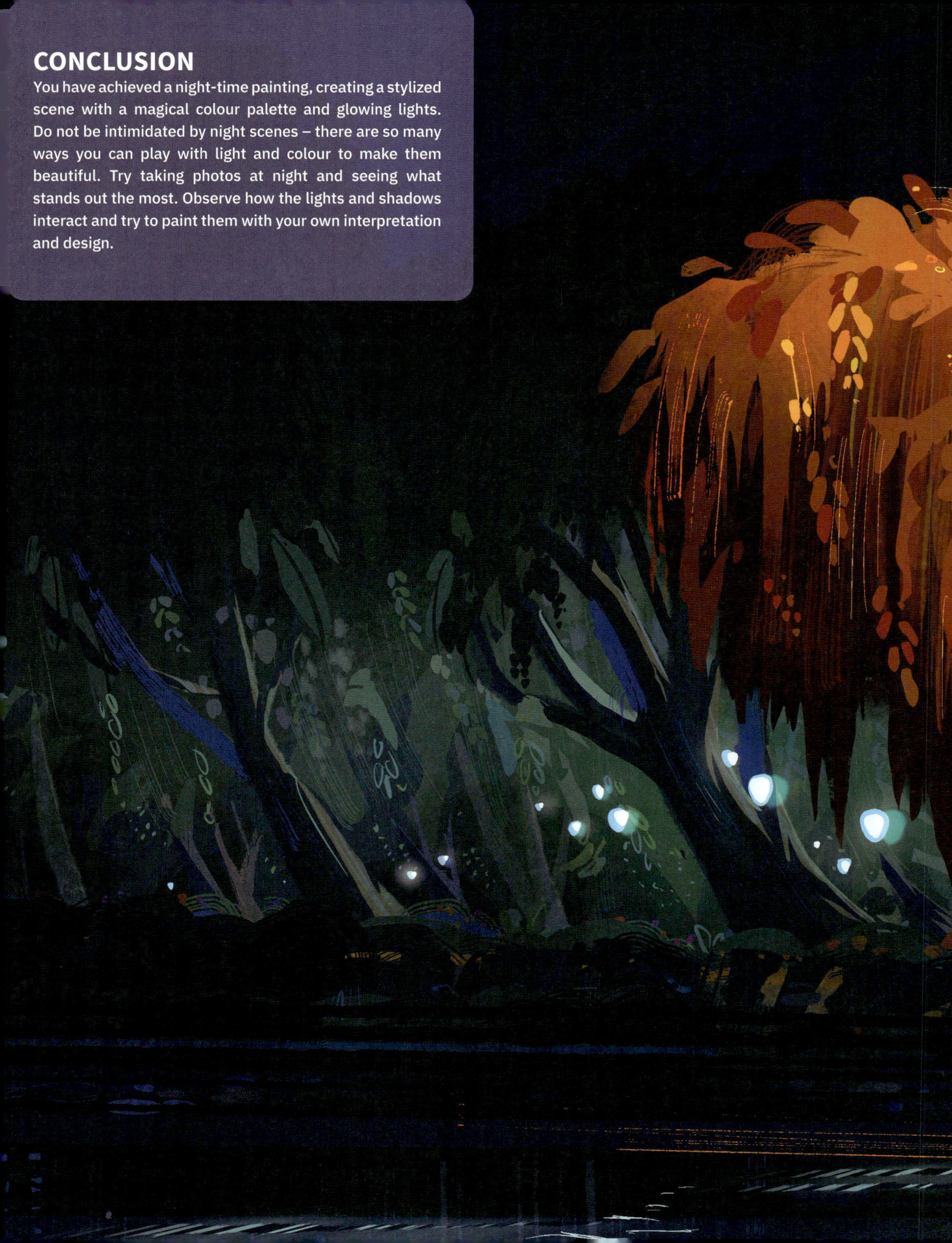

CONCLUSION
You have achieved a night-time painting, creating a stylized scene with a magical colour palette and glowing lights. Do not be intimidated by night scenes – there are so many ways you can play with light and colour to make them beautiful. Try taking photos at night and seeing what stands out the most. Observe how the lights and shadows interact and try to paint them with your own interpretation and design.

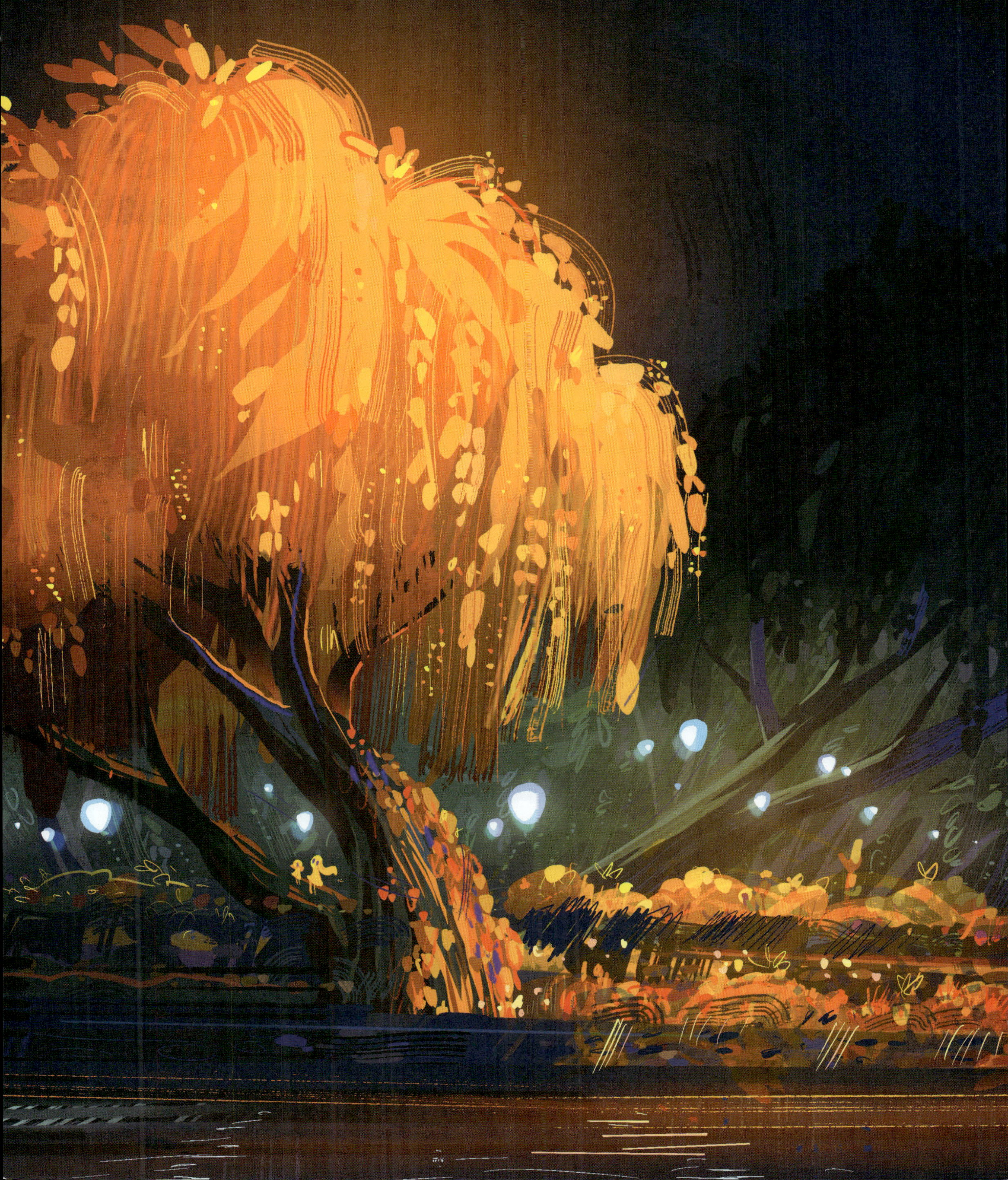

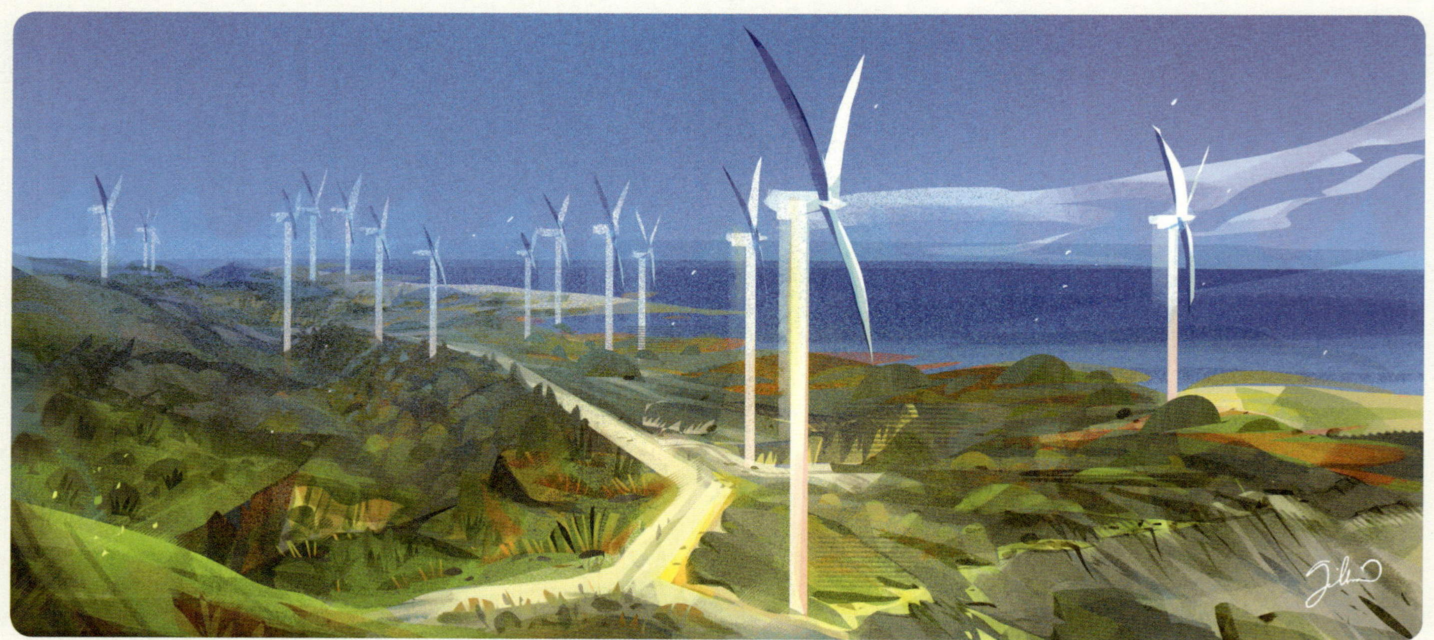

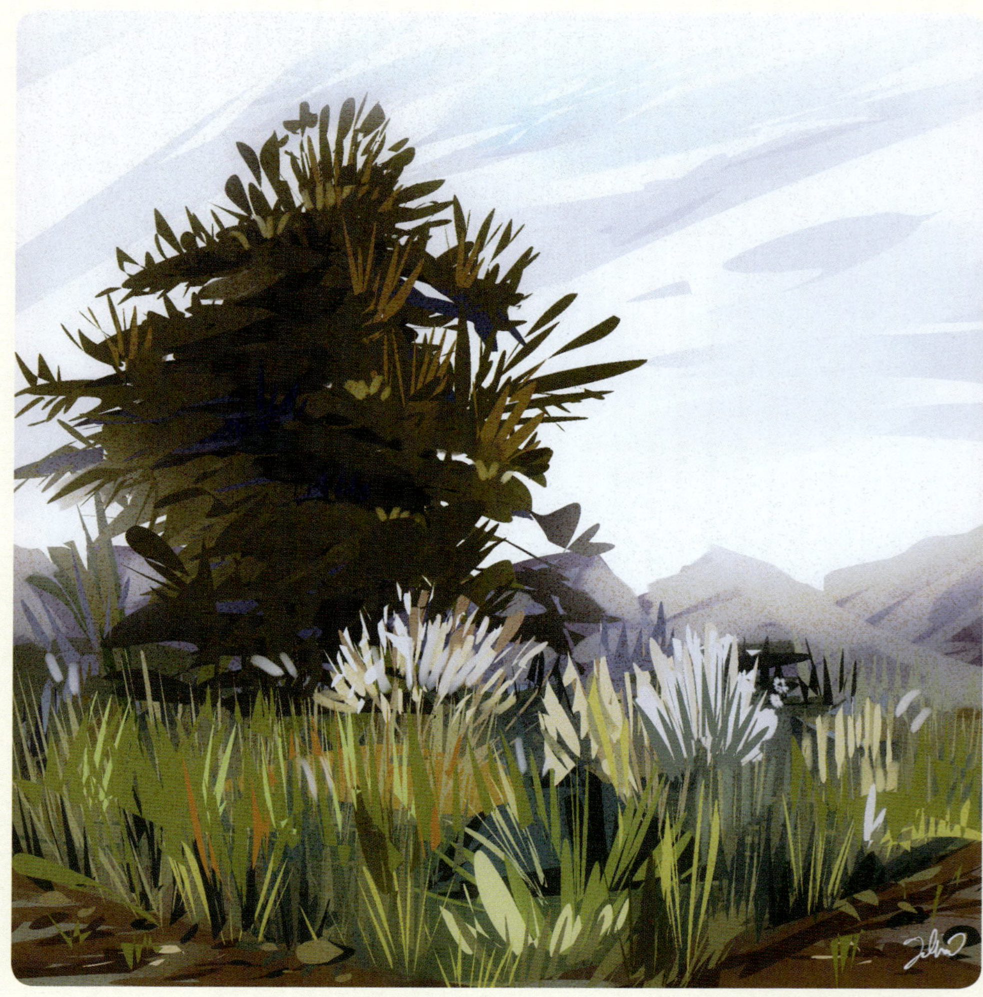

IMAGES © GILLIAN GALANG

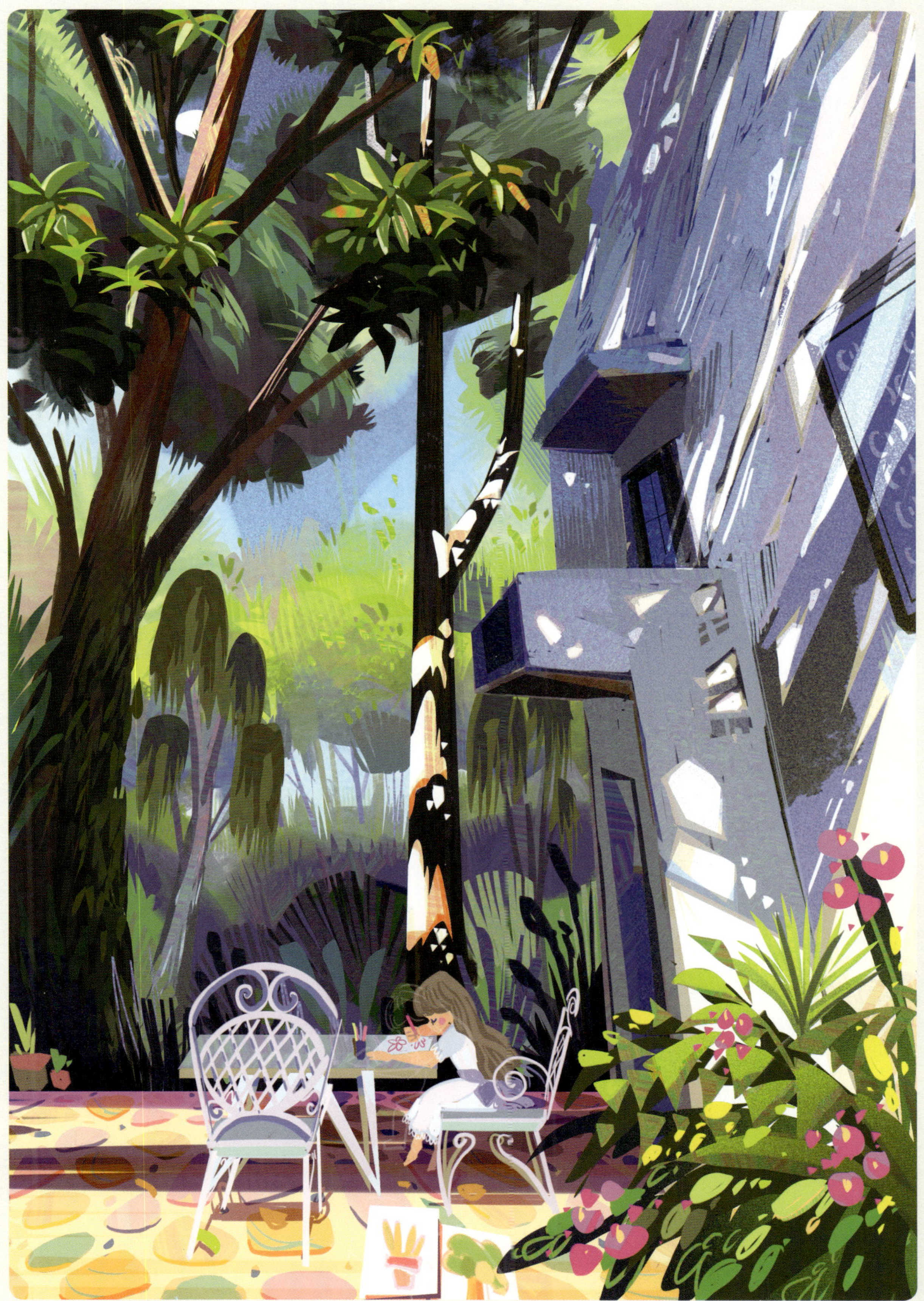

PLEIN-AIR STUDY: I painted this location because I loved the light and shadow in this area; I decided to add a bit of storytelling by adding a girl who's also drawing

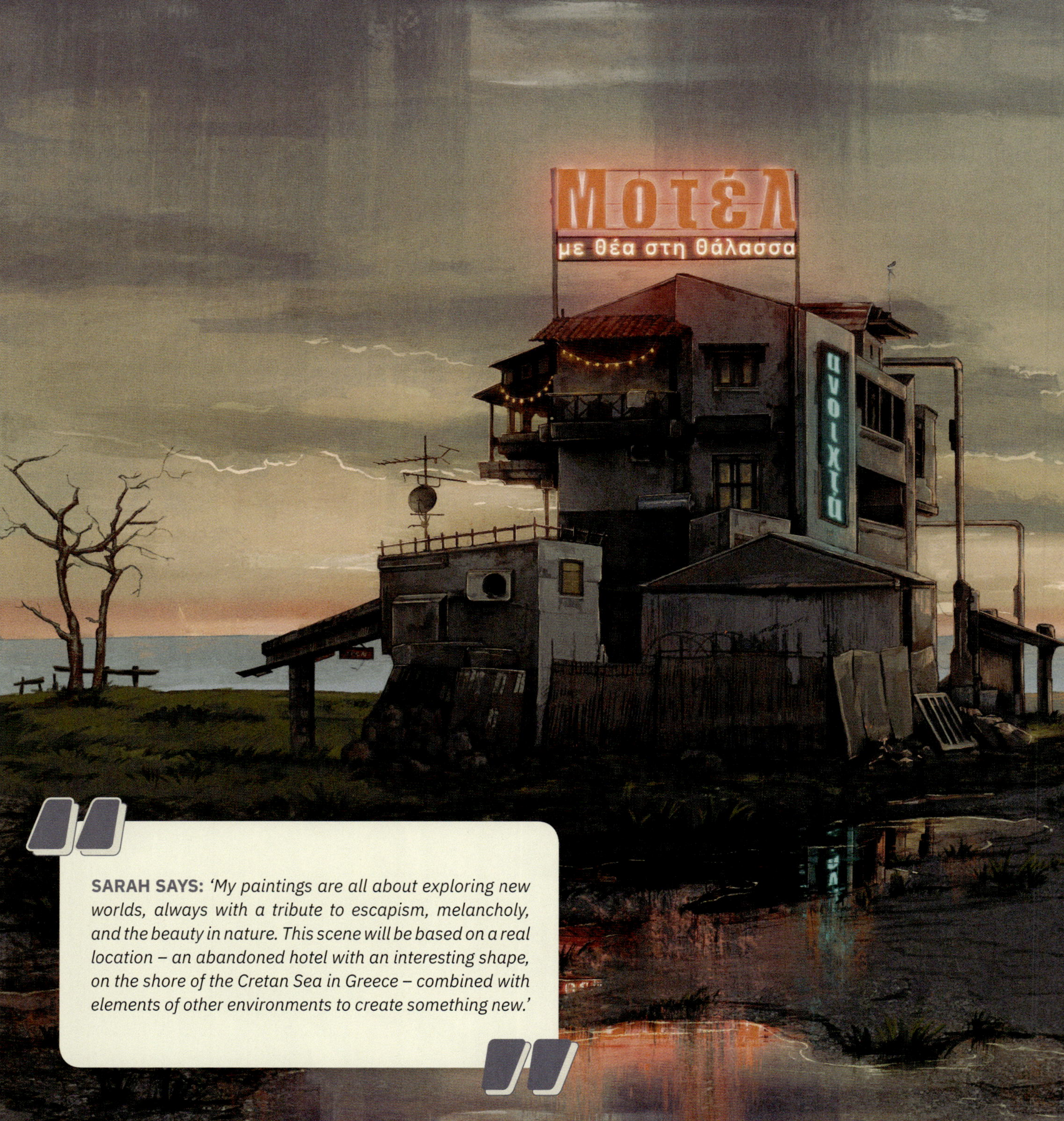

SARAH SAYS: *'My paintings are all about exploring new worlds, always with a tribute to escapism, melancholy, and the beauty in nature. This scene will be based on a real location – an abandoned hotel with an interesting shape, on the shore of the Cretan Sea in Greece – combined with elements of other environments to create something new.'*

- **Combine equal parts reality, reference, and imagination in an environment**

- **Create a new scene using the strongest elements of multiple sources**

- **Create detail efficiently using textured brushes and blend modes**

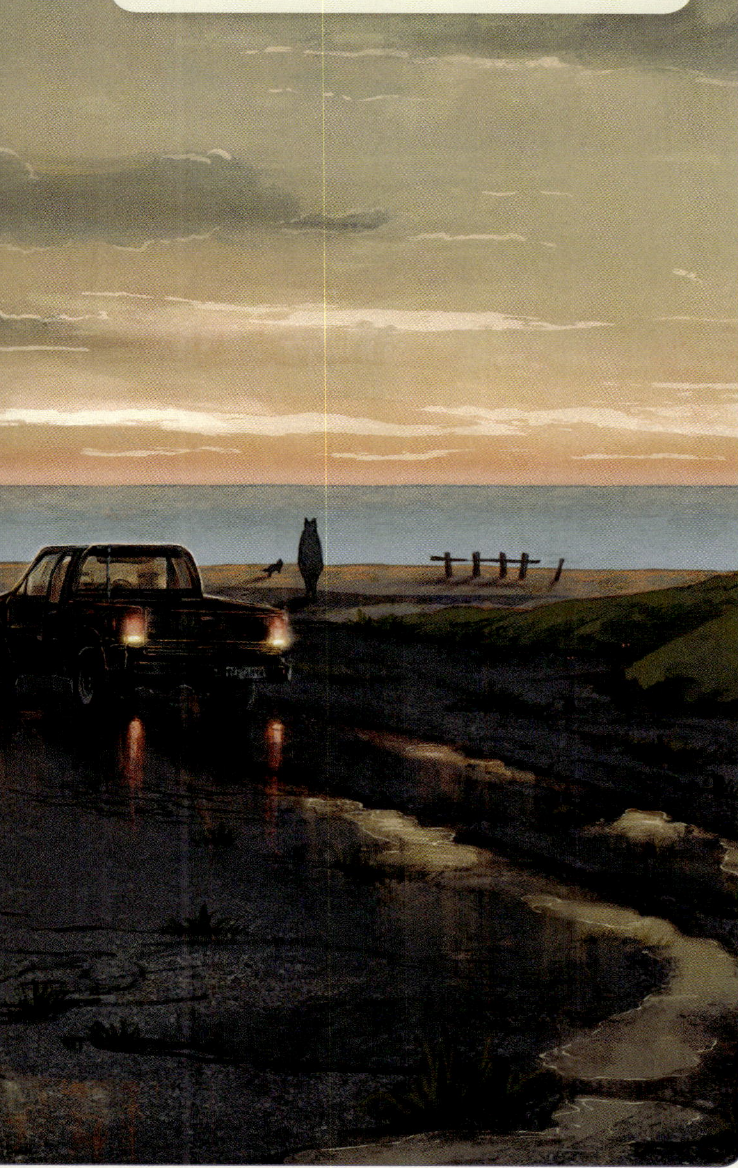

01

Before you begin to draw anything, it is advisable to have a concept ready. Take your time and think about the following things:

- What mood do you want the painting to evoke?
- What story do you want to tell with this scene?
- What kind of composition fits best?

Having these questions in mind will save you a lot of trouble further along in the process, whether you are working from reality, reference, or imagination.

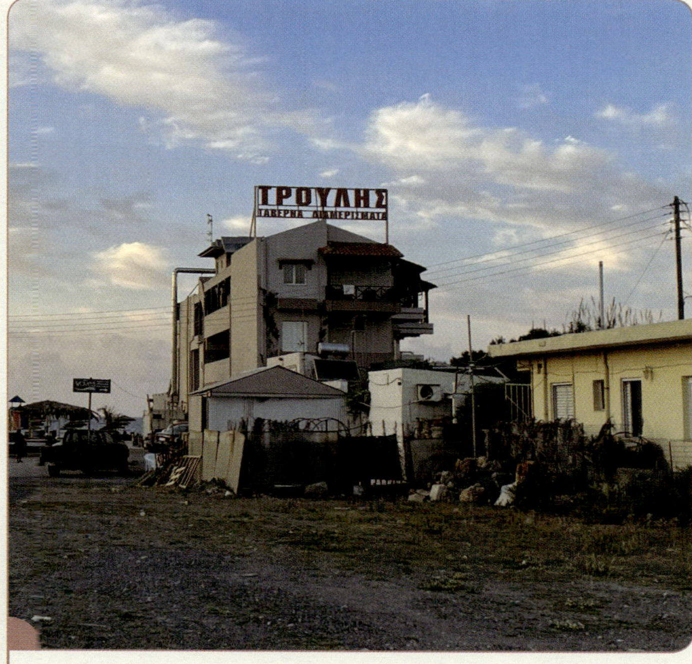

This derelict Greek hotel will be the main reference for the painting

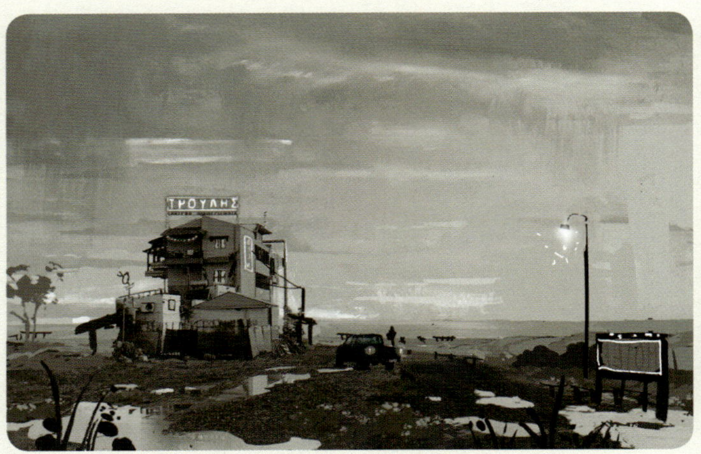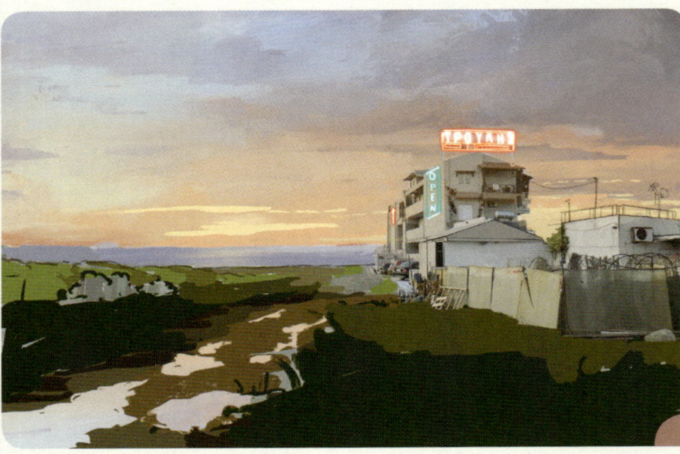

Use the reference photo to create concept sketches; the colour version is discarded in favour of the greyscale idea

02

The objective in this illustration will be to evoke a dark, mysterious mood, similar to the style of the *Twin Peaks* TV series. It will focus on the most interesting structure, the abandoned hotel, and emphasize the dereliction and eeriness that is less apparent in daylight with people nearby. Aside from the street and the ocean in the background, all the excess elements and clutter will be removed. The car parked outside the hotel will remain, but changing its placement will make a stronger composition and help invent a story. The time of day will change from a mild, sunny evening to a late, rainy sunset – this will be the biggest change from reality, but the objective in this chapter is less of a pure study and more of an exercise in creating a new mood and narrative inspired by this intriguing location.

As mentioned at the beginning, having a strong concept in mind will help you stay on track. When working from reference photos, you can take your time to collage together some simple sketches and thumbnails until you find a strong idea.

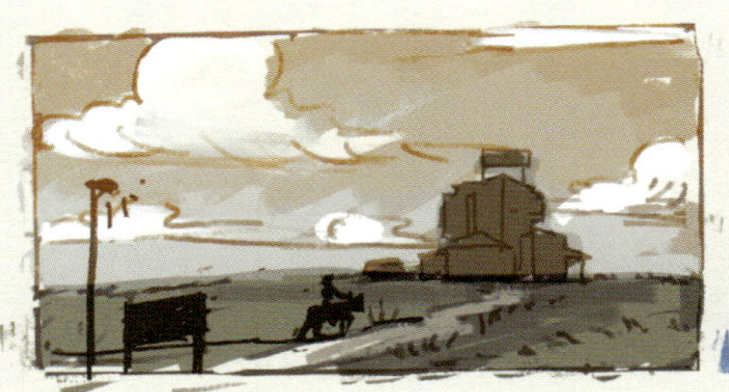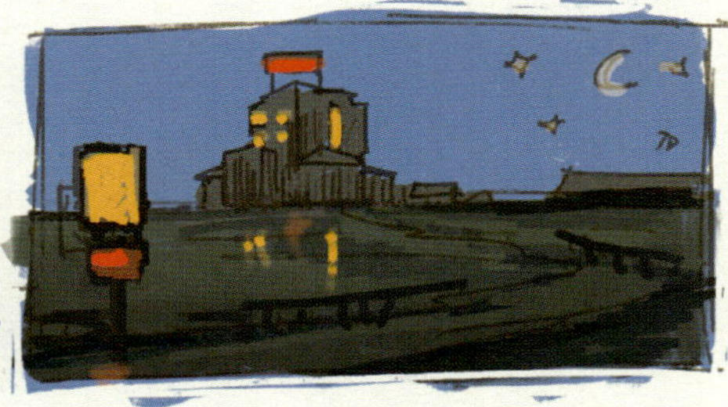

03

Now it's time to think about the visual implementation of your ideas. The most important part of the planning process is deciding how the elements in the painting will be arranged. Drawing thumbnails helps you implement ideas quickly, without fully committing to one just yet. In this case, the main focus is the abandoned building and the dramatic sky that constitutes almost two thirds of the painting.

At the thumbnail stage you can determine aspects such as the composition, arrangement of elements in the scene, and approach to colour and light. It's a good idea to play around with different concepts, so you can choose the version that offers the best execution of your concept. You can do this on a canvas of any size – just keep in mind the proportions you intend for the full-size scene.

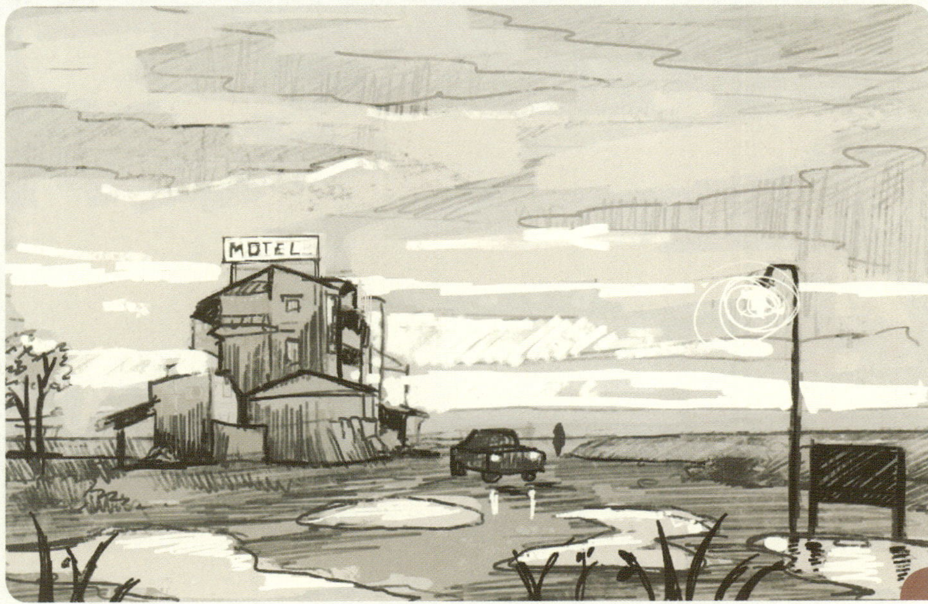

Choose the strongest option out of many thumbnails

04

After devising a concept, you are now ready to create a base for your painting. In this case, it will be an uncoloured sketch drawn on a canvas around 5,080 pixels wide × 3,300 pixels high. Use the **SKETCHING > HB PENCIL** brush and keep the sketch simple. To help you focus on the main content of the scene, avoid using colour and texture right away. The focus is on the abandoned hotel, which is kept accurate to the real building; emphasize the wide road, pot-holed terrain, and ocean view; a couple of distant fictional figures will add some life to the painting, creating a bit of story with the truck parked outside the hotel. The goal here is to create a solid construct for your painting without getting distracted by colour, mood, and rendering. You can add a subtle grey value on a layer underneath the sketch, to make it easier to look at as you draw.

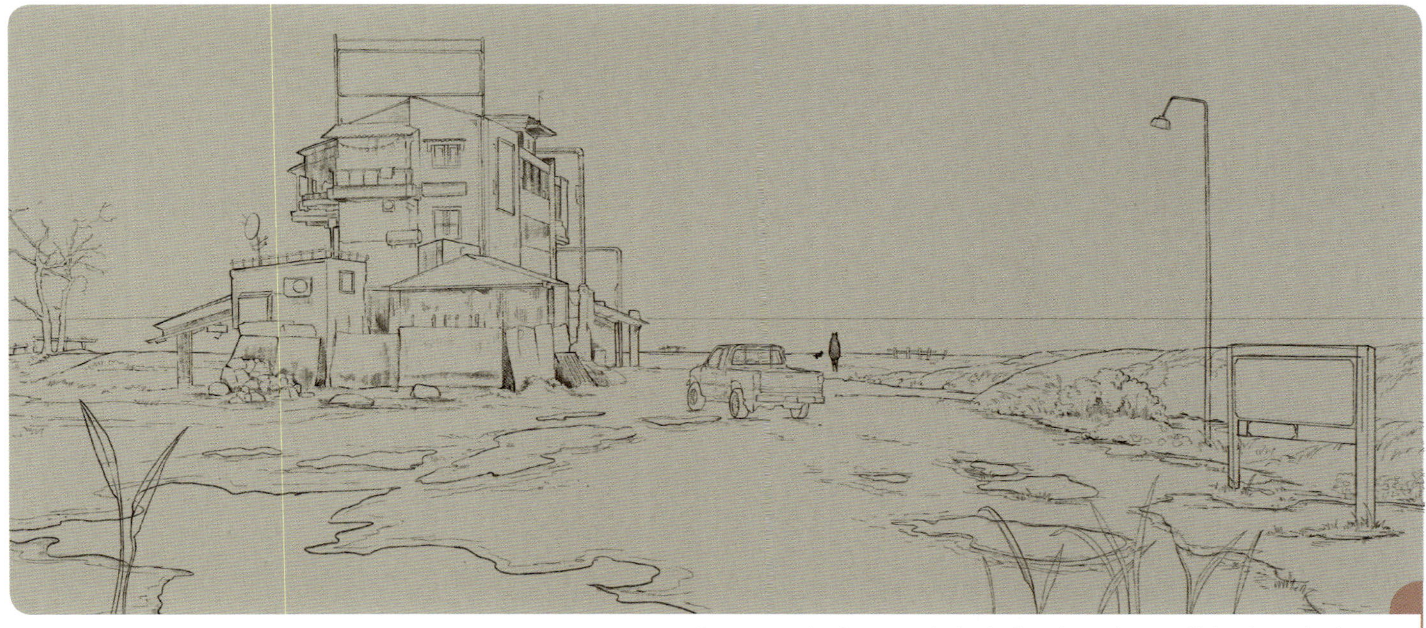
Create a setting for your painting by focusing only on outlining the main elements

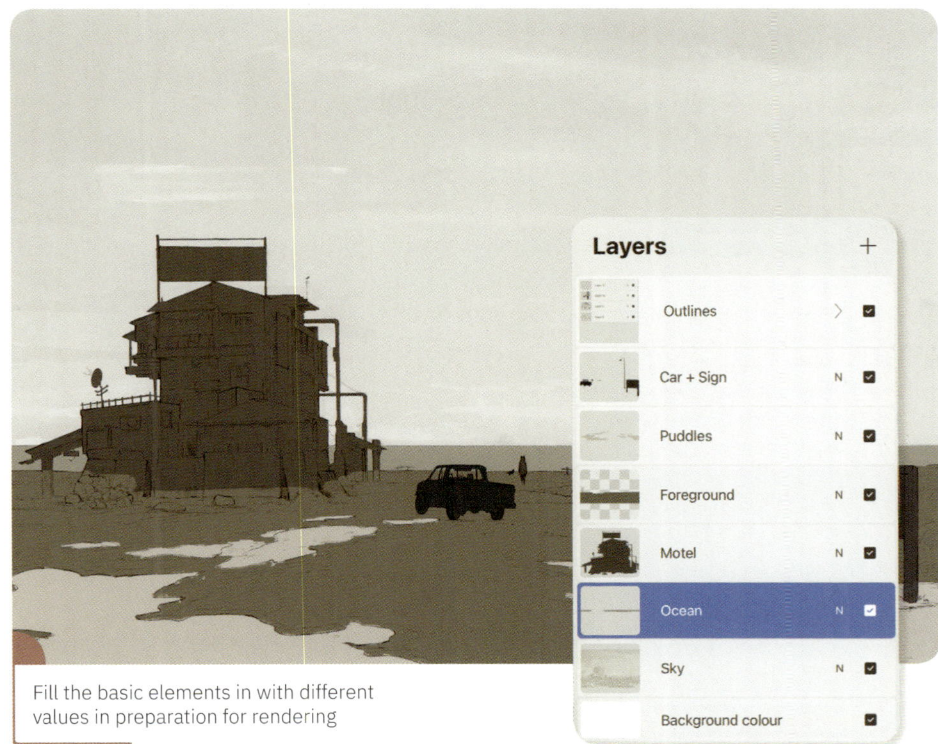

Fill the basic elements in with different values in preparation for rendering

05

To prepare for the upcoming rendering process, start to fill in the basic elements by painting underneath your outline layer. As you can see here, a different value is chosen for each of the different elements, with the points of interest being darkest. Paint each element on a different layer: the car, building, sign, ocean, and the base of the foreground as well as the puddles. At this stage of the process, the priority is to create a clear separation between the elements. While choosing the base values, a handy trick is to utilize an effect called 'atmospheric perspective', in which elements become gradually lighter the further they recede from the viewer. However, remember that this effect depends on the weather conditions of your painted scene, which brings us to the next step.

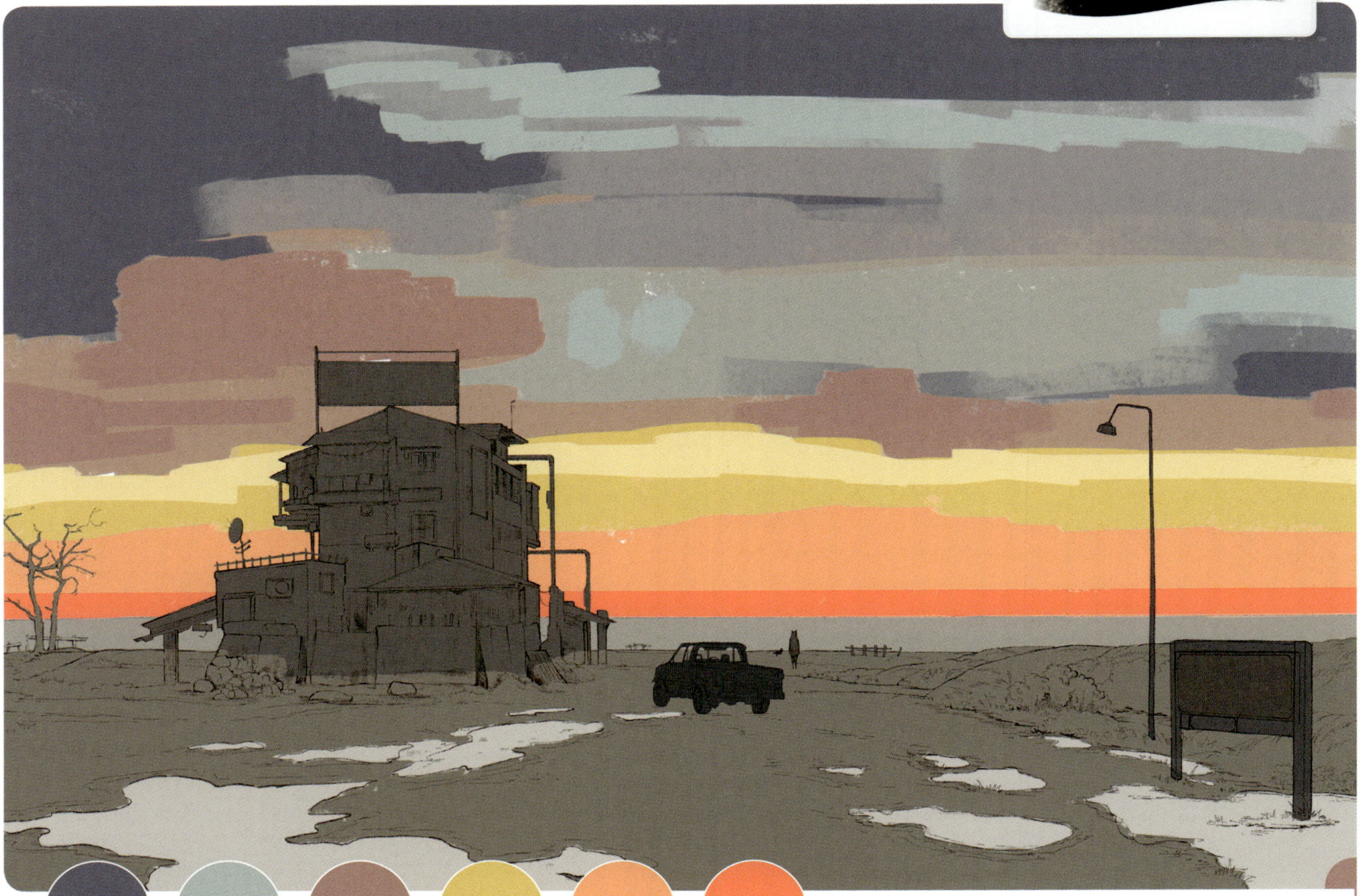

Block out a new sky from reference using the Nikko Rull brush

06

Now it's time to paint the sky. You can do this by hiding the grey sky layer and painting on a new layer at the bottom of the layer stack. Select a thick, textured brush such as **PAINTING > NIKKO RULL**, which can cover the area with wide strokes. Start by adding a few local colours that fit the mood you want to convey in the scene: a dramatic sunset sky. In this case, the colours are going from cool tones on the top (blues, purples) to warmer ones (oranges, peaches) towards the bottom. If you struggle to find the right colours, look at reference images of sunsets to find a solution that complements your scene. If you can go out and capture your own sunset photos, like the ones below, even better!

Remember that you can always have fun and play around with different colours. It can be helpful to keep different sky colours on different layers so you can test or adjust new hues. You don't need to recreate the reference – instead, exaggerate the areas you find most interesting. It is always great to see your own individual take on a commonly painted subject, such as an evening sky.

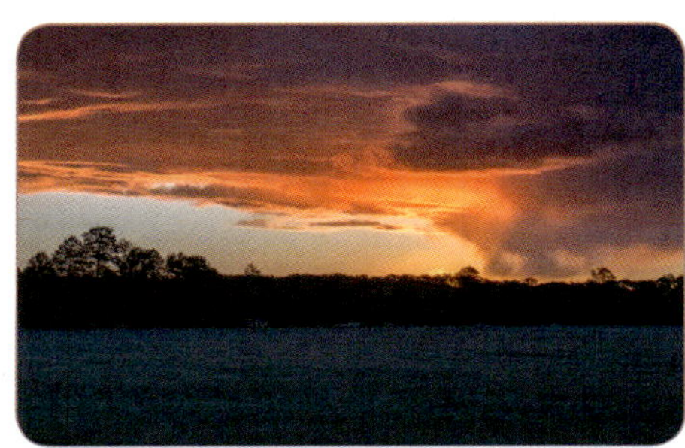
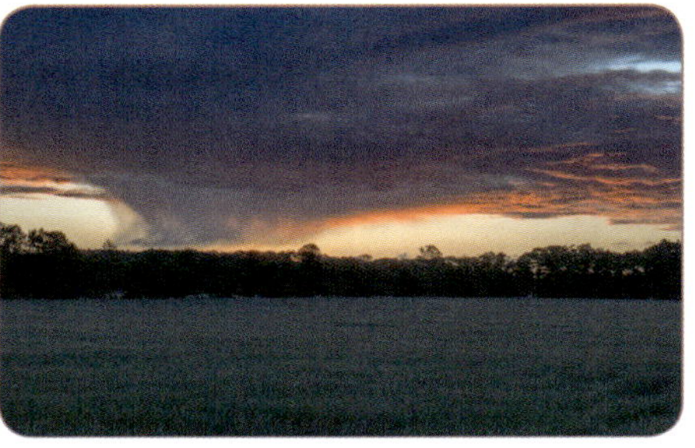
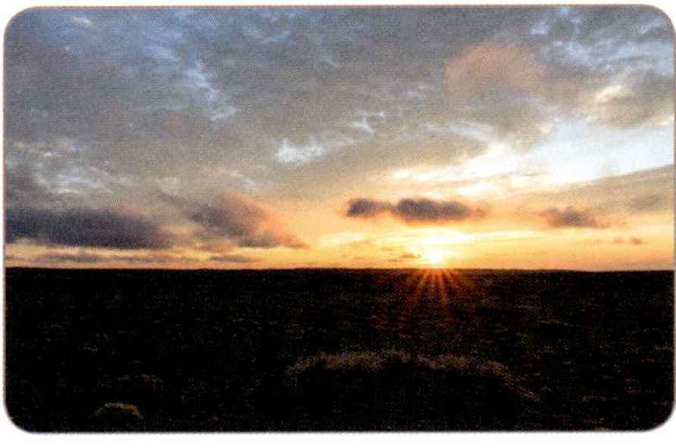

PHOTOGRAPHS © JAN NOACK

07

If you have multiple sky layers, merge them together now, ready for blending. You may want to create a duplicate as a backup before you proceed. Begin smudging over the harsh sky strokes by using the Smudge tool set to **PAINTING > DRY BRUSH**. Dynamic movements and high pressure will create a very interesting painterly, almost traditional look. Your movement controls the way the colours mix together and determines which textures evolve from it.

You could boost the dark atmosphere with a heavy rain cloud on the upper left. Again, it is a good idea to create a backup copy of the sky, as the cloud will be painted and blended directly onto your sky colours. Block out the loose shape of a cumulus cloud, using a much darker colour than the sky, and then smudge it from top to bottom. Repeat this step several times until you create a gradient in which the strokes from the dry brush are still visible.

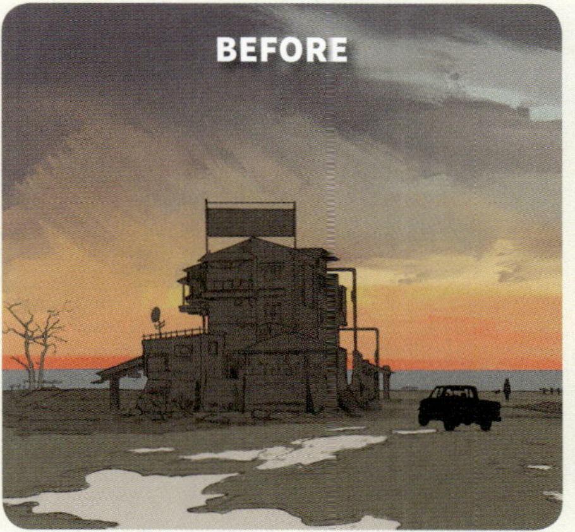

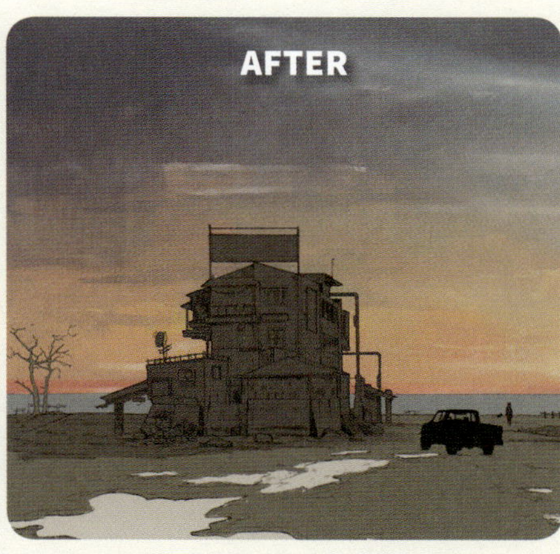

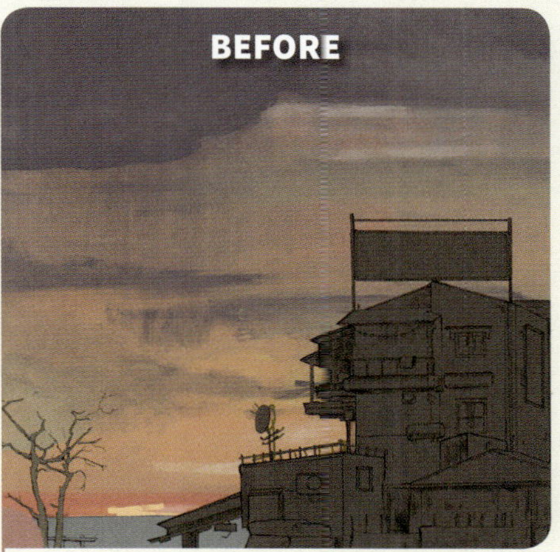

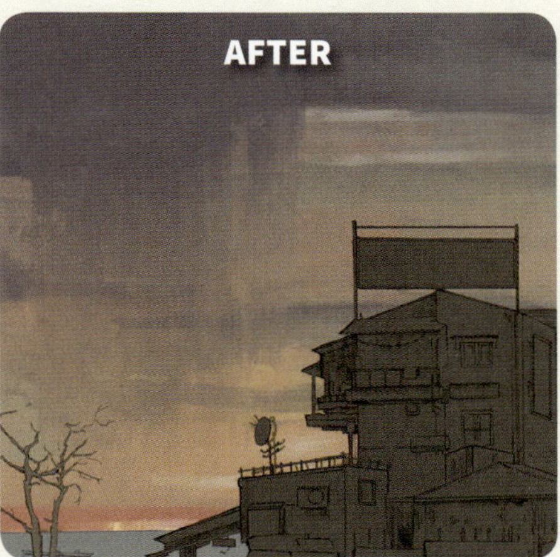

Smudge the sky with a textured brush and add a rain cloud

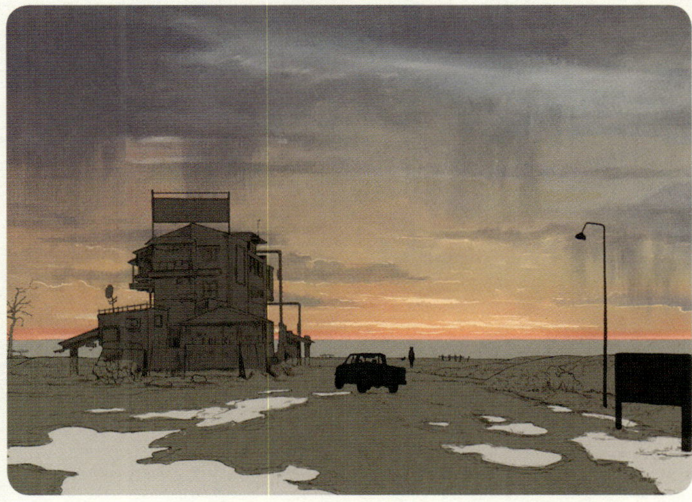

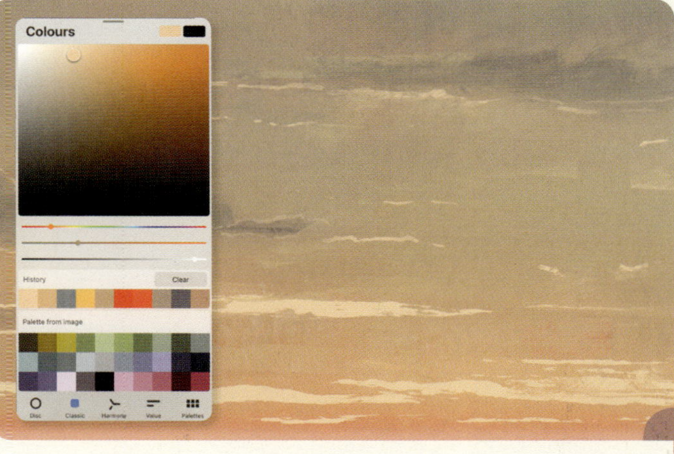

Use the Bamboo brush to add light-orange cloud highlights near the horizon

08

If you have ever seen a sunset in real life, or looked at reference images of sunsets, you will have seen that the brightest parts are found above the horizon, closest to where the sun is going down. Choose a light, bright, saturated orange colour for this. It is important that the colour you choose for highlights has a very light value, but is never pure white. For the brightest parts of the sky, paint a few long strokes with the **ORGANIC > BAMBOO** brush, using a side-to-side horizontal motion. Then use a smaller brush size to outline the clouds that are closest to the light source (the sun below the horizon). If some strokes appear too dominant, you can always smudge over them so they fade naturally into the canvas.

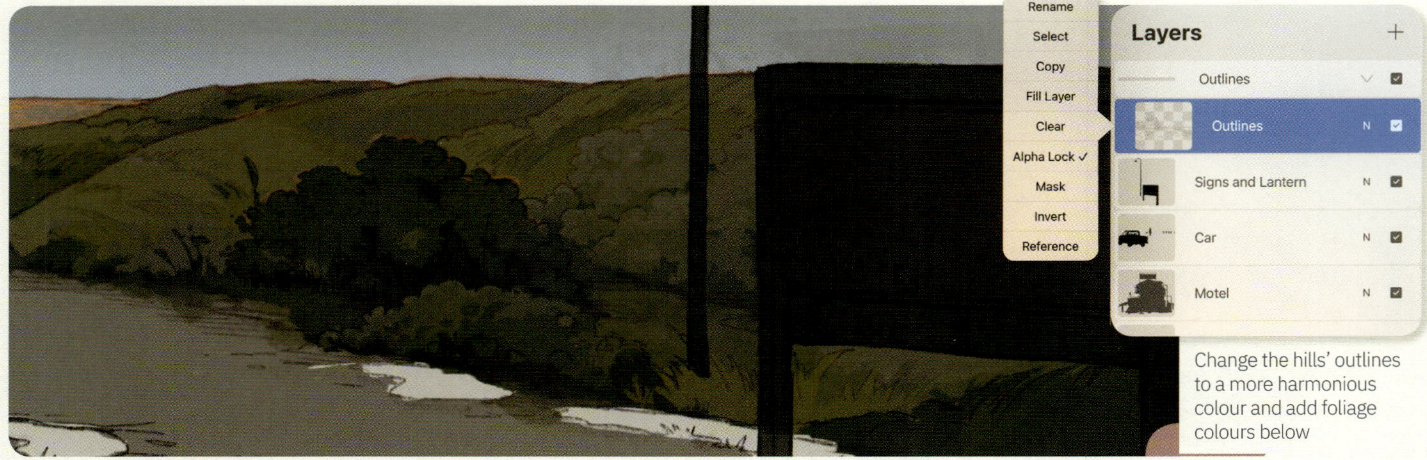

Change the hills' outlines to a more harmonious colour and add foliage colours below

09

You can colour your black outlines to make them more harmonious. Tap on your outline layer in the Layers menu and select the Alpha Lock option. Go over the outlines of the hills and grass areas with a brown-orange colour to soften them.

Select **AIRBRUSHING > HARD BRUSH** and go to the foreground base-colour layer. Begin painting the hills using three to five local colours: add shadows and lights to the foliage and enhance the volume of the bushes and hills, using strokes that follow the forms of the line art. When painting foliage, apply a lighter colour on top and a darker one at the bottom. Use the Eraser in combination with the Hard Brush to create a more natural pattern. Do this for all the grass areas on that foreground layer.

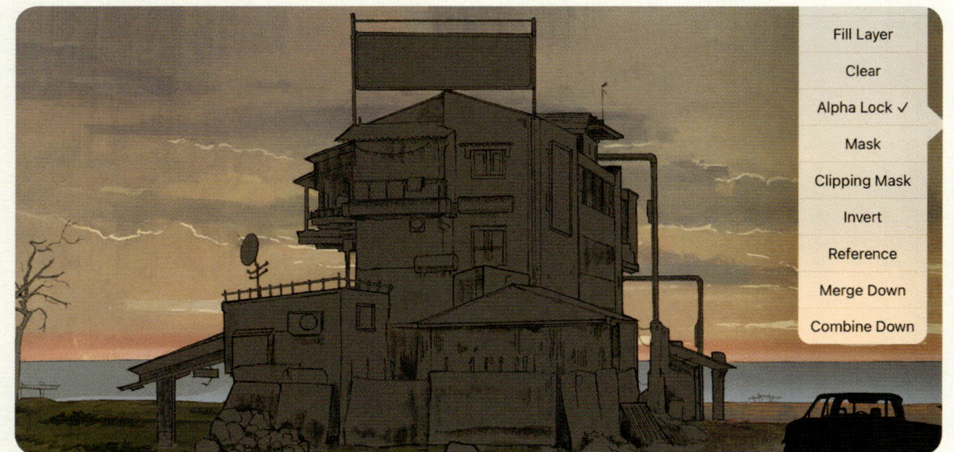

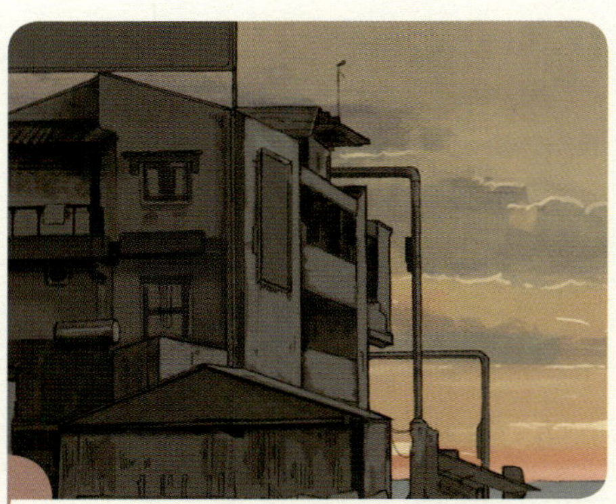

Define the motel's light and shadows in greyscale, using the Nikko Rull brush for a natural, painterly look

10

Now it's time to paint the motel. First, duplicate the layer containing its grey base and enable Alpha Lock. Observing the reference photo will make it easier for you to apply the shadows and lighter parts correctly. Using the **PAINTING > NIKKO RULL** brush, start with rough strokes before building your way up to smaller details, working only in grey values for now. Painting values first makes it easier to focus on achieving a three-dimensional look, planning out the lights and shadows without getting distracted by colour.

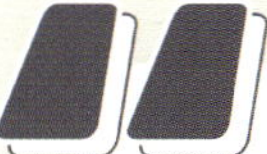

SARAH SAYS: *'At this stage of the painting you have already accomplished a lot! You have learned about the importance of thumbnail sketching and how to methodically approach a new project, breaking down the process from the initial sketch, to blocking in base colours, to rendering the elements with different brush techniques. Getting inspired by and making use of reference photos is also a skill that will be useful for any of your future projects. Finally, the technique of smudging with a textured brush is a convenient way for you to achieve a painterly style in any future image.'*

11

In reality, the derelict motel was seen during the day, with a sign on top that had probably not been illuminated for years. In this version, it will have a big neon sign lit up on top. Remember that the writing on a neon sign is usually formed by a contour – a bright light that often appears white. Here, the writing will have a highly saturated, vibrant red glow around it, on the inside as well as the outside.

To lay the groundwork for the sign, set your colour to black, go to **ACTIONS > ADD TEXT**, and type your choice of motel name and font. Tap the layer in the Layers menu, select Rasterize, and then Alpha Lock. Fill the letter shapes with a bright red. Duplicate this layer, turn off Alpha Lock, and apply **ADJUSTMENTS > GAUSSIAN BLUR** with 15% intensity to create a red glow. Set the layer to Add mode to make it very vibrant. You can also play around with **ADJUSTMENTS > HUE, SATURATION, BRIGHTNESS** to adjust the colours a little – for example, adding a slight pinkish hue, as shown here.

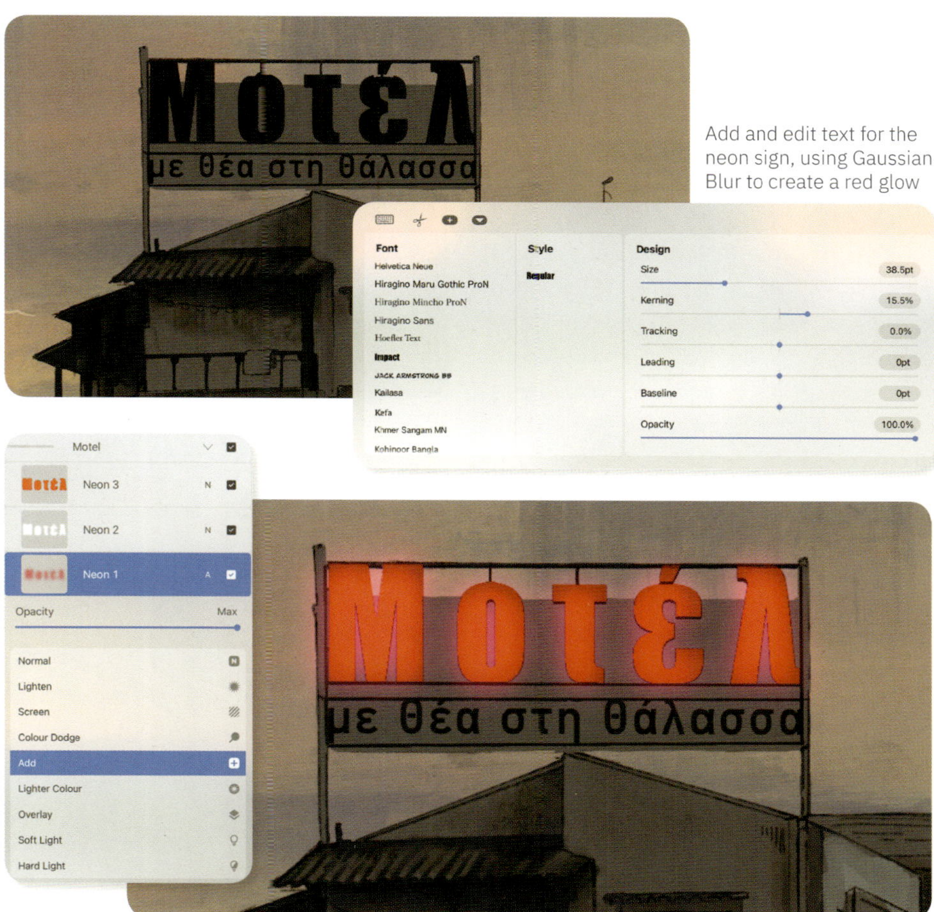

Add and edit text for the neon sign, using Gaussian Blur to create a red glow

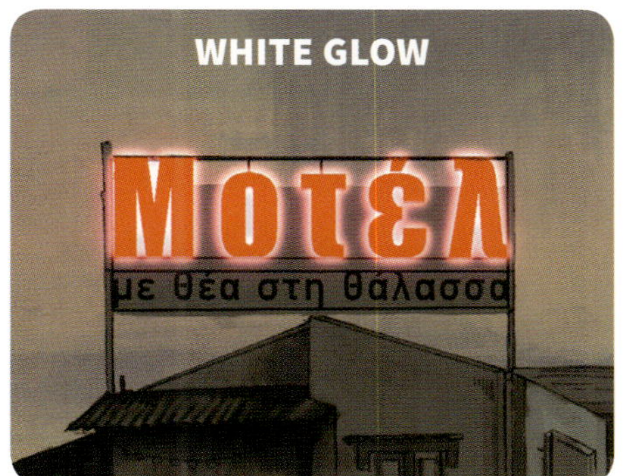

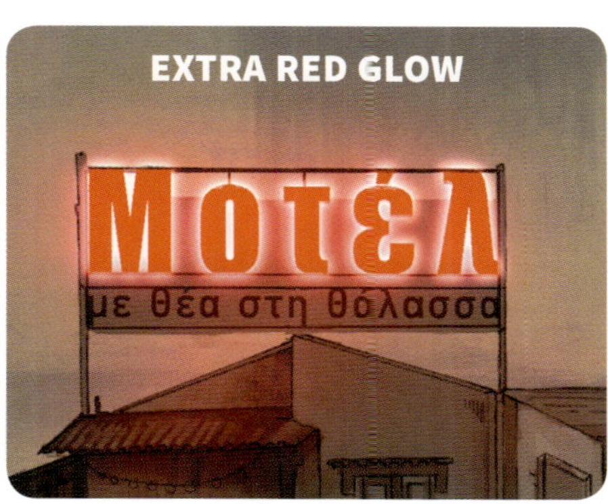

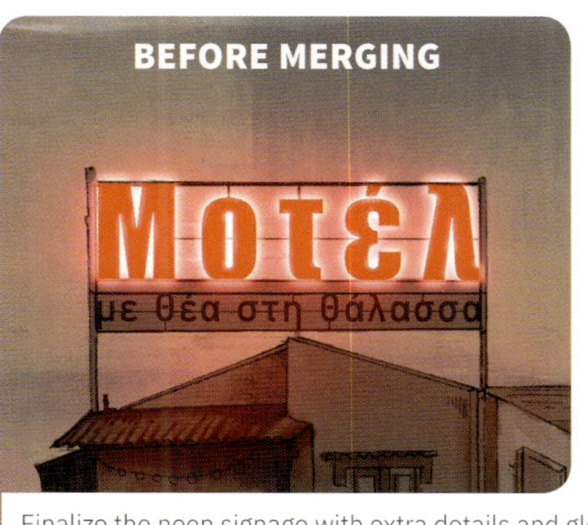

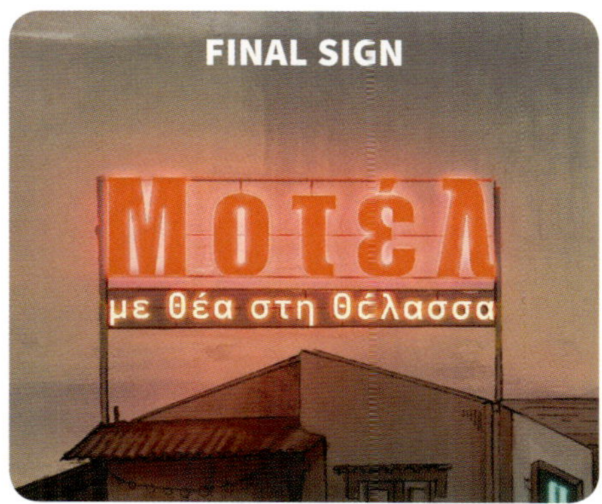

Finalize the neon signage with extra details and glow

12

The sign is still missing the white contour that will really sell its neon look. Duplicate the base text layer again and fill the shape with white. With Alpha Lock turned off, apply **ADJUSTMENTS > GAUSSIAN BLUR** – just a small amount, around 5%. Set this layer to Add mode and place it beneath the red text layer. Duplicate the bright red glow and move it to above the white text. Set its blend mode to Add as well. Finally, create a new layer and set its blend mode to Add. Select **AIRBRUSHING > SOFT BRUSH** and paint a dark red colour over the sign and the top part of the motel. You can always change the intensity of the red glow by reducing the layer's opacity. To keep organized, you can merge some or all of the neon layers, but this may remove or alter their blend modes. Try merging the layers a couple at a time to preserve your desired effect as much as possible – you may have to tweak the results again after merging.

13

You can repeat steps 11 and 12 with different colours and text to add further neon signs. Once they are finished, you can continue working on the building. On a new layer, use **SELECTION > FREEHAND** to lasso the area that you want to focus on. This will make it easier to build up textures without having to repaint other areas. Use the **PAINTING > STUCCO** brush and apply it like a stamp, in single taps rather than strokes. Reduce the texture layer's opacity to between 25% and 40%, so it fades more naturally into the wall. If you are feeling confident, you can paint textures directly onto the motel base layer, simply turning on Alpha Lock and lowering the brush opacity, but keep a backup if you do. Repeat this for the whole motel until you have added weathered greyish textures to the whole exterior. Add a string of yellow bulbs, with a layer of blurry glow as you did for the neon lights, to give the motel a slightly more welcoming look.

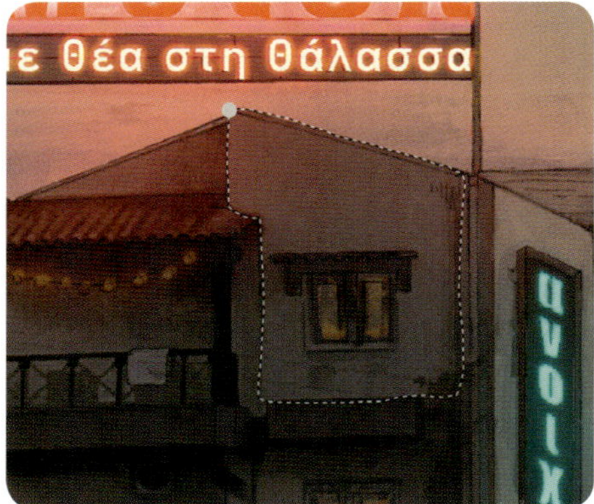
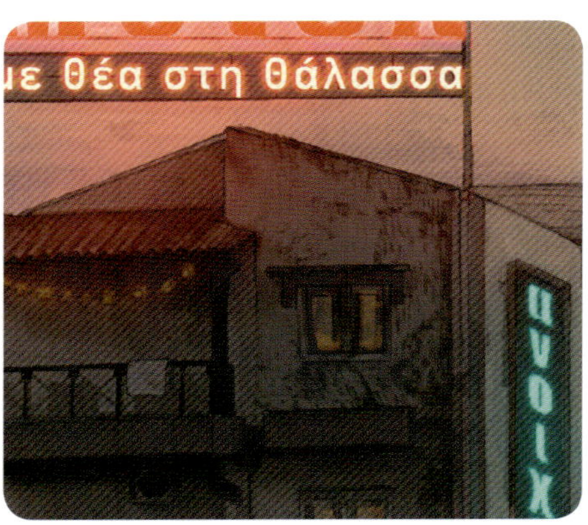
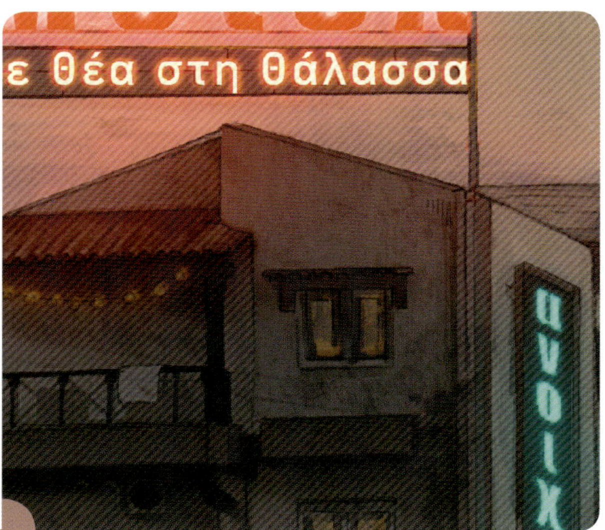
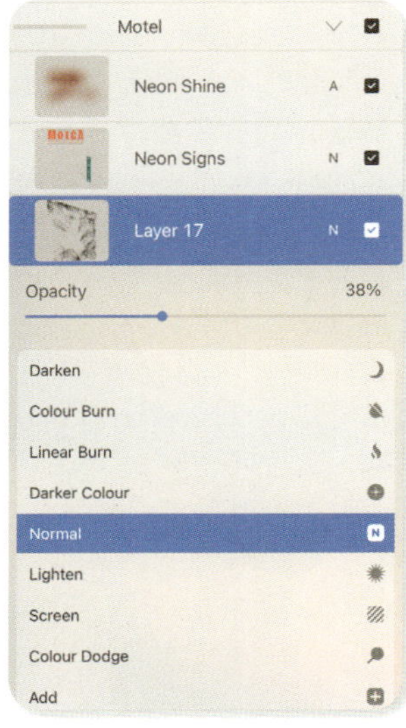

Use the Stucco brush as a texture stamp to detail the weathered motel walls

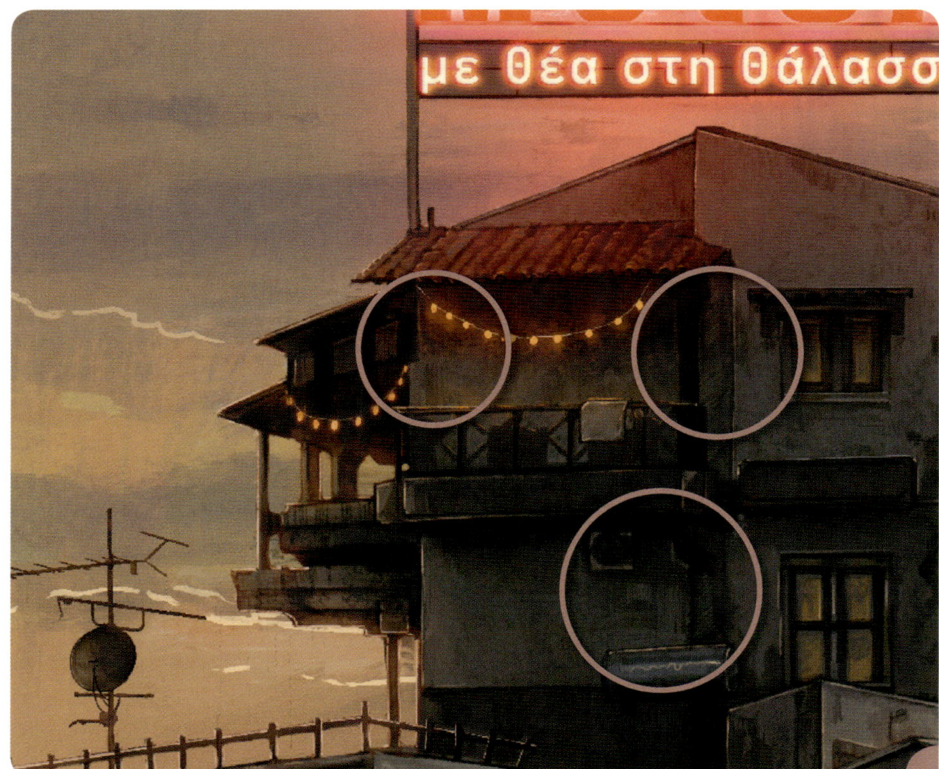

14

Use a basic round brush, such as **PAINTING > ROUND BRUSH** or the smoother **AIRBRUSHING > HARD BRUSH**, for the further rendering process. Textured brushes can save you hours of work rendering the dirty walls of a house; if you want to avoid repeating patterns, however, varying your brushes and application techniques will help achieve a more 'hand-painted' style. Use the Round Brush to paint over the textures and give the surfaces some visual variety. A round brush can be used for many things, such as adding highlights, drawing sharp edges, and applying colour in a clean, controlled way. Take your time lightly painting and blending the motel textures until the whole building has a more painterly look.

Finish the motel with some round-brush detailing

15

Now you can begin adding texture to the rest of the environment. Return to the foreground base-colour layer, making sure it's set to Alpha Lock, and begin painting the trees with SKETCHING > TECHNICAL PENCIL set to the maximum brush size. The pencil brush's natural graphite texture looks very similar to the structure of tree bark. Apply more paint on the edges to create volume.

Still on the same foreground colour layer, add some texture to the road using the same method you used for the motel walls – adding texture before painting extra details with a round brush. Another very useful brush is SKETCHING > SHALE BRUSH. Its shape is similar to a single blade of grass, which makes it ideal for painting fields, weeds, and meadows. Use this to add layers of grass on a new layer above the ground and puddles.

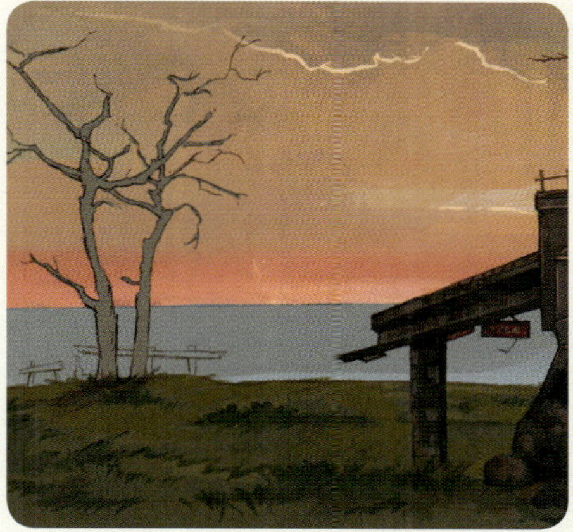
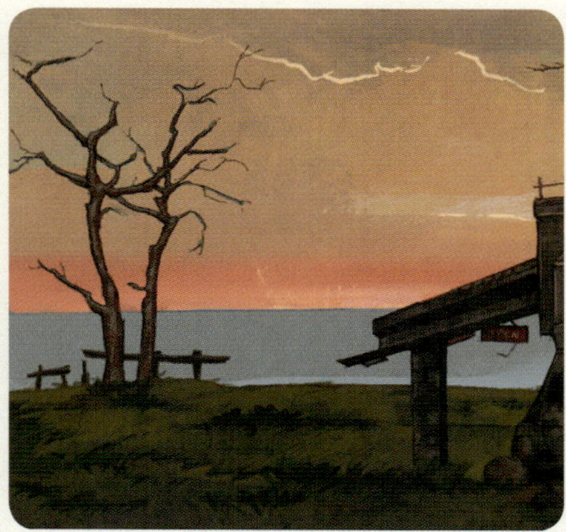

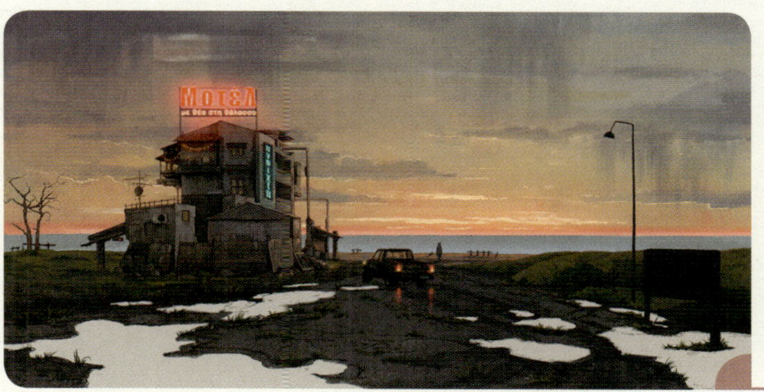

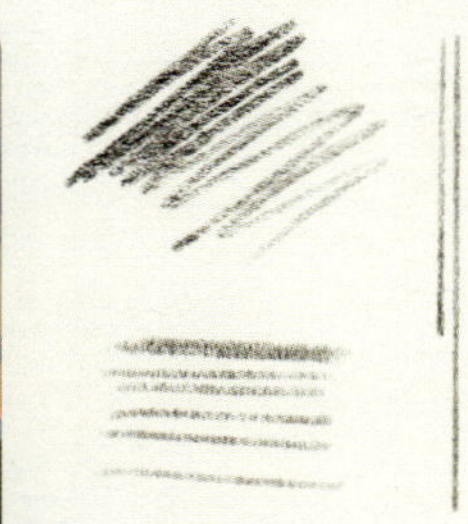

Use textured pencil brushes to paint the trees and grass

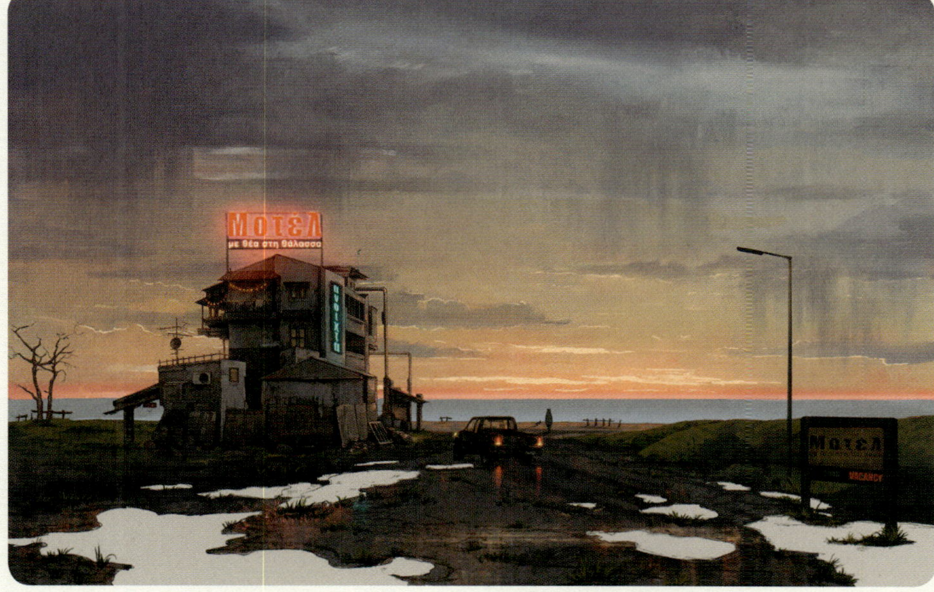

16

Since this scene is happening on a rainy day, you need to add more indicators of the weather aside from just the distant rain clouds in the sky. After rainfall, water usually accumulates on the ground in the form of puddles or a wet film. This water reflects all light sources above. To achieve that reflection effect, use the PAINTING > STUCCO brush on a new layer above the ground. Select the colour that is supposed to be reflected and draw over the ground with a vertical motion, from top to bottom. You can also use this brush in conjunction with the Eraser tool. For example, for the information sign on the right, you can create weathered text by inserting and rasterizing text, and then erasing parts of the letters with the Eraser set to the Stucco brush.

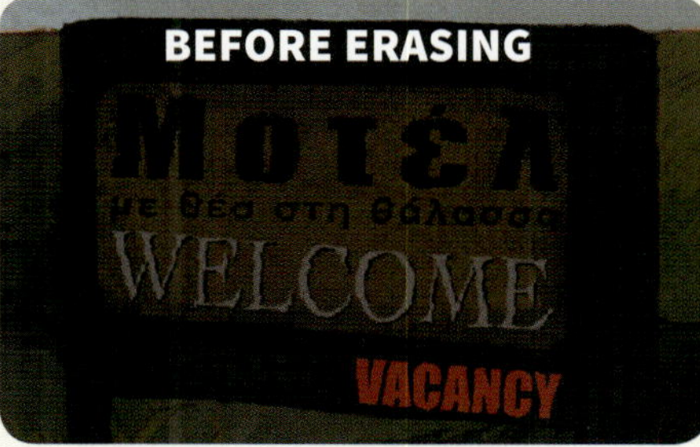

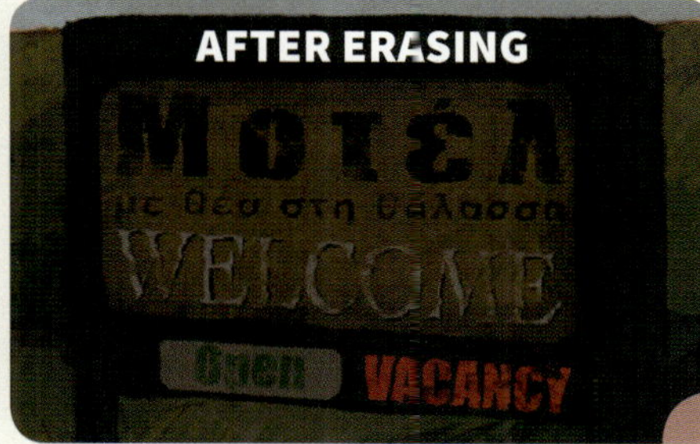

Add atmosphere-building details such as wet ground and weathered signage

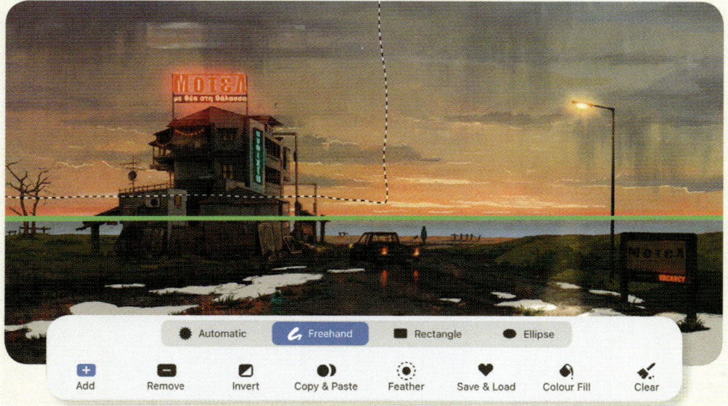

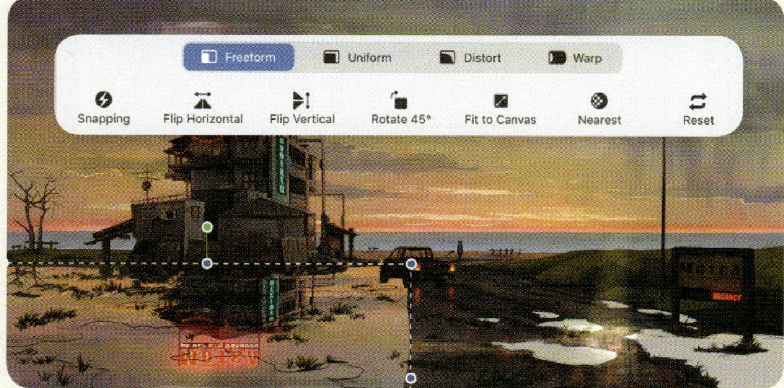

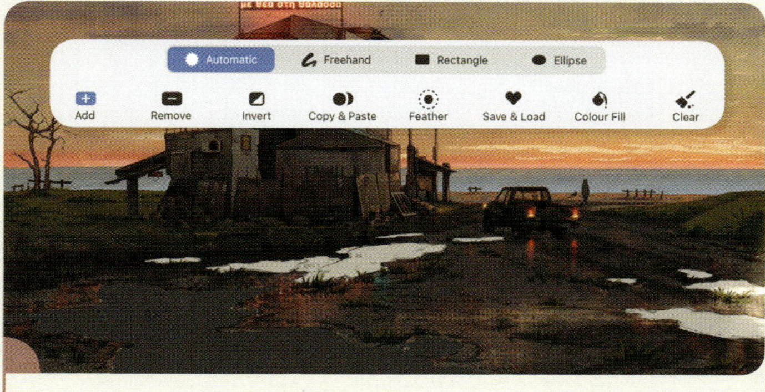

Create a flipped image and cut out parts of it to form reflections in the puddles

17

Now it's time to add reflections to the puddles. Go to **ACTIONS > COPY CANVAS** and **ACTIONS > PASTE** to insert a copy of the whole painting. Use **SELECTION > FREEHAND** to select the part of the scene above the left-hand puddles (above the horizon, which is marked in green). Tap Copy & Paste to duplicate the selected area onto a separate layer, then go to **TRANSFORM > FLIP VERTICAL**. Switch to either **TRANSFORM > AUTOMATIC** or **TRANSFORM > DISTORT** to slightly flatten the flipped image and give it more believable perspective.

You will create the reflections by cutting out shapes to fill the puddles. To do this, turn off the visibility of the reflections layer for now. Go to the layer containing the puddles' base tones, enable **SELECTION > AUTOMATIC**, and tap each puddle to select it. Tap Invert on the bottom menu to select everything outside the puddles instead. Return to the reflections layer, turn on its visibility, and erase all the areas of the mirrored layer that are now selected. This way, only the shapes of the puddles will remain, and you have successfully created a water reflection! You can use the Eraser set to **PAINTING > ROUND BRUSH** to lightly soften the edges where the puddles are shallower. Repeat this process for the other puddles in the scene.

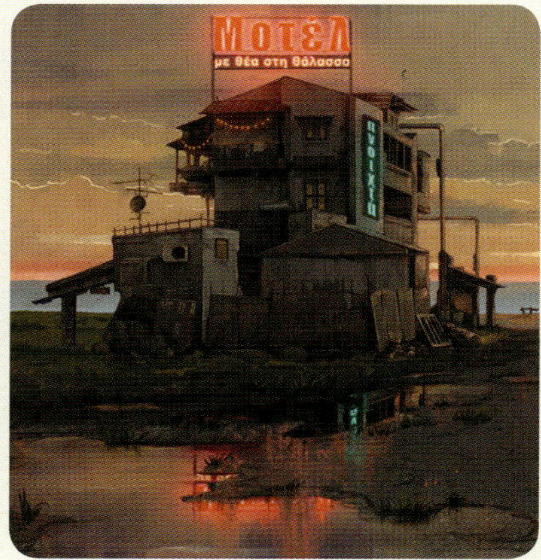

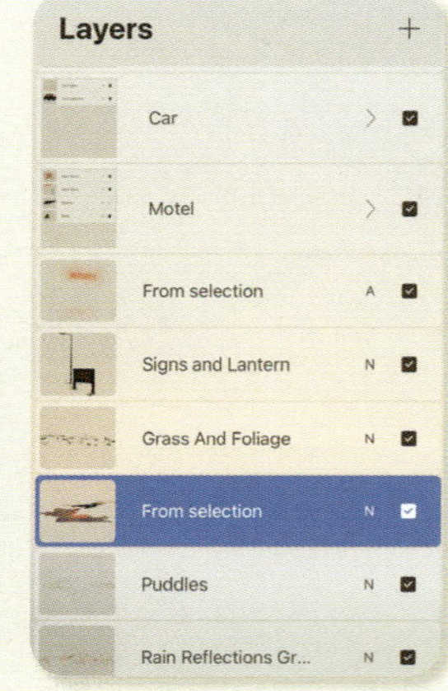

18

To show that the puddles are really part of the environment, they need a bit more fine-tuning: some movement in the water to give an indication of wind, especially under these weather conditions. You can do this by smudging vertically over the reflections using the Smudge tool set to **PAINTING > DRY BRUSH**. But be careful – don't smudge too much! A few delicate brushstrokes are enough. Then, on a new layer, use **SKETCHING > PROCREATE PENCIL** and a pale yellow colour to add some fine strokes around the edges of each puddle, forming ripples of highlight reflected from the sky. You can also add a subtle shadow to the puddles, to avoid flatness. To do this, use a soft brush in a dark colour to paint over the upper parts of the puddles and give them a hint of volume. This will also soften the transition between ground and water.

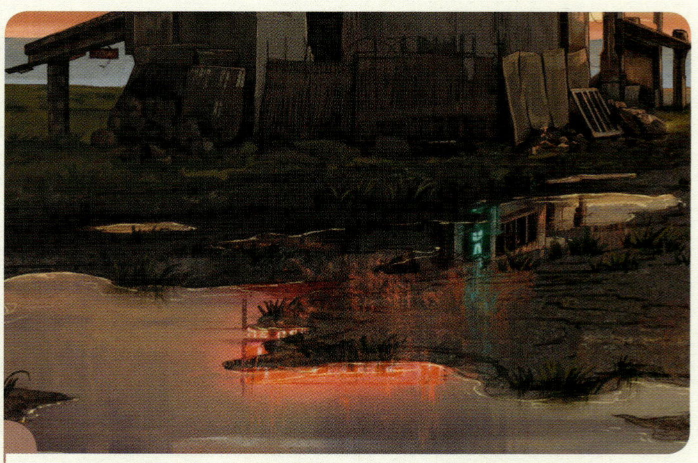

Add smudges and highlights to the puddles to create movement

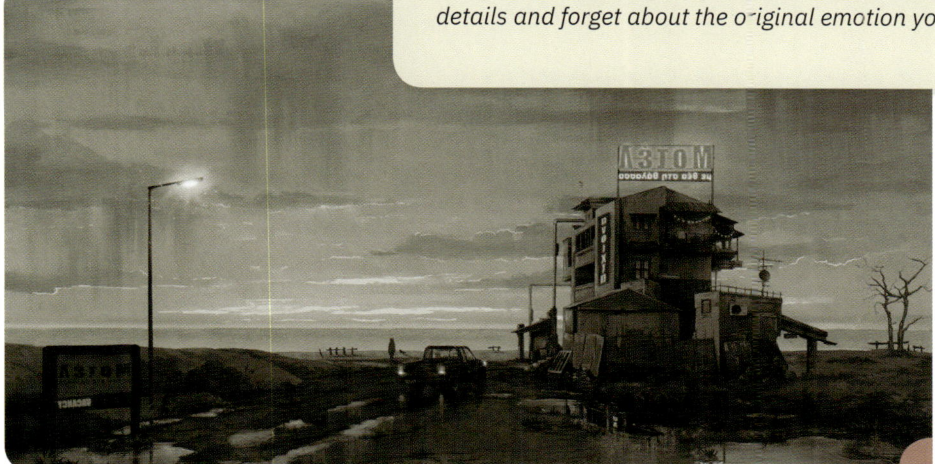

Making a greyscale or mirrored version of your image will help you detect any imbalances in composition and values

19

Before you begin to wrap up the image, you will usually have to fix some mistakes that have come up during the rendering process. Procreate offers many potential ways to help you detect imbalances in an image. One of them is creating a black and white version of your painting. You can do this by using **ACTIONS > COPY CANVAS** again, and converting the pasted image into black and white by reducing its saturation to 0%. You can even go to **TRANSFORM > FLIP HORIZONTAL** to flip the image for an even newer view. Your eyes are not accustomed to seeing the mirrored version, which makes it easier to spot mistakes.

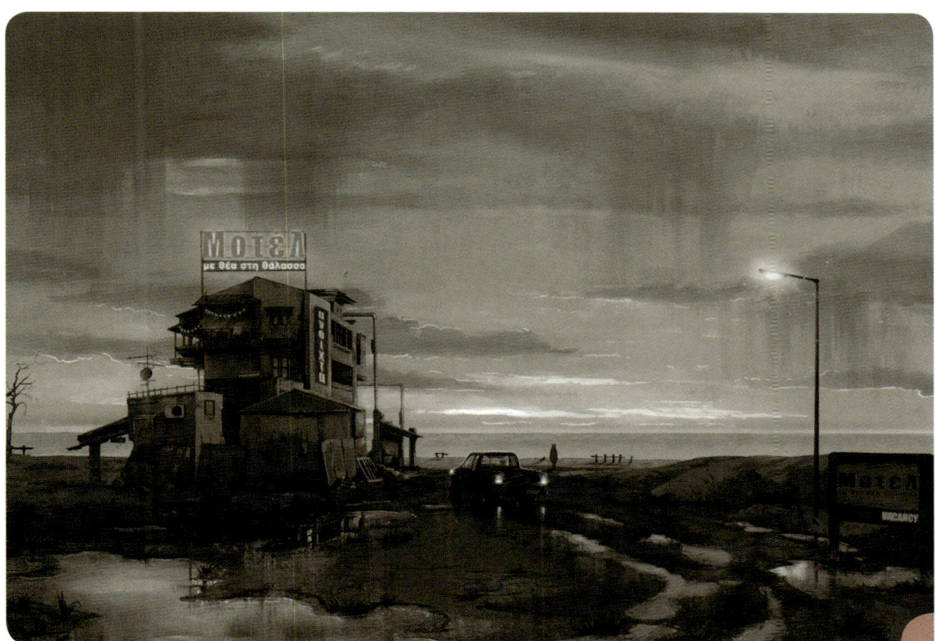

20

Now you are able to check the values of your painting as well as the arrangement of elements with fresh eyes, without the distraction of colours. You can even test out some quick revisions on the greyscale copy before returning to the main image. As you can see here, the sky would benefit from a bit more contrast, and consequently the reflections on the ground would as well. Adding extra highlights to the car would help lead the viewer's eye in that direction. Finally, the street lamp on the side is missing a bright reflection in the puddle underneath it.

Identify errors and test out solutions in the greyscale copy

21

Now that you know what adjustments to make in order to improve the scene's readability, hide the greyscale layer and begin making revisions to the relevant layers. Add contrast to the clouds and ground and add the reflections of the additional lights. Check that the reflections line up believably with the objects above – for example, the blue neon reflection here was incorrectly placed, needing to be moved slightly to the right. Some of the deep tyre tracks on the road were dry – you can paint a few simple patches of reflected sky to add small puddles there.

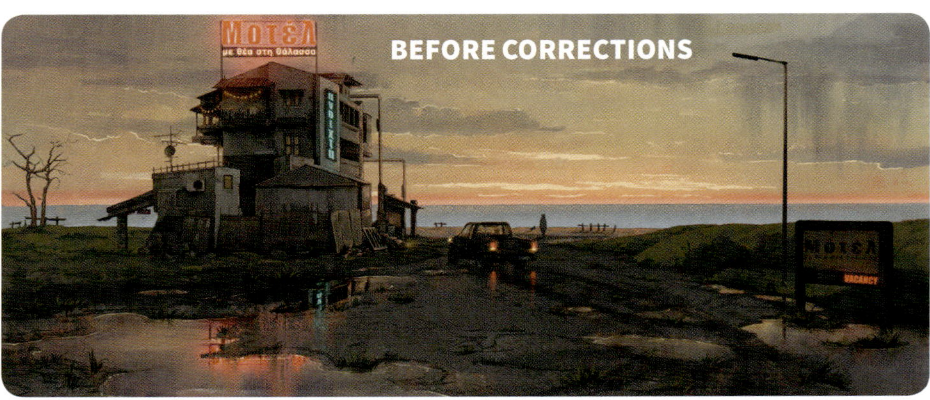

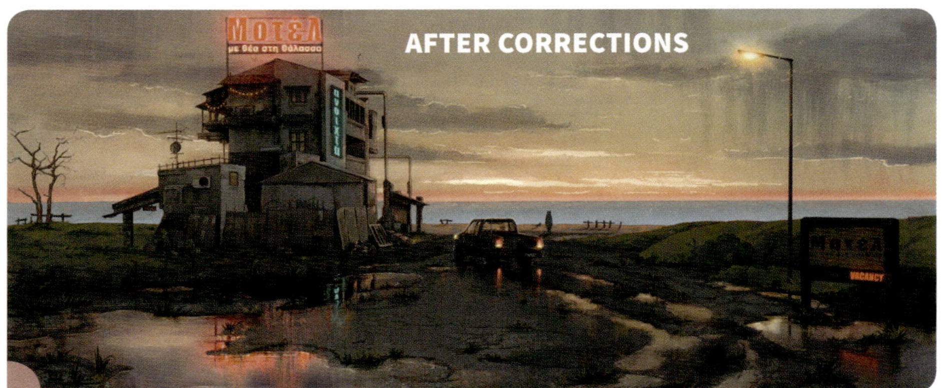

The image before and after revising the contrast and lighting details

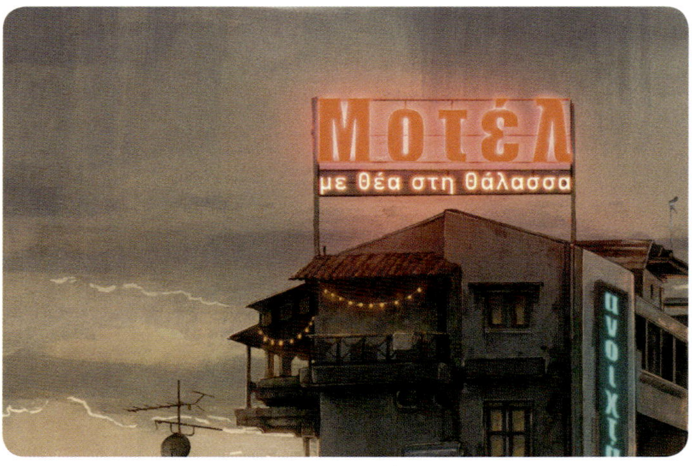

22

Before the painting is completely finished, you can enhance the mood with a few adjustments. One of them is adding noise. If you have references for the mood and emotion of your early concept, you should refer back to them now. One of the main inspirations for this artwork was the ambient retro style of thrillers or series of the early nineties, such as *Twin Peaks*. To emphasize that retro atmosphere, go to **ADJUSTMENTS > NOISE** and slide your finger across the screen to add a subtle 5% Noise adjustment to the painting. You can also go to **ADJUSTMENTS > COLOUR BALANCE** and reduce the magenta level a little, making the green tones slightly more dominant. This increases the mysterious atmosphere and creates a suspenseful mood.

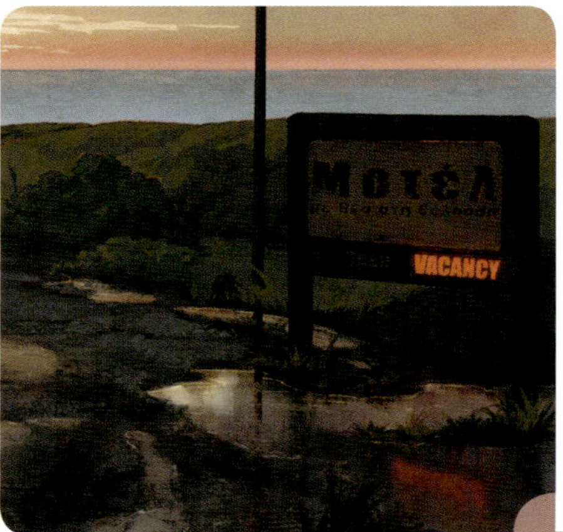

Add a soft Noise adjustment for a retro, cinematic look

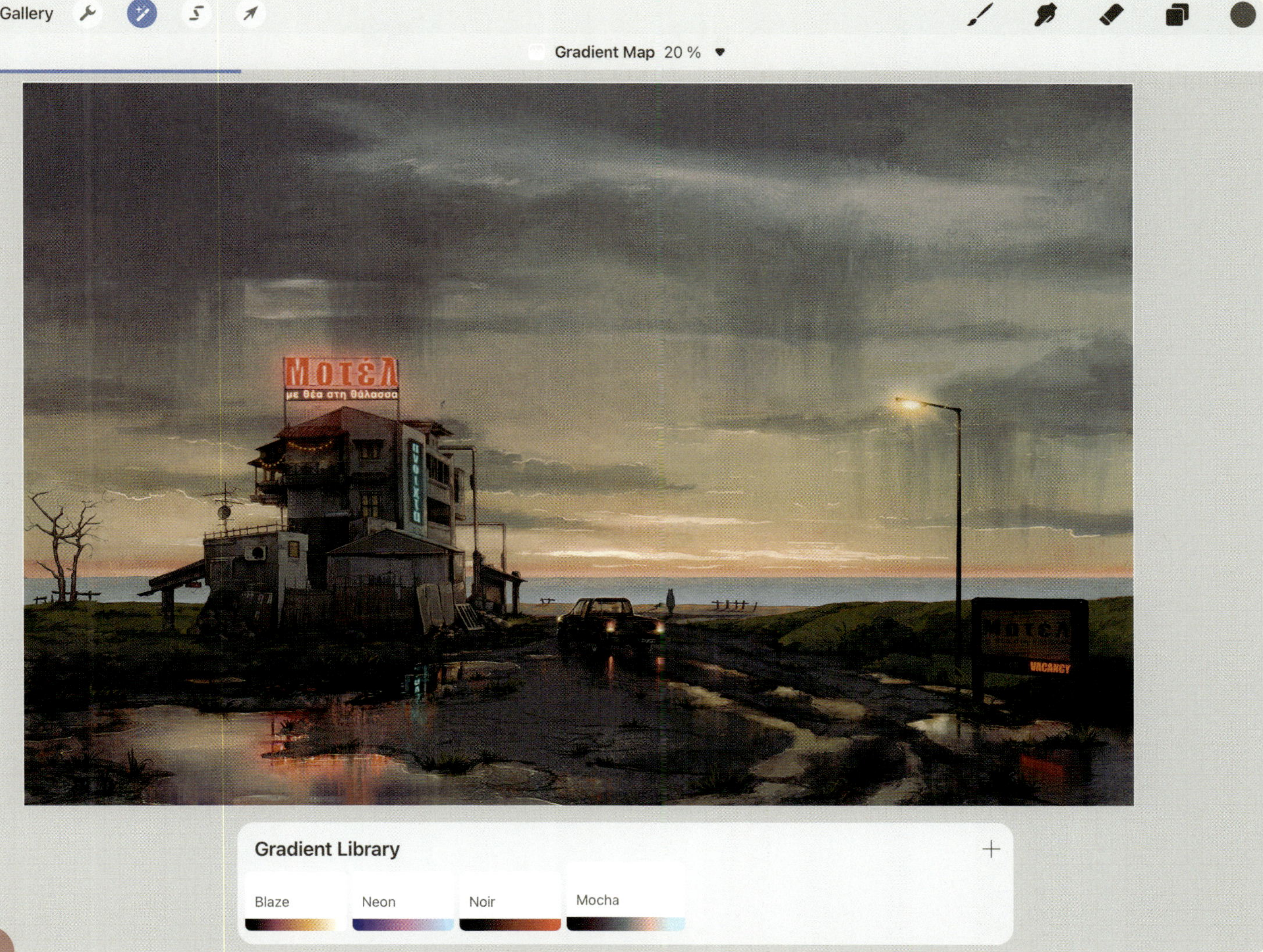

Experiment with Gradient Map options for a final atmospheric colour tweak

> SARAH SAYS: *'Let's have a look at what you have learned so far. You've learned that Procreate can be used for more than "just" painting. To reach your goal, make use of its wide range of tools, such as text, Alpha Lock, and colour correction. Challenges such as creating a neon sign demonstrated the importance of blend modes and how to create light effects with different tools. Trying out rendering techniques with different brushes will help you find your own unique approach. Checks such as creating a mirrored greyscale version of your painting will help you detect mistakes and create balance in the arrangement of your image's elements, as well as improve the composition of your future illustrations.'*

23

Finally, you can play around with Gradient Maps if the colour corrections in the previous step feel like they are still missing something. Procreate offers a well-sorted Gradient Library under **ADJUSTMENTS > GRADIENT MAPS** with many interesting colour combinations to try, but they can be very dominant and are best used very carefully. Try applying the Blaze effect with a very low intensity. Last of all, if the painting needs a bit more brightness after these changes, you can use **ADJUSTMENTS > CURVES** to slightly boost the midtones.

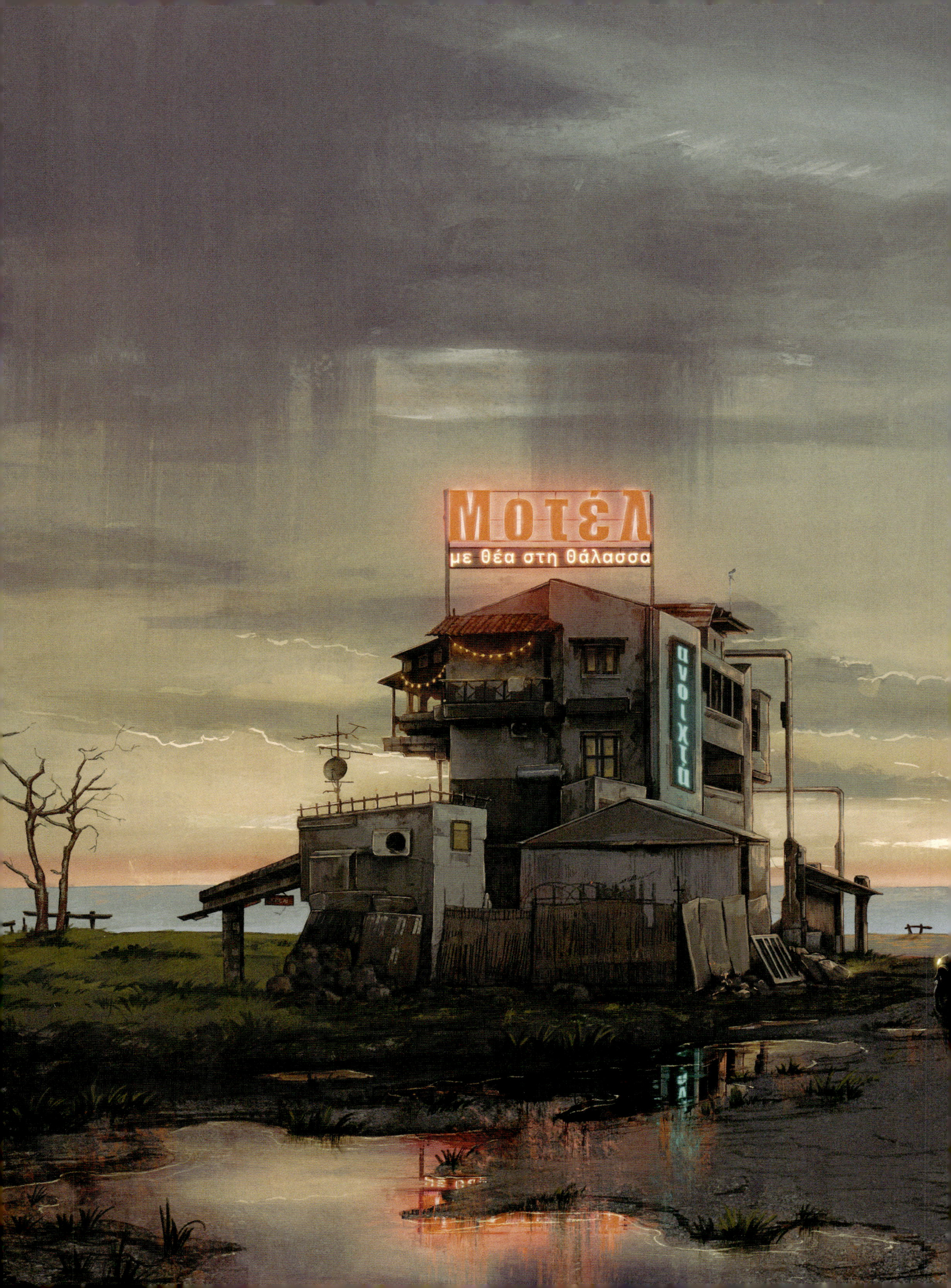

Μοτέλ
με θέα στη θάλασσα
ανοιχτό

CONCLUSION

The illustration is finished at this point. You can be very proud of your endurance and all the new skills and techniques you have opened up for yourself. Now you know how to transform the elements of a real-life photo into a moody, mysterious new scene that tells a story. It is highly recommended to go outside and explore your surroundings – you wouldn't believe how much inspiration you can find out there when you least expect it.

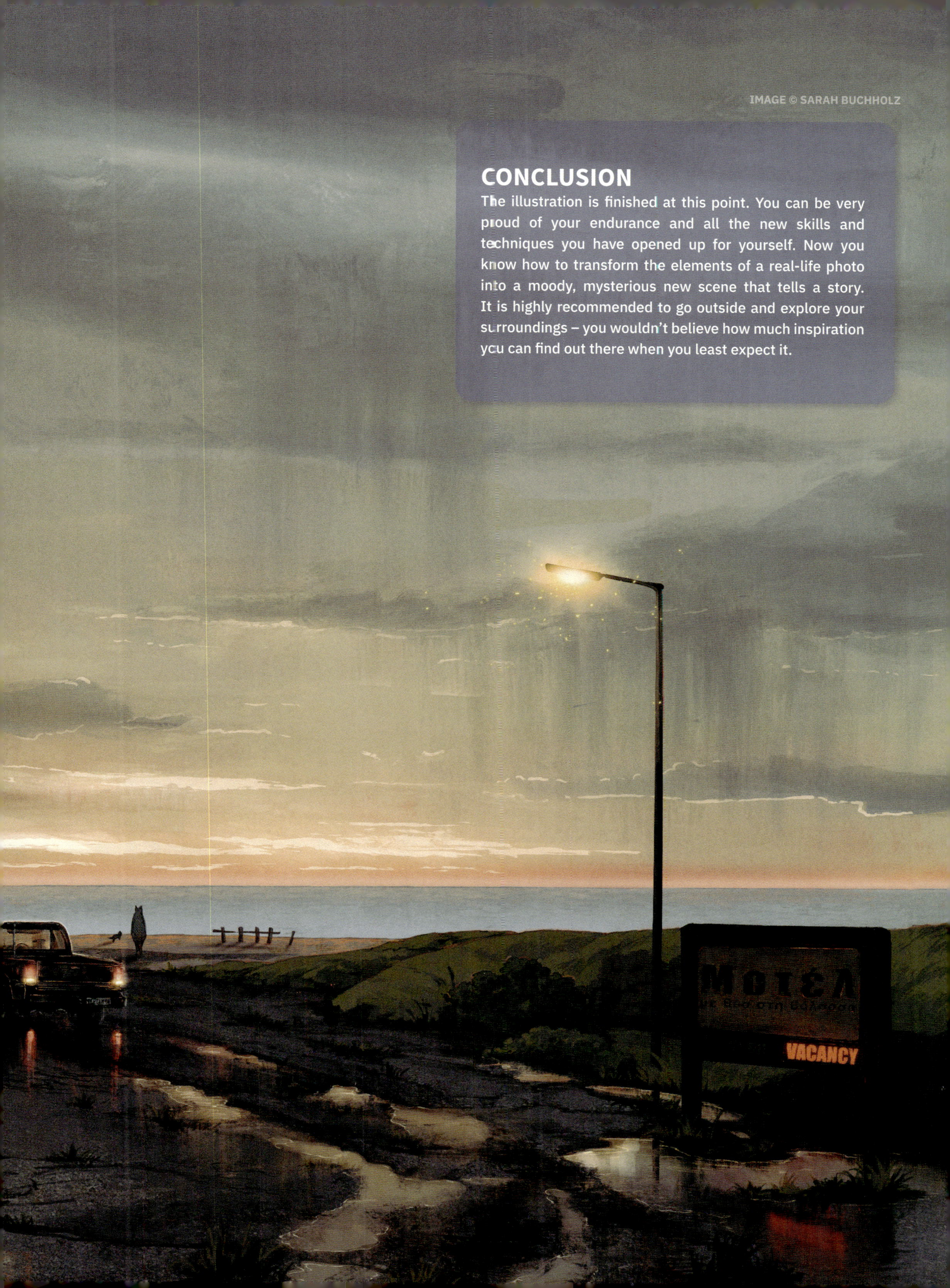

THE ENCOUNTER: This scene takes place in a megacity from my story's universe; the main
character encounters three spirits in the form of antelopes walking across the street

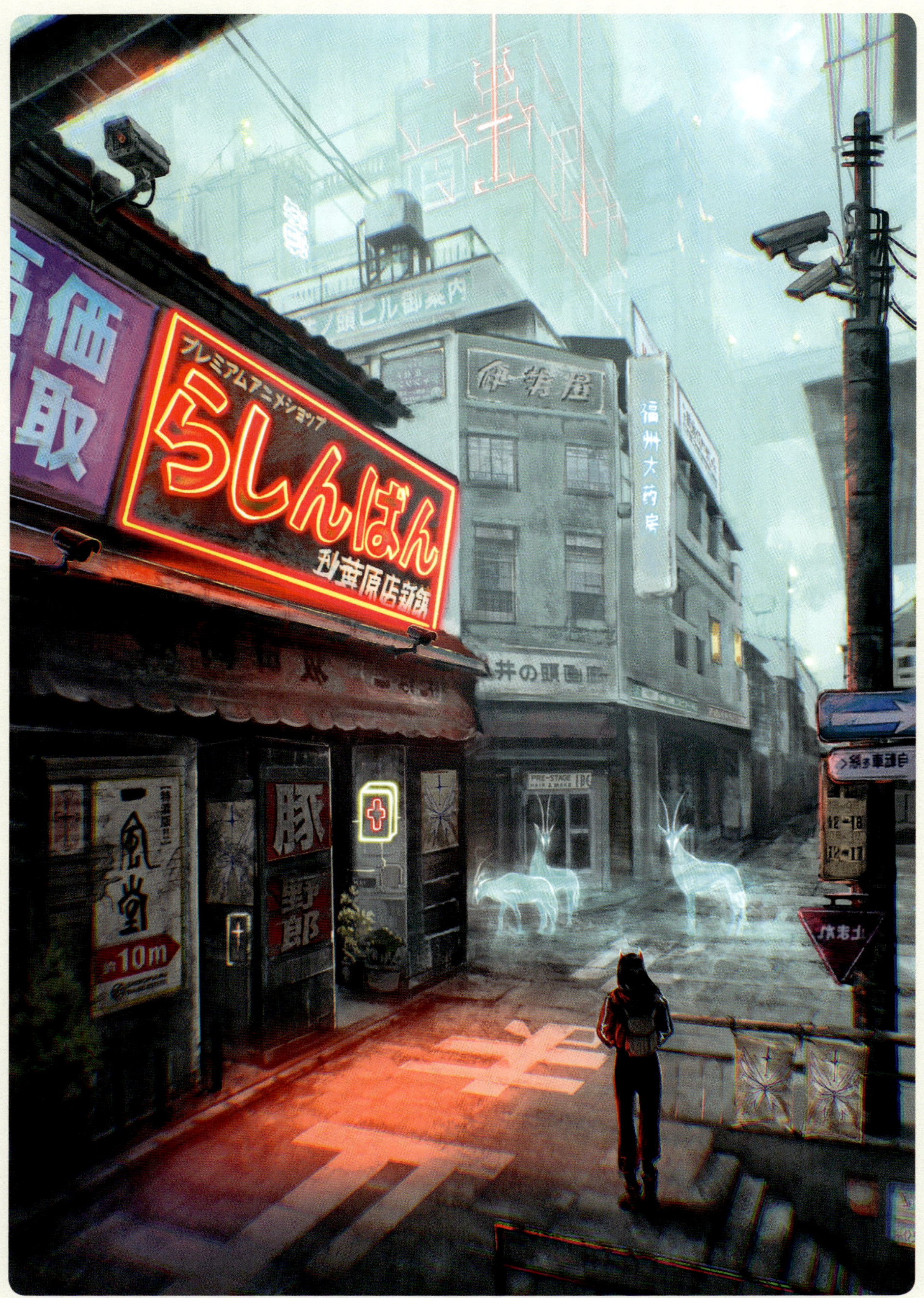

らしんばん
豚
野郎
10m
PRE-STAGE

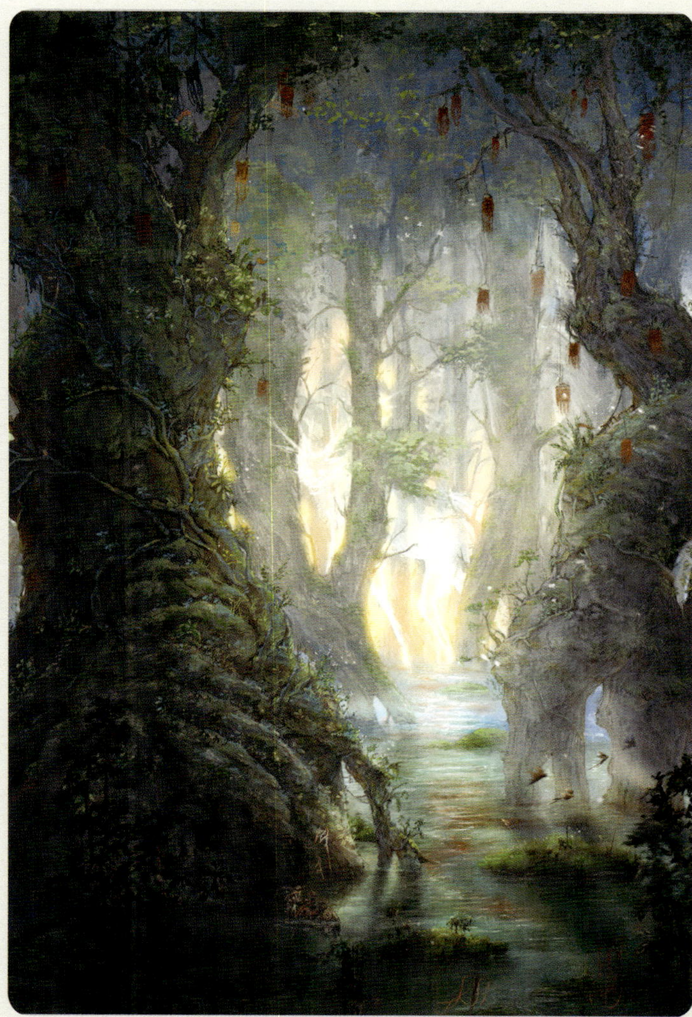

THE RITUAL: This environment was inspired by my favourite Studio Ghibli movie, *Princess Mononoke*; besides its stunning art, I love how the movie depicts humanity's destructive influence on nature and the spirits living in it

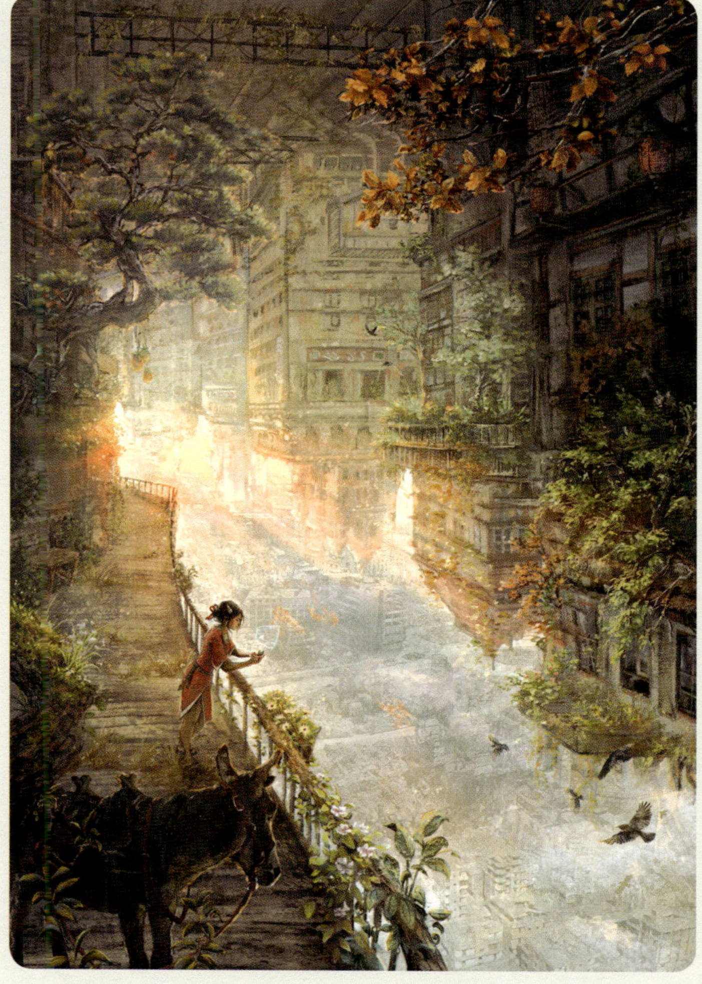

TREASURE HUNT: This scene shows the main character from my story and her donkey companion searching for a cure against demonic possession; she hopes to discover it somewhere in the ruins of what was once a city in the sky

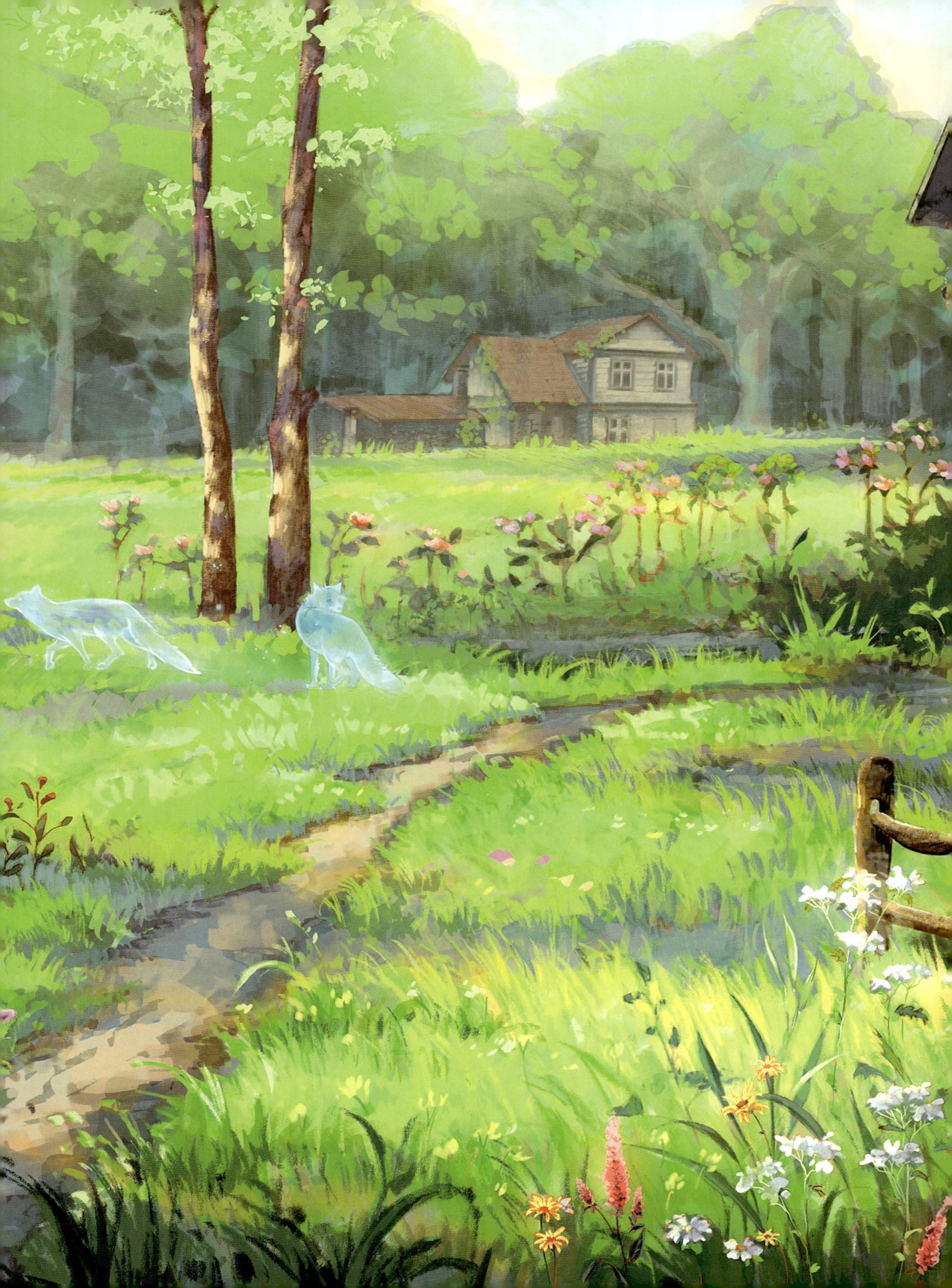

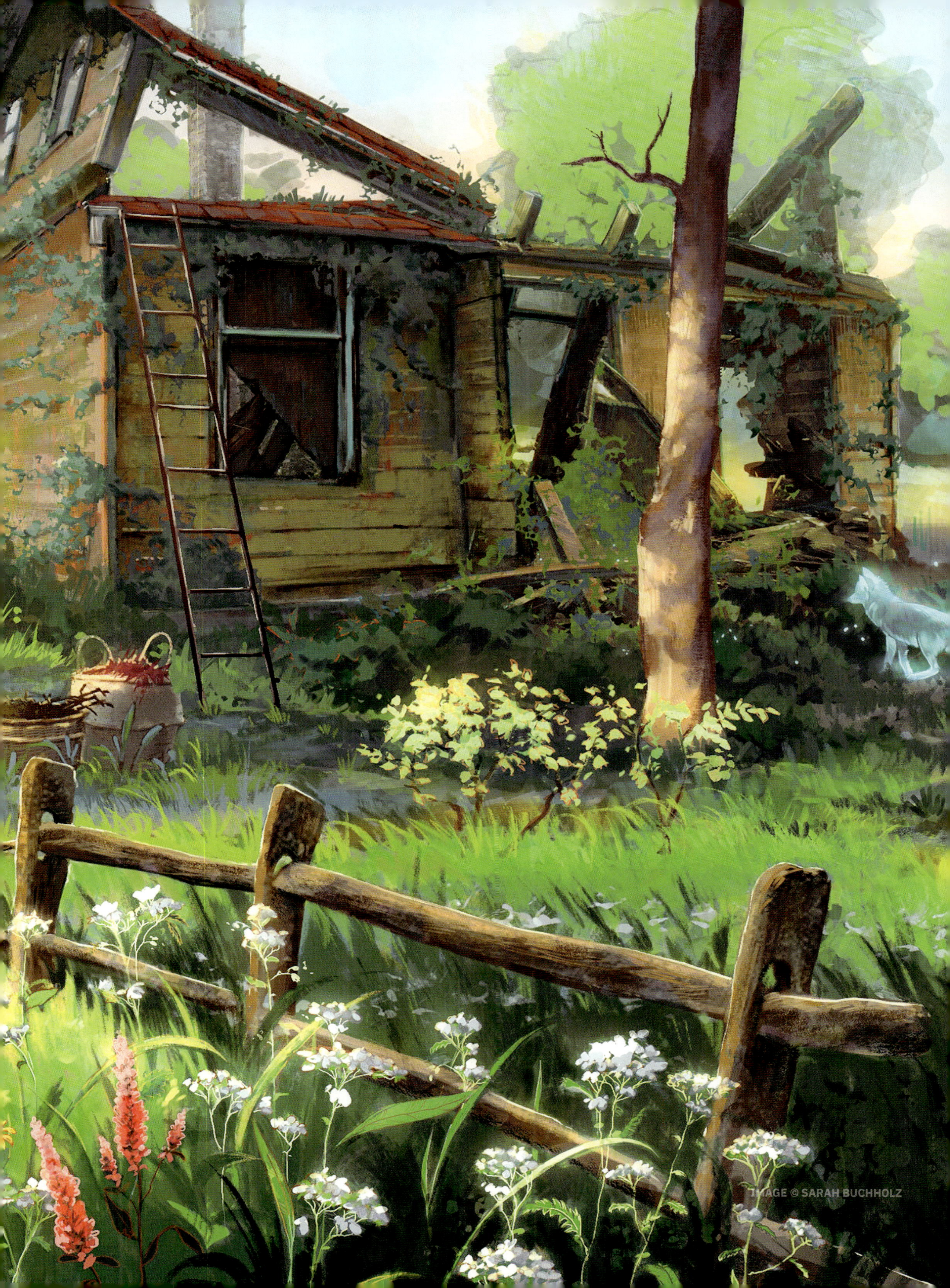

IMAGE © SARAH BUCHHOLZ

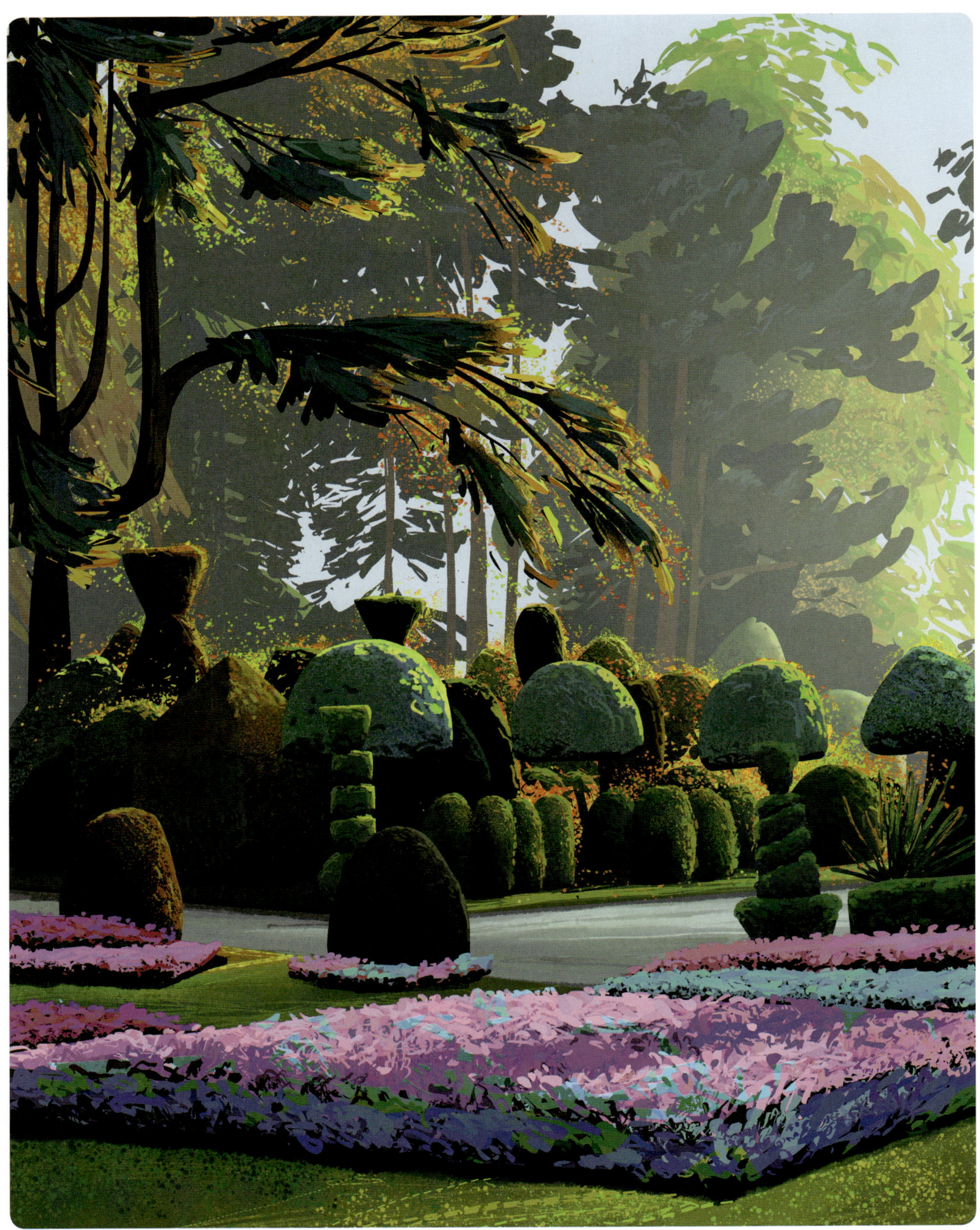

DOWNLOADABLE RESOURCES

Go to *3dtotalpublishing.com/resources* to download these resources. You can import photos into Procreate as a new layer by using **ACTIONS > ADD > INSERT A PHOTO** or **INSERT A FILE** to insert an item from your Camera Roll or Downloads, respectively. You can also open references in a floating window above your canvas by going to **ACTIONS > CANVAS > REFERENCE**, selecting **IMAGE > IMPORT IMAGE**, and navigating to your desired reference photo.

REFERENCE PHOTOS FOR 8 PROJECTS

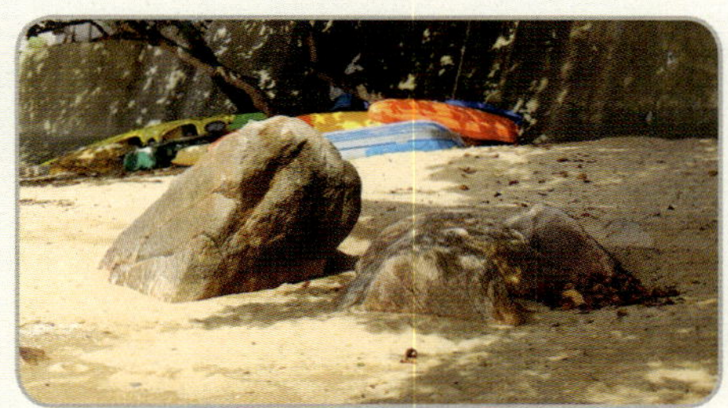 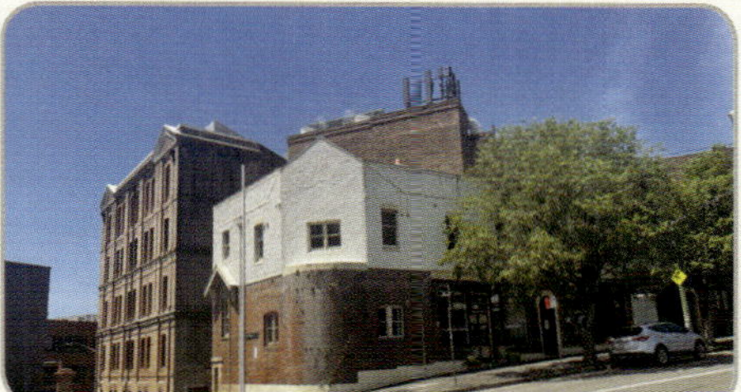 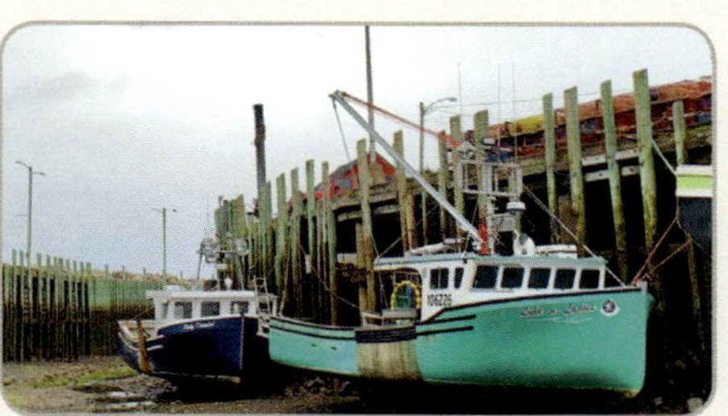

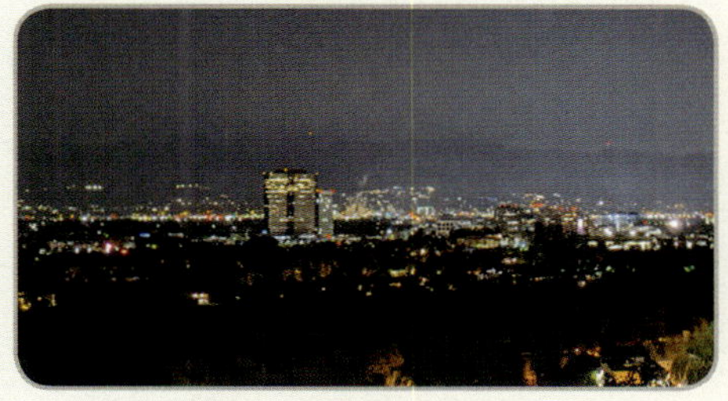 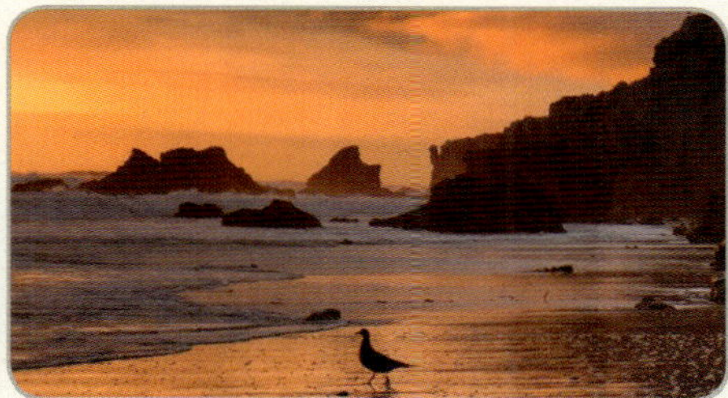 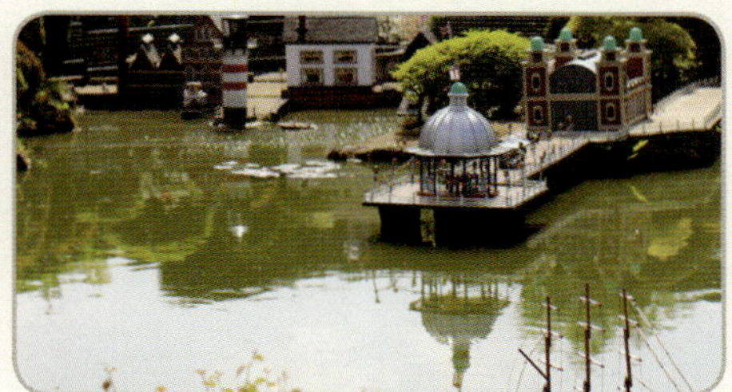

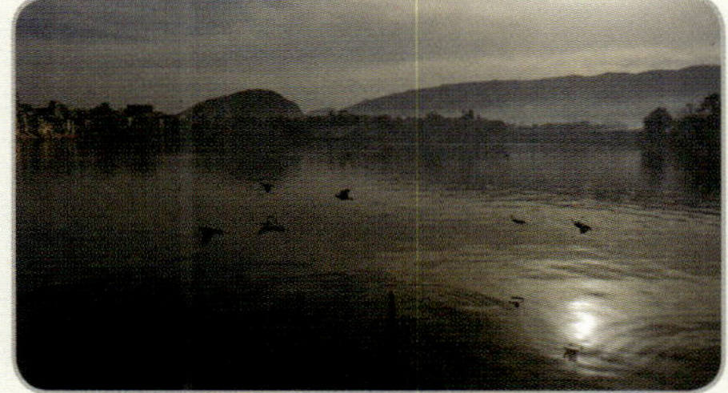 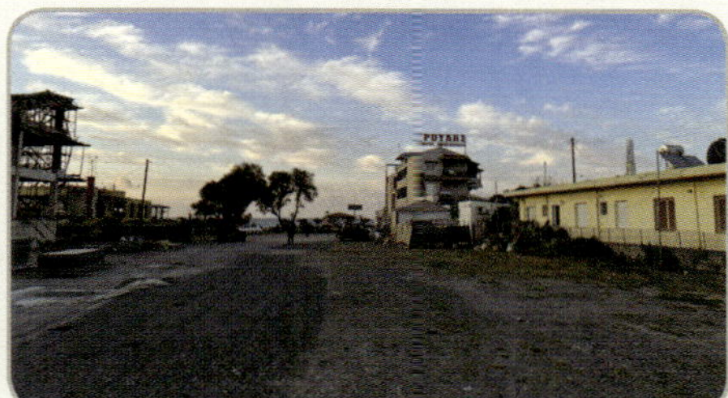 

'JENNIFER'S DEFAULT PACK' BRUSHSET

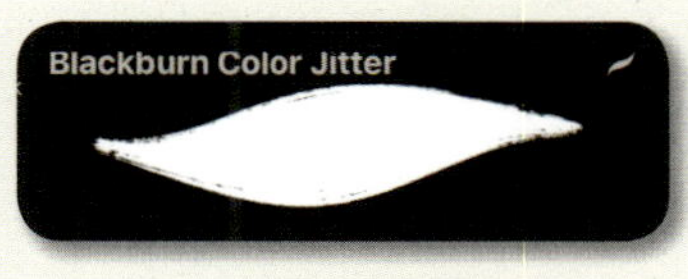

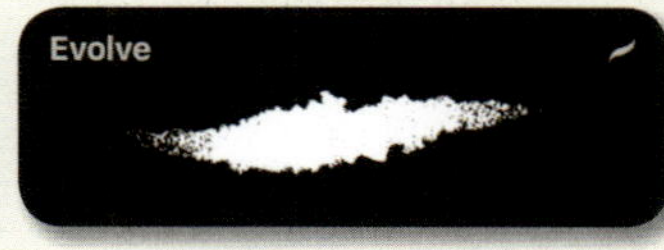

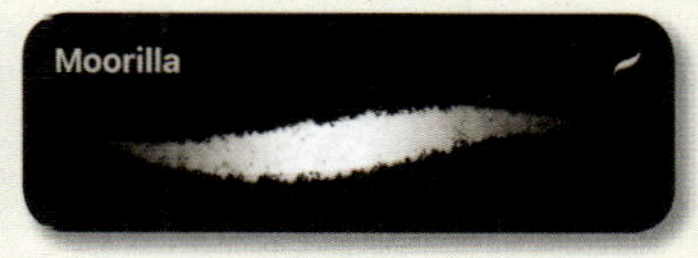

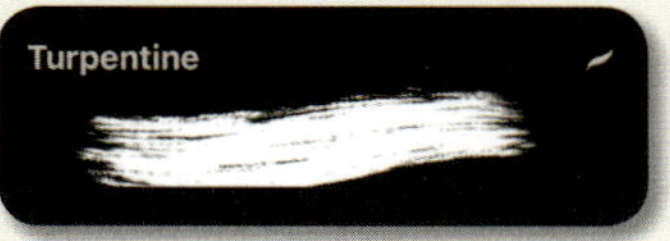

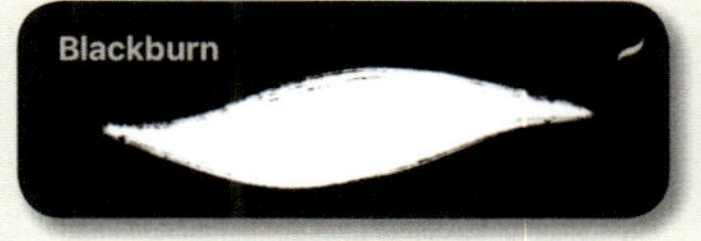

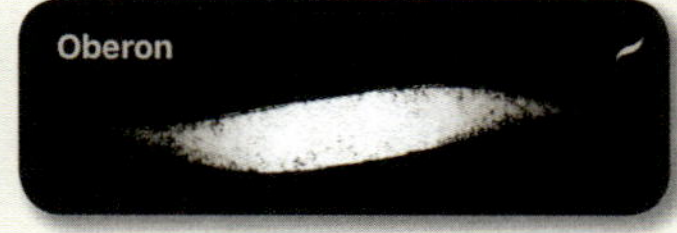

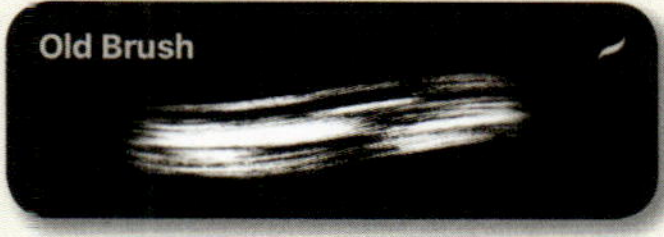

You can also find Mike McCain's 'Free Brush Pack' at *mikemccain.art/store*. Import brushes by opening the Brush Library, tapping the + icon, selecting Import, and navigating to the downloaded brush file.

GLOSSARY

APPLE PENCIL

A stylus developed by Apple exclusively for the iPad. It is the recommended tool for Procreate users, with features including tilt recognition, pressure sensitivity, and side buttons.

BACKGROUND COLOUR LAYER

This non-deletable layer is automatically created for every Procreate file.

BRUSH LIBRARY

Procreate's brush collection, which includes default brushes and any custom brushes you make or download.

BRUSH STUDIO

Procreate's brush-editing suite, which you can open by tapping on a brush in the Brush Library.

CANVAS

Your painting surface, used in both traditional and digital artwork.

EXPORT

To save your artwork out of Procreate for use on your device or in another app.

GALLERY

The Procreate home screen that shows all of your files. You can access your Procreate images and create new canvases from here.

GESTURES

In the context of Procreate and digital tablets, gestures are finger motions that activate tools or effects on your screen.

GRADIENTS

A gradual transition between different values or hues (for example, fading from light to dark).

GREYSCALE

An image that is only in shades of black, white, and grey.

HUE

The general colour 'family' to which a colour belongs, regardless of how light or dark it is. For example, sky blue and navy are both blue hues.

IMPORT

To add a file into Procreate, including brushes, references, or image files from other software.

LAYERS

In digital painting software, layers emulate a stack of transparent sheets that you can edit and manipulate separately. Layers are one of the most important tools in digital painting.

LINE ART

Artwork drawn with lines. It may be an objective in itself or used as a base for a painting.

MIDTONE

A colour or value that falls between the highlights (brightest areas) and shadows (darkest areas) of an image or palette.

OPACITY

An object's level of transparency. In the context of digital painting, it refers to the transparency of your brushstrokes or layers. A layer with low opacity would be see-through, while a layer with high opacity would appear more solid.

PERSPECTIVE

In drawing and painting, perspective is the representation of three-dimensional depth on a flat screen or page.

PRESET

A predefined configuration of settings.

RASTERIZE

The action of converting a vector-based object into a raster (pixel-based) format. For example, if you rasterize a text layer, you will no longer be able to type letters on it, but you will be able to paint on it as a regular layer.

RGB

This is a colour mode that allows you to control a colour by the amount of red, green, and blue.

SATURATION

The purity or vibrancy of a colour. A highly saturated colour appears bold and strong, while a desaturated colour appears more pale and grey.

SOURCE LIBRARY

Specific to Procreate, this library contains a vast number of preset images that can be used to create or alter brushes in the Brush Studio.

STYLUS

A pen-shaped instrument that lets you navigate a touch-sensitive device, such as the iPad.

TAB

One section of a menu. There may be multiple tabs per menu, with each tab listing a different category of options.

THUMBNAILS

Small preliminary versions of your artwork, or small previews of an artwork in a software.

TIME-LAPSE VIDEO

In Procreate, this is a sped-up video recording of your painting process.

WORKFLOW

How you approach the development of a project from start to finish. Every artist develops their own unique workflow over time.

VALUE

In painting, value refers to the lightness or darkness of a colour.

TOOL DIRECTORY

ADJUSTMENTS

A collection of image-editing tools and filters, available via the wand icon on the top left bar.

ALPHA LOCK

A setting that locks transparent pixels on a layer, only letting you paint on the existing filled pixels.

BLOOM

An adjustment that creates a glare or atmospheric glow effect.

BLUR

An adjustment that lets you diffuse the pixels of a layer. The opposite effect is Sharpen.

BRUSH

The main tool used in digital painting, with options that let you simulate different media and effects.

CLIPPING MASK

An option that sets one layer as subordinate to a target layer below. On the subordinate 'clipped' layer, you are not able to paint or edit outside the shape of the target layer.

CLONE

An option that duplicates the selected area.

COLOUR BALANCE

A setting that controls the colour by the amount of red, green, and blue in the image.

COLOUR MENU

This menu, found by tapping the active colour in the top-right corner of the interface, lets you select and edit colour via different modes.

COLOUR SWATCH

The small squares of colour that make up palettes in the Colours menu.

COLOURDROP

A tool used to fill enclosed areas with a flat colour by dragging and dropping it onto the canvas.

CROP

A tool that lets you trim and edit your canvas size.

CURVES

A setting used to manipulate the values and colours through a histogram.

CUSTOM BRUSH

A brush made from scratch by a Procreate user or tweaked from a default one.

DRAWING ASSIST

This tool snaps your lines to the last used Drawing Guide. You can switch it on or off for each layer.

DRAWING GUIDE

A Procreate tool enabling you to create and edit grids to use as guidelines on your canvas.

ERASER

A tool used for deleting pixels from the canvas.

EYEDROPPER

A tool for picking colours from your canvas.

HUE, SATURATION, BRIGHTNESS (HSB)

A Colour menu mode that allows you to control a colour's properties. It is also an adjustment for your image, found under the Adjustments menu.

LAYER BLEND MODES

A setting that determines the interaction between two or more layers, such as brightening or darkening.

LIQUIFY

A tool that lets you manipulate, distort, and reshape the pixels of your canvas.

LOCK

A setting that protects a layer from being edited.

MASK

A non-destructive tool that enables you to hide content without erasing it.

MODIFY BUTTON

The square icon between the two sliders on the sidebar, used to modify tool or gesture behaviour. It is customizable via Procreate's Prefs tab.

NOISE

A setting that adds a textured, grainy effect, similar to an analogue photograph or film.

PALETTES

A fixed collection of colour swatches available in the Colours menu.

QUICKMENU

A menu containing six customizable options summoned through gestures.

QUICKSHAPE

A feature that makes it easy to draw perfect lines and geometry by automatically smoothing your freehand lines.

RECOLOUR

An adjustment that lets you select areas of colour and change them to a preselected one.

SELECTION

A tool found in most digital painting software that allows you to isolate specific areas to edit or manipulate.

SMUDGE

A tool in Procreate that lets you move and smear paint instead of creating or erasing it.

TRANSFORM

A tool that can modify the position, proportions, and scale of the elements in your artwork.

UNDO/REDO

Undo lets you go back a step, and Redo forward a step, in your painting.

CONTRIBUTORS

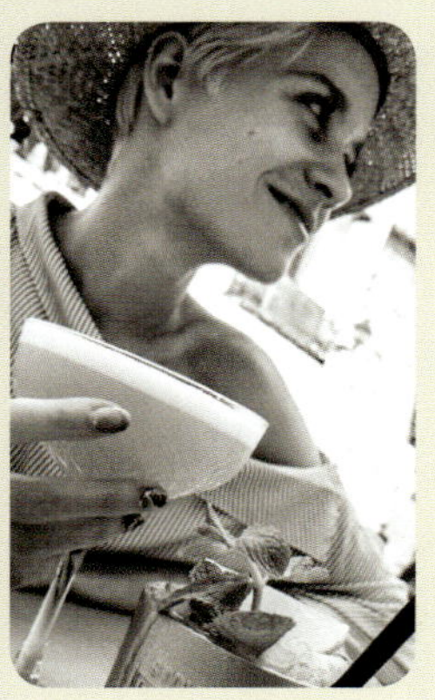

KARIN BRANDENBERG
instagram.com/kbrandenberg

Karin Brandenberg is a Swiss-born artist currently living in Hong Kong. After using 3D tools extensively at work, she enjoys painting plein-air scenes and natural landscapes in her spare time.

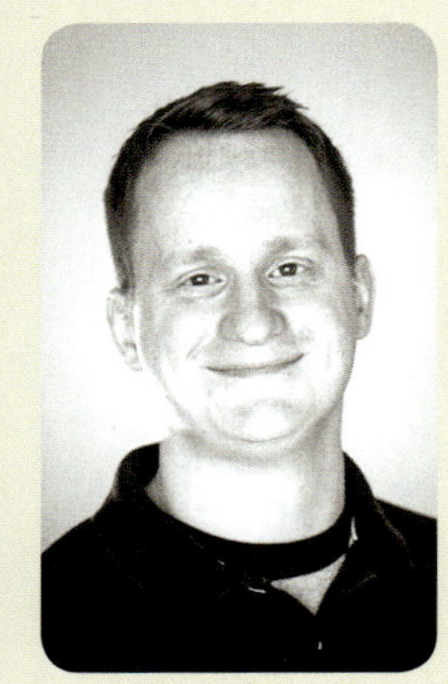

ERIC ELWELL
ericelwellart.com

Eric Elwell is a New-York-based artist focused on concept design and illustration, working in a blend of digital and traditional mediums. He is also the owner of Fantastic Tanks LLC.

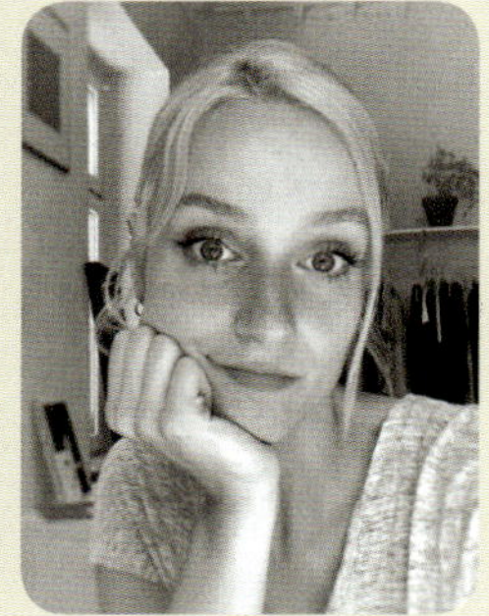

SARAH BUCHHOLZ
sarahbuchholz.com

Sarah Buchholz is currently working as an independent artist in Leipzig, Germany. Her paintings are all about exploring new worlds, always with a tribute to escapism, melancholy, and the beauty found in nature.

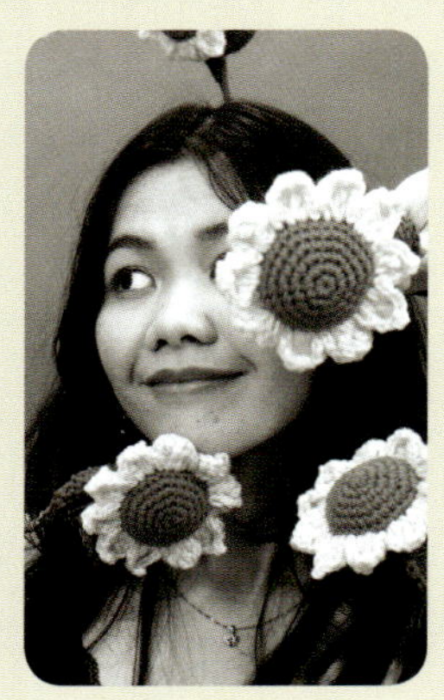

GILLIAN GALANG
instagram.com/gillian3g
twitter.com/gillianthreeg

Gillian Galang is a freelance visual development artist based in the Philippines. In her free time, she loves to play games, travel, and take photos. Her favourite subjects to paint are mountains, shopfronts, and trees.

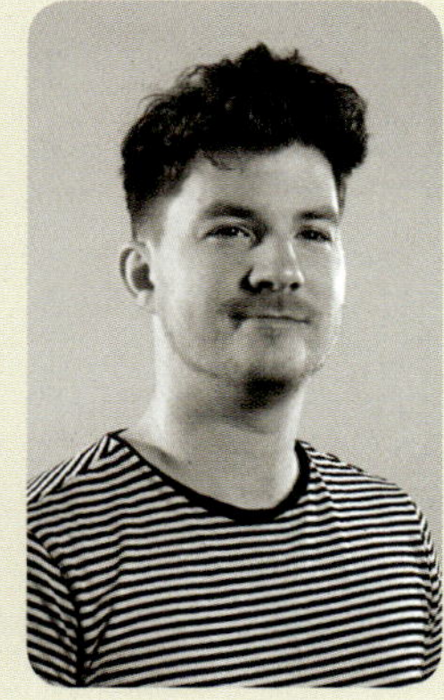

TREVOR CLARE
inprnt.com/gallery/trevorclareart
instagram.com/trevorclareart

Born and raised in Ontario, Canada, Trevor Clare is a multimedia artist with a soft spot for painting local scenes in his home city of Kitchener. He especially enjoys experimenting with the intersection between traditional expressionist painting styles and digital art.

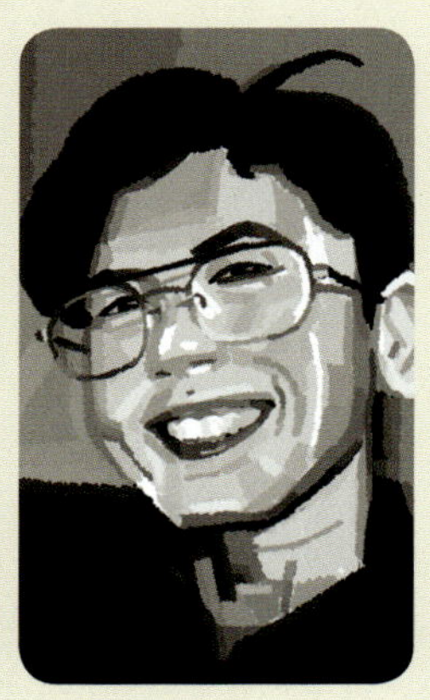

JOJO LU
banditjoj.com

JoJo Lu specializes in concept art, illustration, and animation art. Plein-air painting is one of their favourite ways to experience a place and recall memories of past travels.

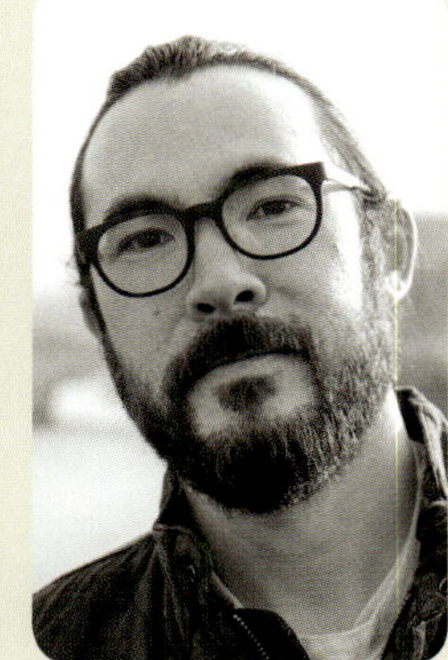

MIKE MCCAIN
mikemccain.art

Mike McCain is a Los-Angeles-based artist fuelled by exploring and painting out in nature, with credits including *The Boy, the Mole, the Fox and the Horse* (Art Director), and *Spider-Man: Across the Spider-Verse* (Visual Development).

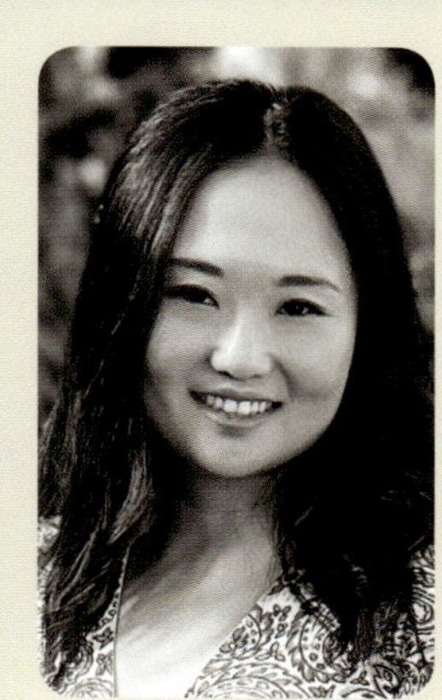

MOMO SUGIMOTO
momoillustration.com

Momo Sugimoto is a Japanese-Australian artist based in Sydney, Australia. She specializes in digital 2D environment art and illustration, and enjoys environment design as well as virtual plein-air painting.

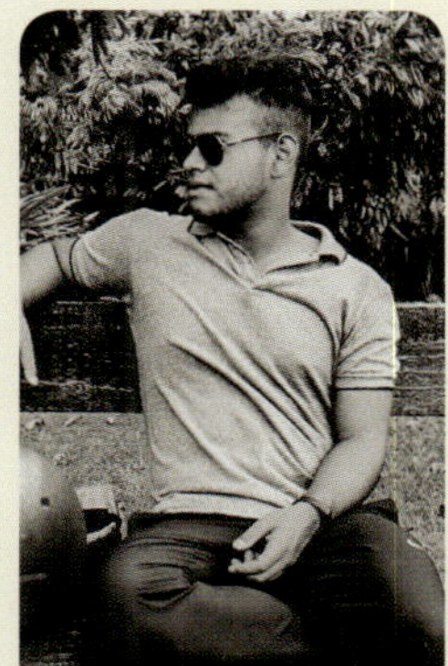

AYAN NAG
artofayan.com

Ayan Nag is an artist from India. He is passionate about exploring, observing, and bringing his own perspective to life through art. He loves creating new worlds, discovering and expressing beauty in the everyday.

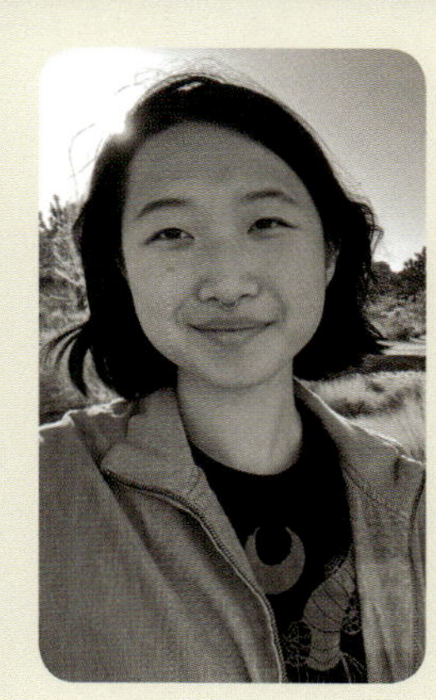

JENNIFER WANG
jenniferwang.art

Jennifer Wang is a plein-air painter living in Los Angeles. She loves exploring the infinite possibilities of colour by bringing her paints and sketchbook to the city's diverse natural realms.

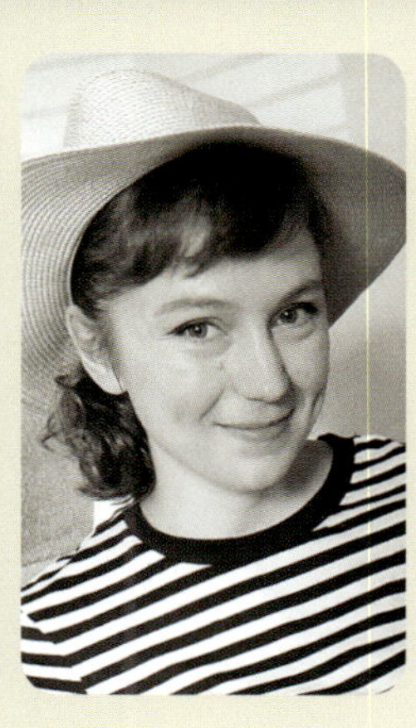

NEVENA NIKOLCHEVA
artstation.com/nen

Nevena Nikolcheva is a freelance concept, visual development, and background artist for the animation and game industry.

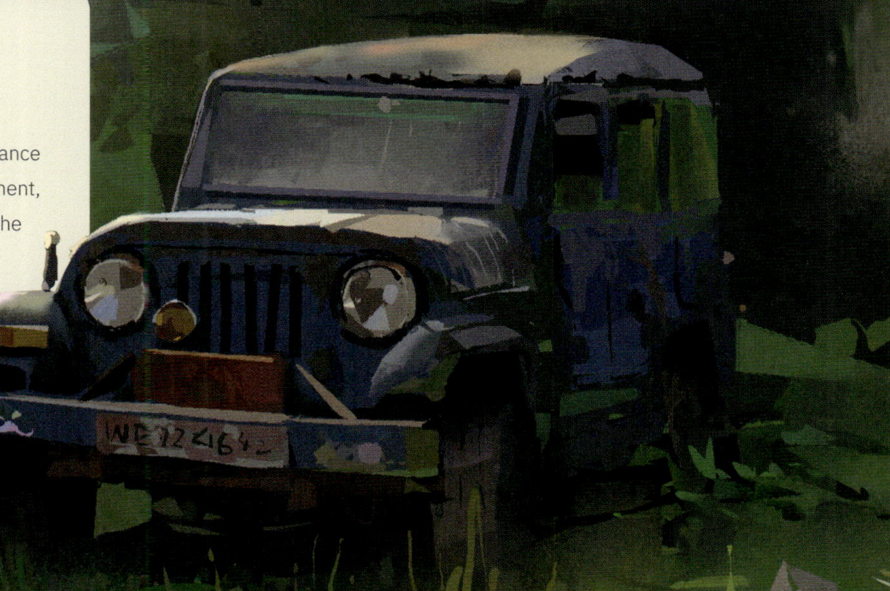

INDEX

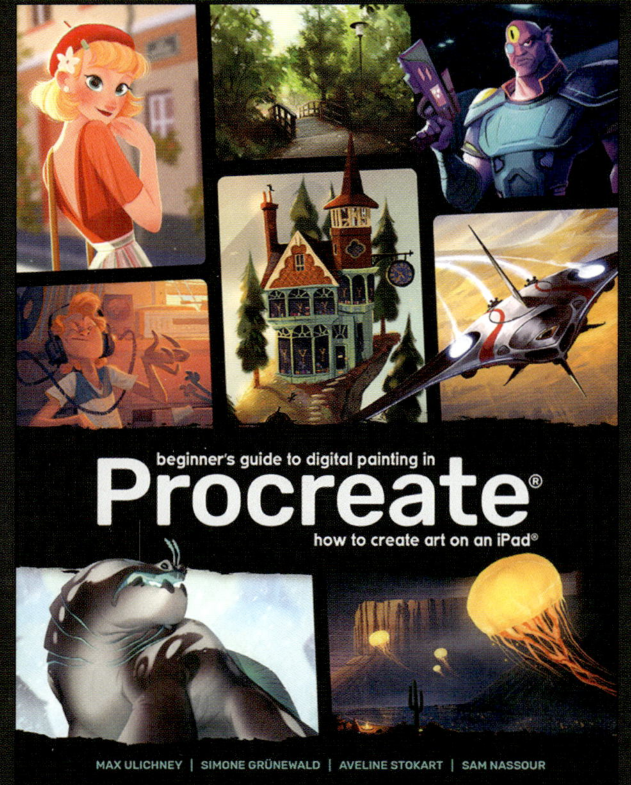

beginner's guide to digital painting in
Procreate
how to create art on an iPad

Learn how to paint on your iPad like the professionals in *Beginner's Guide to Digital Painting in Procreate*, a comprehensive introduction to this industry-standard software. Accessible and versatile, Procreate is an ideal tool for anyone wanting to try digital painting. Step-by-step tutorials, quick tips, and inspiring artwork ensure you'll have all you need to create stunning art quickly and easily.

beginner's guide to digital painting in
Procreate
Characters

Procreate allows you to conceptualize and design straight onto your iPad, and character design benefits hugely from this blend of creativity and convenience. Step by step, you'll learn from experienced and renowned character designers how to manipulate Procreate's intuitive tools, with the focus always on using them to draw and paint compelling characters for all kinds of media.

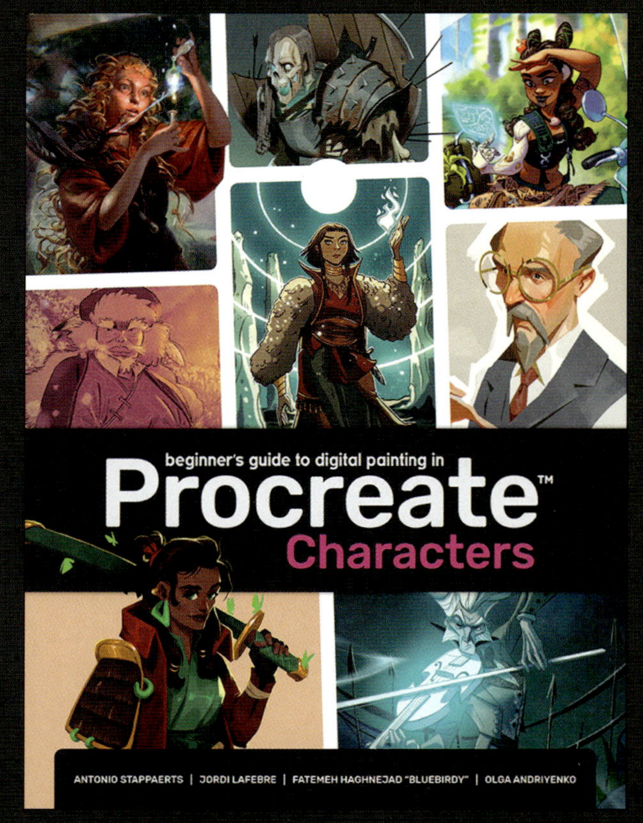

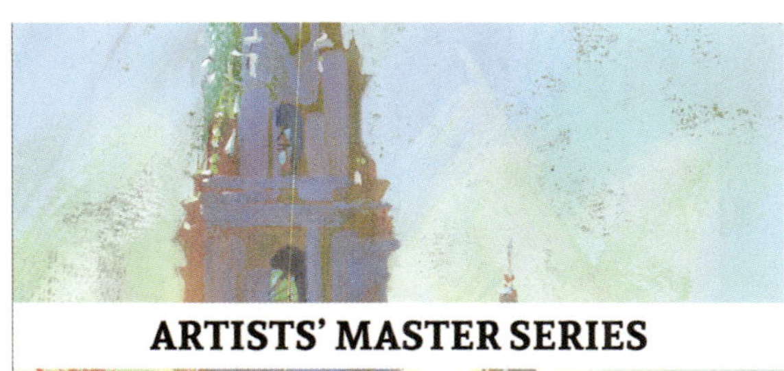

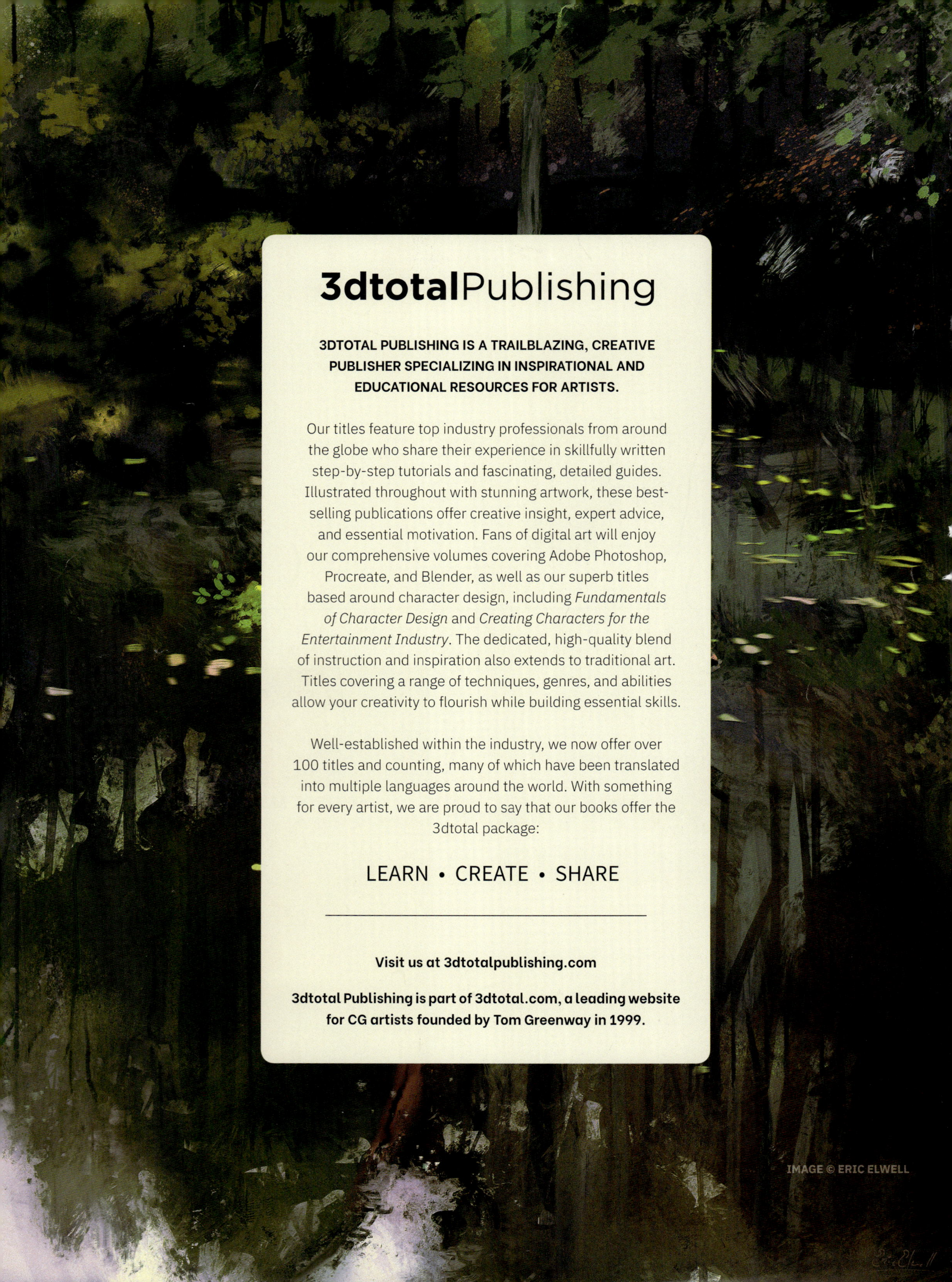

3dtotalPublishing

3DTOTAL PUBLISHING IS A TRAILBLAZING, CREATIVE PUBLISHER SPECIALIZING IN INSPIRATIONAL AND EDUCATIONAL RESOURCES FOR ARTISTS.

Our titles feature top industry professionals from around the globe who share their experience in skillfully written step-by-step tutorials and fascinating, detailed guides. Illustrated throughout with stunning artwork, these best-selling publications offer creative insight, expert advice, and essential motivation. Fans of digital art will enjoy our comprehensive volumes covering Adobe Photoshop, Procreate, and Blender, as well as our superb titles based around character design, including *Fundamentals of Character Design* and *Creating Characters for the Entertainment Industry*. The dedicated, high-quality blend of instruction and inspiration also extends to traditional art. Titles covering a range of techniques, genres, and abilities allow your creativity to flourish while building essential skills.

Well-established within the industry, we now offer over 100 titles and counting, many of which have been translated into multiple languages around the world. With something for every artist, we are proud to say that our books offer the 3dtotal package:

LEARN • CREATE • SHARE

Visit us at 3dtotalpublishing.com

3dtotal Publishing is part of 3dtotal.com, a leading website for CG artists founded by Tom Greenway in 1999.